FORTRAN 77

Donald M Monro

Imperial College of Science and Technology
University of London

Edward Arnold
A division of Hodder & Stoughton
LONDON MELBOURNE AUCKLAND

First published in Great Britain 1982
Reprinted (with corrections) 1983
Reprinted (with further corrections) 1985
Reprinted 1989, 1990

Distributed in the USA by Routledge, Chapman and Hall, Inc.
29 West 35th Street, New York, NY 10001

British Library Cataloguing in Publication Data

Monro, Donald M.
   Fortran 77.
   1. Fortran (Computer program language)
   I. Title
   001.64'24   QA76.73.F25

ISBN 0-7131-2794-5

Printed and bound in Great Britain for Edward Arnold, a division of
Hodder and Stoughton Limited, Mill Road, Dunton Green,
Sevenoaks, Kent TN13 2YA by Athenaeum Press Ltd,
Newcastle upon Tyne.

Preface

FORTRAN 77 is the latest development of the durable computing language FORTRAN. It is the result of many years of labour on the part of an American National Standards Institution subcommittee with the charming, perhaps robotic, name X3J3. It has been adopted as a national standard by most major technological countries and as an international standard by the ISO (the International Standards Organization). Through it FORTRAN gains a new lease of life and will certainly remain as the most important computer language in both Science and Engineering for the foreseeable future. The structure of the language has been improved, many rules have been relaxed, and new facilities have been introduced for text processing which may even extend its influence. It is also now more suitable for structured learning, which is the purpose of this text.

My approach here is based on the belief that experience is the best teacher of programmers, and whether they have learned badly or well has relatively little to do with those who have tried to teach them and a great deal to do with how they have learned. That is why I intend this book not as a teaching aid, but as a learning aid. I endeavour to stress style and efficiency, while introducing many techniques and methods used in the best practice. I take care to point out the commonest pitfalls, and if some of these are overemphasized, it is because I once stumbled badly there myself. To make the book useful as a course text and also as reference material, I introduce syntax and semantics gradually but later summarize in an appropriate place. For example, the control statements GO TO and the logical IF are introduced early but are reiterated in Chapter 6, which covers Program Organization and Control. The order of the early Chapters favours interactive computing because I try to get students doing actual computing, however trivial, as soon as possible. A number of sections and whole Chapters are not central to the learning of FORTRAN 77, but are included because no programmer could claim to be an expert without knowing these things. Essentially, Chapters 2 through 13 are my structured course in elementary FORTRAN 77, with optional sections clearly marked, and with Chapter 12 providing larger programming case studies. Chapters 14 and 15 are enrichment material related to elementary FORTRAN 77, and Chapters 16 to 19 are both an introduction and reference for advanced users.

Some limitations remain which cause the language to fall short of academic respectability, although it is the minor prophets rather than the major ones who seem most bothered. The control structures have been improved greatly in FORTRAN 77, but the missing WHILE construction - proposed but not included - is a great loss. However it is possible to instil a respect for the concepts of good structure, as is done in Chapter 9.

The nature of FORTRAN makes it a tool for numerate people, and so as in my earlier books I emphasize strongly the application of numerical and non-numerical methods of computation to what I know from experience to be practical problems often encountered by Scientists and Engineers. These should not defeat the student who regards them as exercises in computing, not mathematics, with the intention of making the computing interesting, even challenging. This I believe is in contrast with the banality of the examples used in many texts.

The practical help of Duncan Suss and Jerry Yan in the preparation of the manuscript has been vital, and Janet Hill has succeeded in turning my scrawls into excellent line drawings. Many people have typed for me including Nick Davies, Jane Ross, Terrence Theo, and Paul Johnson. Jan Williams has been instrumental in helping me to put the final version together. I extend my grateful thanks to all these people. It has taken longer than it should, and I must particularly apologize to my family for sacrificing their holidays for four summers in order to complete it.

D.M.Monro
Totland Bay
Isle of Wight
September 1981

Contents

1

Introduction

1.1 What is programming?

People in their daily lives are used to giving instructions about all kinds of things - even the meekest person will leave a note for the milkman asking for an extra pint. This is a way of using a written directive to program the milkman. Similarly, programming a computer consists of writing down a list of instructions for the machine to follow. Of course the things computers do are in one way or another concerned with numbers; one is unlikely (just yet) to ask it to draw the curtains, but it is very likely to be asked to add two numbers together. To achieve this a programmer might say:

"Take number A and add it to number B and call the result C".

This is a program of sorts, expressed in the natural language English, and this bit of English could also be a computer language, although as stated it is too verbose. No respectable programmer would tolerate the effort of writing such redundant statements for very long (although some COBOL programmers seem very tolerant). It would be more sensible to say

	LET C=A+B	(BASIC)
or just		
	C=A+B	(FORTRAN)
or possibly		
	c:=a+b	(PASCAL or ALGOL)

Computers provide a range of facilities and programming languages contain constructions which support the use of them. These facilities are sophisticated and many programs instruct the computer to carry out quite complex tasks. The successful completion of a task depends on the instructions, or "recipe" for correctness. Such a recipe is called an algorithm, and programming is the process of expressing an algorithm or computational recipe by means of a programming language.

Because the facilities of computation are very powerful and consequently expensive to use, programmers should be concerned with the efficiency of the algorithms used. However, because programs are often complex, they can be very confusing to any person who tries to understand them; this may even include the original programmer himself. If anything at all worthwhile is done with a computer someone else is bound to be interested. Therefore tricky and/or disorganized programs are always an abomination, and programmers should also be concerned with the style and organization of their programs; in other words, with their structure. Because of this balance between style and efficiency which is required of a good programmer, programming is a craft. The little-known English Philosopher D.D.Burgess has clarified the distinction between artistry and craftmanship in relation to music, and this distinction extends to computer programming: however inspired a programmer may become, the discipline of the craft must have the upper hand.

1.2   About FORTRAN

The name FORTRAN is a result of compressing the two words FORmula TRANslation. FORTRAN began in 1954 as a simpler, more restricted language but after revision in 1958 and again in 1966 it became, as FORTRAN IV, the most common general purpose vehicle for data processing and numerical calculation in science and engineering. Many special purpose languages have sprung up ideally suited to a bewildering variety of tasks, but none presents any particular difficulty in learning after FORTRAN.

Experience in the use of FORTRAN brought an awareness of its shortcomings, particularly in relation to its handling of text (the written word), and because its control statements did not lend themselves very well to present ideas of well structured programs. This new version, FORTRAN 77, goes a long way towards correcting these deficiencies, and assures the language of another epoch in its remarkable endurance. Therefore FORTRAN is still the one computer language which is most useful outside the commercial field (where COBOL prevails).

All languages have rules of construction, or "syntax", which in computing must be precise so that no statement of the language has more than one meaning. FORTRAN 77 relaxes some of the rigid syntax of its predecessors, which is very important in learning it for the first time. From the very first example of Chapter 2 it is possible to write in a natural way things that FORTRAN IV did not allow. This new flexibility allows the learner to concentrate more on the meaning of what he is doing, i.e. the "semantics" of FORTRAN programming. From this point forward, the use of the word FORTRAN means FORTRAN 77.

1.3   About computers

One characteristic of humans is their inventive spirit directed towards the development of tools which can either ease their burden or strengthen their powers. Inevitably each new development will create the need for others; computers have the capacity to automate the repetitive calculations necessitated by earlier inventions and at the same time require the development of the craft of programming.

Every computer is a machine constructed to have a repertoire of simple instructions which it obeys blindly as a result of human guidance. The job of organizing these instructions into a suitable recipe or algorithm has been called programming. The finished list of instructions is called a program and is expressed to the machine in a programming language, often FORTRAN. The computer has no way of knowing whether the instructions given to it make sense or are what the programmer really intended. It interprets them quite literally and could easily get stuck repeating the same meaningless operation until stopped by human intervention or a timing circuit. The person who is trying to get a program to work correctly is capable of many mistakes but (usually) knows his intentions and can deduce what is going wrong. Much of the effort in computer programming is devoted to finding errors in the program.

The machine normally makes no errors but also exercises no judgement. Beginners are quick to blame the computer for making errors when they cannot see them in their own programs. Be warned, however, that in your first few hours as a programmer you will lose count of the your own errors but in a lifetime you may never actually encounter a mistake made by the machine itself.

Provided a computer is instructed properly it can outdistance in seconds or minutes a human lifetime of hand calculation. This is why computers have had a profound effect on a bewildered society. The effects are not always beneficial, particularly when a decision to "computerize" is taken in ignorance of the large overheads and the highly specialized skills involved. But computers can add a million numbers a second and can multiply nearly as rapidly with impressive precision. A computer can store thousands or tens of thousands of results in its memory and recall any one of them in a microsecond.

A vital part of programming is concerned with decision making and so the machine can be given a superficial appearance of intelligent response – but this intelligence originates with the human programmer and the computer's apparent mistakes nearly always have the same origin. It may be interesting to note that the prophets are speaking of a day when computers develop their own intelligence.

For a computer system to be useful, the calculating machine must be supported by devices which feed it information and "systems programs" which guide it through its tasks. The person learning FORTRAN may communicate through a terminal with a keyboard and printer, or less fortunately he may have to submit cards to a "batch service" from which the printed results are returned later.

A computer could have connected to it readers and punches for cards and paper tape, magnetic tape transports, lineprinters, and magnetic disk storage. All these devices provide for input (to the computer) and output (from the computer) of information. Each device has a "driver" program to control it, and there will be a supervisor for the drivers (and probably a program to monitor the supervisor). All these devices and programs make up a computer system before FORTRAN programs can be introduced (Fig.1.1).

Fig. 1.1. A bewildering array of apparatus inhabits the computer room.

1.4   Interactive computing and timesharing

An interactive computer system puts the programmer into direct communication with the computer, usually through a typewriter terminal. Therefore the "turnaround time" for developing new programs and finding and correcting errors is reduced to seconds. The program itself can be written so that the programmer gives it information while the computer is executing it and so he can control the steps of the calculation as it progresses. When FORTRAN is run in an interactive system, programs can be developed rapidly and tested and corrected from a terminal. The learning process is both shortened and made more thorough because the rapid response of the computer and the straightforward nature of the language work in the student's favour and encourage experimentation.

An interactive computer system can be in one of two modes of operation as seen by the programmer. These modes are called "program definition" and "program execution" and are distinguished by whether the programmer or the computer is in control of events as in Fig.1.2. In the program definition mode the programmer will be creating, editing and correcting his program and is himself in control. The main flow of information is from the terminal to the computer and any response by the computer is a result of the programmer's activities. He can enter commands to the system, and the effect of one of these commands might be to submit the program to the computer. If this were done, the system would change to execution mode and the user would then be required to respond only if the program has made specific provision for input from the terminal. The steps carried out by the computer in Fig.1.2 will usually occur in one invisible operation. The major flow of information will be from the computer to the terminal, and the programmer will normally regain control when the program is finished, although he can stop execution manually if necessary.

The computer itself will not understand FORTRAN - the machine code it obeys is a rather nasty series of numbers. A translation program or "compiler" is needed which takes a FORTRAN program and converts it into machine language. Because of the many facilities provided by FORTRAN and the need to check the grammar of a FORTRAN program, the compiler itself is quite a large program. However many years of experience with FORTRAN have enabled people to make very efficient FORTRAN compilers.

The steps in the preparation of a FORTRAN program are illustrated by Fig.1.2, which is the first of many flowcharts that will be used to describe processes, mainly those carried out by computer programs. This one describes the stages in the development of a computer program. The first step will consist of the specification of the problem which is probably the most crucial part, and is one that the programmer must learn to formulate clearly. A procedure is then devised by the method of "stepwise refinement" which is described in Chapter 6. The program is written out in FORTRAN, and then submitted to the computer. The machine compiles the program into its own language, and then loads it into itself and obeys, or "executes", the program. The results are printed and returned. The programmer then decides whether the results are satisfactory or not - a decision is always represented by a diamond-shaped box as in Fig.1.2. If they are incorrect for some reason, the programmer will then revise the program and repeat the submission. It is possible for the revision "loop" to be repeated a large number of times. The difference between batch and timesharing systems lies in the mechanism used and the way in which the machine's part is carried out. A beginner is protected to an extent from the need for detailed knowledge of all this, but FORTRAN is a language that enables the expert to expand into many of the facilities of the system.

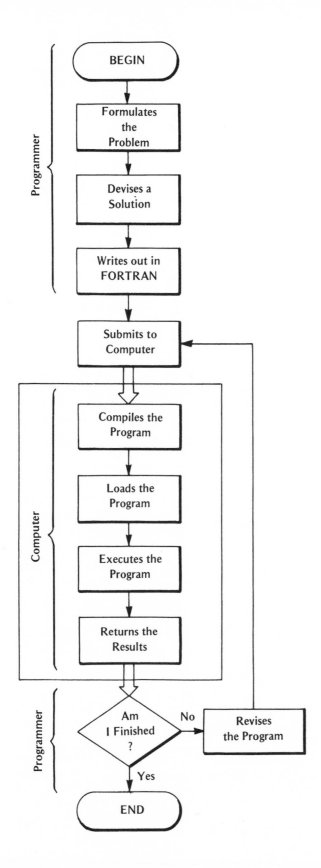

Fig. 1.2. Steps in the development of a FORTRAN program.

1.5 Batch processing

The most likely form of computer service is the batch processing arrangement which, although not ideal for learning, is an efficient system for the production work which accounts for most computer usage. In this kind of bureau, programs are submitted at a central site and are fed to the computer in batches. Some time later, when the machine has completed the batch and moved on to another, the printed results are returned together with the program which will most often have to be corrected and submitted again. The "turnaround" in a batch service is at best a few hours and often overnight even for small jobs and therefore the progress of a person learning FORTRAN can be badly hampered. A service like this requires human intermediaries who organize the input, sort the output and deal with hundreds of moaning users. The user himself is likely to develop a somewhat critical view of the reception department. It should be remembered that delays in processing are unlikely to be the fault of the unfortunates who staff the reception area; many computers seem to have the uncanny ability to develop sick headaches at the worst possible moment.

Some enlightened computer centres mitigate the delays of batch processing by granting the user himself access to enough equipment to run his own "job", and this does tend to create satisfied customers. Once the initial shock at the idea of allowing users to not only see but TOUCH equipment has passed, it is usually found that a well organized "hands-on shop" in which people can read in their own cards and tear off their own output is a success, if untidy at times.

Almost all batch work is done from punched cards, and the deck of cards that makes up a "job" must contain all of the FORTRAN program together with all of the necessary directions to the computer system to make it run, and also any data that the program is then intended to process. These directions, in the form of "control cards" or "job control language", vary widely between different computers as does the manner of organization of the deck of cards. Typically control cards will be needed to initiate translation or "compilation" of the original "source code" (FORTRAN) into machine language, to load this "compiled" program, or "object code", into the computer, search the system libraries for missing bits of program, and set it running, or "executing". The steps are still the same as in Fig.1.2, but the programmer is involved in actual footwork and must spell out the computer's steps in more detail. A benefit of batch processing to the more experienced programmer is the wide range of other facilities available, and this is why the desired steps have to be spelled out in more detail.

1.6   How to use this book

The course is intended to be followed in order from the beginning, doing all the exercises which occur every few pages. The problems at the end of each chapter when taken in order range from easy to difficult and should be used by the student to develop his skills and by the teacher to assess them.

Each section should be read through before the problems associated with it are tried, and even the most tentative solution to a problem written out in advance will save time spent on the computer. It is tragic to watch year after year the amount of time wasted by students in reading the material for the first time and trying to think out solutions at the keyboard; the same people often claim to have had insufficient access.

Some sections will be of interest to more experienced programmers and can be skipped over where indicated without missing any fundamental parts of FORTRAN.

A source of expert advice should be available, firstly about FORTRAN, because people who have made all the mistakes are wise in the ways of spotting them (this is called "experience"), and also about the computer system which is likely to give more trouble at first than the FORTRAN.

2
Calculations with real numbers

2.1 Introduction

A computing machine is directed by a series of instructions telling it exactly what to do at each stage of a calculation; a set of these instructions is called a program. Programming languages are used to express instructions in a way independent of the details of operation of the computer. FORTRAN 77 is called a "high level" language because calculations are expressed in terms familiar to humans rather than to machines. A FORTRAN program uses common English terms and mathematical operations. However, because the communication is with a computer, the instructions given must be precise and no ambiguities can be allowed. Therefore the grammar of FORTRAN, like any other computing language, is constrained by a well defined set of rules which control what grammatical constructions or "syntax" will be understood by the machine.

Programming in FORTRAN is something that nearly everyone can do; experience provides an easy fluency with the language because the rules make sense. This is one of the reasons why FORTRAN is the universal language of scientific calculation and has endured as such for many years. In this chapter enough basic grammar and construction are introduced to allow simple calculations to be undertaken, although some of the material will have to be elaborated on later.

A very simple example of a complete self-contained program serves to introduce the language and point out some of the features of construction. The following is a complete FORTRAN 77 program to calculate and print the easy sum 2.0 + 2.0:

```
PRINT*,2.0+2.0
END
```

There will be things about this program that look familiar, and others that are partly self-explanatory. FORTRAN uses words of English and some recognizable mathematical notation, but it also has very strict rules of punctuation.

The structure of such a simple program is straightforward enough. Each line of the program is called a "statement" of FORTRAN; later it will be seen that some statements are labelled. When a FORTRAN program is obeyed or "executed" by a computer, the order of statements dictates the order in which the instructions given in the program are followed. So the example is executed line by line just as it is read.

The PRINT statement instructs the computer to add together the numbers 2.0 and 2.0 and to print the result somewhere. Given this kind of PRINT statement the machine will print the answer in the obvious place - the terminal in a timesharing system or the lineprinter in a batch environment. The comma after the asterisk is required punctuation.

The END statement signifies the end of the program and when it is reached the computer knows that the job has finished. All programs end with an END statement.

It is often easy to think of programs in terms of flowcharts which explain their structure. A flowchart is shown for this example in Fig.2.1, which gives a graphical guide to the program steps.

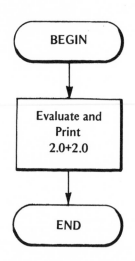

Fig. 2.1. Flowchart for a simple FORTRAN
program which evaluates and prints the expression
2.0 + 2.0.

From the example above it should be
clear that simple calculations can be
undertaken immediately.

EXERCISE:
Deduce the meaning of the following
short programs:

        i)   PRINT*,4.∅-2.∅
              END

       ii)   PRINT*,5.∅+6.∅
              END

      iii)   PRINT*,5.∅/7.∅
              END

       iv)   PRINT*,SQRT(2.∅)
              END

2.2   Basic real constants

The numbers used in the examples of the
previous section are basic real constants.
The most common types of numbers used
in FORTRAN and in real life are those
called integers and real numbers. These
are familiar quantities to all numerate
people, although working with them on
computers can give new insight, particularly in clarifying what is meant by
accuracy and precision. Integers are left
to the next chapter because they have
some rather special characteristics.

A real number is simply a number which
is represented as having decimal places.
If it is written out explicitly as a
number, it is called a basic real constant. Basic real constants are used in
the programs of the previous section.

EXAMPLE:
The following are basic real constants.

3.1416	8.∅∅67
5.∅	−1.
+5.	−2.718284
63.	.∅∅324

Basic real constants are a regular feature
of FORTRAN programs. They are always
written with a decimal point and optionally with a sign. If written without a
decimal point they are integers as will
be seen. The difference between the real
numbers 5.0 or 5. and the integer 5
can be very important in FORTRAN.
Always write an intended real number
with a decimal point. It is not necessary
to write 5. as 5.0 but the latter is
more clear and so is recommended. The
simple programs given in the previous
section did calculations with basic real
constants. This is a rather limited
concept of programming but will be
extended quite a lot in this chapter.

2.3   Arithmetic in FORTRAN — expressions and the slash trap

In FORTRAN, variables and constants can
be combined into what are called
arithmetic expressions which involve the
operations of addition, subtraction, multiplication, division and exponentiation or
"raising to a power". For example, 3.0
+ 4.0 is a real expression whose value
is 7.0. The available operations are:

addition	3.∅+4.∅	real addition, result 7.0
subtraction	3.∅−4.∅	real subtraction, result −1.0
multiplication	3.∅*4.∅	real multiplication, result 12.0
division	3.∅/4.∅	real division, result 0.75
exponentiation	3.∅**4.∅	real number to a real power, result 81.0

(i) ADDITION.
This is very straightforward. The + sign denotes addition but is also used sometimes to denote a positive quantity.

EXAMPLES:

$$14.3+7.6+9.2$$
$$+8.0+1.0$$

(ii) SUBTRACTION.
Again fairly obvious. The - sign also identifies a negative quantity, and so sometimes a bit of care is required because the rules of FORTRAN prohibit more than one operation to appear between two numbers.

EXAMPLES:

$$23.7-13.1$$
$$-16.0+9.5$$
$$-.06-.07$$

It is forbidden to write

$$19.0+-3.0$$

but using brackets, it is possible to write

$$19.0+(-3.0)$$

(iii) MULTIPLICATION.
The asterisk, *, is used to denote the multiplication operation.

EXAMPLES:

$$5.0*4.0$$
$$-19.2*11.0$$

Multiplication can never be implied; the asterisk must be written out. This means that

$$6.0(7.0)$$

is totally forbidden, and should be

$$6.0*(7.0)$$

or

$$6.0*7.0$$

The situation with signed numbers is as before. A programmer is forbidden to write

$$.07*-9.0$$

but instead must use

$$.07*(-9.0)$$

or

$$-9.0*.07$$

(iv) DIVISION.
A slash, /, is the operator signifying division, which with real numbers is carried out as precisely as the machine is able.

EXAMPLES:

$$1.0/8.0$$
$$-42.7/3.21$$

Again the form

$$19.0/-2.0$$

is forbidden and instead should be rendered

$$19.0/(-2.0)$$

A number may not be divided by zero and the computer will detect this if it happens and the program will probably be prevented from continuing.

(v) EXPONENTIATION.
A double asterisk, **, indicates that the number to the left is to be raised to the power of the number on the right, as in the example

$$3.0**2.0$$

In fact a real number raised to an integer power is considered to be a real expression and is sometimes preferred, as will be explained later. This is the only situation in this chapter where an integer number should be used, as in

$$9.0**2$$

With signed powers the correct form again is

$$2.19**(-7)$$

An alert student will now enquire about the meaning of

$$3.0**4.0**5.0$$

Here, the higher exponentiation is done first and so it means

$$3.0**(4.0**5.0)$$

instead of

$$(3.0**4.0)**5.0$$

Two particular kinds of exponentiation are forbidden because they are meaningless. Firstly the number 0 cannot be raised to the power 0 or to any negative power. Secondly a negative number may not be raised to a real power. A computer would detect these when they arose and would probably prevent the program from continuing.

One use of brackets in expressions has already been seen, and another reason for including brackets will become evident as more complicated expressions are formed. It is easily demonstrated that combining these operations into larger expressions creates ambiguities. To a human being the expression

$$4.0+5.0/7.0$$

could mean (4.0+5.0)/7.0 with addition done first or it could mean 4.0+(5.0/7.0) with division done first. FORTRAN operates according to rules which make any expression clear, but this may not always be what a programmer desires and so brackets are used - either to write the expression clearly, or to specify the meaning, or both.

A set of priority rules is used to determine which operations in an expression are done first. The available operations are assigned an order of priority as follows:

High ( ) expressions in brackets
** exponentiation
* or / multiplication or division
Low + or − addition or subtraction

During the evaluation of an expression the operations of highest priority are done first. Therefore exponentiation takes place earlier than multiplication or division and addition or subtraction is done at the end. Expressions in brackets are evaluated first. Normally expressions are evaluated from left to right but exponentation is an exception. A string of exponentiation is done from right to left so that the highest is done first. Therefore

$$3.0**4.0**5.0$$

means

$$3.0**(4.0**5.0)$$

and not

$$(3.0**4.0)**5.0$$

EXAMPLE:
Consider the following real expression

$$3.0+5.0*2.0**4$$

When this is evaluated the order of events would be:

(i) 2.0**4 is calculated (result 16.0)
(ii) This result (16.0) is multiplied by 5.0 (result 80.0)
(iii) 3.0 is added (result 83.0)

So the value of this expression is 83.0.

A careless programmer might well have intended something quite different and written the expression in error. Possible intentions could have been

$3.0+(5.0*2.0)**4$ result 10003.0
$(3.0+5.0)*2.0**4$ result 128.0
$(3.0+5.0*2.0)**4$ result 28561.0

The use of brackets changes the order of calculation and so enables the programmer to make his instructions clear and explicit. Brackets can also make the expression clearer to read. For example the same expression

$$3.0+5.0*2.0**4$$

takes a bit of thought to figure out, and could have been written more clearly as

$$3.\emptyset+(5.\emptyset*(2.\emptyset**4))$$

Here the brackets have been nested, and must always occur as pairs - each "(" must be closed by a ")". In the last example this has caused two closures to be written together, "))".

A final warning to new programmers is in order about the "slash trap". Suppose the desired formula was

$$\frac{4.\emptyset}{2.\emptyset+6.\emptyset}$$

Many, many programmers have written

$$4.\emptyset/2.\emptyset+6.\emptyset$$

when they really mean

$$4.\emptyset/(2.\emptyset+6.\emptyset)$$

This is called the slash trap because it seems never to occur with multiplications, always with divisions.

EXERCISE:
Examine the slash trap carefully: if you do not understand it read the section again.

EXERCISE:
If you have a timesharing system, verify each operation by using simple programs.

EXERCISE:
What is the value of each of the following expressions:

```
3.Ø+1.Ø/2.Ø          3.Ø+(1.Ø/2.Ø)
1.Ø+2.Ø*3.Ø          (1.Ø+2.Ø)*3.Ø
1.Ø/2.Ø+3.Ø          (1.Ø/2.Ø)+3.Ø
1.Ø+2.Ø**3.Ø         (1.Ø+2.Ø)**3.Ø
```

```
        (3.Ø+1.Ø)/2.Ø
        1.Ø+(2.Ø*3.Ø)
        1.Ø/(2.Ø+3.Ø)
        1.Ø+2.Ø**2**3
```

2.4 Real numbers as variables

A great deal of flexibility is gained by allowing a quantity to be referred to by a name rather than a constant value. The purpose of any calculation is to find unknown values from known ones and, just as in algebra, variable quantities in FORTRAN are given names.

Variables in FORTRAN can be given names consisting of several alphanumeric characters, meaning letters and numbers. Used sensibly these are an aid to clear programming since the name given to a variable can help to explain its meaning. As many as six characters can be used. The first character must be alphabetic, but the rest can be a mixture of numbers and letters.

EXAMPLE:
The following are valid variable names of up to six characters (but not necessarily real ones):

```
X           ZERO
Y9          J
THETA       DALEKS
KPRIME      P3264
```

The following are wrong:

```
3XY       (begins with a number)
A$        (contains an illegal character)
VAR7.3 (contains an illegal character)
```

There are several types of variables, but the most common types are real and integer. These two are so common that normally FORTRAN assumes that their type is implied by their spelling. Integer variables must start with the letters I, J, K, L, M, or N, and real variables use the rest of the alphabet. In the prevous example all but KPRIME and J were real variables.

Real variables thus start with the letters A through H and O through Z. Therefore the type real is implied by the first letter of the variable name.

EXAMPLE:
The following are names of real variables:

```
OCTAL      DUMMY
X          P2364
FASTF      WIPE
```

In the previous section the reader had his attention drawn to the requirement that multiplication should always be specified explicitly. With variables this has new importance. In the notation of algebra it is possible to write

xy

meaning x times y. In FORTRAN

XY

is the name of a variable. The multiplication of X by Y would have to be

X*Y

EXERCISE:

Identify the real constants and real variables in the following list:

```
58.3      E1Ø      METOO    B58
154       37       XI       1.
3.E1Ø     PRIME    7.E      3Z
```

2.5 Assignment statements

Anyone following this text with a time-sharing system will already have the experience of trying programs including the PRINT statement in order to evaluate expressions involving constants. Now it will be seen how a variable can be assigned a value, and this will increase the number of things that a program is able to do. Those using a batch system should wait until a few more weapons are added to their programming arsenal before attacking the computer.

All computing languages have assignment statements which call for expressions to be evaluated and the result to be assigned to a variable. The assignment statement in FORTRAN is

variable = expression

for example

$$X=Y+46.\emptyset$$

In this example a real expression is evaluated, Y+46.0, and the real result is assigned to X, replacing whatever value X had before. The assignment statement should not be confused with a mathematical equation. The statement

$$COUNT=COUNT+1.\emptyset$$

is an absurd mathematical proposition but a valid and very useful statement of FORTRAN which has the effect of increasing the value of COUNT by 1.0, whatever it was before.

EXAMPLES:

XSQ=Y*Y+Z*Z

T=4.Ø*PIE

COSA=P/(P*P+Q*Q)**Ø.5

EXAMPLE:

A program can be written to find the trigonometric functions sin, cos and tan for a right angled triangle with sides a and b given, as in Fig. 2.2. From the diagram,

$$\cos \theta = \frac{a}{\sqrt{a^2 + b^2}}$$

$$\sin \theta = \frac{b}{\sqrt{a^2 + b^2}}$$

$$\tan \theta = \frac{b}{a}$$

If the triangle had a=1, b=1, then the program could be

```
A=1.Ø
B=1.Ø
HYP=(A*A+B*B)**Ø.5
CT=A/HYP
ST=B/HYP
TT=B/A
PRINT*,CT,ST,TT
END
```

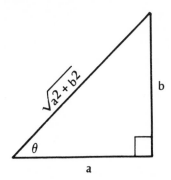

Fig. 2.2. A right angled triangle.

There are other ways of writing this program; it could have all been done in one PRINT statement. However it is much clearer if organized this way. A flowchart is given in Fig. 2.3. First A and B are assigned values, then the hypotenuse and the trigonometric functions can be evaluated. Note how the choice of variable names can be an aid to understanding; HYP for hypotenuse, and CT, ST, and TT for cos θ , sin θ , and tan θ .

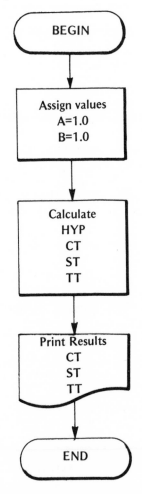

Fig. 2.3. Flowchart of a simple calculation.

EXERCISE:
How would the program accommodate other triangles without changing its structure? If you have a timesharing system, run it.

EXERCISE:
Design a program to find the period of a pendulum given its length. At the surface of the earth, if the length is in metres, the period in seconds for a small amplitude of swing is

$$T = 2\pi\sqrt{\ell/9.81}$$

Note how the square root was accomplished in the given example. Try your program if you are timesharing. Be patient, otherwise.

2.6 Printing captions with results — the PRINT statement

The printed output from a FORTRAN program is immeasurably improved if captions are printed with the results. The PRINT statement can incorporate these very easily; they are simply included in the list of things to be printed. The statement

PRINT*,'HELLO SAILOR'

contains the message 'HELLO SAILOR' in apostrophes, and when it is executed the computer will print

HELLO SAILOR

The caption enclosed by apostrophes is called a "character string constant" and in a later chapter many new facilities of FORTRAN 77 for character manipulation will be introduced. For the present, a character string constant is any string of letters, digits or FORTRAN symbols enclosed by apostrophes. In the next section is found a list of the symbols known to FORTRAN - all but two have been used already.

The apostrophe itself is a FORTRAN symbol and so it must be possible to include it in messages. This is done by writing two apostrophes together in the character string constant to identify it as part of the message. The statement

        PRINT*,'THIS DOESN''T WORK'

will produce as an output when executed

        THIS DOESN'T WORK

and so this method actually does work.

Messages can easily be mixed with results. The triangle calculations of the previous section are improved if the results are printed with explanatory captions as in the following modified version:

```
A=1.0
B=1.0
HYP=(A*A+B*B)**0.5
PRINT*,'GIVEN SIDES ARE ',A,B
PRINT*,'HYPOTENUSE = ',HYP
CT=A/HYP
ST=B/HYP
TT=B/A
PRINT*,'COS = ',CT
PRINT*,'SIN = ',ST
PRINT*,'TAN = ',TT
END
```

Five PRINT statements are used here and if the program were executed its output would be

```
GIVEN SIDES ARE      1.000 1.000
HYPOTENUSE =   1.414
COS =    .707
SIN =    .707
TAN =   1.000
```

showing that each PRINT statement has started a new line.

This is a useful place to pause and explain the PRINT statement. It has been seen in many examples with a * after the word PRINT, in which case it is called a "list directed" PRINT statement. Its form is

        PRINT*[,list]

The square brackets are not part of FORTRAN but are used in this text to denote optional items, therefore the comma and the list are actually optional. "List" is a list of items, separated by commas, which the programmer wishes to

have printed. The items can be variable names, expressions, or character constants as have just been introduced. Since a single constant is a kind of expression, this is permitted as well. A list directed PRINT statement when executed causes the computer to print results, and it will print only what it is instructed to print. The * allows the machine to decide for itself the layout of the printed line. Later a FORMAT directed form of output will be encountered in which the programmer can control the layout exactly. In response to a PRINT statement, the obvious printer is used.

If a PRINT statement is given with no list, in which case there is no comma either, a blank line is printed. It is therefore true to say that every PRINT statement begins a new line. If there is a lot of printing to do the machine may use additional lines.

EXERCISE:
  Improve your pendulum program by the addition of captions.

2.7 Characters recognized by FORTRAN

For reference, all the characters known to FORTRAN are listed here. They all have some meaning in statements of FORTRAN and only these can be used safely in character string constants.

          The letters A - Z

          The digits   0 - 9

          The special symbols:

              Blank

          =   Equals

          +   Plus

          —   Minus

          *   Asterisk

          /   Slash

(	Left parenthesis
)	Right parenthesis
,	Comma
.	Decimal point
$	Currency symbol
'	Apostrophe
:	Colon

The currency symbol may be printed differently in different countries.

2.8 Input of values while running — the READ statement

It is often convenient to provide values to a program while it is running rather than defining them using assignment statements. This is particularly true if the same program is to be run frequently, but with new values each time.

For accepting data during execution of a program , FORTRAN uses the READ statement which is available in a list directed form:

```
READ*[,list]
```

Remember that the square brackets are not part of FORTRAN but denote an optional item. Therefore the comma and the list are optional.

An example is

```
READ*,A,B
```

This causes the computer to refer for input to the obvious place, which is the terminal keyboard for timesharing or the cardreader in a batch system. In timesharing most computers will prompt the user by printing a question mark when it is ready. It is a very good idea in a timesharing system to explain the meaning of each prompt by a PRINT statement before the READ statement, as is done in examples to follow. In this case the user runs his program, waits for the prompt, and then types in his

data. In a batch system, the data follows the program on cards and there is no need for prompting. The details of card deck organization for batch systems vary between computer systems.

This kind of READ statement expects the values to be provided one after the other with spaces and/or commas between them. The easiest way is to give all the necessary data on one line, but things can be arranged in more complicated ways, best illustrated by a series of examples.

EXAMPLE:
Input of a single value. The program will contain

```
PRINT*,'TYPE IN ONE REAL'
READ*,A
END
```

and the programmer wishes to give the value 1.0 to A when he uses the program. This can be done by providing

```
                1.0
```

or

```
                1
```

anywhere in the line of input, be it on cards or on the teletype. Although apparently an integer is provided in the second example the machine will always supply a decimal place at the end unless one is given in the input. This is very easy, but if there is nothing at all in the input line in a timesharing system, the machine will keep trying on new lines until it finds something. A user also has the option of not defining a new value for A. This is done by giving only a series of blanks, or by giving a comma which could be preceded by a series of blanks. It could also be done by providing a / as the only entry, which could again be preceded by a series of blanks. This should only be done if A has already been assigned a value by the program, as it would fail otherwise.

EXERCISE:
Run if you can this program:

```
PRINT*,'INPUT A NUMBER'
READ*,A
PRINT*,'THE SQUARE ROOT IS'
PRINT*,A**Ø.5
END
```

In any case be sure you understand how to provide real data to this program. Try giving it only a comma, or a slash, or a series of spaces, and observe the effect of A being undefined. Try also giving it a value in the exponential form which is defined in the next section - it will work.

EXAMPLE:
Input of two or more values. The program contains

```
PRINT*,'ENTER 2 VALUES'
READ*,X,Y
```

To satisfy this program, two values would normally be given in one line separated by a comma and/or one or more blanks. They could alternatively be given on successive lines. The machine will persist in taking new lines of input until it is satisfied. To make X=5.0 and Y=7.0, satisfactory responses are:

```
5.Ø,7.Ø
5.Ø , 7.Ø
5.Ø 7.Ø
5,7
```

or on successive lines

```
5.Ø
7.Ø
```

By entering only a comma or a series of blanks for an expected value, that value is left unchanged, perhaps undefined. If the above program were given

```
, 7
```

X is left undefined, because the program has never given it a value, and Y is assigned the value 7.0. Similarly the input line

```
, ,
```

leaves both X and Y undefined.

In list directed input, the character "/" can be given. The / terminates the computer's appetite for input and leaves the remainder of the list unaltered - perhaps undefined. It is interesting to note that in this example it is possible to define only X, or neither variable using the /. The input

```
5 /
```

defines X as 5.0 and leaves Y undefined. The input

```
/
```

leaves both X and Y undefined.

EXERCISE:
Here is a program which calculates the hypotenuse of a right angled triangle given the two sides A and B. It assigns "default" values to A and B and then allows you to change them in an input statement.

```
C A PROGRAM TO FIND HYPOTENUSE
C ASSIGN DEFAULT VALUES TO A,B
      A = 1.Ø
      B = 1.Ø
C ASK FOR INPUT
      PRINT*,'INPUT 2 SIDES'
      READ*,A,B
C CALCULATE HYPOTENUSE
      HYP = (A*A+B*B)**Ø.5
C PRINT OUT RESULT
      PRINT*,'THE HYPOTENUSE:'
      PRINT*,HYP
      END
```

Try giving it a / to leave both values unchanged, and then to leave one undefined. Be sure you understand how this is working. The list and comma were said to be optional; if they are not present the computer reads a line or card of input but does nothing with it, which can sometimes be helpful in skipping over cards of input.

EXERCISE:

Develop a program to calculate the total yield y on an investment p at an interest rate of r% over n interest periods. Values of these quantities should be given to the program in response to a READ statement. The formula for the yield is

$$y = p(1+r/100)^n$$

Remember that we are dealing with only real numbers.

2.9 Exponential forms of real numbers

The possible range of real numbers is rather large, and it would not be sensible of FORTRAN to force programmers to write out very small numbers like

0.000 000 000 000 000 000 000 024

when they mean

$$2.4 \times 10^{-23}$$

or very large ones like

30 000 000 000.0

when they mean the speed of light in cm/sec,

$$3 \times 10^{10}$$

Therefore a shorthand is provided; the speed of light could be written

3.ØE1Ø

This is the exponential form of a basic real constant, which is in general

$$y \, E \, n$$

where y is any number and n is an integer exponent; either can be signed. The constant means

$$y \times 10^n$$

EXAMPLE:

The following are basic real constants written in exponential form:

+3.E+1Ø   2.4E-23
-7.2E35   16.35E-4

The exponential form can be used anywhere that a basic real constant can. It can be written in statements of FORTRAN, as

BIG = 6.3E15

or given in response to a READ statement. For its own part the computer may decide to use it in a list directed PRINT, for example

PRINT*,Ø.ØØØØØØØØØØØØØØØØ622

is certain to produce a real number printed with an exponent.

EXERCISE:

Using the hypotenuse program, experiment with real numbers given with exponents. Use them in assignment statements, give them as input, and provoke the computer into printing them.

2.10 Repeating calculations — the GO TO statement and labels

Running a program several times over in order to provide different values as input could be a bit tedious. For this reason the first of many control statements is introduced here.

The GO TO statement is a useful facility which allows the programmer to dictate the order of events in the program, and using it the programs written so far could be made to repeat themselves automatically. Normally a computer follows a FORTRAN program in the order of the statements, one after another. However, certain kinds of statement can change this sequence, and one of these is the GO TO statement. The form of it is

GO TO label

and it causes the execution of the program to jump to the given 'label', which must appear somewhere in the program.

The label is a number of up to five digits put at the front of a statement, with at least one blank between the statement and the label. Labels were once called "statement numbers" but the X3J3 committee which designed FORTRAN 77 have given them a new name. Someone should give the committee a new name before they wind up as robots on a dark planet!

EXAMPLE:

Here is a program to average two numbers whose flowchart, Fig. 2.4, shows clearly the return path created by the GO TO statement.

```
1Ø  PRINT*,'INPUT 2 NUMBERS'
    READ*,XONE,XTWO
    AVG = XONE+XTWO/2.Ø
    PRINT*,'AVERAGE VALUE=',AVG
    GO TO 1Ø
    END
```

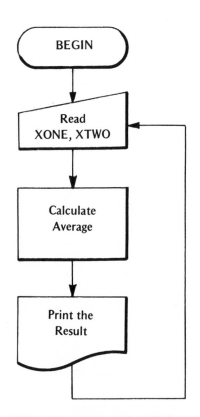

Fig. 2.4. This program repeats the calculation until stopped.

Here the program prompts the user, as it should in timesharing, and then expects to be given two numbers. It calculates and prints the average, and then through the mechanism of the GO TO statement it returns to ask for more.

Any label between 1 and 99999 may be used, but the same label may not be given to more than one statement.

The question of how to stop such a program is bound to arise. The flowchart shows clearly that the "loop" made by the GO TO statement goes on forever. It is actually quite easy to stop a program which requests input each time around. In timesharing, typing in STOP (or some other code) as input in response to READ will terminate the program. In a batch system, if the program runs out of cards to read it will also be terminated. Either way the situation is safe.

EXERCISE:

The program above has a mistake in it. Correct and run it. Be sure you understand it. After the first time around it is safe to enter /. Do you really understand how that works? Modify the program so that it doesn't print the caption after the first time around.

This program is slightly more dangerous:

```
    PRINT*,'BYE-BYE'
1Ø  GO TO 1Ø
    END
```

or this one:

```
    PRINT*,'HA HA YOU CAN''T'
53  PRINT*,'STOP ME...'
    GO TO 53
    END
```

In a batch system you should not try either because they will go on endlessly, or until they run out of paper or time, and that is expensive. On a timesharing system you should be able to stop it with the "break" key, but ask an expert before trying it; it would be as well that you know how because sooner or later you will do something like this by accident. Good luck.

2.11 The structure of simple programs

A feeling for the arrangement of a simple calculation should now have begun to develop and so for the batch people it is possible to put together a program and run it. Those with timesharing have probably had quite a lot of experience already.

Suppose racing drivers complete the Indianapolis 500 mile race in times which are known in hours, minutes and seconds. It is desired to calculate their average speed in miles per hour.

This calculation lends itself to the use of real quantities. If the elapsed time is XH hours, XM minutes, and XS seconds, then the average speed is

$$\frac{500.0}{XH+XM/60.0+XS/3600.0}$$

in miles per hour. The denominator gathers the times together in hours. So the problem has been stated and an attack on the solution formulated. Next a choice of variable names is made. A good choice for hours, minutes and seconds is XH, XM and XS. The time in hours can be called TIME, with the speed called SPEED. A suitable program is

```
C READ TIME HRS, MINS, SECS
 99 READ*,XH,XM,XS
C CALCULATE ELAPSED HOURS
    TIME=XH+XM/60.0+XS/3600.0
C AND THE AVERAGE SPEED
    SPEED=500.0/TIME
C NOW PRINT THE RESULTS
    PRINT*,'TIME FOR 500 MILES:'
    PRINT*,XH,'H',XM,'M',XS,'S'
    PRINT*,'IN HOURS',TIME,'HRS'
    PRINT*,'AVERAGE',SPEED,'MPH'
    GO TO 99
    END
```

FORTRAN programs like this are executed in the order that the statements appear. This program first needs values of the elapsed time, XH hours, XM minutes and XS seconds. In timesharing an explanatory prompt should be added. The total time as one value in hours is calculated and called TIME, and SPEED is

calculated from it. The programmer has chosen to print out the values of all variables in the program; not a bad idea with new programs or ones under development. The program returns endlessly for new values until it is told to stop or it runs out of cards.

The END statement is always the last statement of all - it identifies the end of the program and would also tell the computer to stop executing it, except that in this example it is never reached.

Figure 2.5 is a flowchart for the program. It is good practice always to draw a flowchart; few programs are as simple as this one and these diagrams are an aid to programming and understanding. That is to say, they are helpful in both the synthesis and the analysis of programs.

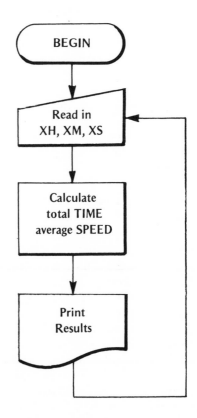

Fig. 2.5. Flowchart of a real program.

There is a new kind of statement in this program. Each line that begins with a C is a COMMENT - not actually a statement but simply the programmer's remarks to help himself remember what he has done on a later reading and to help others to understand his program. Every FORTRAN program should be liberally sprinkled with comments, but not smothered in them.

To get the program executed by the computer it must be entered in some form. The arrangements for doing this are different in batch and timesharing systems.

(a) Batch

Input to a batch system is usually in the form of cards. As well as the FORTRAN program some control cards are necessary to identify the 'job' and instruct the FORTRAN compiler to process the program. The form of control cards varies widely and so local information will be required. The FORTRAN program itself is punched on cards in a layout which is standard. Figure 2.6 shows computer cards with three lines of the example punched in them. The card is divided into 80 columns which are used as follows:

Column 1 - if a C is punched in column 1 the entire card is regarded as a comment and it is not part of the executable program.

Columns 1-5 - are used for labels which are punched anywhere in these columns, if they exist.

Column 6 - is reserved for the special purpose of continuation lines. It sometimes happens that a statement becomes too long for one card and it can be continued on additional cards by punching any standard FORTRAN character other than 0 or blank in column 6 for up to 19 additional cards (which would be rather unusual). Many programmers indicate the first continuation card by a one, the second by a 2, and so on. END statements can never be continued, nor can comments (you simply write additional lines beginning with a C as above). If a numbered statement is continued, the statement number is punched only on the first card. Therefore the columns 1-5 must be blank on a continuation card.

Columns 7-72 - are used for the statements of FORTRAN. Within the statement of FORTRAN blank spaces are ignored except in character string constants, meaning that the statement can be compressed or expanded as desired.

Columns 73-80 are not used by FORTRAN but could be used to identify or serialize the cards.

The FORTRAN program consists of a deck of cards in the correct order, with an END card always as the final one. The program is submitted to the batch service with the necessary control cards, and the cards and printed output are returned. In the deck, data cards if any will follow the program. The precise structure of card decks varies between computer systems.

(b) Timesharing

There are great advantages to time-sharing, particularly when writing and testing small programs. The programmer can enter his FORTRAN program through a terminal, edit out his typing mistakes, try his program, and make corrections. All these operation involve only a few seconds delay. In a timesharing system line numbers will probably be required and these are not the same as the labels - labelled statements have both. The following is the form taken by the example on a timesharing system:

```
00100C READ TIME HRS, MINS, SECS
00110 99 READ*,XH,XM,XS
00120C CALCULATE ELAPSED HOURS
00130    TIME=XH+XM/60.0+XS/3600.0
00140C AND THE AVERAGE SPEED
00150    SPEED=500.0/TIME
00160C NOW PRINT THE RESULTS
00170    PRINT*,'TIME FOR 500 MILES:'
00180    PRINT*,XH,'H',XM,'M',XS,'S'
00190    PRINT*,'IN HOURS',TIME,'HRS'
00200    PRINT*,'AVERAGE',SPEED,'MPH'
00210    GO TO 99
00220    END
```

In each FORTRAN statement, the line number is usually followed by a single blank space to signify the end of the line number. If a label is present, as in statement 99 (line 110) of the example,

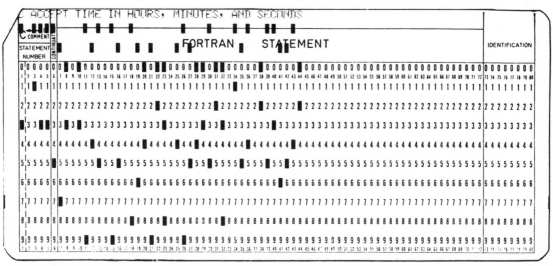

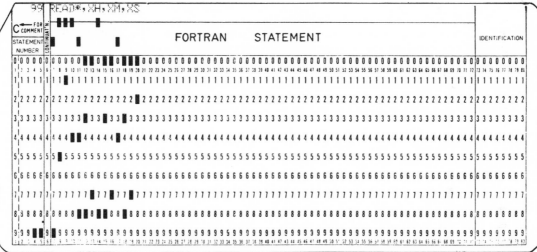

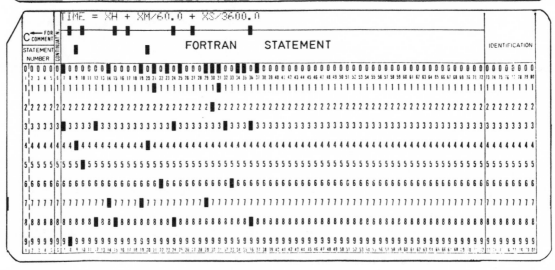

Fig. 2.6. The layout of FORTRAN programs on punched cards.

then it is usually followed by a blank to indicate the end of the statement number. The FORTRAN statement then follows which can have as many blanks scattered through it as desired, meaning that the statement can be expanded or compressed according to the programmer. Blanks in a statement are only significant in character string constants.

A comment is indicated by the letter C immediately following the line number as shown. If a FORTRAN statement is too long for one line, then it may be continued on further lines by placing a plus sign immediately following the line number. If a labelled statement is continued, the label only appears in the first line of the statement.

In using a timesharing system knowledge of certain commands and other arrangements will be necessary, and since these vary widely between installations, this information must be obtained locally.

EXERCISE:
Run this program on your computer. The batch people can now, with with the author's apologies for the priority he has given to timesharing, go back at their own discretion to as many earlier exercises as they feel necessary. Many of them would not be much fun anyway because of the delays in getting results inherent in the batch philosophy.

2.12   Intrinsic functions

For the convenience of programmers, most computing languages have a library of built-in functions which provide a range of useful facilities for the evaluation of often-used functions. FORTRAN is no exception; they are called intrinsic functions and a number are available. Those listed in table 2.1 are the standard ones for operating on real numbers in order to produce real results. In FORTRAN 77 many of these can be referred to by their generic name or their specific name as will be explained in Chapter 4. Most computers will have other functions besides these. It is worth looking carefully at the list as

there are some very useful facilities included.

EXAMPLE:
Here is a program to find the square root of a number:

```
   PRINT*,'SUPPLY A REAL NO.'
10 READ*,X
   Y=SQRT(X)
   PRINT*,'THE SQUARE ROOT OF'
   PRINT*,X,'IS',Y
   GO TO 10
   END
```

This program, when run, will request a value for the variable X, calculate its square root using the SQRT function, and finally print the result.

Functions can be included freely in any arithmetic expression, in assignment or PRINT statements or any of the other places yet to be introduced. Each function operates on one or more values given in parentheses, which are arguments of the function. Arguments themselves can be expressions of varied complexity and can therefore include other functions - and a function may refer to itself. In referring to a function by its generic name the result will be real if the argument is real.

EXAMPLE:
This is a useful way of calculating π. The precision of computers may vary and so the author of a portable computer program will not know how many digits to ascribe to π. He can, however, compute it using the fact that

$$\tan^{-1}(1.0) = \pi/4$$

The program uses the real function ATAN:

```
20 PRINT*,'PIE IS ',4.0*ATAN(1.0)
```

EXERCISE:
Find the value of e, the base of natural logarithms, using the appropriate function.

Generic Name	Specific Name	Meaning
ABS(X)	ABS(X)	The absolute value of X
ACOS(X)	ACOS(X)	Arccos(X), an angle $0 \le a \le \pi$ for which cos(a)=X
AINT(X)	AINT(X)	Integer part of X, i.e. decimal places removed
ANINT(X)	ANINT(X)	X rounded to the nearest whole number
ASIN(X)	ASIN(X)	Arcsin(X), an angle $-\pi/2 \le a \le \pi/2$ for which sin(a)=X
ATAN(X)	ATAN(X)	Arctan(X), an angle $-\pi/2 \le a \le \pi/2$ for which tan(a)=X
ATAN2(Y,X)	ATAN2(Y,X)	Arctan(Y/X),i.e. $-\pi < a \le \pi$ with tan(a)=Y/X
COS(X)	COS(X)	Cosine(X), X in radians
COSH(X)	COSH(X)	Hyperbolic cosine, $(e^x+e^{-x})/2.0$
DIM(X,Y)	DIM(X,Y)	Positive difference X-AMIN1(X,Y)
EXP(X)	EXP(X)	Exponential function e^x
LOG(X)	ALOG(X)	Natural logarithm of X, $\log_e X$
LOG10(X)	ALOG10(X)	Logarithm of X to base 10, $\log_{10} X$
MAX(X,Y,...)	AMAX1(X,Y,...)	Maximum of X,Y,...
MIN(X,Y,...)	AMIN1(X,Y,...)	Minimum of X,Y,...
MOD(X,Y)	AMOD(X,Y)	Remainder of X/Y, i.e. X-AINT(X/Y)*Y
SIGN(X,Y)	SIGN(X,Y)	Transfer of sign, (sign of Y)*ABS(X)
SIN(X)	SIN(X)	Sine of X, X in radians
SQRT(X)	SQRT(X)	Square root of X
SINH(X)	SINH(X)	Hyperbolic sine, $(e^x-e^{-x})/2.0$
TAN(X)	TAN(X)	Tangent of X, X in radians
TANH(X)	TANH(X)	Hyperbolic tangent, $(e^x-e^{-x})/(e^x+e^{-x})$

Table 2.1. Real functions of a real argument from the FORTRAN 77 standard. The specific names are clearly of type real. The generic functions are of type real if given real arguments.

2.13 Problems

These problems, included at the end of each chapter, are intended to give extra practice in FORTRAN programming.

PROBLEM 2.1:
The amount returned after p currency units are invested for n investment periods at r% per period is

$$y=p(1+r/100)^n$$

as in the earlier example. This formula can be turned around in various ways.

(i) Suppose the payments on a car costing 2000 currency units add up to 2400 units over a period of two years. What is the true annual interest rate? (Answer 9.54%)

(ii) A man wishes to save a sum of money for the future. If he needs 1000 units in 16 years, what single sum must he invest now at 6%, 8%, 10% per annum? (Answer 393.65 units at 6%)

(iii) How many full years will it take to at least double an investment at 6%, 8%, 10%, per annum? (Answer 12 years at 6%)

PROBLEM 2.2:
A polynomial

$$ax^3+bx^2+cx+d$$

is to be evaluated over a range of values of x. Write a FORTRAN program which first reads in a, b, c, and d and then evaluates the polynomial as successive values of x are read in. Plot a graph from these calculations of

$$x^3+7.8x^2+18.5x-11.3$$

Approximately where are its roots?

Note: The most efficient way to evaluate a polynomial is to avoid powers of x which the computer evaluates only slowly, and to use

instead a formula like

$$d+x(c+x(b+ax))$$

This requires only additions and multiplications, which computers do very quickly. This arrangement applies to any polynomial and can lead to great economy in computer time.

PROBLEM 2.3:
Write a program which, given the three sides of any triangle, calculates all three angles in degrees using the cosine law for a triangle as in Fig. 2.7.

$$\cos A =(b^2+c^2-a^2)/2bc$$

Note that all the trigonometric functions work in radians. Define the conversion factor between degrees and radians using the ATAN function, based on an idea outlined in an example in section 12 of this chapter.

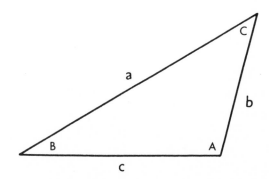

Fig. 2.7. Illustrating the cosine law for any triangle.

PROBLEM 2.4:
In a thin rotating ring or flywheel, the circumferential stress which tries to pull the rim apart is

$$\sigma = \rho r^2\omega^2$$

where σ is in Newtons/metre, ρ is the density in kilograms/metre, r the radius in metres, and ω the rate of spin in radians/second.

Write a program to calculate the maximum safe speed, given the maximum safe stress and other data. From information you can find, identify the material that you can spin fastest. Also find the material that will store the most energy in a flywheel.

PROBLEM 2.5:

Write a program which finds the square root of a number x, but which gives $-\sqrt{|x|}$ if x is negative.

PROBLEM 2.6:

Over the range $-1 \le x \le 1$, e^x can be approximated by a polynomial

$$e^x = 1 + 1.000045 + 1.000022x + .499199x^2$$
$$+ 0.166488x^3 + 0.043794x^4$$
$$+ .008687x^5$$

which is one of the type known as Chebyshev polynomials. Compare this approximation with the EXP function and with the use of 6 terms of the series

$$e^x = 1 + x + \frac{x^2}{2} + \frac{x^3}{6} + \frac{x^4}{24} + \frac{x^5}{120} + \ldots$$

itself a polynomial. Use the efficient method of polynomial evaluation described in Problem 2.2.

PROBLEM 2.7:

Another method of finding e^x uses the continued fraction:

$$e^x = 1 + \cfrac{x}{1 - \cfrac{x}{2 + \cfrac{x}{3 - \cfrac{x}{2 + \cfrac{x}{5 - \cfrac{x}{2 + \cfrac{x}{7 - \cfrac{x}{2 + \text{etc.} \ldots}}}}}}}}$$

which in practice has to stop somewhere because it would be programmed from the bottom up. Investigate the use of this formula as a means of finding e^x.

3

Working with integers

3.1 Introduction

Real numbers as introduced in the previous chapter are the workhorses of calculation, whereas integers are used in specialized and often subtle ways. As everyone will know, integers are numbers which take on exact whole number values and so their values are absolutely precise, as compared to the real quantities in FORTRAN which are generally approximations. Integers are therefore useful as counters and indices.

The mystical qualities of integers have fascinated mathematicians for millenia; indeed the word algorithm, which now applies to any computational recipe, in the middle ages meant any use of Arabic numerals and is a corruption of the name of a ninth century Arabic mathematician, Al Khowarizimi, whose work was important in bringing Arabic numbers to the West. Before the computer was invented the word came to be associated with Euclid's algorithm for finding the greatest common divisor of two integers, which itself points to the usefulness of the remainder in integer division. Homage to Euclid's algorithm is mandatory in any introduction to integer calculations.

3.2 Integers in FORTRAN — constants and variables

An integer constant in FORTRAN is simply a number, either positive or negative, written without a decimal point. The maximum allowed size of integers varies between computers, as discussed in Chapter 4.

EXAMPLE:
The following are integer constants:

$$5 \qquad\qquad -53$$
$$+1\emptyset24 \qquad\qquad 36\emptyset\emptyset\emptyset\emptyset$$

An integer variable in FORTRAN is written exactly as a real one would be, except that the type "integer" is implicit in the spelling of the variable name. Normally the name of an integer variable begins with the letters I, J, K, L, M, or N. An integer variable name has up to six alphanumeric characters, but the first is always a letter.

EXAMPLE:
The following are integer variable names:

$$\text{NUTS} \qquad \text{L}$$
$$\text{KPRIME} \qquad \text{I73}$$
$$\text{JOHN} \qquad \text{MI5}$$

It is vital to appreciate the difference between reals and integers because their misuse in FORTRAN can cause trouble. This is why they are considered as separate cases before their joint use is examined in Chapter 4. Integers are exact whole numbers which carry no decimal places and are useful as counters and indicators. Their arithmetic, particularly in relation to division, has special characteristics. Reals, on the other hand, carry decimal places and have a wide range of values and so are useful in numerical calculation. There are further special types of variables or constants which are described in later chapters.

EXERCISE:
Classify the following as integer or real and variable or constant. For example, 5 is an integer constant.

```
154     B52     XI      PRIME
E1Ø     57.3    1.      1ØØØ
METOO   37      3.E1Ø   3Z
C3PØ    X3.3    JXYZ    R2D2
```

3.3 Arithmetic with integers

Integer expressions are formed in exactly the same way as real expressions except that all the variables and constants involved must be integers, and the result is also an integer. The arithmetic and priority of operations is exactly as described in the previous chapter except that the result of an integer division, because it must be an integer, is perhaps unexpected. Accordingly,

$$14+27 \text{ is } 41$$
$$39-49 \text{ is } -1Ø$$
$$-6*9 \text{ is } -54$$
$$3**3 \text{ is } 27$$

but

$$22/7 \text{ is } 3$$

When an integer division is carried out, the result could be exact, for example

$$81/9 \text{ is } 9$$
$$-26/13 \text{ is } -2$$

If the result is not exact, it is "truncated", i.e. it is the integer of the correct sign but the next lowest absolute value. For example,

$$41/5 \text{ is } 8$$
$$-65/7 \text{ is } -9$$
$$5/7 \text{ is } Ø$$

A FORTRAN programmer quickly gets used to this and indeed it is not a nuisance at all but of great value.

EXAMPLE:
You have a total of JUNK tons of valuable merchandise to send in containers which hold 13 tons each. You are only going to send full ones because the cost of sending a container is fixed regardless of its contents. The rest can go next time.

So you must send JUNK/13 containers. If JUNK=71, then JUNK/13 is 5 with 8 tons left over.

It is also quite easy to get the value of the bit left over. Suppose JUNK is to be divided by IDIV. The result of the division is

$$IQUOT=JUNK/IDIV$$

but the remainder can be retrieved quite easily as

$$IREM=JUNK-IQUOT*IDIV$$

or $IREM=JUNK-(JUNK/IDIV)*IDIV$

The expression (JUNK/IDIV)*IDIV is not equal in value to JUNK unless IDIV happens to divide JUNK exactly - the parentheses force the division to be carried out first.

In general, to put JUNK back together

$$JUNK=IQUOT*IDIV+IREM$$

or $\qquad j=q*d+r$

and this fact will be used in the next section.

The assignment statements employed above evaluate integer expressions and assign the result to an integer variable. Thus assignment statements have the same form

$$\text{variable=expression}$$

as before but in this chapter both the variable and the expression are integers. Please do not mix reals and integers in this chapter - this slight discipline is important and necessary.

3.4 Euclid and the integer remainder

The problem of finding the greatest common divisor of two numbers is one of the classical examples of integer arithmetic. Given two integers i and j, the largest integer which can be divided exactly into each is sought; this will be called "d" for clarity but it should be borne in mind that it is an integer.

There is an obvious brute force approach to this problem; it is easy to try dividing i and j by all the integers from 2 up to the smallest of i-1 and j-1 to get the answer.

EXAMPLE:

i=21 and j=35

Try i=1,2,3,4,5, etc. and it will be found eventually that both i/7 and j/7 give zero remainder. Therefore 7 is the greatest common divisor of 21 and 35.

However this is a poor solution. The first thing to observe would be that 4 will not work if 2 didn't, 6 won't work if 2 and 3 didn't, and so on so that the only numbers worth trying are those with no divisors themselves. These are called the prime numbers.

EXAMPLE:

This program will calculate the remainder for you and allow you to search for the greatest common divisor. Its flowchart is Fig.3.1.

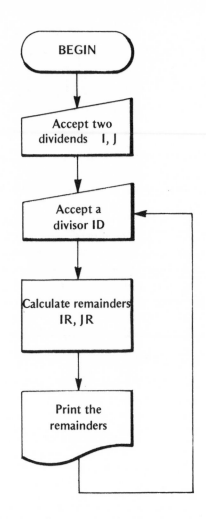

Fig. 3.1. Program to calculate remainders.

```
C PROGRAM TO FIND REMAINDERS
C OF I AND J DIVIDED BY ID
C
C FIRST ACCEPT I AND J
      PRINT*,'INPUT 2 INTEGERS '
      READ*,I,J
      PRINT*,'DIVIDENDS ',I,' AND ',J
C THEN ACCEPT ID
      PRINT*,'INPUT THE DIVISOR '
   1Ø READ*,ID
C CALCULATE REMAINDERS
      IR1=I-(I/ID)*ID
      IR2=J-(J/ID)*ID
C PRINT RESULTS AND GO BACK
      PRINT*,I,' DIVIDED BY ',ID
      PRINT*,'REMAINDER IS ',IR1
      PRINT*,J,' DIVIDED BY ',ID
      PRINT*,'REMAINDER IS ',IR2
      GO TO 1Ø
      END
```

In this program it can be seen that integer variables are allowed in list directed READ and PRINT statements. While executing the PRINT statement, the computer will decide how to arrange the output. In response to the READ statement, the user must decide whether he is expected to provide reals or integers, or both. He must then supply data of the required type in the required order according to the list of variables in the READ statement.

EXAMPLE:
Try this out. Remember how to stop it. How many steps does it take you to find the greatest common divisor of 22261 and 26329?

Actually the above program is still in a brute force state; a person who followed the method and didn't try 2 will have found the answer at the 29th prime number. Euclid knew that if d divides i and j, it also divides i-j because

$$\frac{i}{d} - \frac{j}{d} = \frac{i-j}{d}$$

Therefore the greatest common divisor of i and j is the same as that of i-j and j. So if i>j, j is subtracted from i and the problem is a new one. So that i is always the larger number, i and j may have to be swapped round occasionally. Eventually i-j becomes equal to j and the problem is solved.

EXAMPLE:
Find the greatest common divisor of 28 and 77.

```
First   i=77  and  j=28 , i-j=49
Second  i=49  and  j=28 , i-j=21
Third   i=28  and  j=21 , i-j= 7
Fourth  i=21  and  j= 7 , i-j=14
Fifth   i=14  and  j= 7 , i-j= 7
```

and the problem is finished - the greatest common divisor of 28 and 77 is 7. This is much better - the answer is found in 5 steps.

Patience! This is still not Euclid's algorithm. But it would be a great leap forward to notice something strange about the first three steps and the last two. At the beginning 28 was subtracted twice and the second time round the answer was 21. But the remainder of 77/28 is 21. Further, the final amount 7 appeared in the third stage but was not confirmed until 7 was taken away twice more. But the remainder of 28/21 is 7! So it can all be done more quickly by remainders.

EXAMPLE:
Find the greatest common divisor of 28 and 77.

First: The remainder of 77 over 28 is 21.
Second: The remainder of 28 over 21 is 7.
Third: The remainder of 21 over 7 is 0.

The answer has been found when there is no remainder. Euclid's algorithm has been rediscovered after only 2250 years!

EXERCISE:
Write a program to exploit this.

Do you have a sudden sinking feeling? Have you followed the argument and still do not know what to do? One of the great problems with modern education is that it is based on analysis, i.e. the principle that anything the teacher can explain is OK. The opposite to this is synthesis, a process of creating. It can only be done with experience and this you must acquire.

What you want is a program which allows you to type in i and j and which will find for you the remainder when i is divided by j. You can do this repetitively by re-entering new values of i and j. It is similar to the program of Fig. 3.1, but not the same.

Find the greatest common divisor of 22261 and 26329 by this method. Easy, really.

Soon, in this chapter, you will learn how to automate this calculation totally.

3.5 Counting and stopping — the logical IF statement

Because integer numbers are exact, they are ideal for counting. This is easily arranged in FORTRAN, but the question of how to stop counting arises immediately.

First the counting. To do this a variable is set aside for the purpose of keeping track of the count. Often counting is started from 1, but not always - a different initial value is possible. To assign an initial value of 1 a statement is used like

$$I=1$$

and clearly other initial values are set just as easily. To increment the count another assignment statement is used such as

$$I=I+1$$

which is most interesting. It makes no sense as an equation of mathematics, but of course it isn't one. An assignment statement causes the evaluation of the expression on the right hand side and this value is assigned to the variable on the left, replacing whatever it was before. So here the value of I is increased by 1.

Using a counter, a loop can be set up as shown in Fig. 3.2. The following has the structure of Fig. 3.2, and counts forever.

```
    PRINT*,' NOW WE LEARN TO COUNT'
    I=1
1Ø  PRINT*,I
    I=I+1
    GO TO 1Ø
    END
```

Now the question of how to stop it can be raised. A control statement is required which can examine the value of I and make a decision, something like

IF (something) THEN do something

Indeed the statement which would be used is the logical IF statement which can send the program back to statement 10 or not, depending on the value of I. Suppose the count was to be stopped after 8, then it would be possible to write

IF(I.LE.8) GO TO 1Ø

which means "if I is less than or equal to 8, go to 10". Using this statement the program could be made to count to 8, and along the way to work out the sum 1+2+3+...+8. This would require a second variable to be initialized beforehand and incremented inside the loop; observe how it is done:

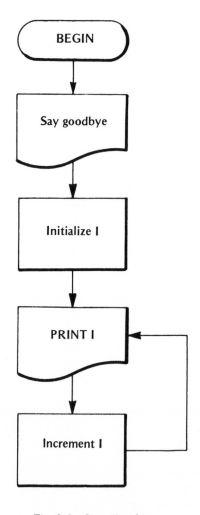

Fig. 3.2. Counting forever.

```
    ISUM=0
    I=1
10  ISUM=ISUM+I
    I=I+1
    IF(I.LE.8)GO TO 10
    PRINT*,'THE SUM TO 8 IS ',ISUM
    END
```

The program illustrates the fundamental outline of a loop or repeated calculation containing processing, initialization, incrementing, and testing as in Fig. 3.3. It is important to be completely familiar with this structure.

EXERCISE:
Run the above program. Find the sum of 100 and 201 numbers. Work out formulae for the sum of n integers for even and odd n. Notice how integer division allows one formula for both.

The logical IF statement can do much more than stop a counter. The statement consists of:

$$\text{IF} \ (\begin{array}{c} \text{logical} \\ \text{expression} \end{array}) \ \begin{array}{c} \text{executable} \\ \text{statement} \end{array}$$

The "logical expression" is something that can be TRUE or FALSE. If it is TRUE then the executable statement is obeyed. If it is FALSE then the program continues with the next statement which follows the logical IF. The "executable statement" might be almost any executable statement of FORTRAN; refer to Chapter 6 for restrictions.

The logical expression can be quite complicated and will be described in detail in Chapter 6. The simplest and most common form it takes is called a "relational expression" and consists of

arithmetic   relational   arithmetic
expression   operator   expression

The types of the arithmetic expressions need not be the same as will be seen, but in this chapter only integer expressions are being used.

Several relational operators are available as follows:

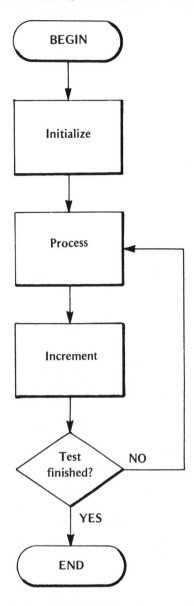

Fig. 3.3. The standard structure of a counting loop.

.GT. greater than
.LT. less than
.EQ. equal to
.GE. greater than or equal to
.LE. less than or equal to
.NE. not equal to

It is evident that all possible combinations are catered for. This is a very useful facility.

EXAMPLES:
Relational expressions

$$\text{I.GT.0}$$

is TRUE if I>0 or FALSE if I≤0.

$$2.\emptyset*THETA.LE.PIE$$

is TRUE if 2.0*THETA≤PIE or FALSE if 2.0*THETA>PIE.

$$AINT(X+Y).LT.J-1$$

is TRUE if the integer part of (X+Y) is less than J-1, otherwise FALSE.

Logical IF statements

$$IF(I.NE.J)PRINT*,I,J$$

If I and J are not the same they are printed. The program then continues with the next statement in sequence.

$$IF(L.LT.\emptyset)M=M+1$$

If L is negative, M is incremented by one and the program then carries on in sequence.

$$IF(B*B-4.\emptyset*A*C.LT.\emptyset.\emptyset)GO\ TO\ 5\emptyset$$

This is evidently the test of the discriminant b^2-4ac of a quadratic expression ax^2+bx+c. If the discriminant is negative the program will jump to statement 50, otherwise the next statement will be the one that follows in sequence. Note the use of B*B instead of B**2. It is more efficient to square a number this way - computers do multiplication more quickly than exponentiation.

EXERCISE:
Go back a few pages to the program for finding the greatest common divisor by Euclid's algorithm. Automate it fully so that only two numbers are entered and the result is printed when the final remainder becomes zero. Before the test that returns the program to the remainder calculation you will have to redefine i as what used to be j, and j as the remainder just calculated. This will require careful organization. An example of this in a different problem occurs in the next section.

3.6 Another example — number systems

The number system used in everyday life is the decimal system, based on 10, which happens to be the number of fingers on two hands by no accident. The symbols 0 to 9 are assigned meanings as digits, and beyond 9 the number system is multidigit. The meaning of a decimal system is well known; the rightmost digit is the number of units (or ones), the next is the number of tens, and so on as in Fig. 3.4.

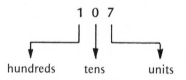

(a) A decimal number.

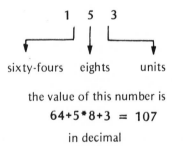

the value of this number is
$$64+5*8+3 = 107$$
in decimal

(b) The octal version of the same number.

Fig. 3.4. Decimal and octal numbers.

Now consider the possibility of a different number system, based on 8 say. This would be the octal system, and in fact is a very useful one. Here the rightmost digit again stands for units, but only counts from 0 to 7. The number next after seven is what is called 8 in decimal, but would be written 10 in octal, because the '1' in '10' now stands for eights rather than tens, as in Fig. 3.4. The usefulness of octal in computing is that each octal digit breaks down easily into binary which is the natural system for computers. Binary is too long winded, so octal is often used instead as illustrated by Fig. 3.5. Hexadecimal (base 16) is also used a great deal.

Octal	Binary				
0	000	or	○	○	○
1	001		○	○	●
2	010		○	●	○
3	011		○	●	●
4	100		●	○	○
5	101		●	○	●
6	110		●	●	○
7	111		●	●	●

Fig. 3.5. The octal digits 0 - 7 and their binary equivalents.

EXAMPLE:

The decimal number: 27

27 = 2 tens + 7 units

is the same as

The octal number: 33

33 = 3 eights + 3 units

Now consider how to convert from decimal to octal. Given an integer number i, then the number is

$$i=j*8+r$$

where j is the integer quotient i/8, and r the remainder. Therefore j is the number of eights and r the number of units. In other words the number of units is the remainder after division by 8. Now consider the eights digit. There are j eights, but j might well be greater than or equal to eight and so another remainder is taken. And so on.

EXAMPLE:

Convert 107 decimal to octal.

107/8	=	13 remainder 3
13/8	=	1 remainder 5
1/8	=	0 remainder 1

Consequently 107 decimal is the same as 153 octal.

A computer program could be written to do this. It reads in the decimal number and proceeds to convert it to octal, printing each digit as it finds it. This means that the digits are printed in reverse order but for the time being that is acceptable. The program, whose flowchart is Fig. 3.6, is

```
      PRINT*,'TYPE IN DECIMAL NO.'
      READ*,I
      PRINT*,'OCTAL EQUIVALENT FOLLOWS'
      PRINT*,'DIGITS IN REVERSE ORDER'
10    J=I/8
      K=I-J*8
      PRINT*,K
      I=J
      IF(I.NE.0)GO TO 10
      END
```

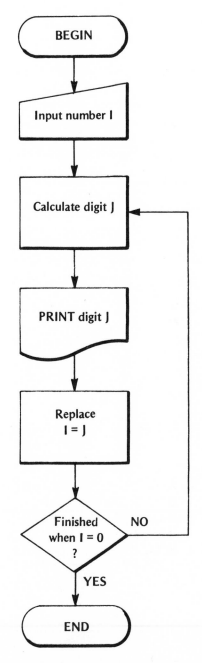

Fig. 3.6. Flowchart for the conversion of decimal numbers to another base.

Note that as each digit is calculated, the quotient becomes the dividend for the next stage. This is similar to the redefinition of i and j referred to in the previous exercise. If it gave difficulties then, it should be clear now.

EXERCISE:
   Write a program to convert a decimal number to any base from 2 to 9.

3.7 Intrinsic functions for integers

FORTRAN provides functions giving integer results for integer values. There are relatively few of these, but some are very useful. Of particular note is the MOD function which calculates exactly the remainder after integer division that has been used so often in this chapter. Thus

$$I-(I/J)*J$$

is the same as

$$MOD(I,J)$$

The full list is given in Table 3.1. In full FORTRAN 77 the generic name should be used - as long as the argument is integer the result will be integer.

EXERCISE:
   Rewrite the programs for the Euclid algorithm and base conversion by using the MOD function.

3.8 Calendars

Of the many fascinating applications of integer arithmetic, the last to be considered here is the problem of calculations in the calendar we are using now. Calendars are complicated by the need to divide the solar year, which is the length of time taken for the earth to circle the sun, into days, each of which is the mean time of rotation of the earth about its axis, in such a way that the new year always falls on the same date. This is complicated by the historical grouping of days into weeks, and into months for essentially super-stitious reasons. The problems are even more intricate when the period of the moon has to be taken into account, as can be discovered in one of the problems at the end of this chapter.

(i) Day of the Year

Perhaps the simplest calendar calculation is to find the "day number" given the date ID,IM,IY as the day of the month, month, and year. Normally day number 1 would be taken as January 1, but to avoid the leap year problem temporarily, it can be assumed that day 1 is March 1. Represent the month by a false value

---

* If the reader thinks this is all too academic for words, this section may be omitted without missing any FORTRAN.

Generic Name	Specific Name	Meaning
ABS(I)	IABS(I)	Absolute value of I
DIM(I,J)	IDIM(I,J)	Positive difference I−MIN(I,J)
MAX(I,J,...)	MAX0(I,J,...)	Maximum value of I,J,...
MIN(I,J,...)	IMIN(I,J,...)	Minimum value of I,J,...
MOD(I,J)	MOD(I,J)	Remainder of I/J, i.e. I−(I/J)*J
SIGN(I,J)	ISIGN(I,J)	Transfer of sign; sign of J times ABS(I)

Table 3.1. Intrinsic integer functions of integer arguments.

M1 which counts March as month 1. The day of the month is called ID. Hence June 10 would be ID=10 and M1=4.

The day number of the beginning of each month behaves as follows:

April 1	is March 1	+28+3
May 1	is April 1	+28+2
June 1	Is May 1	+28+3
July 1	is June 1	+28+2
August 1	is July 1	+28+3
September 1	is August 1	+28+3
October 1	is September 1	+28+2
November 1	is October 1	+28+3
December 1	is November 1	+28+2
January 1	is December 1	+28+3
February 1	is January 1	+28+3

A German gentleman by the name of Zeller* (1824-1899) discovered that the irregular digit in this sequence adds on

$$(13*M1-1)/5-2$$

extra days from the months before M1, and so the number of days counting from March 1 is

$$ID+28*(M1-1)+(13*M1-1)/5-2$$

Now for this to work in practice, the false number M1 for the month has to be calculated. Recalling that the real number of a month is IM, then

$$M1=MOD(IM+9,12)+1$$

To calculate the day number, simply take the day of the month, ID, add 28 days for each month and Zeller's congruence for the irregular days:

---

*This wonderful amateur number theorist is often referred to as the Rev. Zeller but it is the opinion of the splendid amateur digital historian P.W.Throsby that this is the result of a mistranslation and confusion with a different Zeller. Our man, Christian Zeller, was a school inspector and director of a Womens Teacher Training College (Lehrerinnen Seminars). His classic paper, very short and in Latin, was presented on 16 March 1883 and is printed in the Bulletin of the Mathematical Society of France.

```
M1=MOD(IM+9,12)+1
I1=(13*M1-1)/5-2
IDAY=ID+59+28*(M1-1)+I1
```

Unfortunately January and February are treated like part of next year. To get around this, it is necessary to subtract 365 days if the month is January or February, as follows:

$$IDAY=IDAY-365*(M1/11)$$

Note how the term M1/11 makes this happen. The only thing left is to take account of the possibility that the year, IY, is a leap year.

For any year in the 20th century, a year is a leap year if the year number can be divided exactly by 4, i.e. if MOD(IYR,4) is zero, where IYR is the year. This means that one day has to be added to the day number for leap years, and at first glance this might suggest an IF statement. However, looking at it another way, it would be just as correct to add 1 on to all years and take it away again in non-leap years except in January and February; actually this is more efficient. It is possible to form a number NOLEAP:

$$NOLEAP=MIN(1,MOD(IYR,4))$$

which is 0 in a leap year and 1 otherwise. Similarly the value JORF

$$JORF=M1/11$$

is 1 for the months January or February and 0 otherwise. Here, then, is the clever procedure for calculating the day number of any day in any year except exact centuries:

```
READ*,ID,IM,IYR
M1=MOD(IM+9,12)+1
I1=(13*M1-1)/5-2
JORF=M1/11
IDAY=ID+60+28*(M1-1)+I1-366*JORF
NOLEAP=MIN(1,MOD(IYR,4))
IDAY=IDAY-NOLEAP+NOLEAP*JORF
PRINT*,'DAY NO. THIS YEAR',IDAY
```

(ii) Leap Years

The Gregorian calendar, now universally used, was formulated in 1582, and caused a number of interesting effects when implemented, the most famous being riots in England in 1752 because some people believed their lives would be shortened by the removal of 11 days. In most of Europe the Gregorian Calendar was adopted in 1582 but in England, not until 1752. Because the Julian and Gregorian Calendars treat exact centuries differently, they started 10 days apart, but became 11 days apart on 29 Feb 1700 which occurred in the Julian Calendar but not in the Gregorian one. Since the introduction of the Gregorian Calendar, common years have consisted of 365 days and leap years 366 days. Every year divisible by 4 is a leap year except centuries, which are leap years only if divisible by 400. Quite often one is interested in the number of elapsed days between two events which may be in different years. So it is useful to reformulate the day number calculation to calculate the number of days elapsed since, say, March 1 1600 and any other date. The number of days, NDAYS will be

```
NDAYS = 365 * no. of years
          + no. of leap years
          + no. of days this year
```

To implement this, first get the number of full years between 1 March 1600 and the last March, which is:

$$NYR=IYR-1600-M1/11$$

The number of leap years that have occurred in that period will be:

$$LEAPS=NYR/4-NYR/100+NYR/400$$

The number of days since the last March is easily extracted from the previous calculation, to give the final result

```
M1=MOD(IM+9,12)+1
I1=(13*M1-1)/5-2
IDAY=ID+28*(M1-1)+I1
NYR=IYR-1600-M1/11
LEAPS=NYR/4-NYR/100+NYR/400
NDAYS=IDAY+365*NYR+LEAPS
```

The choice of 1 March 1600 as a reference is a happy one since 1600 was the first centurial leap year after the calendar was reformed (the next one is 2000, coming soon). It might be useful to add 2,415,079 to NDAYS which would make the day numbers the same as in the Julian Calendar, in which the day numbers are counted from the official begining of the world. Some computers are unable to accommodate the large integers which may arise in this calculation.

(iii) Day of the Week.

All the hard work has been done to enable the day of the week to be extracted. 1 March 1600 was a Wednesday, and every seventh day since has been as well. It is fairly obvious that the remainder of NDAYS/7 was 1 on that day, and would be 1 again every 7 days forever afterwards. Therefore if Sunday through Saturday are numbered 0 to 6, then the day of the week is:

$$IWK=MOD(NDAYS+2,7)$$

The following program uses this information to tell the user the day of the week.

```
C WORK OUT THE DAY OF THE
C WEEK FOR ANY GREGORIAN DATE
C FROM 1 MARCH 1600
C
C ASK FOR DATE
C
  10 PRINT*,'ENTER DATE ID,IM,IYR'
     READ*,ID,IM,IYR
     M1=MOD(IM+9,12)+1
     I1=(13*M1-1)/5-2
     IDAY=ID+28*(M1-1)+I1
     NYR=IYR-1600-M1/11
     LEAPS=NYR/4-NYR/100+NYR/400
     NDAYS=IDAY+365*NYR+LEAPS
     IWK=MOD(NDAYS+2,7)
     PRINT*,'WEEKDAY IS ',IWK
     GO TO 10
     END
```

EXERCISE:

On the planet OCTAVIAN there are eight days in a week and eight months in a year. Unfortunately the year is 271.1328125 days long. Devise a calendar for these people who, incidentally, count their years in the octal number system. Actually, this is quite easy, particularly if you put their leap year in Octember and note the simple decomposition of that nasty fraction. Write a program to find the number of days between two dates, and print the weekday of both given dates. Computer programmers have it easy on OCTAVIAN. However, there are eight moons and eight sexes which makes Easter a rather complicated festival.

3.9 Problems

PROBLEM 3.1:

Write a program to find the least common multiple of two numbers. It would be wise to start by relating this to the greatest common divisor.

PROBLEM 3.2:

Another interesting kind of number is the prime number. This is an integer which cannot be divided exactly by any smaller integer except, of course, 1. The first few primes are 1, 2, 3, 5, 7, 11, 13, 17, ... The brute force method to find out if a number is prime is to try dividing it by all integers less than itself except 1. In fact it is sufficient to try 2 and the odd ones up to the square root of the number. Write a program to find out if a number is prime.

PROBLEM 3.3:

The same problem, from a different point of view. Find all factors of a number N. Each time a factor is found, say I, then N is replaced by N/I and the search continues starting with I again. This way only the prime factors will be found. Think about where it should stop.

PROBLEM 3.4:

Three calendar calculations. By turning the calculations around, can you calculate:

(i) The date, given the day number from 1 March 1600?

(ii) The dates on which a given weekday will occur in a given month and year - e.g. on what dates do Thursdays occur in March 1984?

(iii) The years in which a particular date will fall on a given weekday, e.g. in what years will your birthday fall on a Sunday? It had better be limited to a given century.

PROBLEM 3.5:

Fermat's last theorem stated that there were no integer solutions other than 0 to

$$x^n + y^n = z^n$$

for $n>2$. Various proofs have been claimed and no-one has ever found a solution which disproves it. So don't waste your time trying to find a solution of

$$x^3 + y^3 = z^3$$

but find all solutions of the right angled triangle with integer sides

$$x^2 + y^2 = z^2$$

with $z<100$. For example

$$3^2 + 4^2 = 5^2$$

is a solution known and used in surveying since ancient times.

PROBLEM 3.6:

A perfect number is one whose factors other than itself add up to itself, i.e.

6=1+2+3
28=1+2+4+7+14

Euclid rather spoiled things by giving a formula for all the even ones. Find an odd perfect number.

PROBLEM 3.7:

The "Chinese Remainder Theorem" is a useful encoding method. Take a set of positive integers which are mutually prime in pairs, i.e. for which the greatest common divisor is one. For example, 3, 4, and 5. Using these integers a three digit code is formed for any number N by

$$ICODE1=MOD(N,3)$$
$$ICODE2=MOD(N,4)$$
$$ICODE3=MOD(N,5)$$

which is unique for any range of 3*4*5 successive numbers. This system means, for the given example, that no two numbers from 1 to 60 give the same code.

Write a program to encode a number from 1 to 52 using factors 4 and 13. Suppose this is a deck of cards and N is the order of the cards while

$$ISUIT=MOD(N,4)$$

represents clubs, diamonds, hearts, spades as 0, 1, 2, 3 and

$$ICARD=MOD(N,13)$$

represents 2, 3, ..., J, Q, A.

What order are the cards in?

Now write a program to "decode", i.e. given the suit and the name of the card, calculate its place in the deck. This is more difficult.

PROBLEM 3.8:
Working out the date of Easter is quite a tricky business. By decision of the Council of Nicea in 325, Easter is celebrated on the Sunday immediately following the first full moon which occurs on or after March 21. Being unaware of the earth's rotation, they thought that midnight occurred simultaneously everywhere, whereas in fact a full moon could occur on March 20th in Rome, near midnight, when it was already March 21st in Jerusalem. This could create a month's uncertainty in the date of Easter. Unfortunately, the Church does not apply actual astronomical data to this rule to calculate the date of Easter. Rather, a formula was devised and has been applied blindly ever since. I telephoned the Royal Greenwich Observatory to get the data for this problem and they told me that their (highly scientific) method for predicting the date of Easter was to look in the Book of Common Prayer.

However, the moon was full on Friday, 5 October 1979 at 35.32 minutes past 19:00 Greenwich mean time, and the mean period for the moon's phases can be taken as 29.53059 days.

Devise a method for computing the Gregorian date of Easter for any year, assuming the critical observations are based on Greenwich mean time. To do this, work out the phase of the moon at 00:00 GMT on 21 March, move forward to the next full moon and then move forward to the next Sunday. Recently, Easter was held on the wrong date according to these calculations. When?

4

Using reals and integers together

4.1 Introduction

The previous two chapters have been concerned with the two most common types of numbers, reals and integers, taken in isolation. It has been seen that there are differences in the nature and behaviour of these two types and so the characteristics of each are exploited in different ways by FORTRAN programmers. Because real numbers carry decimal places, they are used in calculations which require variables to take on a continuous range of values, i.e. any number on the number line of Fig.4.1 - although this is not quite so, as discussed later in this chapter. Integers, on the other hand, take on only exact whole numbered values; in theory between any two integers there are an infinite number of reals. Integers lend themselves naturally to counting and indexing. Also, integer numbers behave in a useful way under the operation of division, and this with the concept of the remainder or MOD function has powerful applications. A few were discussed in Chapter 3.

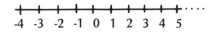

Fig. 4.1. The real number line.

Now the use of integers and reals together is considered and it will be found that the conversion from one to the other is another useful operation. This idea leads to a consideration of the expressions containing mixtures of both reals and integers and how FORTRAN deals with them. A number of questions arise about the nature of numbers and arithmetic on computers and this again leads to some useful ideas about FORTRAN programming.

4.2 More about variables

The use of FORTRAN variables has been demonstrated many times. It is now familiar, or should be, that a variable in FORTRAN has a name, of up to 6 alphanumeric characters, meaning letters and digits, and that the first is always a letter.

Every variable also has a type. Most FORTRAN programs employ real and integer types, but there are others with special uses which are introduced later on. The type of a variable name is implied by its spelling; there are ways of changing this. For the present it is correct to consider that variable names beginning with the letters I, J, K, L, M, or N are of type integer. A variable name beginning with any other letter is of type real.

Every variable has a value. This value could be defined or it could be undefined. A value could come to be defined in many ways, for example in an assignment statement. At the beginning of a program every variable is undefined unless special steps have been taken to predefine it. It must be defined before its first use in a context referring to its value; for example, it cannot appear on the right hand side of an assignment statement until it has been defined. So far only two ways of defining the value of a variable have been introduced.

These are:

(i) In an assignment statement

variable = expression

The "variable" is defined as the value of "expression", which must not refer to any undefined values.

(ii) In a list directed READ statement

READ*, list

The variables in "list" will be redefined by the input unless the user has deliberately avoided redefining them by an empty input field or a /. This could leave variables undefined if they had not been previously defined.

4.3 Functions for type conversion — generic functions explained

Tables 2.1 and 3.1 listed all the functions specified in the FORTRAN 77 standard which are real functions of real arguments and integer functions of integer arguments. A number of other functions are for conversion of type and once they have been introduced all the standard functions for reals and integers are known. There are more to come, however, because the types character, complex, and double precision all have access to functions. Table 4.1 lists all the conversion functions for reals and integers.

Under certain circumstances a programmer may decide, in the course of writing an expression, that he wants the type of an expression converted, and these functions are for that purpose. The conversion from real to integer is available in two forms:

(i) Truncation

The INT function truncates or chops the decimal places away from a real number in order to convert it. Therefore

INT(63.8) is 63
INT(-19.7) is -19

There are situations in which a programmer may not want this but would wish to find the next lowest integer. He could achieve this in various ways, for example

MIN(INT(X),INT(X+SIGN(1.∅,X)))

Perhaps the reader could devise something simpler. AINT (in Table 2.1) does the same truncation as INT but produces a real result.

(ii) Rounding

The function NINT is used to take a real number to the nearest whole integer, and this is the familiar rounding operation. Accordingly,

Generic Name	Specific Name	Meaning
INT(X)	INT(X) IFIX(X)	Conversion of real X to integer by truncation. INT(5.2)=5; INT(-3.5)=-3.
NINT(X)	NINT(X)	Nearest integer to X, i.e. this function rounds X. INT(X+SIGN(0.5,X)).
REAL(I)	REAL(I) FLOAT(I)	Conversion of integer I to a real value.

Table 4.1. Conversion functions of FORTRAN for reals and integers. X is a real argument, I is an integer argument.

```
NINT(63.8)   is    64
NINT(63.1)   is    63
NINT(-19.4)  is   -19
NINT(-19.7)  is   -2Ø
```

and in fact

```
        NINT(X)
```

is the same as

```
        INT(X+SIGN(Ø.5,X))
```

It is quite likely that some readers are puzzled by the use of generic and specific names of functions. The FORTRAN 77 standard recommends that users of the full language should begin to refer to functions by their generic names, which are introduced to FORTRAN 77 for the first time, with the objective that the specific names will eventually be abolished.

The essence of a generic name is that the one name covers the equivalent operation for all types of arguments. Taking the ABS function as a simple example, and just for a moment considering types which are not introduced yet, the language provides

```
Generic    Specific
Name       Name

ABS(a)     ABS(X)     Real X
           IABS(I)    Integer I
           CABS(C)    Complex C
           DABS(D)    Double Precision D
```

The generic name is supposed to cover all specific uses. Therefore

```
        ABS(X)   is a real function of
                 the real variable X
```

```
        ABS(I)   is an integer function of
                 the integer variable I
```

although the specific name IABS could be used instead. Therefore although ABS would appear at first sight to be the name of something real, it is in fact something real, or integer, or double precision depending on the type of its argument. However not every generic function covers every possible type. For example SQRT can have a real, complex, or double precision argument, but not an integer one. That is why SQRT does not appear in Table 3.1 (integer functions of integer arguments). If an argument is an expression, then it becomes important to know how to predict the type of an expression, and this is the topic of the next section.

It is important to realize one further thing about generic functions. Although the type of the argument is now left up to the programmer, some of the functions take several arguments and these must all be of the same type. Therefore

```
        MOD(I,J)   is an integer function
                   of integer arguments
```

```
        MOD(X,Y)   is a real function
                   of real arguments
```

```
        MOD(I,X)
        MOD(X,J)   are both forbidden
```

All this is very well unless your computer is restricted to the allowed subset of FORTRAN 77, in which case the types of the function and its arguments must be specific, and so the specific names must be used.

4.4 The type of expressions

Another facility that should have become familiar in Chapters 1 and 2 is the formation of expressions combining both variables and references to functions with the arithmetic operations available in FORTRAN. It should come as no surprise that every expression also has a type. Discussion of this has been delayed deliberately so that this important attribute can be considered from a point of view which is informed about the distinction between reals and integers for constants, variables and functions.

Clearly an expression involving only integer terms is of type integer, or to use the correct terminology, an integer expression. Similarly an expression involving only real terms is a real expression. A term of an expression could be a variable, or a constant, or a function, and knowledge of the types of these is therefore important. It should be recalled that the result of raising a real number to an integer exponent is considered to be real, i.e.

$$X**7 \quad \text{is real}$$

Furthermore, raising an integer to a real power, which was once forbidden, is now permitted and is real - the integer is converted to real first and so the result has meaning.

$$I**SQRT(2.\emptyset) \text{ is real}$$

It remains to define what happens if an expression is a mixture of real and integer terms. In this case it is always a real expression. How it comes to be evaluated is an important question to be considered very shortly.

EXAMPLES:
The following expressions involve only integer terms and are therefore integer expressions:

$$I-(I/J)*J$$

$$4*I1+MOD(I2,7)$$

$$ABS(MAX(I,\emptyset)-MIN(I,J))$$

The latter is a generic function which is integer because it uses an integer argument.

EXAMPLES:
The following expressions involve only real terms and are therefore real expressions:

$$B*B-4.\emptyset*A*C$$

$$Y+SQRT(Z)$$

$$X**2+Y**2$$

$$LOG(X)-LOG(Y)$$

The latter expression is real by virtue of its use of LOG with a real argument.

EXAMPLES:
The following expressions are real because they contain real terms among the integer terms:

$$X+4$$

$$-4-SQRT(16-4*A*C)/(2*A)$$

$$4+MOD(X,Y)+MOD(I,J)$$

$$4**SQRT(2.\emptyset)$$

In the above, the use of MOD with real arguments implies a real result. An integer to a real power is a real term.

4.5 Evaluation of expressions

The way that FORTRAN evaluates its arithmetic expressions is really quite straightforward. Programmers are allowed to mix real and integer terms in expressions but this freedom allows them to make some very fundamental mistakes where division is concerned and so the careful programmer always thinks of the type of his expressions as he writes them. Of course an expression which includes real and integer terms will always wind up as a real expression, but along the way integer operations can occur and so a programmer must be sure that when he writes an integer division he really means it.

Before an expression is evaluated all variables involved in it must be defined. If they are not, first of all the result of the expression is unpredictable and secondly the computer is likely to reject it. It will also be rejected if impossible operations are called for, such as division by zero, raising a zero valued quantity to a zero or negative power, and the raising of a negative number to a real power. If these catastrophes occur there is something very wrong with the program, and this is a programmer's fault.

The computer may actually reorganize the order of an expression in order to evaluate it more efficiently. It is possible that a programmer has written his expression in a special order for reasons of accuracy or to control the size of the values taken as the expression develops. For example, he may write

$$X=A+B-C$$

knowing that there will be no trouble but that doing A-C first could produce an accuracy problem as is discussed later.

However the computer is permitted to do

$$X=A-C+B$$

and this would cause that particular program to do what the programmer knows is wrong. This problem can be avoided by knowing that the computer is not permitted to violate the integrity of parentheses, in other words given

$$X=A+(B-C)$$

it must evaluate (B-C) before adding it to A.

In evaluating an expression, an integer quantity will be converted to a real value if it is about to be involved in an operation and the other operand is real. Bearing in mind the usual priority of operations, in which exponentiation comes before multiplication or division, which in turn come before addition or subtraction, a programmer can work out how the conversions are going to take place.

EXAMPLES:
In the expression

$$I**2/2.0$$

the term I**2 will be carried out as an integer operation, with the result converted to a real before being divided by 2.0. This is a consequence of the priority of exponentiation over division and has nothing to do with the order in which the terms were written.

Given

$$X*J**Y$$

J**Y is a real expression by definition, and J is converted to real before the exponentiation occurs.

This one

$$4*J+X$$

presents no problems either. 4*J will be done as integers, the result converted to real and added to X.

Here a program may be in trouble:

$$Y+INDEX/7$$

It depends on what is intended. The term INDEX/7 is done as an integer division and so the result may be truncated. If this was intended, so be it. However the programmer might just be careless. Perhaps he meant

$$Y+INDEX/7.0$$

in which case he should have written it like that. We hope he didn't mean

$$(Y+INDEX)/7.0$$

A discussion of program efficiency occurs later in this chapter and it will be seen there that writing

$$X/7$$

is rather a silly way of saving the effort of writing

$$X/7.0$$

and so a moral principle can be put forward:

> DO NOT WRITE INTEGER CONSTANTS IN REAL EXPRESSIONS UNLESS YOU REALLY MEAN IT

Why? Because it is inefficient and in the case of division it could be catastrophic.

4.6 Applications of conversion and truncation

The author is aware that he has devoted several pages to an important but partly philosophical discussion of the implications of type in forming arithmetic expressions. This will shortly be put right. In this section some useful applications of conversion will be explored. The generic functions REAL, INT, and NINT have been introduced. The two functions for real to integer conversion, INT and NINT, truncate the real numbers they are converting in two different ways. NINT is the one whose usefulness is more immediately obvious as it rounds its real argument to the nearest whole number. The expression

$$NINT(X)$$

is the same as

$$INT(X+SIGN(\emptyset.5,X))$$

as has already been described. However, conversion can be done in another way, using instead an arithmetic statement. The proper description of the assignment statement

$$variable = expression$$

is the following: the "expression" is evaluated according to the rules of FORTRAN and then its value is assigned to the "variable" after conversion to the same type as the variable if necessary. Conversion in this case is the same as would be obtained from

$$INT(expression)$$

and so the statement

$$J=X$$

gives exactly the same result as the statement

$$J=INT(X)$$

Therefore there are two ways of obtaining the same truncation. Similarly an assignment statement can be used to obtain the same result as NINT would give.

EXERCISE:
  Work out:

(i) an assignment statement without using INT or NINT gives the same result as

$$NINT(X)$$

(ii) an assignment statement which truncates to the next lower integer. Perhaps you can think of a better way of doing it than in section 3 of this chapter.

EXAMPLE:
  Back on the Indianapolis racetrack, suppose the average speed of a car has been announced and of course the race is over 500 miles. A spectator wants to work out the total elapsed time in hours, minutes and seconds.

It is easy to get the hours, called HOURS. This is just

$$HOURS=5\emptyset\emptyset.\emptyset/SPEED$$

And so you know the time in hours, TH:

$$TH=INT(HOURS)$$

although since you want it in integer form it would be just as well to call it IH;

$$IH=HOURS$$

which is the same thing because of the conversion that will take place in the assignment statement. Now you want the bit left over. There are several ways of getting it; here are two:

$$REST=HOURS-INT(HOURS)$$

or

$$REST=HOURS-IH$$

The second looks simpler and involves less work for the computer. Why?

Now REST is a fraction of an hour and should be converted minutes. You do that and call it XMIN. Then if you write

```
IM=XMIN
REST=XMIN-IM
```

you now have REST as a fraction of a minute. You convert this to seconds, XSEC, and finally the program says

```
PRINT*,'TIME WAS ',IH,IM,XSEC
```

How clever. What you have actually done is take a decimal number in hours and convert it to a mixed base system where whole units are in decimal and fractions are in 1/60ths and 1/3600ths.

EXERCISE:

Code this into a nice program with prompts, comments and a flowchart. You will find that you want to combine some of the operations. Run it and check that for 180 mph you get 2 hours 46 minutes and 40 seconds.

You may at this point like to glance at the Problems 4.1 to 4.3. You should feel confident in your ability to do them. Fine, then select one and do it now.

4.7 What is an integer, really?

(i) Question Answered

The answer to this question is that an integer in a computer is actually an integer. The computer has in its memory a large number of storage cells of a fixed length, and one or more of these side by side make up the integer. The cells are made up of smaller cells called bits which are either on or off. The memory of a computer is just like an array of lights that can be turned on or off - that is how the machine defines the value of an integer. The computer

---

* If you don't care, skip it. The next section with vital information about FORTRAN in it is 4.10.

works in the binary number system with on=1 and off=0. Suppose for simplicity that a cell has 8 bits and this is the size of an integer. If this were the case, it would usually be said that the computer was "byte" organized and that the integer was one byte long. Fig.4.2 illustrates the integer in binary. Each bit stands for a digit of the binary number except that the one on the left is reserved for the special purpose of telling the machine when the integer is negative. If the leftmost, or "most significant" bit is 1, the number is negative.

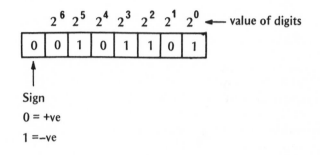

Fig. 4.2. A one byte integer.

The value of the number illustrated by Fig.4.2 can be worked out by reading from left to right and counting the digits which are turned "on":

$$2^5+2^3+2^2+2^0$$

$$= 32+8+4+1 = 45$$

This should illustrate why computers are called digital computers and why the binary number system is so important to them.

This also means that in FORTRAN the range of an integer is limited by the number of bits used to store it. This 8-bit example can count in positive numbers up to

$$2^6+2^5+2^4+2^3+2^2+2^1+2^0 = 127$$

before invading the sign position and spoiling the result. In general, the largest integer allowed in a computer is

$$2^{n-1}-1$$

where n is the number of bits used by the computer for integers. If n is not known it is possible to find out by running a FORTRAN program:

```
C FIND SIZE OF INTEGERS
C TURN ON SMALLEST BIT
      ITEST=1
      NBITS=1
C DOUBLE TILL TROUBLE
   10 NBITS=NBITS+1
      ITEST=ITEST*2
      IF(ITEST.GT.0)GO TO 10
C PRINT THE ANSWER
      PRINT*,'NO. OF BITS ',NBITS
      PRINT*,'OVERFLOW IS ',ITEST
      END
```

This starts with the number 1 which is 2^0 and by doubling it, moves that bit left until it enters the sign position. The cell size is then printed and so is the value of the negative number that is represented by the first bit on and all others off, which will be important. A flowchart is given in Fig.4.3.

It is interesting that most well behaved computers will reveal their secrets to this program although this is an example of a machine dependent program.

One thing to observe, and this is generally true, is that multiplying by 2 is the same as shifting to the left all bits, with zero coming in at the right hand end. This is easily understood if it is realized that each bit represents a digit, $2^{**}K$ say, that becomes $2^{**}(K+1)$ when multiplied by 2. Actually this has been demonstrated only for positive numbers and may not be the case for negative ones as will be seen. It is also true that dividing a positive number by 2 moves it to the right and loses the right hand bit.

(ii) Multiplication of Integers

Computers perform addition using circuitry which is inexpensive and fast; subtraction is much the same. But multiplication is more complicated because it is always a process of repeated addition. Suppose I is to be multiplied by J. The answer is either I added up J times or J added up I times, starting with 0. It is easy to conceive of a computer which cannot multiply in any way except through successive addition. Here, therefore, is a program to multiply I by J:

```
C MULTIPLY BY BRUTE FORCE
C ACCEPT I AND J TO MULTIPLY
      PRINT*,'GIVE TWO INTEGERS'
      READ*,I,J
      I1=MIN(I,J)
      I2=MAX(I,J)
      IPROD=0
C ACCUMULATE THE PRODUCT
   10 IPROD=IPROD+I2
      I1=I1-1
      IF(I1.GT.0)GO TO 10
C PRINT THE RESULT
      PRINT*,'PRODUCT IS ',IPROD
      END
```

Two things are immediately striking. One, a side issue: Fig.4.4 is rather like Fig.4.3 and so are many other programs of the form initialize, calculate until finished, end. Consequently it is assumed that you can by now read simple programs like these without referring to flowcharts. Secondly, the program has its faults - it will not work for the number 0 or negative ones although one good idea is used in the choice of I1 and I2. It is left to the reader to discover why.

Before rushing into the question of extending this program to negative numbers, it is instructive to look again at how it works. Suppose I=5 and J=10. Then we have added J five times. So the answer is

$$IPROD=5*J$$

which is the same as

$$(2^2+2^0)*J$$

$$=2^2*J+J \quad =4*J+J$$

Now this would involve only two additions if it were possible to discover how to do it. Well, it is easy, for

If I is odd add J
If I/2 is odd add J*2
If I/4 is odd add J*4

and so on until I disappears to zero. In FORTRAN:

```
C MULTIPLY BY SHIFTING
C POSITIVE NONZERO NUMBERS
C ACCEPT I AND J TO MULTIPLY
      PRINT*,'GIVE TWO INTEGERS'
      READ*,I,J
      I1=MIN(I,J)
      I2=MAX(I,J)
      IPROD=Ø
```

```
1Ø LSB=MOD(I1,2)
      IF(LSB.EQ.1)IPROD=IPROD+I2
      I1=I1/2
      I2=I2*2
      IF(I1.GT.Ø)GO TO 1Ø
C PRINT THE RESULT
      PRINT*,'PRODUCT IS ',IPROD
      END
```

Here, I1 is shifted to the right by division by 2 and I2 to the left by multiplication by 2. This is begging the

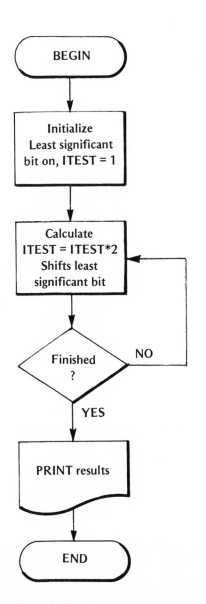

Fig. 4.3. Finding the integer size.

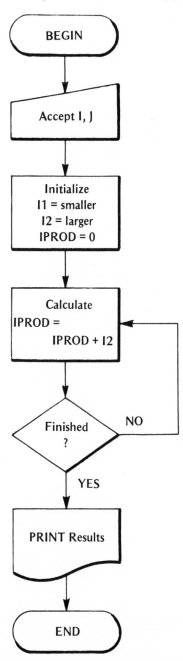

Fig. 4.4. Multiply two numbers.

question slightly because to multiply with adding involves multiplication and division by 2. This, however, is how all computers do multiplication; expensive ones with circuitry and inexpensive ones with hidden programs which have special shift instructions. Whenever an expression in FORTRAN includes a *, this is what happens, at least for positive numbers.

One final comment about this multiplication is that it is quite possible to multiply two modest integers together and produce an answer which is too large. In the 8-bit representation of Fig.4.2, the largest positive number was 127. This means that if 45 were multiplied by 3 a disaster would occur. In real life, as can be discerned by running the program to probe for the largest number, the largest number is usually much bigger. Even so, if the computer uses n bits for integers, two numbers which are $2^{**}(n/2)$ or bigger will always overflow when multiplied together.

```
YOUR COMPUTER WILL NOT TELL
YOU WHEN THIS HAPPENS IN
AN INTEGER MULTIPLICATION
SO WATCH IT !
```

The computer will not complain if a program does this. Why not? Because some people do it on purpose as will the program in Section 4.8.

(iii) Division of Integers

Now division. This is a process of successive subtraction although when it starts the program has no way of knowing how many times to do this — that after all is the answer. Here it is:

```
C DIVISION BY BRUTE FORCE METHOD
C ACCEPT NUMERATOR,DENOMINATOR
      PRINT*,'GIVE TWO INTEGERS'
      PRINT*,'FIRST NUMERATOR'
      PRINT*,'THEN DENOMINATOR'
      READ*,ITOP,IBOT
```

```
      IQUOT=-1
1Ø    IQUOT=IQUOT+1
      ITOP=ITOP-IBOT
      IF(ITOP.GT.Ø)GO TO 1Ø
      ITOP=ITOP+IBOT
      PRINT*,'QUOTIENT ',IQUOT
      PRINT*,'REMAINDER ',ITOP
      END
```

EXERCISE:
Since this whole section is optional, it follows that this exercise is too. However, you have here the chance to discover how computers do division. Consider what happens overall and devise a shifting scheme to reduce the work. Multiplication or division by these methods involves at most n steps for an n-bit integer, which is vastly better than the brute force method. Admittedly the division step is a bit more complicated.

(iv) Negative Numbers

It has already been shown that a negative integer has a sign in the highest digit; the test program provided graphic evidence of this. Now it so happens that computers have three methods of representing negative numbers; the best way is the one that seems most complicated but isn't. Consider the number 45 again. What would appear to be the simplest representation is the "sign and magnitude" form, which according to numerologist D. M. Brookes is most like the way people think about numbers. The number 45 in binary was

$$00101101$$

and so in sign and magnitude notation, -45 is

$$10101101$$

All very well, but this has disadvantages that are easily recognized:

(i) The value of 0 is ambiguous because it can be +0 or -0. FORTRAN requires that there should be no such distinction; 0 is considered positive, for example in the SIGN function. This does not prevent the use of FORTRAN on such a computer but it makes life difficult for the compiler writer and the people who make the functions.

(ii) Division by two is not a simple shift - the sign bit has to be left where it is and the rest shifted.

(iii) In binary arithmetic using sign and magnitude form the difference I-J is not the same as I+(-J), in other words the positive and negative integers are not continuous. One should be able to add 1 to -1 by binary addition and get 0. This means that the circuitry of the sign and magnitude machine is more complex.

You can tell if your computer is a sign and magnitude machine by examining the printout from the program that found the number of bits in an integer. The value of the variable ITEST was also printed, and its binary pattern at that point was

$$100\ldots000$$

which a sign and magnitude machine thinks is 0 (or -0).

The next best method resolves two of these problems. Suppose a negative number is the same as a positive one with all the 1's changed to 0's and all the 0's changed to 1's. This is a bit like a photographic negative. Therefore looking at the number 45 again

$$45 = 00101101$$

$$-45 = 11010010$$

This representation is called 1's complement. Here it is easily seen that adding a positive and a negative number together gives the right answer. If 1 was added to -45, the process is:

$$-45 + 1 = 11010010 + 00000001$$

$$= 11010011 = -44$$

as can be verified by complementing the answer and adding up the digits. Actually the size of the number can be deduced by adding up the 0's as if they were 1's:

$$11010011$$

$$= -\left\{2^5 + 2^3 + 2^2\right\}$$

$$= -\left\{32 + 8 + 4\right\}$$

$$= -44$$

It is already know that adding two positive numbers works, but look at two negative ones in Fig. 4.5.

$$(-44) + (-1)$$

End carry	11010011	-44
	11111110	- 1
	11010001	-46 !!
	1	+1
	11010010	-45

Fig. 4.5. Addition of two negative 1's complement numbers.

The carries that arose in the addition have been marked. Although the answer is wrong, it can be corrected by adding one back in as can be seen. A computer which works in this form has circuitry to detect the end carry and add 1 if necessary. In fact, the end carry is added back in, and is called an end-around carry. This is not so expensive as all that, but it is inherently slower.

The division by two problem is cured but there are still two versions of 0,

$$0 = 00000000$$

$$-0 = 11111111$$

You can tell if your computer is a 1's complement one if the value of ITEST printed by that probing program was large and odd, in fact

$$-2^{n-1} + 1$$

where n is the bit length.

Finally to improve things still further, the best method for machines but the most difficult for humans is the 2's complement form. The 2's complement form is the 1's complement plus 1;

Find 2's complement of 45:

$$45 = 0\ 0\ 1\ 0\ 1\ 1\ 0\ 1$$

form 1's complement $1\ 1\ 0\ 1\ 0\ 0\ 1\ 0$

add 1 $\underline{\qquad\qquad 1}$

$$-45 = 1\ 1\ 0\ 1\ 0\ 0\ 1\ 1$$

in 2's complement

Find 2's complement of -45:

$$-45 = 1\ 1\ 0\ 1\ 0\ 0\ 1\ 1$$

form 1's complement $0\ 0\ 1\ 0\ 1\ 1\ 0\ 0$

add 1 $\underline{\qquad\qquad 1}$

$$45 = 0\ 0\ 1\ 0\ 1\ 1\ 0\ 1$$

Fig. 4.6. Finding the 2's complement.

It is easily verified that the addition of all kinds of numbers now works and so the end carry can be ignored. Furthermore adding one to any number produces the next one along (this wasn't true in 1's complement - try adding 1 to -0) so it is a method in which the integers form a continuous sequence from biggest negative to largest positive. Actually if 1 is added to the largest, it produces the biggest negative one again and so they "wrap around". FORTRAN will not stop you from doing this, so care is always required with integers particularly if the bit length of integers is not not so large.

In 2's complement form there is only one representation of 0;

$$1 \text{ is } 00000001$$

$$0 \text{ is } 00000000$$

$$-1 \text{ is } 11111111$$

You can tell if your computer is a 2's complement machine by the number that was printed when doubling forced your bit into the sign position. If the value printed was a large negative number that is even, you are the lucky user of a 2's complement machine. In fact the number is

$$-2^{n-1}$$

So is there any disadvantage? Yes; people have more trouble understanding it, and shifting a negative number to the right is not the same as the FORTRAN definition of division by 2.

This section ends with some practical results.

Let the number of bits per integer be n.

First: The range of integers is limited. On all types of computer the largest integer is

$$2^{n-1} - 1$$

On 2's complement machines the smallest is

$$-2^{n-1}$$

On the other types the smallest is

$$-2^{n-1} + 1$$

Second: The 2's complement is the 1's complement plus 1. This works either way round.

There is an alternative definition:

$$1\text{'s complement of } I = 2^{n-1} - I$$

$$2\text{'s complement of } I = 2^{n} - I$$

Third: shifting of the bits in a binary number is closely related to multiplication and division by 2. A shift in which the sign of the number remains the same is called an Arithmetic Shift. In an Arithmetic Shift the sign is propagated, i.e.

$$00011010 \text{ shifts to } 00001101$$

$$11100101 \text{ shifts to } 11110010$$

In any kind of left shift zeros enter the right hand end, i.e.

$$00011010 \text{ shifts to } 00110100$$

$$11100101 \text{ shifts to } 11001010$$

For positive numbers any kind of right shift is division by 2 and any kind of left shift is multiplication by 2.

For negative numbers it depends on the kind of arithmetic. In sign and magnitude form the arithmetic shift as defined above is not very useful. Multiplication and division by 2 shift everything but the sign.

In 1's complement division by two is the same as a right shift. Multiplication by two is not the same as a left shift; consider:

$$(-1)\qquad\qquad (-3)$$
11111110 shifted left is 11111100

$$(-2)\qquad\qquad (-4)$$
11111101 shifted left is 11111010

i.e. a shift can be achieved by multiplying by 2 and then subtracting 1. The following expression will do a left shift on a 1's complement machine of the number I:

    I=I*2+MIN(Ø,SIGN(1,I))

For a 2's complement machine the shifting situation is reversed. Multiplication by 2 now does work for left shifting:

$$(-1)\qquad\qquad (-2)$$
11111111 shifted left is 11111110

$$(-2)\qquad\qquad (-4)$$
11111110 shifted left is 11111100

but division does not work for right shifting of an odd number,

$$(-3)\qquad\qquad (-2)$$

11111101 shifted right is 11111110

and in FORTRAN on a 2's complement machine shifting right for all numbers I is like

    I=(I+MIN(Ø,MOD(I,2)))/2

EXERCISE:
Write these shifts out again using IF statements and decide which you prefer.

EXERCISE:
If you are still here, you can see why multiplication and division with signed numbers was not undertaken. Now try to generalize the multiply program for all cases. Perhaps it is a good thing that FORTRAN has the * operation to multiply for you, even if your computer has to do it the hard way.

4.8 A random number generator

It may come as a surprise that a very satisfactory method of producing a series of numbers that appear to be unrelated is to use a very predictable procedure. In many applications users wish to obtain a series of numbers which are unrelated. The simplest case is what is called a "rectangular distribution" in which the chance of any number occurring in a given range is the same as that of all the others.

Such numbers are easily generated using integer multiplication which is intentionally permitted to produce results which are too large for the machine. Let the random integer be I, and take a number called the "seed", ISEED, which is large, positive and odd. Then the next random number J is

$$J=I*ISEED$$

If I was originally also large and odd, the product is rubbish. But to a very good approximation doing this over and over again with a suitable choice of the seed causes the rubbish to appear to be a series of random numbers.

The complication is that the sign bit is quite likely to be left on by the "overflowing" multiply and this has to be got rid of - on a computer with n bits in each integer the random number is taken only from the last n-1 bits.

This is in general not quite the same as taking the absolute value because, as was seen in the previous section the pattern would be complemented. What is done depends on the type of the machine. On a sign and magnitude machine, simply take the absolute value

$$J = ABS(I*ISEED)$$

On a 1's complement machine, to get rid of the sign bit, do this:

$$IF(J.LT.\emptyset) \quad J = \left\{ 2^{n-1} - 1 \right\} + J$$

The constant $2^{n-1} - 1$ is precalculated. On a 2's complement computer this is not right (it would be catastrophic - do you know why?) and it should be:

$$IF(J.LT.\emptyset) \quad J = \left(\left\{ 2^{n-1} - 1 \right\} + J \right) + 1$$

with the parentheses used to control the order of evaluation, because the number $2^{n-1} + 1$ is too big for the machine. After doing this J is the new random number in the range 0 to $2^{n-1} - 1$ used to calculate the next one along.

The choice of seed is actually quite important and the whole question of the best random number generator is a topic of research. But a safe choice is always the largest power of 5 the machine can hold.

Random number generators must be machine dependent, because to make them work the number of bits in an integer and the type of machine must be known. The little program at the beginning of the previous section gives both pieces of information and so a "do it yourself random number kit" can be defined:

(i) The word length is n.

(ii) Work out $2^{n-1} - 1$ and call it IBIG.

(iii) Work out the seed. You seek to find k such that

$$5^k < 2^{n-1}$$

taking logs

$$k \log 5 < (n-1) \log 2$$

from which

$$k < (n-1) \log 2 / \log 5$$

in other words

```
K=(N-1)*LOG(2.Ø)/LOG(5.Ø)
ISEED=5**K
```

(iv) With IBIG and ISEED precalculated, the loop

```
      NEW=ISEED
1Ø    NEW=NEW*ISEED
2Ø    IF(NEW.LT.Ø)NEW=(IBIG+NEW)+1
      PRINT*,'NEXT NO. IS',NEW
      GO TO 1Ø
```

will produce an endless stream of random numbers on a 2's complement machine. On a 1's complement machine change statement 20 to

```
2Ø    IF(NEW.LT.Ø)NEW=IBIG+NEW
```

and on a sign and magnitude machine leave it out altogether but take the absolute value of NEW.

EXERCISE:
Install this kit on your computer. On most computers it should work, but it is assumed in all of this that when a multiplication exceeds the range of a computer, the 'rubbish' left over is a truncated (chopped off) form of the correct answer. If the computer does not work this way, a more sophisticated approach is needed.

If the method fails, use instead the following program, which should be safe on any 2's complement machine with at least 16 bits per integer. On a 1's complement machine, change IBIG to 16383, and it should again be safe.

```
C MAKE RANDOM NUMBERS IN RANGE
C 1 - 16383, SHOULD WORK ON ANY
C TWOS COMPLEMENT COMPUTER
      IBIG=16384
      ISEED=15625
      NEW=ISEED
```

```
C MULTIPLY UP TO NEW NUMBER
   1Ø NEW=NEW*ISEED
      NEW=MOD(NEW,16384)
C CORRECT IF NEGATIVE
      IF(NEW.LT.Ø)NEW= IBIG+NEW
      PRINT*,'NEXT NUMBER ',NEW
      GO TO 1Ø
      END
```

The disadvantage of this "safe" program is that the integer range is assumed to be limited. All random number generators will repeat eventually, and limiting the range of integers unnecessarily shortens the repetition length.

4.9 What is a real, really?

The answer to this question is going to be a surprise, and it mustn't be allowed to create massive disillusionment. In Section 4.7 it was seen that a computer is made up of words of fixed length. In a fixed number of bits, there is no way that a computer can actually represent all irrational or rational numbers. It can only represent some rational numbers. The answer to the question is

A REAL IS REALLY AN INTEGER

Now, don't cry please. If you can't take it, pretend it was never said; believe in reals and skip to Section 4.10.

A real number is really an integer, times an exponent. In other words the representation in the memory of the computer resembles the exponential form that can be used to write a real number in FORTRAN. In a 32-bit machine, one 8-bit byte is normally reserved for the exponent and the remaining 24 bits used for the integer part. In fact the integer part is always interpreted as a fraction and the number is considered as

---

* Again optional, although after the previous sections you should really feel enriched even if bothered and bewildered. Reals are even more complicated but this section does not delve very deeply.

$$\text{fraction x } 2^{\text{exponent}}$$

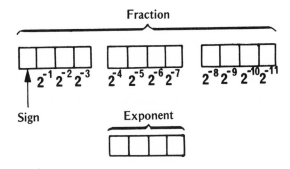

Fig. 4.7. Representation of Real Numbers in a computer.

A simplified diagram is shown in Fig.4.7, of only 16 bits in all. It can be seen that the bits of the fraction (apart from the sign bit) are used to represent

$$2^{-1}, \ 2^{-2}, \ 2^{-3}, \dots$$

$$\text{i.e. } 1/2 \ , \ 1/4 \ , \ 1/8 \ , \dots$$

Real numbers are usually stored so that the 1/2 position is filled and this way a 24-bit fraction always carries 23 bits of precision in the arithmetic of real numbers. It fact this is not as precise as all that, about 6 decimal digits, and for this reason many machines have longer representations. In FORTRAN the type called double precision allows twice the number of bits to be used, as revealed in Chapter 17.

EXAMPLES:

$$0.375 = 1/4 + 1/8 = 2^{-2} + 2^{-3}$$

and would be represented by

$$(2^{-1} + 2^{-2}) * 2^{-1}, \text{ i.e.}$$

$$0110 \ 0000 \ 0000 * 2^{-1}$$

in the representation of Fig. 4.7,

$$17 = 16 + 1 = 2^4 + 2^0$$

$$= (2^{-1} + 2^{-5}) * 2^5 , \text{ i.e.}$$

$$0100 \ 0100 \ 0000 * 2^5$$

In 2's complement, the number -1 is written:

$$1111\ 1111\ 1111 * 2^0$$

Note that it is not precise as it would take infinitely many digits to represent it properly as

$$-1/2\ -1/4\ -1/8\ -1/16...$$

EXERCISE:

Discover the range of real numbers allowed by your computer by starting with 2.0 and squaring until the number goes out of range. You are doubling the exponent each time you do that. When it overflows, search around for the actual maximum exponent. This is complicated by the fact that FORTRAN prints results in decimal so a bit of conversion is required (mentally). What does this tell you about the number of bits in the exponent? Now find the smallest exponent by square rooting around.

EXERCISE:

Now discover the precision of your real numbers. Take 0.0 and add on 1/2, 1/4, 1/8, etc. until the sum ceases to change. You now know how many bits the machine uses for the fraction.

It may be interesting to consider briefly how a computer goes about doing real arithmetic. To add or subtract is a bit tricky. The sum

$$n_1 \times 2^{e_1} + n_2 \times 2^{e_2}$$

is difficult to do if $e_1 \neq e_2$ because the fractions don't line up. Suppose $e_1 < e_2$; then the computer increases the exponent e_1, shifting n_1 right until it has

$$\left(\frac{n_1}{2^{e_2 - e_1}}\right) \times 2^{e_2} + n_2 \times 2^{e_2}$$

and it can then add the fractions. But bits of n_1 have been thrown away in the process. After doing this, it reshifts the result if necessary until the 1/2 position is filled. This is called normalization. Why this is done has already

been described. It is possible to lose a lot of precision by adding a small number to a large one, as in the exercise above, or equally by subtracting two real numbers which are nearly the same. Addition and subtraction of real numbers either requires expensive circuitry or takes a lot of time. A good measure of the likely price of a computer is that it varies inversely as the time taken to do real addition, other factors being equal, i.e.

$$\$ \propto 1/t_a$$

where $\$$ = the price, and t_a = the time taken to add two reals.

Multiplication and division are actually easier. For consider

$$n_1 \times 2^{e_1} \times n_2 \times 2^{e_2}$$

$$= n_1 \times n_2 \times 2^{\{e_1 + e_2\}}$$

which means that two real numbers are multiplied by multiplying the fractions and adding the exponents. Division is similar: divide fractions and subtract exponents, (the right way round, of course).

4.10 Accuracy

In this section the problems of accuracy that arise in calculations are discussed very briefly. It is essential that everyone who submits programs for computers in the real world should recognize that these problems exist, if only to be sure that they are not going to ruin their calculations.

With integers it is known that the results of integer arithmetic are absolutely precise and that as long as the meaning of integer division in FORTRAN is appreciated, no problem of precision arises. However there are problems of range, as discussed in Section 4.7, and the multiplication of two integers of unremarkable size can produce a result which is in error because it has exceeded the range of the computer. Less likely, but still possible, is the chance that a sum of two quite large integers of the same sign will go out of range and produce rubbish. In neither of these cases does the machine issue a warning - it simply carries on quietly.

With real numbers, the range is much greater and normally a calculation does not run into trouble - although it can. What is much more likely is that problems of precision will arise. The machine has a fixed and limited number of digits in its representation of a real number and this limits the accuracy that can be achieved. Hazardous calculations are not all that rare. To add numbers A and B which are widely different in size is dangerous and two examples are offered.

EXAMPLE:

The resonant frequency of an electrical circuit of resistance R and capacitance C in series (Fig. 4.8) is

$$f = f_0 \sqrt{1 - \frac{\pi^2}{Q^2}}.$$

where

$$2\pi f_0 = \frac{1}{\sqrt{LC}}$$

and

$$Q = \frac{2\pi f_0 L}{R}$$

f_0 is what the resonant frequency would be with no resistance and so the expression

$$f = f_0 \sqrt{1 - \frac{\pi^2}{Q^2}}$$

gives the new frequency caused by the presence of a resistance R. In many applications Q is large. For a crystal a Q of 10^7 is possible. On a computer of, say, 6 digits precision, it is not possible to compute f precisely using

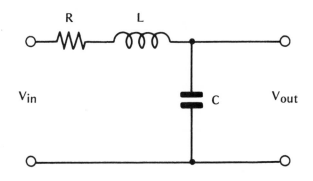

Fig. 4.8. Series RLC circuit.

$$f = f_0 \left(1 - \frac{\pi^2}{Q^2} \right)^{\frac{1}{2}}$$

or any other method. It is, on the other hand, possible to compute the shift in frequency using the binomial approximation

$$f = f_0 - \frac{\pi^2}{2Q^2} f_0 + \cdots$$

So that the frequency shift is

$$\Delta f = \frac{f_0 \pi^2}{2Q^2}$$

with no problems of precision.

To put some numbers to this, suppose $L = 10^{-2}/4\pi^2$ and $C = 10^{-12}$ so that the resonant frequency is

$$f_0 = 10 \text{ MHz } (10^7 \text{ cycles/sec.})$$

If $Q = 10^6$ then

$$\Delta f = \frac{10^7 \pi^2}{2 \times 10^{12}} \approx 5 \times 10^{-5} \text{ Hz}$$

To compute $f_0 + \Delta f$ would require a computer with 14-digit accuracy and is therefore dangerous to say the least. On the other hand Δf can be calculated on its own quite easily.

EXAMPLE:

Heating a metal bar produces a change in length which is small but can produce great stress in a structure. If the original length is ℓ_0 the new length is

$$\ell = \ell_0(1 + \alpha \Delta T)$$

where ΔT is the change in temperature and α is the coefficient of expansion of the metal, for example for steel about 1.2×10^{-5} per °C. For small temperature changes a program in a computer with limited precision could fail to compute ℓ as being any different from ℓ_0. However, observing that

$$\ell = \ell_0 + \Delta \ell$$

with

$$\Delta \ell = \alpha \Delta T$$

it is quite easy to compute $\Delta \ell$. For a 1 metre steel bar a temperature change of 1 °C produces a length change of 1.2×10^{-5} metres. If the computer's precision is only 6 digits, $\ell_0 + \Delta \ell$ is an inaccurate sum.

EXERCISE:

This one is more subtle. The expression

$$6x^4 - 9.8x^3y - 2.7x^2y^2 + 9.8xy^3$$
$$+ 6y^4 - 43.6x^3 + 18.2x^2y + 64.2xy^2$$
$$+ 38.2y^3 + 83.6x^2 + 110.6xy + 82.5y^2$$
$$+ 18x + 73y + 52 = 0$$

looks innocent enough but at

$$x = 1 \quad, \quad y = -2$$

the x and y partial derivatives are 0, as can easily be verified. Near this point the function is very flat and its derivatives are difficult to compute. Try it.

4.11   Reals, integers, and IF statements

Before proceeding to further facilities of FORTRAN, it is useful to consider more carefully some implications of the logical IF statement as far as the type of expressions being compared are concerned. In the comparison

$$IF\left(\begin{matrix} \text{first} \\ \text{expression} \end{matrix} .EQ. \begin{matrix} \text{second} \\ \text{expression} \end{matrix}\right)\text{statement}$$

exact equality of the two expressions is required for the "statement" to be executed. However with expressions involving real variables and real arithmetic, exact equality is unlikely to be achieved. This is because although real arithmetic preserves as many digits of significance as possible, it is not exact. The two statements

$$X = \emptyset.3$$
$$X = X + 1.3$$

might not produce a result of exactly 1.6; it is likely to be something like 1.5999999... which is not quite the same thing. Therefore a statement like

$$IF(X.EQ.1.6)GO\ TO\ 2\emptyset$$

or even

$$IF(X.GE.1.6)GO\ TO\ 2\emptyset$$

could fail to behave as the programmer intended. Therefore as a general rule it is unwise ever to expect exact equalities using reals.

An implication of this general rule is that real variables are unsuitable for counting. To state this in positive terms: it is best to use integers for counting. This is because integer variables always have exact integer values and so will not present the programmer with any nasty surprises in IF statements.

> You can only expect exact equality when comparing two integers.

EXERCISE: Verify that for some values of X, the expression

$$(X/2.\emptyset)*2.\emptyset$$

is not equal to X in your computer.

4.12 Efficiency

The cost of a computation which mainly involves calculation and not too much input/output is related to the product of the time used and the size of the program. Later in this book methods of reducing the amount of space taken by variables will be discussed and, of course, the space occupied by a program is related to the number of statements in the program. Good programmers have the cost of resources in mind when designing and developing programs and try to write concise FORTRAN which is efficient.

Of course it is wrong to be obsessed with these factors because human re-sources are expensive too. If an employer gets on average more than one line of program for every five dollars he pays his programmers then he is doing very well, because designing, writing, developing and documenting the programs is a labour intensive business. Therefore the amount of time spent optimizing a program has to be offset against the computational savings that might eventuate.

However it is easy to learn how to write effective expressions and a good programmer does this naturally. First of all he should realise that there are some operations which are inherently efficient:

Efficient:
    Addition
    Subtraction
    Multiplication
    Division

It is acceptable to consider these operations as having about the same cost and the more expensive the computer, the more likely this is to be true. It is also worthwhile to consider that on a large machine there is little to choose between reals and integers, while on small computers these approximations may be wildly wrong. It is in fact very likely that on small computers, integer operations are much faster than real ones.

Inefficient:
    Exponentiation
    Function references
    Unnecessary conversions

In fact these all boil down to the same thing. They are all multistage processes which are not done "naturally" by computers , i.e. as part of their fast repertoire, and they are all effectively functions. Therefore some things to avoid can be listed:

(i) Expressions mixing reals and integers can be very inefficient if a lot of separate conversions are implied. If you must mix them, group the integers together to minimize the conversions. For example in the expression

$$I*X*J*Y*K$$

the program could be forcing the computer to make three conversions*, and it is much better to use

$$X*Y*(I*J*K)$$

with only one conversion.

Another example of this is the series of assignment statements

$$IWET=I+SOGGY$$
$$JWET=J+SOGGY$$

in which four conversions are necessary in all, compared to

$$KWET=SOGGY$$
$$IWET=I+KWET$$
$$JWET=J+KWET$$

with only one.

(ii) If functions have to be used try to group things efficiently or think of forms

---

* On the other hand the machine itself may optimize the expression - but don't count on it.

with the minimum number of references to them. In Section 4.7 a right shift function was devised for 2's complement numbers. Three choices are

$$I=I/2+MIN(\emptyset,SIGN(ABS(MOD(I,2)),I))$$

$$I=(I+MIN(\emptyset,MOD(I,2)))/2$$

$$IF(I.LT.\emptyset)I=I+1$$
$$I=I/2$$

The version with two functions is clearly better than with three, but on the other hand the IF statement might be faster, and of course there could be a better way still.

(iii) Always write exponentiation to integer powers if possible. For example

$$X**7 \quad or \quad X**I$$

is preferred to

$$X**7.\emptyset \quad or \quad X**Z$$

and up to a reasonable power

$$A*A \quad or \quad A*A*A \quad or \ even \ A*A*A*A$$

is better than

$$A**2 \quad or \quad A**3 \quad or \ even \ A**4$$

Some FORTRAN compilers may spot these and rearrange them for you provided the power was an integer constant.

Finally a programmer can spot simplifications in his arithmetic and arrange it judiciously. An example is in precalculating frequently used quantities such as π or e:

$$PIE=4.\emptyset*ATAN(1.\emptyset)$$

$$EEE=EXP(1.\emptyset)$$

so that if they are used several times they are not recalculated.

It is often possible to spot groups of terms common to a series of calculations; to find in succession

$$X, \ X**2/2, \ X**3/2*3, \ X**4/2*3*4..$$

it would be wise to write something like

```
TERM1=X
TERM2=TERM1*X/2.Ø
TERM3=TERM2*X/3.Ø
TERM4=TERM3*X/4.Ø
```

Indeed this example is one that is returned to later. It is one that strongly suggests what is called a recurrence relationship.

4.13 Problems

PROBLEM 4.1:
In the old British currency system there were 4 farthings to the penny, 12 pence to the shilling and 20 shillings to the pound. Now the currency is decimalized, and is expressed as pounds with two decimal places. There are 100 new pence to the pound, i.e. 4.27 is four pounds and 27 new pence. Write programs to:

(i) Convert old currency to new, rounding down;

(ii) Convert new currency to old, rounding up.

PROBLEM 4.2:
Perhaps the old British currency system was quaint but get this! In one part of the world distances are measured in miles, yards, feet, and inches where:

1 mile = 1760 yards
1 yard = 3 feet
1 foot = 12 inches

A very logical system indeed. Now if 1 mile is 1.609344 kilometres, write programs to:

(i) Convert this silly system to metres.

(ii) Convert kilometres to miles, etc.

PROBLEM 4.3:
The Earth has a period of revolution of 31558150 seconds. Convert this to days, hours, minutes, and seconds.

PROBLEM 4.4:

It is possible in theory to find the value of π by repeatedly dropping a needle onto a piece of paper with two parallel lines ruled upon it. Suppose, as in Fig. 4.9, the lines are one unit apart and the needle is one unit long. If the needle always falls with one end between the lines and all distances y and angles θ are equally possible, then the probability that the other end of the needle crosses one of the lines is $2/\pi$. This is called Buffon's needle experiment, and is said to have been performed during the French revolution as a recreation by people awaiting the guillotine.

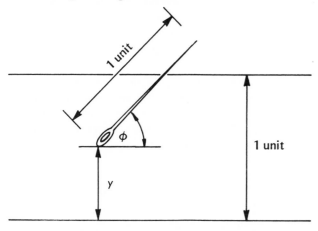

Fig. 4.9. Buffon's needle experiment.

The random number generator developed in this chapter can be used to simulate this experiment. Using the generator, obtain random values of y between 0 and 1, and θ between 0 and 2π radians. If the total number of trials is recorded along with the total number of crossings, their ratio can be used to find π.

Yes, it is begging the question because the value of π is involved in the angle calculation, but it demonstrates a principle. Find π in this way, but don't let it run on for ever. How many trials are needed to get two significant digits? Three? Four? Be sure the computer time can be afforded.

PROBLEM 4.5:

The operation of shifting the bits of an integer one place to the left or the right was discussed in Section 4.7.

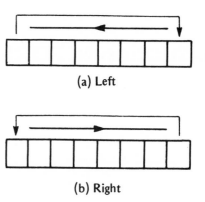

(a) Left

(b) Right

Fig. 4.10. Rotating a binary number.

Another operation that is useful is called "bit rotation", as illustrated by Fig. 4.10. Whereas in shifting bits were lost at one end, in rotation the bit that drops out of one end is tucked in at the other. Devise methods of rotating the bit patterns of integers one place to the left or the right. You will have to know the integer bit length and kind of arithmetic used in your computer; the method of finding out was outlined in Section 4.7.

PROBLEM 4.6:

The raising of any number to an integer power is, of course, a process of successive multiplication. To raise X to the positive power IPOW, it would be possible to write

```
      ANS=1.Ø
 1Ø   ANS=ANS*X
      IPOW=IPOW-1
      IF(IPOW.GT.Ø)GO TO 1Ø
```

However IPOW can be broken down into a series of powers of 2, and so the whole process can be greatly simplified by successively squaring X and multiplying ANS by only those powers of X that are necessary. For example:

$$X^{13} = (X^1)*(X^4)*(X^8)$$

because $13 = 2^0 + 2^2 + 2^3$.

This is similar to the description of integer multiplication in Section 4.7. Do this.

5

Introduction to FORMAT

5.1 Introduction

Until the introduction of FORTRAN 77, FORMAT directed input and output was the only means of reading data from cards and printing results. In list directed form the PRINT and READ statements were introduced some chapters ago, and it was seen that the computer itself decides how to arrange printed output, and the user has a certain flexibility in organizing the input as well. With FORMAT the layout is specified exactly, and it will be shown that the PRINT and READ statements take a more general form. The programmer has to work a bit harder to use FORMAT directed statements but for printing the improvement in presentation can be substantial and standardization of his input is efficient for large scale production runs.

FORTRAN is organized around lines of input or output. In a batch system a line of input is normally a computer card and a line of output usually appears on a lineprinter. In the timesharing environment, input and output will be from a teletype or a similar device. In either case the output is in the form of a printed line. A FORTRAN program can initiate input with a READ statement and output with a WRITE or PRINT statement; both these terms are self-explanatory if it is remembered that the action is taken from the point of view of the computer.

A list directed PRINT statement is already familiar:

```
PRINT*,I,J,K
```

It is the asterisk which causes the computer to arrange the output itself. To place the layout under control of the program, the * is replaced by a reference to a FORMAT specification, such as

```
PRINT 22,I,J,K
```

which asks that the three integer variables listed should be printed under contol of a separate statement whose label is 22. This new statement is a FORMAT statement defining the layout, such as

```
22 FORMAT(1X,3I3)
```

which specifies that three integers are to be printed, each occupying three spaces; this is accomplished by the field specification 3I3. The line of output is to begin with a blank space, called for by the field specification 1X.

Taken together, these two statements mean that the values of these variables, I, J and K, are to be printed according to the FORMAT with label 22. The FORMAT dictates that the printed line is to contain one space with the three integer values following, each occupying three spaces.

As an alternative the PRINT statement may contain the FORMAT specification itself as in

```
PRINT'(1X,3I3)',I,J,K
```

which is exactly equivalent in its effect to the previous example.

Here the means provided by FORMAT direction for laying out real and integer variables and for printing captions will be described. First, however, the statements which initiate output are discussed. This chapter only introduces these facilities and simplifies some of them; there is much more to come, and it is all eventually summarized for easy reference in Chapter 18.

5.2 Arranging output — the PRINT and WRITE statements

For printed output, the programmer has a choice of the PRINT statement already encountered or the WRITE statement which has more facilities. There is an equivalent of every PRINT statement. For example, the statements

PRINT*,list

and   WRITE(*,*)list

are the same. The PRINT statement uses the obvious printer, and in the WRITE statement the first * also tells the computer to use the obvious printer. The * in PRINT and the second * in the WRITE statement instruct the computer to use list directed processing and to decide for itself how to organize the layout.

Both these statements exist in a more general form:

WRITE(unit,f)list

or   PRINT f,list

Here 'unit' identifies the output device to be used by the WRITE statement. It could be a * for the obvious system printer, or it could be the integer number of some other device upon which information can be written in list directed or format directed form; more about this in Chapter 18. The obvious printer is often unit number 6.

'f' is a FORMAT identifier. In either of these statements, giving an asterisk ,*, for 'f' calls for list directed output. 'f' can also identify a FORMAT specification either by its label as in

WRITE(6,22)list

or   PRINT 22,list

or can itself be a character constant enclosed by apostrophes which specify a FORMAT directly, as in

PRINT'(1X,3I3)',list

or   WRITE(6,'(1X,3I3)')list

Note that the enclosing brackets are part of the FORMAT specification.

There are two further forms that 'f' might take, as outlined in Chapter 16. These will allow the FORMAT to be decided by the program as it executes rather than being decided by the programmer in advance as he writes it.

Therefore if the FORMAT identifier 'f' is not a *, then there must be a FORMAT specification given, in which case the program dictates the layout.

5.3 The FORMAT specification

As the previous section stated, the FORMAT specification can be given either in a separate FORMAT statement or directly as a character constant in the WRITE or PRINT statement. It is used to specify the exact layout of a printed line, and does this by listing the editing information in 'fields', one field for each quantity to be printed. A FORMAT statement is a useful way of doing this because any number of PRINT, READ or WRITE statements can use the same FORMAT statement. The FORMAT statement can be anywhere in the program except after the END statement and as will be seen, there are some statements that have to be put at the very beginning. Apart from these, the FORMATs can be put anywhere within a program unit; some programmers group them for easy reference either near the beginning of the program unit or just before the END.

The PRINT and WRITE statements are "executable statements" which cause action to take place and therefore their position in a program is important. When they refer, by its label, to a FORMAT statement it must be somewhere in the program. Because the FORMAT statement is there only to be referred to by input/output statements, it is "non-executable" and its presence at a particular place causes no action to be taken. This is why it can be put nearly anywhere. To examine the same example again, the statement

PRINT 22,I,J,K

requires that a FORMAT with label 22 should be somewhere in the program. The FORMAT might be

22 FORMAT(1X,3I3)

and hence the "fields" of output are dictated by the editing descriptions 1X and 3I3.

(i) I or Integer editing

The I or Integer edit description is one of several possible types. The description

kIm

calls for k integer fields, each occupying m spaces; in a FORMAT statement several I descriptions can be given with commas between. If k is one it can be left out. Printing takes place in one-to-one correspondence between the variables mentioned in the WRITE or PRINT statement and the fields specified in the FORMAT.

(ii) X or Spaces editing

The X description indicates blank spaces, so that a field

nX

calls for n blanks to appear in the printed line.

EXAMPLE:
The statements

WRITE(*,30)I

or   PRINT 30,I

both mean the same thing, and the associated FORMAT could take many forms, for example

30 FORMAT(3X,I2)

might appear in the same program and would produce the value of I printed in the fourth and fifth spaces of the output line, preceded by three blanks. It is entirely possible that the variable I has too large a value for the field, I2; any positive integer greater than 99 or a negative one less than -9 will not fit. In this situation the number will not appear and the computer will print asterisks in place of the offending number.

The statements

WRITE(*,'(3X,I2)')I

or   PRINT'(3X,I2)',I

are exactly equivalent to the above except that the FORMAT specification is not available for the use of other input/output statements because it is embedded in those particular statements.

Each PRINT or WRITE statement begins a new line of printed output. It is therefore impossible in FORTRAN to continue printing along the same line with more than one output statement (although it is possible to overprint lines, which is not quite the same thing).

EXAMPLE:
Suppose the variables I=1, K=-53 and J=1024 are to be printed. Then the statement

WRITE(*,43)I,K,J

with 43 FORMAT(1X,I4,1X,I3,I5)

will produce the printed line

```
    1 -53 1024
..............
```

The dots in these examples indicate the spacing of the printed line and are not actually printed.

The statements

```
    WRITE(*,43)I
    WRITE(*,43)J
    WRITE(*,43)K
```

or

```
    PRINT 43,I
    PRINT 43,J
    PRINT 43,K
```

in a program with the same FORMAT would produce the output on separate lines, as

```
    1
.....
 1024
.....
  -53
.....
```

If there are too many numbers given in the WRITE or PRINT list for the number of fields in the FORMAT specification, then the FORMAT is used again on new lines until all the numbers have been printed.

EXAMPLE:
With I=1, K=-53 and J=1024 as above, the statement

```
    WRITE(*,44)I,K,J
```

with

```
 44 FORMAT(1X,I4)
```

would produce the printed lines

```
    1
.....
  -53
.....
 1024
.....
```

(iii) F editing for real numbers

Editing descriptions for real numbers are

also available; for example the F description which is a bit complicated. F stands for Fixed-point and is used to print real variables with the position of the decimal point fixed.

The statement

```
    PRINT'(1X,F10.5)',X
```

causes variable X to have its value printed in spaces 2-11 of the output line, with five decimal places; the decimal point is printed.

In general the field

$$kF\ell.j$$

prints k real numbers in ℓ spaces each with j decimal places. If the value does not fit the field is printed with ℓ asterisks.

No conversion from real to integer or integer to real is implied by the FORMAT fields. Thus the variables listed in the WRITE statement must be in one-to-one correspondence according to type and position with the fields of the FORMAT; FORTRAN is strict on this point.

EXAMPLES:
Suppose I=1, J=-53, K=1024, X=1.5, Y=-36.73, Z=3.14159265. Then the statements

```
    WRITE(*,41)I,Z,J,K
 41 FORMAT(1X,I4,F10.4,2I5)
```

would produce

```
    1    3.1416  -53 1024
...........................
```

The statement

```
WRITE(*,'(1X,I4,F7.2)')J,Y,I,X,K,Z
```

will produce

```
 -53 -36.73
...........
    1   1.50
...........
 1024   3.14
...........
```

by repeating the FORMAT three times on new lines.

The statements

```
    WRITE(*,43)I,X
    WRITE(*,43)J,Y
 43 FORMAT(1X,I4,F7.2)
```

would print

```
     1   1.50
. . . . . . . . . . . .
   -53 -36.73
. . . . . . . . . . .
```

The statement

```
  PRINT'(1X,I1Ø)'I,X,J,K
```

would result in an error condition because an attempt is made to print X, which is real, according to an Integer field description.

Special note:

Always begin output FORMATs with a space (1X) until further notice. Where a lineprinter is involved failure to do this will result in unpopularity. Reason: lineprinters regard the first space as "carriage control" and have a nasty tendency to jump to a new page if something other than a blank occurs as the first space. An amazing amount of paper can be wasted by careless people. Trees are becoming a scarce resource.

The list directed PRINT* and WRITE(*,*) statements take care of this automatically.

5.4 Arranging input — the READ statement

The list directed READ statement is already familiar:

```
  READ*,list
```

This statement also exists in forms which are FORMAT directed:

```
  READ f,list
```

or

```
  READ(unit,f)list
```

where, as before, "f" is a FORMAT identifier which can be a *, the label of a FORMAT statement, or a character constant which will give the FORMAT directly. The FORMAT description, as with WRITE and PRINT, can consist of a number of fields in I, F, or X editing whose types match the corresponding data values in the input/output list. The data is required to conform exactly to the given FORMAT, and so the value given to each variable in the list must lie within the stated space. If it does not, the program will fail either by giving incorrect results or by being terminated.

Again in these arrangements, FORTRAN is organized around lines of data; each READ statement calls for a new line of information. In a batch system this will probably be a computer card and in a timesharing environment a line typed into a terminal. The meanings of the field specifications are as before, although there is an additional nuance to the F specification.

EXAMPLE:
The statements

```
    READ(5,2Ø)I,J
 2Ø FORMAT(2I5)
```

are a request for values of the integer variables I and J to be taken from input unit 5 which is usually the number of the "obvious" input card reader or terminal.

The FORMAT can be used by other READ, WRITE or PRINT statements which refer to its label, 20. The FORMAT requires that the value of I should lie in spaces 1-5 of the input line, and J in spaces 6-10. FORTRAN will normally ignore blank spaces in numerical fields, therefore the numbers 12 and 50 could be entered in several ways, such as

```
   12   5Ø
. . . . . . . . . .
```

or

```
  12  5Ø
. . . . . . . . . .
```

Were the data misplaced, as in

12 ..5∅
• • • • • • • •

they would be interpreted as 1 and 25. On punched cards it is easy to be sure that data is correctly aligned; however on teletypes in a timesharing system great care must be taken over exact spacing. Figure 5.1 shows these numbers correctly punched on a computer card.

Real numbers can be entered using the familiar F specification. However, FORTRAN permits some flexibility in placing the decimal point. If the specification of a field is

$$F\ell.j$$

then the decimal point can be either omitted, in which case the computer places it before the last j digits, or it can be placed explicitly anywhere in the field of ℓ spaces. In this way the specification can actually be overridden by the data by moving the decimal point about within the field. However, the number must still fall entirely within the field of ℓ spaces. As another option the number could be entered in exponential form - which also has its own FORMAT, as described in section 7 of this chapter.

EXAMPLE:
The integer value 12 and the real value 3.14 are to be entered to a program which asks for them with the statement

READ'(I5,F5.2)',I,X

This information could be entered with the decimal point of X implied, as

12 314
• • • • • • • • •

or with it given explicitly as either

12 3.14
• • • • • • • • •

or

123.14
• • • • • • • • •

These numbers are shown in punched cards in Fig. 5.2.

It is often wise to WRITE or PRINT values again after they have been entered as a check that they are correct. It is not necessary to begin lines of input with a space, although the X specification can be used in input FORMATs, to identify fields which are ignored.

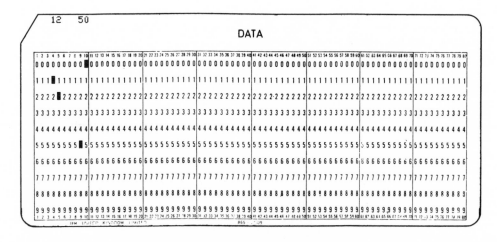

Fig. 5.1. The integer values 12 and 50 punched
correctly according to the FORMAT (2I5).

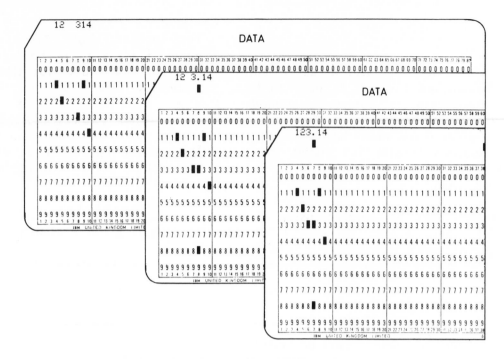

Fig. 5.2. Three correct ways of presenting the
integer value 12 and the real value 3.14 according
to the FORMAT (I5,F5.2).

The / is not allowed in the input data
in FORMAT directed reading, so that it is
always necessary to give enough data to
satisfy all of the list in the READ
statement.

5.5 Captions in FORMAT directed output

The most sophisticated computer program
is of no use unless its results are
presented in an acceptable form. It is
always true that clear presentation is
improved by appropriate titles and captions. Most people who write computer
programs for a living have to produce
results for someone else, and managers
are at least as impressed by good
presentation as by efficient programming. With list directed printing, captions can be included in the printed
output, and they can be written by
FORMAT directed statements as well.

To print captions it is best to include
them in the FORMAT as a field on their
own - this is different from what is
done in list directed output. The
statements

```
PRINT*,'HELLO SAILOR'
```

and

```
WRITE(*,75)
75 FORMAT(1X,'HELLO SAILOR')
```

print the same message. The second one
is interesting - the list of the WRITE
statement is not there, but the
statement is still executed. The 1X has
been specified directly, but the space
which is necessary on a lineprinter could
have been incorporated into the message:

```
75 FORMAT(' HELLO SAILOR')
```

As the examples show, the FORMAT can
include character constants in parentheses
among its editing descriptions. Here is a
little program to work out an integer
quotient and remainder and print them:

```
C FIND QUOTIENT AND REMAINDER
C ACCEPT NUMERATOR, DENOMINATOR
      PRINT 22
 10 READ 23,IN,ID
      PRINT 24,IN
      PRINT 25,ID
      PRINT 26,IN/ID
      PRINT 27,MOD(IN,ID)
      GO TO 10
```

```
22 FORMAT(' GIVE INTEGERS, 2I5')
23 FORMAT(2I5)
24 FORMAT(' NUMERATOR   =',I5)
25 FORMAT(' DENOMINATOR =',I5)
26 FORMAT(' QUOTIENT    =',I5)
27 FORMAT(' REMAINDER   =',I5)
   END
```

This program first tells the user what to provide - on a batch system he would not be there to see this message and so it could be left out. It then reads two values according to FORMAT 23, and the user has to be sure that the values are spaced correctly in his input. The given numerator and denominator are printed out, or "echoed", immediately to allow the user to confirm in his output that they were correct. The desired results are then printed. The FORMATs labelled 24 to 27 have character and integer fields.

It would not have been correct to write

```
PRINT 26,' QUOTIENT =',IN/ID
```

with the FORMAT

```
26 FORMAT(I5)
```

because this FORMAT gives a layout for the printed line which has no space for the character constant in the PRINT list. It can be done with a special kind of FORMAT editing described in Chapter 16, but even then would not be convenient for this purpose.

In FORMAT directed output, put your captions in the FORMAT.

In list directed output, put your captions in the list.

There is another description of messages in FORTRAN, the H or Hollerith constant. This is described in Chapter 18, and will be found in many old FORTRAN programs. It is now likely to fall into disuse.

5.6 An example — more about FORMAT — slashes

It is now possible to prepare programs which can print nicely tabulated results, and this is quite a common requirement in real life. The table printed here has its uses.

If one unit of currency is invested in such a way that it earns i% in each accounting period, then the value of the investment after n accounting periods is

$$(1 + i/100)^n$$

The program given in Fig.5.3 prints a table of values for interest rates from 5% to 10%, rounded to the nearest 1/100 unit. First a title and caption to head the columns are printed, then the table is printed with one line for each accounting period from 1 to 10.

The actual printed result after execution of this program is shown in Fig. 5.3. The user will probably wish to improve the layout by inserting blank lines, for example to space out the title from the table. It is possible, of course to do this with PRINT or WRITE statements with empty lists and empty FORMATS. Any one of the combinations:

```
PRINT*         WRITE(*,*)

PRINT21        WRITE(*,21)
21 FORMAT( )   21 FORMAT( )

READ*          READ 21
               21 FORMAT( )

READ(*,*)      READ(*,21)
               21 FORMAT( )
```

will cause an empty line. However there is a more convenient way, by using the character '/' (slash) in the FORMAT.

Every READ, WRITE or PRINT statement begins a new line or card as a matter of course. However it is often desirable to start a new line (or card) in the middle of a list, or to give extra blank lines, or even to skip past a few cards in the input card reader. The character

```
C PRINT A YIELD TABLE FOR SEVERAL INTEREST RATES
C FIRST PRINT THE TITLES
      PRINT 41
      PRINT 42
      PRINT 43
C THEN WORK OUT THE YIELDS
      N=5
   1Ø Y1=(1.Ø5)**N
      Y2=(1.Ø6)**N
      Y3=(1.Ø7)**N
      Y4=(1.Ø8)**N
      Y5=(1.Ø9)**N
C PRINT A LINE OF THE TABLE
      PRINT 44,N,Y1,Y2,Y3,Y4,Y5
      N=N+1
      IF(N.LT.1Ø)GO TO 1Ø
   41 FORMAT(13X,'YIELD TABLE')
   42 FORMAT(13X,'***********')
   43 FORMAT(5X'RATE = 5    6    7    8    9')
   44 FORMAT('PERIOD',I2,2X,5F5.2)
      END
```

	YIELD TABLE				
	***********				
RATE =	5	6	7	8	9
PERIOD 5	1.28	1.34	1.40	1.47	1.54
PERIOD 6	1.34	1.42	1.50	1.59	1.68
PERIOD 7	1.41	1.50	1.61	1.71	1.83
PERIOD 8	1.48	1.59	1.72	1.85	1.99
PERIOD 9	1.55	1.69	1.84	2.00	2.17

Fig. 5.3. Computer printed interest table.

'/' (slash) encountered in a FORMAT forces a new line or card. The presentation of the interest table is improved if blank lines are given with the titles and between the lines of the table, which makes the result more attractive, as in Fig. 5.4. This is still a somewhat awkward program because five variables are used for the yields. A further refinement will be seen in Chapter 13, when a subscripted variable is used in a similar example to print a table of loan repayments. A new line or card can be obtained in one of three ways:

(i) an empty PRINT, READ, or WRITE
(ii) a FORMAT repeated because the list referring to it has more items than the FORMAT
(iii) a slash, '/', in the FORMAT

or by a combination of (ii) and (iii).

It should be noted carefully that the / has entirely different meanings in list directed and FORMAT directed operations.

In list directed input the / can be given instead of data in response to a READ statement as described in Chapter 2. It causes the termination of input and leaves some values unchanged, perhaps undefined. It does not occur in list directed output.

In FORMAT directed input or output the / is used in the FORMAT to indicate new lines or cards. It cannot be given as input data when a number is asked for.

5.7 Exponential real editing in FORMAT

The exponential form of real constants was encountered in Chapter 2. It can be used to write very large or very small numbers with a multiplying exponential, i.e.

$$3.ØE1Ø \text{ meant } 3 \times 10^{10}$$

$$16.35E-4 \text{ meant } 0.001635$$

Sometimes very large or very small real numbers are expected from calculations and these would not be convenient to print using the F field. FORTRAN supports an exponential form of input or

```
C PRINT A YIELD TABLE FOR SEVERAL INTEREST RATES
C FIRST PRINT THE TITLES
      PRINT 41
      PRINT 42
      PRINT 43
C THEN WORK OUT THE YIELDS
      N=5
   1Ø Y1=(1.Ø5)**N
      Y2=(1.Ø6)**N
      Y3=(1.Ø7)**N
      Y4=(1.Ø8)**N
      Y5=(1.Ø9)**N
C PRINT A LINE OF THE TABLE
      PRINT 44,N,Y1,Y2,Y3,Y4,Y5
      N=N+1
      IF(N.LT.1Ø)GO TO 1Ø
   41 FORMAT(13X,'YIELD TABLE')
   42 FORMAT(13X,'***********'//)
   43 FORMAT(5X'RATE = 5      6      7      8      9'/)
   44 FORMAT('PERIOD',I2,2X,5F5.2/)
      END

      YIELD TABLE
      ***********
```

	RATE = 5	6	7	8	9
PERIOD 5	1.28	1.34	1.40	1.47	1.54
PERIOD 6	1.34	1.42	1.50	1.59	1.68
PERIOD 7	1.41	1.50	1.61	1.71	1.83
PERIOD 8	1.48	1.59	1.72	1.85	1.99
PERIOD 9	1.55	1.69	1.84	2.00	2.17

Fig. 5.4. Computer printed interest table.

output, the E field. It is written in the FORMAT description as:

$$kEm.n$$

where
k is the number of repetitions of the field,
m is the total width of the field, and
n is the number of decimal places.

A number printed in this way contains many extra symbols; blanks or signs, a decimal point and the letter E. There are so many of these that m should be greater than n by at least 7. The printing of E fields often comes out as

$$sØ.ddd..ddEsdd$$

where s is a sign and d are the digits. It can be seen that there are n+7 printed symbols. To allow for blanks between E fields and for three digit exponents which may sometimes occur, a difference of 10 between m and n is practical.

EXAMPLES:
Using a field E15.5, the following numbers could be printed as shown.

3×10^{10}	$Ø.3ØØØØE+11$
16.35×10^{-4}	$Ø.1635ØE-Ø2$
-7.32×10^{24}	$-Ø.732ØØE+25$
-4.28×10^{-15}	$-Ø.428ØØE-14$

As with F fields, FORTRAN allows considerable variations on the exact alignment of input data. First of all the information which is to be read in the E form can be moved about within the field of m spaces, and as long as the decimal point and exponent are given no trouble will be encountered. Therefore the number 3×10^{10} could be read in by the statements:

```
      READ(*,21)X
  21 FORMAT(E15.5)
```

in several ways including

```
      Ø.3ØØØØE+11
. . . . . . . . . . . . . . . . .
      3.Ø E +1Ø
. . . . . . . . . . . . .
            3.E+1Ø
. . . . . . . . . . . . .
```

The letter E can be left out and the exponent indicated only by its sign:

```
      3.Ø+1Ø
. . . . . . . . . . . . . .
      3. + 1Ø
. . . . . . . . . . . . .
```

The decimal point can also be left out and is then assumed to precede the n digits of the mantissa:

```
          3ØØØØE+11
. . . . . . . . . . . . . .
3ØØØØ+11
. . . . . . . . . . . . .
```

Finally the exponent need not be given at all and the data given as any real number. If neither a decimal point nor an exponent are given, then the number has 5 decimal places counting from the right end of the field just as in F editing. In fact both E and F editing accept the same data which can be in the F form described in Section 5.3 or in the E form described here. Therefore E and F data are completely interchangeable in the response to a FORMAT directed READ statement.

5.8 Repeating FORMAT descriptions

There are three ways of making FORMAT descriptions repeat. Some types of field descriptions are repeatable themselves, it is quite possible to repeat groups of FORMAT descriptions, and the FORMATs automatically repeat if they run out before the input/output list is satisfied.

(i) Repeating Field Descriptions

The editing descriptions for numeric data are repeatable in the descriptions

$$kI$$

$$kF\ell.j$$

$$kEm.n$$

where k is the number of repetitions; k can only be an integer constant.

EXAMPLE:
The statements

```
      PRINT 66,I,J,K,P,Q,R,S,X,Y
  66 FORMAT(3I3,4F5.2,2E1Ø.2)
```

use repetition of all of the three editing descriptions to print the nine variables in 49 spaces.

The description nX, /, and captions are not repeated in this way, but can be repeated as parts of groups.

(ii) Repeating Groups

Any part of a FORMAT description can be placed in parentheses and repeated:

$$k(group)$$

Here the group is repeated k times; k can only be an integer constant.

EXAMPLES:
The statements

```
      PRINT 21
  21 FORMAT(1X,5Ø('*'))
```

print a row of 50 asterisks - a useful thing to be able to do. The statement

```
      PRINT'(1X,5Ø(''*''))'
```

does the same thing - note the double quotation marks because the FORMAT description '*' is part of a character constant.

The statements

```
      WRITE(*,5Ø)X,Y
  5Ø FORMAT(1Ø(/),1X,2F1Ø.5)
```

print their results after 10 blank lines, which is the same as

```
50 FORMAT(//////////,1X,2F10.5)
```

An example of a repeated group in a READ statement is

```
   READ 20,INUM,I1,X1,I2,X2,I3,X3
20 FORMAT(I5,3(/,I5,F15.5))
```

which reads INUM from the first card or line of input, and then three further cards with an integer and a real on each.

In a similar vein, the statements

```
   WRITE(*,33)X,Y,P,Q,R,S
33 FORMAT(' RESULTS',3(2F8.3,2X))
```

produce the message and all six results on one line, whereas by writing

```
   WRITE(*,33)X,Y,P,Q,R,S
33 FORMAT(' RESULTS'/3(2X,2F8.3))
```

the message comes on one line with the six results on the next line. Note that the 2X has been moved to keep the first space of each line clear.

(iii) Repeating (most of) the FORMAT

It has already been said that when the end of the FORMAT is reached with quantities left in the list, a new line is begun and the FORMAT is reused. With repeated groups in the FORMAT, this is not strictly correct. The true situation is that the FORMAT is reused (on a new line) from the group ending on the last embedded right bracket if there is one, otherwise from the beginning.

EXAMPLES:
As described earlier, the statements

```
     PRINT 40,X,Y,P,Q,R,S
  40 FORMAT(1X,2F10.5)
```

print on three lines by repetition. With embedded brackets, the statements

```
     PRINT 56,I,J,K,L,M,N
  56 FORMAT(1X,2I5,(2I5))
```

print on two lines, with four results on the first and two on the second.

Finally the statements

```
     WRITE(*,33)X,Y,P,Q,R,S
  33 FORMAT(' RESULTS'/(2X,2F8.3))
```

print a message on the first line and results on the following three.

5.9 When to use FORMAT

With list directed input and output, it is easy for a programmer never to use FORMAT directed forms, but good program design is not always for the convenience of the programmer alone.

FORMAT should be used:

(i) when attractive presentation of results is important;

(ii) when the arrangements for input are to be standardized, for example for processing large amounts of data from cards or tape.

5.10 Problems

PROBLEM 5.1:
The factorial of a positive integer is the product of all numbers from 1 to n, written

$$n! = n(n-1) \ldots (2)(1)$$

Write a program to find the factorial using integers. As can be seen from the definition, the factorials of numbers of even modest size are large. Find out how large a factorial your computer can find using integer arithmetic. It will not tell you when it goes wrong. You will have to devise some form of inspection, automatic or manual.

PROBLEM 5.2:
Now working with reals, find out how large a factorial the computer can calculate. Print the results in exponential format.

PROBLEM 5.3:

Stirling's approximation to the factorial of a large number is

$$n! \approx \sqrt{2\pi n} \left\{ \frac{n}{e} \right\}^n$$

Write a program to evaluate this and compare its accuracy with a factorial calculated directly using real arithmetic as in problem 5.2.

PROBLEM 5.4:

The library functions will usually give an accuracy which is close to the limits of the machine's capabilities. Because of these limits it is incapable of storing the exact result even if you try to supply it in your program.

(a) Use the ATAN function to find π. How accurately does your computer evaluate it, given that

$$\pi = 3.14159\ 26535\ 89793\ 23846$$

(b) Use the EXP function to find e. How accurately does your computer find it, given that

$$e = 2.71828\ 18284\ 59045\ 23536$$

PROBLEM 5.5:

In a similar vein to problem 5.4, investigate carefully the accuracy of the $SIN(x)$ function over the range $-\pi < x < \pi$.

PROBLEM 5.6:

Investigate the accuracy of SQRT over the entire range of real numbers on your machine.

6

Program control

6.1 Introduction

Much of the power and all of the flexibility of computers is derived from their ability to make decisions which alter the sequence of events in a computer program. Two control statements have already been introduced - the GO TO which forces a change of direction in a computer program and the logical IF statement which can formulate a logical proposition and take a decision based on the outcome. These are summarized again here.

It may cheer the reader to be told that by now he knows enough to do almost anything with FORTRAN; the essentials of arithmetic and organization have been covered. The remainder of the book is concerned with sophistication and refinement - if a programmer tried to invert a matrix or sort a list of numbers into order on the basis of what he knows now the programs would be repulsive, but it could be done.

A new feature introduced in FORTRAN 77 is the block IF statement which is very popular for reasons which will become clear. This statement is important because it enables FORTRAN programs to be written in a way more harmonious with modern ideas of good structure. There are also some less frequently used facilities to be found in the 'FORTRAN museum' which forms part of this chapter. Finally the use of END and its companion STOP will be described.

6.2 Review of familiar control statements

The earliest control statement, introduced in Chapter 2, was the GO TO statement:

```
GO TO label
```

which causes an immediate jump to the statement whose label is "label", which must exist in the program unit.

In Chapter 3, the logical IF statement was introduced:

```
IF(logical expression) statement
```

for example

```
IF(I.GT.3) GO TO 99
```

This statement examines the logical expression and if it is .TRUE., executes the statement which quite sensibly can be any FORTRAN executable statement except for the following:

(i) Another logical IF
(ii) an END statement
(iii) A statement from the block IF facility (this chapter)
(iv) a DO statement (Chapter 7)

The simplest kind of logical expression is the relational expressions in which the relational operators are

.GT.	greater than
.GE.	greater or equal
.EQ.	equal to
.LE.	less or equal
.LT.	less than
.NE.	not equal

It is not necessary for the arithmetic expressions to be of the same type, but if one is real and the other integer, the comparison is made by subtracting them as reals. As was pointed out in Chapter 4, it is foolish to rely on equality when the comparison is made with real numbers.

Occasionally a new programmer writes an IF statement in a program which creates a bad program structure. The worst example is something like

```
    IF(logical expression)GO TO 1Ø
    GO TO 2Ø
1Ø something
    .
    .
    GO TO 3Ø
2Ø something else
    .
    .
3Ø next
```

where an IF ... GO TO is followed by a GO TO. This is never necessary and is downright ugly. Any relational expression (or logical expression) has an opposite, and the same objective is achieved in a less mind bending way by

```
        IF(opposite) GO TO 2Ø
        something
            .
            .
        GO TO 3Ø
    2Ø something else
            .
    3Ø next
```

although the block IF will improve this further. For example

```
        IF(I.GT.3) GO TO 1Ø
        GO TO 2Ø
    1Ø J=43*I
        GO TO 3Ø
    2Ø J=-73*K
    3Ø etc...
```

is appalling; a better combination to achieve the same objective is:

```
        IF(I.LE.3) GO TO 2Ø
        J=43*I
        GO TO 3Ø
    2Ø J=-73*K
    3Ø etc...
```

The opposite of every relational operator is another relational operator, as listed below.

Relational Operator	Relational Opposite
.LT.	.GE.
.LE.	.GT.
.EQ.	.NE.
.GE.	.LT.
.GT.	.LE.
.NE.	.EQ.

Alternatively, the opposite of a logical expression is

```
        .NOT. logical expression
```

or some simplification, as will be seen in the next section; one would use the simplest logical expression that suits.

> A good program never follows an IF ... GO TO with a GO TO

6.3 More complicated logical expressions

Only the simplest logical expressions have so far been used in logical IF statements. In addition FORTRAN allows the use of five logical operators in forming more complicated expressions: .NOT., .AND., .OR., .EQV. and .NEQV.. They are used as

```
            logical
    .NOT. expression
```

This "inverts", i.e. if the logical expression is .TRUE. the .NOT. makes the result .FALSE. and vice versa.

```
    logical          logical
    expression .AND. expression
```

This is .TRUE. if both logical expressions are .TRUE., otherwise .FALSE..

```
    logical          logical
    expression .OR. expression
```

This is the "inclusive OR" operation and is .TRUE. if either or both of the logical expressions are .TRUE., otherwise .FALSE..

logical   logical
expression .EQV. expression

This operation gives the result .TRUE. if both logical expressions are the same, i.e. either both .TRUE. or both .FALSE., otherwise (when both expressions are different) the result is .FALSE..

logical   logical
expression .NEQV. expression

This is the "exclusive OR" operation. The result is .TRUE. if the logical expressions are different, i.e. one .TRUE. and the other .FALSE.. Otherwise it is .FALSE.. It is the opposite of the .EQV operation.

A truth table for these operators is given in Fig. 6.1. The rules for their application depend mainly on common sense. As before, the type of an arithmetic expression can be important when using the relational operators .GT., .GE., .EQ., .LE., and .NE.. However the result of a relational operation is either .TRUE. or .FALSE., i.e. it is no longer real or integer but logical. Logical type is, in fact, a type of FORTRAN. As might be expected, expressions operated on by these logical operators must already be logical. Therefore a correct expression is one like

I.GT.J.OR.X.LE.3.14

whereas the following is wrong through misuse of .AND. and dangerous because it expects a real comparison to produce an exact equality, which it may not:

A.AND.B.LT.75.0

Logical expressions can be compounded, but then as with ordinary arithmetic, the meaning of expressions can be unclear unless brackets are used or the hierarchy is defined. For example, does the expression

MARK.GT.7.OR.LESLIE.EQ.5
.AND.JOHN.LE.15

mean

(MARK.GT.7.OR.LESLIE.EQ.5)
.AND.(JOHN.LE.15)

Logical expression a	Logical operator	Logical expression b	Logical result
	.NOT.	.TRUE. .FALSE.	.FALSE. .TRUE.
.TRUE. .TRUE. .FALSE. .FALSE.	.AND.	.TRUE. .FALSE. .TRUE. .FALSE.	.TRUE. .FALSE. .FALSE. .FALSE.
.TRUE. .TRUE. .FALSE. .FALSE.	.OR.	.TRUE. .FALSE. .TRUE. .FALSE.	.TRUE. .TRUE. .TRUE. .FALSE.
.TRUE. .TRUE. .FALSE. .FALSE.	.EQV.	.TRUE. .FALSE. .TRUE. .FALSE.	.TRUE. .FALSE. .FALSE. .TRUE.
.TRUE. .TRUE. .FALSE. .FALSE.	.NEQV.	.TRUE. .FALSE. .TRUE. .FALSE.	.FALSE. .TRUE. .TRUE. .FALSE.

Fig.6.1. Truth table for the logical operations of FORTRAN 77.

or does it mean instead

(MARK.GT.7).OR.
(LESLIE.EQ.5.AND.JOHN.LE.15)

These interpretations give different results in a situation such as MARK = 8, LESLIE = 6, JOHN = 16. It turns out that the second version is correct. The order of priority among logical operations is:

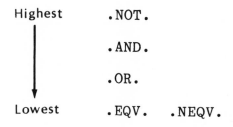

Highest   .NOT.

            .AND.

            .OR.

Lowest   .EQV.   .NEQV.

Examination of this table shows that .AND. is performed before .OR., which explains the earlier expression.

6.4 The block IF statement

Very often in writing a program a person with a natural sense of good structure will feel uncomfortable with a simple logical IF because it allows him only one statement for the .TRUE. condition, whereas he may wish to use several. For example, he may wish to follow a procedure called A if a logical expression is .TRUE. It is easy enough if A is a single statement:

    IF(logical expression) A

but very messy if A is a block of several statements:

    IF(logical expression) GO TO A
    GO TO next

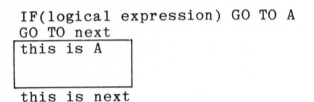

    this is next

which is an ugly structure; the following is better:

    IF(opposite) GO TO next

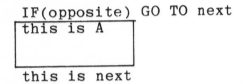

    this is next

The situation is even worse if there is a completely different procedure called B to be followed if the logical expression is .FALSE. as illustrated by the flowchart of Fig.6.2. In this case a programmer using the logical IF statement has no choice but to write something like

    IF(logical expression) GO TO A

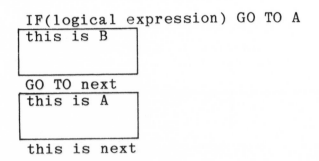

    GO TO next

    this is next

which makes the program difficult to read and is downright repugnant to a good programmer.

The block IF statement allows a more natural program structure than any of these. In the simplest case, a procedure A is to be followed if a logical expression is .TRUE.. Here a programmer should write

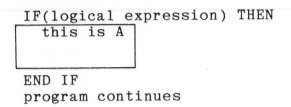

    END IF
    program continues

in which the block IF statement appears, which resembles the logical IF but has the word THEN in place of a statement. Block A consists of all the statements until the END IF statement occurs.

EXAMPLE:

    IF(J.EQ.Ø) THEN
      PRINT*,' PROVIDE MORE DATA'
      READ*,X,Y,Z
      J=3
    END IF
    program carries on

It is a good idea to write the statements of an IF block indented as shown; the labels, if any, have to stay where they are but the statements themselves can be indented.

In the case where there are alternate procedures to execute for the .TRUE. and .FALSE. conditions, the ELSE statement is useful:

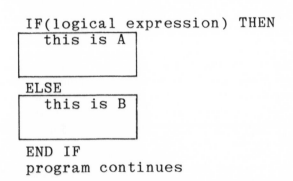

    END IF
    program continues

This corresponds to the structure shown in the flowchart of Fig.6.2. Here, only block A is executed if the expression is .TRUE. If it is .FALSE. the ELSE condition is taken and block B is executed.

EXAMPLE:

```
    IF(FX2.EQ.SIGN(FX2,FXØ)) THEN
C ON THE XØ SIDE, REPLACE XØ
    D=ABS(X2-XØ)
    XØ=X2
    FXØ=FX2
    ELSE
C ON THE X1 SIDE, REPLACE X1
    D=ABS(X2-X1)
    X1=X2
    FX1=FX2
    END IF
```

This is taken from the "False Position" program of the next section. The relational expression used in the IF statement seems to violate the moral principle of never expecting two real quantities to be equal. The statement is testing to see if FX2 has the same sign as FX0 and is safe, although as always there may be a better way. This example should be compared with Fig.6.2 so that the structure is fully understood. This kind of structure occurs often.

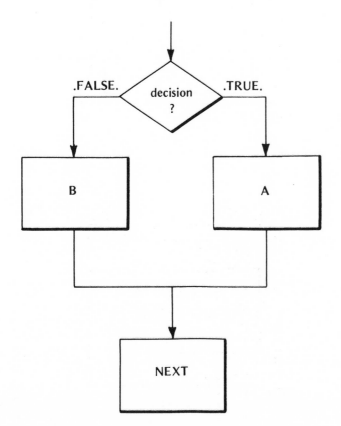

Fig. 6.2. The choices presented by a logical IF statement result in an awkward program structure.

It could be that block B would naturally begin with an IF statement to check another proposition before executing block B. It could be written that way,

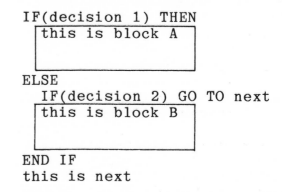

```
IF(decision 1) THEN
    this is block A

ELSE
    IF(decision 2) GO TO next
    this is block B

END IF
this is next
```

but a more readable structure is obtained with the ELSE IF statement,

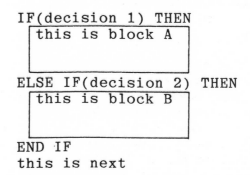

```
IF(decision 1) THEN
    this is block A

ELSE IF(decision 2) THEN
    this is block B

END IF
this is next
```

in which block B is only executed if the ELSE IF is .TRUE..

This can then be followed by more ELSE IF blocks, and as a final block only one optional ELSE until finally an END IF is encountered.

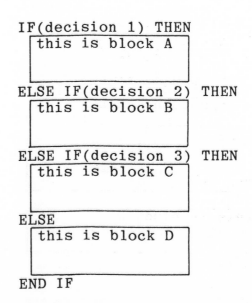

```
IF(decision 1) THEN
    this is block A

ELSE IF(decision 2) THEN
    this is block B

ELSE IF(decision 3) THEN
    this is block C

ELSE
    this is block D

END IF
```

Here, block A is executed if decision 1 is .TRUE. Block B is obeyed if decision 1 is .FALSE. and decision 2 is .TRUE. Block C is executed if decision 1 is .FALSE. and decision 3 is .TRUE. Block D is followed only if decision 1, decision 2, and decision 3 are all .FALSE.

> Only one block is ever executed

To summarize, a block IF structure:

(i) begins with IF...THEN;
(ii) is followed by any number of optional ELSE IF statements;
(iii) is finally followed by only one optional ELSE statement;
(iv) must be closed by an END IF.

IF blocks can be "nested", that is within any block IF structure a new block IF structure can begin. If this is done, the inside block must end before the next clause of the outer one. This means that within an IF block, all ELSE IF, ELSE and END IF statements belong to the most recent IF...THEN. A bad programmer might think otherwise, or even write an impossible structure.

EXAMPLES:
A permitted structure is

```
IF(decision 1) THEN
    IF(decision 2) THEN
        this is block A
    ELSE·IF(decision 3) THEN
        this is block B
    ELSE
        this is block C
    END IF
ELSE
    this is block D
END IF
```

such as

```
IF(HUNGER.GT.4.3) THEN
    IF(TIME.GT.17.Ø) THEN
        EAT=SAVOY
        WEAR=TUX
        PRINT*,EAT,WEAR
    ELSE IF(TIME.GT.12.5) THEN
        EAT=PUB
        PRINT*,EAT
    ELSE
        EAT=EGG
    END IF
ELSE
    EAT=Ø.Ø
    WORK=WORK+1.Ø
END
```

A forbidden structure is

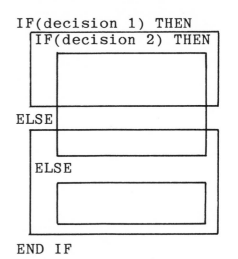

such as

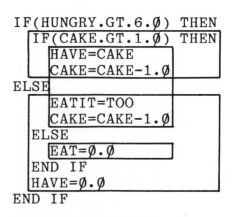

An outer IF block is at level 1, the first nested one at level 2, and so on. An IF block must always be ended by an END IF before the program can return to a lower level. This rule for the nesting of blocks is a common sense one, as is the restriction that an IF block or any clause of it cannot be entered from outside. This means that a control statement like GO TO is not permitted to jump inside the boundary of any IF block. It cannot jump in from outside, nor from another clause at the same level, nor from another level.

EXAMPLE:

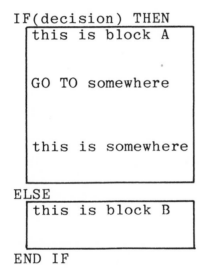

This is permitted because it does not cross a block boundary. It is probably bad structure within block A, but it is not forbidden.

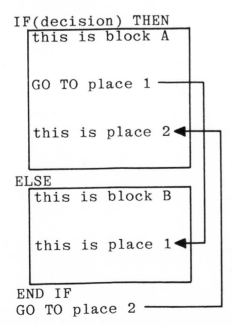

These GO TO statements are forbidden because they jump across the block boundaries. The structure is pretty ugly as well.

Common sense restrictions on the relationships of IF blocks and DO statements also exist; these are outlined in the next chapter.

6.5 An example — method of False Position — flowcharts

Given the program control methods that have been introduced, it is possible to write quite complicated procedures for sophisticated calculations. As an illustration a classical method for solving for the roots of an equation in one variable is developed into a FORTRAN program in this section. The procedure, called the method of False Position, is very straightforward, although its implementation is discussed in some detail (as a computer exercise, not as a problem in mathematics).

Suppose a real distinct root is sought of an equation

$$f(x) = 0$$

The method of False Position turns two rough guesses at the answer into an improvement on one of the guesses. By doing this over and over a 'good answer' is eventually found.

If there are two guesses at the answer called x_0 and x_1, which are known to be on opposite sides of it as in Fig. 6.3, then $f(x_0)$ and $f(x_1)$ will be of opposite sign for an uncomplicated function. The False Position method assumes that $f(x)$ is a straight line between the two guesses, and calculates x_2, which is where the root would be if the straight line assumption were true. A bit of algebra would reveal that

$$x_2 = x_0 - \frac{x_0 - x_1}{f(x_0) - f(x_1)} f(x_0)$$

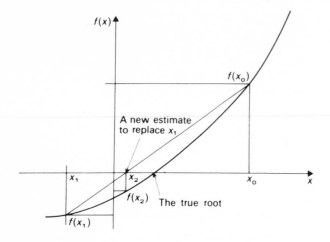

Fig. 6.3. The method of False Position. x_0 and x_1 are initial estimates on opposite sides of the root. x_2 is a new estimate which in the illustration would replace x_1 because it is on the same side of the root.

which is unlikely to be the correct answer, but it must be a better answer than whichever of x_0 and x_1 is on the same side of the root, as can be seen in Fig. 6.3.

Therefore x_2 can replace x_0 if $f(x_2)$ has the same sign as $f(x_0)$; otherwise x_2 can replace x_1. The procedure can then be repeated to find better and better estimates until the program is satisfied with them.

It is desired that this should be made into a computer program. The steps in the program will be:

(i) Establish initial guesses x_0 and x_1

(ii) Calculate an improved guess x_2

(iii) Replace either x_0 or x_1 by x_2

(iv) Return to step (ii) if further improvement is desired.

An outline flowchart for this process is given by Fig. 6.4.

The process of translating this procedure into a FORTRAN program begins with an elaboration of the details.

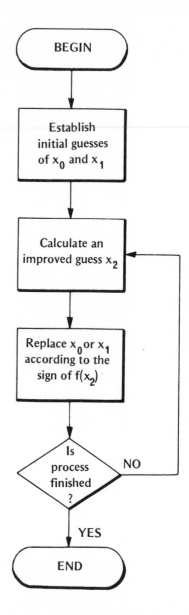

Fig. 6.4. Outline flowchart for the method of False Position.

(i) Establish the initial guess.

It is apparently desirable that x_0 and x_1 should be chosen so that $f(x_0)$ and $f(x_1)$ are of opposite sign. The program could interact with the user who would provide values of x_0 and x_1 until this condition is met. By implication, therefore, this program is intended for use on an interactive system.

It is necessary to decide when $f(x_0)$ and $f(x_1)$ are of opposite sign. Casting around for a means of doing this, the SIGN function suggests itself. The relational expression

$$f(x_0).EQ.SIGN(f(x_0),f(x_1))$$

is .TRUE. when the signs are the same and this will be used to return to the user for the next guess. Fig. 6.5 is a finished description of this stage.

(ii) Calculate an improved guess x_2.

This simply follows the formula

$$x_2 = x_0 - \frac{x_0 - x_1}{f(x_0) - f(x_1)}\, f(x_0)$$

(iii) Replace either x_0 or x_1 by x_2.

To decide which of x_0 or x_1 is to be replaced, the sign of $f(x_0)$ is compared to the sign of $f(x_1)$. As in step (i), this uses a relational expression

$$f(x_2).EQ.SIGN\ (f(x_2),f(x_0))$$

which is .TRUE. when the signs are the same, in which case x_2 replaces x_0. Otherwise x_2 replaces x_1, and similarly $f(x_2)$ replaces either $f(x_0)$ or $f(x_1)$. This suggests a structure like Fig. 6.2. Fig. 6.6 combines this stage and the previous one.

(iv) Is further improvement desired?

Such a simple question unfortunately has a complicated answer if it is done properly. The usual procedure is to see how much of a change is represented by the new estimate and stop if it is small enough. The complications arise in deciding what is small enough. When a new value x_2 has been calculated the absolute value of the change is

$$\Delta = |x_2 - x_0| \quad \text{or} \quad \Delta = |x_2 - x_1|$$

depending on which side is chosen. Stopping of the process could be based on this. For a smallish root, less than 1 say, it might be sensible to say

$$IF(\Delta.GT.1E{-}5)\ go\ back$$

and the change of 10^{-5} probably implies an error around 10^{-4} in the answer.

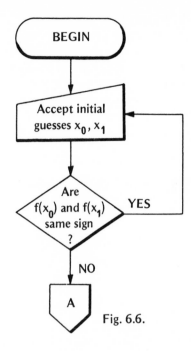

Fig. 6.6.

Fig. 6.5. Flowchart for establishing initial guesses in the method of False Position.

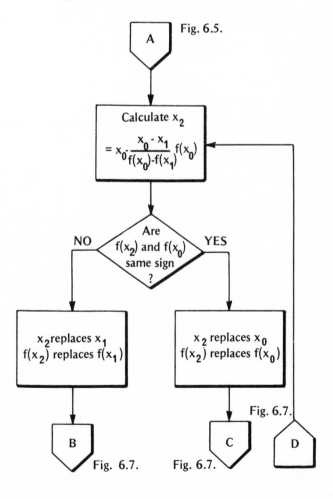

Fig. 6.6. Flowchart of stages (ii) and (iii) in the method of False Position.

However this is nonsense if the root is large. Suppose the root was $x = 10^9$, then to ask that Δ should be less than 10^{-5} is expecting the change to be less than one part in 10^{-14}. This would probably be ridiculously strict and it is unlikely that the computer would have that much precision in the first place.

It is better to 'normalize' the step size as, for example,

$$IF(ABS(\Delta/x_2).GT.1E-5) \text{ go back}$$

except that here the opposite problem could arise for tiny roots. As a compromise use

$$IF(\Delta.GT.1E-5) \text{ go back}$$

if the absolute value of the root x is apparently less than 1 (x_2 is the best guess of it) and

$$IF(ABS(\Delta/x_2).GT.1E-5) \text{ go back}$$

if the absolute value of x_2 is greater than 1. The remainder of the program is accordingly shown by Fig. 6.7.

If the explanation of the procedure is inadequate or confusing, then according to the principle that a picture is worth a thousand words, the complete flowchart of Fig. 6.8 is worthy of study. The reader should be convinced by now of the value of flowcharts as an aid to documentation for his own understanding and as a means of communication with others. Fig. 6.8 is a much better explanation of the method of False Position than any written description.

Various flowchart symbols have been used already in the text, and the meanings of some of the standard symbols are shown in Fig. 6.9.

It only remains to 'code' the False Position algorithm into FORTRAN. Of course up to this point the discussion relates to this algorithm in any language. As a first step, suitable variable names are chosen for the important quantities. In FORTRAN the names can and should be chosen to clarify their meaning in relation to the document-

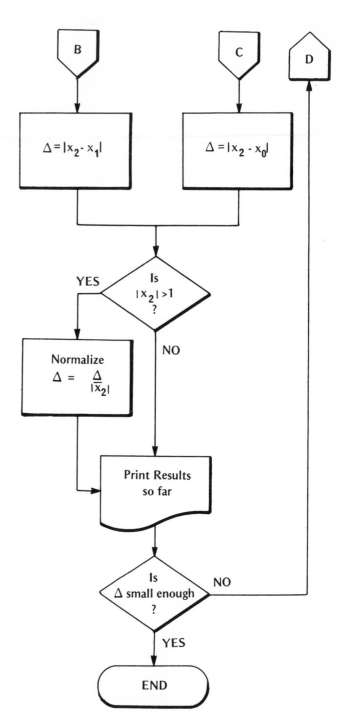

Fig. 6.7. Flowchart of the final stage in the False Position algorithm.

ation. A choice could be

X$\emptyset$	for x_0
X1	for x_1
X2	for x_2
FX$\emptyset$	for $f(x_0)$
FX1	for $f(x_1)$
FX2	for $f(x_2)$
D	for Δ

Suppose now that

$$f(x)=x^3-7.8x^2+18.5x-9.1$$

then the program comes out as

```
C FIND ROOT BY FALSE POSITION
C ESTABLISH AN INITIAL GUESS
      PRINT 100
 10 READ*,X0,X1
C CALCULATE GIVEN FUNCTION VALUES
      FX0=((X0-7.8)*X0+18.5)*X0-9.1
      FX1=((X1-7.8)*X1+18.5)*X1-9.1
      PRINT 110,X0,FX0
      PRINT 120,X1,FX1
C TRY AGAIN IF FX0, FX1 SAME SIGN
      IF(FX0.EQ.SIGN(FX0,FX1))THEN
         PRINT 130
         GO TO 10
      END IF
C CALCULATE THE NEW ESTIMATE X2
 20 X2=X0-FX0*(X0-X1)/(FX0-FX1)
      FX2=((X2-7.8)*X2+18.5)*X2-9.1
      PRINT 140,X2,FX2
C WHICH SIDE ARE WE ON
      IF(FX2.EQ.SIGN(FX2,FX0))THEN
C ON THE X0 SIDE, REPLACE X0
         D=ABS(X2-X0)
         X0=X2
         FX0=FX2
         PRINT 150
      ELSE
C ON THE X1 SIDE, REPLACE X1
         D=ABS(X2-X1)
         X1=X2
         FX1=FX2
         PRINT 160
      END IF
C NORMALIZE D IF ABS(X2) GT 1.0
      IF(ABS(X2).GT.1.0)D=D/ABS(X2)
      PRINT 170,D
C REPEAT UNTIL D IS SMALL
      IF(D.GT.1E-5)GO TO 20
      PRINT 180,X2
 100 FORMAT(' GIVE TWO GUESSES')
 110 FORMAT(' X0, FX0 ARE',2F9.5)
 120 FORMAT(' X1, FX1 ARE',2F9.5)
 130 FORMAT(' TRY AGAIN')
 140 FORMAT(' X2, FX2 ARE',2F9.5)
 150 FORMAT(' X2 REPLACES X0')
 160 FORMAT(' X2 REPLACES X1')
 170 FORMAT(' DELTA = ',F9.5)
 180 FORMAT(' SUITABLE ROOT',F9.5)
      END
```

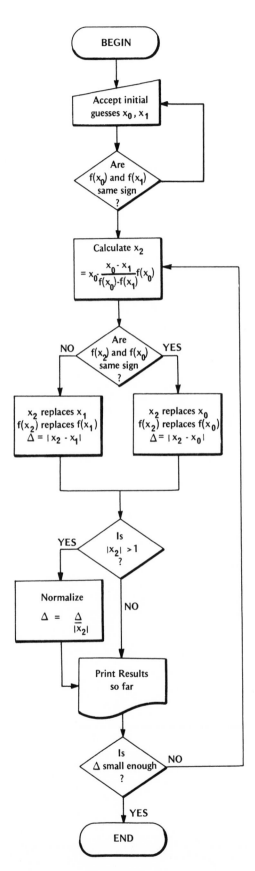

Fig. 6.8. Completed flowchart for the method
of False Position.

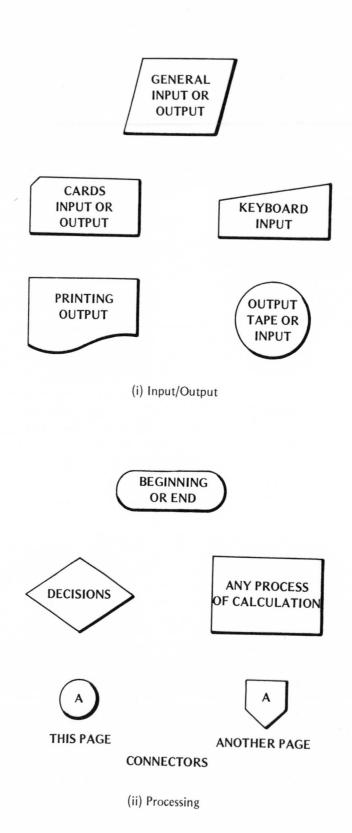

(i) Input/Output

(ii) Processing

Fig.6.9. Conventional flowchart symbols.

EXERCISE:
   Try this program. Does it work? Can you improve it? No program is ever perfect.

EXERCISE:
   Supposedly x_0 and x_1 were initially on opposite sides of the answer. Is this necessary?

Summary

The steps in the preparation of this program have been:

   (i) A statement of the problem

   (ii) An outline of the method (Fig. 6.4)

   (iii) Elaboration of the details (Figs 6.5,6.6,6.7)

   (iv) Finalization of the algorithm

   (v) A choice of reasonable names

   (vi) Translation into FORTRAN

   (vii) Testing and improvement

Careful programmers follow similar steps in developing programs. Although errors are always possible, there will be fewer if a programmer is systematic in his development. Although this may seem an obvious way to organize a programming task, it has been given a name: Stepwise Refinement. The programmer works from the general to the particular, deciding how each part of the task is done in detail after the general outline is known. It is a good principle, but by no means a law. It is not infallible; a wrong decision at an early stage is just as difficult to unravel however systematically it has been made. The most difficult part of programming occurs when a program, however carefully devised, clearly does not work and the errors in it have to be found. They could be errors in conception, design, details, coding or (very unlikely) the computer system. The author will admit that the job of finding errors is the nearest programming comes to being an art rather than a craft; a bit of inspiration always helps.

6.6 The FORTRAN museum — some other control statements

It may not be totally fair to these neglected statements to relegate them to the status of museum pieces, because each has its own uses, but they are infrequently used. The arithmetic IF statement has been largely superseded as a means of branching. The computed GO TO statement is useful in a particular sort of program construction, as is the assigned GO TO.

(i) The Arithmetic IF Statement

The quaint arithmetic IF statement was the only IF statement in early versions of FORTRAN. It considers the result of an arithmetic expression and takes one of three branches depending on whether the expression is positive, negative, or zero. This is not, of course, quite the way that programmers think about decisions and so in practice the logical or block IF is nearly always used. The form of the arithmetic IF is:

$$IF(expression) \quad label_1, label_2, label_3$$

Here, "expression" is an arithmetic expression, and "label1", "label2" and "label3" are three statement labels which must exist. The program jumps to one of these as follows:

   "label1" if "expression" is negative
   "label2" if "expression" is zero
   "label3" if "expression" is positive

The order is easy to remember as "minus, zero, plus" or some polite rhyme to go with this. If "expression" is real, a zero result is unlikely except by accident as this is the same as expecting an exact equality among reals.

The statement immediately following the IF should be one of "label1", "label2", or "label3"; otherwise an ugly structure is a certainty. If it has no label at all it cannot be reached by the program in any way.

EXAMPLE:
   The statement

$$IF(B*B-4.\emptyset*A*C)2\emptyset,3\emptyset,4\emptyset$$

is quite obviously the test of the discriminant in a quadratic expression ax^2+bx+c. This is an obvious situation where the arithmetic IF would be used.

(ii) The Computed GO TO Statement

The computed GO TO statement allows a large number of destinations to be chosen from a list, where the choice depends on the value of an integer expression. It is written

$$GO \ TO \ (\underset{1}{label},...)[,] \ \underset{expression}{integer}$$

where the comma in square brackets is optional. The computer will jump to "label1" if the value of the integer expression is 1, to "label2" if 2, and so on. Clearly the integer expression when evaluated usually gives a result between one and the number of destinations. If it lies outside this range, the program continues with the statement which follows. The same label can appear several times in the list. Every label in the list must occur in the same program unit as the computed GO TO.

EXAMPLE:

    GO TO(1∅,3∅,2∅,1∅),INT(X*X+Y*Y)

Note the use of INT to convert a real expression to integer - a useful trick. The transfer is to

    Label 1∅ if INT(X*X+Y*Y) is 1
    Label 3∅ if INT(X*X+Y*Y) is 2
    Label 2∅ if INT(X*X+Y*Y) is 3
    Label 1∅ if INT(X*X+Y*Y) is 4

The program continues if INT(X*X+Y*Y) is outside the range 1 to 4.

It will be found in the discussion of program structures in Chapter 9 that the computed GO TO is the FORTRAN method of achieving the "CASE OF" construction.

(iii) The Assigned GO TO and the ASSIGN Statement

Finally, FORTRAN has the ASSIGN statement and the assigned GO TO statement which together allow a programmer to change the destination of a GO TO. Some people find this useful, but the author never uses it because it makes programs difficult to follow.

The assigned GO TO is

$$GO \ TO \ iv \ , \ (\underset{1}{label},\underset{2}{label},...)$$

"iv" is an integer variable name, which has been assigned as the label of the destination of the GO TO. This value can only be defined properly by an ASSIGN statement. Not only is the comma optional before the list of labels, but the list itself is optional. If the list "label1", "label2",... is given it must spell out all the possible values that the program might assign to "iv". This may make the option of giving the list sound unattractive, but as a safety measure it is valuable.

The ASSIGN statement

    ASSIGN label TO iv

is the only way of establishing the destination of an assigned GO TO. In a program with ASSIGN statements it is vital to be aware that assigning a statement label is not the same as defining a integer value.

When defined as a statement label

    ASSIGN 1∅ TO I

the variable I does not have the integer value 10; in fact it must not be used as an integer value while it has a label assigned to it. It can be redefined as an integer value

$$I=1\emptyset$$

after which it does not have the label 10 assigned to it. A variable cannot carry a label and an integer value at the same time.

EXAMPLE:

    ASSIGN 34 TO JOHN
    .
    .
    .
    GO TO JOHN (1∅,2∅,16,34,99)

This combination results in a jump to the statement labelled 34 - there must be one.

It is also possible to use the ASSIGN statement to set up the label of a FORMAT statement as will be shown later.

```
You can stop your program
           with
     STOP  or   END
You must end your program
           with
          END
```

6.7 PAUSEing, STOPping, and ENDing

The PAUSE statement is available to bring a temporary halt to a program. How this is implemented in a given computer will vary. On a little machine with one user, the computer may actually halt until someone presses a button. On a huge machine this is unlikely to be the case, for to allow anyone to bring the installation to a grinding halt would be inviting 'computer vandals' to cause disruption. Every computer has its vandals; they are young, bright, immature and love to play tricks and games.

The PAUSE statement is

PAUSE [n]

where n is a string of up to 5 digits or a character constant. The value of n is available during the pause, but what this means depends on the machine.

The STOP statement is very practical; it is an alternative to the END statement for stopping a program, i.e. finally terminating its execution. The difference is that it can be put anywhere in a program whereas END has to be the last statement in the program unit.

The STOP statement is

STOP [n]

The END statement is

END

and must be the last statement of a program unit. In a main program it executes as STOP. In a subprogram it executes as RETURN as will be seen.

6.8 The remaining control statements

There remain a few control statements:

(i) The DO statement and its friend CONTINUE are so important that they rate Chapter 7 all to themselves.

(ii) The RETURN statement is used in FUNCTION and SUBROUTINE subprograms and is described in Chapter 8.

(iii) The CALL statement is used to call a SUBROUTINE and is described in Chapter 10.

Here is a full list of control statements:

```
 1 GO TO
 2 Computed GO TO
 3 Assigned GO TO
 4 Arithmetic IF
 5 Logical IF
 6 Block IF
 7 ELSE IF
 8 ELSE
 9 END IF
10 DO        (Chapter 7)
11 CONTINUE
12 STOP
13 PAUSE
14 END
15 CALL      (Chapter 10)
16 RETURN    (Chapter 8)
```

6.9 Problems

PROBLEM 6.1:
Use the method of False Position to solve:

(i) $\ln(x) + 1 = 0$
(the answer is of course $1/e$ or .3679)

(ii) $x^3 - 3x^2 + 2.5x - 0.5 = 0$
(there are three roots, all real)

Observe the speed of convergence (i.e. how fast it gets to the answer from some reasonable starting position).

PROBLEM 6.2:
The Newton-Raphson method will converge more rapidly than the method of False Position, if it converges. This method requires only a single guess, x_1 and uses the slope of the function to predict an improved root. In Fig. 6.10,

$$x_2 = x_1 - \frac{f(x_1)}{f'(x_1)}$$

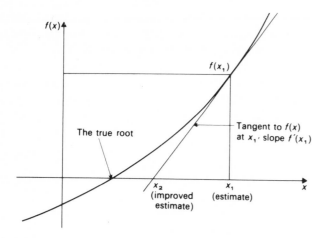

Fig. 6.10. The Newton-Raphson iteration. The improved estimate x_2 is found using the slope of the function at the earlier estimate x_1.

If you don't know how to calculate the slope, f'(x), ask someone who knows more mathematics than you do to work out the formula for f'(x) for you.

Write a nicely stuctured program and solve by this method:

(i) ln(x) +1 = 0

(ii) $x^3 - 3x^2 + 2.5x - 0.5 = 0$

Investigate how fast it converges compared to the False Position method. For the second function investigate how the choice of initial guess affects the stability of the method (i.e. its ability

to get on the right track for each root).

PROBLEM 6.3:
Don't be afraid of this one - tackle it systematically.

The speed of convergence of some numerical methods can be improved by a procedure known as Aitken's delta-squared extrapolation. If three successive improved estimates of a quantity are known, say x_1, x_2 and x_3 then a further improvement is

$$z = \frac{x_1 x_3 - x_2^2}{x_3 - 2x_2 + x_1}$$

This acceleration can easily be built into the method of False Position. The complication is that x_1, x_2 and x_3 must be estimates from the same side of the root. Integer variables can be used to count how many estimates are available on each side and so the extrapolation can be used at the right point. Each time the Aitken formula is used, the improved estimate z becomes x_1 for the next round. Therefore the Aitken formula is used after the first three False Position estimates (on a given side of the root) and then after every further two False Position estimates on that side. The whole procedure can be added to the flow diagram of Fig. 6.8 as a simple elaboration, i.e no major change to the program structure is required.

Using the method of False Position incorporating Aitken's extrapolation solve:

(i) ln(x) + 1 = 0

(ii) $x^3 - 3x^2 + 2.5x - 0.5 = 0$

Again, compare the speed of convergence and stability with the programming methods you used in Problems 6.1 and 6.2. Which of the three would you use for tackling an unknown function? If you have done these three problems well you now have quite a useful function solving kit.

PROBLEM 6.4:

Digital plotting machines are widely used to produce various forms of drawings, graphs and other pictorial results. Most such machines can move their pens only in certain directions, usually as single steps in the X or Y direction or both. A typical machine would move in one of the eight directions shown in Fig. 6.11. Smooth curves are made up of a very large number of single steps in these eight directions.

Programs which control these devices have to be very efficient; although the algebra of the pen motion lends itself to the use of trigonometric functions, these would be too slow in practice. Instead carefully organized logic and arithmetic are used involving the minimum of computation.

(i) Write a program without trigonometric functions which "encodes" the integer co-ordinates of the endpoints in Fig. 6.11 into a number from 0 to 7.

(ii) Write a program without trigonometric functions which decodes a number from 0 to 7 into the integer co-ordinates of the endpoints in Fig. 6.11.

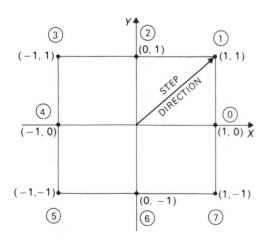

Fig. 6.11. Digital drawing machines can move their pens in single steps from the centre towards eight possible positions on the box. Programs are desired to encode, decode, and rotate the direction of pen motion.

(iii) Write programs for rotation of the step direction: given integer end co-ordinates calculate new ones from them directly for rotations of 45° or 135° clockwise or anticlockwise. The most efficient schemes would not use the encoding and decoding method.

PROBLEM 6.5:

Many games can be devised to be played with the computer. With complex games such as chess, no optimum strategy is known and programming these is a deep study. However for many simple games optimum strategies are possible. Such a game is NIMB, which can always be won by the first player. Write a program to play the simplified version described below. A good program will issue instructions and information as the game proceeds. Furthermore it will never lose if given the first move or if the opponent makes a mistake.

The game in a simplified version begins with the number 15, which could represent, for example, 15 matches on a table. Each of the two players in turn must remove one, two or three from the number available. The loser is the player forced to remove the last one. The winning strategy is very simple.

PROBLEM 6.6:

If NIMB was mastered without difficulty, try noughts and crosses (X's and O's). Here, either player can force a draw. If a player makes a mistake, the other can win. This would be easier with array variables introduced later on. However 'it was said that any problem can now be solved, so do this one the hard way.

PROBLEM 6.7:

Mastermind has been a popular game recently. Here, in its simpler form, four coloured pegs are hidden from sight which are all different and are chosen from 6 possible colours. You could represent these as a choice of four numbers from 1 to 6. The player has to discover the colours and their arrangement by trying to match the combination. He is told how many correct colours he has and how many are in the right place. For example if the hidden code is

4 3 1 5

and the player tries

2 1 3 5

he is told that three colours are correct and one is in the right place.

Write a program in which the computer sets the problem using random numbers (Chapter 4) and you play. The author believes it is always possible to solve the code on the third try if all the colours are different.

PROBLEM 6.8:
Mastermind again. Now you set the code and the computer plays to find the code on the third move.

7
Program loops

7.1 Introduction

A repeated program loop is such a common feature of computer programs that all computer languages have special statements to help in their organization. In this chapter, after a discussion of counting with integers or reals, the DO statement is introduced and its use is described in some detail. There are a number of ways of making repeated calculations as efficient as possible, and these are stressed as well.

7.2 Counting with integers or reals

The structure of a closed loop was first introduced some chapters ago and arises in a program which contains a return path so that a part of the calculation is repeated. These loops can be unconditional, as with a GO TO statement, or conditional as in the method of False Position of Chapter 6, when the calculation was repeated until the error seemed to be small enough.

It is always possible to make a counting loop in which a variable is set aside for counting. This has already been shown for integer counters, as Fig.7.1. Before the loop an integer variable is set to 1, and at the end of the loop 1 is added to it. An IF statement at the end of the loop returns the program to the beginning until it is finished. Such a program is

```
      I=1
  2Ø  PRINT I
      I=I+1
      IF(I.LE.1Ø)GO TO 2Ø
      END
```

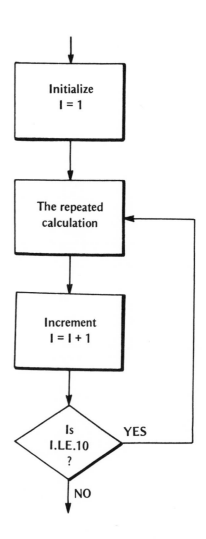

Fig. 7.1. Organization of a counting loop repeated 10 times.

In fact the IF statement might take several forms and still be correct;

```
      IF(I.LT.11)GO TO 2Ø

      IF(I.EQ.11)STOP
      GO TO 2Ø
```

In both these alternatives the machine relies on exact equality of I with the

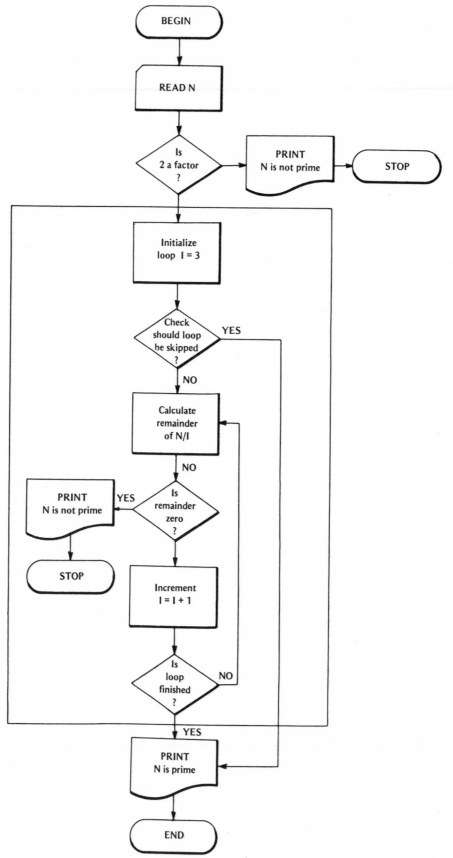

Fig. 7.2. A program to find if N is prime the
hard way.

final value to terminate the loop, which is reliable because I is an integer.

EXAMPLE:

Here is a program to test if a number N is prime by testing all divisors for zero remainder up to SQRT(N). Because it reads the value of N without prompting, it is evidently intended for batch use. Its flowchart is shown in Fig.7.2.

```
C PROGRAM TESTS FOR PRIME NUMBERS
C FOR ANY N GREATER THAN 2
 1Ø FORMAT(I5)
 2Ø FORMAT(I6,' IS NOT PRIME')
 3Ø FORMAT(' YES',I5,' IS PRIME')
C READ IN N FROM CARDS
    READ(5,1Ø) N
C TEST FOR FACTOR OF 2
    IF(MOD(N,2).EQ.Ø) THEN
      PRINT 2Ø,N
      STOP
    END IF
C TRY ODD FACTORS 3 TO SQRT(N)
```
```
C INITIALIZE COUNTER
    IMAX=SQRT(REAL(N))
    I=3
C CHECK OUT THE INITIAL CONDITION
    IF(I.GT.IMAX)GO TO 5Ø
 4Ø IF(MOD(N,I).EQ.Ø) THEN
      PRINT 2Ø,N
      STOP
    END IF
C INCREMENT COUNTER
    I=I+2
C TEST FOR END OF LOOP
    IF(I.LE.IMAX)GO TO 4Ø
```
```
C IF GET TO HERE, N IS PRIME
 5Ø PRINT 3Ø,N
    END
```

The loop to count from 3 to SQRT(N) is contained in a box. Note that a new feature has been added to this loop - before it is begun a test is made to see if it should be executed at all - otherwise the program fails on the prime 3. This initial check is an important feature of the loops using DO statement as will be seen.

EXAMPLE:

It is also possible to count backwards; here is a program to find the factorial of N:

```
C PROGRAM TO FIND FACTORIAL N
C FIRST ACCEPT N AND CHECK IT
 1Ø PRINT*,' PROVIDE +VE INTEGER'
    READ*,N
    IF(N.LT.Ø)GO TO 1Ø
C FORM PRODUCT 1*2*...*N
    IFACT=1
    IF(N.LE.1)GO TO 3Ø
 2Ø IFACT=IFACT*N
    N=N-1
    IF(N.GE.2)GO TO 2Ø
 3Ø PRINT*,'FACTORIAL IS ',IFACT
    END
```

and in its flowchart, Fig.7.3, the same loop structure is found. The factorial of 0 is 1. Does this program work for N=0?

Both these examples show that in some instances it may be undesirable for a loop to be executed at all, and that a check of the counter against the final condition can be used to jump past the loop.

Suppose now that a loop with a real counter is desired. One safe way is actually to use an integer counter and to calculate the real count from it. To count X=0.1, 0.2, ..., 1.0, it is possible to write

```
C COUNT WITH REAL X
    I=1
 1Ø X=REAL(I)/1Ø.Ø
    :
    Calculate
    :
    I=I+1
    IF(I.LE.1Ø)GO TO 1Ø
    Program continues
```

There is no perfectly safe way to control a loop with a real number. It is known that real arithmetic has limited precision and so an exact equality can never be expected. But consider:

```
    X=Ø.1
 1Ø Calculate
    :
    X=X+Ø.1
    IF(X.LE.1.Ø)GO TO 1Ø
    Program continues
```

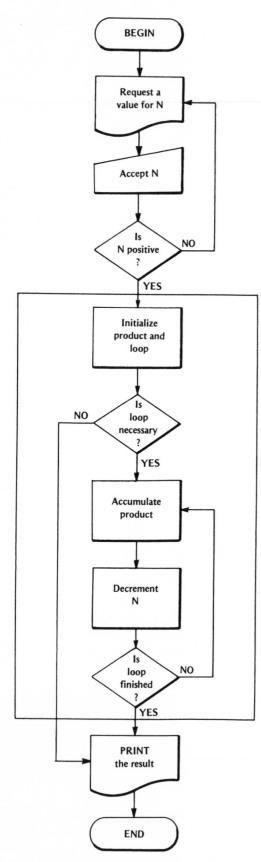

Fig. 7.3. A program to find factorial N the hard way.

As 0.1 is successively added to X, it should either be exact or fall slightly short. Therefore the loop should be done exactly 10 times; the .LE. test should be safe. If the program says

```
IF(X.LT.1.1)GO TO 1Ø
```

then it is asking for trouble, if not in this simple case then in more complicated ones. To count backwards the safest test is .GE.:

```
C COUNT BACKWARDS FROM 4.9 TO 4.1
    COUNT=4.9
 43 Calculate
        :
    COUNT=COUNT-Ø.1
    IF(COUNT.GE.4.1)GO TO 43
    Program continues
```

However, in general it is best to count with integers.

EXAMPLE:

A table of sines is to be calculated for the angles 0°, 10°, ..., 90°. The SIN function must be called with a series of arguments in radians:

$$0, \ \pi/18, \ 2\pi/18, \ ... \ , \ \pi/2$$

A suitable program is

```
C CALCULATE A TABLE OF SINES
    WRITE(6,1Ø)
 1Ø FORMAT(5X,'ANGLE',5X,'SINE')
C INITIALIZE COUNTER AND ANGLES
    TMAX=2.Ø*ATAN(1.Ø)
    TADD=TMAX/9.Ø
    THETA=Ø.Ø
C LOOP AND PRINT SINES
 3Ø WRITE(6,4Ø)THETA,SIN(THETA)
 4Ø FORMAT(1X,2F9.3)
    THETA=THETA+TADD
    IF(THETA.LE.TMAX)GO TO 3Ø
    END
```

You have to try this to be sure that it will repeat the loop the correct number of times.

EXERCISE:

Calculate and print e^x for x=1.0, 0.9, 0.8, ..., -0.9, -1.0.

7.3 Automatic looping with the DO statement

The hard way of organizing loops has been emphasized in various earlier sections, first of all in the hope that the reader will know exactly what a loop is all about, and secondly to emphasize the power and convenience of the DO statement when it is introduced. It is a bit like the nice feeling you get when you stop banging your head against a wall. Repeated sections of a program can be set up with the DO statement, and ended on a labelled statement almost anywhere; however the usual practice is to end loops on the CONTINUE statement. To repeat a calculation 10 times simply write

```
    DO 2Ø I=1,1Ø
       :
    Calculation
       :
 2Ø CONTINUE
```

in which all the statements between DO and CONTINUE form a block which is called the "range" of the DO statement. This block is repeated with the DO variable I taking successive values 1, 2, ..., 10. This simple form of DO statement is

DO label $[,]$ variable = expression1
, expression2

After the DO statement somewhat further down the program there must be a terminating statement with the specified label. All the statements up to and including the terminating statement form a block which is called the "range" of the DO.

The DO variable behaves like a counter whose initial value is "expression1", whose final value is "expression2" and which is incremented each time around the range. A program is not permitted to change the value of the DO variable inside the range of the DO loop.

"Expression1" might not be the same type as the variable in which case the value of "expression1" is converted to the required type, as in

```
    DO 63  X=1,1Ø
       :
 63 CONTINUE
```

or

```
    IMAX=1
    DO 9Ø I=SQRT(REAL(N)),IMAX
       :
 9Ø CONTINUE
```

It could be that "expression2" is less than "expression1", for example, if N were 5 in the above example. In this situation the DO range is jumped over completely. Another example of this would be:

```
    J=1Ø
    DO 3Ø I=J,5
       :
 3Ø CONTINUE
    Program continues
```

The number of repetitions of the loop is predetermined. The machine decides as soon as it hits the DO statement how many times it is required to repeat the DO range and so fooling about with anything connected with the expressions used to determine the number of repetitions will have no effect.* In particular, a program is not permitted to change the value of the DO variable inside the range of the DO loop. The optional comma in the DO statement after the label is not often used.
EXAMPLES:

```
    DO 12Ø IQ=13,27
       :
 12Ø CONTINUE
```

This loop is repeated 15 times with IQ taking the values 13, 14, ..., 27

*Now FORTRAN IV programmers may have to make a major adjustment here. The FORTRAN 77 standard requires loops to be missed out if their parameters indicate this - in FORTRAN IV they were probably done once. This is an area of incompatability which is made worse because FORTRAN IV compilers disobeyed the FORTRAN IV standard. Furthermore, FORTRAN 77 predetermines the number of repetitions and this becomes independent of any changes to the DO variable.

```
      YMIN=15.0
      YMAX=12.0
      DO 130 X=YMIN,YMAX
        :
130   CONTINUE
      Program continues
```

This loop is jumped past. The statement following the CONTINUE is taken next.

```
      M=5
      N=1
      DO 66 K=N,M
      M=10
      N=33
66    CONTINUE
```

This loop is done 5 times.

The CONTINUE statement

CONTINUE

is an executable statement which doesn't do anything. It is used anywhere as a convenient receptacle for a label. Most often programmers will end loops with a CONTINUE because it improves the readability of the program.

EXAMPLE:

I is a positive number and it is desired to obtain the bit-reverse of I. If the binary representation of I is

$$b_N \cdots b_1 \ b_0$$

then the bit-reverse of I is

$$b_0 \ b_1 \cdots b_N$$

For example if I=3 and there are eight bits to be reversed,

```
        I = 3 = 0000 0011
bit-reverse of I = 1100 0000 = 192
```

It can be recalled from Chapter 4 that if I is positive and odd, the least significant bit of I is 1. Furthermore, if I is divided by 2, its bit pattern is shifted to the right. It is therefore possible to examine each bit of I and build up in a variable J the reversed version. Here is the program for reversing 8 bits of I:

```
C OBTAIN THE BIT-REVERSE OF I
      PRINT*,'NUMBER TO REVERSE'
      READ*,I
      J=0
      DO 10 K=1,8
        J=2*J+MOD(I,2)
        I=I/2
10    CONTINUE
      PRINT*,'REVERSE IS ',J
      END
```

This is a practical requirement as will be seen in the Case Study of the fast Fourier transform, Chapter 12. It is interesting that K, the loop variable, has not actually been used within the loop - there is no reason why it should be.

EXERCISE:

Modify this example to calculate the bit-reverse of N bits of a number I, where I and N are read in.

EXAMPLE:

Here is a program to multiply two positive integer numbers, first of all by brute force. The product of I and J is I added to itself J times, or vice versa. Notice the manner of interchanging I and J through an intermediate variable M. Why?

```
C BRUTE FORCE PRODUCT I*J
C READ THEM IN FIRST
      PRINT*,'PROVIDE TWO INTEGERS'
      READ*,I,J
C MAKE I THE SMALLER NUMBER
      IF(I.GT.J) THEN
        M=I
        I=J
        J=M
      END IF
C FORM THE PRODUCT IPROD
      IPROD=0
      DO 10 K=1,I
        IPROD=IPROD+J
10    CONTINUE
      PRINT*,'SILLY PRODUCT ',IPROD
      END
```

Observing that I and J are binary numbers,

$$I = b_0 \times 2^0 + b_1 \times 2^1 + \ldots + b_{N-1} \times 2^{N-1}$$

where its binary representation is

$$b_{N-1} \cdots b_1 \, b_0$$

the multiplication of any two positive numbers can be achieved in at most N steps. For a 32 bit integer, N will be 31 for positive values.

J is added to itself once if b_0 is 1
twice if b_1 is 1
four times if b_2 is 1

etc., or put another way,

J is added if b_0 is 1
$2*J$ is added if b_1 is 1
$4*J$ is added if b_2 is 1

and so on. So here is a much more efficient program:

```
C PRODUCT I*J BY CLEVER METHOD
C READ THEM IN FIRST
      PRINT*,'PROVIDE TWO INTEGERS'
      READ*,I,J
C FORM PRODUCT IPROD
      IPROD=0
      DO 10 K=1,32
        IPROD=IPROD+J*MOD(I,2)
        J=J*2
        I=I/2
        IF(I.EQ.0)GO TO 20
 10   CONTINUE
 20   PRINT*,'CLEVER PRODUCT',IPROD
      END
```

The bits of I are found by successive division of I by 2 - each division shifts the bits of I one place to the right. MOD(I,2) provides the right hand bit each time. The program loop may not be executed the full 32 times because it will stop when successive division provides a zero I. I and J are both subjected here to the process called recursion. Instead of calculating

$$J*2**(K-1)$$

which could be done, J is each time increased by multiplying it, as in

$$J=J*2 \quad \text{i.e.} \quad J_k = J_{k-1}*2$$

and similarly

$$I=I/2 \quad \text{i.e.} \quad I_k = I_{k-1}/2$$

These are recurrence relationships for calculating each new I and J from the previous ones for efficiency. Do be sure you understand this example.

EXERCISE:
Write a program using similar ideas to evaluate X^K, a real number to an integer power. Here K will be shifted right each time as in the example, but X will be squared each time. If the answer is Y, it is multiplied by X each time MOD(K,2) is not zero. If you don't understand this, work at it until you do.

7.4 DO loops with other increments

Increments other than 1 are available in DO loops. It is possible to write

```
      DO 40 I=3,SQRT(REAL(N)),2
```

with an increment of 2, or

```
      DO 20 I=N,2,-1
```

to count backwards, or

```
      DO 30 THETA=0.0,TMAX,TMAX/9.0
```

to make a real variable count by a fractional value. In general the DO statement is (in its final glory):

```
DO label [,]variable=expression1
        ,expression2 ,expression3
```

The optional comma is not generally used. "Expression3" is the increment, and must not be zero. If it is not given, the increment is 1. The properties and rules applying to DO statements are summarised in Section 7.9.

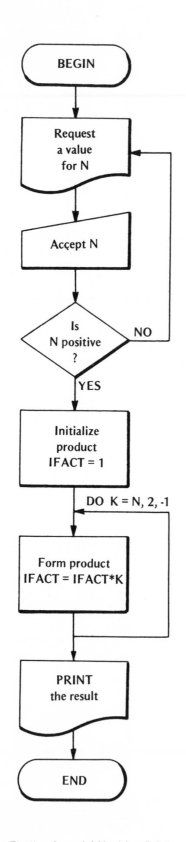

Fig. 7.4. Finding factorial N with a DO loop.

EXAMPLE:
The following loop will be jumped over because the increment is the wrong way round.

    DO 99 JOHN=1,1∅,-1

EXAMPLE:
The program from Section 7.2 to calculate the factorial of integer N is shortened and made more readable by a DO loop running down from N to 1. Note that the loop will not be executed at all if N is less than or equal to 1. The program makes use of this to ensure that the factorial of 0 is 1.

```
C PROGRAM TO FIND FACTORIAL N
C FIRST ACCEPT N AND CHECK IT
  1∅ PRINT*,'PROVIDE +VE INTEGER'
     READ*,N
     IF(N.LT.∅)GO TO 1∅
C FORM PRODUCT N*(N-1)*...*2*1
     IFACT=1
     DO 2∅ I=N,2,-1
     IFACT=IFACT*I
  2∅ CONTINUE
C PRINT THE RESULT
     PRINT*,'FACTORIAL IS ',IFACT
     GO TO 1∅
     END
```

It may surprise the reader to learn that no standard flowcharting method to illustrate DO loops exists. In theory the full flowchart for the DO loop is illustrated by Fig.7.3. In practice, since the DO loop simplifies programming, it would be nice if it was easy to document. The author uses a naughty but simple shorthand flowchart like Fig.7.4. But all the steps of the loop must be borne in mind, as in the full representation of Fig.7.5, including the possibility that it will be jumped over altogether.

EXAMPLE:
The program to calculate and print a table of sines is also amenable to improvement by a DO loop:

```
C CALCULATE A TABLE OF SINES
      WRITE(6,1Ø)
  1Ø FORMAT(5X,'ANGLE',5X,'SINE')
C CALCULATE PI/2
      TMAX=2.Ø*ATAN(1.Ø)
      DO 3Ø THETA=Ø.Ø,TMAX,TMAX/9.Ø
      WRITE(6,4Ø)THETA,SIN(THETA)
  4Ø FORMAT(1X,2F9.3)
  3Ø CONTINUE
      END
```

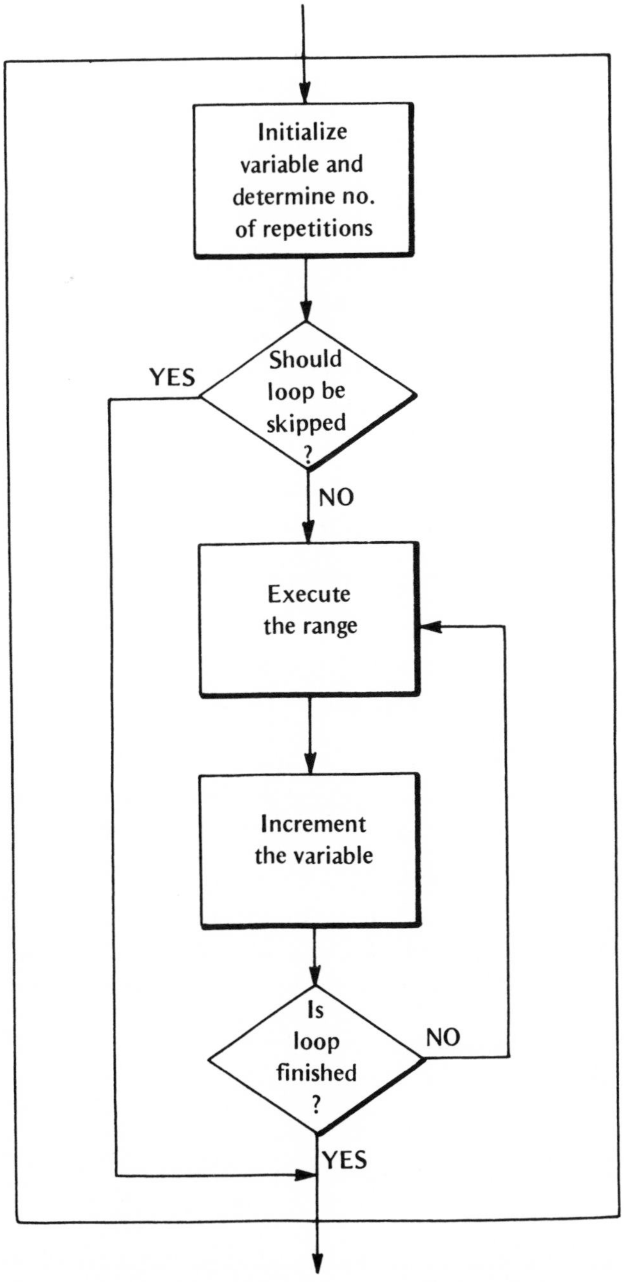

Fig. 7.5. The hidden activity in controlling a DO loop.

As before, you can only be sure that this works by trying it since it aims at an exact equality on the final round.

> It is best to count with integers.

EXERCISE:
Rewrite the program from Section 7.2 to determine whether a number is prime using a DO loop. Consider how you would represent its flowchart.

7.5 Summation

A most important use of the DO loop is in arranging for the calculation of a sum. While the DO loop takes care of the counting, the program has to arrange for accumulation of the sum. For example, these statements sum the numbers between M and N:

```
      ISUM=Ø
      DO 34 K=M,N
      ISUM=ISUM+K
  34 CONTINUE
```

Before the loop, the sum is initialized as zero. Within the loop the sum is accumulated. One would do a similar thing to accomplish a product rather than a sum:

```
      IPROD=1
      DO 37 K=M,N
      IPROD=IPROD*K
  37 CONTINUE
```

Here the initial value is 1 for reasons that should be obvious.

EXAMPLE:
The trapezoidal rule, Fig. 7.6, can be used to find the area under a curve. The area of the shaded trapezoid is

$$\text{Area} = \frac{f(x_1)+f(x_2)}{2}(x_2-x_1)$$

so that applied to integration

$$\int_{x_1}^{x_2} f(x)dx \approx \frac{f(x_1)+f(x_2)}{2}(x_2-x_1)$$

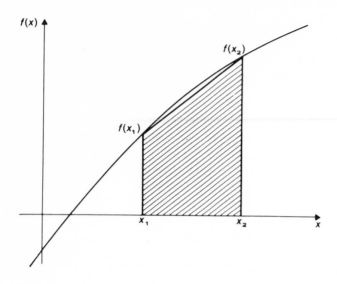

Fig. 7.6. Illustrating the trapezoidal rule

To get an accurate result, the range is divided into N strips whose areas are summed:

$$\int_{x_0}^{x_n} f(x) \approx h \left\{ \frac{f(x_0)}{2} + f(x_1) + \dots \right.$$

$$\left. + f(x_{n-1}) + \frac{f(x_n)}{2} \right\}$$

for N trapezoids of equal width

$$h = \frac{x_n - x_0}{N}$$

One integrand which is only possible numerically, and is a very important one in statistics, is

$$0.5 + \frac{1}{\sqrt{2\pi}} \int_0^x e^{-x^2/2} \, dx$$

Here is a program to integrate this function from 0 to XTOP using the trapezoidal rule in N segments:

```
C TRAPEZOIDAL RULE INTEGRATION
C WORK OUT SCALE FACTOR
      SCALE=1.0/SQRT(8.0*ATAN(1.0))
C GET NO. OF SEGMENTS AND LIMIT
  10 PRINT*,'REAL UPPER LIMIT'
      READ*,XT
      PRINT*,'INTEGER NO. SEGMENTS'
      READ*,N
```

```
C CALCULATE H AND INITIALIZE SUM
      H=XT/FLOAT(N)
      SUM=(1.0+EXP(-XT*XT/2.0))/2.0
C NOW DO THE SUM
      X=H
      DO 20 K=1,N-1
        SUM=SUM+EXP(-X*X/2.0)
        X=X+H
  20 CONTINUE
C INITIAL VALUE AND SCALE FACTOR
      SUM=0.5+H*SCALE*SUM
      PRINT*,'INTEGRAND IS ',SUM
      GO TO 10
      END
```

Note that this program controls the DO loop with an integer counter. To count directly with a real X would be unsafe.

EXERCISE:
Use this program to find the integral from 0 to 1. What value of N gives the result to an accuracy of 0.1%? (The correct answer is 0.8413, within 0.1% when N=5.)

EXAMPLE:
The Fourier series of a function describes how it can be constructed as a sum of sine and cosine waves:

$$f(x) = \frac{a_0}{2} + \sum_{n=1}^{M-1} a_n \cos\left(\frac{2n\pi x}{\ell}\right)$$

$$+ \sum_{n=1}^{M-1} b_n \sin\left(\frac{2n\pi x}{\ell}\right)$$

where it is assumed that f(x) repeats with period ℓ as in Fig.7.7. The numbers a_n and b_n are called the Fourier coefficients of f(x) and can be calculated from

$$a_n = \frac{2}{\ell} \int_0^{\ell} f(x) \cos\left(\frac{2n\pi x}{\ell}\right) dx$$

$$b_n = \frac{2}{\ell} \int_0^{\ell} f(x) \sin\left(\frac{2n\pi x}{\ell}\right) dx$$

In a computer, it is usual to approximate these by the sums over M values of $f(x)$:

$$a_n = \frac{2}{M} \sum_{k=0}^{M-1} f(x_k) \cos\left(\frac{2n\pi x_k}{\ell}\right)$$

$$b_n = \frac{2}{M} \sum_{k=0}^{M-1} f(x_k) \sin\left(\frac{2n\pi x_k}{\ell}\right)$$

Replacing dx by ℓ/M and summing over the values

$$x_k = \frac{k\ell}{M}$$

so that

$$a_n = \frac{2}{M} \sum_{k=0}^{M-1} f(x_k) \cos\left(\frac{2nk\pi}{M}\right)$$

$$b_n = \frac{2}{M} \sum_{k=0}^{M-1} f(x_k) \sin\left(\frac{2nk\pi}{M}\right)$$

In the case of the function illustrated by Fig. 7.7,

$$f(x_k) = \frac{2k}{M} - 1.0$$

and takes up the values

$$-1.0, \ -1.0 + \frac{2}{M}, \ \ldots, \ 1.0 - \frac{2}{M}$$

Here is a program to work out a_n using the sum over M terms:

```
C PROGRAM TO FIND FOURIER COSINE
C COMPONENT A(N) OF RAMP FUNCTION
C BY SUMMATION OVER M TERMS
C
C FIRST GET M AND CALCULATE 2/M
      PRINT*,'FOURIER CALCULATION'
      PRINT*,'ENTER NO. TERMS, M'
      READ*,M
      X2M=2.0/REAL(M)
C NOW ACCEPT N, THE COEFF. NO.
 10   PRINT*,'ENTER COEFF. NO., N'
      READ*,N
```

```
      ANG=X2M*REAL(N)*4.0*ATAN(1.0)
C SUM TO GET THE COEFFICIENT
      SUM=0.0
      DO 20 K=0,M-1
        XK=REAL(K)
C FK IS THE RAMP FUNCTION
        FK=X2M*XK-1.0
        SUM=SUM+FK*COS(XK*ANG)
 20   CONTINUE
C NOW SCALE IT
      AN=SUM*X2M
      PRINT*,'COEFFICIENT IS ',AN
      GO TO 10
      END
```

EXERCISE:

Rewrite this program to find both a_n and b_n, and calculate them for n = 0, 1, 2, 3 and 4 with M = 8 and 16 and 32. Note that the program first establishes M and than works out any number of a_n's for this M. You run it again to change M. Compare the coefficients found this way for different M's by plotting them on the same graph. Which do you suppose are the most correct? There is something peculiar about a_n. Why? What happens if you make the ramp function 0 at K=0?

This program is important because it leads to the case study on the fast Fourier transform in Chapter 12.

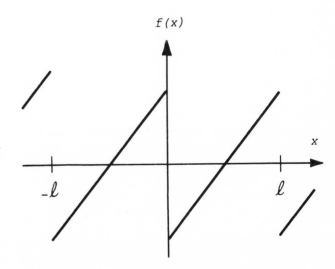

Fig. 7.7. A periodic function can be represented by a Fourier series.

7.6 Recurrence in DO loops

Recurrence is the name given to the process of calculating new values from old ones. The sum

```
        SUM=Ø.Ø
        DO 66 K=1,N
        SUM=SUM+K
    66 CONTINUE
```

is a kind of recurrence in which

$$SUM_n = SUM_{n-1} + n$$

and this kind of equation is called a recurrence relationship. Recurrences, like sums, have to be initialized. A sum is a kind of recurrence..

EXAMPLES:

$$i_n = i_{n-1}/2$$

describes a recurrence in which an old i is divided by 2 to yield a new i. If this is done in FORTRAN with positive integers, the bit pattern of each new i is the old one shifted to the right one place.

Similarly

$$j_n = j_{n-1}*2$$

describes a recurrence which is based on multiplication, which corresponds to shifting positive binary numbers to the left.

The calculation of a factorial is another example of recurrence:

$$n! = n*(n - 1)!$$

Recurrence takes many forms, but in general if a programmer can spot a recurrence relationship in a loop, there is a good chance of a vast improvement in the efficiency of his program. Here, after the reader has been asked to do it several times, is the semi-clever way of calculating X**N where N is positive and less than 32:

```
    ANS=1.Ø
    DO 1Ø K=1,5
        IF(MOD(N,2).NE.Ø)ANS=ANS*X
```

```
        X=X*X
        N=N/2
    1Ø CONTINUE
```

Three recurrence relationships are used here:

(i) $N_k = N_{k-1}/2$ shifts the bits of N right.

(ii) $X_k = X_{k-1}*X_{k-1}$ computes X**2**(K-1) by squaring which is very efficient.

(iii) If N is odd, then the least significant bit of N is 1, in which case $ANS_k = ANS_{k-1} * X$ multiplies the previous version by X.

This is even more efficient without a DO loop at all, because it can be stopped when N becomes zero. This also removes the limit on N:

```
        ANS=1.Ø
    1Ø IF(MOD(N,2).NE.Ø)ANS=ANS*X
        X=X*X
        N=N/2
        IF(N.NE.Ø)GO TO 1Ø
```

This is the semi-clever way, but not the clever way because a polynomial approximation is probably more efficient, as the reader will have the chance to discover in Problem 7.6.

Recurrence is almost always used when evaluating a power series like the one for e^x:

$$e^x = 1 + x + \frac{x^2}{2!} + \frac{x^3}{3!} + \cdots$$

Suppose the evaluation is to be carried out until the absolute value of the latest term is less than 10^{-4}, but to give up if 10 terms is not enough. This suggests a program like:

```
C EVALUATE EXP(X) BY POWER SERIES
        EXPX=1.Ø
        DO 2Ø K=1,1Ø
C WORK OUT FACTORIAL K
        IFACT=1
        DO 1Ø L=K,1,-1
        IFACT=IFACT*L
    1Ø  CONTINUE
```

```
      TERM=X**K/IFACT
      EXPX=EXPX+TERM
      IF(ABS(TERM).LT.1E-4)GO TO 30
   20 CONTINUE
C NOW EXP(X) IS FINISHED
   30 CONTINUE
```

However this method has a recurrence buried in it which is too important to overlook. If the term with x^n in it is called the nth term, then

$$t_n = \frac{x}{n} t_{n-1}$$

for all n greater than zero. A vastly more efficient program is therefore

```
C EVALUATE EXP(X) BY POWER SERIES
C USING RECURRENCE FOR EACH TERM
      EXPX=1.0
      TERM=1.0
      DO 20 K=1,10
       TERM=TERM*X/K
       EXPX=EXPX+TERM
       IF(ABS(TERM).LT.1E-4)GO TO 30
   20 CONTINUE
C NOW EXP(X) IS FINISHED
   30 CONTINUE
```

A curious reader will have asked himself how the computer goes about evaluating such functions as EXP(X) or SIN(X). It is most likely that a method resembling the Chebyshev series of Problem 7.6 is actually used.

EXERCISE:
  Using the above program as a basis, work out some values of e^x and find how big x can be before 10 terms are not enough.

Two more useful types of recurrence are worked out in the following examples:

EXAMPLE:
  Euler's method for solving differential equations is an example of the usual meaning of the term "numerical integration". The usual problem is to solve

$$\frac{dy}{dt} = f(y,t)$$

with an "initial condition" given as

$$y(t_0) = y_0$$

One is required to try and find $y(t)$ for $t > t_0$. One simple (but not brilliantly accurate) method is Euler's method which predicts $y(t+h)$ from $y(t)$. It is known from the Taylor expansion that

$$y(t+h) = y(t) + hy'(t) + hy''(t)/2 + \ldots$$

and the Euler method ignores all terms after the first two to predict

$$y(t+h) \approx y(t) + hy'(t)$$

$$= y(t) + hf(y,t)$$

This is a recurrence, and $y(t_0 + h)$ can be predicted from y, $y(t_0 + 2h)$ from $y(t_0 + h)$ and so on. To solve

$$dy/dt = \cos y$$

from $t = 0$ to $t = \pi$, given that $y(0) = 0.5$, the following program can be used. Note that in solving a differential equation, the response at each step is desired since the user will usually want to see the response develop and plot a graph of it. In this program he can choose the number of steps to use.

```
C SOLUTION OF DY/DT=COS(Y) FROM
C T=0 TO T=PIE BY EULER METHOD
C Y(0)=0.5, NO. OF STEPS VARIABLE
   10 FORMAT('GIVE NO. STEPS, I2')
   20 FORMAT(I2)
   30 FORMAT(7X,'TIME',5X,'VALUE')
   40 FORMAT(1X,2F10.2)
C CALCULATE PIE
      PIE=4.0*ATAN(1.0)
C READ IN NO. OF STEPS
   50 PRINT 10
      READ 20,N
C INITIALIZE THE SOLUTION
      H=PIE/N
      Y=0.5
      PRINT 30
      PRINT 40,0.0,Y
```

```
C NOW DO THE SOLUTION
      DO 6Ø K=1,N
        T=K*H
        Y=Y+H*COS(Y)
        PRINT 4Ø,T,Y
 6Ø   CONTINUE
      GO TO 5Ø
      END
```

EXERCISE:
How many steps must be used before this program appears to give a result with 0.1% accuracy all along the way?

EXERCISE:
Change the program to compute the solution of

$$\frac{dy}{dt} = \frac{1}{\sqrt{2\pi}} e^{-t^2/2}$$

from t = 0 to t = 1 given that the initial value of y(0) is 0.5. Evidently the difference between numerical integration, meaning solving a differential equation, and numerical quadrature, meaning finding the area under a curve, is not so great as all that. Here we can use the Euler method to solve the same integral as with the trapezoidal rule earlier. How do these compare as methods of quadrature? Well, it was never claimed that Euler's method was all that great. If you are looking for really good methods, see Problems 7.4 and 10.6.

EXAMPLE:
This is a very useful recurrence because in a Fourier series or similar calculation it is possible to avoid using the sine and cosine functions except for one value.

Observe that

$$\cos(A+B) = \cos A \cos B - \sin A \sin B$$

and

$$\sin(A+B) = \sin A \cos B + \cos A \sin B$$

In a Fourier series calculation the cos and sin of a number of angles are used,

$$\theta = 0°, \quad 2n\pi/M, \quad 4n\pi/M, \quad \ldots$$

Suppose

$$CA_{k-1} = \cos\left\{\frac{2(k-1)n\pi}{M}\right\}$$

and

$$SA_{k-1} = \sin\left\{\frac{2(k-1)n\pi}{M}\right\}$$

Then it is possible to compute

$$CA_k = CA_{k-1}*CB - SA_{k-1}*SB$$

and

$$SA_k = SA_{k-1}*CB + CA_{k-1}*SB$$

if required, where

$$CB = CA_1 = \cos(2n\pi/M)$$

and

$$SB = SA_1 = SQRT(1.0 - CB*CB)$$

This marvellous recurrence, which you should look at carefully, means that in the Fourier series calculation, the COS function only has to be called once! Here is the program (but again only for a_n) using this recurrence; wonderful isn't it?

```
C PROGRAM TO FIND FOURIER COSINE
C COMPONENT A(N) OF RAMP FUNCTION
C BY SUMMATION OVER M TERMS
C A COSINE RECURRENCE IS USED
C
C FIRST GET M AND CALCULATE 2/M
      PRINT*,'FOURIER CALCULATION'
      PRINT*,'ENTER NO. TERMS, M'
      READ*,M
      X2M=2.Ø/M
C NOW ACCEPT N, THE COEFF. NO.
 1Ø   PRINT*,'ENTER COEFF. NO., N'
      READ*,N
      ANG=X2M*N*4.Ø*ATAN(1.Ø)
C INITIALIZE COSINE RECURRENCE
      CB=COS(ANG)
      SB=SQRT(1.Ø-CB*CB)
      CA=1.Ø
      SA=Ø.Ø
```

```
C SUM FOR THE FOURIER COEFFICIENT
      SUM=0.0
      DO 20 K=0,M-1
C FK IS THE RAMP FUNCTION
      FK=X2M*K-1.0
      SUM=SUM+FK*CA
C RECURRENCE TO GET NEXT COSINE
      TEMP=CA
      CA=CA*CB-SA*SB
      SA=SA*CB+TEMP*SB
  20 CONTINUE
C NOW SCALE IT
      AN=SUM*X2M
      PRINT*,'COEFFICIENT IS',AN
      GO TO 10
      END
```

7.7 Nesting loops — IF blocks too

Not surprisingly, DO loops can be written within DO loops; an example of this was glimpsed in the evaluation of e^x by a power series, although it was dropped from the final version by the use of recurrence. DO loops can be "nested" to any depth so long as they do not cross; this commonsense rule resembles the one for nested IF blocks. Nested loops must use different DO variables; this also makes sense. If these two rules are observed, a program will allow nested loops.

EXAMPLE:

Bit-reverse all the 4-bit numbers from 0 to 15. To do this, the earlier example of bit-reversal is adapted for 4-bit numbers and placed inside a loop which counts from 0 to 15:

```
C OBTAIN THE BIT-REVERSE
C OF NUMBERS FROM 0 TO 15
      PRINT*,'NUMBER   BIT-REVERSE'
      DO 20 N=0,15
         J=0
         I=N
         DO 10 K=1,4
            J=2*J+MOD(I,2)
            I=I/2
  10     CONTINUE
         PRINT'(2I10)',N,J
  20 CONTINUE
      END
```

Note that the outer loop variable N is not used directly for the recurrence in

the inner loop so that its value will be correct the next time around. Modifying N would not change the number of times the loop is done - that is predetermined - but it would cause N to have a silly value the next time around. A better way of doing bit-reverse counting is described in Problem 7.5.

EXAMPLE:

This program finds all the prime numbers from 1 to 100. Knowing that 1, 2 and 3 are prime, all the odd numbers from 3 to 99 are tested and printed if they are prime.

```
C FIND ALL PRIME NUMBERS
C FROM 1 TO 100
      PRINT*,'PRIMES FROM 1 TO 100'
      PRINT 10,1,2
  10 FORMAT(1X,I4)
      DO 30 N=3,99,2
         DO 20 I=3,SQRT(REAL(N)),2
            IF(MOD(N,I).EQ.0)GO TO 30
  20     CONTINUE
C IF GET TO HERE N IS PRIME
         PRINT 10,N
  30 CONTINUE
      END
```

This latter example jumps out of an inner loop but remains within an outer one. This is allowed, although on no account must a program ever jump into a loop from outside. A DO loop is allowed to have an IF block inside it as long as the entire block is contained within it. Similarly an IF block can have a DO loop inside it as long as the loop is entirely inside one IF ... THEN, ELSE IF, or ELSE clause.

EXAMPLES:

Do loops may be nested:

```
Correct    DO 30 K=1,N
              :
              DO 20 L=K,M
                 :
                 DO 10 INDEX=1,4
  10                CONTINUE
                 :
  20           CONTINUE
              :
  30 CONTINUE
```

and can end on the same terminating statement:

```
Permitted        DO 10 I=1,5
                  DO 10 J=1,5
                        :
             10 CONTINUE
```

DO loops must not cross; this is forbidden:

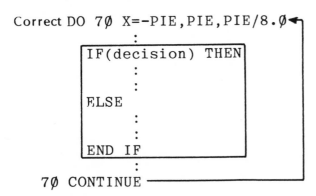

```
Forbidden DO 10 K=1,N
                :
          DO 30 L=K,M
                :
              DO 20 INDEX=1,4
                :
      10 CONTINUE
                :
      20        CONTINUE
                :
      30        CONTINUE
```

A DO loop may contain an IF block:

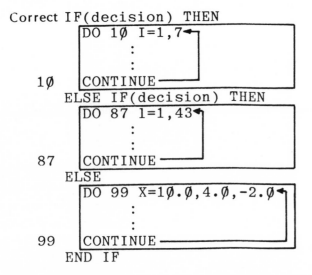

```
Correct DO 70 X=-PIE,PIE,PIE/8.0
                :
        IF(decision) THEN
                :
                :
        ELSE
                :
                :
        END IF
                :
     70 CONTINUE
```

An IF block may contain a DO loop but it must be confined within a clause:

```
Correct IF(decision) THEN
           DO 10 I=1,7
                :
     10    CONTINUE
        ELSE IF(decision) THEN
           DO 87 I=1,43
                :
     87    CONTINUE
        ELSE
           DO 99 X=10.0,4.0,-2.0
                :
                :
     99    CONTINUE
        END IF
```

IF clauses and DO loops must not cross:

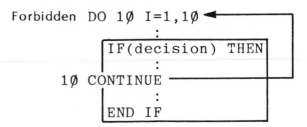

```
Forbidden DO 10 I=1,10
                :
          IF(decision) THEN
                :
      10 CONTINUE
                :
          END IF
```

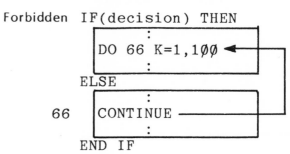

```
Forbidden IF(decision) THEN
                :
          DO 66 K=1,100
                :
          ELSE
                :
      66    CONTINUE
                :
          END IF
```

A program may jump out of a DO loop:

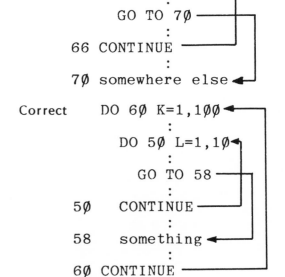

```
Correct    DO 66 K=1,100
                :
           GO TO 70
                :
      66 CONTINUE
                :
      70 somewhere else
```

```
Correct    DO 60 K=1,100
                :
           DO 50 L=1,10
                :
           GO TO 58
                :
      50    CONTINUE
                :
      58    something
                :
      60 CONTINUE
```

It has not jumped into the range of DO 60 because it was within it already.

*A program may not jump into a DO loop:

---

*This is forbidden in FORTRAN 77 - FORTRAN IV programmmers note. If you used to jump out and back, in you can't any more. The IF...THEN structure makes it unnecessary.

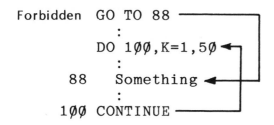

```
Forbidden  GO TO 88
                :
           DO 100,K=1,50
                :
      88   Something
                :
     100   CONTINUE
```

It should be recalled that both these rules apply to IF blocks as well:

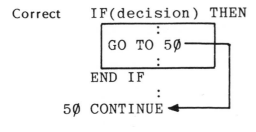

```
Correct    IF(decision) THEN
                :
           GO TO 50
                :
           END IF
                :
      50   CONTINUE
```

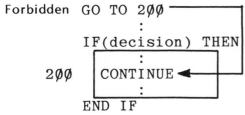

```
Forbidden  GO TO 200
                :
           IF(decision) THEN
                :
     200   CONTINUE
                :
           END IF
```

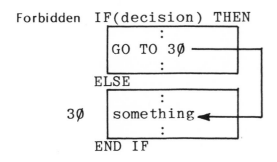

```
Forbidden  IF(decision) THEN
                :
           GO TO 30
           ELSE
                :
      30   something
                :
           END IF
```

EXERCISE:

Modify the Fourier series program to calculate all the M Fourier coefficients $a_0, \ldots, a_M$ and $b_0, \ldots, b_M$, given M. Notice a symmetry in them? If not, you have got it wrong. Notice also that you can use another recurrence for the first cos and sin of each coefficient,/ so you still need only call the COS and SIN functions once each. If this suggestion is beyond you, don't bother. But do calculate the coefficients and observe the symmetry if you are interested in the fast Fourier case study of Chapter 12.

7.8 Efficiency

A good programmer tries to write FORTRAN in such a way that the cleverest compiler in the world is unable to improve upon it. It is not necessary to make a great fuss about this - if you learn from the beginning to recognize inefficient coding, then writing programs in a nearly optimal way comes naturally.

Loops deserve particular attention in this regard, for it makes sense that computers spend most of their time in the innermost loops of programs, and the simplest changes here can improve the efficiency of the program.

In the section on recurrence, it was seen how recognizing a recurrence relationship in the loop saved effort. In the examples given the saving was substantial. In the evaluation of the power series for e^x, the statement

$$TERM=TERM*X/K$$

replaced an inner loop to evaluate a factorial and also eliminated exponentiation, another slow process. The saving of computer time, and therefore money, was vast. It is probable that the program is at least five times faster with the recurrence.

In the evaluation of a Fourier series, the cosine and sine functions seemed to be needed over and over again, but it was possible to eliminate these from the inner loop altogether. At a guess the program is ten times faster this way. Scientists and engineers spend a lot of computer time on Fourier series so this kind of economy in resources is no joke. This is why a case study in Chapter 12 is devoted to the fast Fourier transform in which a kind of recurrence is exploited in the summation that defines the Fourier series.

Another way of optimizing loops is to remove from them "invariant" operations. This has also been used in some of the examples. If an operation inside a loop does not change between repetitions then this operation is "invariant" and hence unnecessary. In the Fourier series program, it was necessary to calculate

$$a_n = \frac{2}{M} \sum_{k=0}^{M-1} f(x_k) \cos\left\{\frac{2nk\pi}{M}\right\}$$

One could have written this out more or less literally:

```
AN=∅.∅
DO 2∅ K=∅,M-1
   ANG=(4.∅*ATAN(1.∅)*N*K)*2.∅/M
   FK=(2.∅/M)*K-1.∅
   AN=AN+FK*COS(ANG)*2.∅/M
2∅ CONTINUE
```

This is quite dreadful. By far the worst feature is that the ATAN function is called every time with exactly the same argument, 1.0. Not only that, but the only thing that varies in this statement is K itself. Furthermore the multiplier 2/M is used in three statements, and every time M and K are used they have to be converted to real. This is why the first revision of that program removed the calculation of 2/M and $2n\pi/M$ from the loop to become (nearly):

```
X2M=2.∅/M
ANG=X2M*N*4.∅*ATAN(1.∅)
AN=∅.∅
DO 2∅ K=∅,M-1
   FK=X2M*K-1.∅
   AN=AN+FK*COS(K*ANG)*X2M
2∅ CONTINUE
```

This is a very good first step, and the most glaring inefficiencies have been removed. However a few less evil redundancies are now evident. The multiplier X2M is used every time around and could be put after the loop. Furthermore K is converted from integer to real twice when once would do. (The author prefers to use an integer DO variable because it is safer and fits his idea of the defining equation better.) With all redundant operations removed from inside the loop the program has become:

```
X2M=2.∅/M
ANG=X2M*N*4.∅*ATAN(1.∅)
SUM=∅.∅
DO 2∅ K=∅,M-1
   XK=K
```

```
   FK=X2M*XK-1.∅
   SUM=SUM+FK*COS(XK*ANG)
2∅ CONTINUE
   AN=SUM*X2M
```

Why can the statement

$$FK=X2M*XK-1.∅$$

not be optimized by the removal of the invariant 1.0?

These were not the steps followed in designing the program; because of the author's experience with loops he wrote it down like this the first time. The recurrence for COS was a later inspiration.

EXERCISE:
Examine the program to find the area under a curve by the trapezoidal rule for evidence that it has been optimized.

DO loops should be optimized by

(i) removing invariant operations where possible;

(ii) the use of recurrences to reduce the number of operations where possible.

7.9 Summary of DO loop rules

The DO statement:

DO label [,] variable = e1, e2, e3

Notes on the DO statement:

(i) The "label" is the label of the terminating statement which follows the DO statement farther along the program. This labelled statement is most often the CONTINUE statement but it can be any executable statement except GO TO, assigned GO TO, arithmetic IF, block IF, ELSE IF, ELSE, END IF, RETURN, END or DO. It can be a logical IF (but this logical IF as pointed out in Chapter 6 cannot itself contain another logical IF, DO, block IF, ELSE IF, ELSE, END IF, or END).

This all makes sense because these are statements which would interfere with the repetition of the DO loop.

> Avoid trouble - use CONTINUE

(ii) The optional comma is never used - forget it.

(iii) The "variable" is the name of the DO variable of type real, integer or DOUBLE PRECISION (Chapter 17).

(iv) The expressions "e1", "e2" and "e3" are of real, integer or DOUBLE PRECISION type but are converted to the type of the DO variable.

The range of a DO statement:

All the statements after DO up to and including the terminating statement belong to the range of the DO.

Rules about range (many examples were given in Section 7.7):

(i) Another DO range may exist if it is completely nested inside this one and uses a different DO variable. It can share the same terminating statement.

(ii) IF blocks may exist if they are totally inside the range, i.e. the IF...THEN follows the DO and the END IF is before the terminating statement of the DO.

(iii) Similarly a DO statement can be inside an IF block, but it must be wholly contained within a single clause.

(iv) A GO TO or similar statement may leave the range of a DO.

(v) No statement is permitted to jump into the range of a DO from outside it (FORTRAN IV programmers take note).

(vi) A program is not permitted to change the value of the DO variable inside the range of the DO loop.

How the DO works:

With reference to Fig. 7.5

(i) "e1", "e2" and "e3" are first evaluated and converted to the same type as the DO variable. If e3 is not present it is taken as unity.

(ii) The DO variable is assigned the initial value e1.

(iii) The number of repetitions is established in advance as

$$n = MAX(INT(e2-e1+e3)/e3,0)$$

(iv) If n is 0 the loop is passed over.

(v) Otherwise the loop is executed n times. It is not possible to change the number of repetitions inside the loop. A program is not permitted to change the value of the DO variable inside the range of the DO loop.

(vi) When the terminal statement has been executed each time the DO variable is incremented by e3, and it should be noted that e3 was predetermined and cannot be changed.

(vii) The loop is repeated until the nth pass, when the program carries on.

The CONTINUE statement

CONTINUE

is an executable statement that does nothing. Its principal use is in terminating DO loops.

It is worth noting that nested loops can share the same terminating statement:

```
      DO 1Ø I=1,1Ø
        DO 1Ø J=1,5
          DO 1Ø K=7,8
          :
          :
   1Ø CONTINUE
```

If several loops terminate on the same statement, inner ones are processed first.

7.10 Problems

PROBLEM 7.1:

A sequence of numbers originated in 1202 AD by Fibonacci is

$$0, \ 1, \ 1, \ 2, \ 3, \ 5, \ 8, \ \ldots$$

in which $F_k = F_{k-1} + F_{k-2}$.

i.e. each Fibonacci number is the sum of the previous two. This series turns up everywhere; Fibonacci himself proposed it as the answer to the problem "how many pairs of rabbits can be produced from a single pair in a year's time?".

Write a program to evaluate this series.

PROBLEM 7.2:

The power series expansions of some common functions are surprisingly efficient, and of some others are surprisingly inefficient. Most can be evaluated using recurrence. Write programs to evaluate:

$$e^x = 1 + x + \frac{x^2}{2} + \frac{x^3}{3!} + \ldots$$

$$\ln(1+x) = x - \frac{x^2}{2} + \frac{x^3}{3} - \frac{x^4}{4} + \ldots$$

$$\sin x = x - \frac{x^3}{3!} + \frac{x^5}{5!} - \frac{x^7}{7!} + \ldots$$

$$\cos x = 1 - \frac{x^2}{2!} + \frac{x^4}{4!} - \frac{x^6}{6!} + \ldots$$

Which of these are efficient and which are inefficient? Do the recurrence relationships give any guidance in estimating the residual errors after n terms and the expected rate of convergence for these series? Would you use any of them if you were asked to write your own functions to give answers correct to 6 decimal places?

PROBLEM 7.3:

Find the date of Easter for every year this century. Refer to Problem 2.8.

PROBLEM 7.4:

A FORTRAN program for finding the area under a curve by the trapezoidal rule was used as an example in Section 7.5.

Simpson's rule provides a better formula for the area under two adjoining segments, as shown in Fig. 7.8.

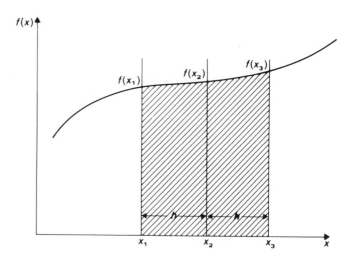

Fig. 7.8. Illustrating Simpson's rule.

Here

$$\int_{x_1}^{x_3} f(x)\,dx \approx \frac{h}{3} \left\{ f(x_1) + 4f(x_2) + f(x_3) \right\}$$

Where a series of segments join, the formula can be turned into a recurrence relationship for greater efficiency. Write a program to find the area under a curve given the starting and finishing points and the number of segments to use. If the number of segments is odd, fill in the end with a trapezoid. Be careful to remove invariant code from your loops.

Using as a test

$$0.5 + \frac{1}{\sqrt{2\pi}} \int_0^1 e^{-x^2/2} \, dx$$

compare the accuracy of this method as a function of the number of steps with the performance of the trapezoidal method.

PROBLEM 7.5:

There is a nice way to do the bit-reverse counting more efficiently than the method used as an example in Section 7.7. It is attributed to

Norman Brenner but appears not to have been published in any journal.

Consider the process of binary addition. Suppose 1 is added to 39, then a series of carries occurs which stops when a binary 0 is encountered, Fig. 7.9.

$$
\begin{array}{r}
1\,0\,0\,1\,1\,1 \\
1 \\
\hline
1\,0\,1\,0\,0\,0
\end{array}
$$

Fig. 7.9. Carries generated in binary addition.

A FORTRAN program can do this backwards, for example the bit-reverse of the same addition is the process illustrated by Fig.7.10. The program has to determine when the carries occur and do the necessary extra additions. In Fig.7.10, adding 32 produces a carry and it is detected because the answer is 64 or greater. The 64 is removed and the bit it represents is put back in the right place by adding 16. This carries again to give a result 32 or greater, so 32 is subtracted and 8 is added which carries again to give a result 16 or greater, so 16 is subtracted and 4 is added at which point no carry occurs and the process is finished. Each carry is detected and turned around.

$$
\begin{array}{r}
1\,1\,1\,0\,0\,1 \\
1 \\
\hline
0\,0\,0\,1\,0\,1
\end{array}
$$

Fig. 7.10. Backward carries in bit-reverse counting.

The carry does not occur at all half the time, extends one place a quarter of the time, 2 places an eighth of the time and so on. In other words the average length of carry is 1/2 of a place.

Write a program to count from 0 to 63 in bit-reverse (6-bit numbers).

PROBLEM 7.6:

The Chebyshev polynomial of Problem 2.6 was an example of an important method of approximation. Over a range $-1 \leqslant x \leqslant 1$ a function $f(x)$ can be approximated by

$$
f(x) = \frac{C_0}{2} + C_1 T_1(x) + C_2 T_2(x) + \cdots + C_{N-1} T_{N-1}(x)
$$

where the quantities C_0, C_1, $\cdots C_{N-1}$ are Chebyshev coefficients and T_0, T_1, $\cdots$, T_{N-1} are Chebyshev polynomials. It is known from theory that

$$
T_0(x) = 1 \quad \text{and} \quad T_1(x) = x
$$

and that the higher order polynomials obey the recurrence

$$
T_{r+1}(x) = 2x T_r(x) - T_{r-1}(x)
$$

so that

$$
T_2(x) = 2x^2 - 1, \quad T_3(x) = 4x^3 - 3x
$$

and so on.

The Chebyshev coefficients are calculated from known values of $f(x)$ at the non-uniformly spaced values

$$
x_k = \cos\left\{ \frac{(2k+1)\pi}{2N} \right\}, \quad k = 0, 1, \cdots, N-1
$$

using the formula

$$
C_n = \frac{2}{N} \sum_{k=0}^{N-1} f(x_k) \cos\left\{ \frac{(2k+1)n\pi}{2N} \right\}
$$

Therefore a polynomial like the one given in Problem 2.15 can be obtained by deciding how many terms to use and calculating the Chebyshev coefficients. These are combined with the Chebyshev polynomials and by bringing together like powers of x a polynomial is obtained. The precision of the approximation may be determined by the precision of the coefficients and the number of terms used.

Investigate the Chebyshev polynomial for calculating:

(i) e^x over the range $-1 \leqslant x \leqslant 1$.

(ii) $\cos x$ to cover the range $-\pi \leqslant x \leqslant \pi$.

8

Define your own functions

8.1 Introduction

Many algorithms naturally express themselves as producing a single result, and therefore suggest strongly that they should be a function. With an algorithm organized as a function, a programmer can communicate his function to others and use it freely in other programs. SQRT is a function intrinsic to FORTRAN. Why shouldn't a programmer express the calculation of a factorial, or the area of a triangle in a similar way? This chapter shows how.

8.2 Statement functions

Many functions are simple enough to be expressed in a single assignment statement, and so the most elementary kind of defined function is the statement function which can be included in any program. It can be used within the program unit that defines it just as if it were an intrinsic function.

EXAMPLE:
A function SUMSQ is defined in a program

$$SUMSQ(X,Y)=X*X+Y*Y$$

whose purpose is to find the sum of squares of its arguments. X and Y in this statement are called the "dummy arguments" and this statement is sufficient to define the function. This defining statement belongs at the beginning of the program and is itself not an executable statement - it does nothing unless another statement refers to it.

Later on the program could say, in an executable statement

$$Z=SUMSQ(P,Q)$$

or

$$PRINT*,SUMSQ(A,B)$$

or refer to the function SUMSQ as a term of any expression at all. When it does so, the actual values of the arguments are substituted for the dummy arguments.

SUMSQ(X,Y) is a real function of two real arguments. It can only be used with real arguments, and so the statement

$$IF(SUMSQ(I,J).EQ.\emptyset)GO\ TO\ 31$$

is rubbish.

A function and its arguments have a type which is implied as real or integer by the spelling of the function name. Later it will be seen that statement functions can also be of type COMPLEX, DOUBLE PRECISION, LOGICAL, or CHARACTER.

EXAMPLE:
The statement

$$DISC(A,B,C)=B*B-4.0*A*C$$

defines the statement function DISC which is a real function of three real arguments A, B, and C. This function evidently evaluates the discriminant of a quadratic expression

$$ax^2 + bx + c$$

Therefore the statement

$$IF(DISC(1.\emptyset,1.\emptyset,1.\emptyset))1\emptyset,2\emptyset,3\emptyset$$

uses the DISC function to evaluate the discriminant of

$$x^2 + x + 1 = 0$$

which is negative. In this case the program would jump to statement number 10.

EXAMPLE:
The statement

```
ERF(Y)=CONST*EXP(-Y*Y/2.Ø)
```

defines the function

$$\frac{1}{\sqrt{2\pi}} \, e^{-x^2/2}$$

provided CONST has the value $1/\sqrt{2\pi}$. The program to evaluate

$$\frac{1}{\sqrt{2\pi}} \int_0^1 e^{-x^2/2} \, dx$$

by the trapezoidal rule from Section 7.5, can be rewritten:

```
C TRAPEZOIDAL RULE INTEGRATION
C USING STATEMENT FUNCTION ERF(Y)
C
C DEFINE THE STATEMENT FUNCTION
    ERF(Y)=CONST*EXP(-Y*Y/2.Ø)
C WORK OUT THE SCALE FACTOR
    CONST=1.Ø/SQRT(8.Ø*ATAN(1.Ø))
C GET NO. SEGMENTS AND TWO LIMITS
  1Ø PRINT*,'ENTER REAL LIMITS'
    READ*,XBOT,XTOP
    PRINT*,'INTEGER NO. SEGMENTS'
    READ*,N
C CALCULATE H AND INITIALIZE SUM
    H=(XTOP-XBOT)/N
    SUM=(ERF(XBOT)+ERF(XTOP))/2.Ø
C NOW DO THE SUM
    X=H
    DO 2Ø K=1,N-1
      SUM=SUM+ERF(X)
      X=X+H
  2Ø CONTINUE
C FINALLY SCALE THE RESULT
    SUM=SUM*H
    PRINT*,'INTEGRAND IS ',SUM
    GO TO 1Ø
    END
```

The nice thing about this is that it is now easy to change the function definition and integrate a different function. To make it general some invariant code has sneaked into the DO loop with the function definition. C'est la vie!

This last example raises an interesting point about dummy arguments and the variables used in the function definition. It is time for some rules.

Statement function definitions

must appear at the beginning of the program. Later it will be seen that other statements must appear at the beginning, and that the order of some of these is compulsory. The required order is finally spelled out in Chapter 17.

A statement function takes the form:

name (dummy arguments) = expression

The type of the function is implied by its "name", if not explicitly stated in a type statement as encountered in Chapter 17. The type of the "dummy argument" is specified similarly, and the type of the "expression" is determined according to the usual rules for expressions. There are many possible combinations in the type of the function, its dummy arguments and the expression.

The dummy arguments are names which apply only to the statement function and do not refer to the same names that might be used for variables elsewhere in the program. This is very important. In the example

```
ERF(Y)=CONST*EXP(-Y*Y/2.Ø)
```

Y is used only to define the use of the argument in the function; it is said that its "scope" is limited to the definition. If the name Y is used for a variable elsewhere in the program, it is not the same Y. The dummy Y is not a variable at all, just a name which takes an actual value only when the function is used.

In the same example, the variable CONST does have a meaning in the rest of the program as does any variable name used in the expression which is not a dummy argument. CONST has the scope of the whole program unit.

When the function is referred to, actual arguments are supplied which can be expressions as in the case of intrinsic functions. However these must correspond with the dummy arguments according to type.

The function itself has the scope of the whole program unit. For the moment this is anywhere up to the END statement; the possibility of other program units arises later in this chapter.

It is possible for a statement function to have no arguments. In this case, the brackets in the definition are required, as in

$$PIE()=4.0*ATAN(1.0)$$

and brackets are also required when referring to it, as in

$$ANG=X2M*N*PIE()$$

EXAMPLE:
A function YIELD evaluates the yield on an investment of X units for N periods at I percent. It is a real function of one real and two integer arguments.

$$YIELD(X,N,I)=X*(1.0+I/100.0)**N$$

The statement

$$PRINT*,YIELD(1.0,2,10)$$

prints the answer

$$1.21$$

EXAMPLE:
The conversion from Cartesian (X,Y) co-ordinates to polar (r,θ) co-ordinates as illustrated by Fig. 8.1 is defined by two functions

$$RADIUS(X,Y)=SQRT(X*X+Y*Y)$$
$$ANGLE(X,Y)=ATAN2(Y,X)$$

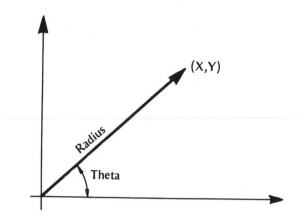

Fig.8.1. Polar and Rectangular Co-ordinates.

and the inverse relationship by

$$XCORD(R,THETA)=R*COS(THETA)$$
$$YCORD(R,THETA)=R*SIN(THETA)$$

There is the possibility that one statement function may wish to refer to another. This is permitted if they are defined in the correct order; a function can only refer to one that was previously defined.

EXAMPLE:
A function to evaluate a polynomial

$$ax^3+ bx^2+ cx + d$$

could be

$$POLY(A,B,C,D,X)=((A*X+B)*X+C)*X+D$$

and the program could be intended to integrate any old function which it calls FNC. To avoid rewriting the program you could use

$$FNC(Y)=POLY(1.0,-7.8,18.5,-11.3,Y)$$

To make this more complex, the program could actually be looking for the maximum of two functions

$$XMAXY(Z)=MAX(FNC(Z),FND(Z))$$

where

$$FND(Z)=POLY(1.0,-4.0,2.3,5.0,Z)$$

Provided it was written in the following way, it would work quite nicely, although the example is not all that practical.

```
POLY(A,B,C,D,X)=((A*X+B)*X+C)*X+D
FNC(Y)=POLY(1.Ø,-7.8,18.5,-11.3,Y)
FND(Z)=POLY(1.Ø,-4.6,2.3,5.Ø,Z)
XMAXY(Z)=MAX(FNC(Z),FND(Z))
```

It is perhaps a pity that a function cannot call itself, directly or indirectly. If it were possible, the function would be called "recursive". FORTRAN functions are not recursive, and some people think that this is a pity. Programs are not allowed to say things like

$$IFACT(I)=I*IFACT(I-1)$$

to define a factorial, nor may they contain a loop of function references:

$$FNA(X)=X*FNB(X-1.\emptyset)$$
$$FNB(X)=X*FNA(X-1.\emptyset)$$

EXERCISE:
   The method of False Position had in it three separate evaluations of the polynomial that was being solved, and if Problem 6.3 was attempted, two calculations of the Aitken extrapolation. Make these into statement function references so that you can change the function being solved more easily.

   Solve

   (i) x + sin x = 0.5

   (ii) $e^x = 2x^2$

EXERCISE:
   You have just improved one half of your equation solving "kit", assuming Problem 6.2 was done. Finish the job.

8.3 FUNCTION subprograms — the FUNCTION and RETURN statements

The statement function described above is clearly useful but has its obvious limitations; some one line jokes are good but much funnier things can be done with more space. FORTRAN has the facility to create multiple line functions and incorporate any combination of FORTRAN statements. This will allow a programmer to write a function in a separate

"subprogram" which makes a distinct module or "program unit" beginning with a FUNCTION statement and ending with its very own END statement.

Here is a function to evaluate the integer factorial of an integer number; after looking at this the reader will be aware that many previous examples would make very useful little functions rewritten in this way:

```
      FUNCTION IFACT(N)
C
C A FUNCTION FOR FACTORIAL N
C CHECK TO SEE IF N IS LEGAL
      IF(N.LT.Ø)THEN
C ILLEGAL, PRINT RUDE MESSAGE
C AND RETURN THE RESULT ZERO
      PRINT*,'ILLEGAL FACTORIAL'
      IFACT=Ø
      RETURN
      ELSE
C CALCULATE THE FACTORIAL
      IFACT=1
      DO 1Ø K=2,N
      IFACT=IFACT*K
 1Ø   CONTINUE
      END IF
      END
```

Notice how the correct answer is returned for the factorials of 0 or 1 by jumping round the DO loop.

The FUNCTION statement defines the name of the function and its arguments:

```
FUNCTION name([dummy arguments])
```

The type of the function and of its dummy arguments (it needn't have any) is implicit in the spelling as usual. The dummy variables are names that have values assigned when another program refers to this function, just as in the case of intrinsic functions and statement functions. IFACT is therefore an integer function of one integer argument. As with statement functions, these arguments must agree in order, number and type with the actual arguments given when the function is used.

The FUNCTION statement is followed by a FORTRAN program of any complexity which works out the value of the function. At least once in the program the value must be assigned by a statement of the form

name=expression

and the completion of the function is signalled either by a RETURN statement (there could be several in a complicated function):

RETURN

or by an END, which must be the last statement of the function:

END

One useful aspect of the FUNCTION is the way variable names are treated. The FUNCTION IFACT is a separate program unit, and all the variable names which appear as dummy arguments are given actual values by another program which uses the function. These are the only values which are shared. Thus in IFACT only N is a value from the "main program". All the other names are "local names" whose scope is limited to IFACT. Therefore the variable K is a private variable to IFACT, totally unrelated to any variable K which may exist in the program which uses IFACT.

This makes IFACT highly portable – anyone can use it in any program knowing that it will not interfere with any K used elsewhere. This is one of the strengths of FORTRAN - subprograms do not intefere with other program units. (It will be found later that variables can also be shared by deliberately putting them into a shared region called COMMON.)

How then is this function used? The FUNCTION subprogram and the "main program" which uses it are presented to the computer together. The main program usually comes first with its own END, followed by the FUNCTION statement, and the rest of the function up to and including its own END statement. Other functions could then follow, as could other kinds of subprograms including SUBROUTINEs which are introduced later. Each of these parts is called a program

unit. Fig. 8.2 illustrates the usual structure of a FORTRAN program which includes subprograms. In batch systems some computers require separate "control cards" between the modules; it is beyond the scope of this book to describe them all.

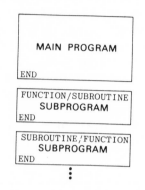

(a) As a listing on a timesharing system.

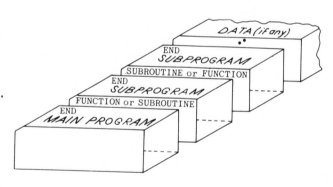

(b) As a card deck for batch work.

Fig. 8.2. The layout of a FORTRAN program with subprograms.

A main program using the function IFACT to evaluate and print all the factorials from 0 to 10 is then:

```
C A MAIN PROGRAM TO GET ALL
C FACTORIALS FROM 1 TO 1Ø
C
      DO 2Ø K=1,1Ø
C FACTORIAL FROM FUNCTION IFACT
      IJ=IFACT(K)
      WRITE(*,1Ø)K,IJ
1Ø FORMAT(I4,'! IS ',I1Ø)
2Ø CONTINUE
      END
```

In both the FUNCTION and the main program a variable K has been used. Because they are separate programs they are not the same; they are "local" variables which means that they are completely unrelated. In practice this means that a FUNCTION subprogram does not interfere with any variables of the main program because they are not shared. Thus if these programs are used together, the values 1, 2, ..., 10 taken by K are used in the factorial subroutine as the values of the dummy variable N.

Therefore it follows - and this is very important - that if N were adjusted or changed in the subprogram, then this change would be carried back as a change in the main program variable K. It is unusual and altogether too fancy to do this deliberately in a FUNCTION subprogram, although as will be seen it is quite usual in subroutines.

It is possible to get into serious and elusive trouble if a subprogram, by adjusting one of its arguments, turns out to have adjusted a constant instead of a variable! The main program is, in effect, wrecked. The following program destroys itself:

Main Program

$$X=BLOW(1.\emptyset)$$
$$\vdots$$

Subprogram

```
FUNCTION BLOW(Z)
   :
Z=Z+1.Ø
   :
BLOW=5.Ø
END
```

Here, BLOW is defined safely, but the function has added 1.0 to Z, which now turns the constant 1.0 to 2.0. Every time this careless programmer uses 1.0 he gets 2.0 instead. This could be baffling.

The people who wrote the FORTRAN 77 standard have taken great care to spell out what can happen if a function changes one of its arguments which is a variable at an embarrassing moment, for example in the middle of an input/output list. I suggest that this is bad programming.

A FUNCTION subprogram need have no arguments. If it has no arguments, the brackets are required in the FUNCTION statement:

```
FUNCTION EEUGH()
EEUGH=EXP(1.Ø)
END
```

In referring to a FUNCTION subprogram with no arguments, brackets are used:

$$YILSL=EEUGH()**2$$

It is strongly suggested that the purpose of a FUNCTION is to return a single result in the proper manner, and that no FUNCTION should modify its arguments; SUBROUTINEs should be used for that purpose.

```
DO NOT WRITE A FUNCTION
THAT MODIFIES ITS ARGUMENTS
```

A FUNCTION subprogram can have statement functions inside it. If this is the case, they belong (for the present) immediately following the FUNCTION statement. There are a number of other statements which have to go in a special order as is finally spelled out in Chapter 17.

EXAMPLE:
For a particular application it is found that the SIGN function is inconvenient, and the programmer would rather have a function

$$MYSIGN(J)=SIGN(1,J)*MIN(1,ABS(J))$$

which gives him 1 if the argument is positive, 0 if it is zero and -1 if it is negative. This will be put to practical use in an example to follow.

EXAMPLE:
The area of a triangle can be found directly from its co-ordinates, as illustrated by Fig. 8.3, in which

$$Area = \frac{1}{2}\left| y_2(x_3-x_1)+y_1(x_2-x_3)+y_3(x_1-x_2) \right|$$

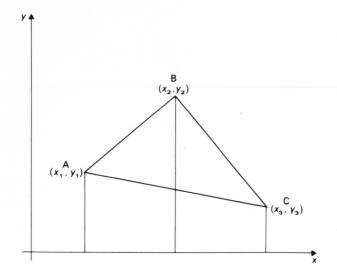

Fig. 8.3. The area of a triangle can be calculated from the co-ordinates of its vertices.

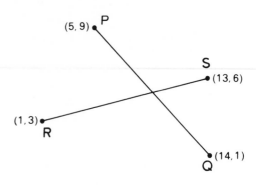

(a) Line segments which intersect.

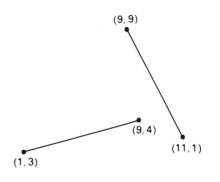

(b) Line segments which do not intersect.

Fig. 8.4. Illustrating Problem 4.10. The line segments are specified by their end co-ordinates.

Clearly a statement function could be written to calculate this. In addition a very interesting fact is that the expression

$$y_2(x_3 - x_1) + y_1(x_2 - x_3) + y_3(x_1 - x_2)$$

has a positive sign if the co-ordinates are taken in clockwise order and negative if anticlockwise. This can be very useful. A statement function to give the area for integer co-ordinates is

```
IARA(IX1,IY1,IX2,IY2,IX3,IY3)
   =IY2*(IX3-IX1)+IY1*(IX2-IX3)
      +IY3*(IX1-IX2)
```

and to find the sign of this in the way described above, one could write

```
MYSIGN(IARA(IX1,IY1,IX2,IY2,
              IX3,IY3))
```

EXAMPLE:
The end co-ordinates of two line segments are known, and it desired to know if they intersect, as illustrated by Fig. 8.4.

The signed triangle idea is just the thing, for observe in Fig.8.4 that if PQ intersects RS, P and Q are on opposite sides of RS and at the same time R and S are on opposite sides of PQ. This means that the triangles RPQ and SQP and QRS and PSR all have the same signs. Here then is a FUNCTION INTR which returns 0 for no intersection and 1 for an intersection. Note that an end touching or lines co-linear are not counted as intersections.

```
      FUNCTION INTR(IP,JP,IQ,JQ,IR,JR,IS,JS)
C FUNCTION TO DECIDE IF LINE (IP,JP) TO (IQ,JQ)
C INTERSECTS WITH THE LINE (IR,JR) TO (IS,JS)
C RETURNING THE VALUE Ø IF NO, 1 IF YES
C
      IARA(I,J,K,L,M,N)=L*(M-I)+J*(K-M)+N*(I-K)
      MYSIGN(J)=ISIGN(1,J)*MIN(1,ABS(J))
      ITEST=MYSIGN(IARA(IR,JR,IP,JP,IQ,JQ))
     + +MYSIGN(IARA(IS,JS,IQ,JQ,IP,JP))
     + +MYSIGN(IARA(IQ,JQ,IR,JR,IS,JS))
     + +MYSIGN(IARA(IP,JP,IS,JS,IR,JR))
      INTR=ABS(ITEST/4)
      END
```

A final word is in order about the names of functions. Clearly a named function in some cases could be an intrinsic function, or a FUNCTION sub-program and it is important to know which is used. The answer is that

(i) a statement function is used if it is present;

(ii) failing that a FUNCTION subprogram is used if it is part of a user's program; or

(iii) failing that one or more libraries are searched including the one which contains the intrinsic functions.

This means, for example, that the user is permitted to write his own SQRT function either in a statement function, in which case his own SQRT will be used only in in program units which define it, or as a FUNCTION subprogram in which case all program units will use it.

Once a name has been used for a function the same name cannot be given to a variable or to anything else in that program unit (except a COMMON block, Chapter 13).

EXERCISE:
Using the original triangle idea, write a FUNCTION subprogram to tell if a point whose integer co-ordinates are given is inside or outside a given triangle. Return 0 for no, 1 for yes.

8.4 Multiple entries to subprograms — the ENTRY and SAVE statements

The ENTRY statement permits a programmer to refer to a subprogram in different ways which start at distinct places in the subprogram, or to gather similar subprograms into one program unit.

EXAMPLE:
Suppose the programmer wishes to combine a FUNCTION to calculate the area of a triangle with one to determine the order of co-ordinates and another to find whether two lines intersect. This program could be

```
      FUNCTION TAREA(IA,IB,IC,ID,IE,IF)
C FUNCTION WORKS OUT TRIANGLE AREA
      IAR(I,J,K,L,M,N)=L*(M-I)
     +          +J*(K-M)+N*(I-K)
      MYS(J)=SIGN(1,J)*MIN(1,ABS(J))
      X=IAR(IA,IB,IC,ID,IE,IF)
      TAREA=Ø.5*ABS(X)
      RETURN
C ENTRY GETS CO-ORDINATE DIRECTION
      ENTRY KO(I1,J1,K1,L1,M1,N1)
      KO=MYS(IAR(I1,J1,K1,L1,M1,N1))
      RETURN
C ENTRY DETECTS INTERSECTION
      ENTRY INTR(IP,JP,IQ,JQ,
     +            IR,JR,IS,JS)
      IT=MYS(IAR(IR,JR,IP,JP,IQ,JQ))
     +   +MYS(IAR(IS,JS,IQ,JQ,IP,JP))
     +   +MYS(IAR(IQ,JQ,IR,JR,IS,JS))
     +   +MYS(IAR(IP,JP,IS,JS,IR,JR))
      INTR=ABS(IT/4)
      END
```

*This is a bit advanced and can safely be left out at first study.

The above program is the simplest case because the function references do not interact at all but are simply grouped to make use of the same statement functions; they could just as easily have been separate program units. However it does illustrate the basic arrangements. The FUNCTION statement is first, and with its dummy arguments is a real function of six integer arguments. The ENTRY statements can be placed anywhere between FUNCTION and END, and the position then defines where execution of their particular FUNCTIONs begins.

For compatibility with the rules about DO loops and IF blocks, the ENTRY cannot be inside one of these because this would be the same as jumping into the range or block from outside.

Accordingly, in the previous example, KO is an integer function of integer arguments which returns 1 for a clockwise triangle, 0 for a zero area triangle and -1 for an anticlockwise triangle. INTR is the same integer function as before. Notice that these functions do not call each other. This would be forbidden.

More complicated situations arise when the arguments and names of the different entries interact with each other and with arithmetic statement functions. To understand why the rules exist, it is necessary to know how variables become defined and undefined in subprograms.

In FORTRAN programs, all variables are initially undefined unless special steps have been taken to predefine them - these methods have not yet been introduced. A variable becomes defined in various ways which make common sense - through an assignment or READ statement for example. When a FUNCTION is referred to, the quantities that make up its arguments must already be defined, and so when the function is entered the dummy arguments of that entry have been given actual values. But the dummy arguments of another entry, if they are different, have not. Furthermore when the FUNCTION is finished and RETURNs to the program which invoked it, all values are lost including the values of the dummy arguments - they become unde-

fined. therefore the following illustrations are all incorrect:

```
FUNCTION DEMO(X,Y)
DEMO=X+Y+Z
ENTRY SILLY(Z)
SILLY=X-Y-Z
RETURN
END
```

This is doubly wrong. The statement

```
DEMO=X+Y+Z
```

uses Z which is certainly undefined. Therefore FORTRAN forbids the use of a dummy argument before the entry that defines it. Furthermore

```
SILLY=X-Y-Z
```

will not work for ENTRY SILLY, because if the function is entered at SILLY, X and Y are certainly undefined.

Care is required in using statement functions as well. Observe that in

```
FUNCTION EXAMPL(X,Y)
JUNK(P)=X*X+Y*Y+Z*Z
EXAMPL=JUNK(X)
RETURN
ENTRY NOTON(Z)
NOTON=JUNK(Z)
RETURN
END
```

the same rule is violated because whichever entry is used, some of the variables referred to in the arithmetic statement function JUNK are undefined. The point of all this is that dummy arguments of different entries cannot interact.

As with FUNCTION names, ENTRY names may not be used for any other purpose in the program unit. The ENTRY statement is:

```
ENTRY name([dummy arguments])
```

FORTRAN 77 allows a program to force the values of local variables to be saved for future references to the FUNCTION. Therefore, although dummy arguments cannot interact, the program obeyed on one entry can leave information behind to be used by other entries. This is done by the SAVE statement:

> SAVE list

which gives a list of variables whose values are to be saved to use in future references to the function. The list must not include any dummy arguments. If there is no list as in

> SAVE

all local variables are saved.

The SAVE statement belongs near the beginning of the program, after the FUNCTION statement but before any executable statement. SAVE itself is not an executable statement.

EXAMPLE:

A function is written to find the arcsin, arccos, and arctan of an angle. Of course FORTRAN has these built in but they work in radians. This function will work in either degrees or radians. Provided SWITCH has been used the function operates on a stored conversion factor. The programmer can also ask JWITCH to tell him which way the function is operating:

```
      FUNCTION SWITCH(ISW)
C A VERSATILE ANGLE FINDER IN
C DEGREES OR RADIANS. SWITCH(ISW)
C SETS RADIANS IF ISW=Ø, DEGREES
C OTHERWISE
      SAVE KSW,CON
      KSW=ISW
      CON=1.Ø
      IF(ISW.NE.Ø)CON=45.Ø/ATAN(1.Ø)
      SWITCH=CON
      RETURN
      ENTRY AMYTAN(X)
C ARCTAN IN DEGREES OR RADIANS
      AMYTAN=CON*ATAN(X)
      RETURN
      ENTRY AMYCOS(X)
C ARCCOS IN DEGREES OR RADIANS
      AMYCOS=CON*ACOS(X)
      RETURN
      ENTRY AMYSIN(X)
C ARCSIN IN DEGREES OR RADIANS
      AMYSIN=CON*ASIN(X)
      RETURN
```

```
      ENTRY JWITCH
C INTERROGATES THE SWITCH
      JWITCH=KSW
      RETURN
      END
```

It is noticed that the the FUNCTION SWITCH returns the value CON because the rules require that it must return something. Also the ENTRY JWITCH has no argument. It would be correct to write either

> ENTRY JWITCH()

or

> ENTRY JWITCH

but in referring to it brackets must be given:

> IF(JWITCH().EQ.Ø) GO TO 55

8.5 Giving names to constants — the PARAMETER statement

Up to this point all constants have been written out each time they are used, for example

> SUM=EXP(-XTOP*XTOP/2.Ø)/2.Ø

There are advantages in being able to give constants a name, for example in calling 2.0 by the name TWO. Firstly a programmer may get tired of writing out a constant with a lot of digits many times, and secondly in making a program portable a programmer may wish to make it easy for a constant to be changed. When it is written only once in a PARAMETER statement this is obviously much easier than changing it many times throughout a program. There is a subtle reason behind this as well - one computer may have less precision than another and so it may be necessary to add extra digits to a constant or even to make it DOUBLE PRECISION (Chapter 17), and the PARAMETER statement makes this easier. Clearly one of its virtues is as an aid to program portability. Indeed for publication some journals ask that all real constants be given names for this reason - authors find themselves writing ONE for 1.0 all the time.

The PARAMETER statement is

PARAMETER(name=con[,name=con,..])

and is not executable, meaning that it gives the program preliminary information but does not do anything more as a program executes.

"Name" is the symbolic "name" that is going to be used for the constant, and "con" is the value it is going to stand for. If necessary "con" is converted to the type of "name". Once "name" is identified with a constant it cannot be used as a variable or for any other purpose. It is important not to regard the PARAMETER statement as a means of giving initial values to variables, because the program will not allow the value to be changed. And if it is changed the sneaky way - through a subprogram - it is a constant that has been changed which can cause a lot of trouble.

> PARAMETER defines constants.

EXAMPLES:

        PARAMETER (ONE=1.0,TWO=2.0)

defines ONE and TWO.

        PARAMETER (X=5,PIE=3.1416)

gives the value 5.0 to X (after conversion) and 3.1416 to PIE. The author prefers to define π through the ATAN function as the reader will be well aware by now.

        PARAMETER (ONE=1.0)
        PARAMETER (IONE=ONE)

This illustrates the use of the name of a constant in a later PARAMETER statement. ONE has the value 1.0 and IONE has the integer value 1. It could have been done as

        PARAMETER (ONE=1.0,IONE=ONE)

but not as

        PARAMETER (IONE=ONE,ONE=1.0)

because the value of ONE is not known when IONE is defined.

The placing of the PARAMETER statement within a program is important. Up to this point, a number of statements have been introduced whose positions within a FORTRAN program are constrained in some way. These are summarised as follows:

	FUNCTION Statement	
COMMENTS can go anywhere before END	FORMAT and ENTRY	PARAMETER and SAVE
		Statement Function Definitions
		Executable Statements
END Statement		

As can be seen, this is a process of grouping together the informative non-executable statements at the beginning of the program, and will be continued as other statements are introduced. The final word on the ordering of statements is in Chapter 17.

EXAMPLE:
    A program shifts numbers right or left one place on any twos complement machine, but is easily converted to ones complement just by changing a PARAMETER statement.

```
    FUNCTION ISHFR(I)
C FUNCTION TO SHIFT I RIGHT
    PARAMETER (ISUBR=1,ISUBL=0)
    J=I
    IF(I.LT.0)J=J-ISUBR
    ISHFR=J/2
    RETURN
    ENTRY ISHFL(I)
    J=I*2
    IF(I.LT.0)J=J-ISUBL
    ISHFL=J
    RETURN
    END
```

To install this on a ones complement machine, change the PARAMETER statement to:

        PARAMETER(ISUBR=0,ISUBL=1)

8.6 Problems

PROBLEM 8.1:
A programmer has come to realize that the definition of integer division and the remainder in FORTRAN can be a nuisance in certain cases. In number theory, the definition of integer division is based on

$$n = q*d + r$$

where n is a number, d is a divisor, q is a quotient and r is the remainder. The trouble with the way FORTRAN does things is that in a lot of applications involving negative numbers it is more convenient to have a positive remainder. For consider numbers 7 apart:

$$16 = 2*7+2$$
$$9 = 1*7+2$$
$$2 = 0*7+2$$
$$\text{but } -5 = 0*7-5$$

Steps of -7 along the number line, Fig. 8.5, should, logically, produce the same remainder and quotients differing by one. But as we pass zero in FORTRAN there is a crunch.

If this were a calendar problem, a programmer would be happy to know that the 16th, 9th and 2nd were all Tuesdays but not too happy to move back a week from the 2nd and be in day -5.

In other word he really wants

$$-5/7 \text{ to be } -1$$

and MOD(-5,7) to be 2, so that

$$9 = 1*7+2$$
$$2 = 0*7+2$$
$$-5 = -1*7+2$$
$$-12 = -2*7+2$$

and so on.

Write statement functions MYQUOT and MYMOD to do integer division and remaindering this other way.

Fig. 8.5. On the number line integers 7 apart ought to give decreasing quotients and the same remainder modulo 7. FORTRAN does a nasty as it passes 0.

PROBLEM 8.2:
Write function subprograms IPERM and ICOMB to find the number of permutations of n objects taken r at a time:

$$nPr = n!/(n-r!)$$

and the number of combinations of n objects taken r at a time:

$$nCr = n!/r!(n-r)!$$

If done efficiently it is not just a simple matter of taking factorials. The value of n! becomes too big for the computer for quite modest n. You should be able to get nCr for larger n than that.

PROBLEM 8.3:
Write a function subprogram RANDY to produce random numbers according to the methods discussed in Chapter 4. Provide entries RANGE to set a range other than 0.0 - 1.0 and SEED to replace the built-in seed by your own.

PROBLEM 8.4:
The sum of twelve successive random numbers in the range 0.0 to 1.0 is almost indistinguishable from a Gaussian distribution with mean 6 and unit standard deviation. Take away six and you have zero mean. Write a function to produce a new Gaussian number every time it is called based on 12 calls to RANDY. If you know enough about statistics to be aware of the effects of scaling, give it an entry STAND through which you define the standard deviation.

PROBLEM 8.5:

The Poisson distribution is easily obtained also. Suppose a sequence of numbers is desired with mean e^{-m}. Using RANDY find a random number x_1. If $x_1 < e^{-m}$, the new Poisson number is 1. If not, find another random number and if $x_1 x_2 < e^{-m}$, the new Poisson number is 2, and so on. In general keep using RANDY until $x_1 x_2 \ldots x_k < e^{-m}$ after which the new Poisson number is k.

Write a function subprogram POISS to generate Poisson numbers in this way. Provide an entry point XMEAN to set the mean.

PROBLEM 8.6:

Write function subprograms:

IDAY for the day of the week given the date,
IEAST for the date of Easter given the year.

Refer to Chapter 3 for the methods. You may find MYMOD (Problem 8.1) is quite useful.

PROBLEM 8.7:

Write a function IBITRV (I,N) to give the reverse of N bits of the number I. Refer to Section 7.3 for the method.

PROBLEM 8.8:

Write a function IRCNT(I,N) to add 1 in bit-reverse count to I considered as an N bit number. Refer to Problem 7.5 for the method.

9
Structured programming

9.1 Introduction

This chapter is concerned with current ideas about organizing a well structured program. The basic idea behind structured programming is that any program, however complex, should be written in such a way that it can be read by a human who starts at the beginning and follows it through from top to bottom. Computer scientists have identified a fundamental set of control structures which make this possible. It is clear that an obvious feature of a well structured program is that it does not contain a lot of jumps from here to there. In other words the GO TO statement is used sparingly if at all.

FORTRAN IV is a very difficult language to write structured programs in - it was designed before the ideas of structured programming fully matured. Some of the most important innovations of FORTRAN 77 are those which help in structured programming - principally the block IF facility. There are a few constructions not supported by statements of FORTRAN 77, and in those cases a GO TO statement is used as part of the realization of the structure.

A programmer should aim to organize his program according to the structures outlined here. Any use of the GO TO statement should be consciously part of one of the accepted structures. And it is very important that a FORTRAN IV programmer who has fallen into bad habits should try to reform. Therefore this chapter is about writing good programs in any language, and although it is not essential to the learning of the FORTRAN language, it is of some importance in its usage.

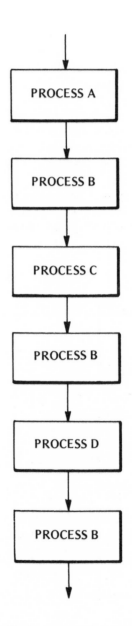

Fig. 9.1. A perfectly respectable sequential structure containing a repeated process.

9.2 Sequence

The simplest and most obvious structure occurs when a series of operations are carried out one after the other, in sequence. A FORTRAN program is obeyed in the order that the statements occur, and so a series of statements with no branching or jumping forms a sequence. Such a straightforward idea is an important part of "top-down" readability, and is ruined by too much branching.

Consider the structure of Fig. 9.1; the process illustrated can be of any complexity and could contain any control structure within itself. This is clearly a sequential structure and so a good one, but it may be overlong because the process labelled B is performed three times. In order to shorten programs like this, programmers have been known to abuse structures terribly. In Fig. 9.2, a few statements are filled in to show how this crime might be committed - and the culprit is the GO TO statement. And just where in the program does procedure B go? It is just as bad wherever it is

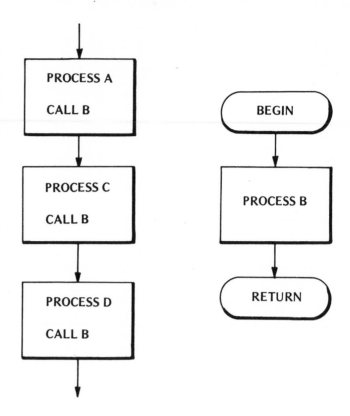

Fig. 9.3. How to shorten the program of Fig. 9.1 without ruining its structure — use a subprogram.

put. This is an ugly structure and can be avoided by making B into a subprogram or possibly a statement function, as in Fig. 9.3. If a programmer finds that an identical procedure is being used in various places, and is more than a few statements long, he should consider making it a FUNCTION subprogram, as described in Chapter 8, or a SUBROUTINE subprogram, as described in Chapter 10.

EXAMPLE:

Here is a program intended to evaluate the binomial coefficient nCr, which is the number of combinations of n things taken r at a time:

$$_{n}C_{r} = \frac{n!}{r!\,(n-r)!}$$

Suppose the procedure to be followed is

   (i) Evaluate n!
   (ii) Evaluate r!
   (iii) Evaluate n-r!
   (iv) Combine the results to form nCr as illustrated by Fig.9.4, which of course resembles Fig.9.1.

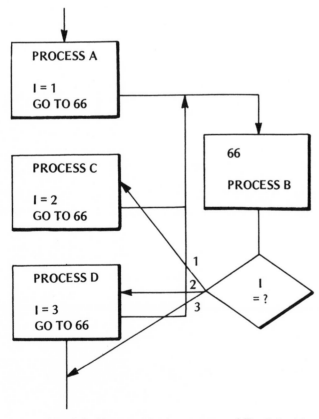

Fig. 9.2. How to ruin the program of Fig. 9.1 with GO TO statements.

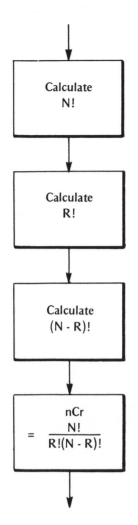

Fig. 9.4. A possible way to calculate $_nC_r$.

The following is a well structured program for nCr, although it does more work than is actually necessary.

```
C EVALUATE BINOMIAL COEFF NCR
C IN AND IR ARE ALREADY DEFINED
C GET THE FACTORIAL OF IN
      IFN=1
      DO 10 K=2,IN
        IFN=IFN*K
   10 CONTINUE
C GET THE FACTORIAL OF IR
      IFR=1
      DO 20 K=2,IR
        IFR=IFR*K
   20 CONTINUE
C GET THE FACTORIAL OF IN-IR
      IFNR=1
      DO 30 K=2,IN-IR
        IFNR=IFNR*K
   30 CONTINUE
C AND FINALLY MAKE THE ANSWER NCR
      NCR=IFN/(IFR*IFNR)
```

On the other hand, some programmers have been known to write things like:

```
C EVALUATE BINOMIAL COEFF NCR
C IN, IR ARE ALREADY DEFINED
C GO GET FACTORIAL IN
      I=1
      IF=IN
      GO TO 66
   10 NCR=IFCT
C GO GET FACTORIAL IR
      I=2
      IF=IR
      GO TO 66
   20 NCR=NCR/IFCT
C GO GET FACTORIAL IN-IR
      I=3
      IF=IN-IR
      GO TO 66
   30 NCR=NCR/IFCT
      GO TO 68
C HERE EVALUATE FACTORIAL IFCT
   66 IFCT=1
      DO 67 K=2,IF
      IFCT=IFCT*K
   67 CONTINUE
      GO TO (10,20,30)I
   68 Here the program continues
```

This doesn't even save statements and is a horrible structure - observe the confusion created by all those GO TO statements. In fact it has the appalling structure of Fig.9.2. The programmer in a misguided way is trying to write a subprogram inside the program, which is used by setting up some variables and reached with a GO TO. It is possible to rationalize this program without destroying the structure, as:

```
C EVALUATE BINOMIAL COEFF NCR
C IN, IR ARE ALREADY DEFINED
C GET FACTORIAL IN
      IFIN=IFACT(IN)
C GET FACTORIAL IR
      IFIR=IFACT(IR)
C GET FACTORIAL IN-IR
      IFNR=IFACT(IN-IR)
      NCR=IFIN/(IFIR*IFNR)
```

where the function IFACT is found in Section 8.3. Most people of any experience would, of course, have seen the need for a function immediately in this unlikely example; it was chosen to illustrate what can happen (and frequently does) in larger programs. Naturally enough, this example reduces to

```
NCR=IFACT(IN)/(IFACT(IR)
          *IFACT(IN-IR))
```

which still is not the solution to Problem 8.4 because steps (i) and (ii) of this procedure have something in common.

EXERCISE:
Write a FUNCTION subprogram to evaluate nCr in a more efficient way. Plenty of hints have been dropped about how to do this; you want to get the smallest number of multiplications without ruining the structure. Examine the formula for nCr and you will see that some of the multiplications are common for the numerator and denominator.

9.3 Selection by conditional clauses

Given the opportunity to make decisions, or select his next move, a programmer can do many powerful things. In terms of structured programming he could do them badly or he could do them well. The conditional structure is expressed as

```
IF condition DO procedure
```

which rather resembles a logical IF statement - but note that the word "DO" is not the DO statement. Fig. 9.5 illustrates the structure.

In FORTRAN this structure can be realized in two ways, depending on the complexity of the procedure. If the procedure can be expressed as a single statement, the logical IF statement is used:

```
IF(condition)executable statement
```

as in the error normalization of the method of False Position in Section 6.5

which shows the structure clearly in its flowchart, Fig. 6.7 or 6.8.

If the procedure is longer, a block IF statement is used,

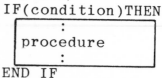

```
          IF(condition)THEN
             :
           procedure
             :
          END IF
```

as it was in the following extract from a brute force multiplication program in Section 7.3:

```
C MAKE I THE SMALLER NUMBER
    IF(I.GT.J) THEN
       M=I
       I=J
       J=M
    END IF
```

Here it was necessary that of two given numbers, I and J, I should be the smaller, unless they are equal, when it doesn't matter. It should be obvious what M was for! The same might have been achieved as follows:

```
C MAKE I THE SMALLER
    IF(I.LE.J)GO TO 20
       M=I
       I=J
       J=M
 20 etc...
```

This is what a FORTRAN IV program would have done, but it is an inferior structure.

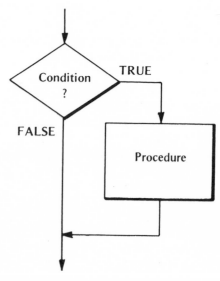

Fig. 9.5. The structure of a conditional clause.

9.4 Selection by alternative clauses

It is very likely that a program will make a choice of two alternatives; this is an obvious extension of the conditional clause. The structure is usually described as

```
IF condition THEN procedure 1
             ELSE procedure 2
```

which certainly bears a strong resemblance to the block IF statement. A flowchart describing it is shown in Fig. 9.6. This structure would be achieved by a block IF statement with an ELSE clause, as

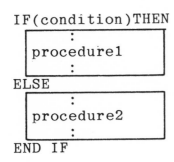

```
IF(condition)THEN
     :
   procedure1
     :
ELSE
     :
   procedure2
     :
END IF
```

As an example, the method of False Position described in some detail in Section 6.5, used the alternative clause,

```
C WHICH SIDE ARE WE ON
     IF(FX2.EQ.SIGN(FX2,FXØ))THEN
C ON THE XØ SIDE, REPLACE XØ
       D=ABS(X2-XØ)
       XØ=X2
       FXØ=FX2
       PRINT 15Ø
     ELSE
C ON THE X1 SIDE, REPLACE X1
       D=ABS(X2-X1)
       X1=X2
       FX1=FX2
       PRINT 16Ø
     END IF
```

which as Figs 6.2 and 6.3 showed, is the same structure as Fig.9.6.

It is instructive to compare this to the awkward syntax:

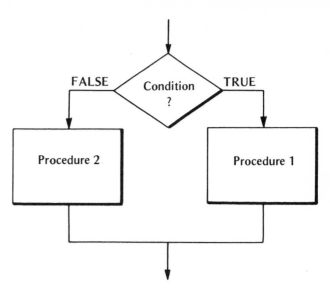

Fig. 9.6. The structure of an alternative clause.

```
C WHICH SIDE ARE WE ON
     IF(FX2.NE.SIGN(FX2,FXØ))GO TO 3Ø
C ON THE XØ SIDE, REPLACE XØ
       D=ABS(X2-XØ)
       XØ=X2
       FXØ=FX2
       PRINT 15Ø
     GO TO 4Ø
  3Ø CONTINUE
C ON THE X1 SIDE, REPLACE X1
       D=ABS(X2-X1)
       X1=X2
       FX1=FX2
       PRINT 16Ø
  4Ø CONTINUE
```

which is what would have been done in FORTRAN IV. Note the use of GO TO.

9.5 Selection by choice clauses

As a generalization of the conditional and alternative structures, it is sometimes very useful to have a choice of a number of procedures. A structure which achieves this is described by:

```
CASE i OF p1,p2,...pn
```

where i is an integer and p1, p2, ..., pn are procedures. When i is 1, p1 is to be followed; when i is 2, p2 is to be executed; and so on. The structure of this, Fig. 9.7, is easy to achieve with the computed GO TO statement

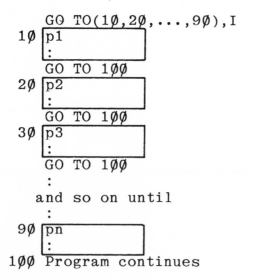

Fig. 9.7. The structure of selection by case or choice.

```
GO TO(p1,p2,...,pn),i
```

where p1, ..., pn are now the labels of the desired procedures, except that GO TO statements are required to get to the end of the case block. Hence FORTRAN achieves this structure but requires the GO TO,

```
      GO TO(1Ø,2Ø,...,9Ø),I
1Ø  p1
    :
      GO TO 1ØØ
2Ø  p2
    :
      GO TO 1ØØ
3Ø  p3
    :
      GO TO 1ØØ
    :
    and so on until
    :
9Ø  pn

1ØØ Program continues
```

It would also be possible to do this in an extended IF block:

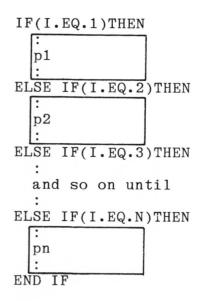

```
IF(I.EQ.1)THEN
  :
  p1
  :
ELSE IF(I.EQ.2)THEN
  :
  p2
  :
ELSE IF(I.EQ.3)THEN
  :
  and so on until
  :
ELSE IF(I.EQ.N)THEN
  :
  pn
  :
END IF
```

Here the ELSE IF statements select the necessary block. The computed GO TO would be preferred if the number of different procedures was large; if there were only a few, the ELSE IF may be more readable. The IF block is more versatile than the case structure itself because ELSE IF statements are clearly not restricted to decisions based on consecutive integers.

9.6 Iteration and repetition

As is well known from earlier chapters, most FORTRAN programs involve some kind of looping. The structure of any loop can be described by the WHILE construction:

WHILE condition DO procedure

illustrated in Fig.9.8. FORTRAN 77 does not have this feature; it was proposed but not included. The WHILE structure is much more powerful than the DO loop. In fact the DO loop is an unsophisticated WHILE. The DO loop

```
      DO 3Ø I=1,1Ø
       :
       procedure
       :
 3Ø   CONTINUE
```

is the same as saying

```
      I=1
      WHILE(I.LE.1Ø)DO
       :
       procedure
       :
       I=I+1
      END WHILE
```

There are, accordingly, two ways that a WHILE structure may be organized in FORTRAN. It might be a DO loop, or using the logical IF statement:

```
 1Ø   procedure
       :
       :
      IF(.NOT.condition)GO TO 1Ø
```

It may be noticed that once again the GO TO is required to achieve the desired control structure. This appeared in many earlier examples. For example, in the method of False Position in Section 6.5, the process was repeated until D was less than 10^{-5}; this is a WHILE structure:

```
      D=1.Ø
      WHILE (D.GT.1E-Ø5) DO
       Procedure
       for
       Method
```

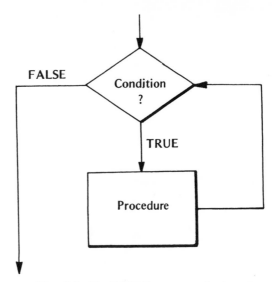

Fig. 9.8. The WHILE structure for iteration.

```
       of
       False
       Position
      END WHILE
```

that has been expressed as

```
 2Ø   Procedure
       for
       Method
       of
       False
       Position
      IF(D.GT.1E-Ø5)GO TO 2Ø
```

Similarly, in the clever method for multiplying two positive numbers in Section 4.7,

```
C MULTIPLY BY SHIFTING
C POSITIVE NONZERO NUMBERS
C ACCEPT I AND J TO MULTIPLY
      PRINT*,'GIVE TWO INTEGERS'
      READ*,I,J
      I1=MIN(I,J)
      I2=MAX(I,J)
      IPROD=Ø
 1Ø   LSB=MOD(I1,2)
      IF(LSB.EQ.1)IPROD=IPROD+I2
      I1=I1/2
      I2=I2*2
      IF(I1.GT.Ø) GO TO 1Ø
C PRINT THE RESULT
      PRINT*,'PRODUCT IS ',IPROD
      END
```

the procedure is repeated while I1 is greater than 0. If this is compared to the same program using an IF statement to escape from a DO loop in Section 7.4, the former has the better structure.

9.7 When to use GO TO

Some computer scientists have been known to refer to structured programming as programming without GO TO, meaning in the case of FORTRAN that the GO TO statement should only be used to simulate a program control structure, as described in connection with the CASE and WHILE constructions. It is certainly true that GO TO statements tend to make programs difficult to read, because a well structured program is one which can be followed easily by the human mind, meaning that it should not skip around a good deal. In extreme cases GO TO statements can make programs incomprehensible.

In practice there are a few situations where a GO TO is not as bad as all that. Firstly a GO TO is useful to escape from a DO loop or IF block to somewhere further down the program. It should then never transfer in an upwards direction against the flow of the program except where a WHILE construction is being simulated. This permissible use is illustrated in the program to find all the primes from 1 to 100 which was described in Section 7.7.

```
C FIND ALL PRIME NUMBERS
C FROM 1 TO 100
      PRINT*,'PRIMES FROM 1 TO 100'
      PRINT 10,1,2
 10   FORMAT(1X,I4)
      DO 30 N=3,99,2
        DO 20 I=3,SQRT(REAL(N)),2
          IF(MOD(N,I).EQ.0)GO TO 30
 20     CONTINUE
C IF GET TO HERE N IS PRIME
        PRINT 10,N
 30   CONTINUE
      END
```

Throughout this book, the preferred structures are used, and the GO TO is only used to simulate them (in WHILE constructions), or to escape from a loop.

9.8 Problems

PROBLEM 9.1:
The saturating ramp function illustrated by Fig. 9.9 is

$$f(x) = -1 \text{ for } x < -1$$
$$f(x) = x \text{ for } -1 \leqslant x \leqslant 1$$
$$f(x) = 1 \text{ for } x > 1$$

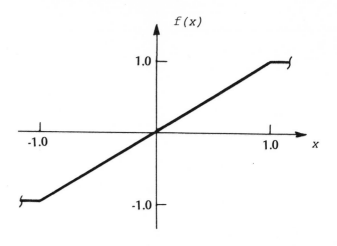

Fig. 9.9. A nice symmetric saturating function.

Write a subprogram RAMP(X) to evaluate this. How would you achieve the function of Fig. 9.10 where

$$f(x) = -a \text{ for } x < -b$$
$$f(x) = c \text{ for } x > d$$
$$f(x) = \text{straight line for } -b \leqslant x \leqslant d?$$

PROBLEM 9.2:
This one was inevitable. Write a program to find the roots of the quadratic equation

$$ax^2 + bx + c = 0$$

covering all cases.

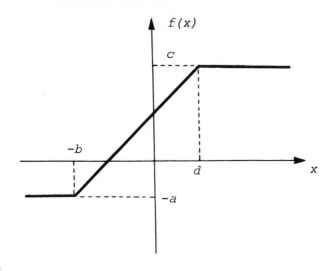

Fig. 9.10. A non-symmetric saturating function.

PROBLEM 9.3

Write a function to evaluate the cosine of an angle given in radians:

(i) by constructing a fifth order Chebyshev polynomial (Problem 7.6);

(ii) by using five terms of the power series expansion (Problem 7.2);

In either case it is only necessary to evaluate over the range $-\pi$ to π after first reducing the angle to this range. How? Compare the errors in these two methods against something you would trust, and decide which method you would use if you had the job of designing the COS function.

PROBLEM 9.4

Write a function subprogram to evaluate the Bessel function of the first kind of order n:

$$J_n(x) = x^n \sum_{m=0}^{\infty} \frac{(-1)^m x^{2m}}{2^{2m+n} \, m! \, m+1!}$$

It is not as difficult as it looks.

PROBLEM 9.5

The Gamma function is like a generalized factorial. It is known that

$$n! = n(n-1)!$$

for integers > -1. The Gamma function

$$\Gamma(x) = (x-1)\,\Gamma(x-1)$$

has a similar property for all x. In particular, if x is an integer

$$\Gamma(x) = \Gamma(x-1)!$$

There are several formulae for it:

(i) $$\Gamma(x) = \frac{1}{x} \prod_{n=1}^{\infty} \frac{\left\{1 + \frac{1}{n}\right\}^x}{1 + \frac{x}{n}}$$

(ii) $$\Gamma(x) = \int_0^{\infty} e^{-t} \, t^{x-1} \, dt \qquad \text{for } x>0$$

(iii) $$\Gamma(x) = \sqrt{2\pi} \; x^{x-\frac{1}{2}} \, e^{-x} \left\{ 1 + \frac{1}{12x} + \frac{1}{288x^2} - \frac{139}{51840x^3} - \cdots \right\}$$

This last equation extends Stirling's approximation. Develop a function to evaluate $\Gamma(x)$ to suitable accuracy for your computer.

10
Subroutines

10.1 Introduction

FORTRAN in its various forms has endured for many years as the principal computing language for scientific and technical calculation, and one of the major reasons for this is found in its superior facilities for defining and using functions and subroutines. It is a great convenience to programmers that they can generalize algorithms into independent program units. But even more important is the way these units can be communicated through program libraries in order to be of use to other people. Subroutines for thousands of applications are available to help a FORTRAN programmer to benefit from the work of others.

10.2 Subroutines — the SUBROUTINE and CALL statements

The subroutine is a very popular facility of FORTRAN. Although a FUNCTION subprogram can in theory do most of the same things as a subroutine, in practice it is used most often for the obvious purpose of providing a single numerical result as part of an expression. The subroutine is used for more general purposes, such as operating upon its list of arguments, or performing input/output operations. The intelligent use of functions and subroutines enables a good programmer to simplify his programs and improve their structure by identifying modular tasks and forming them into subprograms. This can greatly improve and shorten a program if it contains the same calculations at different places. However it can be overdone, and over-zealous programmers can end up creating an incomprehensible maze of subprograms.

As always, good programming is clear programming.

EXAMPLE:
In Chapter 8, it was recommended that functions should not modify their arguments. If this advice is followed, a function can provide only a single result. To return several results, a subroutine should be used.

Functions for conversion from rectangular to polar Cartesian co-ordinates as in Fig. 10.1 were given in Chapter 8:

```
RADIUS(X,Y)=SQRT(X*X+Y*Y)
ANGLE(X,Y)=ATAN2(Y,X)
```

A conversion from (X,Y) to (RADIUS, ANGLE) required two functions. It may be more convenient to use a subroutine like

```
      SUBROUTINE POLAR(ARG1,ARG2)
C CONVERT CARTESIAN (ARG1,ARG2) TO
C POLAR (RADIUS,ANGLE) WITH ANGLE
C IN RADIANS. RESULT (ARG1,ARG2)
      X=SQRT(ARG1*ARG1+ARG2*ARG2)
      ARG2=ATAN2(ARG2,ARG1)
      ARG1=X
      END
```

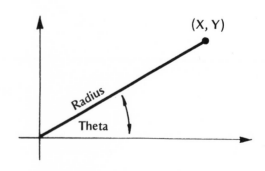

Fig. 10.1. Polar and Cartesian co-ordinates.

This subroutine, called POLAR, has two real arguments, ARG1 and ARG2. It converts these to polar form, and when it finishes their values have been changed. It should be noticed that in the conversion an intermediate variable X has been used to store what eventually becomes the new value of ARG1. This is necessary because the original value of ARG1 is required for the calculation of both new values; it cannot be replaced until ARG2 has been calculated.

To use a subroutine, a CALL statement is inserted in the program that is to use it.

EXAMPLE:

In a main program or in another subroutine a statement like the following could appear:

CALL POLAR(X,Y)

Here X and Y are arguments of the CALL and are used as the values of ARG1 and ARG2 in the subroutine. Hence a subroutine uses the same dummy argument idea in just the same way as does a function. This subroutine changes the values of X and Y, and so the arguments of this call must be variables.

A subroutine differs from a function in that its name does not stand for a result and so it does not have a type associated with it.

To generalize, a subroutine begins with the SUBROUTINE statement, has an END statement as its last line, and may contain various RETURN statements. The name and list of dummy arguments are defined in in the first statement:

SUBROUTINE name[(dummy variables)]

"name" is the name given to the subprogram, but in this case there is no significance to its spelling; the notion of type (real or integer) does not apply to subroutine names.

"dummy variables" is a list of variable names separated by commas. Their type is implied by the spelling.

The SUBROUTINE statement is followed by the body of the subprogram which, using the facilities of FORTRAN, can do such things as manipulate the values of the dummy variables, initiate input or output, or call on other subprograms. If statement functions are desired they must be defined locally, following the SUB-ROUTINE statement (which is not executable) and before the first executable statement.

The order in which statements must appear in subroutines is the same as in FUNCTION subprograms. The subroutine is a separate program unit, bounded by the SUBROUTINE statement and the END statement. Of the statements known so far, the order must be:

	SUBROUTINE Statement	
COMMENTS can go anywhere before END	FORMAT and ENTRY	PARAMETER and SAVE
		Statement Function Definitions
		Executable Statements
END Statement		

More statements are to be introduced in later chapters which belong in a specific order. A summary of the required order appears in Chapter 17.

The subroutine is a separate program unit. As described so far a program unit could be a main program, a subroutine, or a function. One further kind of program unit is introduced in Chapter 13.

Any variables which are not specified as dummy variables in the SUBROUTINE statement are local to the subroutine, that is they are not known to other parts of the program. This extremely important concept applies just as it would to functions, and is the reason why FORTRAN subroutines are so portable. A subroutine which is used correctly does not interfere with the program which called it.

Within the subprogram either the END statement or a RETURN statement will indicate the completion of the subroutine and will cause a return to the program which called it.

Subroutines are used by the CALL statement:

    CALL name[(arguments)]

'name' is the name of the subroutine.

'arguments' is the list of variables, constants or expressions to be operated on by the subroutine, separated by commas. They must be in one-to-one correspondence in type with the dummy variables of subroutine 'name'. The subroutine uses the arguments as the actual values of the dummy variables. If a dummy variable is assigned a new value or changed in any other way by the subroutine, then the corresponding argument must not be a constant or expression; otherwise the program will destroy itself.

A subroutine which has no arguments can be defined and called with or without brackets. This was not the case with function references which had to include brackets.

EXAMPLE:
The subroutine POLAR could be called by a statement:

    CALL POLAR(X,Y)

and the subroutine would return the results in X or Y. This is safe as long as X and Y are variables. However any one of the following would cause disaster:

    PARAMETER(ONE=1.Ø,TWO=2.Ø)
    CALL POLAR(ONE,TWO)

or   CALL POLAR(1.Ø,2.Ø)

or   CALL POLAR(X*X,Y*Y)

because each would destroy the calling program. In designing and using subroutines it is essential to understand that constants or expressions may not be used as arguments if they correspond to dummy variables that are modified in the subroutine. Were the subroutine instead

    SUBROUTINE POLAR(X,Y,RAD,ANG)
C CONVERT CARTESIAN(X,Y) TO POLAR
C (RAD,ANG) WITH ANG IN RADIANS
    RAD=SQRT(X*X+Y*Y)
    ANG=ATAN2(Y,X)
    END

then a call like

    CALL POLAR(1.Ø,2.Ø,P,Q)

would be acceptable. A programmer has to keep account of these finer points of usage himself. The FORTRAN compiler will not save him and the likely result is wrong answers. Note that in the second case the result can be calculated without using intermediate variables to save part of the answer. This is because the result does not replace the given data.

EXAMPLE:
The following 'main program' calls a subroutine ANGLES to find the three angles A1, A2 and A3 of a triangle whose three sides S1, S2 and S3 are known:

```
C FIND OPPOSITE ANGLES A1,A2,A3
C TRIANGLE WITH SIDES S1,S2,S3
C FIRST READ IN THE SIDES
    READ'(3F1Ø.5)',S1,S2,S3
C CALL SUBROUTINE FOR ANGLES
    CALL ANGLES(S1,S2,S3,A1,A2,A3)
    WRITE(*,1Ø)
 1Ø FORMAT(' SIDE OPP.ANG')
    WRITE(*,2Ø)S1,A1,S2,A2,S3,A3
 2Ø FORMAT(2F7.2)
    END
```

The subroutine ANGLES should check for impossible triangles, and it could be

```
      SUBROUTINE ANGLES(X,Y,Z,A,B,C)
C CALCULATE ANGLES A,B,C IN
C DEGREES OPPOSITE SIDES X,Y,Z
C FIRST GET CONVERSION FACTOR
      FAC=45.Ø/ATAN(1.Ø)
C USE COSINE LAW TO FIND COS(A)
      CA=(Y*Y+Z*Z-X*X)/(2.Ø*Y*Z)
C IS THIS TRIANGLE POSSIBLE
      IF(ABS(CA).LE.1.Ø) THEN
C YES, GET THE REQUIRED ANGLES
      A=ACOS(CA)*FAC
C USE RATIO X/SINA = Y/SINB FOR B
      THING=Y*SQRT(1.Ø-CA*CA)/X
      B=ASIN(THING)*FAC
      C=18Ø.Ø-A-B
      ELSE
C IMPOSSIBLE TRIANGLE, BE RUDE
      WRITE(*,2Ø)X,Y,Z
  2Ø  FORMAT(' BAD SIDES',3F1Ø.5)
      A=Ø.Ø
      B=Ø.Ø
      C=Ø.Ø
      END IF
      END
```

A flow diagram for this subroutine is given in Fig. 10.2. In the main program given earlier, the CALL to ANGLES uses arguments S1, S2, S3, A1, A2 and A3. The subroutine in execution will use the values of S1, S2 and S3 as its dummy variables X, Y, and Z. It calculates the angles A, B, and C, but in this example these are dummies for A1, A2, and A3.

Therefore when the subroutine returns to the main program, new values of A1, A2 and A3 have been calculated.

The variables FACTOR and COSA are only known within subroutine ANGLES. If these names happened to appear in the main program or in other subprograms they would not refer to the same variables - those in ANGLES are local to the subroutine.

In the CALL statement the three angles A1, A2 and A3 must be variables as in this example because they are replaced within the subroutine. The three sides S1, S2 and S3 could be variables, constants, or expressions since they are not modified by the subroutine. All six arguments must be real.

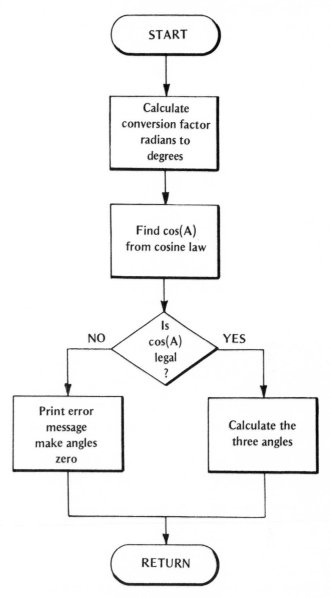

Fig. 10.2. Flowchart of a subroutine to find the angles of a triangle given the sides.

10.3 Two useful subroutines

In this section some examples of subroutines are given. In each case the subroutine is used not because it is necessary, but because the programmer has identified it as a procedure that he might well use again, or one that he feels might be of use to others.

(i) Recursive sine and cosine generation.

Many calculations use a series of sines and cosines that are equally spaced; the calculation of a Fourier series is a good example of a series that uses a great many. It was seen in Chapter 7 that it is not necessary to use the intrinsic COS or SIN function more than once provided that all the angles are equally spaced, because

$$\cos(A+B)=\cos(A)\cos(B)-\sin(A)\sin(B)$$

and

$$\sin(A+B)=\sin(A)\cos(B)+\cos(A)\sin(B)$$

Therefore if CA and SA are the cosine and sine of A, and CB and SB are the cosine and sine of B, then the statements

```
TEMP=CA
CA=CA*CB-SA*SB
SA=SA*CB+TEMP*SB
```

perform the recurrence, i.e. they calculate $\cos(A+B)$ and $\sin(A+B)$ from $\cos(A)$, $\cos(B)$, $\sin(A)$ and $\sin(B)$.

If there are a great many angles to calculate, errors slowly accumulate. It has been found that these errors can be reduced if the recurrence is slightly reorganized to avoid loss of precision:

```
D=CB-1.0
Z=CA+D*CA-SA*SB
SA=SA+D*SA+CA*SB
CA=Z
```

One or other of the cos or sin could be small, so they are calculated separately, and the results are then corrected to ensure that

$$\sin(A+B) + \cos(A+B) = 1.0$$

This method tends to accumulate errors more slowly.

Here, therefore, is a subroutine SWING to calculate $\cos(A+B)$ and $\sin(A+B)$. It is assumed that A is to be the new angle, and so CA and SA are replaced by $\cos(A+B)$ and $\sin(A+B)$:

```
      SUBROUTINE SWING(CA,SA,CB,SB)
C
C CORRECTED SIN + COS RECURRENCE
C
C CA=REAL VARIABLE, INPUT COS(A)
C                   OUTPUT COS(A+B)
```

```
C SA=REAL VARIABLE, INPUT SIN(A)
C                   OUTPUT SIN(A+B)
C CB=REAL VALUE, INPUT COS(B)
C SB=REAL VALUE, INPUT SIN(B)
C
      PARAMETER(HALF=0.5,ONE=1.0)
      PARAMETER(ONE5=1.5)
      D=CB-ONE
      Z1=CA+D*CA-SA*SB
      Z2=SA+D*SA+CA*SB
      T=ONE5-HALF*(Z1*Z1+Z2*Z2)
      CA=T*Z1
      SA=T*Z2
      END
```

This little subroutine has served the author very well indeed in Fourier calculations and using Chebyshev polynomials. It is an indispensable part of the fast Fourier calculation used as a case study in Chapter 12.

An example of the use of SWING is given here in calculating the Fourier coefficients of a function by the traditional, slow method. This subroutine, SLOWF1, calculates the Nth Fourier coefficients using M values of a periodic function which is defined by a FUNCTION subprogram FUNC over a range 0.0 to x1. The coefficients are calculated according to the definitions:

$$A_N = \frac{2}{M} \sum_{k=0}^{M-1} f(x_k) \cos \frac{2Nk\pi}{M}$$

$$B_N = \frac{2}{M} \sum_{k=0}^{M-1} f(x_k) \sin \frac{2Nk\pi}{M}$$

```
      SUBROUTINE SLOWF1(N,M,X1,AN,BN)
C
C EVALUATE NTH FOURIER COEFFS
C AN + BN FOR THE USER'S FUNCTION
C FUNC OVER THE RANGE 0.0 TO X1
C
C N=INPUT VALUE, NO. OF
C                DESIRED HARMONIC
C M=INPUT VALUE, NO. OF
C                POINTS USED IN SUM
C X1=INPUT VALUE, FUNCTION PERIOD
C AN=OUTPUT COSINE COEFFICIENT
C BN=OUTPUT SINE COEFFICIENT
```

```
C SET UP CONSTANTS
      PARAMETER(ZERO=Ø.Ø,ONE=1.Ø)
      PARAMETER(TWO=2.Ø)
      X2M=TWO/M
      THING=X1/M
      ANG=X2M*N*4.Ø*ATAN(1.Ø)
C SET UP COS + SIN RECURRENCE
      CA=ONE
      SA=ZERO
      CB=COS(ANG)
      SB=SIN(ANG)
C SUM TO GET NTH FOURIER COEFFS
      SUMA=ZERO
      SUMB=ZERO
      DO 1Ø K=Ø,M-1
        FX=FUNC(K*THING)
        SUMA=SUMA+CA*FX
        SUMB=SUMB+SA*FX
C GET NEXT COS AND SINE
        CALL SWING(CA,SA,CB,SB)
   1Ø CONTINUE
      AN=SUMA*X2M
      BN=SUMB*X2M
      END
```

The function FUNC(X) must calculate the values of the function whenever it is referred to by SLOWF1. The range 0.0 to X1 must represent one period of the function, as illustrated by Fig. 10.3.

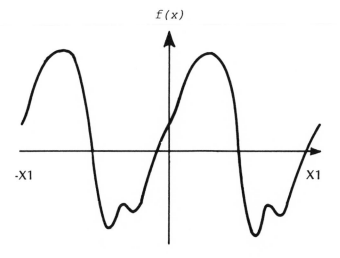

Fig. 10.3. A periodic function whose Fourier series can be found.

EXERCISE:

Devise some functions and test this program. Can you invent functions for which BN is always zero? What about AN?

(ii) The area under a function.

Here a subroutine called STRAP is given which will find the area under a function by the trapezoidal rule. The limits of the integration are given to the subroutine as BOT and TOP, and so is the desired accuracy DELTA. The subroutine evaluates

$$\int_{BOT}^{TOP} f(x)\ dx$$

which is illustrated in Fig.10.4, by the trapezoidal rule:

$$\int_{BOT}^{TOP} = h\left\{\frac{f_0}{2} + \left\{f_1 + f_2 + \ldots + f_{N-1}\right\} + \frac{f_N}{2}\right\}$$

where

$$h = (TOP-BOT)/N$$

and the function is evaluated at the N+1 points

$$f = f(BOT)$$
$$f = f(BOT+h)$$
$$\vdots$$
$$f = f(TOP)$$

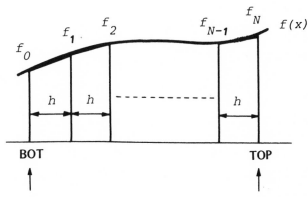

Fig. 10.4. Illustrating the trapezoidal rule.

The user supplies the function to be integrated as the FUNCTION subprogram FUNC(X), which STRAP can use for as many values of X as it needs. The subroutine tries two slices, four slices, eight slices, and so on until it thinks

```
      SUBROUTINE STRAP(BOT,TOP,DELTA,ANSWER,NSTRIP)
C
C SUBROUTINE FOR QUADRATURE BY TRAPEZOIDAL RULE
C INTEGRATES FUNCTION FROM BOT TO TOP, DOUBLING
C NUMBER OF STRIPS UNTIL ERROR IS LESS THAN DELTA
C THE USER SUPPLIES THE INTEGRAND AS FUNCTION FUNC
C
C BOT - INPUT VALUE, THE LOWER LIMIT OF INTEGRATION
C TOP - INPUT VALUE, THE UPPER LIMIT OF INTEGRATION
C DELTA - INPUT VALUE, THE DESIRED ERROR BOUND
C ANSWER - OUTPUT VARIABLE, THE CALCULATED INTEGRAND
C NSTRIP - OUTPUT VARIABLE, THE NUMBER OF STRIPS USED
C
C SET UP LOCAL VARIABLES FOR EFFICIENCY
      XDELTA=4.0*DELTA
      XTOP=TOP
      XBOT=BOT
C INITIALIZE
      NST=1
      H=XTOP-XBOT
      SOLD=(FUNC(XBOT)+FUNC(XTOP))*H/2.0
C MAKE THE NEW SUM
   10 X=XBOT+H/2.0
      NST=NST*2
      SNEW=0.0
      DO 20 K=1,NST,2
         SNEW=SNEW+FUNC(X)
         X=X+H
   20 CONTINUE
C FORM NEW INTEGRAND AND ESTIMATE ERROR
      H=H/2.0
      SNEW=SNEW*H+SOLD/2.0
      CHANGE=ABS(SOLD-SNEW)
      SOLD=SNEW
C DO AGAIN WHILE ERROR.GT.4.0*DELTA
      IF(CHANGE.GT.XDELTA)GO TO 10
C FINISHED, RETURN RESULTS
      ANSWER=SOLD
      NSTRIP=NST
      END
```

the error is less than DELTA. How does it decide this? Well, the error in the trapezoidal rule is approximately proportional to h^3, and so each time the number of points is doubled, the error should decrease by a factor of four. It is therefore reasonable to assume that when the calculated area changes by less than 4*DELTA when the step size is halved, the latest value is good enough. The program returns the area as ANSWER and the number of strips as NSTRIP. The repeated calculation resembles the WHILE structure described in Chapter 9.

A number of things have been done to make this program efficient. One of these is new. Inside the subprogram the dummy variables BOT, TOP, and DELTA are used a number of times - DELTA in particular is used every time around the calculation. Now it just happens that a computer has to work harder to refer to one of its dummy arguments than to a local variable. Therefore, at the beginning of the subroutine, the values have to be assigned to local variables, and in the case of DELTA, the subprogram is actually interested in 4.0*DELTA. In addition, values are not assigned to the results until they are finally known, for the same reason. It is a good rule to

```
┌─────────────────────────────────────┐
│  USE LOCAL VARIABLES IN PREFERENCE   │
│   TO DUMMY VARIABLES IF THEY ARE     │
│     REFERRED TO SEVERAL TIMES        │
└─────────────────────────────────────┘
```

In addition a recurrence has been noticed in the calculation which means that the number of terms added up is no more than if the number of strips was known in advance! In the calculation, each time H is halved, the new area is half the old one plus the new points in between the old ones:

New area = (old area)/2 + (new sum)*h

The subroutine has been carefully organized to exploit this fact. The author has chosen to control the summing loop with an integer K because he trusts this; with H being halved so many times, he is worried that using X as the loop variable might not work. Is it possible that a statement

DO 2∅ X=XBOT+H/2.∅,XTOP-H/2.∅,H

might give the wrong number of repetitions?

EXERCISE:
   All the same ideas can be used to make an even better subroutine for quadrature based on Simpson's rule (see Problem 7.4). In this case the error is proportional to h^4 and therefore it is going to need fewer strips than the trapezoidal rule. You must use this fact to revise your estimate of the error. Do this and evaluate

$$\int_0^{\pi/2} \frac{dx}{\sqrt{1 - \frac{\sin^2 x}{4}}}$$

by both the trapezoidal rule and Simpson's rule, comparing the number of steps required for a given accuracy. Which method do you prefer for your program library?

10.4 Multiple entries to subroutines

As with functions, the ENTRY statement provides a way of entering a subroutine at more than one place by using different CALL statements. This can be a useful facility but its operation inevitably contains pitfalls which are an open invitation to disaster if the programmer has an incomplete understanding of the use of dummy arguments. The form of the ENTRY statement is

ENTRY name[(arguments)]

where
   "name" is the name of the entry point
   "arguments" are the dummy arguments for the entry.

The ENTRY statement is not an executable statement. It may appear anywhere in a function or subroutine except in the range of a DO loop or inside an IF block. Obviously a subroutine must not call itself, and so a subroutine may not call one of its own entries.

When a CALL or function reference is made to the entry "name", control passes to the function or subroutine at the ENTRY statement. There must be the usual one-to-one correspondence by type and position between the calling arguments and the dummy arguments of the ENTRY statement. These need not bear any relationship to the subroutine or function arguments or to those of any other entry. When the entry point is called, its dummy arguments are given the values of the arguments of the CALL throughout all parts of the function or subroutine; this is useful but caution is required.

EXAMPLE:
   One use of multiple entries is to initialize constants within a subroutine. Suppose a subroutine RECT for conversion of polar to rectangular Cartesian co-ordinates is to be used for angles given in either degrees or radians. Entry points are provided so that it can be initialized or switched.

   The local variables of a subroutine become undefined as soon as the subroutine returns control to the main program, and so the SAVE statement is used in subroutines to cause variables to remain defined for another CALL.

```
      SUBROUTINE RECT(RAD,ANG)
C
C CONVERT POLAR (RAD,ANG) TO
C RECTANGULAR (X,Y). RESULT
C REPLACES (RAD,ANG). RADIANS
C OR DEGREES MUST FIRST BE
C SPECIFIED THROUGH ENTRIES
C RADIAN OR DEGREE. THEY CAN
C LATER BE SWITCHED.
C
      SAVE CONST
      X=RAD*COS(ANG*CONST)
      ANG=RAD*SIN(ANG*CONST)
      RAD=X
      RETURN
C ENTRY TO SPECIFY ANG IN RADIANS
      ENTRY RADIAN
      CONST=1.∅
      RETURN
C ENTRY TO SPECIFY ANG IN DEGREES
      ENTRY DEGREE
      CONST=ATAN(1.∅)/45.∅
      END
```

Before using a CALL to RECT, CONST must be defined through a call to either DEGREE or RADIAN. It is then preserved for later calls because of the SAVE statement.

EXERCISE:
  Add the subroutine POLAR to convert rectangular co-ordinates to polar form as another entry to the same subprogram.

Interaction between different entries can get a program into trouble if the programmer is unaware of whether dummy variables are defined or undefined. A dummy argument of an ENTRY must not be referred to earlier in the program than an entry point that defines it. This is allowed:

```
      SUBROUTINE A(X)
         :
         :
      ENTRY B(Y)
         :
      Z=SQRT(Y)
         :
      END
```

wheras this is illegal:

```
      SUBROUTINE A(X)
         :
         :
      Z=SQRT(Y)
         :
      ENTRY B(Y)
         :
      END
```

A statement function cannot use a dummy argument of any entry unless the definition of the statement function follows that entry. This is permitted:

```
      SUBROUTINE A(X)
      FUNC(Z)=Z*X
         :
      ENTRY B(Y)
         :
      END
```

while this is wrong:

```
      SUBROUTINE A(X)
      FUNC(Z)=Z*Y
         :
      ENTRY B(Y)
         :
      END
```

The program forgets the values of dummy arguments when it returns from the subroutine. As dummy arguments cannot be used in SAVE statements, a programmer has to use common sense.

This is legal but certain to fail:

```
      SUBROUTINE A(X)
         :
         :
      RETURN
      ENTRY B(Y)
      Z=X+Y
         :
         :
      END
```

When the assignment statement for Z is reached, one or the other of X or Y must be undefined, and so the program fails.

10.5 Alternate returns — or how to spoil the structure of a program

A feature of subroutines (but not of functions) is an ability to return to a different part of the calling program - in other words to jump directly to some place in the calling program that is not the statement after the CALL. This is described here mainly for the sake of completeness and its use is not highly recommended - it does not fit at all the ideals of structured programming.

In a SUBROUTINE statement, one or more asterisks can be given in the list of dummy arguments:

```
SUBROUTINE VULG(X,Y,*,*)
```

and this indicates that alternate returns may be used. In the subroutine the statement

```
RETURN
```

returns to the normal place - the next statement after the CALL. But a statement

```
RETURN integer expression
```

could cause an alternate return if the value of the integer expression is suitable. It behaves rather like a computed GO TO. If the integer expression is 1, the first alternate return is taken, using the first asterisk; if 2, the second, and so on. If the integer expression is less than 1, or greater than the number of asterisk dummy arguments, the return is a normal one.

The information about the returns is given in the CALL statement, as in

```
CALL VULG(P,Q,*1Ø,*2Ø)
```

in which case the first alternate return is to statement 10, and the second to statement 20.

The practical use of this could lie in an escape from a DO loop, as in:

```
      :
      DO 66 K=1,1Ø
         CALL PT1Ø9(X,Y,*7Ø)
66    CONTINUE
      This is the ordinary
      continuation after
      completion of the DO
         loop
      :
      :
7Ø    This is the alternate
      return from PT1Ø9 -
      escapes from DO loop
      :
      :
```

where the subroutine PT109 contains:

```
SUBROUTINE PT1Ø9(R,S,*)
   :
   :
IF(ERROR.LT.1E-Ø6)RETURN 1
   :
   :
END
```

Another use might be in the return to a special error routine when a fault is detected, as in the main program:

```
      :
      CALL ROOT3(A,B,C,D,
               DELTA,ANSWER,*9Ø)
      Normally the subroutine
      would return to here
      :
      :
C COME TO HERE IF ERROR
9Ø    PRINT*,'YOU BLEW IT',FX
      STOP
      :
```

using a subroutine like:

```
      SUBROUTINE ROOT3(A,B,C,D,
               DELTA,ANSWER,*)
      :
      :
C UNSUCCESSFUL COMPLETION
      ANSWER=FX
      RETURN 1
      :
      :
C SUCCESSFUL COMPLETION
      ANSWER=FX
      END
```

10.6 About RETURN and END

It will be recalled that in a main program, the END statement must be the last statement of the program, but it also behaves like a STOP statement in terminating the program. STOP could appear anywhere.

In a subprogram, END must again be the last statement of the program unit, and it also behaves like a RETURN statement in returning control to the program that called a subroutine or referred to a function. RETURN can appear anywhere. The END statement cannot specify an alternate return; that has to be done with

RETURN integer expression

Subprograms end with
END
Subprograms return with
RETURN or END
Alternate returns are nasty

10.7 Documentation of subroutines

The suggestions for documentation made here apply in a general way to all programs - but the chances are that any FORTRAN programs a person wishes to communicate or publish are either functions or subroutines. It is important that a program should be both well written and well written up. A programmer who has any self-respect will have taken the trouble to write an efficient, well structured and easily understood program. But FORTRAN does not always read like a natural language (nor do the other computing languages that are supposed to). Therefore the first requirement is a description of the program in words:

(i) A description of the program.

Aim to describe fully the purpose of the program and all the methods used, explaining any theory beyond the most elementary algebraic facts. Most programs have limitations and these should be described. State what is required of the user in the way of input values, and what is returned in the way of results. Make it very clear which variables are modified by the program so that the user does not fall into the trap of using constants in his call which are destroyed.

(ii) A list of the arguments with explanation.

This description is known as the "calling sequence". In the case of a main program give an explanation of the data input and output. Make it absolutely clear which arguments are for input, which are for output, and which are for both. The type of each should be stated; it is suggested that the distinction should be made between arguments which must be variables only, and those which can be any kind of value (variables, constants, or expressions).

(iii) A flowchart of any but the simplest program.

(iv) A "listing" of the program itself with suitable comments. It is a good idea to summarize (i) and (ii) in comments at the beginning of the program.

Some journals have special ideas about the layout of programs. One journal may insist that every subroutine should check against every conceivable fault in its arguments and return fault parameters. Another may wish all constants to be assigned names in PARAMETER statements to aid in the portability of programs. Most will insist on statement labels being in sequence, which is unlikely to be the case after a program has been worked over a few times. Some have specific requirements for indentation of DO loops and IF blocks. Check these out beforehand - there are computer programs which will tidy up your computer programs.

EXAMPLE: Documentation to the Monro Minimum Standard (MMS)

The subroutine and entry ROT135 and ROT45 perform rotations of the directed search vector found in contour plotting algorithms. As in Fig.10.5, the vector is directed from the origin to the sides or corners of a square. The end of the vector is represented by the integer co-ordinates IX and IY, and it is the purpose of ROT45 to rotate this vector 45° if ISENS is +1 and -45° if it is -1, replacing IX and IY. ROT135, on the other hand, is intended to rotate -135° if ISENS is +1 and +135° if it is -1, - the opposite way to ROT45.

Both entries assume correct values of IX,IY, and ISENS. A rotation of +45° is accomplished by the matrix multiplication:

$$IX = IX - IY$$
$$IY = IX + IY$$

i.e.

$$\begin{matrix} IX \\ IY \end{matrix} = \begin{pmatrix} 1 & -1 \\ 1 & 1 \end{pmatrix} \begin{matrix} IX \\ IY \end{matrix}$$

and for -45°

$$IX = IX + IY$$
$$IY = -IX + IY$$

i.e.

$$\begin{matrix} IX \\ IY \end{matrix} = \begin{pmatrix} 1 & 1 \\ -1 & 1 \end{pmatrix} \begin{matrix} IX \\ IY \end{matrix}$$

For 135°, the direction is first swung 180°

$$IX = -IX$$
$$IY = -IY$$

and then swung back 45°. The length of the vector increases by $\sqrt{2}$ on each 45° rotation and the program then reduces non-zero co-ordinates to unity values.

The calling sequence is:

    CALL ROT135(IX,IY,ISENS)

or

    CALL ROT45(IX,IY,ISENS)

where in both cases

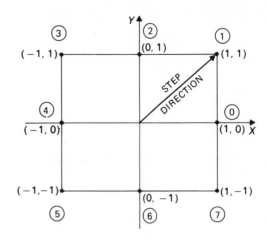

Fig. 10.5. Possible orientation of a directed search vector for contour plotting.

IX = integer variable
   input: the X co-ordinate before rotation
   output: the X co-ordinate after rotation

IY = integer variable
   input: the Y co-ordinate before rotation
   output: the Y co-ordinate after rotation

ISENS: integer value controlling the direction of rotation

   if ISENS=1 ROT45 rotates +45°
                 ROT135 rotates -135°
   if ISENS=-1 ROT45 rotates -45°
                 ROT135 rotates +135°
   The subroutine malfunctions for other values of ISENS.

A flowchart is shown in Fig.10.6.

Note that there is no return before the ENTRY ROT45. Therefore if ROT135 has been called both parts of the program are used.

```
      SUBROUTINE ROT135(IX,IY,ISENS)
C SUBROUTINE TO ROTATE (IX,IY)
C
C IX=INTEGER VARIABLE
C    INPUT X CO-ORDINATE,
C    OUTPUT SAME ROTATED
C IY=INTEGER VARIABLE
C    INPUT Y CO-ORDINATE,
C    OUTPUT SAME ROTATED
C ISENS=INTEGER VALUE
C    INPUT +1 FOR -135 DEGREES
C    INPUT -1 FOR +135 DEGREES
C FIRST ROTATE 18Ø DEGREES
      IX = -IX
      IY = -IY
      ENTRY ROT45 (IX,IY,ISENS)
C ENTRY FOR 45 DEGREE ROTATION
C ISENS=+1 FOR +45 DEGREES
C ISENS=-1 FOR -45 DEGREES
      IXX = IX-ISENS*IY
      IYY = IX*ISENS+IY
      IX = IXX/MAX(1,IABS(IXX))
      IY = IYY/MAX(1,IABS(IYY))
      END
```

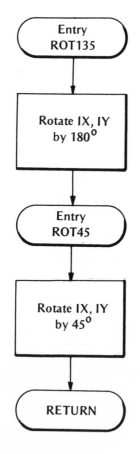

Fig. 10.6. Flowchart of subroutine ROT135 with entry ROT45.

10.8 Problems

Many examples and problems using subroutines are found in the remainder of this book.

PROBLEM 10.1:
Write a subroutine which, given two pairs of integer co-ordinates on a straight line, finds a, b, and c in the equation of that line:

$$ax + by + c = 0$$

with a=1 where possible.

PROBLEM 10.2:
Write a subroutine to find all the roots of a cubic polynomial. Use the False Position method to find one real root, and calculate the coefficients of the quadratic that is left over. Calculate the remaining two roots using the usual formula, covering all cases. Find the roots of

$$x^3 - 7.8x^2 + 18.5x - 11.3 = 0$$

PROBLEM 10.3:
Write a program to find a root of any function FUNC provided by the user, by the method of False Position accelerated by the Aitken extrapolation (Problem 6.3). Devise some way of getting initial guesses that make sense.

Solve

$$(i) \quad x + \sin(x) = 0.5$$

$$(ii) \quad e^x = 2x^2$$

PROBLEM 10.4:
The Newton-Raphson method is a very fast method without the stability of the method of False Position. It perhaps has not been given the prominence it deserves in this text. Make up for that by getting into it deeply now. It was defined for you in Problem 6.2. Find out what it is that causes the stability problem and write a program that starts off by the method of False Position without acceleration but switches to Newton-Raphson when it gets going. It may

have to switch back again temporarily. When you have finished you can decide which procedure you prefer; accelerated False Position or False Raphson (Newton Position?). Tidy and document your choice and send it to someone.

PROBLEM 10.5:

Write a subroutine for solving a differential equation

$$dy/dt = f(y,t)$$

in which the user supplies $f(y,t)$ in a FUNCTION subprogram. Use Euler's method, described in an example in Section 7.6. Solve

$$dy/dt = \cos y$$

PROBLEM 10.6:

A more accurate method for solving differential equations is the popular Runge-Kutta procedure, which involves several stages of calculation. Write a subroutine for this, and observe its accuracy for different step lengths. How do you know when the solution is correct?

Given the value y_0 at time t_0, you seek the value y_1 at $t_0 + h$, where h is a time step. To do this calculate in succession the quantities

$$k_0 = h\ f(y_0, t)$$

$$k_1 = h\ f(y_0 + k_0/2, t_0 + h/2)$$

$$k_2 = h\ f(y_0 + k_1/2, t_0 + h/2)$$

$$k_3 = h\ f(y_0 + k_2, t_0 + h)$$

and then put these together to find

$$y = y_0 + 1/6\left\{k_0 + 2k_1 + 2k_2 + k_3\right\}$$

In fact there is a whole range of similar methods. This is the commonest fourth order Runge-Kutta procedure.

Write a program to solve first order differential equations by this method. The main program should read in the starting values, the step size h, and the number of steps desired. A subroutine should then be used to do the calculation. Because $f(y,t)$ is used so often, and to make the program general, either a function or a subroutine should be used for $f(y,t)$.

Solve

$$dy/dt = \cos y$$

from $t=0$ to $t=2\pi$ given $y(0)=0.5$. Compare its accuracy as a function of h with the Euler method. How can you tell what the correct answer is anyway? How about its stability, i.e. what happens as h gets large?

11
Arrays and subscripts in one dimension

11.1 Introduction

Subscripted variables are extensively used in both scientific and commercial computing. Indeed, although their introduction comes halfway through this book, it is rare to find a program in practice without some use of arrays in it. Consequently the FORTRAN facilities for defining and using array variables with subscripts are widely used. This Chapter introduces arrays with one subscript and therefore a large number of examples and applications are given. In the next Chapter extended consideration is given to a number of array based operations which are both of some practical significance.

11.2 Introducing arrays and subscripts — the DIMENSION statement

Until now, a variable name has stood for a single value; these have been scalar quantities which can only contain one value. Using arrays a name can be given to a list of values which can be referred to by their subscripts.

For example, the number of people living in a house could be called IFOLK and have an integer value. However, suppose there was a row of houses, say 8 of them as in Fig.11.1. It would be rather tedious to use different variable names for the number of people in each house. However, if IFOLK were a subscripted variable, then it would be possible to refer to the number of people in the first house as IFOLK(1), in the second as IFOLK(2), and so on. Working with the figures then becomes relatively easy. To find the total number of occupants in the row of houses, one would write something like:

```
ISUM=∅
DO 22 K=1,8
    ISUM=ISUM+IFOLK(K)
22 CONTINUE
```

Here, the sum is accumulated in the DO loop as the subscript K is varied, until ISUM holds the result when the DO is satisfied. This kind of summation should be a familiar process by now. The array IFOLK represents an ordered list of integer quantities; in FORTRAN it is called an integer array.

It will be noticed that each reference to IFOLK(K) resembles a reference to a function. The computer must have some way of distinguishing array references from functions, so the programmer tells it about the array in a special statement at the beginning of the program. It also has to know how much space the array is going to occupy, and so the same statement includes this information. The statement used is the DIMENSION statement which, for the occupants of the houses in this example, is

```
DIMENSION IFOLK(8)
```

This states that 8 spaces are to be reserved for the array called IFOLK. IFOLK is an integer array as is implied by the spelling of its name. Any use of this name with a subscript refers to a member of the array. Once given to an array in a particular program unit, the name will always refer to that array, and so a function of the same name cannot be used. If the name is used without a subscript, it refers to the first member of the array. The computer may not permit this in expressions.

Two forms of confusion about arrays cause common FORTRAN errors. The first of these arises when an arithmetic expression is intended to include multiplication but the * has been left out - a perfectly natural mistake. If there are brackets nearby FORTRAN could mistake the expression for either a function or an array. The statements

$$\text{DEATH=WAGES(IFIX(SIN))}$$

and $\text{DEATH=WAGES*(IFIX(SIN))}$

mean very different things. The first is either an array reference or a function reference depending on whether WAGES was mentioned in a DIMENSION statement or not. If it was not, FORTRAN will expect to find a function called WAGES.

Similarly any use of subscripts will cause confusion if the DIMENSION information was not given. The statement

$$\text{X=THING(I,J)}$$

could refer to either an array (of two dimensions) or a function called THING; the program must contain either a DIMENSION statement or a statement function definition. Otherwise FORTRAN will expect a FUNCTION subprogram to be given.

11.3 Some examples — searching, shuffling, and sieving

Vast numbers of useful manipulations are possible with arrays, and before delving into the formalities, a number of typical operations are described.

EXAMPLE:
Finding the largest value.

In the neighbourhood illustrated by Fig. 11.1, there are a number of searches that a computer program might wish to do.

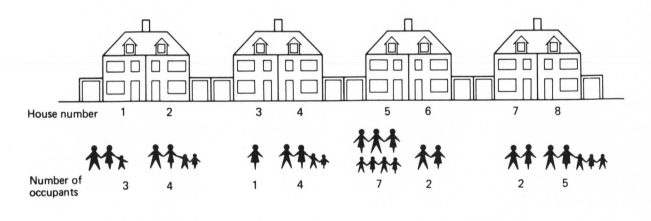

IFOLK(1)=3	WAGES(1)=9000.0
IFOLK(2)=4	WAGES(2)=11580.0
IFOLK(3)=1	WAGES(3)=5600.0
IFOLK(4)=4	WAGES(4)=14400.0
IFOLK(5)=7	WAGES(5)=22800.0
IFOLK(6)=2	WAGES(6)=9600.0
IFOLK(7)=2	WAGES(7)=14800.0
IFOLK(8)=5	WAGES(8)=18000.0

Fig. 11.1. The inhabitants of Anystreet showing how many occupy each of the eight houses and the total family incomes. The numbers of inhabitants are arranged in the integer array IFOLK and the incomes in the real array WAGES.

(i) Find the largest number of inhabitants:

```
    IMAX=0
    DO 60 K=1,8
    ITST=IFOLK(K)
      IF(ITST.GT.IMAX)IMAX=ITST
60 CONTINUE
```

To perform this search successfully, the variable IMAX must be given an initial value which is less than or equal to the maximum eventually found. In the above case 0 was chosen because it is the minimum that could ever occur. It might be better to use IFOLK(1) as the initial value, however - that would be safe and would also reduce the number of comparisons by one:

```
    IMAX=IFOLK(1)
    DO 60 K=2,8
      ITST=IFOLK(K)
      IF(ITST.GT.IMAX)IMAX=ITST
60 CONTINUE
```

(ii) Find the house number with the largest number of inhabitants:

```
 IHOUS=1
 DO 60 K=2,8
   JTST=IFOLK(K)
   IF(JTST.GT.IFOLK(IHOUS))IHOUS=K
60 CONTINUE
```

This is not quite the same, and it will be slower than the previous example because it compares two subscripted values each time. Referring to arrays involves the computer in more work than referring to ordinary variables. Consequently the first kind of search is probably more efficient. What happens in each case if the largest number of inhabitants is the same in two houses?

EXAMPLE:
Find the smallest value:

```
    IMIN=IFOLK(1)
    DO 70 K=2,8
      ITST=IFOLK(K)
      IF(ITST.LT.IMIN)IMIN=ITST
70 CONTINUE
```

Related arrays can be defined to hold other information about the families in Fig.11.1. The total income of each family could be stored in a real array WAGES, as the Figure shows.

EXAMPLE:
  (i) Find the smallest gross income:

```
    DIMENSION IFOLK(8),WAGES(8)
        :
        :
    WMIN=WAGES(1)
    DO 400 K=2,8
      WTST=WAGES(K)
      IF(WTST.LT.WMIN)WMIN=WTST
400 CONTINUE
```

(ii) Find the lowest income per person for any house in the street:

```
    ZMIN=WAGES(1)/IFOLK(1)
    DO 66 K=2,8
      ZZ=WAGES(K)/IFOLK(K)
      IF(ZZ.LT.ZMIN)ZMIN=ZZ
66 CONTINUE
```

Here information from both arrays is used - it would not work too well if one of the houses was empty. If this is a possibility an IF statement must prevent it:

```
    ZMIN=WAGES(1)
    DO 66 K=1,8
     IFLK=IFOLK(K)
     IF(IFLK.NE.0)THEN
       ZZ=WAGES(K)/IFLK
       IF(ZZ.LT.ZMIN)ZMIN=ZZ
     END IF
 66 CONTINUE
```

Observe the steps that have been taken to minimize references to the array as in all these examples.

EXAMPLE:
Rotate the families.

Particularly in applications verging on the commercial field, it is often the case that information has to be moved about within arrays.

(i) The families are rotated up the street. Family 1 moves into house 2, family 2 into house 3, and so on; family 8 moves to house 1. They take their wages with them. It would be a disaster to try:

```
      DO 9Ø L=2,8
        IFOLK(L)=IFOLK(L-1)
        WAGES(L)=WAGES(L-1)
   9Ø CONTINUE
```

because, on thinking about it, it is easy to see that family 1 has moved into every house on the street and the others have been obliterated. Before moving family 1 in, family 2 has to be taken out into temporary lodgings. A hardworking but not too clever programmer might try:

```
      ITEMP1=IFOLK(1)
      WTEMP1=WAGES(1)
      DO 9Ø L=2,8
        ITEMP2=IFOLK(L)
        WTEMP2=WAGES(L)
        IFOLK(L)=ITEMP1
        WAGES(L)=WTEMP1
```

```
        ITEMP1=ITEMP2
        WTEMP1=WTEMP2
   9Ø CONTINUE
      IFOLK(1)=ITEMP1
      WAGES(1)=WTEMP2
```

which is awkward and hard to follow, but correct. Unfortunately the movers have been kept rather busy; in fact families 2 to 8 have each been moved three times and family 1 twice. Why not start with family 8? This is the recommended method, as illustrated by Fig.11.2:

```
      ITEMP=IFOLK(8)
      WTEMP=WAGES(8)
      DO 1ØØ L=8,2,-1
        IFOLK(L)=IFOLK(L-1)
        WAGES(L)=WAGES(L-1)
  1ØØ CONTINUE
      IFOLK(1)=ITEMP
      WAGES(1)=WTEMP
```

Note that it still requires temporary storage.

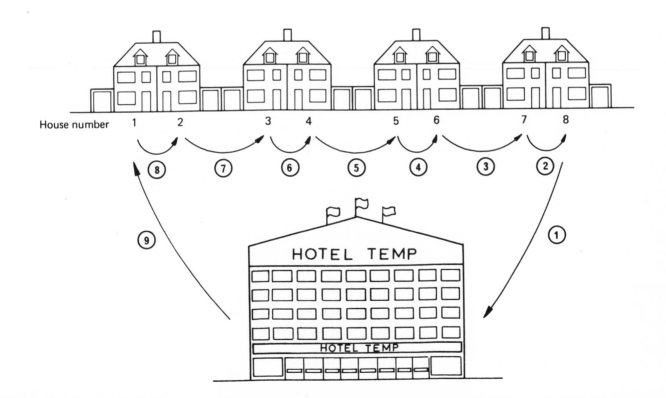

Fig. 11.2. The sequence of moves in rotating the families to the right.

(ii) They can be rotated down the street as well; here it is correct to start with family number 1 as in Fig.11.3:

```
      ITEMP=IFOLK(1)
      WTEMP=WAGES(1)
      DO 200 L=1,7
         IFOLK(L)=IFOLK(L+1)
         WAGES(L)=WAGES(L+1)
200   CONTINUE
      IFOLK(8)=ITEMP
      WAGES(8)=WTEMP
```

This is quite a common thing to have to do. Remember:

> To move everyone up,
> start at the top.
> To move everyone down,
> start at the bottom.
> In both cases,
> temporary storage is needed.

EXAMPLE:
Finding prime numbers.

If the working space is available, the Sieve of Eratosthenes is a wonderfully efficient way to find prime numbers by eliminating all the numbers that are not primes. The previous method to find all the primes less than $\sqrt{N}$ required each of the $N/2$ odd candidates to be individually tested by every odd divisor up to N, or until it failed. (In fact if N was 1000, well over half the numbers would have failed by the time they were tested with 7, so it was not all that bad.)

To use the sieve, store every odd number between 3 and N in an array. All multiples of 3 are first eliminated by replacing them with 0 - in fact every third number in the list is a multiple of 3. Then move to the next number (5). If nonzero it is a prime (not a multiple of a lower odd

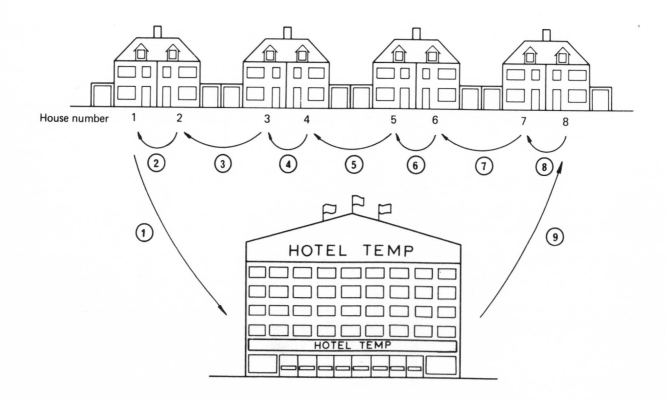

Fig. 11.3. The sequence of moves in rotating the families to the left.

number), so print it, and remove all its multiples (every 5th number is a multiple of 5). And so on, as in Fig. 11.4 except that sieving can cease at $\sqrt{N}$, after which all nonzero entries are prime. This program will work for any N up to 2000; its flowchart is given in Fig.11.5. It contains a good example of nesting with IF blocks and DO loops:

```
C SIEVE OF ERATOSTHENES
      PARAMETER(NMAX=2000)
      DIMENSION NUMBS((NMAX-1)/2)
C ESTABLISH LIMIT OF SEARCH
      PRINT*,'FIND ODD PRIMES'
      PRINT*,'BELOW N, MAX 2000.'
   10 PRINT*,'ENTER A VALUE FOR N'
      READ*,N
      IF(N.GT.NMAX)GO TO 10
      PRINT*,'ODD PRIMES TO',N
C INITIALIZE
      NTOP=(N-1)/2
      ISQRN=SQRT(REAL(N))
C SET UP ARRAY OF ODD NUMBERS
      DO 20 L=1,NTOP
         NUMBS(L)=2*L+1
   20 CONTINUE
C COMMENCE SEARCH FOR PRIMES
      DO 40 L=1,NTOP
         KTES=NUMBS(L)
         IF(NUMBS(L).NE.0) THEN
C FOUND A PRIME, PRINT IT
            PRINT*,KTES
```

```
C IF .LT. SQRT(N) DO THE SIEVE
            IF(KTES.LT.ISQRN) THEN
               LOLM=L+KTES
               DO 30 M=LOLM,NTOP,KTES
                  NUMBS(M)=0
   30          CONTINUE
            END IF
         END IF
   40 CONTINUE
      GO TO 10
      END
```

There are 168 prime numbers less than 1000, not counting 1 or 2. In sieving the 499 stored odd numbers, the unwanted 331 are removed by the time the largest prime less than $\sqrt{1000}$ - which is 31 - is reached. A number may be sieved more than once - 15 for example is sieved by 5 and by 3 - but the total number of sieves is only 461. Only 10 odd primes are less than 31!

EXERCISE:

In the sieving program, the statements

```
      IF(KTES.LT.ISQRN) THEN
         LOLM=L+KTES
         DO 30 M=LOLM,NTOP,KTES
            NUMBS(M)=0
   30    CONTINUE
      END IF
```

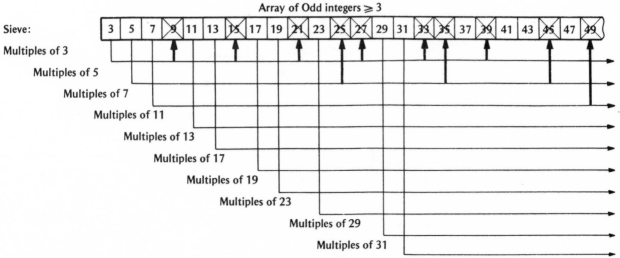

Fig. 11.4. The sieve of Eratosthenes. Of the 49 numbers shown, the sieve is complete at the third prime found, 7. The ten primes to 31 are sufficient to sieve all the way to 1023. All the numbers not crossed out are prime.

are unnecessary after a relatively small number of repetitions of the outer loop. This suggests that a slightly longer program would be more efficient. Break the loop

```
DO 4Ø L=1,NTOP
    .
    .
    .
4Ø CONTINUE
```

into two consecutive ones - the first with a sieve and the second without. You have to think a bit about the limits of these loops. The statement:

```
IF(KTES.LT.ISQRN) THEN
```

and its END IF disappear altogether. What a nice program!

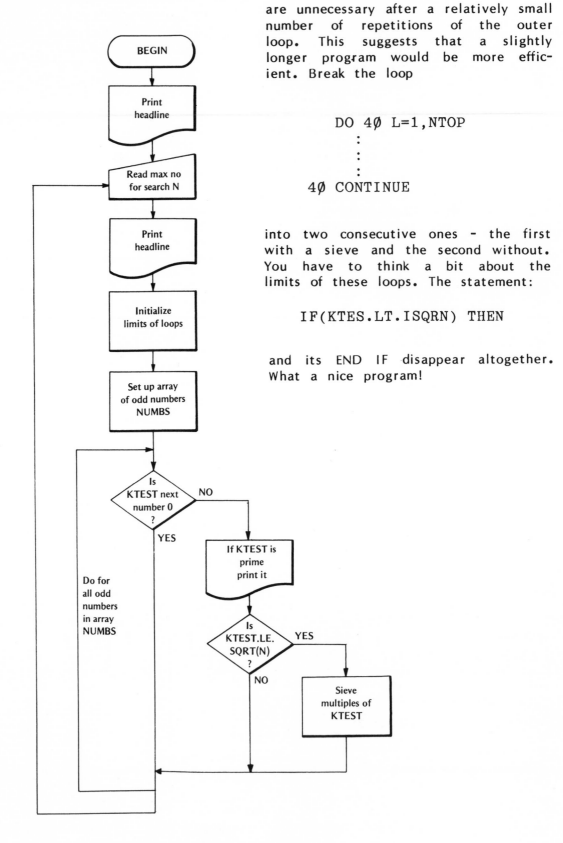

Fig. 11.5. Flowchart for a program to find prime numbers by the sieve of Eratosthenes.

11.4 Some rules about arrays

Actually the rules are not complicated. The DIMENSION statement is used to identify the arrays and indicate the space taken by each, and in it there are a few different ways of indicating the range of subscripts that the program wishes to use. In actually using an array, there are some regulations about the subscripts.

The DIMENSION statement has the form:

DIMENSION $\begin{array}{c} \text{array} \\ \text{name} \end{array} \left(\begin{array}{c} \text{subscript} \\ \text{limits} \end{array} \right) [, \ldots]$

The "array name" is a name obeying the usual rule about symbolic names in FORTRAN - a maximum of 6 alphanumeric characters and the first is a letter. It identifies the name of an array, and the type of that array is normally implied by the spelling of the name. Once a name is given to an array, it cannot be used for anything else, meaning an ordinary variable, the name of a function or subroutine, or the name of a constant in a PARAMETER statement.

The "subscript limits" tell the computer over what range the program intends to use subscripts for the array and this, of course, also tells it how much space the array takes. In the simplest form only the upper limit is given, as in the example

    DIMENSION IRAY(1000),XRAY(64)

In this case the lower limit is 1, and so from this statement the computer learns that IRAY is an integer array of size 1000, and that the program will only use subscripts in the range 1-1000. XRAY is a real array of size 64 with subscripts from 1 to 64.

Often it may be convenient to use subscripts which are zero or negative. If this is the case, the subscript limits may be given in the form:

    lower limit : upper limit

in which naturally enough the upper limit

must be greater than or equal to the lower limit, as the size of array is

    upper limit - lower limit + 1

Therefore in the statement

    DIMENSION XRAY(0:63),IBIX(-5:5)

XRAY is a real array of size 64 whose subscripts may range from 0 to 63. IBIX is an integer array of length 11 whose subscripts are from -5 to 5.

Any number of DIMENSION statements is allowed but they must go at the beginning of the program unit. The size of an array cannot be changed and so the language will only allow an array name to appear once in the DIMENSION statements of a program unit. As with ordinary variables, an array is known only to the program unit that defines it - but it can be communicated to subprograms. A later section of this Chapter discusses the use of arrays in subprograms, and there are special facilities for telling a subprogram about the length of arrays that are dummy arguments.

In a main program, the subscript limits can be expressions as long as everything in them is an integer whose value is defined - but because the DIMENSION statement has to go before any executable statements, this limits the expressions to ones containing integer constants. However the DIMENSION statements can be mixed in with the PARAMETER statements, and so the name of an integer constant could be used if the PARAMETER statement defining it is put first.

EXAMPLES:

    DIMENSION X(17*12/7:34*6-3)

This is of course a bit silly; the program would read better if the expressions were worked out, and it would then be found that the real array X had bounds 32 and 201, and so had length 170.

```
PARAMETER (NMAX=2000)
DIMENSION NUMBS((NMAX-1)/2)
```

This combination was seen in the program for the sieve of Eratosthenes and is useful. A user of this program can adjust the space it uses and its limits according to his requirements.

Once an array has been declared in a DIMENSION statement, it can be used like any other variable in most statements of FORTRAN. The DO statement is the important exception - none of the parameters in a DO statement may be array names.

The rule about subscripts is very straightforward: a subscript must be an integer expression whose value lies within the limits for that array. As it can be any integer expression it can contain variables, array references, and function references. If a programmer is silly enough to use a function to modify its arguments (and other things) it is possible to can make a real mess of subscripts - such a foolish person had

better memorize the whole FORTRAN 77 Standard. Otherwise the only thing to remember is to stay within the array bounds.

EXAMPLES:
Assuming a suitable DIMENSION has been given, the following expressions use valid subscripts:

```
IF(BRONX(3*J+4).LT.0) THEN
```

```
ITEM(MOD(IPOINT,7))=19
```

The following is illegal:

```
READ*,SERENE(3*X)
```

but could be legalized:

```
READ*,SERENE(INT(3*X))
```

There are certain situations in which an array name may be used without a subscript to refer to the whole array, as will be seen. Otherwise the use of the name without a subscript refers to the first element of the array - if the compiler permits it.

The required order of statements in programs is now:

COMMENTS can go anywhere before END	FORMAT and ENTRY Statements	FUNCTION or SUBROUTINE Statements
		PARAMETER, DIMENSION or SAVE Statements
		Statement Function Definitions
		Executable Statements
END Statement		

11.5 Printing of arrays — the implied DO loop

The names of arrays can be used in several ways in READ, WRITE and PRINT statements. The most obvious use would be with a subscript; for example

```
DIMENSION XAMP(3)
DO 10 K=1,3
   XAMP(K)=K
10 CONTINUE
PRINT 20,XAMP(1),XAMP(2),XAMP(3)
20 FORMAT(1X,3F10.5)
END
```

would print

```
1.00000    2.00000    3.00000
```

with the numbers on one line, or

```
DIMENSION IZMP(3)
DO 10 K=1,3
   IZMP(K)=K
10 CONTINUE
PRINT 20,IZMP(1),IZMP(2),IZMP(3)
20 FORMAT(1X,I5)
END
```

would produce

```
1
2
3
```

with a new line for each number. This is a bit limiting. However, if the array name is used without a subscript the whole array is printed, as for example in

```
DIMENSION IRAY(0:9)
DO 10 K=0,9
   IRAY(K)=K
10 CONTINUE
PRINT*,IRAY
END
```

which prints

```
0  1  2  3  4  5  6  7  8  9
```

In planning the FORMAT, take account of the size of the array so that the correspondence between the output list and the FORMAT editing specifications is preserved. Therefore

```
DIMENSION IFOLK(8),WAGES(8)
        :
        :
WRITE(*,30)IFOLK,WAGES
30 FORMAT(1X,8I6/1X,8F6.0)
        :
        :
```

would print correctly, but

```
WRITE(*,60)IFOLK,WAGES
60 FORMAT(8(1X,I10,F10.5/))
```

is wrong. The rules for repeating FORMAT statements persist. One could say

```
DIMENSION XSQ(10)
DO 10 K=1,10
   XSQ(K)=K*K
10 CONTINUE
WRITE(*,'(1X,10F7.0)')XSQ
END
```

and get the results all on one line, but

```
WRITE(*,25)XSQ
25 FORMAT(' SQUARES'/(1X,F10.5))
```

gives the results on ten lines because the FORMAT is repeated ten times from the first embedded bracket, each time on a new line.

EXAMPLE:
In the example of the previous Section, after sieving you can print the entire array of zeros and primes by inserting

```
PRINT 50,NUMBS
50 FORMAT(1X,20I4)
```

after the statement labelled 40. The printout takes 50 lines with 20 numbers on each.

There is another facility which applies to printing of all kinds, but is particularly useful in printing arrays. Without it, printing only part of an array is awkward. The awkward way is to use a DO loop, as in

```
      PARAMETER(NMAX=2000)
      DIMENSION NUMBS((NMAX-1)/2)
             :
             :
      DO 60 K=NMAX/4,NMAX
         PRINT*,NUMBS(K)
   60 CONTINUE
```

which uses a new line for every PRINT statement. It is possible to write a structure known as an "implied DO loop" within the list of an input or output statement. To repeat a group, write

```
    (group,variable=min,max,inc)
```

in brackets as shown.

The implied DO loop behaves just like an ordinary DO loop and is subject to similar rules.

"group" is any input/output list which can itself contain other implied DO loops.
"variable" is the DO variable which must not be in use by any other loop when it is used.
"min" is the first value of the variable.
"max" is the stopping value.
"inc" is the increment.

"min", "max", and "inc" are any expressions, and the loop behaves exactly like a DO loop. The "variable" can appear in the group to be printed in an output statement, but quite sensibly cannot appear as a value to be defined by a READ statement.

Therefore to realize the printing described above write

```
    PRINT 66,(NUMBS(K),K=NMAX/4,NMAX)
 66 FORMAT(20I5)
```

An example of the variable appearing in the output list is:

```
      DIMENSION XSQ(10)
      DO 10 K=1,10
         XSQ(K)=K*K
   10 CONTINUE
      PRINT 20,(K,XSQ(K),K=1,10)
   20 FORMAT(1X,I4,' **2 =',F5.0)
      END
```

or even:

```
      PRINT 20,(K,K*K,K=1,10)
   20 FORMAT(I5,' SQUARED IS',I5)
      END
```

which is a complete program. An example of the variable not being used at all except to control the printing is:

```
    PRINT*,('*',K=1,25)
```

with a very pretty output. Here, a variable number of characters can be printed across the terminal or line-printer. This is very suggestive of some interesting applications of graph plotting as will be developed in some examples in Chapter 16.

EXAMPLE:
In the program for the sieve of Eratosthenes, it is probably desirable to print only the part of the array that is actually being used. To print the array of zeros and primes after sieving is complete, insert

```
    PRINT*,(NUMBS(L),L=1,NTOP)
```

after the statement labelled 40. In this, the first NTOP values from the array NUMBS are printed.

EXAMPLE:
It is required to evaluate and print the binomial coefficients

$$nCr$$

in the form known as Pascal's triangle, Fig.11.6. If 10 lines are to be printed, then it is desired to place $_0C_0$ in the middle of the first line, $_1C_0$ and $_1C_1$ nicely disposed on the next and so on. Suppose the computer in response to the list-directed statement

```
    PRINT*,I
```

uses n spaces for a moderate sized value of I. The program wants to start printing each line n/2 spaces back from the previous one. On the author's terminal the middle space is column

36, and each integer uses 8 spaces. His complete program to print Pascal's triangle using a function NCR to obtain nCr (Chapter 9) is

```
C PROGRAM PRINTS PASCAL TRIANGLE
C USING COEFFICIENT FUNCTION NCR
C MID IS THE MIDDLE OF THE PAGE
C MAD IS NO. OF SPACES TO MOVE
C EACH NEW LINE BACK FROM MIDDLE
C
      PARAMETER(MID=36,MAD=4)
      DO 10 N=0,9
        IPLACE=MID-N*MAD
        PRINT*,(' ',K=1,IPLACE),
               (NCR(N,IR),IR=0,N)
10  CONTINUE
      END
```

Using an array, no function is needed at all. This is because

$$_nC_r = {}_{n-1}C_{r-1} + {}_{n-1}C_r$$

i.e. each coefficient is the sum of the two above it in the triangle. Therefore a more efficient program is

```
C PROGRAM PRINTS PASCAL TRIANGLE
C USING RECURRENCE FOR COEFFS
C MID IS THE MIDDLE OF THE PAGE
C MAD IS NO. OF SPACES TO MOVE
C EACH NEW LINE BACK FROM MIDDLE
C
      PARAMETER(MID=36,MAD=4)
      DIMENSION ICF(0:10)
      DO 10 K=1,9
        ICF(K)=0
10  CONTINUE
      ICF(0)=1
      DO 30 N=0,9
        DO 20 IR=N,1,-1
          ICF(IR)=ICF(IR-1)+ICF(IR)
20    CONTINUE
        IPLACE=MID-N*MAD
        PRINT*,(' ',K=1,IPLACE),
+               (ICF(K),K=0,N)
30  CONTINUE
      END
```

in which an expression for a subscript is used for the first time. Recall that a subscript can be any integer expression. Both these programs print the same result.

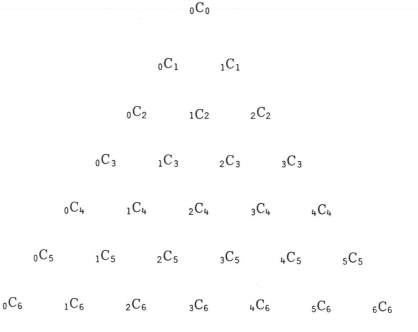

Fig. 11.6. Arrangement of binomial coefficients in Pascal's triangle.

EXERCISE:

Run both programs to make Pascal's triangle.

It is important to realize that this is the only way that a program can move numbers around freely on a line of output. The variable number of spaces used can only be achieved using an implied DO loop in a list-directed statement. There is another way of doing this for character data as will be seen in Chapter 16.

All the above facilities apply to input as well. An entire array can be read (from 20 cards probably) by writing

```
    DIMENSION XSTUF(16Ø)
        :
        :
    READ(5,66)XSTUF
66 FORMAT(8F1Ø.Ø)
        :
        :
```

or part of it

```
    DIMENSION XSTUF(16Ø)
        :
        :
    READ(5,66)(XSTUF(L),L=MIN,MAX)
66 FORMAT(8F1Ø.Ø)
        :
        :
```

but an implied DO loop cannot be permitted to read the value of the DO variable - for obvious reasons

```
    DIMENSION RUBBSH(1ØØ)
        :
        :
    READ 2Ø,(K,RUBBSH(K),K=1,1ØØ)
        :
        :
```

is forbidden. What the programmer probably wants is

```
    READ 2Ø,(K,RUBBSH(K),L=1,1ØØ)
```

which is correct.

11.6   Defining variables in advance — the DATA statement

There are many situations where a programmer may wish to set up a list of variables with values known at the beginning of the program. The only way to do this until now would have been through a tedious list of assignment statements like those suggested by Fig. 11.1. The PARAMETER statement has already been met for giving names to constants. Now there is a facility for giving values to variables - not the same thing! In fact the numbers of inhabitants of Anystreet and their incomes could have been set up using the DATA statements:

```
DIMENSION IFOLK(8),WAGES(8)
DATA IFOLK/3,4,1,4,7,2,2,5/
DATA WAGES/9ØØØ,1158Ø,56ØØ,144ØØ,
1    228ØØ,96ØØ,148ØØ,18ØØØ/
```

which assign the required variables before the program is actually executed. In general a program can contain any number of DATA statements, which belong after DIMENSION statements and before the values are used:

```
DATA variables /values/ [,] [...]
```

There must be exactly the same number of variables in each "list" as there are values following it and the values are assigned in one-to-one correspondence. If necessary, conversions from real to integer or vice versa are carried out, and the same variable can only be defined once. Only constant values are permitted, with the important exception described a bit later in connection with implied DO loops. As a result, any symbolic name appearing in the value list must have been assigned to a constant in a PARAMETER statement. The name of an array given without a subscript refers to the entire array, starting from its lower limit of subscripts.

EXAMPLES:

```
DATA PIE/3.14159/,E/2.71828/
```

assigns the real value 3.14159265 to PIE and 2.71828182845 to E. So does

```
PARAMETER(APIE=3.14159265)
PARAMETER(AE=2.71828182845)
DATA PIE,E/APIE,AE/
```

but it is important to realize that whereas PIE and E are variables, the names APIE and AE stand for constants.

```
DATA I,J,K,L/17,23,29,31/
```

assigns the integer values 17,23,29 and 31 to integer variables I,J,K and L.

```
DATA X,Y/1,2/I,J/14.5,27.3/
```

causes conversions to be carried out in assigning the values.

It can be convenient to assign the same value to several variables. To make I,J and K all zero it is possible to write

```
DATA I,J,K/3*0/
```

Here the asterisk does not imply multiplication - it causes the constant to be repeated three times. An entire array can be assigned initial values in this way:

```
DIMENSION ONES(25),NINES(9)
DATA ONES/25*1.0/,NINES/9*9/
```

But only a single constant can be repeated - it is wrong to write:

```
DIMENSION ONETWO(10)
DATA ONETWO/5*(1,2)/
```

In subroutines the values of local variables can be initialized, but not those of dummy arguments, because dummy arguments have no value until a subroutine is called. Therefore

```
SUBROUTINE SILLY(X,Y,I,J)
DATA P,Q,K,L/2*2.0,4,3/
```

is correct but

```
SUBROUTINE WRONG(P,Q,K,L)
DATA P,Q,K,L/4*1/
```

is wrong.

Arrays have already been seen in DATA statements; values can be assigned to a whole array as in

```
DIMENSION ONES(25)
DATA ONES/25*1.0/
```

or to individual elements, like

```
DIMENSION SMALL(4)
DATA SMALL(2),SMALL(3)/2*1.0/
```

In fact, implied DO loops can be used, in a restricted way which makes common sense. It is possible to write

```
DIMENSION BIGUN(-7:7)
DATA (BIGUN(K),K=-2,2)/5*4.36/
```

or

```
DIMENSION NICE12(20)
DATA (NICE12(K),K=1,19,2)/10*1/
DATA (NICE12(K),K=2,20,2)/10*2/
```

or in general

```
DATA (group,variable=min,max,inc)
```

where "group" could have inner loops as long as "min", "max" and "inc" are expressions involving only constants or the variables of outer implied DO loops:

```
DIMENSION LILLY(12)
DATA((LILLY(K+3*L),K=1,3),L=0,3)
1    /1,2,3,1,2,3,1,2,3,1,2,3/
```

assigns the values 1, 2, 3, 1, 2, 3, 1, 2, 3, 1, 2, 3, to the array LILLY.

As the above examples imply, the DO variable can appear in the subscript of an array being defined. The subscript must be an integer expression involving only constants or a DO variable if it is in the range of that DO. An inner DO can use the DO variable of an outer DO in its expressions for "min", "max", and "inc". The implied DO loop does not give the DO variable itself an initial value; hence in

```
DIMENSION I(30)
DATA (I(K),K=1,10)/10*5/
DATA (I(K),K=11,20)/10*10/
DATA (I(K),K=21,30)/10*15/
```

K is not given an initial value, whereas in

```
DIMENSION IN(5)
DATA(IN(K),K=1,5),K/6*∅/
```

or even in

```
DIMENSION IN(5)
DATA K,(IN(K),K=1,5)/6*∅/
```

it is given the initial value zero.

11.7   The order of statements so far

In this Chapter the DIMENSION and DATA statements have been introduced, so it is necessary to bring the table of statement order up to date once again. Of the statements known so far, DIMENSION can be put anywhere before END, but must follow any PARAMETER statements which define constants used by it. The rules so far are summarized by the table given here.

11.8   More examples — sorting

Sorting is the operation which takes an array of values in unknown order and rearranges them in (usually ascending) order, along with associated arrays. The values in the array used to define the sequence are called the keys.

This would seem to be a simple idea, but a great deal of work has been done on sorting because it is actually quite difficult to do efficiently in little space - and as the cost of computation is related to the product of time and space, efficient sorting is an important problem. Commercial installations spend more time sorting their records into order than doing anything else and because commercial computers outnumber scientific ones, to invent a better sort is to help the economy of the world.

Not surprisingly, a case study in the next Chapter is devoted to an important sorting method. Here some basic principles are discussed.

(i)   Bubble sorting

An attractive little algorithm is the bubble sort, which unfortunately is hopelessly inefficient. Suppose an array of disordered values exists, as in Fig.11.7. To do a bubble sort, the first and second values are compared and switched if they are out of order. Then the second and third are treated the same way, and so on. Sooner or later the largest value will be picked up and be carried to the end where it belongs, and along the way various little sequences will be partially ordered. After this pass, the array is more ordered than it was, and another pass is made. As the Figure shows, although the process begins at the beginning of the array each time, it need go no further than the last swap of the previous pass. It is called the bubble sort because the biggest values bubble to the top.

COMMENTS can go anywhere before END	FUNCTION or SUBROUTINE Statements		
	FORMAT and ENTRY Statements	PARAMETER, DIMENSION or SAVE Statements	
		DATA Statements	Statement Function Definitions
			Executable Statements
END Statement			

Begin:	86	82	54	2	32	76	94	29
First pass	82	54	2	32	76	86	29	94
Second pass	54	2	32	76	82	29	86	94
Third pass	2	32	54	76	29	82	86	94
Fourth pass	2	32	54	29	76	82	86	94
Fifth pass	2	32	29	54	76	82	86	94
Sixth pass	2	29	32	54	76	82	86	94
Seventh pass	2	29	32	54	76	82	86	94
Finished

Fig. 11.7. Bubble sorting 8 random numbers. The list becomes gradually more ordered and complete from the right hand end.

The attractive thing about this is the ease of programming and the fact that all the sorting is done by exchanging two values so no extra storage is required. Here is a little program to read from cards, first the size of the sort, maximum 100, then to read the keys, and to sort them into order:

```
C BUBBLE SORT OF DATA FROM CARDS
C MAX 100 KEYS - AND THAT IS SLOW
C
      DIMENSION IRAY(100)
C DETERMINE SORT SIZE
      READ(5,10)NSORT
 10 FORMAT(8I10)
C READ IN KEYS
      READ(5,10)(IRAY(K),K=1,NSORT)
C COMMENCE SORTING
      NTOP=NSORT
 20 NSTOP=0
      DO 30 K=1,NTOP-1
        KEY1=IRAY(K)
        KEY2=IRAY(K+1)
        IF(KEY1.GT.KEY2) THEN
C SWITCH AND REMEMBER WHERE
          IRAY(K)=KEY2
          IRAY(K+1)=KEY1
          NSTOP=K
        END IF
 30 CONTINUE
      NTOP=NSTOP
      IF(NSTOP.GT.1)GO TO 20
      WRITE(6,40)(IRAY(K),K=1,NSORT)
 40 FORMAT(1X,8I10)
      END
```

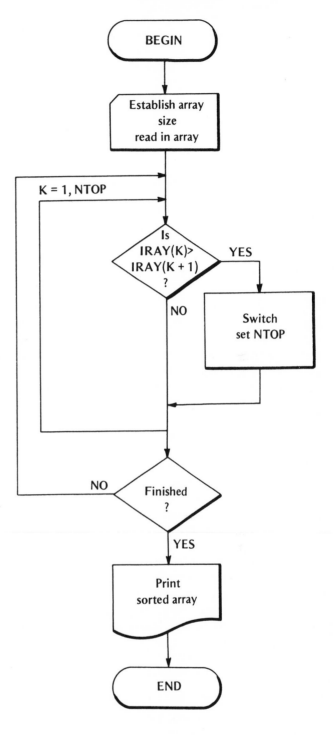

Fig. 11.8. Flowchart of bubble sort from cards.

The flowchart for bubble sorting is given in Fig.11.8.

The efficiency of a sort is usually expressed in terms of the number of comparisons made, which on average is twice the number of exchanges. In bubble sorting, the best case is the situation where the file is already in order, when only N comparisons are made, and the worst is when N-1 passes of average length N/2 are made - the number of passes is then

$$N(N-1)/2$$

which contains N^2, and is therefore pretty bad. The general case is rather difficult to analyse theoretically but the expression for average performance still contains $N^2/2$ which is not very good. A few refinements are possible but there are none known which make bubble sorting better than:

(ii)   Insertion Sorting

An insertion sort is generally considered to be more efficient than the bubble sort. Certainly there are fewer comparisons to do, but on the other hand the operation of insertion involves moving the data around quite a lot.

Fig.11.9 illustrates the stages of an insertion sort. The algorithm begins by examining the second element of the array and deciding where it belongs in the first two elements. The third number is examined and placed in the right place among the first three, and so on. Each key as it is examined will be inserted somewhere to the left of its original position and everything that belongs above it has to be moved up one place. This insertion resembles the rotation examples near the begin-

ning of this Chapter. In this program for insertion sorting, the place to insert each value is found by searching from the beginning of the array:

```
C INSERTION SORT OF CARD DATA
C MAXIMUM OF 100 KEYS PERMITTED
C
      DIMENSION IRAY(100)
C DETERMINE SORT SIZE
      READ(5,10)NSORT
 10 FORMAT(8I10)
C READ IN DATA
      READ(5,10)(IRAY(K),K=1,NSORT)
C SORT THE DATA - TAKE NEXT VALUE
      DO 40 K=2,NSORT
      IVAL=IRAY(K)
C SEARCH FOR ITS PLACE
      DO 30 L=1,K-1
      IF(IVAL.LT.IRAY(L))THEN
C INSERT AT L, ESCAPE FROM SEARCH
      DO 20 M=K,L+1,-1
      IRAY(M)=IRAY(M-1)
 20      CONTINUE
      IRAY(L)=IVAL
      GO TO 40
      END IF
 30   CONTINUE
 40 CONTINUE
      WRITE(6,50)(IRAY(K),K=1,NSORT)
 50 FORMAT(1X,8I10)
      END
```

Fig.11.9 is a flowchart of the insertion sort. A more efficient method of searching is added later in this Chapter.

A sorting operation is said to be stable if equal values remain in the same order after sorting. Both the bubble and insertion sort have been carefully programmed to be stable. For example, in the insertion sort, the value is inserted to the left of the first array element which is greater than it, and so equal values retain their order.

In this insertion sort the number of comparisons is on average

$$N(N-1)/4$$

and it is therefore about twice as fast as a bubble sort if the rotations in

Begin	86 82 54	2 32 76 94 29
Second Point	82→86 54	2 32 76 94 29
Third Point	54→82→86	2 32 76 94 29
Fourth Point	2→54→82→86	32 76 94 29
Fifth Point	2 32→54→82→86	76 94 29
Sixth Point	2 32 54 76→82→86	94 29
Seventh Point	2 32 54 76 82 86 94 29	
Eighth Point	2 29→32→54→76→82→86→94	

Fig. 11.9. Insertion sort of 8 random numbers.

inserting are neglected. It still contains a term in $N^2/4$ which is unacceptably slow. If space is not at a premium, a dramatic improvement is offered by:

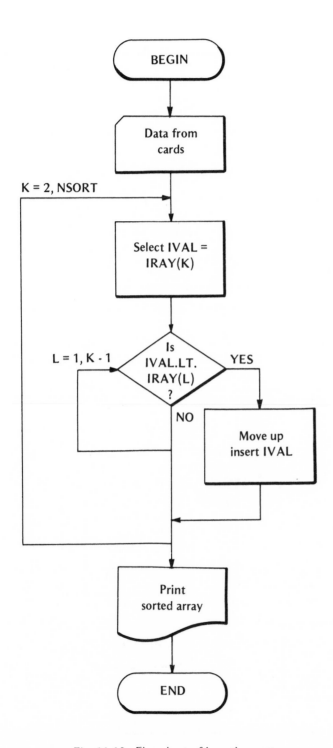

Fig. 11.10. Flowchart of insertion sort.

(iii) Merge Sorting

The operation of taking files or arrays which are already in sequence and putting them together into a large ordered file is called merging. It requires the original arrays and an array for merging into.

It is possible to sort in this way by first merging files of length 1 into files of length 2, then 2 into 4, and so on. Sorting two files in this way is called a two-way merge sort. Fig. 11.11 illustrates the steps.

Begin:	86 82	54 2	32 76	94 29
Two-merged	82 86	2 54	32 76	29 94
Four-merged	2 54 82 86		29 32 76 94	
Eight-merged	2 29 32 54 76 82 86 94			

Fig. 11.11. Two-way merge.

As can be seen, this is spectacularly more efficient. It uses exactly N comparisons in each stage, and there are $\log_2 N$ stages. Consequently this method uses $N\log_2 N$ steps as compared to kN^2 for insertion or bubble sorting. The operation of merging two arrays into one is not difficult if approached carefully. Consider Fig.11.12 in which two segments of A and B are to be merged into C. Variables IA and IB are used to point at the files to be merged, and IC points at C. To merge, A(IA) is compared with B(IB). If A(IA) is less than or equal to B(IB), A(IA) is transferred and IA incremented for the next step. Otherwise B(IB) is

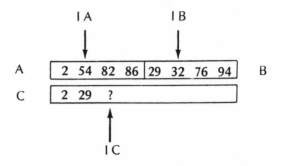

Fig. 11.12. The merging operation.

transferred and IB is incremented. This ensures that equal values remain in the same order because they are taken by preference from the lower half. When one of IA or IB hits its upper bound, the merge is completed by transferring the remaining values from the other half.

The merge operation is illustrated by the flowchart of Fig.11.13. In the two-way merge sort this operation is needed from A to C, and from C to A alternately. This suggests strongly the use of a subroutine. Before the example can be completed satisfactorily, it is necessary to find out how to pass array names as arguments to subroutines and functions.

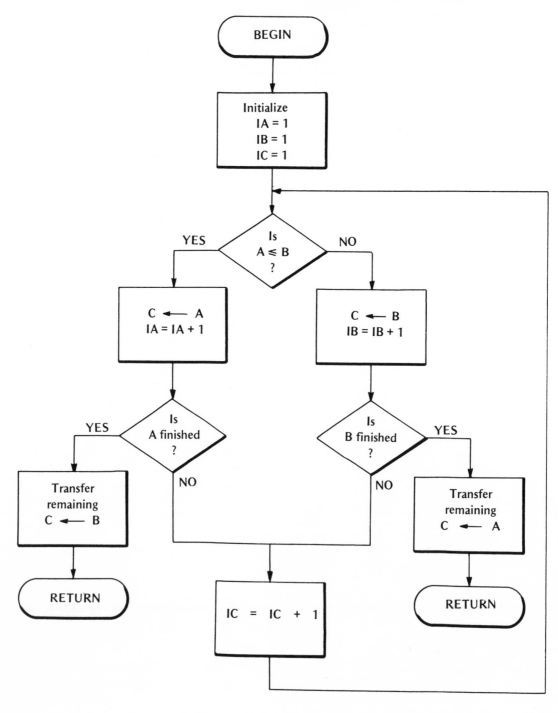

Fig. 11.13. Flowchart for the merging operation.

11.9 Using arrays in subprograms — adjustable dimensions

Between program units arrays behave in much the same way as ordinary variables. If an array is defined in a program unit, then its name is known only within that program unit. The same name can be used in a different program unit but the two are separate - the scope of an array name is a program unit, unless of course it is used as the argument of a function or subroutine. The complication with arrays is that their dimensions have to be communicated as well. The easiest way is to state a fixed size, but this is inflexible. It would be possible to say

```
SUBROUTINE MRG(IRA,IRB,IRC)
DIMENSION IRA(50),IRB(50),IRC(50)
```

but this means that the array size really must be 50. This inhibits the portability of subroutines. Much better would be

```
SUBROUTINE MRG(IRA,IRB,IRC,NA,NB)
DIMENSION IRA(NA),IRB(NB)
DIMENSION IRC(NA+NB)
```

which is in fact allowed. This is called an adjustable dimension. Using this the merge subroutine left over from the previous section can be written

```
   SUBROUTINE MRG(IRA,IRB,IRC,NA,NB)
C ROUTINE MERGES IRA, LENGTH NA
C AND IRB, LENGTH NB, INTO IRC
C
      DIMENSION IRA(NA),IRB(NB)
      DIMENSION IRC(NA+NB)
C INITIALIZE ARRAY POINTERS
      IA=1
      IB=1
      IC=1
C HERE IS THE MERGE OPERATION
C NEXT ENTRY FROM IRA OR IRB
   10 IF(IRA(IA).LT.IRB(IB)) THEN
C TAKE FROM ARRAY A
         IRC(IC)=IRA(IA)
         IA=IA+1
C HAS END BEEN REACHED
         IF(IA.GT.NA) THEN
C TRANSFER REMAINING IRB AND EXIT
            DO 20 K=IB,NB
               IC=IC+1
               IRC(IC)=IRB(K)
```

```
   20       CONTINUE
            RETURN
         END IF
      ELSE
C TAKE FROM IRB
         IRC(IC)=IRB(IB)
         IB=IB+1
C HAS END BEEN REACHED
         IF(IB.GT.NB) THEN
C TRANSFER REMAINING IRA AND EXIT
            DO 30 K=IA,NA
               IC=IC+1
               IRC(IC)=IRA(K)
   30       CONTINUE
            RETURN
         END IF
      END IF
      IC=IC+1
      GO TO 10
      END
```

In the above subroutine, the arrays IRA and IRB are merged into an array IRC. The sizes of the arrays to be used are communicated to the subroutine as NA, NB, and NC. The merging operation proceeds as was illustrated by Figs 11.12 and 11.13.

To perform a real merge sort, this subroutine must be called repeatedly to merge fragments of a longer list of keys, as was illustrated by Fig. 11.11. To do this, a little subroutine called STAGE could be written. Its purpose is to call MRG as many times as are necessary to combine subfiles of length IW from an array K1 into K2. It can be seen in STAGE that in the call to MRG, the actual array arguments are subscripted variables which point MRG at particular fragments of K1 and K2. These two subroutines are worth careful study as they illustrate the very flexible arrangements possible in FORTRAN for the use of arrays as subroutine arguments. Note how the IF block in subroutine STAGE takes care of the possibility that a single fragment of K1 is left over at the end.

```
      SUBROUTINE STAGE(K1,K2,IW,NS)
C SUBROUTINE ORGANIZES A MERGE
C SORT STAGE. SUBFILES LENGTH
C IW ARE MERGED FROM K1 TO K2.
C
      DIMENSION K1(NS),K2(NS)
```

```
      ISPAN=2*IW
   DO 2Ø K=1,NS,ISPAN
     KSP=K+IW
     IF(KSP.LE.NS) THEN
       IWIBE=MIN(IW,NS-KSP+1)
       CALL MRG(K1(K),K1(KSP)
               ,K2(K),IW,IWIBE)
     ELSE
       DO 1Ø L=K,NS
         K2(L)=K1(L)
 1Ø      CONTINUE
     END IF
 2Ø  CONTINUE
     END
```

To do an actual sort, arrays must be merged back and forth with the fragment width IW in subroutine STAGE increasing each time. Here is the merge sort "master" subroutine MERGE to do it all. Note how the alternating use of arrays IRYA and IRYB is accomplished by interchanging the arguments between the two calls to STAGE. Merging is done beginning with subfiles of length 1, doubling this length until it exceeds the number of keys NK, when the sort is finished. If the result happens to be in the array IRYB, then it is copied back to IYRA. It should be noted that the use of subfiles whose lengths are powers of two does not restrict the procedure to sorting numbers of keys that are powers of two. STAGE and MRG have been written to take care of odd length fragments, and so any number of keys can be sorted by subroutine MERGE.

```
      SUBROUTINE MERGE(IRYA,IRYB,NK)
C MERGE SORT MASTER SUBROUTINE
C IRYA = INTEGER ARRAY OF NK KEYS
C          FOR SORTING IN ASCENDING
C          ORDER. THE RESULT IS
C          ALSO RETURNED IN IRYA.
C IRYB = INTEGER ARRAY LENGTH NK
C          USED FOR WORKSPACE.
C NK   = INTEGER VALUE GIVING NO.
C          OF KEYS FOR SORTING AND
C          ARRAY LENGTHS.
C
      DIMENSION IRYA(NK),IRYB(NK)
      IW=1
C MERGE SUBFILES WIDTH IW
C FIRST IRYA INTO IRYB
 1Ø IF(IW.LT.NK) THEN
       CALL STAGE(IRYA,IRYB,IW,NK)
```

```
     ELSE
       RETURN
     END IF
C THEN IRYB INTO IRYA
     IW=IW*2
     IF(IW.LT.NK) THEN
       CALL STAGE(IRYB,IRYA,IW,NK)
     ELSE
C MUST COPY RESULT BACK TO A
       DO 2Ø K=1,NK
         IRYA(K)=IRYB(K)
 2Ø    CONTINUE
       RETURN
     END IF
     IW=IW*2
     GO TO 1Ø
     END
```

Here is a main program to exercise this merge sort. Here a fixed dimension of 1000 for KEYA and KEYB limits the number of keys that can be sorted by this particular main program. It is always necessary for an actual size to be given to an array in the program unit that originates it, in this example the main program. Taken together, this program and its subroutines are a real, useful application.

```
C MERGE SORT, MAXIMUM 1ØØØ KEYS
      DIMENSION KEYA(1ØØØ)
      DIMENSION KEYB(1ØØØ)
C DETERMINE SORT SIZE
      READ(*,1Ø)NSOR
 1Ø FORMAT(8I1Ø)
C READ IN DATA FOR SORTING
      READ(*,1Ø)(KEYA(K),K=1,NSOR)
C CALL MERGE TO DO THE SORT
      CALL MERGE(KEYA,KEYB,NSOR)
C AND PRINT THE RESULT
      WRITE(*,5Ø)(KEYA(K),K=1,NSOR)
 5Ø FORMAT(1X,16I5)
      END
```

The searching part of the insertion sort from the previous Section might be a good thing to use as a function subprogram. This function locates the place for insertion:

```
      FUNCTION LOCATE(KEYS,IRAY,NK)
C LOCATE INSERTION PLACE FOR KEYS
C IN ORDERED ARRAY IRAY OF LENGTH
C NK. RETURN NK+1 IF NOT FOUND.
C
      DIMENSION IRAY(NK)
```

```
      LOCATE=NK+1
      DO 1Ø L=1,NK
        IF(KEYS.LT.IRAY(L)) THEN
          LOCATE=L
          RETURN
        END IF
 1Ø   CONTINUE
      END
```

and the whole insertion sort can be made a subroutine:

```
      SUBROUTINE INSORT(IRAY,NSORT)
C INSERTION SORT OF NSORT VALUES
C IN THE INTEGER ARRAY IRAY
C
      DIMENSION IRAY(NSORT)
      DO 2Ø K=2,NSORT
        IVAL=IRAY(K)
C FIND OUT WHERE IT GOES
        LPLACE=LOCATE(IVAL,IRAY,K-1)
C AND INSERT IT AT LPLACE
        IF(LPLACE.LT.K) THEN
          DO 1Ø M=K,LPLACE+1,-1
            IRAY(M)=IRAY(M-1)
 1Ø       CONTINUE
          IRAY(LPLACE)=IVAL
        END IF
 2Ø   CONTINUE
      END
```

which can be used by the program:

```
C DO AN INSERTION SORT
C MAXIMUM 1ØØ VALUES
      DIMENSION IRAY(1ØØ)
C DETERMINE SORT SIZE
      READ(*,1Ø)NSOR
 1Ø   FORMAT(8I1Ø)
      READ(*,1Ø)(IRAY(K),K=1,NSOR)
      CALL INSORT(IRAY,NSOR)
      WRITE(*,2Ø)(IRAY(K),K=1,NSOR)
 2Ø   FORMAT(1X,8I1Ø)
      END
```

An adjustable dimension in FORTRAN, like everything else, has rules about its usage. In a DIMENSION statement in a subprogram, either or both of the DIMENSION bounds can be an adjustable size, which is any expression involving only integers, which may be constants or dummy arguments. The only arrays that can be treated in this way are ones that are dummy arguments of the sub-program. Local arrays must be given constant array bounds in exactly the way that arrays are dimensioned in main programs.

EXAMPLE:

Here is an example of a "digital filter". Data in a real array X can be "smoothed" by applying an equation to it such as

$$Y_n = 0.25\ X_{n-2} + 0.75\ X_{n-1} + X_n$$

$$+ 0.75\ X_{n+1} + 0.25\ X_{n+2}$$

where Y_n is a smoothed value corresponding to the rough value X_n. Here is a subroutine with a local array COEF giving the filter coefficients. This calculates a smoothed version XOT of an input array XIN. Because XIN and XOT are dummy arguments, they can have adjustable dimensions. Because COEF is a local array, it must have constant dimensions. The smoothing equation involves previous and later input values, and because of this the first two values and the last two values of the output array XOT have not been defined by this subroutine.

```
      SUBROUTINE SMUTH(XIN,XOT,LEN)
C SMOOTH AN ARRAY OF DATA
C XIN = INPUT REAL ARRAY FOR
C       SMOOTHING, LENGTH LEN
C XOT = OUTPUT REAL ARRAY WITH
C       RESULT, LENGTH LEN
C LEN = NO. OF VALUES TO SMOOTH
C
      DIMENSION XIN(LEN),XOT(LEN)
      DIMENSION COEF(-2:2)
      DATA COEF/.25,.75,1.,.75,.25/
      DO 2Ø K=3,LEN-2
        SUM=Ø.Ø
        DO 1Ø L=-2,2
          SUM=SUM+XIN(K+L)*COEF(L)
 1Ø     CONTINUE
        XOT(K)=SUM
 2Ø   CONTINUE
      END
```

A number of forms would violate the rules - as always these are based on common sense.

```
      SUBROUTINE IDIOT(X,Y,N)
      DIMENSION DATA(N)
```

is forbidden because DATA is not a dummy argument and cannot therefore have an adjustable dimension.

```
SUBROUTINE FASTF(XREAL,XIMAG,N)
DIMENSION XREAL(ABS(N))
DIMENSION XIMAG(ABS(N))
```

is illegal because the adjustable dimension can have only integer terms which are constants or dummy arguments of the call. Function references are not allowed:

```
FUNCTION ROTTEN(XRAY)
DIMENSION XRAY(ILL)
```

is wrong because the adjustable dimension ILL is not a dummy argument.

In a CALL statement or function reference that wishes to communicate an array to a subprogram, several forms are permitted. The array name might be given without a subscript, in which case the subroutine dummy argument points to the beginning of the array.

EXAMPLE:

```
DIMENSION J(25)
     :
     :
CALL INSORT(J,25)
     :
     :
END
SUBROUTINE INSORT(IRAY,NSORT)
DIMENSION IRAY(NSORT)
     :
     :
END
```

The above is the most straightforward case, but consider:

```
DIMENSION X(11)
     :
     :
CALL FILTER(X)
     :
     :
END
SUBROUTINE FILTER(FILT)
DIMENSION FILT(-5:5)
     :
     :
END
```

which is a correct reference, as would be:

```
DIMENSION X(-5:5)
     :
     :
CALL FLITER(X,5)
     :
     :
END
SUBROUTINE FLITER(FLIT,N)
DIMENSION FLIT(-N:N)
     :
     :
END
```

EXAMPLE:
One cannot leave the question of sorting and searching without an introduction to the binary search. This is a spectacularly fast method of finding a

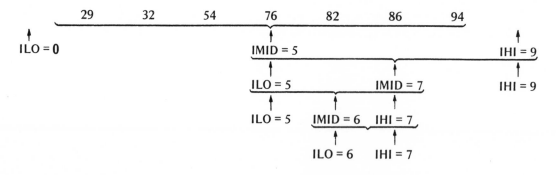

Here it is !

Fig. 11.14. A binary search closes in on its target with amazing speed. Three comparisons have found the place to insert the value 84.

desired place in an array provided the array is in order. In the insertion sorting example, the ordered part of the array was searched from the beginning each time to find where the new value belonged. This operation was removed to a function LOCATE a few pages back. In fact LOCATE can be made wildly more efficient.

Consider an ordered array of length N as in Fig. 11.14 for N=8. A programmer wishes to search for the value 4 without knowing in advance where it is, but knowing that the array is in order. He looks at the middle of the array, and immediately knows which half the value 4 is in. Going to that half, he divides it in two and knows which quarter it is in, and so on until the right place is found in a maximum of $\log_2 N$ comparisons, as compared to an average of N/2 using a linear search. The array length does not need to divide into exact halves, quarters etc. for it to work. Two pointers ILO and IHI are used to indicate the lowest and highest subscripts that are possible. A comparison is made between the key and the arrray element (ILO+IHI)/2. The program rapidly closes in on the right place. In the function LOCATE, recall that the subscript of the first member which is greater than the key is sought. Thus as soon as ILO and IHI differ by one, IHI is the answer. This is an important method, but the function could need modifying for different applications, for example if an array is being searched for the occurrence of the key. A flowchart of this function is given in Fig. 11.15.

```
FUNCTION LOCATE(KEY,IRAY,NK)
C LOCATE PLACE TO INSERT KEY
C IN INTEGER ARRAY IRAY OF
C LENGTH NK BY BINARY SEARCH
C ANSWER MAY BE NK+1
C
      DIMENSION IRAY(NK)
C INITIALIZE
      ILO=0
      IHI=NK+1
   10 IMID=(ILO+IHI)/2
      IF(KEY.LT.IRAY(IMID)) THEN
C SEARCH GOES LEFT, CHANGE IHI
```

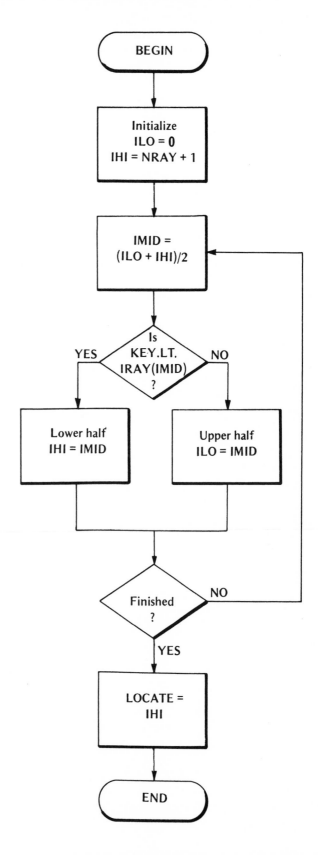

Fig. 11.15. Flowchart of function to do binary search for insertion sort.

```
      IHI=IMID
    ELSE
C KEY GOES RIGHT, CHANGE ILO
      ILO=IMID
    END IF
C IS IT FINISHED
    IF(IHI.GT.ILO+1)GO TO 1Ø
    LOCATE=IHI
    END
```

If the actual argument uses a specific subscript, then when the program calls the function or subroutine, the dummy argument points to the specific array element named, and can begin its dummy array at that point. This is how the merging subroutine works:

```
CALL MRG(IAR(K),IAR(K+IW),IBR(K),
      IW,MIN(IW,MSORT-K+IW))
```

tells the subroutine the beginning of the segments to be merged and the length of each:

```
SUBROUTINE MRG(IRA,IRB,IRC,NA,NB)
DIMENSION IRA(NA),IRB(NB)
DIMENSION IRC(NA+NB)
```

and it is instructive to examine that subroutine to see how it keeps out of trouble when it hits the end of the array if the second segment is shorter than the first.

It should be clear from all the previous examples that the integer dummy arguments used to compute adjustable dimensions are just like any other integers and can be used for other purposes.

EXERCISE:
Write a function LOCMAX to search for the maximum value in a disordered real array and return the integer subscript of the maximum. This suggests that four different searching functions might be useful; real and integer arrays each searched for either maximum or minimum values.

EXERCISE:
Write a subroutine which finds the location and the value of the smallest real value in an array.

EXERCISE:
Write a binary searching function IFIND which searches an ordered integer array for a "key" and returns the subscript value of the highest array element that is equal to the key, or zero if the key does not occur at all.

11.10 Multiple entries

It has already been stated that an array can only appear in one DIMENSION statement in a program unit. This implies some restrictions on subroutines with multiple entries.

A particular array can be used as a dummy argument in both SUBROUTINE and ENTRY statements - but it can only be dimensioned once. Because the DIMENSION statement must know the values of the adjustable dimensions, the array name and any integer variables used in the adjustable dimensions have to appear together whenever they appear at all as dummy arguments; therefore

```
SUBROUTINE PRIMUS(A,B,X,N,M)
DIMENSION A(N),X(M)
    :
    :
ENTRY SCNDUS(A,Z,X,M,N)
    :
    :
END
```

is allowed but

```
ENTRY FIRST(IRAY,N)
DIMENSION IRAY(N)
    :
    :
ENTRY SECOND(IRAY)
    :
    :
END
```

is not because the dimension N is undefined when ENTRY SECOND is used. The SAVE statement cannot help because it cannot save dummy arguments.

11.11 The interaction of SAVE and DATA

Using the DATA statement, any variable which is local to a subprogram can be given an initial value. This is true for any kind of variable. However it is possible that the subprogram may modify the value of such a variable before control is returned to the calling program. What then is the value of this variable if the program is called again?

If there is no SAVE statement, on the second call the unsuspecting user will find that all the values have become undefined. Therefore when a main program like

```
PRINT*,NEXT()
```

calls the function NEXT repeatedly,

```
FUNCTION NEXT()
DATA INXT/1/
NEXT=INXT
INXT=INXT+1
END
```

on the second call INXT is undefined and the program fails. On the other hand, if a SAVE statement is used, the function

```
FUNCTION NEXT()
SAVE
DATA INXT/1/
NEXT=INXT
INXT=INXT+1
END
```

returns the values 1,2,3,.....

11.12 Assumed size arrays in subprograms

There are situations in which a programmer may not wish to state the dimension bounds of an array - and FORTRAN 77 allows the upper bound to be left dangling. If in a subprogram an array (which is a dummy argument) is given the upper bound *, then it is an assumed size array:

```
SUBROUTINE SLOWF2(XREAL,XIMAG,N)
DIMENSION XREAL(Ø:*),XIMAG(Ø:*)
```

A program which calls this may use the array name

```
CALL SLOWF2(ARAY,BRAY,-128)
```

to refer to the whole array, or a subscripted reference

```
CALL SLOWF2(X(1),X(N/2+1),-N)
```

to refer to the part of the array from there to the end.

It should be used only with good reason, because the upper bound is not known to the subprogram. This implies a restriction on the use of the array in input/output. Because it does not know the upper bound, it is not possible to say

```
SUBROUTINE NONSNS(X)
DIMENSION X(*)
    ⋮
    ⋮
PRINT 2Ø,X
    ⋮
    ⋮
END
```

or to refer to the entire array in any other input/output statement. It would be possible to say

```
PRINT 2Ø(X(L),L=NBOT,NTOP)
```

but of course if NTOP was the upper bound, it ought to have been used in the DIMENSION statement.

11.13 A few things to remember

It is hoped that the very large number of examples in this Chapter are helpful in demonstrating the use of arrays in subprograms. Many of the rules depend on common sense, but there are a few (perhaps obvious) points to bear in mind.

(i) An array must originate somewhere.

It has been seen how array names and sizes are passed down through function and subroutine references using dummy arguments and adjustable dimensions. It is important to grasp one basic, obvious fact: every array must originate in some program unit as having a DIMENSION statement with constant bounds. This means that first of all every array used in a main program is given its actual constant dimension (nothing forces the program to use all of it, of course). This was stated as a rule but should now be a perfectly natural fact; the computer has to make space for it somewhere and that somewhere is where the array originates. The same fact means that any array used in a subprogram has to be given a constant dimension if it is not a dummy argument:

```
SUBROUTINE MGSORT(IARAY,NSORT)
DIMENSION IARAY(NSORT),IBRAY(16)
            :
            :
CALL MRG(IARAY(K),IARAY(KSP),
         IBRAY(K),IW,IWIBE)
            :
            :
```

IARAY clearly originates in a calling program. IBRAY originates in subroutine MGSORT. Both are passed to subroutine MERGE in fragments:

```
SUBROUTINE MRG(IRA,IRB,IRC,NA,NB)
DIMENSION IRA(NA),IRB(NB)
DIMENSION IRAC(NA+NB)
```

(ii) DATA statements.

An array can only be used in a DATA statement to give it initial values in the program unit where it originates. This, it will be remembered, is a consequence of the way dummy arguments work; no dummy argument can be mentioned in a DATA statement.

(iii) Adjusting adjustable dimensions.

This can't be done. In a subprogram, the subscript bounds are defined when the program is first entered. In the example

```
SUBROUTINE FIDDL(X,N)
DIMENSION X(N)
    :
    :
N=N+13
```

the fiddling about with N hasn't changed the nature of the array. This does not have much importance with arrays of one dimension, but misguided people can try to change the nature of higher dimensioned arrays and get in trouble. There is nothing wrong with changing N as long it was a variable in the CALL or function reference, but it has no effect on the dimension bounds. This is reminiscent of the non-influence on DO loops of fiddling about with the DO parameters inside the loop. Once inside it is too late.

(iv) Respect the array bounds.

Arrays occupy a certain amount of space in the memory of a digital computer and the purpose of a DIMENSION statement is to ensure that the correct amount of space is created and that the subscripts address it properly. In fact the space around arrays is also used by other arrays, variables, constants and the instructions of the computer program itself. For this reason a program that steps outside the bounds of an array by accident is going to fail in a way that a programmer cannot possibly predict; it could be a catastrophic, obvious failure or a subtle, puzzling one. Therefore a subscript should not exceed the array bounds, and in most cases the computer is not going to check this for each subscript because of the cost in efficiency that would be involved.

For the same reason, a subprogram cannot increase the size of an array that originates outside it. If a program had

```
DIMENSION A(100)
    :
    :
CALL SUBB(A,200)
    :
    :
END
SUBROUTINE SUBB(A,N)
DIMENSION A(N)
    :
    :
```

it may fool the computer but the programmer is only fooling himself if he thinks he is picking up extra space.

(v) Those confusing rules about subscript expressions summarized.

A subscript may be any integer expression but its value should lie within the array bounds, for example:

ARAY(3*J+INT(X))

A constant dimension must be used where an array originates and is an expression involving only integer constants, and simple arithmetic (no functions), for example:

DIMENSION A(1ØØ+2*3/7)

PARAMETER(M=6)
DIMENSION RAZZ(M*14)

or DIMENSION SIMPLE(4)

An adjustable dimension occurs only in subprograms, and only for arrays that are given dummy arguments. It can be an integer expression involving constants or dummy arguments which are integers using simple arithmetic (no functions), for example:

SUBROUTINE MUD(SLING,M,N)
DIMENSION SLING(M+3*N)

Actually it may involve something else - another kind of integer whose value may be defined at the commencement of a subprogram is one contained in a COMMON block as will be encountered in Chapter 13.

SUBROUTINE ADVANC(X,Y,Z)
COMMON M,N
DIMENSION X(M),Y(N),Z(M+N)

11.14 Problems

PROBLEM 11.1:
Write a program to convert a number given to any base into any other base. Use an array to hold the digits

of the first number and another to hold the digits of the result. The result can now be printed in the correct order!

PROBLEM 11.2:
Write a subroutine, SLOWF2, which calculates the Fourier series of tabulated values. With a limited number N of tabulated values, there are only N coefficients that can be calculated. If the tabulated values are called F, then the coefficients Y can be calculated from

$$Y_n = \frac{2}{N} \sum_{k=0}^{N-1} F_k \, e^{\frac{-j2\pi kn}{N}}$$

$$\text{for } n = 0,1,\ldots,N\text{-}1$$

which is called by the misleading title "Discrete Fourier Transform." Each Y_n has a real part and an imaginary part; use separate arrays for these. The real part resembles the cosine coefficient of the Fourier series (Chapter 10). The reconstruction of F from Y is

$$F_k = \frac{1}{2} \sum_{n=0}^{N-1} Y_n e^{\frac{j2\pi kn}{N}}$$

$$\text{for } k = 0,1,\ldots,N\text{-}1$$

Make use of the subroutine SWING from Chapter 10.

PROBLEM 11.3:
The Chebyshev series, Problem 7.6, is also often calculated from tabulated values, and can also make good use of SWING, but in a more involved way. Write subroutine CHEBY to calculate the Chebyshev coefficients of an array of tabulated values.

PROBLEM 11.4:
The Clenshaw recurrence calculates the values of a function from its Chebyshev coefficients. This is an important method of interpolation. The Chebyshev coefficients are calculated as in Problem 11.3, and the Clenshaw recurrence can then be used to recover whatever intermediate values of the function are desired.

To find f(x), first take

$$a_{N+1} = 0$$

$$a_N = 0$$

and then form $a_{N-1}, \ldots, a_1$ according to

$$a_k = 2xa_{k+1} - a_{k+2} + C_k$$

where C_k is a Chebyshev coefficient. Note that you don't have to hold all the a values in an array — only the most recent two are needed in the recurrence.

Finally

$$a_0 = 2xa_1 - a_2 + C_0/2$$

after which

$$f(x) = a_0 - a_1 x$$

Make a subroutine CLENSH to do this. Try interpolating the data of Fig. 11.16.

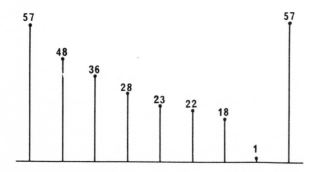

Fig. 11.16. Interpolate this data by a Chebyshev series.

PROBLEM 11.5:

Form a histogram of the relative occurrence of random numbers from the random number generator of Chapter 4, which you made into a function in Problem 8.3 (didn't you?) In doing so, design a good histogram-making subroutine.

PROBLEM 11.6:

Make a subroutine for quadrature, i.e. finding the area under a curve, which works on tabulated data.

PROBLEM 11.7:

This is actually quite tricky, although if you think very clearly there is a neat way through it. You have an array of values, and the length of the array is an even number. Rearrange the data in the array so that all the data values that were at odd subscripts are now in the bottom half of the array, and all the data from even subscripts are in the top half, as illustrated in Fig.11.17. The difficulty is that the rearrangement is to be done without using an extra array, i.e. by moving one value at a time within the array. You are being asked to do a "cyclic permutation".

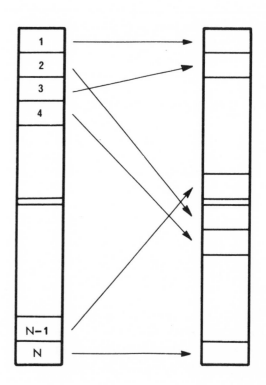

Fig. 11.17. Achieve this even-odd re-ordering in place.

12

Two case studies

12.1 Introduction

In this chapter, two extended examples are considered which involve the use of arrays of one dimension. Many of the examples in earlier chapters have necessarily been limited illustrations of particular relevance to aspects of FORTRAN. These case studies, apart from being very useful programs, are an opportunity to see what is involved in the development of real programs to do serious work.

Sorting is the most important non-numerical problem in computation, and is widely used in commercial data processing. In Section 12.2 a complex but important method of sorting is described which approaches the efficiency of merge sorting without the extra array storage required by an ordinary merge sort.

The fast Fourier transform, described in Section 12.3, is a 'numerical' algorithm of great importance in signal processing, and is used for a broad spectrum of scientific purposes.

12.2 A merge-exchange sorting program

In both of Chapters 10 and 11, much emphasis was placed on examples of sorting using FORTRAN 77. The merge sorting program of Chapter 11 is one of the fastest known methods of sorting, requiring $N \log_2 N$ comparisons of keys to sort completely N keys if N is a power of 2 - N comparisons in each of $\log_2 N$ stages. In terms of pure speed, there is no faster way. However, the cost of a computation is related to the amount of memory used as well as to the amount of time taken. Even though memory is always getting cheaper, it will remain reasonable to regard the cost of computation as being the product of the memory used and the time taken. The efficient merge sorting program required an array of length N for the keys and a further array into which a stage of the sort was made. The 'cost' was then something like $2N \log_2 N$. It is possible that a slower method using less storage could cost less.

There are very many different methods of sorting, some of them extremely clever. All merge-exchange methods achieve sorting by merging without requiring additional storage. Even merge-exchange sorting comes in various flavours - the simple and efficient method described here is a form of Batcher's algorithm, presented by K.E. Batcher to the Spring Joint Computer Conference in 1968.

To merge by exchanging, start with two ordered files of length N/2 which are to be combined into one ordered file of length N. This is a similar requirement to the ordinary merging described in Chapters 10 and 11. However, to make this one work, the two files, called A and B, are actually alternating within one long array, as illustrated by Fig. 12.1.

Suppose for the moment that N is a power of 2, as in Fig. 12.1. The first operation is to scan through the file making each entry in the A file less than the entry just next to it in the B file, as shown by Fig. 12.2.

When this has been done it is easy to see that each number is within N/4 places of its correct position in the merged file. Furthermore, each number in the A file can only move up and each

File A	File B	Array Containing A and B	Merged Result
13		13	7
	7	7	13
52		52	36
	36	36	38
64		64	50
	38	38	51
73		73	52
	50	50	64
76		76	73
	51	51	76
77		77	77
	88	88	77
77		77	88
	91	91	89
89		89	91
	95	95	95

Fig.12.1. Merge–exchange sorting works by merging file A and file B, both already in order, which alternate within the same array.

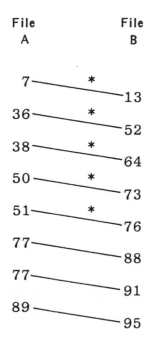

Fig.12.2. Corresponding members of the two files have been ordered – exchanges have been made where marked by asterisks.

number in the B file can only move down. We can always give every number the chance to move to the correct place by comparing numbers in the A file with numbers further up in the B file. A very remarkable thing happens if we scan completely through the files comparing numbers a certain fixed distance apart and exchanging them whenever the number in A is less than the one in B. This remarkable thing is that both the files remain in order after every scan like this, and furthermore each number in A stays less than the one next to it in B! This is important enough to offer a simple proof, as follows:

Suppose that in Fig. 12.3, a(i) is compared to some b(j) which is further up the list. The two are exchanged if a(i) < b(j) and this is done from top to bottom of the file.

Remarkable Fact (1): The files remain in order.

If two numbers are switched, then b(j) becomes smaller and a(i) gets larger. Provided the A file was in order up to that point, it remains so. As b(j) gets smaller, can it be less than b(j-1), so ruining the B file? There are two cases:

(i) Either a(i-1) was switched with b(j-1) and the B file remains in order;
(ii) or a(i-1) was not switched with b(j-1) in which case b(j-1)≤a(i-1)≤new b(j), and the B file remains in order. This works for b(1) and hence for the entire file.

Remarkable Fact (2): a(j) remains ≤ b(j) and a(i) remains ≤ b(i).

Suppose a(i) is changed with b(j). b(j) will decrease but remain greater than a(j) because the new value comes from a(i) which is always greater than or equal to a(j).

Similarly a(i) will increase but remain ≤ b(i) because of where the new a(i) comes from, i.e. b(j)≤b(i).

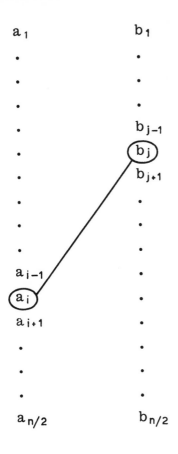

a_1 b_1

b_{j-1}

b_j

b_{j+1}

a_{i-1}

a_i

a_{i+1}

$a_{n/2}$ $b_{n/2}$

Fig.12.3. Illustrating a scanning stage in the merge–exchange sort.

The importance of these facts is that after every such scan, the files are ready for another scan in which the B values can again only move down and the A values up. We simply have to choose a series of scans which allow any value to move as much as N/4 places overall. One could be silly and do N/4 scans, with i=j+1; this would be slower than bubble sorting. However, because of the Remarkable Facts, it can't hurt to move values too far, because after every scan it is still true that the keys in the B file can only move down while those in the A file can only move up. Scanning with a 'reach' j-i of N/4 places, followed by N/8, N/16,...,1, will always allow any key to move any number of places. After the last scan, with i=j+1, the merge is complete. Fig.12.4 shows all of this in merging the 16 numbers we started with. Note that no switches are made when the reach is N/4 - this is an unlikely event in any case.

To implement this in a FORTRAN 77 program, first it is seen that all the reordering scans are similar, even the one that makes each a(i) less than b(i). So first a subroutine is written to scan through the array of values, comparing values IREACH apart and exchanging them if necessary. This subroutine is called EXPASS, meaning 'exchanging pass'. For each K from MINI to MAXI, stepping by ISTEP, the keys are exchanged if the value of KEYS(K) is greater than or equal to KEYS(K-IREACH). Here it is:

```
      SUBROUTINE EXPASS(KEYS,MINI,MAXI,ISTEP,IREACH)
C
C SUBROUTINE FOR A SINGLE PASS AT AN ARRAY OF KEYS,
C COMPARING VALUES IREACH APART AND SWITCHING IF
C NECESSARY, SO KEYS(K) IS .GE. KEYS(K-IREACH)
C            FOR K = MINI,MAXI,ISTEP
C
C KEYS = INTEGER ARRAY, LENGTH MAXI TO BE REORDERED
C MINI,MAXI,ISTEP = INTEGER VALUES CONTROLLING SEARCH
C IREACH = INTEGER VALUE GIVING SPACING OF THE PASS
C
      DIMENSION KEYS(MAXI)
      DO 10 K=MINI,MAXI,ISTEP
        IF(KEYS(K).LT.KEYS(K-IREACH)) THEN
          IT=KEYS(K)
          KEYS(K)=KEYS(K-IREACH)
          KEYS(K-IREACH)=IT
        END IF
   10 CONTINUE
      END
```

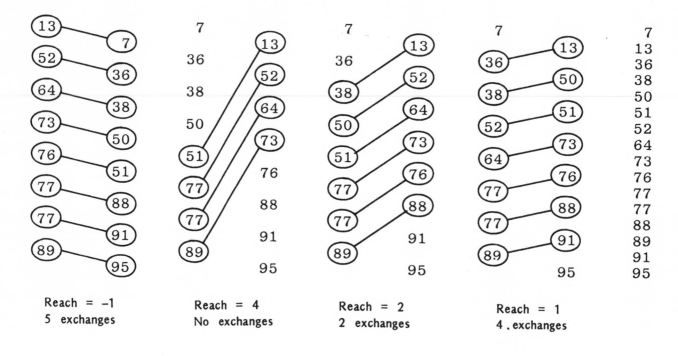

Reach = –1   Reach = 4   Reach = 2   Reach = 1
5 exchanges   No exchanges   2 exchanges   4 . exchanges

Fig.12.4. All the stages in merging two interleaved files
of length 8 into one file of length 16.

The first pass in sorting an array of values is to make each member of the A file less than the member of the B file just above it. To do this for the 16 numbers shown in Fig. 12.4, we write:

CALL EXPASS(KEYS,2,16,2,-1)

This causes EXPASS to switch KEYS(2) with KEYS(1) if KEYS(2) is less than KEYS(1), then deal with KEYS(4) and KEYS(3), and so on. The next stage uses EXPASS the other way around, with a reach of 4:

CALL EXPASS(KEYS,9,16,2,4)

Here, KEYS(9) is compared with KEYS(13) and so on. Next,

CALL EXPASS(KEYS,5,16,2,2)

and finally

CALL EXPASS(KEYS,3,16,2,1)

To automate this process completely, a subroutine is required which will merge two files of any length, deciding what stages to use. In order to make this into a completely general sorting procedure, it is necessary that the merging subroutine should be able to deal with A and B files which are still alternating within the array of keys, but which are spaced out - there might be other files in between as will be seen. Therefore the subroutine MERGEX is used to merge two files which are contained as alternating values within an array called KEYS, with the values spaced by KSPAN. The A file is in KEYS(1), KEYS(2*KSPAN+1),... and the B file is in KEYS(KSPAN+1), KEYS(3*KSPAN+1),... The number of keys in the A and B files combined is N, ignoring the values in between which do not form part of either A and B.

In MERGEX, the actual length of the array of keys used in the merge is 1+(N-1)*KSPAN - this allows all the space for the unused keys in between. The DIMENSION statement reflects this:

```
DIMENSION KEYS(1+(N-1)*KSPAN)
```

Note that every value used in the dimension bound is either a constant or a dummy argument of the subroutine as required by the rules of FORTRAN 77. The first call to EXPASS sets each a(i) less than or equal to the b(i) next to it.

```
CALL EXPASS(KEYS,KSPAN+1,LAST1,
            2*KSPAN,KSPAN)
```

It is then necessary to choose the reach for the scan through the keys that is to follow. For any value of N, the next power of 2 less than N/4 is taken as the first reach. Observe the statements:

```
      LSPAN=1
   10 IF(LSPAN.LT.N) THEN
         LSPAN=LSPAN*2
         GO TO 10
      END IF
      LSPAN=MAX(1,LSPAN/4)
```

Here the MAX function ensures that the subroutine does not blow up for files of length 2 or 3, the smallest that could ever be encountered. For N=2, the scanning DO loop in MERGEX is jumped over, while with N=3 it is done once - both are correct. LSPAN is the value of the reach as was illustrated by Fig. 12.4, but it does not take account of the extra numbers in the array which are not involved in this particular merge. The value assigned to IREACH does take account of this.

```
      SUBROUTINE MERGEX(KEYS,N,KSPAN)
C
C     MERGE TWO FILES WHICH ALTERNATE WITHIN
C     THE ARRAY KEYS SPACED BY KSPAN, INTO ONE
C     FILE OF N VALUES, BY MERGE-EXCHANGE METHOD
C
C KEYS = INPUT INTEGER ARRAY OF KEYS, LENGTH AT LEAST
C        1+(N-1)*KSPAN. THE ELEMENTS 1, 2*KSPAN+1,
C        4*KSPAN+1,... MAKE UP FILE A WHICH IS ALREADY
C        ORDERED. THE ELEMENTS KSPAN+1, 3*KSPAN+1,...
C        MAKE UP FILE B WHICH IS ALSO ALREADY ORDERED.
C
      DIMENSION KEYS(1+(N-1)*KSPAN)
      LAST1=1+(N-1)*KSPAN
C THE FIRST PASS MAKES EACH A(I).LE.B(I)
      CALL EXPASS(KEYS,KSPAN+1,LAST1,2*KSPAN,KSPAN)
C NOW BEGIN REORDERING STAGES WITH REDUCING
C REACH. GET FIRST LSPAN AS NEXT LOWER POWER OF 2
      LSPAN=1
   10 IF(LSPAN.LT.N) THEN
         LSPAN=LSPAN*2
         GO TO 10
      END IF
      LSPAN=MAX(1,LSPAN/4)
C SET UP THE LOOP
   30 MINI=1+2*LSPAN*KSPAN
      MAXI=LAST1
      ISTEP=2*KSPAN
      IREACH=KSPAN+2*KSPAN*(LSPAN-1)
C DO THE EXCHANGES FOR THIS STAGE
      CALL EXPASS(KEYS,MINI,MAXI,ISTEP,IREACH)
C GET THE NEXT VALUE OF REACH
      IF(LSPAN.LE.1) RETURN
      LSPAN=(LSPAN+1)/2
      GO TO 30
      END
```

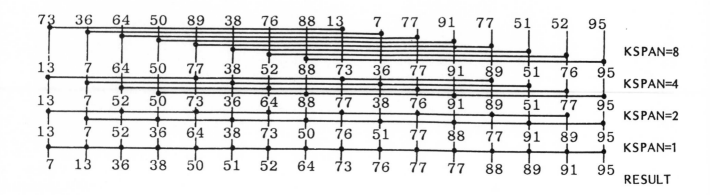

Fig.12.5. How to organize the sorting of a file of 16 disordered
keys using a succession of merge-exchange steps. Note how the
value 36 moves half way up the array and then back again.

This merge-exchange procedure can now be organized into a program to sort any number of keys. Suppose, as in Fig. 12.5, there are 16 totally disordered numbers. In the ordinary merging example of Chapter 11, files were merged which were initially end to end. Here, the numbers are going to be considered as interleaved files. To sort them, first order all 8 possible subfiles of length 2, spaced by 8 places as the Fig. 12.5 shows. These are then merged into 4 subfiles of length 4, spaced 4 apart, each now in order. The next stage produces 2 ordered files of length 8 which are spaced 2 apart. These two files are the same numbers used to illustrate the process of merging by

exchanging, and the last stage merges them into one file of 16 values.

This is clearly not too difficult to organize. However, it is necessary to cope with perfectly general lengths of arrays to make this method really useful.

Suppose the array length is M. The first stage always works on subfiles of length 2, spaced apart by the power of 2 which is next below M. But if M is not a power of 2, there will not be M/2 of these files. Fig. 12.6 follows the sorting of 13 numbers through all stages. Here there are 5 subfiles of length 2 spaced 8 apart in the first stage - the remaining 3 numbers are held over to the next

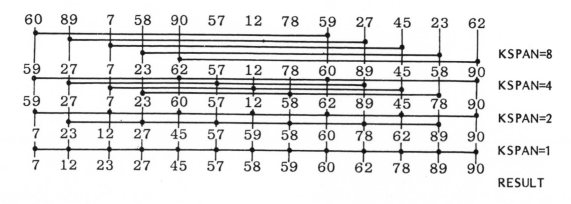

Fig.12.6. How to organize the sorting of a file of 13 disordered
keys using a succession of merge-exchange steps. Note the
irregularities in the subfile lengths.

stage. In the second stage there is only one subfile of length 4 spaced 4 apart, but there are three other subfiles of length 3 spaced 4 apart. In general, for M keys sorted into subfiles spaced NSPAN apart, there are NSPAN subfiles. Some of these are of length $1+(M-1)/NSPAN$ - there are always $MOD(M,NSPAN)$ of these (or NSPAN of them if M is an exact multiple of NSPAN). The rest of the subfiles are of length $(M-1)/NSPAN$. There are several examples of this in Fig. 12.6.

Now the master sorting routine can be written. Subroutine SORT arranges M keys in order. First the power of 2 next below M is found as the first value of NSPAN. Subroutine MERGEX is called for all the subfiles spaced by NSPAN, in two DO loops because there are two different subfile lengths, as explained above. Then a new value of NSPAN is obtained, and the process is repeated with NSPAN halved each time. The sort is complete when the stage with NSPAN = 1 is finished. This subroutine will work for any value of M greater than zero.

```
      SUBROUTINE SORT(KEYS,M)
C
C MASTER SUBROUTINE FOR MERGE-
C           EXCHANGE SORTING
C KEYS = INPUT INTEGER ARRAY, KEYS
C        TO BE SORTED, LENGTH M.
C        OUTPUT, THE SORTED KEYS
C M = INPUT INTEGER VALUE, THE
C        NUMBER OF KEYS TO SORT
C
      DIMENSION KEYS(M)
C GET NEXT LOWEST POWER OF 2 AS
C THE FIRST SPACING OF THE FILES
      NSPAN=1
  10  IF(NSPAN.LT.M) THEN
         NSPAN=NSPAN*2
         GO TO 10
      END IF
      NSPAN=NSPAN/2
      IF(NSPAN.EQ.0) RETURN
C DO A GROUP OF SORTS LENGTH NO
  20  NO=1+(M-1)/NSPAN
      ILONG=MOD(M,NSPAN)
      IF(ILONG.EQ.0)ILONG=NSPAN
      DO 30 L=1,ILONG
  30  CALL MERGEX(KEYS(L),NO,NSPAN)
C AND REMAINDER LENGTH NO-1
      KO=NO-1
      IF(KO.GT.1) THEN
         DO 40 L=ILONG+1,NSPAN
  40     CALL MERGEX(KEYS(L),KO,NSPAN)
      END IF
      NSPAN=NSPAN/2
      IF(NSPAN.GT.0)GO TO 20
      END
```

The number of comparisons made in sorting can easily be counted if M is a power of 2. In one stage of the sort, first the corresponding $a(i)$ and $b(i)$ values are ordered. This requires $M/2$ comparisons to cover all the subfiles of length NSPAN. The remaining scans require

$$(M/2-M/4) + (M/2-M/8) +...+ (M/2-1)$$

comparisons. There are $\log_2(M/NSPAN)-1$ terms in the above sum. Adding all this up gives

$$M/2\left\{\log_2(M/NSPAN) -1\right\} + NSPAN$$

for all merges in the stage using spacing NSPAN.

Subroutine SORT passes through $\log_2 M$ merging stages with NSPAN taking the values $1,2,...,M/2$. Adding these stages up gives a grand total of

$$M/4 \ (\log_2 M)^2 - M/4 \ \log_2 M + M - 1$$

which for moderate to large values of M is approximately

$$M/4 \ (\log_2 M)^2$$

This is possibly disappointing. Ordinary merging using two arrays, as in Chapter 11, has a cost of $2M \log_2 M$ units, taking the product of the memory used and the comparisons made as the cost. For small values of M, the merge-exchange sort is going to be more economical. However, above some M, straight merging is less costly - assuming of course that the memory is available. The break-even point is when

$$M/4 \ (\log_2 M)**2 = 2M \ \log_2 M$$

which is clearly when $\log_2 M=8$, or $M=256$. Beyond 256 keys, the straight merging routine of Chapter 11 is more economical.

EXERCISE:

That, of course, is not the whole story. In sorting a large file, most of the work is done in the closing stages, when the merge-exchange procedure has to work through a lot of different values of NSPAN. However, if you were to look at the exchanges that actually get made, you will see that much of this work is unnecessary. As a file which was originally disordered becomes more and more ordered through the merging stages, the keys move, on average, very close to their final positions at quite an early stage. If you are a statistical whizz, work out for what length of subfile it would be worth making an extra scan through in advance, to determine what initial value of reach to use.

12.3   The fast Fourier transform

The fast Fourier transform, or FFT, was discovered, or re-discovered, through a paper in the journal 'Mathematics of Computation' by J.W.Cooley and J.W. Tukey in 1965, entitled 'An algorithm for the machine calculation of complex Fourier series.' Many, many people want to take a table of M complex numbers $\{X\}$, called

$$X_0, X_1, \ldots, X_{M-1}$$

and transform them into a different series of complex numbers $\{Y\}$ by an equation

$$Y_n = \frac{2}{M} \sum_{k=0}^{M-1} X_k \, e^{\frac{-j2\pi kn}{M}} \qquad (12.1)$$

for n=0,1,...,M-1

This is called the discrete Fourier transform, or DFT. A program was given earlier to calculate part of this transformation which followed this definition exactly, and used the clever little

subroutine SWING to produce the necessary cosines without calling the COS function more than once. Now, using arrays it is possible to calculate all the results $\{Y\}$ from tabulated values of $\{X\}$. You should not attempt to follow this case study without first understanding subroutine SLOWF1 in Section 10.3. It would also be useful to have tried Problem 11.2.

If you have the values of $\{Y\}$ calculated as in equation 12.1, you can get back to the original values of $\{X\}$ by

$$X_k = \frac{1}{2} \sum_{n=0}^{M-1} Y_n \, e^{\frac{j2\pi kn}{M}} \qquad (12.2)$$

for k = 0,1,...,M-1

The interpretation and properties of these transforms have to be left to more specialized textbooks. However, it is easy to see that a program which evaluates equation 12.1 by following the definition does a sum of M operations - with what is meant by an 'operation' being effectively a complex multiplication and addition. Along the way, the same values of $\{X\}$ are used over and over again, and they may be multiplied by the same sine or cosine several times in different sums.

The clever person who invented the FFT found a way of breaking the DFT down into something like

$$Y_{c+\frac{M}{2}d} = \frac{2}{M} \sum_{a=0}^{1} e^{\frac{-j2\pi ad}{2}} e^{\frac{-j2\pi ac}{M}}$$

$$\sum_{b=0}^{\frac{M}{2}-1} e^{\frac{-j2\pi bc}{M/2}} X_{a+2b} \qquad (12.3)$$

'the Cooley-Tukey method.'

Now this looks awful, but is not as bad as it seems. The values of n and k in equation 12.1 have been split up by using

$$k = a + 2b$$
for $a = 0,1$
and $b = 0,1,\ldots,M/2-1$

and $n = c + M/2\ d$
for $c = 0,1,\ldots,M/2-1$
and $d = 0,1$

If you were to make the substitution for k and n, you would be able to get the same result quite easily. There is another split, which is known as the Sande-Tukey method.

The brilliant part of this lies in realizing that this horrid equation suggests a new way of evaluating $\{Y\}$. First you evaluate all the M possible results of the inner sum:

$$Z_{c+\frac{M}{2}a} = \sum_{b=0}^{\frac{M}{2}-1} e^{\frac{-j2\pi bc}{M/2}} X_{a+2b} \quad (12.4)$$

for $c = 0,1,\ldots,M/2-1$
first with a=0 and then with a=1

You can see that this is the same as doing the DFT of every second number in $\{X\}$, first the even ones when a=0 and then the odd ones when a=1.

To finish, calculate all the possible results of

$$Y_{c+\frac{M}{2}d} = \frac{2}{M} \sum_{a=0}^{1} e^{\frac{-j2\pi ad}{2}} e^{\frac{-j2\pi ac}{M}} Z_{c+\frac{M}{2}a} \quad (12.5)$$

for $c = 0,1,\ldots,M/2-1$
and $d = 0,1$

This is easier than it looks because both a and d can only be 0 or 1. The term

$$W_{ac} = e^{\frac{-j2\pi ac}{M}}$$

has a=0 half the time, and therefore has the value 1.0 as the first half of the sum. Also the term

$$e^{\frac{-j2\pi ad}{2}} = \cos(\pi ad) - j\ \sin(\pi ad)$$

is always 1 or -1. Actually equation 12.5 is the same as making a lot of little DFTs of length 2 except for the intervention of W, which is called the 'twiddle factor'. Yes, really!

Therefore, ignoring the factor 2/M for now, equation 12.5 is like

$$Y_c = X_c + W_{ac} X_{c+M/2}$$
$$Y_{c+M/2} = X_c - W_{ac} X_{c+M/2}$$
$$(12.6)$$

and this rather simple pair of equations holds the key.

So what has been saved? In evaluating equation 12.4, not very much (yet). In 12.4 there are M possible results, each involving M/2 terms, for a total of $M^2/2$ - half the effort involved in 12.1. But in 12.5 there are also M results, each involving essentially two terms. So the other half of the effort of 12.1 has been reduced from $M^2/2$ to 2M, a great saving. To achieve this, M has to be an even number. Further big savings are gained if equation 12.4 is itself broken down again and again, until the whole process is made into a series of DFTs of length 2 and twiddle factors.

As an illustration, take the simple case of four numbers. Often drawings known as 'butterfly diagrams' are used to illustrate how the procedure works. Fig. 12.7 shows the original complex numbers X, the intermediate sums Z, the twiddle factors W, and the final results Y. From equation 12.4,

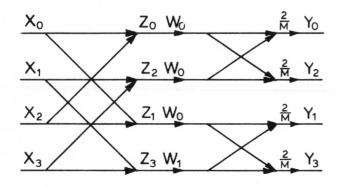

Fig.12.7. Butterfly diagram for
FFT of length 4.

$$Z_0 = X_0 + X_2$$

$$Z_1 = X_0 - X_2$$

$$Z_2 = X_1 + X_3 \qquad (12.7)$$

$$Z_3 = X_1 - X_3$$

and so in the butterfly, a rising line represents combination by adding, a falling one subtracting. Then, noting that $W_0 = 1.0$,

$$Y_0 = Z_0 + Z_2$$

$$Y_1 = Z_1 + W_1 Z_3$$

$$Y_2 = Z_0 - Z_2 \qquad (12.8)$$

$$Y_3 = Z_1 - W_1 Z_3$$

The best result in the general case is obtained when M is a power of 2. If this is so, the FFT becomes a lot of little steps which are all nice easy DFTs of length 2, done by adding and subtracting with twiddle factors in between, just like equation 12.6. For example, if there are 8 numbers, there are three stages:

(i) 4 different DFTs of length 2 on data spaced 4 apart (M=2 in equation 12.5).

(ii) These are combined to make 2 different DFTs of length 4 on data spaced 2 apart (M=4 in equation 12.5).

(iii) These are combined to make the final DFT of length 8 (M=8 in equation 12.5).

Every step is based on equation 12.5, and produces two sums assuming that the values of Z have already been produced, as they have by the previous step. Fig. 12.8 shows the butterfly diagram for a FFT of length 8. To do it there are three stages of 8 operations, a total of 24 operations compared to 64 if the DFT had been done the conventional way. With even larger transforms, the savings become truly spectacular. There is one important complication. In both of Figs 12.7 and 12.8 it will be noticed that the results come back in the wrong order and get disordered progressively with each stage. This is because we want to use the same FORTRAN array for the results as for the data. In doing equation 12.5, we would want to take the values of Z from c + M/2 a as if they had come from equation 12.4. However, looking at equation 12.4 reveals that this is not possible, because the X data were taken from a + 2b and so can only go back to a + 2c. Furthermore, in Fig. 12.8, it can be seen that the twiddle factors occur in the wrong order as we move down the butterfly diagram. To get them in the right order, it is necessary to take the index c out of order. This is very inconvenient. However, refer to Fig. 12.9. Here, we scramble the data before the transform, so that after each stage the results get unscrambled progressively, and it turns out that every value is precisely where we want it as the transform progresses. You could spend many happy hours studying these drawings.

Let us suppose that the data are pre-scrambled. We now wish to create a FORTRAN program based on equation 12.5. Suppose the actual total FFT length is N, a power of 2. In equation 12.5, M will be the lengths of the intermediate DFTs produced at a particular stage. The procedure will start

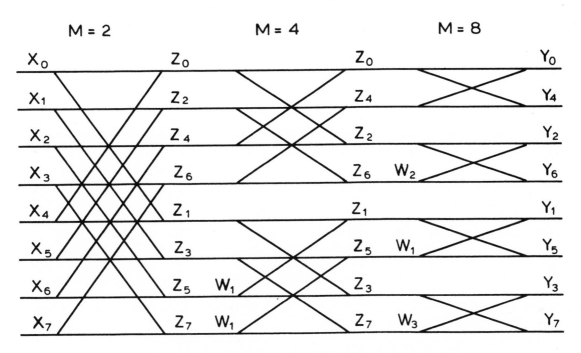

Fig.12.8. Butterfly diagram for the FFT of length 8 on data originally in natural order.

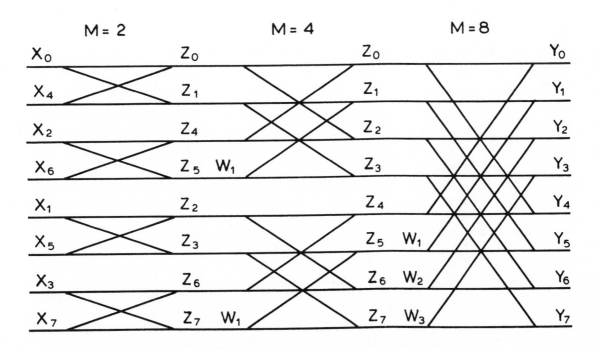

Fig.12.9. Butterfly diagram for the FFT of length 8 on data prescrambled into bit–reverse order. The results appear in natural order.

with M=2, and double it each time until at the last stage M is the same as N. There are $\log_2 N$ stages. In each stage there are N/M different DFTs of length M to be produced, from data that are N/M apart. The total number of operations in the entire FFT is effectively $N \log_2 N$, which is spectacularly more efficient than the N^2 implied by equation 12.1.

To achieve this for pre-scrambled data, we obtain the beginning of the M/N different transforms in a stage using

$$KFORM=\emptyset, M, 2*M, \ldots$$

and then obtain the M/2 values of c as

$$INDEXC=\emptyset, 1, \ldots, M/2-1$$

The required Z values are

```
ZØ=X(KFORM+INDEXC)
Z1=X(KFORM+INDEXC+M/2)
```

Apply the twiddle factor to Z1, and

```
YØ=ZØ+W*Z1
Y1=ZØ-W*Z1
```

and put the results back in the array.

To actually do this in FORTRAN, it is necessary to realize that we are working with complex numbers. Therefore the data arises in two arrays, XR and XI. In the subroutine, the value of π will be referred to, as will the real constants 0.0, 1.0, 2.0, and 4.0. Therefore the subroutine begins as follows:

```
       SUBROUTINE FASTG(XR,XI,N)
C
C COMPLEX DISCRETE FAST FOURIER
C TRANSFORM, PRESCRAMBLED DATA
C
C XR = INPUT REAL ARRAY REAL
C        PARTS TO BE TRANSFORMED,
C        OUTPUT REAL PART OF
C        RESULT, LENGTH N
C XI = INPUT REAL ARRAY IMAGINARY
C        PARTS TO BE TRANSFORMED,
C        OUTPUT IMAGINARY PART OF
C        RESULT,LENGTH N
C  N = INTEGER VALUE, LENGTH OF
C        TRANSFORM, A POWER OF 2
```

```
       DIMENSION XR(Ø:N-1),XI(Ø:N-1)
       PARAMETER(ONE=1.Ø,TWO=2.Ø)
       PARAMETER(FOUR=4.Ø)
       PIE=FOUR*ATAN(ONE)
```

We begin with M=2, and cycle through the necessary transforms:

```
       M=2
C SELECT THE N/M TRANSFORMS
 1Ø DO 2Ø KFORM=Ø,N-1,M
       DO 2Ø INDEXC=Ø,M/2-1
          IØ=KFORM+INDEXC
          I1=IØ+M/2
          ZRØ=XR(IØ)
          ZIØ=XI(IØ)
          ZR1=XR(I1)
          ZI1=XI(I1)
```

and carry out the actual calculation:

```
C  CALCULATE TWIDDLE FACTOR
          ANGL=TWO*PIE*INDEXC/M
          TWIDR=COS(ANGL)
          TWIDI=SIN(ANGL)
C APPLY TWIDDLE FACTOR
          TT=TWIDR*ZR1+TWIDI*ZI1
          ZI1=TWIDR*ZI1-TWIDI*ZR1
          ZR1=TT
C FLUTTER BY
          XR(IØ)=ZRØ+ZR1
          XI(IØ)=ZIØ+ZI1
          XR(I1)=ZRØ-ZR1
          XI(I1)=ZIØ-ZI1
 2Ø CONTINUE
```

Finally the next value of M is selected, and the process is repeated while M≤N. At the end the scaling factor 2/N is applied:

```
C SELECT M FOR NEXT STAGE
       M=M*2
       IF(M.LE.N)GO TO 1Ø
C APPLY SCALE FACTOR TO RESULT
       FACTOR=TWO/N
       DO 3Ø K=Ø,N-1
          XR(K)=XR(K)*FACTOR
          XI(K)=XI(K)*FACTOR
 3Ø CONTINUE
       END
```

EXERCISE:

Although the program given above is not yet refined to its full beauty, there are a number of things in its implementation that are worth thinking about. Examine this program to determine:

(i) why are the subscripts I0 and I1 precalculated?
(ii) why are TWIDR and TWIDI used? Could you just include the COS and SIN functions where you need them? And what about ANGL?
(iii) What is the purpose of the real variable TT?
(iv) What has happened to the step

$$Y\emptyset=Z\emptyset+W*Z1$$
$$Y1=Z\emptyset-W*Z1$$

In doing the above FFT, the COS and SIN functions are each used N log N times. With the clever subroutine SWING from Section 10.3, this can be very much reduced. The twiddle factors in each stage always start with

$$TWIDR=1.\emptyset$$
$$TWIDI=\emptyset.\emptyset$$

and advance through angles equally spaced by $2\pi/M$ as INDEXC increments. Therefore SWING can be used. Before each stage compute

$$CB=COS(2\pi/M)$$
$$SB=SIN(2\pi/M)$$

and at the end of the loop which changes INDEXC, get a new twiddle factor using SWING:

CALL SWING(TWIDR,TWIDI,CB,SB)

Indeed, there is no reason not to change the order of nesting of the loops to reduce the number of times that the twiddle factor is computed. Also, the case c=0 occurs often enough to make it worthwhile skipping over the multiplication by the twiddle factor when this occurs. Finally there is a certain amount of invariant coding within the inner loop which can be removed. Here, then, is the subroutine FASTG, serenely beautiful, yet efficient:

```
      SUBROUTINE FASTG(XR,XI,N)
C
C COMPLEX DISCRETE FAST FOURIER
C TRANSFORM, PRESCRAMBLED DATA
C
C XR = INPUT REAL ARRAY REAL
C        PARTS TO BE TRANSFORMED,
C        OUTPUT REAL PART OF
C        RESULT, LENGTH N
C XI = INPUT REAL ARRAY IMAGINARY
C        PARTS TO BE TRANSFORMED,
C        OUTPUT IMAGINARY PART OF
C        RESULT,LENGTH N
C  N = INTEGER VALUE, LENGTH OF
C        TRANSFORM, A POWER OF 2
C
      DIMENSION XR(Ø:N-1),XI(Ø:N-1)
      PARAMETER(ZERO=Ø.Ø,ONE=1.Ø)
      PARAMETER(TWO=2.Ø,FOUR=4.Ø)
      PIE=FOUR*ATAN(ONE)
      M=2
   1Ø TWIDR=ONE
      TWIDI=ZERO
      ANGL=TWO*PIE/M
      CB=COS(ANGL)
      SB=SIN(ANGL)
      MBY2=M/2
      DO 3Ø INDEXC=Ø,MBY2-1
        DO 2Ø IØ=INDEXC,N-1,M
          I1=IØ+MBY2
          ZRØ=XR(IØ)
          ZIØ=XI(IØ)
          ZR1=XR(I1)
          ZI1=XI(I1)
          IF(INDEXC.NE.Ø)THEN
C APPLY TWIDDLE FACTOR
            TT=TWIDR*ZR1+TWIDI*ZI1
            ZI1=TWIDR*ZI1-TWIDI*ZR1
            ZR1=TT
          END IF
          XR(IØ)=ZRØ+ZR1
          XI(IØ)=ZIØ+ZI1
          XR(I1)=ZRØ-ZR1
          XI(I1)=ZIØ-ZI1
   2Ø   CONTINUE
C GET THE NEXT TWIDDLE FACTOR
        CALL SWING(TWIDR,TWIDI,CB,SB)
   3Ø CONTINUE
C SELECT M FOR NEXT STAGE
      M=M*2
      IF(M.LE.N)GO TO 1Ø
C APPLY SCALE FACTOR TO RESULT
      FACTOR=TWO/N
      DO 4Ø K=Ø,N-1
        XR(K)=XR(K)*FACTOR
        XI(K)=XI(K)*FACTOR
   4Ø CONTINUE
      END
```

EXERCISE:

FASTG operates on scrambled data. In fact they are in bit-reverse order; $\log_2 N$ bits of each subscript should be reversed to give the scrambled subscript. The reversal can be done by exchanging values in pairs according to the method outlined in Problem 7.5. You want to write a subroutine

    SUBROUTINE SCRAG(XRAY,N)

which bit reverses the given real array XRAY of N elements, where N is a power of 2. A proper FFT could then be done by subroutine FASTG, as follows:

```
    SUBROUTINE FASTF(XR,XI,N)
C
C COMPLEX DISCRETE FAST FOURIER
C TRANSFORM, PRESCRAMBLES DATA
C
C XR = INPUT REAL ARRAY REAL
C       PARTS TO BE TRANSFORMED,
C       OUTPUT REAL PART OF
C       RESULT, LENGTH N
C XI = INPUT REAL ARRAY IMAGINARY
C       PARTS TO BE TRANSFORMED,
C       OUTPUT IMAGINARY PART OF
C       RESULT, LENGTH N
C  N = INTEGER VALUE, LENGTH OF
C       TRANSFORM, A POWER OF 2
C
C FIRST GET THEM SCRAMBLED
    CALL SCRAG(XR,N)
    CALL SCRAG(XI,N)
C THEN THE TRANSFORM ITSELF
    CALL FASTG(XR,XI,N)
    END
```

If you can't write SCRAG using Brenner's bit-reverse counting, it is more or less done for you in Section 7.7 by a less efficient method.

This is not, of course, the end of the story. There is the question of the inverse transform, easily solved. To do an inverse transform from $\{Y\}$ to $\{X\}$, conjugate $\{Y\}$, i.e. change the sign of the imaginary parts, and then use the forward transform. The scale factor will be wrong. Actually, if you use the forward transform to do an inverse transform without touching the data beforehand, you get the correct result (apart from the scale factor) in reverse order.

This FFT program has depended on the decomposition of the DFT into stages using operations of length 2. This is called a radix 2 FFT. The radix 4 butterfly of Fig.12.7 can be implemented very easily just by writing out the operations. Therefore a further, less dramatic, improvement in efficiency can be obtained by using a decomposition into operations of length 4, a radix 4 transform. Indeed radix 8 and radix 16 transforms are known. However to allow N to be any power of 2, a higher radix transform may have to finish off with stages of smaller radix; therefore these programs can be a bit long.

In addition, FFTs have been developed to give greater efficiency in cases where all the data are real, not complex. In fact there is a way of applying the FFT to data of any length N, using an intermediate calculation called the Chirp transform. Once introduced to the delights of the FFT, it can go on for a lifetime. Most people, however, are more interested in using them than in developing their own! For that reason, you will find subroutine SCRAG in a little Appendix after Chapter 19. But don't tell the others.

13
Multidimensional arrays and storage

13.1 Introduction

The two previous Chapters have concentrated a great deal of attention on arrays of one dimension and the use of subscripts with them. It will come as no surprise now to find that it is possible to have arrays of higher dimension whose members are addressed by using between two and seven subscripts. Often in dealing with multidimensional arrays, the subscripts are being varied in complicated ways, usually in nested DO-loops, and even experienced programmers have to be very careful in understanding and organizing their calculations. There is no point in leaping into multidimensional arrays unless the concepts of arrays and subscripts are firmly established for the case of one dimension. If in doubt, go back over Chapter 11.

13.2 Arrays and subscripts in main programs

As explained in earlier Chapters, arrays of one dimension have space assigned to them by the DIMENSION statement

DIMENSION name(subscript limits),...

where the array called 'name', whose type is normally implied by its name, is given the space requested by the subscript limits. The size of the array and the range of allowed subscripts are both defined by the subscript limits which in a main program must be expressions which involve only integer constants. In the simplest form, if the size is given by a single integer constant expression, then the lower subscript bound is one. There are special facilities for dimensioning in subroutines

and these will be revealed in a later section of this Chapter.

EXAMPLE:
 The statements

PARAMETER(ISIX=6)
DIMENSION STATS(13),EAGLES(Ø:1Ø)
DIMENSION JAYS(-ISIX:ISIX)

define three arrays of one dimension. STATS is a real array of length 13, whose subscripts can have the range 1 to 13. EAGLES is a real array with 11 elements and subscript range 0 to 10, and JAYS has 13 elements subscripted from -6 to 6.

A subscript used with an array can be any integer expression whose value falls within the bounds for that array.

EXAMPLES:
 The following references may be made to the above arrays:

STATS(8)	is valid
STATS(Ø)	is incorrect because lower bound is 1
STATS(I*3-J)	is valid if $1 \leq I*3-J \leq 13$
EAGLES(Ø)	is valid
JAYS(K)	is valid if $-6 \leq K \leq 6$

When using arrays of two or more dimensions the situation is very similar. Then the DIMENSION statement simply specifies bounds for each subscript; arrays can have up to seven dimensions, but applications of more than two are somewhat rare. The DIMENSION statement in its most general form is then

DIMENSION name(integer bounds
      [,integer bounds,...]),...

where up to seven sets of bounds can be given for each name. An array of two dimensions has two sets of bounds, one of three dimensions has three sets and so on.

EXAMPLES:

The following statements define multi-dimensional arrays.

```
DIMENSION TWODEE(5,5),THIN(0:9,4)
DIMENSION WIDE(2,23),P(4,5,6)
DIMENSION RAVER(2,3,2,3,2,3,2)
```

Once a multidimensional array is established, it must always be used with the correct number of subscripts, as must an array of only one dimension. The array TWODEE defined above is an array of two dimensions, and both subscripts can run from 1 to 5. The size of the array is therefore 25 elements. In general the size of a multidimensional array is the product of the sizes of its individual subscript bounds. RAVER is therefore a seven dimensional array which has 432 members despite the modest looking size of its individual bounds. Multidimensional arrays can get very big!

Conceptually, an array of one dimension can form either a vector or a list. This interpretation as a vector has some importance in the next Chapter. Similarly a two dimensional array will form a table or a matrix. For example, suppose that a geographical area is divided into a 5x6 grid, as in Fig. 13.1, and the birth rate is recorded for each sector. Then it is possible (and logical) to hold this data in an array of two dimensions, called BIRTH, say, as illustrated by Fig.13.1. Space could be set aside for the array by a DIMENSION statement like

DIMENSION BIRTH(5,6)

Using such an array is very easy. For two dimensions it is convenient to think of the first subscript as the row number and the second as the column number. BIRTH(I,J) is therefore in row I and column J. With experience this identification becomes automatic, but there is a trap to avoid which will be seen later in this Chapter.

Suppose the mean birth rate for the entire district is desired. It may be easy enough to find it in one dimension, but what about two? Setting aside the question of assigning the values by a DATA statement until the next section, the part of the program which finds the average birth rate is

```
      SUM=0.0
      DO 2 I=1,5
      DO 1 J=1,6
      SUM=SUM+BIRTH(I,J)
    1 CONTINUE
    2 CONTINUE
```

Here, the program in nested DO-loops runs through the entire array and adds up the values, then finds the average in the variable AVG. Note that the index which is associated with each dimension has respected the bounds. Index I has addressed 5 rows and J has referred to 6 columns, and so the whole array has been covered.

EXERCISE:

Write the FORTRAN statements to find the largest birth rate and its position in the array.

An array of three dimensions could be considered as a block. There is no standard conceptual layout, but two are suggested. The simplest is to consider that the third dimension adds depth to a normal two dimensional array, as is illustrated by Fig.13.2a. Here, supposing X is a 5x5x5 array, a subscript X(I,J,K) refers to row I, column J, level K and the corners are as labelled; the hidden corner is X(5,1,5).

An alternative might be to follow the mathematical x,y,z directions as in Fig. 13.2b, in which the hidden corner is X(1,1,1).

Beyond three dimensions the physical interpretation, if any, of the layout of an array is up to the user.

EXAMPLE:

A special array, called a unit matrix, is a square two dimensional array in which all members are zero except the ones along the diagonal of the square, as illustrated below.

$$\begin{bmatrix} 1.0 & 0.0 & 0.0 & 0.0 & 0.0 \\ 0.0 & 1.0 & 0.0 & 0.0 & 0.0 \\ 0.0 & 0.0 & 1.0 & 0.0 & 0.0 \\ 0.0 & 0.0 & 0.0 & 1.0 & 0.0 \\ 0.0 & 0.0 & 0.0 & 0.0 & 1.0 \end{bmatrix}$$

The efficient way to define this in a program is to write the program as if the whole array were being set to zero in a doubly nested loop, except that after each row is cleared, the diagonal of that row is set to one. Here is the program:

```
      DIMENSION UNIT(5,5)
      DO 2 I=1,5
      DO 1 J=1,5
      UNIT(I,J)=0.0
  1   CONTINUE
      UNIT(I,I)=1.0
  2   CONTINUE
```

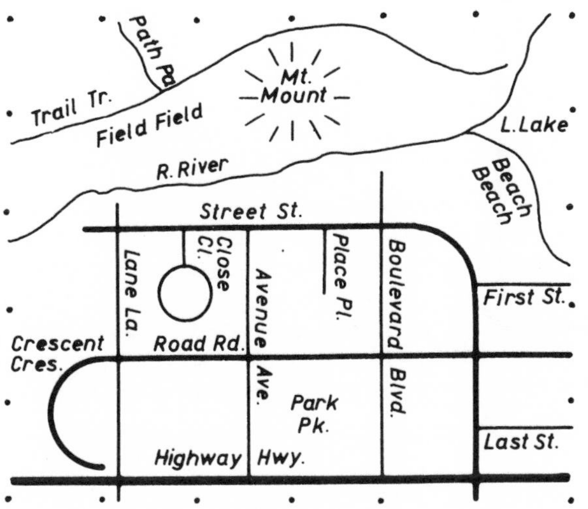

(a) County County

2.57	4.69	3.60	3.17	3.10	4.83
3.50	4.20	4.49	2.81	4.55	4.85
4.76	3.60	3.29	4.71	3.79	3.62
2.95	4.96	4.38	4.47	3.12	3.51
4.53	3.79	3.21	2.52	3.10	3.93

(b) The grid and birth rates

BIRTH(1,1)	BIRTH(1,2)	BIRTH(1,3)	BIRTH(1,4)	BIRTH(1,5)	BIRTH(1,6)
2.57	4.69	3.60	3.17	3.10	4.83
BIRTH(2,1)	BIRTH(2,2)	BIRTH(2,3)	BIRTH(2,4)	BIRTH(2,5)	BIRTH(2,6)
3.50	4.20	4.49	2.81	4.55	4.85
BIRTH(3,1)	BIRTH(3,2)	BIRTH(3,3)	BIRTH(3,4)	BIRTH(3,5)	BIRTH(3,6)
4.76	3.60	3.29	4.71	3.79	3.62
BIRTH(4,1)	BIRTH(4,2)	BIRTH(4,3)	BIRTH(4,4)	BIRTH(4,5)	BIRTH(4,6)
2.95	4.96	4.38	4.47	3.12	3.51
BIRTH(5,1)	BIRTH(5,2)	BIRTH(5,3)	BIRTH(5,4)	BIRTH(5,5)	BIRTH(5,6)
4.53	3.79	3.21	2.52	3.10	3.93

(c) The array BIRTH

Fig.13.1. The birth rate per 1000 of population in County County arranged as the real array BIRTH.

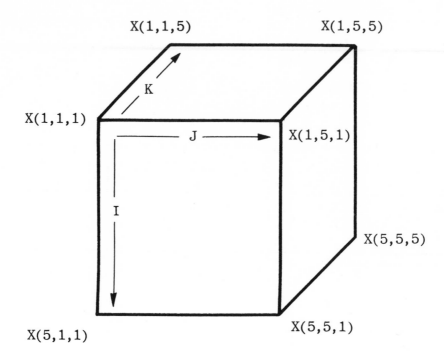

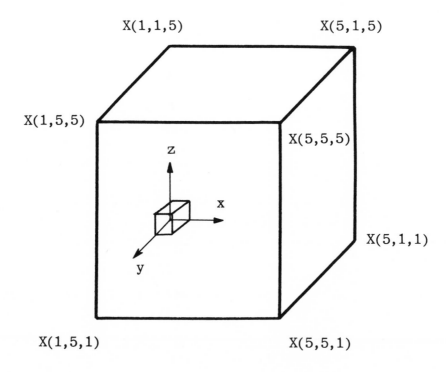

Fig. 13.2. Two possible interpretations of a three
dimensional array.

As this is a simple but important example in using an array of two dimensions, it is vital that every step of it should be understood, otherwise many of the things that follow will be complete mysteries.

EXAMPLE:

To help the reader to manage his financial affairs, a table of loan repayments is calculated. It is assumed that XLOAN units of currency are borrowed, to be repaid over N periods at an interest rate of INT% per period.

Theory: Whenever regular payments are made, whether it is savings or loan repayments, a geometric series is then formed. If you borrow an amount XLOAN, and make a repayment at the end of the first period, called PMT, then after that first payment you owe

$$XLOAN*FACTOR-PMT$$

where

$$FACTOR=1.0+FLOAT(INT)/100.0$$

is the magnification of your loan by the interest charged in each period. During the second period, what you owe is magnified again, and at the end you make another repayment. Then you owe

$$(XLOAN*FACTOR-PMT)*FACTOR-PMT$$

You will find that after N periods you owe

$$XLOAN*FACTOR**N$$

$$-PMT*(FACTOR**(N-1)+FACTOR**(N-2)$$

$$+...+FACTOR+1.0)$$

which sums to

$$XLOAN*FACTOR**N$$

$$-PMT*(1.0-FACTOR**N)/(1.0-FACTOR)$$

The loan is repaid when this falls to zero.

The part

$$XLOAN*FACTOR**N$$

represents how much you would owe if you made no repayments at all, and the part

$$PMT*(1.0-FACTOR**N)/(1.0-FACTOR)$$

represents the accumulated value of your payments. This could be used on its own to calculate how much can be saved by regular investment.

The reader will probably agree that this is complicated enough to be worth presenting as a table, and although he does not yet know how to print a table, a program is given here. The table is printed to cover a loan of 100 units at rates of 4%, 8%, 12% and 16%, and to cover loans lasting for between 1 and 25 periods. This is calculated in an array of size 25 by 4.

```
C CALCULATE LOAN REPAYMENTS TABLE
      DIMENSION PMT(25,4)
C FOUR DIFFERENT INTEREST RATES
      DO 10 I=1,4
      INT=4*I
      FACTOR=1.0+FLOAT(INT)/100.0
C TWENTY-FIVE DIFFERENT PERIODS
      DO 10 N=1,25
      OWING=100.0*FACTOR**N
      TOP=1.0-FACTOR
      BOT=1.0-FACTOR**N
      PMT(N,I)=OWING*TOP/BOT
  10  CONTINUE
C PRINT THE TABLE
      PRINT'(13X,''PAYMENT TABLE'')'
      PRINT'(17X,''RATES'')'
      PRINT 20,(4*L,L=1,4)
  20 FORMAT(' PERIODS',4I6)
      DO 30 K=1,25
      PRINT 40,K,(PMT(K,L),L=1,4)
  30 CONTINUE
  40 FORMAT(3X,I2,4X,4F6.1)
      END
```

EXERCISE:
Run this program.

EXERCISE:

Using the same approach, work out how to calculate the amount still owing after each repayment on a loan of 1000 units over N periods at i%. Write a program to produce a set of tables. Do this in an array of three dimensions.

13.3 The storage of arrays — DATA statements

Before multidimensional arrays can be given values in DATA statements, or used for input and output, it is helpful to know how they are arranged in the storage of a computer. When a FORTRAN program is executed, the memory of the computer holds the "compiled" version of the program along with all its variables and constants. The ordinary variables of a program represent single values and occupy a particular amount of space in the memory which will be called one "location". Array variables occupy an amount of space which is the size specified for the array in the DIMENSION statement. An array such as BIRTH of dimensions 5 by 6 occupies 30 locations. The memory is actually ordered and, not surprisingly, the space reserved for an array is a continuous block in the memory.

An array of one dimension is stored so that its subscripts refer to consecutive spaces; in Fig. 13.3 a possible storage scheme is shown for a program with the DIMENSION statement

DIMENSION ICOEFF(∅:1∅)

which also refers to ordinary variables N, IR, and K and to the integer constants IMID (value 3), IMAD (value 4), 0, 1, and 9. In fact this could be the program for calculating and printing the binomial coefficients which was used as an example in Section 5 of Chapter 11. Within the array ICOEFF, the memory locations will be grouped together in 11 successive spaces as might be expected.

Now consider a DATA statement used with an array. The statements

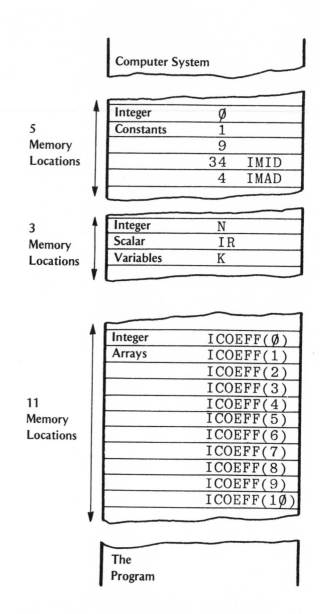

Fig. 13.3. Arrangement of variables in the memory of a typical computer including the integer array of one dimension ICOEFF.

DIMENSION NUMBS(1∅)
DATA NUMBS/1,2,3,4,5,6,7,8,9,∅/

produce a block of storage which is reserved and which has values assigned to it in advance, as in Fig. 13.4.

For multidimensional arrays, the memory locations used are also consecutive, but it is important to know exactly how the multidimensional subscripts map onto the computer's memory, which is only one dimensional. In fact it is the first subscript which varies most rapidly. This

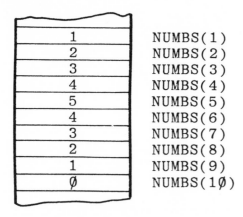

Fig. 13.4. The array NUMBS with values assigned by a DATA statement.

means that an array of two dimensions is stored in column order, so that a DATA statement which refers to a two dimensional array must assign values to the array by going down successive columns. Fig. 13.5 shows the values defined by the statements

```
DIMENSION IQ(3,3)
DATA IQ/1ØØ,13Ø,16Ø,11Ø,14Ø,17Ø,
        12Ø,15Ø,18Ø/
```

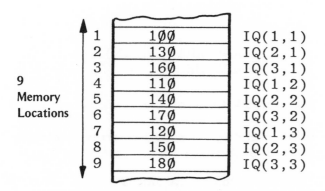

Fig. 13.5. Arrangement of the 3 x 3 array IQ in memory showing initial values defined by a DATA statement.

If a DATA statement is given an array name, there must be a value given for each array element. The special array which has zeros everywhere but on the diagonal, as used in an example in the last section, could be defined by the statements

```
DIMENSION UNIT(5,5)
DATA UNIT/1.Ø,5*Ø.Ø,1.Ø,5*Ø.Ø,
        1.Ø,5*Ø.Ø,1.Ø,5*Ø.Ø,1.Ø/
```

This is not a better or worse way than before, merely different. Either might be useful in different circumstances.

Of course, implied DO-loops could be used nested to change the order. The following statements define the array THINGS in row order:

```
DIMENSION THINGS(-3:3,3)
DATA((THINGS(I,J),J=-3,3),I=1,3)/
        7*1.Ø,7*2.Ø,7*3.Ø/
```

EXERCISE:
    Draw a memory map of the array THINGS similar to Fig. 13.5.

For higher dimensions than two the idea of rows or columns disappears, and it is necessary to remember the rule:

> The first subscript varies most rapidly

It is then logical that the second subscript varies the second most rapidly, and so on.

Thus, the array defined by

$$\text{DIMENSION XRAY}(2,3,4)$$

is stored as shown in Fig. 13.6, and it could be given the values shown by the statement

```
DATA(((XRAY(I,J,K),K=1,4),J=1,3),
        I=1,2)/12*1,12*2/
```

EXAMPLE:
    The array BIRTH used in the previous section can be defined by a series of DATA statements. For clarity, it is often a good idea to do it this way - and very much easier to make changes.

```
DATA (BIRTH(1,K),K=1,5)/2.57,4.69,3.60,3.17,3.10,4.83/
DATA (BIRTH(2,K),K=1,5)/3.50,4.20,4.49,2.81,4.55,4.85/
DATA (BIRTH(3,K),K=1,5)/4.76,3.60,3.29,4.71,3.79,3.62/
DATA (BIRTH(4,K),K=1,5)/2.95,4.96,4.38,4.47,3.12,3.51/
DATA (BIRTH(5,K),K=1,5)/4.53,3.79,3.21,2.52,3.10,3.93/
```

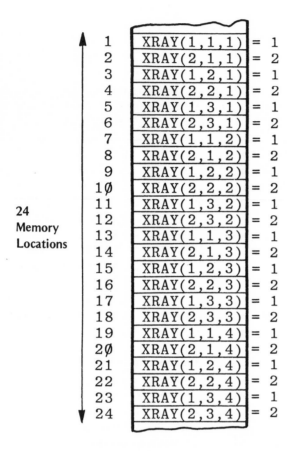

24
Memory
Locations

Fig. 13.6. Arrangement of the 2 x 3 x 4 array XRAY in
the memory of a typical computer.

13.4 Reading and printing of arrays —
the transposition syndrome

Arrays of one dimension were easy to
use in the input and output statements
of FORTRAN. To obtain the entire array,
the name was given in an input/output
list. A single element was printed if a
subscript was used, and a range of
subscripts could be covered by an implied
DO-loop. In any event, if a FORMAT was
used, the correct number and type of
FORMAT specifications had to be given.

The situation with multidimensional arrays
is similar. Given an array XRAY defined
by

```
       DIMENSION XRAY(2,3,4)
```

a single member could be read by

```
       READ*,XRAY(1,2,3)
```

or printed by

```
    WRITE(6,'(1XF10.5)')XRAY(1,K,1)
```

The statements

```
       DO 2 I=1,2
       DO 2 J=1,3
       DO 2 K=1,4
       PRINT 1,XRAY(I,J,K)
     1 FORMAT(1XF10.5)
     2 CONTINUE
```

are probably not useful because each
repetition of the PRINT statement begins
a new line; similarly

```
       DO 1 I=1,2
       DO 1 J=1,3
       DO 1 K=1,4
       READ*,XRAY(I,J,K)
     1 CONTINUE
```

asks for 24 lines or cards of input.

More usefully, the entire array could be
printed by writing

```
       PRINT 20,XRAY
    20 FORMAT(1X,6F10.5)
```

to get the output on 4 lines, and here
it is important to remember the rule:

> The first subscript varies
> most rapidly

This can be changed by the use of
implied DO-loops as in

```
WRITE(6,2Ø)(((XRAY(I,J,K),
         K=1,4),J=1,3),I=1,2)
2Ø FORMAT(1X,4F1Ø.5)
```

which prints on 6 lines.

In a similar way an implied DO-loop can be used to address only part of the array

```
READ(5,2Ø)(XRAY(1,1,K),K=1,4)
2Ø FORMAT(4F15.8)
```

A problem arises called the 'transposition syndrome' when using arrays of two dimensions; it causes a lot of confusion among programmers, usually novices, but it can also affect some surprisingly experienced people. FORTRAN varies its first subscript most rapidly, in contrast to the long established notation used by mathematicians for arrays. The usual mathematical shorthand for a 3x3 array is

$$A = \begin{bmatrix} A(1,1) & A(1,2) & A(1,3) \\ A(2,1) & A(2,2) & A(2,3) \\ A(3,1) & A(3,2) & A(3,3) \end{bmatrix}$$

so for consistency a programmer should remember that A(I,J) refers to row I and column J.

Unfortunately, as was discussed above, FORTRAN was originally designed so that it will read and write arrays of two dimensions in column order. Suppose that A was defined by

```
DIMENSION IA(3,3)
DATA IA/1,4,7,2,5,8,3,6,9/
```

or alternatively by

```
DATA((IA(I,J),J=1,3),I=1,3)/
        1,2,3,4,5,6,7,8,9/
```

then in either case it contains

$$\begin{bmatrix} 1 & 2 & 3 \\ 4 & 5 & 6 \\ 7 & 8 & 9 \end{bmatrix}$$

In a given input or output statement, FORTRAN will vary the first subscript most rapidly and will therefore print the columns across the paper; the unwary could then mistake these columns for rows. Thus,

```
WRITE(6,1)IA
1 FORMAT(1X3I5)
```

would print

```
    1     4     7
............
    2     5     8
............
    3     6     9
............
```

which is not what is wanted.

This is the transposition problem. It is easy for a novice to get his FORTRAN confused with his mathematics and make a lot of errors unless he adopts a consistent approach to this problem. It is all too easy unwittingly to transpose data in error because of this. Similarly a READ statement like

```
READ*,IA
```

expects its data in column order.

The best way around this problem, in the author's opinion, is to adopt as correct the mathematical notation, and then to develop the habit of always writing input and output statements by using implied DO-loops where arrays of two dimensions are concerned. It is best to write

```
WRITE(6,1)((IA(I,J),J=1,3),
                    I=1,3)
1 FORMAT(1X3I5)
```

and get the desired result

```
    1     2     3
............
    4     5     6
............
    7     8     9
............
```

A similar problem arises with tensors, and the solution is the same.

Similarly for input, write

    READ*,((A(I,J),J=1,3),I=1,3)

so that values are read in row order. This takes a bit more effort to write but it is a habit which helps to keep programmers away from some common traps.

EXAMPLE:

In the X,Y plane, a lump whose height is

$$h_1 = 25\sqrt{9 - x^2 - y^2}$$

sticks up through the surface whose height is

$$h_2 = (x - 1)^2 + (y - 1)^2$$

Looking down from above, the higher of these two surfaces would be seen. Here is a program to calculate and print the height seen from above. Where h includes a negative square root, it is taken as zero.

    DIMENSION HEIGHT(-5:5,-5:5)
    DO 10 IX=-5,5
       DO 10 IY=-5,5
          HH=MAX(0,9-IX*IX-IY*IY)
          H1=25.0*SQRT(HH)
          H2=(IX-1)**2+(IY-1)**2
          HEIGHT(IY,IX)=MAX(H1,H2)
    10   CONTINUE
       PRINT 20,((HEIGHT(I,J),
          J=5,-5,-1),I=5,-5,-1)
    20 FORMAT(1X,11F4.0)
       END

EXERCISE:

Obtain the result from this program, and draw on it by hand lines of equal height in the manner of a topographical map. You will see that the lump is in the correct place.

13.5 Multidimensional arrays in subroutines

Just as with arrays of one dimension, there are a number of ways in which multidimensional arrays can be used in subroutines. It is of course possible to use an array which is local to the subroutine, and it is also possible to state the size of the array explicitly. In the subroutine that begins with

    SUBROUTINE BOING(A,B)
    DIMENSION A(5,10),B(5,10),C(5,10)

the real arrays A and B are passed down by the subroutine CALL and so they must originate in a main program, or in another subroutine, which is where their space is set aside. The real array C, on the other hand, is local to subroutine BOING, known only within it and has its memory set aside by this DIMENSION statement. However the three arrays are used in BOING, the true size of each array is 5 x 10 and that is what the dimensions of A and B must have been when they originated.

However suitable this arrangement may be in some circumstances, it is not very general because the subroutine BOING is limited to 5 x 10 arrays. However, it is already known that adjustable dimensions can be passed to a subroutine. The statements

    SUBROUTINE VIEW(PICT,IAX,JAX,KAX)
    DIMENSION PICT(IAX,JAX,KAX)

arrange that the subroutine VIEW does not need to know the values of the three dimensions of the array PICT until it is called, at which time values are given to the dummy arguments IAX, JAX, and KAX.

EXAMPLE:

Here is the subroutine TRANSP to transpose the square array IRAY which is variable in size. To transpose a square array, the element IRAY(I,J) is switched with IRAY(J,I) over the whole array. It is not necessary to do the diagonal members.

```
      SUBROUTINE TRANSP(IRAY,ISIZE)
C
C TRANSPOSE A SQUARE ARRAY IRAY
C
C IRAY = INTEGER ARRAY TO BE
C           TRANSPOSED, DIMENSIONS
C           ISIZE BY ISIZE
C
      DIMENSION IRAY(ISIZE,ISIZE)
      DO 1 I=1,ISIZE-1
        DO 1 J=I+1,ISIZE
          IHOLD=IRAY(I,J)
          IRAY(I,J)=IRAY(J,I)
          IRAY(J,I)=IHOLD
    1 CONTINUE
      RETURN
      END
```

This is another nice example of the use of two subscripts to run through an organized set of operations. Why did the programmer not write

```
      DO 1 I=1,ISIZE
      DO 1 J=1,ISIZE
```

Why is the variable IHOLD used?

Here is a program to use this subroutine; note that the true size of the array originates in the main program.

```
      DIMENSION IA(3,3)
      DATA IA/1,4,7,2,5,8,3,6,9/
      PRINT*,' HERE IS ARRAY BEFORE'
      PRINT 1,((IA(I,J),J=1,3),I=1,3)
    1 FORMAT(1X,3I3)
      CALL TRANSP(IA,3)
      PRINT*,' AND AFTERWARDS'
      PRINT 1,((IA(I,J),J=1,3),I=1,3)
      END
```

Finally, an assumed size can be used, but only for the last subscript. It is possible to write

```
      SUBROUTINE MAD(WILD,N)
      DIMENSION WILD(3*N,*)
```

or

```
      SUBROUTINE CRAZED(LOCO,INUM,JNUM)
      DIMENSION LOCO(INUM,INUM+JNUM,*)
```

but in both of these cases, only the final dimension is assumed. In the next section some trouble is taken to explain this point, and also to show why it is wrong to give an incorrect size for an array, except in very special circumstances (which are poor style anyway).

EXAMPLE:
A programmer wishes to search part of an array for the largest value. This is done in a function which is told the actual size of the first subscript but not the second. All rows are searched but not all columns; the programmer specifies the column limits as JLO and JHI.

```
      FUNCTION FIND(ARAY,N,JLO,JHI)
C
C SEARCH ALL N ROWS OF THE ARRAY
C ARAY FOR THE LARGEST VALUE IN
C COLUMNS JLO TO JHI, WHICH IS
C THE VALUE GIVEN TO THE FUNCTION
C
      DIMENSION ARAY(N,*)
      FIND=ARAY(N,JLO)
      DO 10 I=1,N
        DO 10 J=JLO,JHI
          IF(ARAY(I,J).GT.FIND)THEN
            FIND=ARAY(I,J)
          END IF
   10 CONTINUE
      END
```

13.6 Addresses, subscripts, and telling the truth

The way arrays are arranged in memory has already been described. Following the memory in order, the first subscript varies most rapidly, the second subscript is next, and so on until the last varies least rapidly. Some examples of this are shown in Figs 13.3 to 13.6.

FORTRAN has to calculate the memory address of the array element from the subscripts. It is instructive to know how this is done.

---

* This section can be omitted but some tricky uses of EQUIVALENCE can get you in trouble if you don't know about this.

Consider a two dimensional array defined by

```
DIMENSION IQ(3,3)
DATA IQ/100,130,160,110,140,170,
        120,150,180/
```

and illustrated by Fig. 13.7. Note that the DATA statement assigns values in column order and follows the storage. Since the storage arrangement is known, it is easy for a FORTRAN program to find a given array element in storage, provided it knows the dimensions. A member IQ(I,J) is to be found I+(J-1)*3 locations along the array. This is an important fact because it suggests that for every array of two dimensions there is an equivalent array of one dimension which could be used in its place. In Fig. 13.7,

IQ(I,J) is equivalent to

IQQ(I+(J-1)*3)

and the two programs listed here are equivalent:

```
        DIMENSION IQ(3,3)
        IVAL=100
        DO 30 I=1,3
          DO 30 J=1,3
            IQ(I,J)=IVAL
            IVAL=IVAL+10
30 CONTINUE
```

```
        DIMENSION IQQ(9)
        IVAL=100
        DO 30 I=1,3
          DO 30 J=1,3
            IQQ(I+(J-1)*3)=IVAL
            IVAL=IVAL+10
30 CONTINUE
```

Both programs will define the values of the array as illustrated by Fig. 13.7, although of course in practice a DATA statement would be preferred.

Consider a more general case:

```
SUBROUTINE EXAMPL(ARAY,ID1,ID2)
DIMENSION ARAY(ID1,ID2)
```

1	100	IQ(1,1)	IQQ(1)
2	130	IQ(2,1)	IQQ(2)
3	160	IQ(3,1)	IQQ(3)
4	110	IQ(1,2)	IQQ(4)
5	140	IQ(2,2)	IQQ(5)
6	170	IQ(3,2)	IQQ(6)
7	120	IQ(1,3)	IQQ(7)
8	150	IQ(2,3)	IQQ(8)
9	180	IQ(3,3)	IQQ(9)

Fig. 13.7. Arrangement of the 3 x 3 array IQ in the memory of a typical computer showing an equivalent storage arrangement for the array of one dimension IQQ.

For simplicity, the lower subscript bounds are both 1. This array whose dimensions are ID1 by ID2 would be equivalent to an array of one dimension ID1*ID2, so that it would always be possible to use

```
SUBROUTINE EXAMPL(ARAY,ID1,ID2)
DIMENSION ARAY(ID1*ID2)
```

instead. In this case every two dimensional subscript (I,J) would be replaced by I+(J-1)*ID1 in one dimension; therefore

(I,J) corresponds to address

I+(J-1)*ID1

This may not sound too practical, but there was a time when FORTRAN II and some versions of FORTRAN IV did not support adjustable dimensions, and this meant that subroutines could only be made general by writing them out in one dimension. There is still an important point to be gained from all this as will be seen shortly.

EXAMPLE:
The subroutine TRANSP to transpose a square array was given in the previous section. Here is the same subroutine which still transposes the square array, but which internally pretends that it is of one dimension.

```
      SUBROUTINE TRANSP(IRAY,ISIZE)
C
C TRANSPOSE A SQUARE ARRAY IRAY
C
C IRAY = INTEGER ARRAY TO BE
C            TRANSPOSED, DIMENSIONS
C            ISIZE BY ISIZE
C THIS VERSION USES EQUIVALENT
C ARRAY OF ONE DIMENSION
C
      DIMENSION IRAY(ISIZE*ISIZE)
      DO 1 I=1,ISIZE-1
        DO 1 J=I+1,ISIZE
          IHOLD=IRAY(I+(J-1)*ISIZE)
          IRAY(I+(J-1)*ISIZE)=
                  IRAY(J+(I-1)*ISIZE)
          IRAY(J+(I-1)*ISIZE)=IHOLD
    1 CONTINUE
      END
```

The interest in this example is mainly historical. Because one dimension has been used, the DIMENSION statement could be

$$\text{DIMENSION IRAY}(*)$$

exploiting the fact that the address is worked out explicitly and the dimension is not necessary. In early FORTRAN this was not allowed, but programmers would use

$$\text{DIMENSION IRAY}(1)$$

and this was the only way to make the subroutine general for any matrix size.

This has provided two items of practical importance to FORTRAN 77. First, recall that a subscript (I,J) corresponds to an equivalent address given by $I+(J-1)*ID1$ (still assuming lower bounds of 1 on the subscripts). This tells us that the second dimension, ID2, is not needed in working out the address, and this is the reason why FORTRAN now permits this size to be assumed, but not ID1. Therefore, instead of

```
SUBROUTINE EXAMPL(ARRAY,ID1,ID2)
DIMENSION ARRAY(ID1,ID2)
```

it is possible to write

```
SUBROUTINE EXAMPL(ARRAY,ID1)
DIMENSION ARRAY(ID1,*)
```

The other practical message is that it should now be clear why the true value of ID1 must be given to the subroutine. If the array really has a first dimension which is different to ID1, the addresses will be calculated incorrectly. Therefore, extending this argument to all arrays:

(i) Only the final dimension can be assumed.
(ii) All the others must be given truthfully.

For convenience, the address calculation for all arrays is summarized in Table 13.1, in the completely general case where the lower bounds on the subscripts may not be 1.

Dimensions of Array	Subscript	Equivalent One Dimension Subscript Value
(ILO:IHI)	(I)	$1+(I-ILO)$
(ILO:IHI, JLO:JHI)	(I,J)	$1+(I-ILO)$ $+(J-JLO)*(IHI-ILO+1)$
(ILO:IHI, JLO:JHI, KLO:KHI)	(I,J,K)	$1+(I-ILO)$ $+(J-JLO)*(IHI-ILO+1)$ $+(K-KLO)*(JHI-JLO+1)*(IHI-ILO+1)$

and so on for a maximum of 7 subscripts.

Table 13.1. How to calculate the equivalent address in one dimension for arrays in FORTRAN 77. The equivalent subscript in one dimension has a lower bound of 1, as if it were an assumed size array with a dimension declaration of (*).

EXAMPLE:

It is shown here how a general array of two dimensions may be transposed on top of itself. At first glance this may seem to be an impossible problem, although it was simple enough when used as an example a few pages back for the square array in which both dimensions were the same. Suppose now that you have an array ONE of dimensions M, N

        DIMENSION ONE(M,N)

and that you want it to be transposed; you could have another array TWO

        DIMENSION TWO(N,M)

and you could copy one array to the other. Although these two arrays are not the same shape if M is different from N, they are the same size. The following subroutine would suffice:

```
     SUBROUTINE TRANS2(ONE,TWO,M,N)
     DIMENSION ONE(M,N),TWO(N,M)
C
C TRANSPOSE M BY N ARRAY ONE
C INTO N BY M ARRAY TWO. IT WILL
C NOT WORK IF ONE AND TWO ARE
C THE SAME ARRAY (EQUIVALENCED)
C
     DO 10 I=1,M
       DO 10 J=1,N
         TWO(J,I)=ONE(I,J)
 10  CONTINUE
     END
```

You could very easily use this subroutine as follows:

```
C THIS IS A MAIN PROGRAM
     DIMENSION ONE(7,3),TWO(3,7)
     DATA((ONE(I,J),I=1,7),J=1,3)
       /1,2,3,4,5,6,7,8,9,10,11,12,
       13,14,15,16,17,18,19,20,21/
     PRINT*,' HERE IT IS BEFORE'
     DO 1 K=1,7
  1  PRINT*,(ONE(K,L),L=1,3)
     CALL TRANS2(ONE,TWO,7,3)
     PRINT*,' AND THEN AFTER'
     DO 2 K=1,3
  2  PRINT*,(TWO(K,L),L=1,7)
     END
```

But suppose you want the two arrays to use the same block of memory, as in the main program

```
C THIS IS A MAIN PROGRAM
     DIMENSION ONE(7,3),TWO(3,7)
     EQUIVALENCE(ONE,TWO)
     DATA((ONE(I,J),I=1,7),J=1,3)
       /1,2,3,4,5,6,7,8,9,10,11,12,
       13,14,15,16,17,18,19,20,21/
     PRINT*,' HERE IT IS BEFORE'
     DO 1 K=1,7
  1  PRINT*,(ONE(K,L),L=1,3)
     CALL TRANS2(ONE,TWO,7,3)
     PRINT*,' AND THEN AFTER'
     DO 2 K=1,3
  2  PRINT*,(TWO(K,L),L=1,7)
     END
```

Unfortunately this wouldn't work. The EQUIVALENCE statement is described in Section 13.8, and is a request for ONE and TWO physically to occupy the same memory. Fig. 13.8 shows the storage layout for M = 7 and N = 3. It is easily seen that you can't copy ONE into TWO, or even switch ONE(I,J) with TWO(J,I), because two other memory locations are involved.

However with a bit of thought it is still possible, although the method is somewhat more complicated. Look at ONE(2,1). It is the second memory location and should be taken to the 4th position. This 4th position corresponds to ONE(4,1) which should move to position 10, which in turn moves to position 8, which moves to position 2 where it all started. These arrangements form a cycle. It is possible in some arrays for the rearrangement to be one long cycle, as would be found in a 6 by 2 array for example. It is more likely that the cycles will be shorter. For this example the cycles are

```
 1   --> 1
 2   --> 4   --> 10 --> 8   --> 2
 3   --> 7   --> 19 --> 15 --> 3
 5   --> 13 --> 17 --> 9   --> 5
 6   --> 16 --> 6
11 --> 11
12 --> 14 --> 20 --> 18 --> 12
21 --> 21
```

ARRAY ONE	MEMORY ADDRESS	ARRAY TWO
ONE(1,1)	1	TWO(1,1)
ONE(2,1)	2	TWO(2,1)
ONE(3,1)	3	TWO(3,1)
ONE(4,1)	4	TWO(1,2)
ONE(5,1)	5	TWO(2,2)
ONE(6,1)	6	TWO(3,2)
ONE(7,1)	7	TWO(1,3)
ONE(1,2)	8	TWO(2,3)
ONE(2,2)	9	TWO(3,3)
ONE(3,2)	1Ø	TWO(1,4)
ONE(4,2)	11	TWO(2,4)
ONE(5,2)	12	TWO(3,4)
ONE(6,2)	13	TWO(1,5)
ONE(7,2)	14	TWO(2,5)
ONE(1,3)	15	TWO(3,5)
ONE(2,3)	16	TWO(1,6)
ONE(3,3)	17	TWO(2,6)
ONE(4,3)	18	TWO(3,6)
ONE(5,3)	19	TWO(1,7)
ONE(6,3)	2Ø	TWO(2,7)
ONE(7,3)	21	TWO(3,7)

Fig. 13.8. Memory arrangement of equivalent arrays ONE (7 x 3) and TWO (3 x 7).

and in the general case a cycle

$$a_0 \rightarrow a_1 \rightarrow \ldots \rightarrow a_{k-1} \rightarrow a_k \rightarrow \ldots \rightarrow a_0$$

obeys the law

$$a_k - 1 = \frac{a_{k-1} - 1}{m} + n * \mathrm{mod}(a_{k-1} - 1, m)$$

or going the other way

$$a_{k-1} - 1 = \frac{a_k - 1}{n} + m * \mathrm{mod}(a_k - 1, n)$$

(you could enjoy yourself by showing where these equations come from).

Two interesting points:

All cycles return to the starting place (always).
No cycles overlap (ever).

There are still problems. When you come to do the whole rearrangement how do you avoid messing up the result by repeating cycles you have already done? The answer lies in the way they have been listed above, in which each cycle always moves to addresses which are higher than the starting place. Therefore you could try every starting place in order, and generate the cycles on each. If the cycle returns without going below the starting place, then do it, but if it encounters a lower address than the starting one, then don't. Consider this program:

```
      SUBROUTINE TRANS2(ONE,M,N)
C
C VERY CLEVER ROUTINE TRANSPOSES
C ANY M BY N ARRAY ONE IN PLACE
C
      DIMENSION ONE(M*N)
      DO 3Ø K=1,M*N-2
C CHECK THROUGH THIS CYCLE
      KLAS=K
 1Ø   KLAS=KLAS/M+N*MOD(KLAS,M)
C IF A BACKWARDS MOVE, QUIT
      IF(KLAS.LT.K)GO TO 3Ø
C IF IT IS FORWARDS, GO ON
      IF(KLAS.GT.K) GO TO 1Ø
C ONLY GET TO HERE AT SUCCESSFUL
C END OF CYCLE, SO DO IT
      KLAS=K
      SAVED=ONE(K+1)
 2Ø   KNEX=KLAS/M+N*MOD(KLAS,M)
      SAVE=ONE(KNEX+1)
      ONE(KNEX+1)=SAVED
      SAVED=SAVE
      KLAS=KNEX
      IF(KNEX.NE.K)GO TO 2Ø
 3Ø   CONTINUE
      END
```

This subroutine tries all the starting addresses between 2 and M*N-2 (it is obvious that 1 and M*N must already be in place). The new position is then calculated and followed through the cycle. If a lower address than K is ever encountered, the cycle has been done before. Otherwise the cycle will return to K, and it is then known that it is a new one which will be recomputed and carried out.

EXERCISE:

I know how to do this without so much computation (boasting again). No, it doesn't involve saving the addresses in an array - in the very worst case the array would have to be M*N-2 elements long and that isn't much use. But try this:

Consider each address in turn. If it is meant to move up in memory, switch it with the data which is already there. If it is meant to move down in memory, then it must have been switched already (possibly more than once). In this case follow it back until you find it (further up the array) or the cycle ends, in which case you do nothing.

13.7 The COMMON area

Much of the flexibility of the FORTRAN language arises from the use of dummy arguments to transmit values between program units such as main programs, functions, and subroutines. A programmer does not have to associate his variables with particular areas of memory and is allowed to use the same subroutine to process different arguments.

However, this is not always what the programmer wants. Sometimes he may wish to have an area of memory where the space is shared by program and subprograms. Some flexibility is lost, but as will be seen an ability to use the same space for different purposes is gained and the lists of subroutine arguments can be shortened or eliminated. The COMMON statement allows this to be done. In addition to this, 'labelled' common areas can be created in which only specified subprgrams can share the space.

The COMMON area can only be created in the main program by the COMMON statement

COMMON variables

and this will cause an ordered area of memory to be reserved for the named variables. The COMMON statement can be used in addition to, or instead of, a DIMENSION statement; for example

```
DIMENSION A(5,5)
COMMON X,Y,Z,A
```

or

```
COMMON X,Y,Z,A(5,5)
```

These alternatives have exactly the same effect, and space is set aside in COMMON for the ordinary variables X, Y, and Z and the array A. Therefore, a total of 28 memory locations are reserved, and in order as illustrated in Fig. 13.9. Here, therefore, is a statement which implies a relationship with memory.

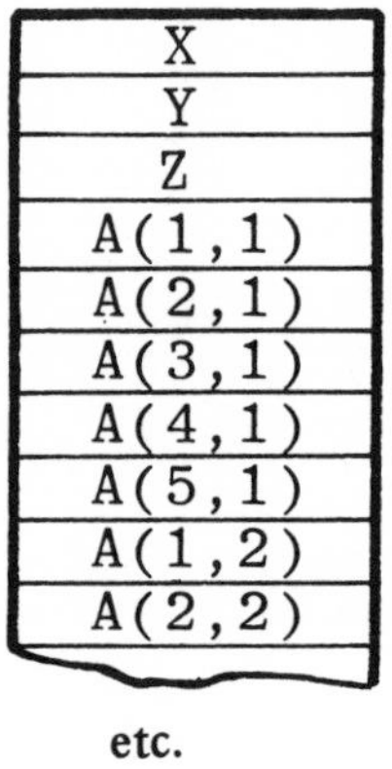

X
Y
Z
A(1,1)
A(2,1)
A(3,1)
A(4,1)
A(5,1)
A(1,2)
A(2,2)

etc.

Fig. 13.9. Illustrating a COMMON area.

You can DIMENSION using COMMON but not vice versa

Once a COMMON area has been created by a main program, all subroutines or functions can make use of it if they have their own COMMON statements. In a subprogram, the COMMON statement tells where in COMMON the variables are to be found. A function could refer to the COMMON area of Fig. 13.9; for example the subroutine INVENT could be used to define $A(I,J)$ as $X + Y**I + Z**J$.

```
main program

    COMMON X,Y,Z,A(5,5)
    X=1.Ø
    Y=2.Ø
    Z=3.Ø
```

```
CALL INVENT
PRINT*,A
END
```

subroutine

```
SUBROUTINE INVENT
PARAMETER (ISZ=5)
COMMON P,Q,R,S(ISZ,ISZ)
DO 2 I=1,ISZ
  DO 1 J=1,ISZ
    S(I,J)=P+Q**I+R**J
1   CONTINUE
2 CONTINUE
END
```

Notice that subroutine INVENT refers to these variables by different names from the main program. The subroutine does not need to know the names in the main program, only the arrangement of values to be used. The COMMON statement has been used to associate variables with a particular part of memory, the COMMON area, and therefore with other variables of the main program and other subroutines.

EXERCISE:
The above example is inefficient: work out how to make use of recurrence to accomplish the task required of the subroutine.

It has been seen above that a COMMON statement in a subprogram tells where in the COMMON area values may be found. In the process their names and even their type can change, but only in a one-to-one correspondence with the space set aside in the main program. However, it is not necessary for the COMMON blocks to be the same size.

EXAMPLE:
This is legal; the subroutine uses less than the full COMMON area.

main program

```
COMMON AREA(25)
```

subroutine

```
COMMON IDATA(1Ø)
```

EXAMPLE:
This is also allowed. The subroutine extends COMMON beyond its size as determined in the main program.

main program

```
COMMON I,J,X,Y,DATA(8)
```

subroutine

```
COMMON I,J,P,Q,VALUES(12)
```

EXAMPLE:
The subroutine that creates the special array (unit matrix) referred to earlier could operate in COMMON.

main program

```
DIMENSION ARAY(5,5)
COMMON ARAY
CALL UNIT
   :
   :
```

subroutine

```
SUBROUTINE UNIT
COMMON UNIT(5,5)
DO 35 K=1,5
  DO 36 L=1,5
    U(K,L)=Ø.Ø
36   CONTINUE
  U(K,K)=1.Ø
35 CONTINUE
RETURN
```

An interesting use of COMMON, referred to in Chapter 11, is to transmit the variables used in adjusting the size of an array. In transmitting an array to a subroutine, in which the dimensions are adjustable, instead of writing

main program

```
DIMENSION ARAY(-5:6)
CALL SHARK(ARAY,-5,6)
   :
   :
```

with

```
subprogram

SUBROUTINE SHARK(ARAY,M,N)
DIMENSION ARAY(M:N)
      :
      :
```

a programmer could put

```
main program

COMMON M,N
DIMENSION ARAY(-5:6)
M=5
N=6
CALL SHARK(ARAY)
      :
      :
```

with

```
subprogram

SUBROUTINE SHARK(ARAY)
COMMON M,N
DIMENSION ARAY(-M,N)
```

This is of limited usefulness, and is probably bad style, because the array itself cannot be in COMMON. One cannot write

```
main program

COMMON M,QUAD(3,3)
M=3
   :
   :
Y=SUNK()
```

with

```
subprogram

FUNCTION SUNK      (illegal)
COMMON INDEX,BOATS
DIMENSION BOATS(INDEX,INDEX)
```

because an array in COMMON cannot have an adjustable dimension.

It is important to realize what is gained and what is lost in using the COMMON area. What is gained is the ability to shorten or eliminate the argument list of a subroutine, which can make a program easier to read. Also, the programmer has the ability to reduce the amount of space taken by his program by having workspace shared by different parts of the program which may be used in totally different ways; an example of this will be seen later. There is no need for the variables in COMMON to be of the same type between program units; a big real array used as workspace by one subroutine could be used for integer values by another. Of course the programmer has to keep track of what unit uses the space at what time.

Generality is lost in using COMMON - there is no way of making an array in COMMON variable in length, and a subroutine which is operating on COMMON operates only on a particular part of memory. Naturally a variable in COMMON can be passed as an argument to a subroutine if the subroutine doesn't know it is in COMMON, as in:

```
main program

COMMON BIG(25),BIGGER(35)
      :
      :
CALL LOUDLY(BIG,25)
      :
CALL LOUDLY(BIGGER,35)
      :
      :
```

```
subroutine

SUBROUTINE LOUDLY(XRAY,NSIZE)
DIMENSION XRAY(NSIZE)
      :
      :
```

However, it is forbidden to have a variable named both in COMMON and as the dummy argument in the same subroutine, because terrible conflicts would be possible:

```
SUBROUTINE ROTTEN(X,Y)
COMMON X(33)
```

It is easy to understand why this is illegal; suppose a main program tried to call the subroutine ROTTEN with

CALL ROTTEN(GARBGE,CAN)

where GARBGE is not in COMMON. How then could ROTTEN know what to do? Any number of COMMON statements can be included, and the COMMON area is defined by taking these in the order they occur. Therefore the COMMON area of Fig. 13.9 could have been defined by

```
COMMON X
COMMON Y
COMMON Z
COMMON A(5,5)
```

Finally it must be said that it is not possible to define values for COMMON by using a DATA statement, which again prevents conflicts between main programs and subroutines - who wins if both try to define values for the same   part of memory? These two rules are easy to forget - it is quite possible that the reader will forget them until his first unfortunate blunder. As a reminder:

> (i) Don't try to define a part of COMMON using a DATA statement.
>
> (ii) In a subroutine, don't have the same name in COMMON and also as a dummy argument.

It will be seen later that there is a special facility for assigning pre-defined values to 'labelled' COMMON.

The COMMON statement is another statement whose position in a program is restricted. It must be placed with the DIMENSION statements and can be mixed with them. Indeed, both COMMON and DIMENSION are examples of specification statements. More of these will be introduced in the next few Chapters, and they can all be mixed together. In a later section of this Chapter the rules of statement ordering will be summarized again.

EXAMPLE:
Here is something that may be useful. A program reads an 8 x 8 array and interpolates between the values by a factor of 8 to give a 57 x 57 array; perhaps for graphical representation. Later on a case study will present a program for contour drawing. Suppose that a civil engineer who has an array of survey data wants to interpolate this to a larger number to get smooth contours drawn. A subroutine MAP may be used for this purpose.

The method is first to interpolate the 8 rows of the data to 57 values each, and then the 57 columns as illustrated by Fig. 13.10. The interpolation is by cubic segments, Fig. 13.11. Between adjacent values a cubic segment joins up nicely so that the slopes match at the ends. It is easy to show that if the cubic is

$$f(u) = a + bu + cu^2 + du^3$$

and if the given values are f(0) and f(1) and the slope f'(0) and f'(1), then the constants a, b, c, and d are

```
a = f(0)
b = f'(0)
c = 3f(1) - f'(1) - 3a - 2b
d = f(1) - a - b - c
```

The only problem is to calculate the slopes. In the middle of a row or column this task is quite easy; a respectable differentiation formula is

$$f'(k) = \frac{f(k-2)-8f(k-1)+8f(k+1)-f(k+2)}{12}$$

which uses two values on either side, as in Fig. 13.12, where k is from 3 to 6.

However, different formulae are needed at and near the edges; for example

$$f'(1) = \frac{-25f(1)+48f(2)-36f(3)+16f(4)-3f(5)}{12}$$

$$f'(2) = \frac{-3f(1)-10f(2)+18f(3)-6f(4)+f(5)}{12}$$

$$f'(7) = \frac{3f(8)+10f(7)-18f(6)+6f(5)-f(4)}{12}$$

$$f'(8) = \frac{25f(8)-48f(7)+36f(6)-16f(5)+3f(4)}{12}$$

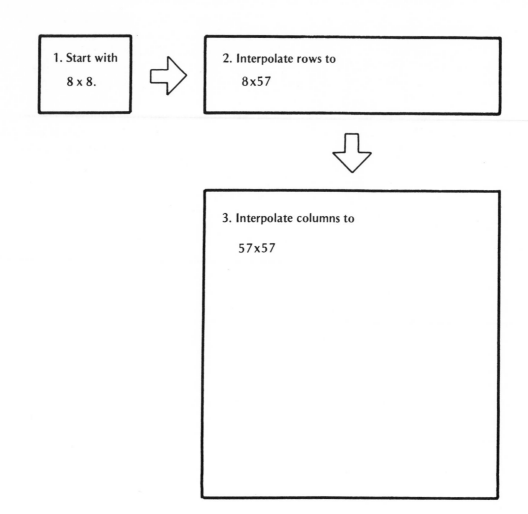

Fig. 13.10. An interpolation scheme in two dimensions.

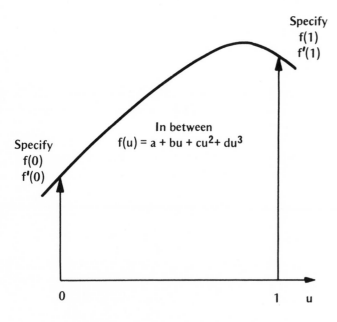

Fig. 13.11. Interpolation by cubic segments.

It might seem strange that a two dimensional interpolation is achieved by one dimensional means, but this procedure works very well; try it and see.

First of all, a main program to read the 8 x 8 array and call the mapping subroutine MAP.

```
C MAIN PROGRAM FOR MAPPING
C
      COMMON ARAY(8,8),BIGM(57,57)
C READ 8 X 8 MEASUREMENT ARRAY
      READ(5,1Ø)((ARAY(I,J),
                J=1,8),I=1,8)
  1Ø FORMAT(8F1Ø.5)
C CALL THE MAPPING SUBROUTINE
      CALL MAP
```

```
C PRINT THE RESULTS
      WRITE(6,20)((BIGM(I,J),
               J=1,57),I=1,57)
  20 FORMAT(' RESULT, ROW BY ROW'/
               57(1X,8F10.5/)/)
      END
```

Subroutine MAP will organize the calculation.

```
      SUBROUTINE MAP
C
C PREPARE 57 X 57 MAP FROM 8 X 8
C
C ARRAY = INPUT REAL ARRAY OF
C          8 X 8 VALUES IN COMMON
C  BIGM = OUTPUT REAL ARRAY OF
C          57 X 57 INTERPOLATION
C          ALSO IN COMMON
C
      COMMON ARAY(8,8),BIGM(57,57)
      DIMENSION W1(8),W2(8),W3(57)
C FIRST DO THE ROWS - GET ROW J
      DO 3 J=1,8
        DO 1 K=1,8
          W1(K)=ARAY(J,K)
   1    CONTINUE
C GET THE SLOPES FOR THIS ROW
        CALL DIFFN(W1,W2,8)
C AND CALL CUBIC TO INTERPOLATE
        CALL CUBIC(W1,W2,W3,8,8)
C SAVE THE RESULT IN BIGM ROW J
        DO 2 K=1,57
          BIGM(J,K)=W3(K)
   2    CONTINUE
   3  CONTINUE
```

```
C NOW TACKLE THE COLUMNS
      DO 5 K=1,57
C GET COLUMN K
        DO 4 J=1,8
          W1(J)=BIGM(J,K)
   4    CONTINUE
C GET THE SLOPES FOR THIS COLUMN
        CALL DIFFN(W1,W2,8)
C INTERPOLATE STRAIGHT INTO BIGM
        CALL CUBIC(W1,W2,BIGM(1,K),
     +              8,8)
   5  CONTINUE
      END
```

In MAP there are three local working arrays, W1, W2, and W3. The rows are interpolated first. To do this row J is copied into the workspace W1. Subroutine DIFFN is used to calculate the slopes at each point of W1, with the slopes returned in W2. Subroutine CUBIC is then used actually to interpolate, given W1, W2, and returning the interpolated row in W3. The interpolated rows are stored in BIGM - and so the first step of Fig. 13.10 has been accomplished.

The columns are done in exactly the same way except that because each column in storage consists of 57 consecutive memory locations, subroutine CUBIC places the answers directly in the columns of BIGM, because it associates its argument BIGM(1,K) with the beginning of a 57 location array of

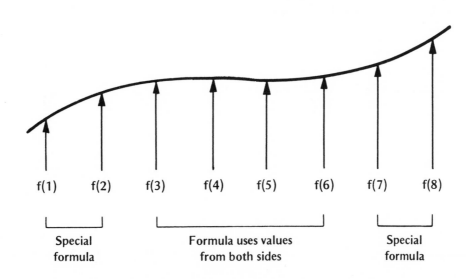

Fig. 13.12. How to differentiate a row or column.

one dimension. This kind of association can often help in multidimensional calculation, but to use it the arrangement of arrays in storage has to be understood.

Most of the hard work is done in one dimension. Subroutine DIFFN calculates the derivatives exactly as is described earlier:

```
      SUBROUTINE DIFFN(F,DF,N)
C GET SLOPES DF FOR ARRAY F
C OF LENGTH N (MINIMUM 5)
C USING FIFTH ORDER FORMULAE.
C
C F  = INPUT REAL ARRAY, VALUES,
C       DIMENSION N
C DF = OUTPUT REAL ARRAY, SLOPES,
C       DIMENSION N
C N  = INPUT INTEGER VALUE, THE
C       LENGTH OF F AND DF. MUST
C       BE 5 OR GREATER.
C.
      REAL F(N),DF(N)
C FIRST TWO POINTS OWN FORMULA
      DF(1)=(-25.0*F(1)+48.0*F(2)
             -36.0*F(3)+16.0*F(4)
             -3.0*F(5))/12.0
      DF(2)=(-3.0*F(1)-10.0*F(2)
             +18.0*F(3)-6.0*F(4)
             +F(5))/12.0
C INSIDE VALUES USE A LOOP
      DO 10 K=3,N-2
        DF(K)=(F(K-2)
               +8.0*(F(K+1)-F(K-1))
               -F(K+2))/12.0
10    CONTINUE
C LAST TWO POINTS OWN FORMULA
      DF(N-1)=(3.0*F(8)+10.0*F(7)
             -18.0*F(6)+6.0*F(5)
             -F(4))/12.0
      DF(N)=(25.0*F(8)-48.0*F(7)
             +36.0*F(6)-16.0*F(5)
             +3.0*F(4))/12.0
      END
```

The subroutine CUBIC makes the interpolation:

```
      SUBROUTINE CUBIC(F,DF,ANS,N,
                       INTRP)
C
C INTERPOLATE N VALUES OF F INTO
C F INTO ANS USING SLOPES DF
C
```

```
C F  = INPUT REAL ARRAY, VALUES,
C       DIMENSION N
C DF = INPUT REAL ARRAY, SLOPES,
C       DIMENSION N
C ANS = OUTPUT REAL ARRAY, RESULT,
C       DIMENSION INTRP*(N-1)+1
C N  = INPUT INTEGER VALUE, THE
C       NUMBER OF ORIGINAL VALUES
C INTRP=INPUT INTEGER VALUE, THE
C       FACTOR OF INTERPOLATION
C       INTRP*(N-1)+1 NEW VALUES
C       OBTAINED FROM N ORIGINALS
C
      DIMENSION F(N),DF(N)
      DIMENSION ANS(INTRP*(N-1)+1)
C INITIAL VALUES AND CONSTANTS
      KBIG=1
      DU=1.0/INTRP
C SELECT INTERVAL F(K) TO F(K+1)
      DO 20 K=1,N-1
        A=F(K)
        ANS(KBIG)=A
        KBIG=KBIG+1
        B=DF(K)
        Q=F(K+1)-A
        C=3.0*Q-DF(K+1)-2.0*B
        D=B+DF(K+1)-2.0*Q
        U=0.0
        DO 10 L=1,INTRP-1
          U=U+DU
          ANS(KBIG)=((D*U+C)*U+B)*U+A
          KBIG=KBIG+1
10      CONTINUE
20    CONTINUE
      ANS(KBIG)=F(N)
      END
```

Both subroutines DIFFN and CUBIC are perfectly general - they could be used to differentiate any array and interpolate by cubics as long as the sizes are related by:

```
LARGE SIZE = 1 + (SMALL SIZE - 1)
             *INTERPOLATION FACTOR
```

13.8 Storage association — the EQUIVALENCE statement

Use of the COMMON statement enabled one association in each program unit with a shared block of memory. Use of an EQUIVALENCE statement provides the ability to associate variables of different names with each other, either using local variables within a program unit, or with COMMON.

It can often happen with a large or complicated FORTRAN program that the programmer works at different times with different arrays, and in order to save space he wishes to put several arrays in the same place in memory. If knows how an array is stored, he can be quite cunning about this. In one program unit the same space can be used for arrays of different dimensions at different times; they may even share values. To make this easy, the EQUIVALENCE statement allows the association together of several variables, each of which can have a different name, a different number of subscripts, and can even be of different type.*

EXAMPLE:

Three arrays can be made to share the same space by the statements:

```
DIMENSION ICOEFF(0:10),IQQ(3,3)
DIMENSION XRAY(2,3,4)
EQUIVALENCE (ICOEFF,IQ,XRAY)
```

This results in the storage association shown in Fig. 13.13. Since the arrays are not all of the same length, the total space taken is dictated by the largest, XRAY.

The programmer is free to refer to any of these arrays at any time by their separate names using the correct number of subscripts. But as with all powerful weapons, this has to be used with care. Because these arrays share the same physical memory space, it is necessary to be sure that their different uses do not interfere. This means that the programmer must always know what he is doing. If he changes XRAY(2,2,1), for

example, he is destroying IQ(1,2) and ICOEFF(4). They are destroyed, and not merely redefined, because a real value is placed there which has no meaning if referred to as an integer. The statements

$$XRAY(2,2,1)=1.0$$

or

$$XRAY(2,2,1)=1$$

both place a real value in memory, the second by conversion as the assignment is done. This is not the same as

$$IQ(1,2)=1$$

because the integer value 1 does not resemble the real value 1.0 in memory. In this latter case, the values of IQ(1,2)

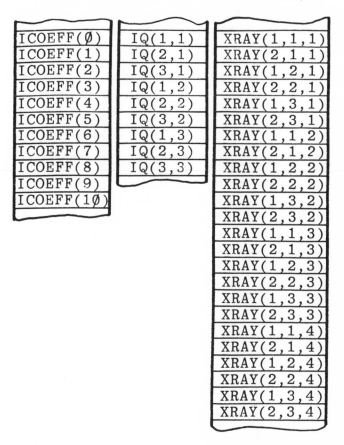

Fig.13.13. Alignment of arrays of one, two, and three dimensions in memory using an EQUIVALENCE statement. It is assumed here that real and integer values each use the same space.

---

* The assumption is made here that real and integer variables use the same space as the FORTRAN 77 standard requires. However, many small computers will have two integers occupying the space of one real, and some large ones allow this to be done - both these things are non-standard. If this were so, then the association of variables is more complicated.

and ICOEFF(4) become 1, and XRAY(2,2,1) is destroyed. It is not safe to use the EQUIVALENCE facility unless this is fully understood.

The general form of the EQUIVALENCE statement is

```
EQUIVALENCE (variables)
            [,(variables),...]
```

The groups of variables enclosed within brackets are made to line up in memory. The variables can be scalar or array names with or without subscripts, as in the earlier example; in this case the first member of the array is intended.

The EQUIVALENCE statement forces all the named variables to occupy the same memory location, so the earlier example as illustrated by Fig. 13.13 has the beginnings of the four arrays aligned, and the remainder of the arrays line up accordingly. It may be necessary in some cases actually to draw a sketch of the memory layout to understand it - indeed where either COMMON or EQUIVALENCE (or both) are concerned a memory map is a valuable part of documentation.

A programmer could specify an impossible arrangement; for example

```
DIMENSION X(9),INCA(2,2)
EQUIVALENCE (X(2),INCA)
EQUIVALENCE (X(7),INCA(1,2))
```

Here, he had intended to align X(2) with INCA(1,1) at the same time as X(7) with INCA(1,2). This does not work because, as Fig. 13.14 shows, they do not line up that way and arrays cannot be broken into pieces.

An arrangement that would be allowed is

```
DIMENSION ICOEFF(Ø:1Ø),IQ(3,3)
DIMENSION XRAY(2,3,4)
EQUIVALENCE (IQ,XRAY)
EQUIVALENCE (ICOEFF,XRAY(1,3,2)
```

in which, compared with Fig. 13.13, the array ICOEFF has been moved down so that it does not overlap the array IQ. This new alignment is as illustrated in

Fig. 13.15; note that XRAY(2,2,2) is not associated with either of the other two, nor is anything after XRAY(1,2,4).

There are a few things which cannot be done with EQUIVALENCE. It will be recalled that an array name that is the same as a function name would confuse the FORTRAN language because in arithmetic expressions there is no way of distinguishing the two. Similarly, even though it is permitted that an ordinary

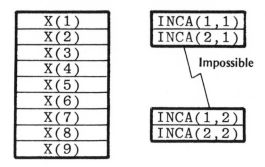

Fig. 13.14. An impossible attempt to violate the addressing of the array INCA through an EQUIVALENCE conflict.

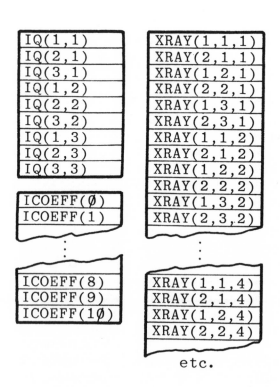

etc.

Fig. 13.15. Another illustration of allowable association by the EQUIVALENCE statement.

variable could have the name of a function, such a variable cannot be used in an EQUIVALENCE statement. Since it would be terribly bad style to name a variable after a function in the first place, a good programmer should not have trouble with this:

illegal

    EQUIVALENCE (X,ATAN)

Another restriction is that a subroutine cannot refer in an EQUIVALENCE statement to one of its dummy arguments. This is forbidden:

    SUBROUTINE LINDA(X,Y)
    EQUIVALENCE (X,P)

EQUIVALENCE is a specification statement, like DIMENSION or COMMON. Its position in the program is constrained in the same way as any other specification. COMMON, DIMENSION, and EQUIVALENCE statements can be mixed together at the beginning of the program unit. The rules of ordering statements so far are summarized again in Section 11 of this Chapter.

13.9 EQUIVALENCE and COMMON together

The EQUIVALENCE statement can be used to associate some variables with others which are declared to be in COMMON, and if this is done they all wind up in COMMON. A simple example of this is

    PARAMETER (INK=5)
    COMMON INCLE(-INK:INK)
    DIMENSION UNCLE(11)
    EQUIVALENCE (INCLE,UNCLE)

Here, 11 memory spaces in COMMON are shared by the arrays INCLE and UNCLE. The PARAMETER statement has assigned the name INK to the constant 5; and the COMMON statement is not using an adjustable dimension.

To understand the alignments that occur when using combinations which are more complicated, it is necessary to remember that it is the COMMON statements which will specify the order and layout of the COMMON area. The EQUIVALENCE state-

ments will simply associate other variables with COMMON. Consider the statements

    COMMON X,Y,Z
    DIMENSION X(2),Y(2),Z(2)
    COMMON INDEX(3)
    DIMENSION ZIPPY(4),NUTTY(3)
    EQUIVALENCE (ZIPPY,X),(NUTTY,Z(2))

Here the DIMENSION and EQUIVALENCE statements have not influenced the layout of COMMON, as shown by Fig. 13.16.

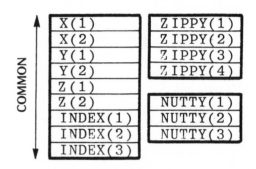

Fig. 13.16. Using COMMON and EQUIVALENCE together.

However, an EQUIVALENCE statement may have the effect of making the COMMON area longer, as in

    DIMENSION MORE(1Ø)
    COMMON I,J,IRAY(5)
    EQUIVALENCE (J,MORE)

which, as shown in Fig. 13.17, extends the COMMON area. If there were another COMMON statement, it would add to the end of IRAY, not MORE.

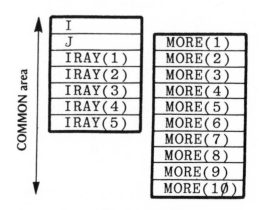

Fig. 13.17. The COMMON area may be extended by an EQUIVALENCE association.

It is, however, illegal to extend the COMMON area backwards as the statement

$$EQUIVALENCE \ (I,MORE(3))$$

would attempt to do, as shown in Fig. 13.18.

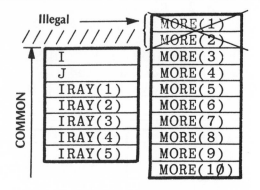

Fig. 13.18. An EQUIVALENCE statement may not extend the COMMON area backwards.

The same COMMON area as defined above in a main program could be referred to in a subroutine such as

```
SUBROUTINE SILKY
COMMON MUCK(2),MYRAY(6)
```

which specifies the locations in COMMON of two integer arrays. Whenever the two program units are used together, these arrays are associated with parts of MORE and with I,J, and IRAY, as shown in Fig.13.19.

Main Program COMMON Area

| I |
| J |
| IRAY(1) |
| IRAY(2) |
| IRAY(3) |
| IRAY(4) |
| IRAY(5) |

| MORE(1) |
| MORE(2) |
| MORE(3) |
| MORE(4) |
| MORE(5) |
| MORE(6) |
| MORE(7) |
| MORE(8) |
| MORE(9) |
| MORE(1∅) |

Subroutine SILKY COMMON Area

| MUCK(1) |
| MUCK(2) |
| MYRAY(1) |
| MYRAY(2) |
| MYRAY(3) |
| MYRAY(4) |
| MYRAY(5) |
| MYRAY(6) |

Fig. 13.19. Variables also become associated through COMMON and EQUIVALENCE between main programs and subroutines.

In Chapter 15, a case study on the solution of equations and matrix inversion by triangular factorization will make use of an equivalencing arrangement in which different parts of a given two dimensional array are referred to by different names. In effect, three arrays will be stored in the same space but are given different names for clarity. This is rather a close-knit example of equivalencing as the whole array is always in use.

13.10   Named COMMON and the BLOCK DATA subprogram

Named COMMON is another kind of shared COMMON area, but it is not necessarily shared by all program units. It has the advantage that it need not be defined in the main program and also that initial values can be assigned to it using DATA statements in a special program unit known as the BLOCK DATA subprogram. However, it has the slight disadvantage that all named COMMON areas which have the same name must be specified with exactly the same length in all program units that refer to it.

The name is defined between slashes in the COMMON statement; in fact named and blank COMMON areas can be intermixed in the same statement, but this is confusing and is therefore poor style. The name of a COMMON area must not be the same as any subprogram name (and this restriction includes the generic or specific names of intrinsic functions such as ATAN).

EXAMPLES:
   Ordinary COMMON, which is sometimes called blank COMMON

$$COMMON \ HORSE(1\emptyset),GONE(1\emptyset)$$

A named COMMON, called BOLT

$$COMMON/BOLT/ \ STABLE(5),DOOR(5)$$

Both in the same program unit

```
COMMON HORSE(10),GONE(10)
COMMON/BOLT/STABLE(5),DOOR(5)
```

or

```
COMMON HORSE(10),GONE(10),
        /BOLT/STABLE(5),DOOR(5)
```

or

```
COMMON HORSE(10),GONE(10),
        /BOLT/STABLE(5),DOOR(5)
```

or

```
COMMON/BOLT/STABLE(5),DOOR(5)//
              HORSE(5),DOOR(5)
```

or

```
COMMON/BOLT/STABLE(5),DOOR(5),//
              HORSE(5),DOOR(5)
```

Notice how the switch is made from named back to blank COMMON and that there is an optional comma between the block names. If blank COMMON is given first, there is no need to name it. Each omitted block name refers to blank COMMON, and if blank COMMON appears first, then the name is usually omitted. The most general form of the COMMON statement is:

$$\text{COMMON } [/ \begin{smallmatrix} block \\ name \end{smallmatrix} /] \text{ variables } [,]$$

$$[/ \begin{smallmatrix} block \\ name \end{smallmatrix} /] \text{ variables } ...$$

It is not permitted for variables in two COMMON blocks to be associated by EQUIVALENCE statements; the blocks must remain separate.

illegal:

```
COMMON/PARTS/X(10),/PAR2/I(10)
EQUIVALENCE (X,I)
```

EXAMPLE:

A main program calls two subroutines, SETUP and CRANK. These subprograms share an array QUITE with each other through the COMMON area named TURN, and QUITE is not shared by the main program. However, the main program does share some variables with both programs through blank COMMON.

The main program:

```
COMMON A(3,3),Y(3),STEP
        ⋮
        ⋮
CALL SETUP
        ⋮
        ⋮
CALL CRANK(DRIVE)
        ⋮
        ⋮
END
```

Subroutine SETUP:

```
SUBROUTINE SETUP
COMMON A(3,3),STUF(3),H
COMMON/TURN/SET(3,3)
        ⋮
        ⋮
END
```

Subroutine CRANK:

```
SUBROUTINE CRANK(DRIVE)
COMMON RUSH(9),Y(3),H
COMMON/TURN/QUITE(3,3)
        ⋮
        ⋮
END
```

The storage arrangement known to all these programs is illustrated in Fig. 13.20.

One disadvantage of using blank COMMON is that normal DATA statements are never allowed to refer to it. Data may never be entered during compilation to blank COMMON. However, a named COMMON block can have its initial values assigned by a BLOCK DATA subprogram. A BLOCK DATA subprogram begins with a BLOCK DATA statement, and ends with an END statement. It does not contain any executable statements. The BLOCK DATA subprogram contains all the named COMMON statements, DIMENSION or type statements if necessary, and DATA statements which refer to any variables in the named COMMON area. Several named COMMON blocks can be referred to. More than one BLOCK DATA subprogram is permitted, but if all or part of an area is redefined then the last reference to it in a BLOCK DATA subprogram is used for the initial value. The sole purpose of the BLOCK DATA subprogram is to assign values to variables in named COMMON.

EXAMPLE:

The array NUMBRS in the COMMON area COUNT is to be defined. Other variables in the same named COMMON are not initialized. The entire subprogram is

```
BLOCK DATA
DIMENSION A(4),B(4)
DIMENSION NUMBRS(1Ø),ARAY(5,5)
COMMON/COUNT/A,B,C,I,J,K
COMMON/COUNT/NUMBRS,ARAY
DATA NUMBRS/1,2,3,4,5,6,7,8,9,Ø/
END
```

13.11 Keeping values defined through COMMON

In Chapters 8 and 10, the use of the SAVE statement to force a subprogram to preserve the status of all or some of its variables between one CALL and the next was described. COMMON blocks provide a useful way of making this happen without a SAVE statement. Once they have been defined in the first place, all variables in blank COMMON remain defined through all the units that make up a program. Therefore a programmer need never worry about the definition status of variables in blank COMMON.

	Main Program	Subroutine CRANK	Subroutine SETUP
Blank COMMON	A(1,1) ↔	RUSH(1) ↔	A(1,1)
	A(2,1)	RUSH(2)	A(2,1)
	A(3,1)	RUSH(3)	A(3,1)
	A(1,2)	RUSH(4)	A(1,2)
	A(2,2)	RUSH(5)	A(2,2)
	A(3,2)	RUSH(6)	A(3,2)
	A(1,3)	RUSH(7)	A(1,3)
	A(2,3)	RUSH(8)	A(2,3)
	A(3,3)	RUSH(9)	A(3,3)
	Y(1)	Y(1)	STUFF(1)
	Y(2)	Y(2)	STUFF(2)
	Y(3)	Y(3)	STUFF(3)
	STEP	H	H
Local Variables	DRIVE		
/TURN/ Labelled COMMON	(not known)	QUITE(1,1) ↔	SET(1,1)
		QUITE(2,1)	SET(2,1)
		QUITE(3,1)	SET(3,1)
		QUITE(1,2)	SET(1,2)
		QUITE(2,2)	SET(2,2)
		QUITE(3,2)	SET(3,2)
		QUITE(1,3)	SET(1,3)
		QUITE(2,3)	SET(2,3)
		QUITE(3,3)	SET(3,3)

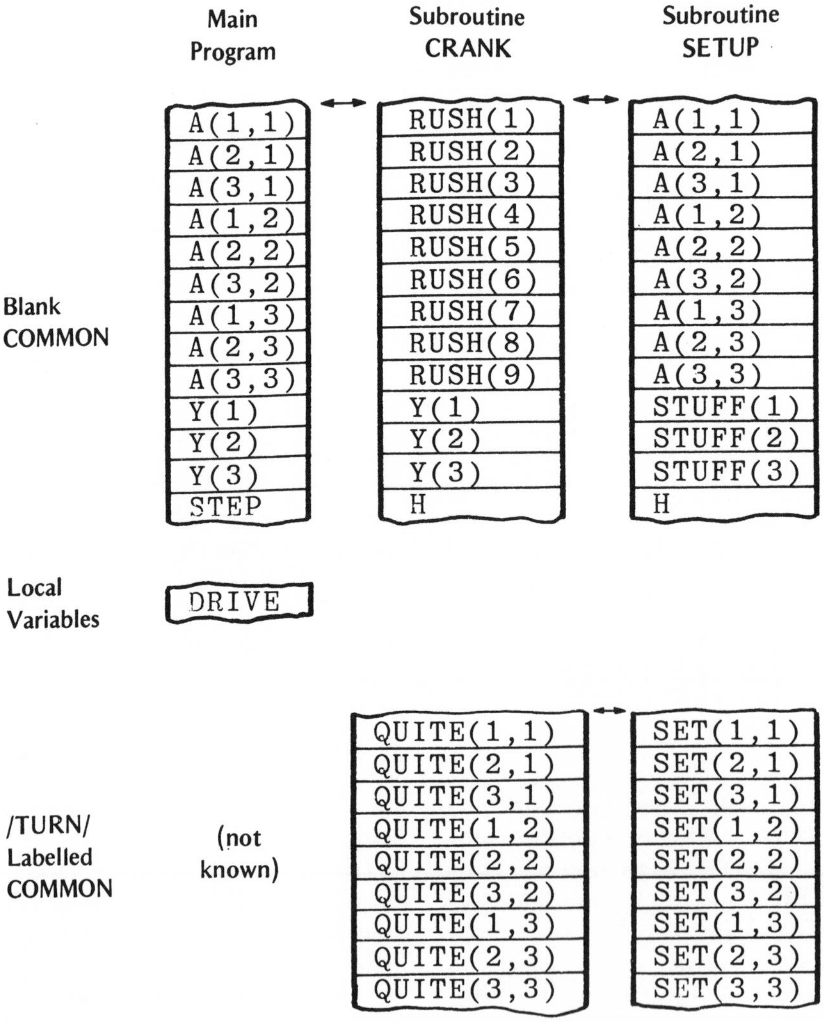

Fig. 13.20. Illustrating a storage arrangement involving blank and labelled COMMON.

This is not quite true of a named COMMON block. If it appears in a main program, then it remains defined provided that more than one subprogram uses it. If it appears in only one subprogram, then it is treated like a local variable, and becomes undefined when the subprogram is finished. In that situation a SAVE statement may be necessary.

EXAMPLES:
(i) X and Y are always defined.

main program

```
COMMON X,/BLOK/Y
```

(ii) In this one I is always defined but J is undefined after the RETURN unless COMMON /SPLOG/ exists in a unit which is calling DEMMY either itself or through a chain of calls.

```
SUBROUTINE DEMMY
COMMON I,/SPLOG/J
J=5
I=3
END
```

Of course a SAVE statement could be used:

A labelled COMMON block not defined in a main program is lost on a RETURN if there is then no unit in the chain of calls using it. The safe way to keep a labelled COMMON defined is to use the SAVE statement. SAVE cannot specify individual items from any kind of COMMON but the name of a labelled COMMON block given with slashes around it preserves the entire block:

```
SUBROUTINE DURHAM
COMMON/DUKE/BARR,SPACH,
COMMON/DUKE/GIDDEN,MILLER
SAVE/DUKE/
    :
    :
```

It is only necessary to use SAVE with a labelled COMMON block that exists in one subprogram only.

13.12 The order of statements

In this Chapter several new statements have been introduced which belong at the beginning of program units. Here the rules regarding ordering are summarized (again) for the statements of FORTRAN as they are known so far. Fig. 13.21 shows the ordering. The specification statements

Comments can go anywhere before END	SUBROUTINE, FUNCTION, PROGRAM or BLOCK DATA Statements		
	FORMAT and ENTRY	PARAMETER Statements	Specification Statements COMMON DIMENSION EQUIVALENCE
		DATA Statements	Statement Function Definitions
			Executable Statements
END Statement			

Fig. 13.21. The actual FORTRAN 77 rules about statement ordering (so far).

used so far are COMMON, EQUIVALENCE, SAVE, and DIMENSION. Note that the PARAMETER statement is shown mixed with the specification statements, and that the DATA statements have flexibility in their position as well.

13.13 Problems

Many problems involving arrays of two dimensions actually present themselves in the form of equations or matrices. That is why the following Chapter is devoted entirely to this subject. However, these concepts are too mathematical for some people. For this reason, a few problems are given here which do not involve the concept of an array as a matrix.

PROBLEM 13.1:
The Chebyshev series was introduced in Problem 7.6, and was also the basis of Problems 11.3 and 11.4. Compare the use of the Chebyshev series as an interpolating method in two dimensions with the simple spline method used as an example earlier in this Chapter. The comparison is subtle. If you decide that the Chebyshev interpolation is a useful method, work up a Chebyshev version of SUBROUTINE MAP, which was given in Section 13.7.

PROBLEM 13.2:
Refer back to Problem 11.4, which is a cyclic permutation of an array in one dimension. In view of what was said earlier in this Chapter about cyclic permutations, can you now do a better job of it?

PROBLEM 13.3:
Now consider the possibility that the array length used in Problems 11.4 and 13.2 is a power of 2. Look at the subscripts as actual binary addresses, and recall that the question of bit-reversing an address was dealt with in Chapter 12.

PROBLEM 13.4:
Consider the question of transposing an M x N array on top of itself if both of the dimensions M and N are powers of 2.

PROBLEM 13.5:
The Laplace partial differential equation in a plane:

$$\frac{\partial^2 u}{\partial x^2} + \frac{\partial^2 u}{\partial y^2} = 0$$

is very important because it describes a number of practical problems in all branches of science and engineering. This problem explores what is called a finite difference approach to solving this equation numerically. An approximation to the equation is made, which is good enough if the problem is divided into enough tiny elements. Consider a model in which $U_{m\,n}$ is the solution in the interior of a grid with uniform spacing h in both directions, illustrated by Fig. 13.22. The second derivatives in the Laplace equation are approximately:

$$\frac{\partial^2 U_{m\,n}}{\partial x^2} \approx \frac{1}{h} \left\{ \frac{\partial U_{m\,n+1}}{\partial x} - \frac{\partial U_{m\,n}}{\partial x} \right\}$$

$$\approx \frac{1}{h^2} \left\{ \left\{ U_{m\,n+1} - U_{m\,n} \right\} - \left\{ U_{m\,n} - U_{m\,n-1} \right\} \right\}$$

$$= \frac{1}{h^2} \left\{ U_{m\,n+1} - 2U_{m\,n} + U_{m\,n-1} \right\}$$

and similarly

$$\frac{\partial^2 U}{\partial y^2} \approx \frac{1}{h^2} \left\{ U_{m+1\,n} - 2U_{m\,n} + U_{m-1\,n} \right\}$$

So that a model for the entire Laplace equation is

$$U_{m\,n+1} + U_{m\,n-1} + U_{m+1\,n} + U_{m-1\,n}$$

$$= 4U_{m\,n}$$

from which

$$U_{m\,n}$$

$$= \frac{U_{m\,n+1} + U_{m\,n-1} + U_{m+1\,n} + U_{m-1\,n}}{4}$$

The mathematics of this result are not important here; this last equation can be used to solve any physical problem involving the Laplace equation.

Fig.13.23 illustrates an electrical prob-

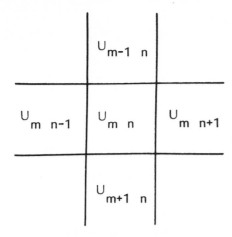

Fig. 13.22. Using an array of two dimensions to model a plane in the solution of Laplace's equation.

lem in which a long electrical cable runs in a long conducting duct. The electrical potential in the duct obeys the Laplace equation, and the drawing shows this expressed as a 20 x 40 two dimensional array.

Normally the solution is obtained by iteration. An initial set of values is assumed - anything will do - and the model equation for $U_{m\ n}$ is used over and over to calculate and recalculate the field. The 'boundary condition' of zero potential around the outside and of +100 volts and -100 volts in the cables is respected (i.e. not changed) in the iteration. Eventually the solution will approach the correct answer. If the iteration is applied directly to the array so that new values are

constantly replacing old ones, then you are carrying out what is called the Gauss-Seidel iteration, and this always works for these equations.

The only difficulty is in knowing when the iteration is finished. To observe the progress of the solution, the RMS (root mean square) change for each iteration from the previous one may be easily computed as the iteration is done. This method is slowly converging - which means that it creeps rather gradually towards the answer - and so the actual error will always be larger than this RMS change. It is left to you to discover, by direct observation of your solution, a reasonable stopping condition based on the RMS change.

Solve for the electrical field of Fig. 13.23. There exists a symmetry which makes it possible to do in a 20 x 20 array.

PROBLEM 13.6:
Now in the solution to Problem 13.5 a different iteration is used.

$$U_{m\ n}^{new} = (1-\omega)U_{m\ n}^{old}$$
$$+ \frac{U_{m\ n+1} + U_{m\ n-1} + U_{m+1\ n} + U_{m-1\ n}}{4}$$

Here, ω is called the 'relaxation factor' and in theory the equation has the same solution as the model used in Problem 13.5. If $\omega = 1$, the model is exactly the same, as you can easily see. For $0 < \omega < 1$ this will slow the iteration down, which is not terribly useful. However, for $1 < \omega < 2$, the solution will be speeded up - this is called 'over-relaxation'. However, if ω is too large, the solution will fail by blowing up - having introduced this ω it is no longer possible to say that the iteration is guaranteed to work.

Investigate the use of over-relaxation to speed up the solution. It would be wise to observe the behaviour of the RMS change as it develops from iteration to iteration for various values of ω. There will be a best value of ω - in selecting it there are one or two subtle points.

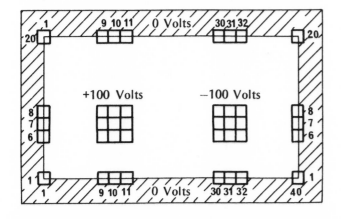

Fig. 13.23. An electrical problem involving solving the Laplace Equation numerically in a 20 x 40 grid. In the problem there is a line of symmetry.

14
Equations and matrices

14.1 Introduction

Arrays of two dimensions are used so often to represent either systems of linear equations or matrices that it is well worth devoting a separate Chapter to describe the notation and to give some important examples. Some of the methods described have a considerable background of mathematics, and no attempt is made to delve into this. It is hoped that the reader will find here a useful collection of facts and techniques, but he will have to look elsewhere if he feels a desire for mathematical fulfillment.

14.2 Arrays as equations

Many problems in virtually any field of human endeavour where numbers are used require the solution of a set of simultaneous linear equations. Schoolchildren first encounter these in terms resembling the following:

"Mum goes to Fortnum's every day and buys a avocados, m mangoes, and p papayas. Market forces cause the prices to vary from day to day. On Monday, each fruit is $1 and she pays $12 for the lot. On Tuesday mangoes have gone up to $2 and papayas to $1.50, and she pays $18.50. On Wednesday, with mangoes at $1.50, papayas at $3 due to a storm at sea, and avocados at $2, she pays $27. Dad sees one of the bills, and the family ceases to eat exotic fruit. How many of each did she buy each day?"

In other words, it is necessary to solve for a, m, and p in the equations

$$
\begin{aligned}
a + \quad m + \quad p &= 12 \\
a + \quad 2m + 1.5p &= 18.5 \\
2a + 1.5m + \quad 3p &= 27
\end{aligned}
$$

Mathematicians have developed a shorthand to describe these equations by writing down a table of coefficients, in the form of an array of two dimensions, and the unknowns and the right hand side as arrays of one dimension:

$$
\begin{pmatrix} 1 & 1 & 1 \\ 1 & 2 & 1.5 \\ 2 & 1.5 & 3 \end{pmatrix} \quad \begin{pmatrix} a \\ m \\ p \end{pmatrix} = \begin{pmatrix} 12 \\ 18.5 \\ 27 \end{pmatrix}
$$

$$\text{coefficients} \qquad \text{unknowns} \qquad \begin{array}{c}\text{right hand}\\\text{side}\end{array}$$

This shorthand could be interpreted as an instruction to substitute the values of a, m, and p in the array of coefficients, and if this were done the results of the right hand side would then be obtained. Therefore the system of equations and its solution (as yet unknown) can be represented by three arrays which could be called A, x, and y so that the equations are now summarized by

$$Ax = y$$

which, for the present, means 'substitute x into A to get y' where

$$A = \begin{pmatrix} 1 & 1 & 1 \\ 1 & 2 & 1.5 \\ 2 & 1.5 & 3 \end{pmatrix}$$

$$x = \begin{pmatrix} a \\ m \\ p \end{pmatrix} \quad \text{the unknowns}$$

$$y = \begin{pmatrix} 12 \\ 18.5 \\ 27 \end{pmatrix}$$

Defining this in this way suggests the data structure specified in these FORTRAN statements:

```
DIMENSION A(3,3),X(3),Y(3)
DATA((A(I,J),J=1,3),I=1,3)
/1.0,1.0,1.0,
 1.0,2.0,1.5,
 2.0,1.5,3.0/
DATA Y/12.0,18.5,27.0/
```

Note how A has been laid out for clarity. This is how the equations are represented in the program, and it is now possible to consider ways of solving them.

14.3 Solving equations by Cramer's rule

It can easily be shown by hand in a few seconds that two equations in two unknowns

$$ax_1 + bx_2 = y_1$$
$$cx_1 + dx_2 = y_2$$

have the solution

$$x_1 = \frac{dy_1 - by_2}{ad - bc}$$

$$x_2 = \frac{dy_2 - cy_1}{ad - bc}$$

(which blows up with mighty force when ad=bc!)

Cramer's rule simply results from noticing the pattern in this. The array shorthand for these equations is

$$\begin{pmatrix} a & b \\ c & d \end{pmatrix} \begin{pmatrix} x_1 \\ x_2 \end{pmatrix} = \begin{pmatrix} y_1 \\ y_2 \end{pmatrix}$$

Notice that in the solution, the denominator is the same both times and is a sort of cross-product from the coefficient array. This is known as the 'determinant' of the array and will be called D.

$$D = ad - bc = \begin{vmatrix} a & b \\ c & d \end{vmatrix}$$

Remember to take the downwards product first and then subtract the upwards one.

Now suppose there is a different determinant which is obtained by replacing the first column by the right hand side. This may seem a strange thing to do, but the result is magical:

$$D_1 = dy_1 - by_2 = \begin{vmatrix} y_1 & b \\ y_2 & d \end{vmatrix}$$

Notice then that

$$x_1 = \frac{D_1}{D}$$

and similarly, if

$$d_2 = ay_2 - cy_1 = \begin{vmatrix} a & y_1 \\ c & y_2 \end{vmatrix}$$

then

$$x_2 = \frac{D_2}{D}$$

This is called Cramer's rule, and once you know it you can solve small systems of equations very quickly. First find the determinant of the coefficient array, D. Then to get the solution belonging to the first column, replace the first column by the right hand side and work out the determinant D_1. Do the same for the second column. Note that if D is zero, the equations are impossible to solve. This means that an impossible set of equations can be recognized instantly! If D is small enough that it approaches the limits of precision of your computer as compared to the typical size of coefficients, then the equations are almost impossible to solve. Nearly impossible, or 'ill conditioned' equations are found to occur with annoying regularity in serious engineering calculations.

Cramer's rule will also work for larger systems of equations provided it is known how to work out the determinants. For the 3x3 array A

$$A = \begin{pmatrix} a_{11} & a_{12} & a_{13} \\ a_{21} & a_{22} & a_{23} \\ a_{31} & a_{32} & a_{33} \end{pmatrix}$$

the determinant is:

$$a_{11} (a_{22}a_{33} - a_{32}a_{23})$$

$$\begin{vmatrix} a_{22} & a_{23} \\ a_{32} & a_{33} \end{vmatrix}$$

$$- a_{12} (a_{21}a_{33} - a_{31}a_{23})$$

$$\begin{vmatrix} a_{21} & a_{23} \\ a_{31} & a_{33} \end{vmatrix}$$

$$+ a_{13} (a_{21}a_{32} - a_{31}a_{22})$$

$$\begin{vmatrix} a_{21} & a_{22} \\ a_{31} & a_{32} \end{vmatrix}$$

It can thus be seen that to find a 3x3 determinant, the coefficients in the top row must be taken one at a time and multiplied by the determinant of the other rows and columns, with the sign altering each time. Therefore any 3x3 determinant is the sum of three 2x2 determinants each multiplied by a coefficient. So Cramer's rule could now be used for three equations. Here is the remainder of the FORTRAN program to solve the fruity problem stated earlier in this Chapter:

```
C SOLVE EQUATION BY CRAMER'S RULE
C
C FIRST GET DETERMINANT OF MATRIX
C NOTE THAT PROGRAM IS NOT PROTECTED
C AGAINST SMALL OR ZERO DETERMINANT
C
      COF1=A(2,2)*A(3,3)-A(3,2)*A(2,3)
      COF2=A(2,1)*A(3,3)-A(3,1)*A(2,3)
      COF3=A(2,1)*A(3,2)-A(3,1)*A(2,2)
      D=A(1,1)*COF1-A(1,2)*COF2+A(1,3)*COF3
C SOLVE FOR X(1)
      CF2=Y(2)*A(3,3)-Y(3)*A(2,3)
      CF3=Y(2)*A(3,2)-Y(3)*A(2,2)
      X(1)=(Y(1)*COF1-A(1,2)*CF2+A(1,3)*CF3)/D
C SOLVE FOR X(2)
      CF1=CF2
      CF3=A(2,1)*Y(3)-A(3,1)*Y(2)
      X(2)=(A(1,1)*CF1-Y(1)*COF2+A(1,3)*CF3)/D
C SOLVE FOR X(3)
      CF1=A(2,2)*Y(3)-A(3,2)*Y(2)
      CF2=CF3
      X(3)=(A(1,1)*CF1-A(1,2)*CF2+Y(1)*COF3)/D
C PRINT THE RESULT
      PRINT*,'MUM USED TO BUY:'
      PRINT*,X(1),' AVACADOS'
      PRINT*,X(2),' MANGOES'
      PRINT*,X(3),' PAPAYAS'
      END
```

For four equations, the procedure is the same. Taking each coefficient from the top row leaves four 3x3 determinants, each evaluated by three 2x2 determinants - a total of 4x3x2 cross-products. And so on.

If Cramer's rule is so simple, why is it not universally used? The answer is that it is easy to see that for n equations there are n! cross-products and for more than three or four equations this is just too large. For a 10x10 system there would be 4,000,000 cross-products, and the method outlined in the next section would be about 4,000 times faster than Cramer's rule.

14.4   The Gauss elimination method

When most people solve equations by hand, they use a systematic elimination method in which chosen variables are eliminated in turn, reducing the number of equations and unknowns until only one equation in one unknown is left. They then work backwards through their equations substituting to get one new part of the solution at a time. This is called the Gaussian elimination method after the German child prodigy and mathematical genius, Friedrich Gauss (1777 - 1855).

Suppose the equations are

$$a_{11}x_1 + a_{12}x_2 + a_{13}x_3 = y_1 \qquad (1)$$

$$a_{21}x_1 + a_{22}x_2 + a_{23}x_3 = y_2 \qquad (2)$$

$$a_{31}x_1 + a_{32}x_2 + a_{33}x_3 = y_3 \qquad (3)$$

The first step carried out in Gaussian elimination would be to eliminate the variable x_1 from equation (2) by subtracting row (1) times a_{21}/a_{11} from row (2) to give a new row (2).

The right hand side of the equation is also operated on to give a new term

$$y_2' = y_2 - (a_{21}/a_{11}) y_1$$

Similarly, variable x_1 is eliminated from equation (3) by subtracting row (1) times a_{31}/a_{11} from row (3) to give a new row (3) and a new right hand side. In

this operation a_{11} is called the pivot. This gives a new set of equations

$$a_{11}x_1 + a_{12}x_2 + a_{13}x_3 = y_1 \qquad (1)$$

$$b_{22}x_2 + b_{23}x_3 = y_2' \qquad (4)$$

$$b_{32}x_2 + b_{33}x_3 = y_3' \qquad (5)$$

The variable x_2 can now be removed from equation (5), using b_{22} as the pivot, and subtracting equation (4) times b_{32}/b_{22} from equation (5) to give a new equation (6). The equations are now

$$a_{11}x_1 + a_{12}x_2 + a_{13}x_3 = y_1 \qquad (1)$$

$$b_{22}x_2 + b_{23}x_3 = y_2' \qquad (4)$$

$$c_{33}x_3 = y_3'' \qquad (6)$$

If the coefficients had originally been arranged in an array A of two dimensions and the right hand side in an array Y of one dimension, then the arrays are transformed as the elimination progresses:

Initially

$$A \qquad\qquad Y$$
$$\begin{pmatrix} a_{11} & a_{12} & a_{13} \\ a_{21} & a_{22} & a_{23} \\ a_{31} & a_{32} & a_{33} \end{pmatrix} \text{ and } \begin{pmatrix} y_1 \\ y_2 \\ y_3 \end{pmatrix}$$

After stage 1

$$\begin{pmatrix} a_{11} & a_{12} & a_{13} \\ 0 & b_{22} & b_{23} \\ 0 & b_{32} & b_{33} \end{pmatrix} \text{ and } \begin{pmatrix} y_1 \\ y_2' \\ y_3' \end{pmatrix}$$

and finally

$$\begin{pmatrix} a_{11} & a_{12} & a_{13} \\ 0 & b_{22} & b_{23} \\ 0 & 0 & c_{33} \end{pmatrix} \text{ and } \begin{pmatrix} y_1 \\ y_2' \\ y_3'' \end{pmatrix}$$

If there were N equations, then the algorithm can be generalized:

```
For each column K from 1 to N-1
  For each row I from K+1 to N
    Operate on Y(I) by letting
    Y(I)=Y(I)-Y(K)*A(I,K)/A(K,K)
```

And also along the row for J from K to N

Operate on A(I,J) by letting

A(I,J)=A(I,J)-A(K,J)*A(I,K)/A(K,K)

In Fig.14.1 is shown the state of the array A with the Gauss elimination procedure frozen when the elimination of coefficients in column K has progressed to row I.

There is a subtle problem in translating this directly into FORTRAN; it will not work exactly as stated because it obliterates A(I,K) while it is still needed. This is fairly easy to see once it is pointed out. Referring to Fig.14.1, the first thing to be done in row I is the elimination of A(I,K) (when J = K in the recipe above). Unfortunately the previous value of A(I,K) is still needed to complete row I (when J proceeds to the values K+1, K+2 ... N in the recipe). It is necessary to preserve the value A(I,K)

somehow. This is quite simple. Before operating on the row for J from K to N, compute and save the value A(I,K)/A(K,K) which is used for the whole of the row. Then the recipe is modified. If

$$Z = A(I,K)/A(K,K)$$

then the row procedure is

$$Y(I) = Y(I) - Y(K)*Z$$

and

$$A(I,J) = A(I,J) - A(K,J)*Z$$

This method also has some advantages in efficiency since there is less arithmetic and subscripting in the innermost loop.

Once the elimination has been completed, the solution to the equation is found by back-substitution:

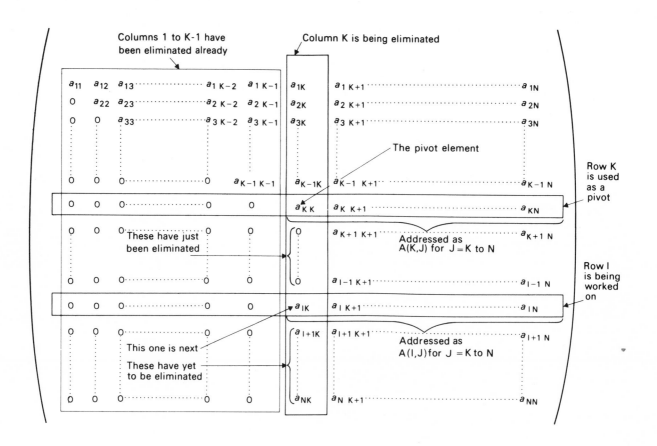

Fig. 14.1. The state of an array in the midst of Gaussian elimination. Row K is used as pivot for the elimination of column K, which has progressed to row I.

$$x_3 = y_3^{\cdot}/c_{33}$$

$$x_2 = (y_2^{\cdot} - b_{23}x_3)/b_{22}$$

$$x_1 = (y_1 - a_{12}x_2 - a_{13}x_3)/a_{11}$$

which can be described in the general case of N equations as first:

$$X(N) = Y(N)/A(N,N)$$

and for each row K from N - 1 to 1

$$X(K) = \left\{ Y(K) - \sum_{J=K+1}^{N} A(K,J)*X(J) \right\} /A(K,K)$$

To prove that the program is not so difficult, here it is as a general purpose subroutine to solve N equations in N unknowns whose coefficients are given in the NxN real array A, with the right hand side in Y and the answer returned in X. A and Y are, of course, modified in the course of the procedure. It has been written in such a way that X and Y could be EQUIVALENCEd by the calling program.

```
      SUBROUTINE GAUSS(A,Y,X,N)
C
C GAUSS ELIMINATION SOLVE AX = Y
C
C A = INPUT REAL ARRAY OF N X N
C     COEFFICIENTS, IS DESTROYED
C Y = INPUT REAL ARRAY, N RIGHT
C     HAND SIDES, IS DESTROYED
C X = OUTPUT REAL SOLUTION ARRAY
C     DIMENSION N
C N = INPUT INTEGER VALUE, NUMBER
C     OF EQUATIONS
C
C X AND Y COULD BE EQUIVALENCED
C
      DIMENSION A(N,N),Y(N),X(N)
C OUTER LOOP - ELIMINATE COLUMN
      DO 30 K=1,N-1
C THIS LOOP - ROW TO OPERATE ON
      DO 20 I=K+1,N
C THIS LOOP ACTUALLY DOES IT
      Z=A(I,K)/A(K,K)
      DO 10 J=K,N
10       A(I,J)=A(I,J)-A(K,J)*Z
C OPERATE ALSO ON Y
20    Y(I)=Y(I)-Y(K)*Z
30 CONTINUE
```

```
C NOW BACK-SUBSTITUTE
      X(N)=Y(N)/A(N,N)
C TAKE ROWS IN REVERSE ORDER
      DO 50 K=N-1,1,-1
C SUM OVER KNOWN RESULTS
      SUM=Y(K)
      DO 40 J=K+1,N
40    SUM=SUM-X(J)*A(K,J)
50 X(K)=SUM/A(K,K)
      END
```

14.5 Pivoting

In such a pretty method as described in the previous section, it is unfortunate that some nasty numerical problems can arise to spoil the results. The essence of this method is the operation

```
10 A(I,J)=A(I,J)-A(K,J)*Z
```

where Z was the value of A(K,K) before column K was tackled. The whole procedure pivots on the value of Z, and so A(K,K) is called the pivot element of the method at the Kth column. What if the pivot element had been zero! Clearly the whole procedure goes pow in your face if some Z somewhere in the process turns up a zero. Indeed if a Z is very small then all the results below it will become very large. The next Z, then, will be large giving a lot of very small results, and so on. The method can start to oscillate in this way and the result is inaccurate results, or even answers that are just plain wrong. What can be done?

First of all, it makes no difference at all in theory to the results if the order of the rows of array A is changed. This is just the same as writing the equations in a different order. Therefore it is possible to look down column K to find the coefficient of largest magnitude, and switch two rows to bring this to A(K,K). You could then divide this new row K by A(K,K) to make the pivot element A(K,K) exactly 1.0. This is going to save a lot of subscripting.

Actually even more than this can be done to ensure the best possible result. If the columns of A are interchanged, the effect is to reorder the unknowns. This would not be a very good idea if, at the end, the program had lost track of the order of the unknowns, but it is possible to record the rearrangements of the columns and to undo the rearrangement at the end. Suppose that in a 5x5 system of equations, an integer array ICOL is used to keep track of the order of the columns. Initially ICOL could contain the values

1   2   3   4   5

Then if columns 2 and 4 of A were exchanged, it would be possible also to switch ICOL(2) with ICOL(4). Then ICOL contains

1   4   3   2   5

which is a record of the new order of the rows.

Therefore it is possible to search all of the rows and columns below and beyond A(K,K) to find the largest coefficient, switch it into the pivot position, and divide the new row K by this to make the crucial value Z always 1.0. At the end, the order of the result has to be changed.

Here is a subroutine SPIV to search for the largest coefficient and to make the switch:

```
      SUBROUTINE SPIV(A,Y,N,K,ICOL)
C
C SUBROUTINE TO PIVOT EQUATIONS A
C
C SEARCH N X N REAL ARRAY A FOR
C LARGEST ABSOLUTE VALUE A(I,J)
C FOR I,J .GE. K. THEN SWITCH
C ROWS AND COLUMNS TO BRING THIS
C TO A(K,K). ALSO SWITCH RIGHT
C HAND SIDE VECTOR Y AND COLUMN
C MEMORY ARRAY ICOL
C
      DIMENSION A(N,N),Y(N),ICOL(N)
      IF(K.GE.N) RETURN
C SEARCH A FOR LARGEST A(I,J)
      ABSMX=0.
      IMAX=K
      JMAX=K
      DO 10 J=K,N
        DO 10 I=K,N
          ABSA=ABS(A(I,J))
          IF(ABSA.GT.ABSMX) THEN
```

```
            ABSMX=ABSA
            IMAX=I
            JMAX=J
          END IF
   10 CONTINUE
C SWITCH ROWS K AND IMAX IN A,Y
      DO 20 J=1,N
        TEMP=A(K,J)
        A(K,J)=A(IMAX,J)
   20 A(IMAX,J)=TEMP
      TEMP=Y(K)
      Y(K)=Y(IMAX)
      Y(IMAX)=TEMP
C SWITCH COLUMNS K,JMAX IN A,ICOL
      DO 30 I=1,N
        TEMP=A(I,K)
        A(I,K)=A(I,JMAX)
   30 A(I,JMAX)=TEMP
      IT=ICOL(K)
      ICOL(K)=ICOL(JMAX)
      ICOL(JMAX)=IT
C SCALE ROW K
      Z=A(K,K)
      DO 40 J=K,N
   40 A(K,J)=A(K,J)/Z
      Y(K)=Y(K)/Z
      END
```

Here is a subroutine which puts things back into the original order at the end. Please note that X and Y now have to be separate arrays.

```
      SUBROUTINE UNPIV(X,Y,N,ICOL)
C
C UNDO COLUMN REARRANGEMENTS
C
C ON INPUT X IS REAL SOLUTION
C VECTOR LENGTH N WHICH HAS BEEN
C REORDERED. INTEGER ARRAY ICOL
C ON INPUT TELLS DESIRED ORDER,
C Y IS USED AS WORKING SPACE. ON
C OUTPUT X IS THE SOLUTION IN
C THE CORRECT ORDER.
C
      DIMENSION X(N),Y(N),ICOL(N)
      DO 10 J=1,N
        ITRUE=ICOL(J)
   10 Y(ITRUE)=X(J)
      DO 20 J=1,N
   20 X(J)=Y(J)
      END
```

Finally, here is the subroutine GAUSS, modified for what is called 'full pivotal condensation'. It will not blow up on 'good' equations, although no amount of fiddling about can prevent ill conditioned or impossible equations from tossing up some nasty numbers when the program reaches the bottom few rows.

```
      SUBROUTINE GAUSS(A,Y,X,ICOL,N)
C
C GAUSS ELIMINATION SOLVE AX = Y
C WITH ROW AND COLUMN PIVOTING
C
C A = INPUT REAL ARRAY OF N X N
C     COEFFICIENTS, IS DESTROYED
C Y = INPUT REAL ARRAY, N RIGHT
C     HAND SIDES, IS DESTROYED
C X = OUTPUT REAL SOLUTION ARRAY
C     DIMENSION N
C ICOL = WORKING INTEGER ARRAY
C     DIMENSION N
C N = INPUT INTEGER VALUE, NUMBER
C     OF EQUATIONS
C
      DIMENSION A(N,N),Y(N),X(N)
      DIMENSION ICOL(N)
C FIRST INITIALIZE ICOL
      DO 5 K=1,N
    5 ICOL(K)=K
C OUTER LOOP - ELIMINATE COLUMN
      DO 30 K=1,N-1
C FIND THE BEST PIVOT ELEMENT
        CALL SPIV(A,Y,N,K,ICOL)
C THIS LOOP - ROW TO OPERATE ON
        DO 20 I=K+1,N
C THIS LOOP ACTUALLY DOES IT
        Z=A(I,K)
          DO 10 J=K,N
   10     A(I,J)=A(I,J)-A(K,J)*Z
C OPERATE ALSO ON Y
   20   Y(I)=Y(I)-Y(K)*Z
   30 CONTINUE
C NOW BACK-SUBSTITUTE
      X(N)=Y(N)/A(N,N)
C TAKE ROWS IN REVERSE ORDER
      DO 50 K=N-1,1,-1
C SUM OVER KNOWN RESULTS
      SUM=Y(K)
      DO 40 J=K+1,N
   40 SUM=SUM-X(J)*A(K,J)
   50 X(K)=SUM
C FINALLY UNDO REORDERING
      CALL UNPIV(X,Y,N,ICOL)
      END
```

14.6 Vectors and matrices

An array of one dimension can be considered to be a vector. Whether it is interpreted as a row or a column vector depends on the programmer.

EXAMPLE:
The program

```
      DIMENSION X(3)
      DO 1 K=1,3
      X(K)=K
    1 CONTINUE
```

could be thought of as defining either the column vector

$$x = \begin{pmatrix} 1 \\ 2 \\ 3 \end{pmatrix}$$

or the row vector

$$x = (1 \quad 2 \quad 3)$$

To print it like a row vector, simply write

```
      PRINT 20,X
   20 FORMAT(1X,3F5.0)
```

to get

```
    1.    2.    3.
```

or as a column vector write

```
      PRINT 30,X
   30 FORMAT(1X,F5.0)
```

which gives

```
    1.
    2.
    3.
```

EXAMPLE:
It is easy to write a subroutine for the inner product of two vectors x and y each of length n. By definition the inner product p is

$$p = \sum_{k=1}^{n} x_k y_k$$

and could be interpreted as the product of their lengths times the cosine between them.

Here it is:

```
      FUNCTION PRODIN(X,Y,N)
C
C FINDS INNER PRODUCT OF REAL
C VECTORS X AND Y, LENGTH N
C
      DIMENSION X(N),Y(N)
      PRODIN=Ø.Ø
      DO 1Ø K=1,N
        PRODIN=PRODIN+X(K)*Y(K)
 1Ø CONTINUE
      END
```

The norm of a vector is its inner product with itself and could be interpreted as the square of its length

```
C
      FUNCTION VNORM(X,N)
C
C FINDS NORM OF REAL VECTOR
C X, LENGTH N, WHICH IS INNER
C PRODUCT OF X WITH ITSELF
C
      DIMENSION X(N)
      VNORM=Ø.Ø
      DO 1Ø K=1,N
        VNORM=VNORM+X(K)*X(K)
 1Ø CONTINUE
      END
```

or of course it would have been possible to use the previous function

```
      VNORM=PRODIN(X,X,N)
```

An array of two dimensions could be regarded as a matrix.

EXAMPLE:
The statement

```
      DIMENSION A(3,4)
```

defines the matrix

$$\begin{pmatrix} a_{11} & a_{12} & a_{13} & a_{14} \\ a_{21} & a_{22} & a_{23} & a_{24} \\ a_{31} & a_{32} & a_{33} & a_{34} \end{pmatrix}$$

and in referring to the element

```
      A(I,J)
```

in a program, the matrix element in row I and column J is accessed. This is the standard notation used by everyone for matrices.

Because of the way FORTRAN stores arrays column by column in memory (as described in some detail in Chapter 13) the unwary programmer is sometimes tricked into unintentional transposition of matrices. The way to print a matrix with the correct layout on paper is to use implied DO loops to force it to be printed row by row:

```
      PRINT 2Ø,((A(I,J),J=1,4),I=1,3)
 2Ø FORMAT(1X4F5.Ø)
```

A column vector of n elements could be an nx1 array:

```
      DIMENSION Y(3,1)
      DATA Y(4.Ø,5.Ø,6.Ø)
```

defines

$$x = \begin{pmatrix} 1 \\ 2 \\ 3 \end{pmatrix}$$

and

```
      DIMENSION X(1,3)
      DATA X/1.Ø,2.Ø,3.Ø/
```

defines

$$y = (4 \quad 5 \quad 6)$$

EXAMPLE:
Two matrices which are the same size can be added or subtracted element by element, according to the definition of matrix arithmetic. Here is a subroutine to add:

```
      SUBROUTINE MADD(A,B,C,M,N)
C SUBPROGRAM FOR MATRIX SUM C=A+B
      DIMENSION A(M,N),B(M,N),C(M,N)
      DO 1Ø I=1,M
        DO 1Ø J=1,N
          C(I,J)=A(I,J)+B(I,J)
 1Ø CONTINUE
      END
```

and another to subtract, which is rather similar

```
      SUBROUTINE MSUB(A,B,C,M,N)
C MATRIX DIFFERENCE C=A-B
      DIMENSION A(M,N),B(M,N),C(M,N)
      DO 1Ø I=1,M
        DO 1Ø J=1,N
          C(I,J)=A(I,J)-B(I,J)
 1Ø CONTINUE
      END
```

EXAMPLE:
Two matrices which "conform" can be multiplied. The product

$$C = AB$$

is possible if the second dimension of A and the first of B are the same.

The definition of the multiplication is

$$c_{ij} = \sum_{k=1}^{r} a_{ik}b_{kj}$$

where r is the common size of A and B.

The product C has the first dimension of A and the second of B. Therefore

$$C \quad = \quad A \quad * \quad B$$

$$m \times n \quad m \times r \quad r \times n$$

Here is a useful little subroutine for matrix multiplication:

```
      SUBROUTINE MMPY(A,B,C,M,IR,N)
C
C FIND MATRIX PRODUCT C=A*B
C
C A = INPUT REAL M X IR MATRIX
C B = INPUT REAL IR X N MATRIX
C C = OUTPUT REAL M X N MATRIX
C M,IR,N = INTEGER ARRAY SIZES
C
      DIMENSION A(M,IR),B(IR,N)
      DIMENSION C(M,N)
      DO 2Ø I=1,M
```

```
        DO 2Ø J=1,N
          SUM=Ø.Ø
          DO 1Ø K=1,IR
            SUM=SUM+A(I,K)*B(K,J)
 1Ø       CONTINUE
          C(I,J)=SUM
 2Ø CONTINUE
      END
```

EXAMPLE:
The product of a matrix with a vector could be achieved by the matrix multiplication program, or by a special purpose one. Here is a program to multiply a column vector by a matrix; there is only one way round to do this:

$$y \quad = \quad A \quad x$$

result	matrix	column vector
size	size	size
m	m x n	n

```
      SUBROUTINE MBYV(A,X,Y,M,N)
C
C MATRIX TIMES VECTOR Y=A*X
C
C A = INPUT REAL M X N MATRIX
C X = INPUT REAL N VECTOR
C Y = OUTPUT REAL M VECTOR
C M,N = INTEGER ARRAY SIZES
C
      DIMENSION A(M,N),X(N),Y(M)
      DO 2Ø I=1,M
        SUM=Ø.Ø
        DO 1Ø K=1,N
          SUM=SUM+A(I,K)*X(K)
 1Ø     CONTINUE
        Y(I)=SUM
 2Ø CONTINUE
      END
```

Referring to the section on linear equations, this multiplication is the same as substituting values of x into the equations whose coefficients are given by A, and similarly a row vector by a matrix:

$$q \quad = \quad p \quad A$$

size	size	size
n	m	m x n

```
      SUBROUTINE VBYM(A,P,Q,M,N)
C
C VECTOR TIMES MATRIX Q=P*A
C
C A = INPUT REAL M X N MATRIX
C P = INPUT REAL M VECTOR
C Q = OUTPUT REAL N VECTOR
C M,N = INTEGER ARRAY SIZES
C
      DIMENSION A(M,N),P(M),Q(N)
      DO 20 J=1,N
        SUM=0.0
        DO 10 K=1,M
          SUM=SUM+P(K)*A(K,J)
 10     CONTINUE
        Q(J)=SUM
 20   CONTINUE
      END
```

The final operation that might be desired is division but this is an operation that is not defined. However there is something very close to this that is extremely important - but not so easy to calculate as the other definitions. First of all there is a very special matrix, the unit matrix, which leaves square (nxn) matrices unchanged under multiplication. This matrix is called I by mathematicians:

$$I = \begin{Bmatrix} 1 & 0 & 0 & . & . & . & 0 \\ 0 & 1 & 0 & . & . & . & 0 \\ . & . & . & & & & . \\ . & . & . & & & & . \\ . & . & . & & & & . \\ 0 & 0 & 0 & . & . & . & 1 \end{Bmatrix}$$

i.e. it is zero everywhere except on the diagonal. It is very easy to see what happens if this is multiplied by another matrix:

$$c_{ij} = \sum_{k=1}^{n} a_{ik}b_{kj}$$

Recalling that these are all n x n, then c_{ij} is the same as a_{ik} if B is a unit matrix, since in making the sum, only b_{jj} is not zero. A similar thing occurs if A is a unit matrix.

Now given any n x n matrix A, the inverse of A, called A^{-1}, is that matrix

which gives the product

$$A A^{-1} = I$$

This is important in many ways, not least as a method of solving linear equations of the form

$$Ax = y$$

since by premultiplying both sides by the inverse of A, then

$$x = A^{-1} y$$

This means that, if A^{-1} can somehow be found from A, then the equations are solved if the right hand side y is substituted in this latest equation, i.e. multiplied by A^{-1}. The next section is devoted to one method of computing this useful result, and another is given as a case study in the next Chapter.

14.7 The Gauss-Jordan matrix inversion

It is desirable to have a systematic procedure to find the inverse A^{-1} of a given matrix A, so that $A A^{-1} = I$. In an earlier section, it was seen that the Gauss Elimination procedure could reduce the coefficients of an array to an upper triangular form:

$$A = \begin{pmatrix} a_{11} & a_{12} & a_{13} \\ a_{21} & a_{22} & a_{23} \\ a_{31} & a_{32} & a_{33} \end{pmatrix}$$

became what could be called

$$U = \begin{pmatrix} u_{11} & u_{12} & u_{13} \\ 0 & u_{22} & u_{23} \\ 0 & 0 & u_{33} \end{pmatrix}$$

In fact, the Gauss Elimination procedure could be modified slightly so that A is reduced to the special unit matrix I. Re-examining the procedure, it is seen that in eliminating column K with a_{kk} as a "pivot", only the elements beneath a_{kk}

were eliminated. It is easy to eliminate the ones above as well. The recipe could be rewritten:

For each column K from 1 to N
For each row I from 1 to N
except row K
Define Z=A(I,K)/A(K,K) and operate along row I for J from 1 to N by letting A(I,J)=A(I,J)-A(K,J)*Z

For clarity the right hand side has been dropped from the procedure. (However you may have noticed that this procedure carried out with the right hand side of an equation included would remove any need for back-substitution.)

What is available now is a method of reducing the matrix A to diagonal form. Suppose N is 3, then

$$A = \begin{pmatrix} a_{11} & a_{12} & a_{13} \\ a_{21} & a_{22} & a_{23} \\ a_{31} & a_{32} & a_{33} \end{pmatrix}$$

becomes

$$D = \begin{pmatrix} d_{11} & 0 & 0 \\ 0 & d_{22} & 0 \\ 0 & 0 & d_{33} \end{pmatrix}$$

The goal of a unit matrix has not quite been achieved, but all that is necessary is to divide row K through by A(K,K) at the end of the recipe for each K. Here therefore is a FORTRAN program which reduces an N by N matrix A to a unit matrix. It incorporates every step required to find the inverse of A, as will be seen in a moment.

```
C SELECT COLUMN K
      DO 40 K=1,N
C DO ALL ROWS EXCEPT ROW K
      DO 20 I=1,N
          IF(I.NE.K)THEN
              Z=A(I,K)/A(K,K)
              DO 10 J=1,N
                  A(I,J)=A(I,J)-A(K,J)*Z
10            CONTINUE
```

```
          END IF
20    CONTINUE
C AND DIVIDE ROW K BY A(K,K)
      Z=A(K,K)
      DO 30 J=1,N
          A(K,J)=A(K,J)/Z
30    CONTINUE
40 CONTINUE
```

To find the inverse of matrix A, it is necessary to start with a unit matrix. This may seem magical, but here is a brief explanation: each step K in the Gauss-Jordan reduction could be expressed as the multiplication of A by some twiddly matrix T_k. An inquisitive reader might like to sort out exactly what that is. The overall result is that A has been multiplied by a series of twiddlies which eventually produce the unit matrix because

$$AT_1 T_2 \cdots T_N = I$$

but

$$A A^{-1} = I$$

defines the inverse. Therefore

$$A^{-1} = T_1 T_2 \cdots T_N$$

and so by doing all the same operations on what starts as a unit matrix, A^{-1} is obtained. Here is a subroutine for matrix inversion by this procedure.

```
      SUBROUTINE GAUSSJ(A,B,N)
C
C INVERT N X N MATRIX A
C
C A = INPUT N X N REAL MATRIX
C B = OUTPUT N X N REAL INVERSE
C N = INTEGER SIZE OF A AND B
C
      DIMENSION A(N,N),B(N,N)
C SET UP B AS UNIT MATRIX
      DO 20 I=1,N
          DO 10 J=1,N
10        B(I,J)=0.0
20    B(I,I)=1.0
C SELECT COLUMN K FOR ELIMINATION
      DO 60 K=1,N
C DO ALL ROWS EXCEPT ROW K
      DO 40 I=1,N
```

```
      IF(I.NE.K) THEN
        Z=A(I,K)/A(K,K)
        DO 3Ø J=1,N
          A(I,J)=A(I,J)-A(K,J)*Z
          B(I,J)=B(I,J)-B(K,J)*Z
3Ø      CONTINUE
      END IF
4Ø   CONTINUE
C AND DIVIDE ROW K BY A(K,K)
      Z=A(K,K)
      DO 5Ø J=1,N
        A(K,J)=A(K,J)/Z
        B(K,J)=B(K,J)/Z
5Ø   CONTINUE
6Ø CONTINUE
   END
```

This program does not use pivoting to reduce the risk of instability as was discussed in the previous section. To incorporate pivoting is presented as a problem at the end of the Chapter - it is a bit more subtle than it was for the ordinary Gauss elimination.

14.8 Some iterative methods

Given a satisfactory method like Gaussian elimination for solving equations, it may seem peculiar that a totally different approach, that of iteration, is often used. Two things all too often affect the elimination methods adversely. The first is the problem of ill conditioning - where the determinant of an equation is small problems arise with the pivot elements that full pivoting cannot avoid in extreme cases - unfortunately most large systems of equations are extreme. Iterative methods can succeed where the Gauss elimination "blows up". Secondly, the elimination methods require N^2 operations to reduce an N by N set of coefficients - and although this is a big improvement over the N! behaviour of Cramer's rule, it is still a lot of work for large N. Iterative methods take N steps for each iteration, and so if the number of iterations is not too large, they can be efficient.

Returning to the matrix shorthand for equations,

$$Ax = y$$

where A is the array of coefficients, y the right hand side vector, and x the unknown solution vector.

The law of multiplication for a matrix by a vector gives

$$y_i = \sum_{j=1}^{N} a_{ij}x_j$$

$$= \sum_{\substack{j=1 \\ j \neq i}}^{N} a_{ij}x_j + a_{ii}x_i$$

This means to take the sum over j except for the term when j=i, and consider it afterwards. This allows a rearrangement:

$$a_{ii}x_i = y_i - \sum_{\substack{j=1 \\ j \neq i}}^{N} a_{ij}x_j$$

which is still true, except that it has an unknown on the right hand side. However if a guess of x was available, then it could be plugged into the right hand side to give a better estimate. This is the basis of any iteration. Let x^k stand for the kth guess, then

$$x_i^{k+1} = \frac{1}{a_{ii}} \left\{ y_i - \sum_{\substack{j=1 \\ j \neq i}}^{N} a_{ij}x_j^k \right\}$$

defines what is known as the Jacobi iteration. It can be proven that it will succeed under suitable conditions. A suitable original guess of x is

$$x_i^o = \frac{y_i}{a_{ii}}$$

which is of course what the answer would be if A were purely diagonal. In fact for the Jacobi interation to work, the absolute value of a_{ii} has to be larger than the sum of the absolute values of all other coefficients in any row or column.

The iteration is carried on until a suitably small change occurs from one iteration to the next - perhaps an RMS change. This method has only linear convergence - meaning that it can creep very slowly towards the solution. Thus the change between iterations could be much smaller than the true error.

Here is a program that does this iteration until the RMS change is less than DELTA, which you define, and has a safety device to stop it anyway after NTRYS iterations rather than running on forever. It is given A, the coefficients, and Y, the right hand side. It returns the answer in X. The array XW is used as workspace, because the definition requires that the old X is used each time in calculating the new one - so none of X can be replaced until an iteration is complete. When the subroutine returns, it tells you how many iterations it used, also in NTRYS, and the latest RMS change in DELTA. Therefore you know if it has succeeded. Since both their values are changed by the subprogram, it is important that DELTA and NTRYS are variables of the calling program, not constants.

```
      SUBROUTINE JACOBI(A,Y,X,XW,
     N,DELTA,NTRYS)
C
C JACOBI ITERATION SOLVES A*X=Y
C
C A = INPUT REAL N X N MATRIX OF
C     COEFFICIENTS, NOT ALTERED
C Y = INPUT REAL N VECTOR RIGHT
C     HAND SIDE. NOT ALTERED.
C X = OUTPUT N REAL SOLUTIONS
C XW = REAL WORKSPACE SIZE N
C N = INPUT INTEGER ARRAY SIZES
C DELTA = REAL VARIABLE. INPUT
C     DESIRED MAX RMS CHANGE IN
C     X FOR STOPPING. OUTPUT
C     THE CHANGE ACHIEVED.
C NTRYS = INTEGER VARIABLE.
C     INPUT MAX NO OF ITERATIONS
C     OUTPUT THE ACTUAL NUMBER
C
      DIMENSION A(N,N),Y(N),X(N)
      DIMENSION XW(N)
```

```
C THE FIRST GUESS
      DO 10 I=1,N
 10   X(I)=Y(I)/A(I,I)
C NOW THE ITERATION
      DO 60 ITER=1,NTRYS
        NITER=ITER
        DO 30 I=1,N
          SUM=Y(I)
          DO 20 J=1,N
            IF(J.NE.I) THEN
              SUM=SUM-A(I,J)*X(J)
            END IF
 20       CONTINUE
          XW(I)=SUM/A(I,I)
 30     CONTINUE
C FORM THE RMS CHANGE
        RMS=0.0
        DO 40 I=1,N
 40       RMS=RMS+(X(I)-XW(I))**2
        RMS=SQRT(RMS/N)
C COPY NEW VALUE INTO X
        DO 50 I=1,N
 50       X(I)=XW(I)
        IF(RMS.LT.DELTA) GO TO 70
 60   CONTINUE
 70   NTRYS=NITER
      DELTA=RMS
      END
```

The above program deliberately refrained from replacing the x solution until the iteration was complete. Now why not? If each new x_i came into force as it was calculated, then the iteration would be

$$x_i^{k+1} = \frac{1}{a_{ii}}\left\{ y_i - \sum_{j=1}^{i-1} a_{ij}x_j^{k+1} - \sum_{j=i+1}^{N} a_{ij}x_j^k \right\}$$

and this is a perfectly good scheme, known as the Gauss-Seidel iteration. As might be expected, it is actually a more powerful (faster) iteration. Interestingly, it will sometimes work when the Jacobi method will not. However both of these are guaranteed to converge to the correct solution if at all. This means that if DELTA is small enough, you know you are in the vicinity of the answer.

EXERCISE:
    Using JACOBI as a model, program GASEID to do the some thing using the Gauss-Seidel iteration. Using the test equations given at the end of this Chapter, compare their speeds.

Both of these methods are capable of being speeded up using either the method of over-relaxation (analogous to that described in Problem 13.6) or Aitken's extrapolation as described in Problem 6.3, applied sparingly (i.e. not after every third iteration, but less often). Opportunities to do this are provided in the problems at the conclusion of this Chapter.

14.9 Arrays as differential equations

Some very simple differential equations were solved as examples in Chapter 7 and given as problems there and in Chapter 10.

Now it is possible, by a very convenient manipulation, to put any set of linear ordinary differential equations into the form of a matrix equation.

Suppose the equation is

$$\frac{d^2y}{dt^2} + 2\frac{dy}{dt} + 5y = 1$$

Define new variables y_1 and y_2 so that y_1 is just y and

$$\frac{dy_1}{dt} = y_2$$

then

$$\frac{dy_2}{dt} = \frac{d^2y}{dt^2} = -5y_1 - 2y_2 + 1$$

By this bit of magic the original second order equation is now two simultaneous first order equations, which can be written in matrix form:

$$\begin{bmatrix} \dfrac{dy_1}{dt} \\[2ex] \dfrac{dy_2}{dt} \end{bmatrix} = \begin{bmatrix} 0 & 1 \\ -5 & -2 \end{bmatrix} \begin{bmatrix} y_1 \\ y_2 \end{bmatrix} + \begin{bmatrix} 0 \\ 1 \end{bmatrix}$$

or

$$\frac{dy}{dt} = Ay + u$$

where A is a matrix and y and u are now vectors. Any nth order ordinary differential equation which has constant coefficients can be treated this way:

$$a_n\frac{d^ny}{dt^n} + a_{n-1}\frac{d^{n-1}y}{dt^{n-1}} + \ldots + a_0 = f(t)$$

becomes

$$\begin{bmatrix} \dfrac{dy}{dt}1 \\[1.5ex] \dfrac{dy}{dt}2 \\[1.5ex] . \\ . \\ . \\ \dfrac{dy}{dt}n \end{bmatrix} = \begin{bmatrix} 0 & 1 & 0 & \ldots & 0 \\ 0 & 0 & 1 & \ldots & 0 \\ . & & & & . \\ . & & & & . \\ . & & & & . \\ -\dfrac{1}{a_n} & -\dfrac{a_{n-1}}{a_n} & & & -\dfrac{a_0}{a_n} \end{bmatrix} y + \begin{bmatrix} 0 \\ 0 \\ . \\ . \\ . \\ f(t) \end{bmatrix}$$

Any of the standard methods for solving differential equations can be adapted. The simplest, Euler's method, was used as an example in Chapter 7. In Euler's method, the solution at a time t+h in the future can be predicted from the 'present' solution at time t:

$$y(t+h) = y(t) + h\frac{dy(t)}{dt}$$

and if the differential equation is in the matrix form

$$\frac{dy}{dt} = A y + u$$

then Euler's prediction is

$$y(t+h) = y(t) + h\left\{Ay + u\right\}$$

where y and u are now vectors and A is the coefficient matrix. A subroutine is required to predict a new value of Y, H seconds in the future, from a present value of Y for a system of N differential equations arranged as described above. The subroutine should be given the NxN array of coefficients A and the driving vector U. Here is such a subroutine:

```
      SUBROUTINE OILY(A,Y,U,N,H)
C
C PREDICT SOLUTION DY/DT = A*Y+U
C FOR ONE STEP BY EULER'S METHOD
C
C A = REAL N X N SYSTEM MATRIX
C Y = REAL ARRAY SIZE N. INPUT
C       THE PRESENT SOLUTION,
C       OUTPUT THE PREDICTION
C U = REAL ARRAY SIZE N, THE
C       FORCING VECTOR. NOT CHANGED
C N = INTEGER VALUE GIVING NUMBER
C       OF EQUATIONS, LIMIT 1Ø
C H = REAL VALUE GIVING THE STEP
C       SIZE FOR THE PREDICTION
C
      DIMENSION A(N,N),Y(N),U(N)
      DIMENSION WORK(1Ø)
      IF(N.GT.1Ø) THEN
      PRINT*,'WORKSPACE EXCEEDED'
      RETURN
      END IF
C MULTIPLY TO GET A*Y
      CALL MBYV(A,Y,WORK,N,N)
C ADD ON U AND MULTIPLY BY H
      DO 1Ø K=1,N
 1Ø   Y(K)=Y(K)+H*(WORK(K)+U(K))
      END
C
      SUBROUTINE MBYV(A,X,Y,M,N)
C COPIED FROM EARLIER EXAMPLE
      DIMENSION A(M,N),X(N),Y(M)
      DO 2Ø I=1,M
      SUM=Ø.Ø
      DO 1Ø K=1,N
        SUM=SUM+A(I,K)*X(K)
 1Ø   CONTINUE
      Y(I)=SUM
 2Ø   CONTINUE
      END
```

Did you realize that solving a differential equation could be so easy? The above subprogram uses an internal working array, WORK, which limits the program to systems of 10 equations. Of course WORK could be increased in size or made an argument of the subroutine with an adjustable dimension. Recall that the calling program would then have to make an actual allocation of space.

Here is a main program which will use OILY to calculate and print the solution of

$$\frac{d^2y}{dt^2} + 2\frac{dy}{dt} + 5\,y = 1$$

given that y and dy/dt are initially zero. The solution is presented for 20 steps with H = 0.1:

```
DIMENSION A(2,2),Y(2),U(2)
   DATA A/Ø.Ø,-5.Ø,1.Ø,-2.Ø/
   DATA U/Ø.Ø,1.Ø/,Y/2*Ø.Ø/
   T=Ø.Ø
   H=Ø.1
   PRINT*,' TIME   Y(1)    Y(2)'
   PRINT 1Ø,T,Y
1Ø FORMAT(1X,3F7.3)
   DO 2Ø K=1,2Ø
     T=T+H
     CALL OILY(A,Y,U,2,H)
     PRINT 1Ø,T,Y
2Ø CONTINUE
   END
```

The Runge-Kutta method of solving differential equations can be treated in a similar way. This method was introduced as Problem 10.6, and should be more accurate than the Euler method, although it can be less stable for large step sizes. Problem 14.6 asks you for the Runge-Kutta solution. Finally in Problem 14.7 will be found a little known method which has the virtue of great stability; its accuracy is better than that of the Euler method although not so good as the Runge-Kutta technique.

14.10 Problems

Here is a system of equations

$$10x_1 - 7x_2 + 3x_3 + 5x_4 = 6$$
$$-6x_1 + 8x_2 - x_3 - 4x_4 = 5$$
$$3x_1 + x_2 + 4x_3 + 11x_4 = 2$$
$$5x_1 - 9x_2 - 2x_3 + 4x_4 = 7$$

The solution is

$$x = \begin{pmatrix} 5.00 \\ 4.00 \\ -7.00 \\ 1.00 \end{pmatrix}$$

and the inverse of the coefficient matrix is

$$\begin{pmatrix} 0.2940 & 0.4390 & -0.0314 & 0.1580 \\ 0.1810 & 0.4110 & 0.0249 & 0.1160 \\ -0.1580 & -0.6160 & 0.00217 & -0.425 \\ -0.0390 & 0.0672 & 0.0964 & 0.1010 \end{pmatrix}$$

A "diagonally dominant" system of equations with the same solution is:

$$10x_1 - 3x_2 + 2x_3 + x_4 = 25$$

$$x_1 + 8x_2 - 2x_3 + 3x_4 = 26$$

$$x_1 + x_2 + 6x_3 + x_4 = -32$$

$$2x_1 + 3x_2 + x_3 + 9x_4 = 24$$

Use these in the following problems.

PROBLEM 14.1:
Write a subroutine to calculate the determinant of a general NxN matrix.

PROBLEM 14.2:
Using the result of Problem 14.1, write a subroutine to solve linear equations by Cramer's rule. Guard against a near-zero determinant.

PROBLEM 14.3:
Pivoting to reduce the risk of failure in the Gauss-Jordan reduction is possible in a limited way. To find the limitation, first develop the matrix equivalent of the elimination process. Implement pivoting as far as possible in a subroutine to find the inverse of an NxN matrix by this method.

PROBLEM 14.4:
Choose either the Jacobi or Gauss-Seidel iteration and develop a method of over-relaxation to apply to it (see Problem 13.6). Investigate the performance under over-relaxation. If you are still keen, do the other method.

PROBLEM 14.5:
Experiment with the application of Aitken's extrapolation to one of the iterative methods of solving equations (see Problem 6.3). Apply it sparingly - develop some way of knowing when the iteration has settled down enough to apply Aitken to it. This is a tricky

but rewarding exercise. If you survive it, try the other method.

Here is a pair of differential equations:

$$\frac{d^2 y_1}{dt^2} = -\frac{2s}{m} y_1 + \frac{s}{m} y_2$$

$$\frac{d^2 y_2}{dt^2} = -\frac{s}{m} y_2 + \frac{s}{m} y_1$$

They describe the motion of a pair of weights of mass m kilograms and springs of stiffness s Newtons/metre, as shown in Fig.14.2. Use this equation in Problems 14.6 and 14.7, making up the initial conditions yourself and picking round numbers for s and m, for example 1.0.

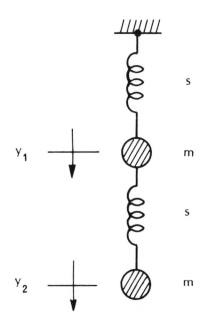

Fig. 14.2. A system of masses and springs for testing differential equation solvers.

PROBLEM 14.6:
The Runge-Kutta method was described in Problem 10.6, and is a popular and useful method for solving differential equations. Implement it for equations of the type

$$\frac{dy}{dt} = Ay + u$$

as described earlier in this Chapter.

Using the springs and weights, compare its accuracy and stability to the Euler method. Pay particular attention to the effect of h, the step length, on accuracy and stability. For simplicity you could take u to be zero.

PROBLEM 14.7:

The Crank-Nicholson method is well known as a way of solving partial differential equations, and is rather closely related to the iteration that was recommended in Problem 13.5 for solving Laplace's equation. It is not so well known that the "model" of the second derivative on which Problem 13.5 was based

$$\frac{d^2 y(t)}{dt^2} \approx \frac{1}{h} \left\{ \frac{dy(t+h)}{dt} - \frac{dy(t)}{dt} \right\}$$

can be used to produce a very nice method of solving ordinary differential equations.

Consider the Taylor expansion of the desired prediction:

$$y(t+h) = y(t) + h \frac{dy(t)}{dt} + \frac{h^2}{2} \frac{d^2 y(t)}{dt^2} + \cdots$$

Substituting for the derivatives up to second order,

$$y(t+h) \approx y(t) + \frac{h}{2} A y(t) + \frac{h}{2} A y(t+h)$$

$$+ \frac{h}{2} \left\{ u(t) + u(t+h) \right\}$$

However it can be solved as

$$\left[I - \frac{h}{2} A \right] y(t+h) =$$

$$\left[I + \frac{h}{2} A \right] y(t) + \frac{h}{2} \left\{ u(t) + u(t+h) \right\}$$

from which by the magic of matrix inversion

$$y(t+h) = \left[I - \frac{h}{2} A \right]^{-1} \left[I + \frac{h}{2} A \right] y(t)$$

$$+ \frac{h}{2} \left\{ u(t) + u(t+h) \right\}$$

$$= C y(t) + F$$

where C is just a matrix that can be calculated from A and h, and F is a modification of the forcing vector. As long as h is constant from one step to the next, C need only be found once, after which the entire solution is a process of very easy successive multiplication. This method is often overlooked, which is a pity because it has admirable stability properties. My program for this has a subroutine SETUP to make the matrix C, and another one CRANK to crank out the solution.

Taking F=0, which simplifies matters somewhat, solve the springs and masses. Once again look at how the accuracy and stability depend on h and compare with the Euler and Runge-Kutta methods.

15
Two more case studies

15.1 Introduction

In this Chapter two more applications of arrays of two dimensions are considered in some detail. The first of these will be another matrix method, which has a certain amount of versatility because it can be used either for solving linear equations or, with a bit of additional work, for matrix inversion without extra storage. The second application introduces the idea of using drawing machines, or 'plotters', with computers, and a program is given for drawing the isolines or contours of a field of data presented as an array of two dimensions.

15.2 The uses of LU factorization

This is a method for matrix inversion or the solution of linear equations. The basic idea is that a matrix can be factored into the product of a lower diagonal matrix L and an upper diagonal matrix U. This is always possible in theory if the square NxN matrix A is nonsingular, i.e. its determinant is nonzero. In practice there is trouble if the determinant is small.

For convenience, the diagonal elements of U can be forced to be 1, with no loss of generality. Therefore the factorization can be expressed as

$$A = LU$$

with

$$A = \begin{bmatrix} a_{11} & a_{12} & a_{13} & \cdots & a_{1n} \\ a_{21} & a_{22} & a_{23} & \cdots & a_{2n} \\ \vdots & & & & \vdots \\ a_{n1} & a_{n2} & a_{n3} & \cdots & a_{nn} \end{bmatrix}$$

$$L = \begin{bmatrix} \ell_{11} & 0 & 0 & \cdots & 0 \\ \ell_{21} & \ell_{22} & 0 & \cdots & 0 \\ \vdots & & & & \vdots \\ \ell_{n1} & \ell_{n2} & 0 & \cdots & \ell_{nn} \end{bmatrix}$$

$$U = \begin{bmatrix} 1 & u_{12} & u_{13} & \cdots & u_{1n} \\ 0 & 1 & u_{23} & \cdots & u_{2n} \\ \vdots & & & & \vdots \\ 0 & 0 & 0 & \cdots & 1 \end{bmatrix}$$

As a preview of its versatility, here is a summary of how it is used.

(a) To Solve Linear Equations

It is desired to solve $Ax = y$.

If first $Lz = y$ is solved for the intermediate vector z, and $Ux = z$ is then solved, what has been found is

$$LUx = y$$

i.e.

$$Ax = y$$

Recipe:
(i) Find L and U.
(ii) Solve $Lz=y$ by a procedure of 'forward substitution'.
(iii) Solve $Ux=z$ by a procedure of back substitution.

(b) To Invert a Matrix

It is desired to invert $A = LU$.

Then
$$AU^{-1} = L$$
$$AU^{-1}L^{-1} = I \text{ (the unit matrix)}$$

Therefore

$$U^{-1}L^{-1} = A^{-1} \text{ (the desired inverse)}$$

Recipe:
  (i) Find L and U.
  (ii) Find L^{-1} and U^{-1}, which turns out not to be too difficult.
  (iii) Find $A^{-1} = U^{-1}L^{-1}$.

As a bonus, it will be seen that each and every step of these procedures can be carried out without using an extra matrix. L and U can be found in the space which is occupied by A, L^{-1} can be calculated on top of L, U^{-1} on top of U, and the product $U^{-1}L^{-1}$ can be formed in the space occupied by U^{-1} and L^{-1} !

15.3 The details of factorization

Consider the law of matrix multiplication as it applies to the factors L and U:

$$A = LU$$

means that

$$a_{jk} = \sum_{i=1}^{N} \ell_{ji}u_{ik}$$

but there are certain zero entries in both L and U which can be exploited. To find column k of L, notice that

$$u_{ik} = 0 \text{ for } i > k$$

and furthermore

$$u_{kk} \text{ is } 1$$

Therefore

$$a_{jk} = \sum_{i=1}^{k-1} \ell_{ji}u_{ik} + \ell_{jk}$$

from which

$$\ell_{jk} = a_{jk} - \sum_{i=1}^{k-1} \ell_{ji}u_{ik} \qquad (1)$$

Since

$$\ell_{jk} = 0 \text{ for } j < k$$

this is calculated only for j from k to N. It is important to observe that the calculation of column k of L uses only values from L in columns before k, and values from U in the first k-1 rows.

Now look at row k of U. As before the law of matrix multiplication could give

$$a_{kj} = \sum_{i=1}^{N} \ell_{ki}u_{ij}$$

but again zero elements are observed in L;

$$\ell_{ki} = 0 \text{ for } k > i$$

Therefore

$$a_{kj} = \sum_{i=1}^{k-1} \ell_{ki}u_{ij} + \ell_{kk}u_{kj}$$

from which

$$u_{kj} = a_{kj} - \sum_{i=1}^{k-1} \frac{\ell_{ki}u_{ij}}{\ell_{kk}} \qquad (2)$$

and since

$$u_{kj} = 0 \text{ for } k > j$$

and

$$u_{kk} = 1$$

this is done only for j from k+1 to N. Again it may be observed that the calculation of row k of U will require the value of ℓ_{kk} , but apart from that values from L up to column k-1 and from U up to row k-1.

Here, therefore, is the complete recipe for LU factorization:

(i) Column 1 of L is the same as column 1 of A (observe this in the equation (1)).

(ii) Row 1 of U is simply obtained using $u_{1j} = a_{1j} / \ell_{11}$ for j from 2 to N; and $u_{11} = 1$.

(iii) For each k from 2 to N

    (a) Find column k of L using the equation (1) for j from k to N.

    (b) Except when k=N, find row k of U using the equation (2).

(iv) Row N of U contains only $u_{NN} = 1$.

This codes very easily into FORTRAN. The following program segment assumes that A, XL, and XU are real matrices of dimensions NxN.

```
C PROGRAM FOR LU FACTORIZATION
C FIRST CLEAR L AND U
      DO 5 J=1,N
        DO 5 K=1,N
          XL(J,K)=0.0
          XU(J,K)=0.0
  5 CONTINUE
C COLUMN 1 OF XL IS COLUMN 1 OF A
      DO 10 J=1,N
 10 XL(J,1)=A(J,1)
C NOW FIND ROW 1 OF XU
      XU(1,1)=1.0
      DO 20 J=2,N
 20 XU(1,J)=A(1,J)/XL(1,1)
C NOW WORK THROUGH THE REMAINDER
      DO 80 K=2,N
C FIND COLUMN K OF XL
        DO 40 J=K,N
          SUM=A(J,K)
          DO 30 I=1,K-1
 30         SUM=SUM-XL(J,I)*XU(I,K)
 40     XL(J,K)=SUM
        XU(K,K)=1.0
```

```
        DO 60 J=K+1,N
          SUM=A(K,J)
          DO 50 I=1,K-1
 50         SUM=SUM-XL(K,I)*XU(I,J)
 60     XU(K,J)=SUM/XL(K,K)
 80 CONTINUE
```

And now comes the black magic! It has already been observed that the calculation of column k of L or row k of U requires only the values of L and U from previous rows or columns. This feature is essential for the method to work in the first place. But it may also be observed that the elements of A, the matrix being factored, are only referred to once each, just as they are about to be replaced. Therefore there is no conflict between A and L or between A and U. Therefore either L or U could use the same space as A. Is there a conflict between L and U? Yes, but it is only the diagonal. However, it is known that all diagonal elements of U are to be 1, so there is no need to store them. Therefore A, L, and U can all occupy the same space.

Here, the three arrays A, XL and XU are associated through an EQUIVALENCE statement in a program which factorizes and prints a trial 4x4 matrix:

```
      DIMENSION A(4,4)
      DIMENSION XL(4,4),XU(4,4)
      EQUIVALENCE (A,XL,XU)
      DATA ((A(I,J),J=1,4),I=1,4)
     /10.0,-7.0,3.0,5.0,
     -6.0,8.0,-1.0,-4.0,
     3.0,1.0,4.0,11.0,
     5.0,-9.0,-2.0,4.0/
      N=4
C COLUMN 1 OF XL IS COLUMN 1 OF A
C NOW FIND ROW 1 OF XU
      DO 20 J=2,N
 20 XU(1,J)=A(1,J)/XL(1,1)
C NOW WORK THROUGH THE REMAINDER
      DO 80 K=2,N
C FIND COLUMN K OF XL
        DO 40 J=K,N
          SUM=A(J,K)
          DO 30 I=1,K-1
 30         SUM=SUM-XL(J,I)*XU(I,K)
 40     XL(J,K)=SUM
C FIND ROW K OF U EXCEPT WHEN K=N
```

```
      DO 60 J=K+1,N
         SUM=A(K,J)
         DO 50 I=1,K-1
 50         SUM=SUM-XL(K,I)*XU(I,J)
 60      XU(K,J)=SUM/XL(K,K)
 80   CONTINUE
      DO 90 K=1,N
      PRINT*,(A(K,L),L=1,N)
 90   CONTINUE
      END
```

In making this into a subroutine, all the references have to be made to A itself because the dummy arguments of a subroutine are not allowed to appear in an EQUIVALENCE statement. Here is a useful subroutine for LU factorization:

```
      SUBROUTINE FACTLU(A,N)
C
C PROGRAM TO FACTORIZE N X N REAL
C MATRIX A INTO LOWER TRIANGLE XL
C AND UPPER TRIANGLE XU WHICH USE
C THE SAME SPACE AS A. DIAGONAL
C OF U IS UNITY AND NOT STORED.
C
      DIMENSION A(N,N)
C COLUMN 1 OF L IS COLUMN 1 OF A
C FIND ROW 1 OF U
      PIV=A(1,1)
      DO 10 J=2,N
 10   A(1,J)=A(1,J)/PIV
C NOW WORK THROUGH THE REMAINDER
      DO 60 K=2,N
C FIND COLUMN K OF XL
      DO 30 J=K,N
         SUM=A(J,K)
         DO 20 I=1,K-1
 20         SUM=SUM-A(J,I)*A(I,K)
 30      A(J,K)=SUM
C FIND ROW K OF U EXCEPT FOR K=N
C DIAGONAL ELEMENTS ARE ASSUMED
      PIV=A(K,K)
      DO 50 J=K+1,N
         SUM=A(K,J)
         DO 40 I=1,K-1
 40         SUM=SUM-A(K,I)*A(I,J)
 50      A(K,J)=SUM/PIV
 60   CONTINUE
      END
```

Note that the loop which terminates on statement 50 is safe in FORTRAN 77; when K=N it will be jumped over. This was not the case in FORTRAN IV.

15.4 Solving equations by LU factorization

As outlined earlier, once a matrix has been factored into the product of lower and upper triangular matrices as in the previous Section, equations of the form

$$Ax = y$$

can be solved by a substitution process. First solve

$$Lz = y$$

for the intermediate vector z, by forward substitution, and then solve

$$Ux = z$$

by back substitution.

To solve

$$Lz = y$$

the law of multiplication of a vector by a matrix is examined. Clearly

$$y_j = \sum_{i=1}^{N} \ell_{ji} z_i$$

but

$$\ell_{ji} = 0 \quad \text{for } i > j$$

Therefore

$$y_i = \sum_{i=1}^{j} \ell_{ji} z_j$$

$$= \sum_{i=1}^{j-1} \ell_{ji} z_i + \ell_{jj} z_j$$

from which

$$z_j = \frac{y_j - \sum_{i=1}^{j-1} \ell_{ji} z_i}{\ell_{jj}}$$

To calculate z_j, only the earlier z values between 1 and $j-1$ are needed. Therefore the z vector can be found, starting with z_1 and working forward. The following fragment of program will accomplish this. Note that when J=1, the inner DO-loop is not executed. You can observe that y is used only in calculating z, and so z and y could use the same storage.

```
      DO 20 J=1,N
        SUM=Y(J)
        DO 10 I=1,J-1
10      SUM=SUM-XL(J,I)*Z(I)
20    Z(J)=SUM/XL(J,J)
```

The procedure for back substitution is similar. It is virtually the same as was used in the previous Chapter following Gaussian elimination, except that here, in the matrix U, the diagonal elements are assumed to be 1.0 and are not stored (because the space is used by the diagonal of L). To solve

$$Ux = z$$

use the fact that

$$z_j = \sum_{i=1}^{N} u_{ji} x_i$$

But $u_{ji}=0$ for $i < j$ and $u_{jj}=1$.

Therefore

$$z_j = \sum_{i=j+1}^{N} u_{ji} x_i + x_j$$

from which

$$x_j = z_j - \sum_{i=j+1}^{N} u_{ji} x_i$$

for j=N, N-1, ..., 1, a process of back substitution. In the following program fragment the inner DO is not executed when J=N. It is again evident that x and z could occupy the same space.

```
      DO 40 J=N,1,-1
        SUM=Z(J)
        DO 30 I=J+1,N
30      SUM=SUM-XU(J,I)*X(I)
40    X(J)=SUM
```

These fragments can now be combined into a complete subroutine for solving the equation

$$Ax = y$$

by these methods. Because z is allowed to overwrite y, and is itself overwritten again by x, only the arrays A and y are required by the program. The solution is returned in the same array Y in which the right hand side is given. The program first calls on FACTLU, the subroutine which forms the L and U factors, and then applies the forward and back substitution process to arrive at the answer.

```
      SUBROUTINE SOLVLU(A,Y,N)
C
C SOLVE LINEAR EQUATIONS A*X=Y
C BY TRIANGULAR FACTORIZATION
C
C A = INPUT REAL N X N MATRIX
C     OF COEFFICIENTS. ON OUTPUT
C     IT HAS BEEN LU FACTORED.
C Y = INPUT REAL N VECTOR, THE
C     RIGHT HAND SIDE. OUTPUT
C     THE SOLUTION X.
C N = INTEGER SIZE OF ARRAYS
C
      DIMENSION A(N,N),Y(N)
C INVOKE FACTORIZATION PROGRAM
      CALL FACTLU(A,N)
C FORWARD SUBSTITUTE FOR Z
      DO 20 J=1,N
        SUM=Y(J)
        DO 10 I=1,J-1
10      SUM=SUM-A(J,I)*Y(I)
20    Y(J)=SUM/A(J,J)
```

```
C BACK SUBSTITUTE FOR X
      DO 4Ø J=N,1,-1
         SUM=Y(J)
         DO 3Ø I=J+1,N
  3Ø     SUM=SUM-A(J,I)*Y(I)
  4Ø  Y(J)=SUM
      END
```

EXERCISE:

Enumerate the steps involved in solving equations by LU factorization. Is there any advantage in speed over the Gauss elimination method? Can you see any other advantage?

15.5 Matrix inversion by LU factorization

As discussed at the beginning of the Chapter, to achieve matrix inversion by this method once L and U have been found, L and U themselves have to be inverted and the product $U^{-1}L^{-1}$ formed.

Consider first the inversion of the upper triangular matrix U. A matrix P is to be found for which

$$UP = I \text{ (the unit matrix)}$$

It can be shown that P itself is also an upper triangle and that its diagonal is also unity. This is rather convenient. The law of matrix multiplication is

$$\sum_{i=1}^{N} u_{ji}p_{ik} = I_{jk} = 0 \text{ for } j < k$$

But

$$u_{ji} = 0 \text{ for } i < j$$

$$p_{ik} = 0 \text{ for } i > k$$

$$u_{jj} = 1 \text{ and } p_{kk} = 1$$

Therefore

$$p_{jk} + \sum_{i=j+1}^{k-1} u_{ji}p_{ik} + u_{jk} = 0$$

From which

$$p_{jk} = -u_{jk} - \sum_{i=j+1}^{k-1} u_{ji}p_{ik}$$

If this evaluation is made in the order

$$j = k-1, k-2, \ldots, 1$$

then each sum will only involve known values from P. Observe also that even though a number of elements of U are involved in the sum, they are not the same subscripts as any values of P that have already been defined. It will therefore once again be possible to work in the same space, this time for P and U. Here is the necessary program fragment - note that the diagonal elements (which are 1.0) are not found.

```
      DO 2Ø K=N,2,-1
        DO 2Ø J=K-1,1,-1
          SUM=-XU(J,K)
          DO 1Ø I=J+1,K-1
  1Ø      SUM=SUM-XU(J,I)*P(I,K)
  2Ø  P(J,K)=SUM
```

A similar development reveals how the lower triangular matrix L may be inverted. This time the diagonals are not 1.0 and must be calculated. To get the inverse, called Q,

$$LQ = I$$

$$\sum_{i=1}^{N} \ell_{ji}q_{ik} = I_{jk}$$

Again it can be shown quite easily that Q is itself a lower triangular matrix. Accordingly,

$$\ell_{ji} = 0 \text{ for } i > j$$

$$q_{ik} = 0 \text{ for } i < k$$

Therefore

$$\sum_{i=k}^{j} \ell_{ji} q_{ik} = I_{jk}$$

On the diagonal, j=k and

$$q_{kk} = \frac{1}{\ell_{kk}}$$

Off the diagonal,

$$\sum_{i=k}^{j-1} \ell_{ji} q_{ik} + \ell_{jj} q_{jk} = 0$$

giving

$$q_{jk} = - \frac{\displaystyle\sum_{i=k}^{j-1} \ell_{ji} q_{ik}}{\ell_{jj}}$$

If this done in the order

$$k = 1, 2, \ldots, N$$

then the sums involve only those values from Q which have already been defined. Furthermore the values from L have subscripts (j,i) which have not yet been used in Q. So again the calculation can be made in place. Here is the program:

```
      DO 5Ø K=1,N-1
        Q(K,K)=1.Ø/XL(K,K)
        DO 5Ø J=K+1,N
          SUM=Ø.Ø
          DO 4Ø I=K,J-1
4Ø        SUM=SUM-XL(J,I)*Q(I,K)
5Ø      Q(J,K)=SUM/XL(J,J)
        Q(N,N)=1.Ø/XL(N,N)
```

The final step is to multiply P by Q to make the inverse, A :

$$A = U^{-1} L^{-1} = PQ$$

But

$$a_{jk} = \sum_{i=1}^{N} p_{ji} q_{ik}$$

But

$$p_{ji} = 0 \quad \text{for} \quad i < j$$

$$p_{jj} = 1 \quad \text{and so is not stored}$$

$$q_{ik} = 0 \quad \text{for} \quad i < k$$

Therefore

$$\bar{a}_{jk} = q_{jk} + \sum_{i=j+1}^{N} p_{ji} q_{ik} \quad \text{if} \quad j \geq k$$

or

$$\bar{a}_{jk} = \sum_{i=k}^{N} p_{ji} q_{ik} \quad \text{if} \quad j < k$$

The last row is in fact the same as the last row of Q.

In this program, the same space can again be used for the result being calculated as for P and Q if the results are calculated in the same order. If you haven't lost the drift of this, do you understand why?

```
      DO 7Ø K=1,N
        DO 7Ø J=1,N-1
          IF(J.GE,K) THEN
            LOLIM=J+1
            SUM=Q(J,K)
          ELSE
            LOLIM=K
            SUM=Ø.Ø
          END IF
          DO 6Ø I=LOLIM,N
6Ø        SUM=SUM+P(J,I)*Q(I,K)
7Ø      A(J,K)=SUM
```

Finally, all these fragments are gathered together into a rather splendid program for inverting an NxN matrix A. FACTLU is used to obtain the factors, and the other steps are exactly as above.

```
      SUBROUTINE INVRLU(A,N)
C
C LU FACTORIZE MATRIX INVERSE
C
C A = INPUT REAL N X N MATRIX
C       OUTPUT THE INVERSE
C N = INTEGER VALUE, SIZE OF A
C
      DIMENSION A(N,N)
C OBTAIN LU FACTORS
      CALL FACTLU(A,N)
C INVERT THE U MATRIX WITHIN A
      DO 20 K=N,2,-1
         DO 20 J=K-1,1,-1
            SUM=-A(J,K)
            DO 10 I=J+1,K-1
 10         SUM=SUM-A(J,I)*A(I,K)
 20      A(J,K)=SUM
C INVERT THE L MATRIX WITHIN A
      DO 50 K=1,N-1
         A(K,K)=1.0/A(K,K)
         DO 50 J=K+1,N
            SUM=0.0
            DO 40 I=K,J-1
 40         SUM=SUM-A(J,I)*A(I,K)
 50      A(J,K)=SUM/A(J,J)
      A(N,N)=1.0/A(N,N)
C FORM PRODUCT U AND L INVERSES
      DO 70 K=1,N
         DO 70 J=1,N-1
            IF(J.GE.K) THEN
            LOLIM=J+1
            SUM=A(J,K)
            ELSE
            LOLIM=K
            SUM=0.0
            END IF
            DO 60 I=LOLIM,N
 60         SUM=SUM+A(J,I)*A(I,K)
 70      A(J,K)=SUM
      END
```

EXERCISE:
  Count the operations involved in this method of matrix inversion. Compared with the earlier Gauss-Jordan program there is clearly a saving in the space occupied by matrices. Can a similar saving be realized in the Gauss-Jordan method? Which has the advantage in speed? What about pivoting?

15.6 Following and drawing contours

Many computer installations have drafting machines of one kind or another for the production of drawings of (generally) high quality. The program developed here is a realization of an algorithm for drawing contours of the data in an array of two dimensions, which was described by M. O. Dayhoff in the Communications of the Association for Computing Machinery in October 1963. This method is most useful for those plotting machines which work by physically moving the paper and/or pen, because it is costly in time on this kind of plotter to jump from one place to another. This contouring algorithm follows a contour from start to finish in one or two continuous movements. Other types of plotters which draw on cathode ray tubes, or which store an entire drawing and then produce it as a continuous stream, do not have the cost problem associated with a lot of jumping around and could use other methods - see Problem 15.3 for a chance to build your own. However, contours drawn continuously have an advantage when it comes to 'line styling' as in Problem 15.2.

The plotter should have with it software which makes the programming of it as simple as possible. Quite a variety of facilities may be provided, such as axes, captions, colours, line thickness and so on. But the fundamental requirement is to be able to draw lines. For various reasons the subroutine PLOT is almost universal and its simplest facilities are the ability to move the pen (or light beam, or whatever) with it 'up', making no trace, or with it 'down' making a line.

Assume that the paper is laid out as in Fig. 15.1. The statement

    CALL PLOT(X,Y,3)

will move the pen to X,Y from wherever it is now, but without drawing a line. Similarly

    CALL PLOT(X,Y,2)

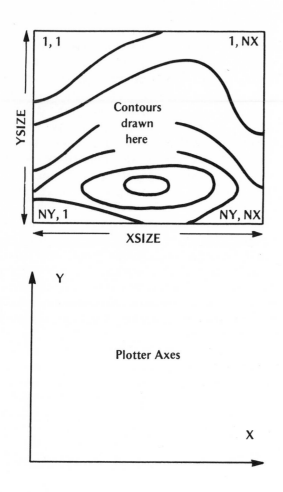

Fig.15.1. A computer directed plotter draws lines in the X,Y plane.

The contour map will be laid out as in Fig. 15.1. The computer has the job of first of all finding, and then drawing the contours.

(i) Finding a Contour

In practice, a given contour or isoline is unlikely to pass exactly through any of the defined array points, but will usually follow a path between them. As an example, Fig. 15.2 shows a contour of level 1.0 passing through some given array points. To find the contour in the first place, it is necessary to scan the array until two points are found with the contour between, as in the top row of Fig. 15.2. When it is found, the coordinates of the array element on the low side of the contour will be called (IX,IY) and those on the high side will be called (IW,IZ). The program will then follow the contour.

There is a complication. After the contour has been followed and drawn, the program must continue scanning for new contours from wherever it left off, since there could be several different contours of the same level in a map. But how then does a program know when a contour is new? This may be solved by having the procedure which follows the contour keep track of all the points lying on the low side, by entering the co-

will move to X,Y with the pen down, so drawing a straight line. This is all that is needed for the contouring subroutine.

The data to be contoured is in an array of two dimensions, and the given data describes a field of information. It could be the elevation of the land, or the depth of the sea, and in this case the contours drawn will be like those on a topographical map. The information might be barometric pressure, in which case a weather map would be intended. There are many other possibilities.

The assumption is made here that the sampling of the array is fine enough to make the contours appear smooth even though they are actually going to be straight line segments. Any array greater than 50x50 is usually satisfactory.

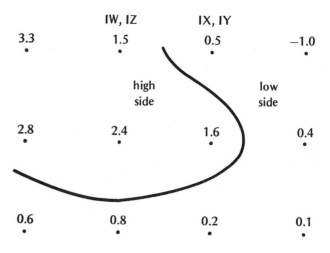

Fig. 15.2. A contour of level 1.0 passing through an array of data.

ordinates into two arrays, IXSTOR and IYSTOR, which become more and more filled as the contours are followed. The number of co-ordinates in them is called KSTOR. When a new contour is found, it has to be checked against this list. However, the list could get very long. Therefore it has to be edited from time to time - in this program at the end of every row of scanning, when everything in the list before the present row can be discarded because there is no danger that it will be scanned again. This keeps the size of these arrays under control. Furthermore, to make the checking of each new contour as efficient as possible, another array called ISCAN always has in it a list of the contours that have crossed row KROW, which is the row being scanned at present. The maximum necessary size of this row is NX, the number of columns, and the number of crossings in it at a particular time is called KSCAN.

Fig. 15.3 is an outline flowchart of this contour searching, without details of the procedure for following the contours. For an array of data called POINTS with dimensions NY by NX, here is the fragment of program which does all of this:

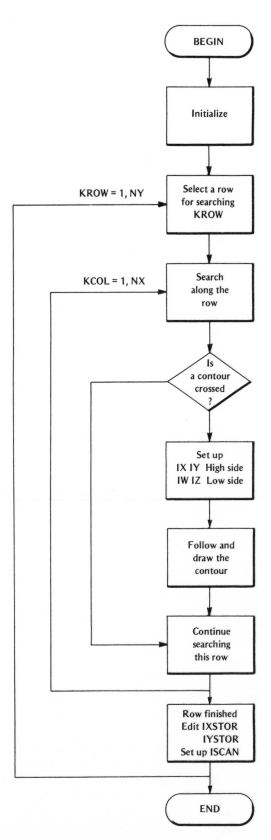

Fig. 15.3. Flowchart for contouring with the emphasis on the searching.

BEGIN

Initialize

KROW = 1, NY → Select a row for searching KROW

KCOL = 1, NX → Search along the row

Is a contour crossed ?

Set up
IX IY High side
IW IZ Low side

Follow and draw the contour

Continue searching this row

Row finished
Edit IXSTOR
IYSTOR
Set up ISCAN

END

```
C INITIALIZE MEMORY POINTERS
      KSTOR=0
      KSCAN=0
C SELECT A ROW TO SEARCH
      DO 110 KROW=1,NY
C SEARCH ALONG THE ROW
      DO 70 KCOL=2,NX
C HAS A CONTOUR BEEN CROSSED
      X=POINTS(KROW,KCOL-1)
      Y=POINTS(KROW,KCOL)
       IF(X.LT.ZLEV.AND.
+          Y.GE.ZLEV) THEN
        IXBEG=KCOL-1
        IWBEG=KCOL
      ELSE IF(Y.LT.ZLEV.AND.
+          X.GE.ZLEV) THEN
        IXBEG=KCOL
        IWBEG=KCOL-1
      ELSE
        GO TO 70
      END IF
      IYBEG=KROW
      IZBEG=KROW
C YES A CONTOUR IS CROSSED
```

```
C LOOK AT ISCAN TO SEE
C IF IT IS A NEW ONE
      DO 1Ø L=1,KSCAN
        IF(IXBEG.EQ.ISCAN(L))
+                            GO TO 7Ø
  1Ø CONTINUE
C
C*******************************
C IF GET HERE CONTOUR IS NEW AND
C THE DRAWING AND FOLLOWING PART
C FOLLOWS (AND DRAWS). THE
C MEMORY OF THE LOW SIDE OF
C ALL CONTOURS IS BUILT UP IN
C THE ARRAYS IXSTOR AND IYSTOR.
C*******************************
C
C AND HERE THE SCAN CONTINUES
C
  7Ø CONTINUE
C SEARCH OF ROW COMPLETE - SET
C UP MEMORY OF NEXT ROW IN ISCAN
C AND EDIT IXSTOR AND IYSTOR
      IF(KROW.LT.NY) THEN
        JSTOR=Ø
        KSCAN=Ø
        NEXT=KROW+1
        DO 1ØØ L=1,KSTOR
          IXT=IXSTOR(L)
          IYT=IYSTOR(L)
C MEMORY OF NEXT ROW INTO ISCAN
          IF(IYT.EQ.NEXT) THEN
            KSCAN=KSCAN+1
            ISCAN(KSCAN)=IXT
C RETAIN MEMORY OF ROWS TO COME
C AND FORGET THE REST
          ELSE IF(IYT.GT.NEXT) THEN
            JSTOR=JSTOR+1
            IXSTOR(JSTOR)=IXT
            IYSTOR(JSTOR)=IYT
          END IF
  1ØØ   CONTINUE
        KSTOR=JSTOR
      END IF
  11Ø CONTINUE
      END
```

(ii) Follow that Contour!

Some of the ideas required in contour following were introduced earlier on. As a result of the searching part described above, the following procedure will know initially the co-ordinates of one point (IX,IY) which is on the low side of the contour, and another (IW,IZ) on the high (or equal) side. The problem now is how to follow it without losing it.

Dayhoff's procedure for doing this is both elegant and simple. In Fig. 15.4, point A is known to be on the low side, and point B is on the high side. To track the contour shown, the line joining A to

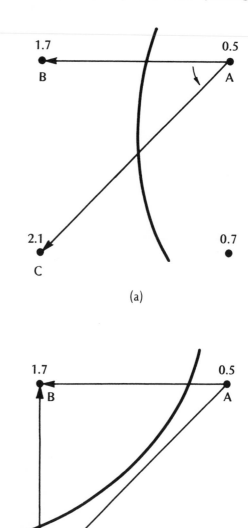

Fig. 15.4. Following a contour through the array of data.

B can be rotated about A by 45°, to the position AC. Only two things can happen; the contour lies between A and C or it does not. If A and C are still on opposite sides as in Fig. 15.4(a) then the program can carry on following. Otherwise the rotation has lost contact with the contour, as in Fig. 15.4(b). If this is so, A and C are both on the low side. However it is known that B is on the high side and so the line CB would still be in contact with the contour. Therefore whenever the following routine loses the contour, the centre of the search rotation is transferred to the new point and the search is then rotated backwards through 135° to re-establish contact. Whatever the orientation, this will always work. The contour memory is added to after every transfer of the centre. Also an indicator called ISTEP is set which the drawing procedure will need.

It just so happens that in Chapter 10 a subroutine for all combinations of 45° and 135° rotations was given in detail! The search direction in this contouring program will be called (IXGO,IYGO). At any time during the search, the low side of the contour is therefore at (IX,IY), while the high (or equal) side is at (IX+IXGO,IY+IYGO); this has already been called (IW,IZ), as shown in Fig. 15.5. The program given in Chapter 10 is used for all the required rotations.

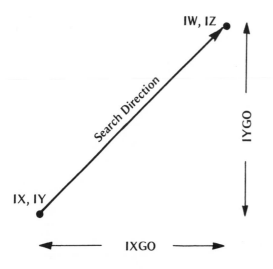

Fig. 15.5. Defining terms in the contour searching program.

Now that a contour can be followed, it is important to consider just what might happen to it. Two things can occur here also. Firstly it could close on itself, as in Fig. 15.16. If this happened, (IX,IY) and (IW,IZ) would go back to their original values, and so closure can be easily detected if the original values are preserved. For this reason, whenever a

contour is detected, the original values of (IX,IY) and (IW,IZ) would be called (IXBEG,IYBEG) and (IWBEG,IZBEG). Before each rotation (except for the first one) the following procedure will check for a closure and resume the search for new contours when a closure occurs. A variable IFIRST indicates the first rotation – otherwise the procedure for following would never get started.

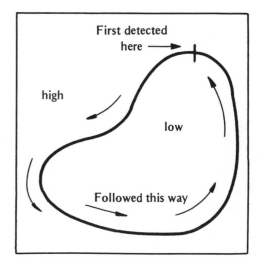

Fig. 15.6. A contour that closes.

The other thing that can happen is that a contour might hit the boundary of the array. After a rotation (but before the check that contact has been maintained with the contour) the point (IW,IZ) may have passed outside the array. If this is so, an end of the contour has been reached. However, it is then necessary to go back to the beginning point and follow the contour the other way until it again leaves the array, as in Fig. 15.7. For this reason the contour following procedure has two phases, controlled by a DO-loop for which the index, IBOUND, takes the values +1 and −1. On the first pass the rotations are anticlockwise while on the second pass they are clockwise. Conveniently, the index IBOUND controls the direction of rotation in the subroutines ROT135 and ROT45. Perhaps this will now explain the peculiar way the sense of rotation differed in these two entries to the same subroutine!

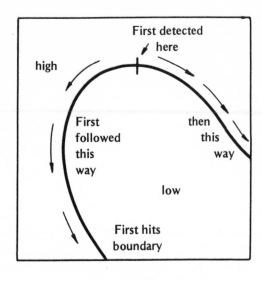

Fig. 15.7. A contour that hits the boundary has to be done in two parts.

The flowchart and program can now be given for contour following – recalling that somehow these contours must also be drawn, and that it is necessary to build up the memory of the (IX,IY) co-ordinates within the arrays IXSTOR and IYSTOR. Fig. 15.8 is the flowchart, with the drawing procedure left vague. Here is the program, designed to fit inside the searching program given earlier:

```
C THE DRAWING AND FOLLOWING
C LOOP PROVIDES BOTH ROTATION
C DIRECTIONS BY VARIABLE IBOUN.
      DO 6Ø IBOUN=1,-1,-2
C SET STARTING POINT AND IFIRST
      IX=IXBEG
      IY=IYBEG
      IW=IWBEG
      IZ=IZBEG
      IFIRST=1
      ISTEP=Ø
C GET THE FIRST SEARCH DIRECTIONS
      IXGO=IW-IX
      IYGO=IZ-IY
  2Ø  CONTINUE
C
C*******************************
C HERE DO THE ACTUAL DRAWING
C*******************************
C
C IF NOT THE FIRST POINT CHECK
C FOR CLOSURE OF THE CONTOUR
```

```
      IF(IFIRST.NE.1.AND.
     +    IX.EQ.IXBEG.AND.
     +    IY.EQ.IYBEG.AND.
     +    IW.EQ.IWBEG.AND.
     +    IZ.EQ.IZBEG) THEN
C
C*******************************
C DO BIT OF DRAWING TO CLOSE
C       THE CONTOUR
C*******************************
C
      GO TO 7Ø
      END IF
      IFIRST=Ø
C NOW THE ROTATION
      ISTEP=Ø
      CALL ROT45(IXGO,IYGO,IBOUN)
      IW=IX+IXGO
      IZ=IY+IYGO
C  IS IT OUT OF BOUNDS
      IF(IW.LT.1) GO TO 5Ø
      IF(IW.GT.NX) GO TO 5Ø
      IF(IZ.LT.1) GO TO 5Ø
      IF(IZ.GT.NY) GO TO 5Ø
C IS CONTACT LOST WITH CONTOUR?
      IF(POINTS(IZ,IW).LT.
     +            ZLEV) THEN
C YES LOST, STEP TO NEW CENTRE
      ISTEP=1
      IX=IW
      IY=IZ
      CALL ROT135(IXGO,IYGO,
     +            IBOUN)
      IW=IX+IXGO
      IZ=IY+IYGO
C AND DO THE CONTOUR MEMORY
      IF(IY.EQ.KROW) THEN
      KSCAN=KSCAN+1
      ISCAN(KSCAN)=IX
      ELSE IF(IY.GT.KROW) THEN
      KSTOR=KSTOR+1
      IF(KSTOR.GT.NSTOR)THEN
      PRINT*,'ABANDON ROW'
      PRINT*,'NEED BIGGER'
      PRINT*,'WORKSPACE'
      GO TO 7Ø
      END IF
      IXSTOR(KSTOR)=IX
      IYSTOR(KSTOR)=IY
      END IF
      END IF
C GO BACK TO DRAW THIS ONE
      GO TO 2Ø
C
  5Ø  CONTINUE
```

```
C
C*******************************
C REACH HERE ONLY IF BOUNDARY
C ENCOUNTERED - DRAW  LAST BIT
C*******************************
C
  60 CONTINUE
```

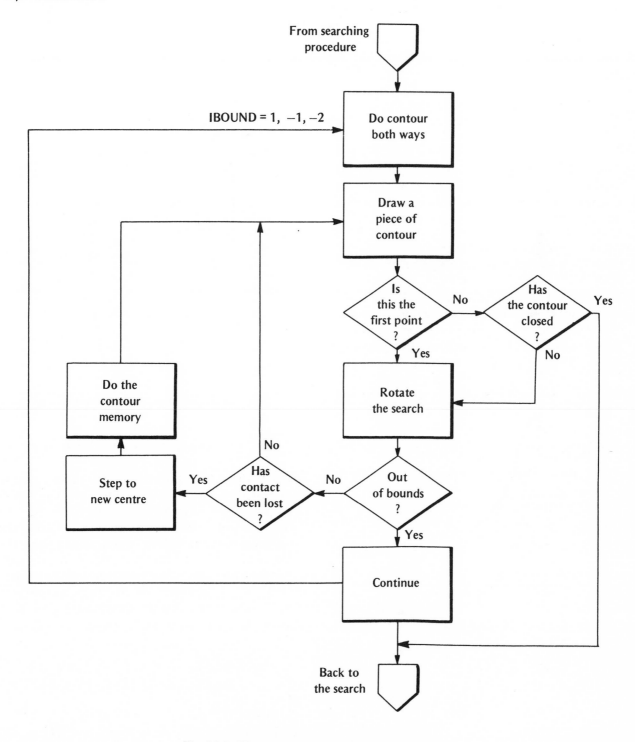

Fig. 15.8. The procedure for following a contour
until it closes. If it hits the array boundary, the
procedure is used twice with opposite directions of
rotation.

(iii) Drawing the Contour

So far, contours have been found and followed. There remains only the small matter of actually drawing them. Referring back to Fig. 15.1, the contour area is to fit a rectangular box which is XSIZE units wide and YSIZE units high. A point having subscript (I,J) in array POINTS corresponds to some place inside the rectangle. First define scaling factors:

$$SCALEX = XSIZE/(NX-1)$$
$$SCALEY = YSIZE/(NY-1)$$

Then, assuming the origin of plotting co-ordinates is at the bottom left hand corner of this rectangle, the paper X-Y co-ordinates of POINTS(I,J) are

$$X = (J-1)*SCALEX$$
$$Y = YSIZE - (I-1)*SCALEX$$

The actual contours in general do not lie on points in the data array, but pass between them. Interpolation must be used to find their actual positions. In Fig. 15.9, if the search direction is non-diagonal, then the distance from the point (IX,IY) is called DX,DY and is very simply

```
DTOP=ZLEV-POINTS(IY,IX)
DBOT=POINTS(IZ,IW)-POINTS(IY,IX)
DIST=DTOP/DBOT
DX=DIST*IXGO
DY=DIST*IYGO
```

except that this is on a scale between 0 and 1 and it will later have to be scaled by SCALEX and SCALEY.

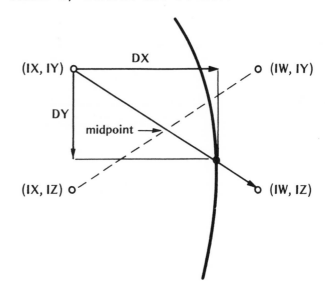

Fig. 15.10. Diagonal interpolation.

If, on the other hand, the search direction is diagonal, as in the Fig. 15.10, then the interpolation is a bit more complicated. The elevation at the midpoint of the rectangle is taken to be the average of the four corners, and the interpolation is then made between the midpoint and a corner. Here is a subroutine for full interpolation of the position of a contour if it is adjacent to IX,IY and the search directions are IXG, IYG:

```
      SUBROUTINE CALC(PTS,NY,NX,
+       ZLEV,IX,IY,IXG,IYG,DIST)
C
C SUBROUTINE TO INTERPOLATE THE
C POSITION OF A CONTOUR WHICH IS
C KNOWN TO BE NEXT TO IX,IY IN
C THE DIRECTION IXG,IYG. THE
C UNSCALED DIST. ALONG IXG,IYG
C IS RETURNED AS DIST, WHICH THE
```

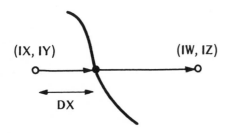

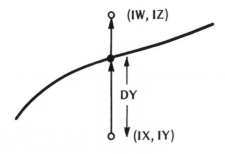

Fig. 15.9. Non-diagonal interpolation.

```
C CALLING ROUTINE WILL MAKE INTO
C ACTUAL CO-ORDINATES.
C
      DIMENSION PTS(NY,NX)
C COMPUTE OTHER CO-ORDINATE
      IA=IX+IXG
      IB=IY+IYG
C DIAGONAL OR NON-DIAGONAL
      IF(IXG.EQ.Ø.OR.IYG.EQ.Ø)THEN
C NON-DIAGONAL - DO THE EASY WAY
        DTOP=ZLEV-PTS(IY,IX)
        DBOT=PTS(IB,IA)-PTS(IY,IX)
        DIST=DTOP/DBOT
      ELSE
C DIAGONAL - COMPUTE MIDPOINT
        PMID=PTS(IY,IX)+PTS(IB,IA)
        QMID=PTS(IB,IX)+PTS(IY,IA)
        ZMID=(PMID+QMID)/4.Ø
C HOW DOES IT COMPARE TO MIDLINE
        IF(ZMID.GE.ZLEV)THEN
C BEFORE OR AT MIDLINE
        DTOP=ZLEV-PTS(IY,IX)
        DBOT=ZMID-PTS(IY,IX)
        DIST=Ø.5*DTOP/DBOT
        ELSE
C BEYOND MIDLINE
        DTOP=ZLEV-ZMID
        DBOT=PTS(IB,IA)-ZMID
        DIST=Ø.5+Ø.5*DTOP/DBOT
        END IF
      END IF
      END
```

After using the above subroutine, the X,Y co-ordinates of the latest contour point can be computed as (XNEW,YNEW):

```
      DX=DIST*IXGO
      DY=DIST*IYGO
      XNEW=(IX-1+DX)*SCALEX
      YNEW=YSIZE-(IY-1+DY)*SCALEY
```

Although this drawing part may seem straightforward enough, there are again two complications. If a non-diagonal step has been made between the searching centres, then two diagonal interpolations will have been made in succession. There is nothing wrong with this if both of these interpolations are 'before the mid-point', but if they are beyond it, as in Fig. 15.11, then the points on the contour have been found in the wrong order and a zigzag will occur in it unless the points are switched. This complicates several things, because to

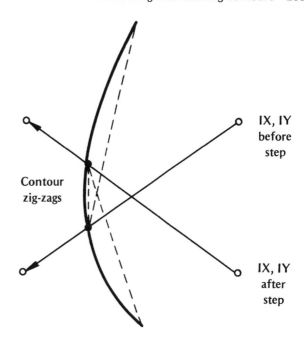

Fig. 15.11. The contour may zig-zag after a non-diagonal step.

allow for it only the last point can be drawn each time, and the new one has to wait until the next time around. This also means that when a boundary is encountered, or when a contour closes on itself, there is still an old point hanging around waiting to be drawn.

The other complication is that when a diagonal change of searching centres is made, an additional interpolation should be done along the opposite diagonal as in Fig. 15.12. This is so that as many

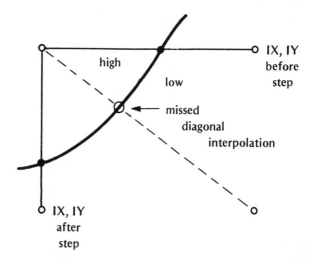

Fig. 15.12. An extra point can be interpolated after a diagonal step.

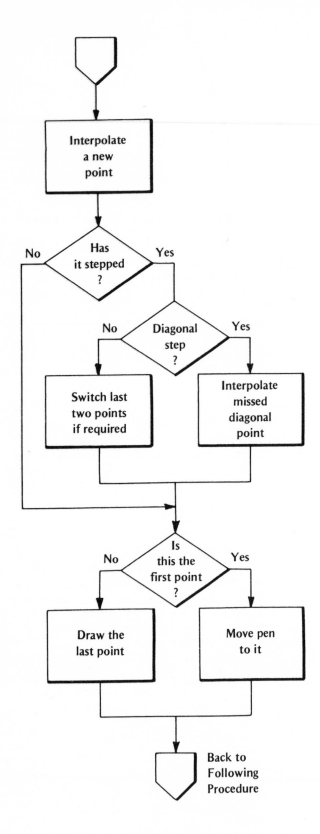

Fig. 15.13. Drawing a piece of contour.

points as possible are always found on a contour, to make it smooth. To get this extra point, subroutine CALC is used to find a contour adjacent to (IW,IZ) and in a direction which is 45° back.

In Fig. 15.13, the flowchart for contour drawing is given. It will be recalled that the system routine for drawing lines is called PLOT, and the full program can now be given. It has been made into a subroutine CONTRS. I hope you like it.

```
      SUBROUTINE CONTRS(POINTS,NY,NX,
     +   ZLEV,XSIZE,YSIZE,ISCAN,
     +   IXSTOR,IYSTOR,NSTOR)
C
C CONTOUR NY X NX REAL ARRAY
C POINTS AT THE LEVEL ZLEV
C
C POINTS = INPUT REAL NY BY NX
C          ARRAY TO BE CONTOURED
C NY     = INPUT INTEGER VALUE
C          NO OF ROWS IN POINTS
C NX     = INPUT INTEGER VALUE
C          NO OF COLS IN POINTS
C ZLEV   = INPUT REAL VALUE,
C          LEVEL OF ISOLINES
C XSIZE  = INPUT REAL VALUE,
C          WIDTH OF CONTOUR AREA
C YSIZE  = INPUT REAL VALUE,
C          HEIGHT OF CONTOUR AREA
C ISCAN  = INTEGER ARRAY, SIZE
C          NX, WORKSPACE
C IXSTOR = INTEGER ARRAY, SIZE
C          NSTOR, WORKSPACE
C IYSTOR = INTEGER ARRAY, SIZE
C          NSTOR, WORKSPACE
C NSTOR  = INPUT INTEGER VALUE.
C          SIZE OF WORKSPACE. IS
C          IMPOSSIBLE TO SPECIFY
C          EXACT REQUIREMENTS.
C          NX*NY/10 IS USUALLY
C          SUFFICIENT.
C
C THE PROGRAMS ASSUME THE SYSTEM
C ROUTINE PLOT IS AVAILABLE. TO
C CALL CONTRS, PLACE ORIGIN OF
C CO-ORDINATES AT THE LOWER LEFT
C CORNER OF THE RECTANGULAR AREA
C SIZE XSIZE BY YSIZE IN WHICH
C ISOLINES ARE DRAWN. GOOD LUCK!
C
C ON EACH CALL TO CONTRS, ONE
C SET OF ISOLINES IS DRAWN AT THE
C LEVEL ZLEV. THIS GIVES THE USER
```

```
C THE FLEXIBILITY (AND THE DUTY)
C OF CHOOSING ANY LEVELS THROUGH
C MULTIPLE CALLS TO CONTRS.
C
      DIMENSION POINTS(NY,NX)
      DIMENSION ISCAN(NX)
      DIMENSION IXSTOR(NSTOR)
      DIMENSION IYSTOR(NSTOR)
C
C SCALE FACTOR FOR DRAWING
      SCALEX=XSIZE/(NX-1)
      SCALEY=YSIZE/(NY-1)
C
C INITIALIZE MEMORY POINTERS
      KSTOR=0
      KSCAN=0
C SELECT A ROW TO SEARCH
      DO 110 KROW=1,NY
C SEARCH ALONG THE ROW
      DO 70 KCOL=2,NX
C HAS A CONTOUR BEEN CROSSED
      X=POINTS(KROW,KCOL-1)
      Y=POINTS(KROW,KCOL)
      IF(X.LT.ZLEV.AND.
   +          Y.GE.ZLEV) THEN
        IXBEG=KCOL-1
        IWBEG=KCOL
      ELSE IF(Y.LT.ZLEV.AND.
   +          X.GE.ZLEV) THEN
        IXBEG=KCOL
        IWBEG=KCOL-1
      ELSE
        GO TO 70
      END IF
      IYBEG=KROW
      IZBEG=KROW
C YES A CONTOUR IS CROSSED
C LOOK AT ISCAN TO SEE
C IF IT IS A NEW ONE
      DO 10 L=1,KSCAN
        IF(IXBEG.EQ.ISCAN(L))
   +                  GO TO 70
 10   CONTINUE
C IF GET HERE CONTOUR IS NEW AND
C THE DRAWING AND FOLLOWING PART
C FOLLOWS (AND DRAWS). THE
C MEMORY OF THE LOW SIDE OF
C ALL CONTOURS IS BUILT UP IN
C THE ARRAYS IXSTOR AND IYSTOR.
C
C THE DRAWING AND FOLLOWING
C LOOP PROVIDES BOTH ROTATION
C DIRECTIONS BY VARIABLE IBOUN.
      DO 60 IBOUN=1,-1,-2
C SET STARTING POINT AND IFIRST
      IX=IXBEG
      IY=IYBEG
      IW=IWBEG
      IZ=IZBEG
      IFIRST=1
      ISTEP=0
C GET THE FIRST SEARCH DIRECTIONS
      IXGO=IW-IX
      IYGO=IZ-IY
 20   CONTINUE
C
C HERE DO THE ACTUAL DRAWING
      CALL CALC(POINTS,NY,NX,ZLEV,
   +        IX,IY,IXGO,IYGO,DIST)
      DX=DIST*IXGO
      DY=DIST*IYGO
      XNEW=(IX-1+DX)*SCALEX
      YNEW=YSIZE-(IY-1+DY)*SCALEY
C HAS A STEP OCCURRED IN SEARCH
      IF(ISTEP.NE.0) THEN
        IF(IXGO*IYGO.EQ.0) THEN
C IT WAS A DIAGONAL STEP SO
C INTERPOLATE MISSED POINT
C ROTATE 45 DEGREES TO GET IT
          IXG=IXGO
          IYG=IYGO
          CALL ROT45(IXG,IYG,IBOUN)
          IA=IW-IXG
          IB=IZ-IYG
          CALL CALC(POINTS,NY,NX,
   +          ZLEV,IA,IB,IXG,IYG,DIST)
C PLOT THE OLD, OLD POINT
          CALL PLOT(XLAS,YLAS,2)
C AND PUT IN THE NEW, OLD POINT
          DX=DIST*IXG
          DY=DIST*IYG
          XLAS=(IA-1+DX)*SCALEX
          YLAS=(IB-1+DY)*SCALEY
          YLAS=YSIZE-YLAS
        ELSE
C STEP WAS NOT DIAGONAL SO
C THIS LAST INTERPOLATION MAY
C BE OUT OF ORDER - FIND OUT
C AND SWITCH IF NECESSARY
          IF(DIST.GT.0.5) THEN
            XT=XLAS
            XLAS=XNEW
            XNEW=XT
            XT=YLAS
            YLAS=YNEW
            YNEW=XT
          END IF
        END IF
      END IF
C DRAW THE LAST POINT - UNLESS
C THE NEW ONE IS THE FIRST
      IF(IFIRST.NE.1) THEN
        CALL PLOT(XLAS,YLAS,2)
      ELSE
```

```
C MOVE PEN TO FIRST POINT
        CALL PLOT(XNEW,YNEW,3)
      END IF
      XLAS=XNEW
      YLAS=YNEW
C
C IF NOT THE FIRST POINT CHECK
C FOR CLOSURE OF THE CONTOUR
      IF(IFIRST.NE.1.AND.
+        IX.EQ.IXBEG.AND.
+        IY.EQ.IYBEG.AND.
+        IW.EQ.IWBEG.AND.
+        IZ.EQ.IZBEG) THEN
          CALL PLOT(XLAS,YLAS,2)
          GO TO 70
      END IF
      IFIRST=0
C NOW THE ROTATION
      ISTEP=0
      CALL ROT45(IXGO,IYGO,IBOUN)
      IW=IX+IXGO
      IZ=IY+IYGO
C  IS IT OUT OF BOUNDS
      IF(IW.LT.1) GO TO 50
      IF(IW.GT.NX) GO TO 50
      IF(IZ.LT.1) GO TO 50
      IF(IZ.GT.NY) GO TO 50
C IS CONTACT LOST WITH CONTOUR?
      IF(POINTS(IZ,IW).LT.
+                 ZLEV) THEN
C YES LOST, STEP TO NEW CENTRE
        ISTEP=1
        IX=IW
        IY=IZ
        CALL ROT135(IXGO,IYGO,
+                    IBOUN)
        IW=IX+IXGO
        IZ=IY+IYGO
C AND DO THE CONTOUR MEMORY
      IF(IY.EQ.KROW) THEN
        KSCAN=KSCAN+1
        ISCAN(KSCAN)=IX
      ELSE IF(IY.GT.KROW) THEN
        KSTOR=KSTOR+1
        IF(KSTOR.GT.NSTOR)THEN
          PRINT*,'ABANDON ROW'
          PRINT*,'NEED BIGGER'
          PRINT*,'WORKSPACE'
          GO TO 70
        END IF
        IXSTOR(KSTOR)=IX
        IYSTOR(KSTOR)=IY
      END IF
      END IF
C GO BACK TO DRAW THIS ONE
      GO TO 20

 50    CONTINUE
C REACH HERE ONLY IF BOUNDARY
C ENCOUNTERED - DRAW  LAST BIT
        CALL PLOT(XNEW,YNEW,2)
 60 CONTINUE
C AND HERE THE SCAN CONTINUES
C
 70 CONTINUE
C SEARCH OF ROW COMPLETE - SET
C UP MEMORY OF NEXT ROW IN ISCAN
C AND EDIT IXSTOR AND IYSTOR
      IF(KROW.LT.NY) THEN
        JSTOR=0
        KSCAN=0
        NEXT=KROW+1
        DO 100 L=1,KSTOR
          IXT=IXSTOR(L)
          IYT=IYSTOR(L)
C MEMORY OF NEXT ROW INTO ISCAN
          IF(IYT.EQ.NEXT) THEN
            KSCAN=KSCAN+1
            ISCAN(KSCAN)=IXT
C RETAIN MEMORY OF ROWS TO COME
C AND FORGET THE REST
          ELSE IF(IYT.GT.NEXT) THEN
            JSTOR=JSTOR+1
            IXSTOR(JSTOR)=IXT
            IYSTOR(JSTOR)=IYT
          END IF
 100    CONTINUE
        KSTOR=JSTOR
      END IF
 110 CONTINUE
      END
```

Here are two examples of the use of this routine. In the first, an array of measurements of the electrical potential measured on a person's body as their heart beats has been interpolated from an array of measurements using almost exactly the same program for interpolating a map given as an example in Section 13.7. In the map contoured in Fig. 15.14, the electrical potentials on the chest are contoured in the right hand box, and the left hand box is a map of the potential on the back. Below the boxes a conventional heart recording is shown, with a vertical line showing the precise instant of the heart map above.

Fig. 15.15 is an automatic contour plot of meteorological data. Here a more

sophisticated version of the same contouring program has been used. Notice
the variety of styles of contour lines,
and the labelling of them. The background map was drawn from the author's
data base.

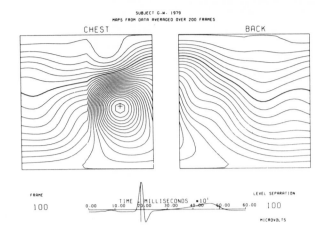

Fig.15.14. Contour diagrams of medical
information.

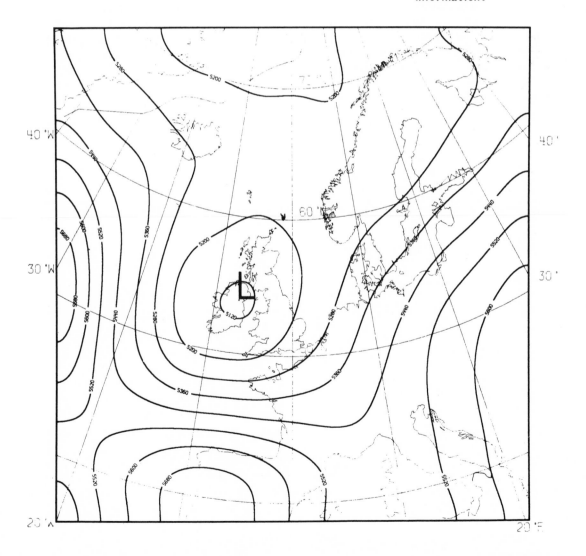

Fig.15.15. Contour diagram of meteorological information.

15.7　Problems

PROBLEM 15.1:

Consider here the possibility of pivoting during the process of LU factorization - it is not necessary in any of the later stages of either equation solving or matrix inversion.

PROBLEM 15.2:

Now consider the possibility of 'line styling' in drawing contours. It may be desirable to label some of the contours with their values, and to draw lines that are dashed. In order to do this well each of the marks and spaces must be laid out to the proper length as the contours are drawn - and this will mean splitting up the segments that are being drawn. It is not good enough to draw each little segment with the pen either up or down (try it and see). Write some line styling facilities into the contouring program.

PROBLEM 15.3:

A different sort of contouring program may be more efficient. If there is little cost attached to dragging the pen about, then it may produce a much simpler and much more efficient program if each little square of four points is considered in isolation, as in Fig. 15.16. A contour which passes through this block can only follow a limited number of possible paths, as indicated. It may therefore be better to consider each little block of the array in turn, drawing the little paths as they are encountered; these paths eventually combine to make the whole picture. Be very careful about contours which hit the corners exactly as there are a number of degenerate cases. The whole job could probably be done in 100 nicely organized statements. The disadvantage of this approach will be that line styling is difficult.

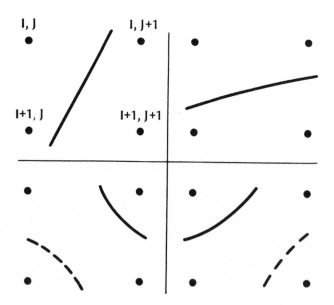

Fig. 15.16. Paths that contours might take through an array cell bounded by four data points.

16

Character data

16.1 Introduction

New facilities which assist in the manipulation of written text have been introduced into FORTRAN 77. These will be of great assistance in a great many applications, both small and large, in which programmers have been forced to deal with text by using cumbersome manipulations. Editing programs for the modification and correction of text are a feature of many timesharing systems. Previously these programs were written in machine language; this may be very efficient but such programs are difficult to write and maintain, and are not portable. However, it is now possible to produce comprehensive text editing programs written in FORTRAN 77, and also 'word processing', report writing, and typesetting programs.

There have been certain problems in introducing the CHARACTER data type because the representation of characters within computers is (unnecessarily) machine dependent, and to some extent these difficulties have been reflected in the new facilities.

16.2 CHARACTER variables, constants and expressions

Previously in this text, only two data types have been introduced - REAL and INTEGER. CHARACTER data is another distinct type, and three further types will be introduced in Chapter 17.

A programmer can declare the intention of using a variable to represent characters by the CHARACTER statement:

CHARACTER names

If this is done, the variables which have been named are reserved exclusively for use with character data throughout the program unit that makes this designation. For the moment their use is described for main programs only, but the very important extension to subprograms will be described later in this Chapter.

The CHARACTER statement is the first one to be introduced of a group known as the 'type statements' - the remaining ones are introduced in the next Chapter. These statements allow the program to dictate the type of a variable. The names of variables in a CHARACTER statement will resemble real or integer names, but they are forced to be of character type and cannot be used as anything else.

A type statement is a kind of specification statement. As is already known, the ordering and position of specification statements in a program is constrained - they also belong near the beginning of a program unit. Therefore the table which shows the recommended order of statements must be further elaborated, as in Fig. 16.1.

A CHARACTER statement will specify how many characters are associated with a particular name. If the length is not specified, then each variable holds one character. The statement

CHARACTER ALPHA

declares a variable ALPHA to be of the type CHARACTER, and it holds only one character. The statement

CHARACTER*4 ITHICK

Comments can go anywhere before END	FORMAT and ENTRY	SUBROUTINE, FUNCTION, PROGRAM or BLOCK DATA statements	
		PARAMETER Statements	Specification Statements COMMON DIMENSION EQUIVALENCE CHARACTER
		DATA Statements	Statement Function Definitions
			Executable Statements
END Statement			

Fig. 16.1. The required order of statements in FORTRAN 77 programs including the statements covered so far.

declares the character variable ITHICK to have four characters in it. In general, one would write

CHARACTER [*len[,]] names

The optional length specification can have any integer constant length, either as an unsigned nonzero integer constant length, as in

CHARACTER*6,GLOB

or as an expression in brackets involving only integer constants or the names of integer constants, which gives a sensible length (positive and nonzero), as in

CHARACTER*(3*4+1) BLOB

or

PARAMETER (L=6)
CHARACTER*(L) THONG

or

PARAMETER (NUM=3,KRUM=4)
PARAMETER (ISUM=KRUM-NUM)
CHARACTER*(NUM*KRUM+ISUM) SLOB

Note that the comma after the length specification is optional; the forms

CHARACTER*2,EGZAM

and

CHARACTER*2 EGZAM

mean the same thing.

Every CHARACTER statement has a length associated with it, either one or greater as is described above, and this length will apply throughout the list of names in the CHARACTER statement. However, an individual name can have its own length which applies to that name only. For example, consider

CHARACTER*4 ALPH1,ALPH2*2,ALPH3

Here ALPH1 and ALPH3 have length 4 characters while ALPH2 has been given a length of 2.

Character constants have already been encountered in output statements. Any string of characters enclosed within apostrophes must be a character constant; for example

        PRINT*,'GOOD GRIEF'

The apostrophes do not count as part of the constant. If one is desired as part of a string, then two must be given together for each one required, as

    PRINT*,'IT WENT ''POW'' IT DID.'

which has length 21 and whose meaning is

        IT WENT 'POW' IT DID.

and

      PRINT*,'THREE '''''' QUOTES'

which has length 16 and meaning

        THREE ''' QUOTES

The messages that have been used in printing until now have been character constants, either in list-directed input or output, or in a FORMAT specification. Characters other than FORTRAN ones are likely to be included in the range of symbols that the computer can handle – this depends upon machine arrangements which are nothing to do with FORTRAN. In this respect, machine dependence persists.

Character constants can be given symbolic names through PARAMETER statements. To do this, a CHARACTER statement must first define the name as being one of type CHARACTER, and then a PARAMETER statement can assign a character constant expression. For example

        CHARACTER FIRST4*4
        PARAMETER (FIRST4='ABCD')

sets the constant value ABCD to be represented by the name FIRST4, which throughout the program unit stands only for that constant value and cannot be changed. In the example

    CHARACTER LEF*3,RIGH*4,LOUD*7
    PARAMETER (LEF='BIG',RIGH='DEAL')

        PARAMETER (LOUD=LEF//RIGH)

the character constant BIGDEAL is formed from two other constants concatenated (this is discussed below). As will be seen, concatenation is the only operation available in character expressions, and so character constant expressions can be no more complicated than the concatenation of a series of constants.

The ordering of the PARAMETER statement and a type statement such as CHARACTER is important. Constants must be defined before they are used, as in

        PARAMETER (NCHARS=8)
        CHARACTER*(NCHARS) WORDS,MUSIC

but the type of a name must be defined before it can be assigned a value as in

        CHARACTER ARTY
        PARAMETER (ARTY='PAINT')

This is why PARAMETER and CHARACTER statements can be mixed, as shown in Fig. 16.1. But in practice the rules illustrated by the previous two examples must be obeyed. The next example obeys both rules:

        PARAMETER (NUMS=5)
        CHARACTER TODAY*(NUMS)
        PARAMETER (TODAY='SUNNY')
        PRINT*,TODAY

while this one is illegal twice over:

        PARAMETER (WEATHR='CLIMATE')
        CHARACTER WEATHR*(LONG)
        PARAMETER (LONG=7)

There is a possible clash of lengths between the PARAMETER statement and the CHARACTER statement. Normally the CHARACTER statement is definitive. In the statements

        CHARACTER DULL
        PARAMETER (DULL='PQRS')

the length of DULL is 1 character (by default). Only the leftmost ones will be taken in the PARAMETER statement, so that DULL has value P. In the statements

CHARACTER *(handwritten)* *
↑
NUMBER OF *(handwritten)*

```
CHARACTER BRIGHT*4
PARAMETER (BRIGHT='RA')
```

the length of BRIGHT is 4 characters, but the PARAMETER statement has defined only two. Here the right hand side is filled with blanks so the value is the same as

```
'RA  '
```

↑
2 blanks

It is easy to remember the general rule: character values are ranged left and are either truncated or filled with blanks as circumstances dictate. The same rule will apply to assignment statements and the reading of input.

There is, however, one special way of allowing the PARAMETER statement to dictate its own length. A length of (*) can be given in the CHARACTER statement. As will be seen, this could mean various things in a subprogram, but in a main program it can only mean that the names which use it must be the names of character constants, and a subsequent PARAMETER statement must define values for them. The length is then implied by the actual value given. For example, in

```
CHARACTER MISTY*(*)
PARAMETER (MISTY='CAN''T SEE')
PRINT*,MISTY
```

the length of the character constant MISTY is 9 characters.

Character expressions are uncomplicated. The only operation allowed is that of 'concatenation', which means the joining together of character strings, and is represented by two slashes.

EXAMPLE:

```
CHARACTER A*5,B*4,C*9
PARAMETER (A='WATER',B='GATE')
PARAMETER (C=A//B)
PRINT*,C
```

defines the character constant C and prints its value:

WATERGATE

For simplicity, the lengths are exactly right.

A character expression can be

$$\begin{array}{ccc} \text{character} & // & \text{character} \\ \text{entity} & & \text{entity} \end{array}$$

and the length of the result is the sum of the constituent lengths. A 'character entity' may be a character variable, or a character constant, or a character expression. There are a few intrinsic functions available as will be seen. No mixing with reals or integers or any other type is permitted and character expressions may not include arithmetic or logical operations because these have no meaning as character expressions in FORTRAN 77. However, the function CHAR, which appears in Table 16.1 and which converts an integer argument to its corresponding character value, is permitted.

16.3 Using character data

Character Assignment Statements

Characters can be used in many of the statements of FORTRAN 77. A character assignment statement is available which is the same as any assignment statement:

$$\begin{array}{ccc} \text{character} & = & \text{character} \\ \text{variable} & & \text{expression} \end{array}$$

However no mixing with REAL, INTEGER, or any other type is allowed, and there is no conversion of type either. The character expression is evaluated and the result, which will always be a character string, becomes the new value of the character variable. If the length of the variable is not exactly right, the same rule is followed as was illustrated for the PARAMETER statement. The characters are ranged left in the character variable, and the string is either truncated or filled out with blanks to the length of the variable. Therefore

```
      CHARACTER CVAR*8
         :
         :
      CVAR='A CONSTA'
```

is the same as

```
      CHARACTER CVAR*8
         :
         :
      CVAR='A CONSTANT TOO LONG'
```

and

```
      CHARACTER*8 TEXT
         :
         :
      TEXT='SHORT'
```

is the same as

```
      CHARACTER*8 TEXT
         :
         :
      TEXT='SHORT   '
                    ↑
              3 blanks
```

Comparing Characters

Comparisons between character quantities are clearly an essential part of the text handling facility. The ordinary relational operators are available, for use in a logical IF statement,

```
   character  relational  character
    entity       operator     entity
```

as for example

```
 CHARACTER*8 TEST
    :
    :
 IF(TEST.EQ.'FINISHED") RETURN
```

or

```
      CHARACTER*4 ONE,OTHER
         :
         :
      IF(ONE.LT.OTHER) THEN
         :
         :
```

The comparison of characters with these facilities is somewhat machine dependent. The .EQ. and .NE. operations of course give no trouble, but the results of the other comparisons depend on what is called the 'collating sequence' of characters on the particular computer. The collating sequence is the order of the hidden integer values used inside the machine to represent characters. Usually the alphabet is stored in order (sometimes broken up, but still in order) as are the numbers. But the interrelation between the letters, numbers, and other symbols could be almost anything.

For this reason, FORTRAN 77 introduces what are called 'lexical comparisons', obviously related to the relational ones, and specifies the collating sequence for them. For portability this is the best way to compare character strings; however they take the form of intrinsic functions. All the character functions are listed in Table 16.1, and the first four are used for lexical comparisons. They are in fact logical functions of character arguments. They have the result .TRUE. or .FALSE. and are used in IF statements as in the following examples.

```
CHARACTER BIG*6
   :
   :
IF(LGT(BIG,'ZZZ')) INDEX=INDEX+1
```

is true if the character value of BIG comes after ZZZ in the ASCII sequence - this is possible.

```
      CHARACTER DATA,STAR
      CHARACTER*3,VAR*6,ONE,TWO
      PARAMETER (ONE='AAA')
      PARAMETER (TWO='BBB')
      PARAMETER (STAR='*')
         :
         :
      IF(LLE(VAR,ONE//TWO)) THEN
         DATA=STAR
         ICOUNT=JCOUNT
         RETURN
```

Function	Meaning
LGE(a,b)	Logical result .TRUE. if a ≥ b in ASCII sequence.
LGT(a,b)	Logical result .TRUE. if a > b in ASCII sequence.
LLE(a,b)	Logical result .TRUE. if a ≤ b in ASCII sequence.
LLT(a,b)	Logical result .TRUE. if a < b in ASCII sequence.
LEN(a)	Integer result: the length of character entity a.
INDEX(a,b)	Integer result: the starting position within character entity a of the first appearance of the shorter string b, or zero if b does not occur.
ICHAR(a)	Integer result: the numerical value of a in the machine dependent sequence. The length of a is 1.
CHAR(I)	Character result: the character (length 1) whose machine dependent numerical value is I.

Table 16.1. Functions for use with character data. Arguments a and b are of type character. I is of type integer.

The collating sequence is the ASCII code, as listed in Table 16.2, which is the national and international standard code for information interchange in many countries. It is very unhelpful that some of the computer manufacturers have adopted other codes of their own devising (for their own reasons, of course).

With either comparison, there is no need for the character strings to be of the same length; the shorter one is extended by blanks. In the ASCII code, blanks have a lesser value than all the alphanumerics. Assuming that this is so in the machine dependent codes, then

'ABC'	is less than	'ABCD'
'MONEY'	is less than	'NOTHING'
'ZZZ'	is less than	'ZZZA'
'LONGER'	is less than	'SHORT'

which is very useful for placing things in alphabetical order.

Character Statement Functions

Character statement functions can be defined. As before, a statement function is established at the beginning of a program unit, in the order permitted by Fig. 16.1, although the full regulations for statement ordering are not available until Chapter 17. It will be recalled that a statement function can be used throughout the program unit that defines it. To define a character statement function, its name and length must be established in a CHARACTER statement. If dummy arguments of the function are also of type CHARACTER, they must be declared also. The function can then be defined.

EXAMPLE:
 (i)

```
CHARACTER COMB*4,ALPHA*2,ALPHB*2
COMB(ALPHA,ALPHB)=ALPHA//ALPHB
```

This is a character statement function for concatenation of the two strings ALEPHA and ALEPHB. This statement function, its dummy arguments, and the defining expression are all of type CHARACTER.

 (ii)

```
CHARACTER*12 CFUNC,RESLT,CCON*(*)
CHARACTER*4 CVAR
PARAMETER (CCON='PLUS')
CFUNC(CVAR)=CVAR//CCON//'MORE'
```

This statement function involves two character constants: one is defined in the statement function itself, and the other is defined in the PARAMETER statement. A statement

```
RESLT=CFUNC(CVAR)
PRINT*,RESLT
```

has the result, called RESLT, of value

Symbol	Decimal Code	Symbol	Decimal Code
Space	32	P	80
!	33	Q	81
"	34	R	82
#	35	S	83
$	36	T	84
%	37	U	85
&	38	V	86
'	39	W	87
(	40	X	88
)	41	Y	89
*	42	Z	90
+	43	[	91
,	44	\	92
—	45	]	93
.	46	^	94
/	47	_	95
0	48	`	96
1	49	a	97
2	50	b	98
3	51	c	99
4	52	d	100
5	53	e	101
6	54	f	102
7	55	g	103
8	56	h	104
9	57	i	105
:	58	j	106
;	59	k	107
<	60	l	108
=	61	m	109
>	62	n	110
?	63	o	111
@	64	p	112
A	65	q	113
B	66	r	114
C	67	s	115
D	68	t	116
E	69	u	117
F	70	v	118
G	71	w	119
H	72	x	120
I	73	y	121
J	74	z	122
K	75	{	123
L	76	|	124
M	77	}	125
N	78	~	126
O	79		

Table 16.2. Printable characters of the ASCII code.

THISPLUSMORE

(iii) Not all quantities in a statement function need to be of type CHARACTER. However, because assignment of a value of any other type to a character result is not permitted, the right hand side must be a character expression.

```
CHARACTER ZAP*6,WHAM*4,POW*6
ZAP(WHAM,I)=WHAM//' '//CHAR(I)
```

Here a blank and character number I from the machine collating sequence are stuck on the end of the dummy argument WHAM. In the program, the reference

```
POW=ZAP('BANG',33)
PRINT*,POW
```

prints the result

    BANG !

if ! is character number 33, as it is in ASCII. Note, however, that ! is not a usual FORTRAN symbol.

The length of the result of a statement function behaves just as with assignment statements. The result is always ranged left, and either filled out with blanks or truncated as required. The lengths of character functions and dummy arguments must always be given explicitly in the CHARACTER statement – an asterisk is never permitted for the length of a character statement function name or a character statement function dummy argument name.

Where a statement function is referred to, its actual arguments can, of course, be expressions. It is recalled that these actual arguments correspond according to their type and position with the dummy arguments of a statement function. In the case of arguments of type character, the actual argument will be some constant or variable, or some more complicated expression. It too has a length, which will be converted to the length of the corresponding dummy argument, before the function is evaluated.

EXAMPLE:

```
CHARACTER COMB*4,ALPHA*2,ALPHB*2
CHARACTER B1*(*),B2*(*),THIS*3
PARAMETER (B1='X',B2='Y')
COMB(ALPHA,ALPHB)=ALPHA//ALPHB
         ⋮
THIS=COMB(B1//'23',B2//'HELLO')
PRINT*,THIS
```

This is not a very useful example, but serves to illustrate the length conversions that might arise. The actual first argument is

B1//'23'

which has the value

X23

However, the associated dummy argument of the character statement function COMB is ALPHA, which has length 2. Therefore before evaluation of the statement function, this argument is shortened to

X2

Similarly, after evaluation, the length of the second argument is shortened to make it

YH

The statement function is then evaluated and has the result

X2YH

which is exactly the right length for the result of the function. However, the character variable THIS has length 3, so the value assigned to it is

X2Y

This can be verified by running the program.

It is not really very difficult to keep track of character lengths, although a sloppy program could certainly lose a lot of characters.

16.4　Character arrays and substrings

Processing of significant amounts of text implies the use of arrays and substrings. Indeed the character facilities are really useful only when dealing with character data in these forms.

A name of type CHARACTER can represent an array. The size of the array can be established using a DIMENSION statement. In the statements

```
CHARACTER*4 GONK
DIMENSION GONK(10)
```

GONK is defined to be a character array. Each array element has a character length of 4, and there are 10 elements in GONK. This makes a total of 40 characters. As can be seen from Fig.16.1 there is no specified order among these statements. DIMENSION and CHARACTER are both specification statements. Therefore an equally valid combination is

```
DIMENSION GONK(10)
CHARACTER GONK*4
```

It is also possible for the CHARACTER statement to specify the size of an array. Of course an array can have its dimensions defined only once. Therefore another possibility is

```
CHARACTER*4 GONK(10)
```

10 × 4 chars

A more complicated specification for a character array TEST is

```
PARAMETER (N1=3,N2=7,LENTH=4)
CHARACTER TEST(N1:N2)*(LENTH)
```

Here, TEST is a character array with subscript bounds from 3 to 7. Each element holds 4 characters. It will be seen in the next Chapter that any type statement is capable of assigning sizes to arrays using constant subscripts, or, in the case of subroutines, variable dimensions and assumed size dimensions.

EXAMPLE:

Suppose that CHARS is a character and CLOOK a character variable, defined by

```
CHARACTER*8 CHARS(2Ø),CLOOK
CHARACTER*8 KEY1,KEY2
```

In the following program fragment the array is examined to see if one of the elements is the same as CLOOK. The integer variable IFIND will give the result; 0 if CLOOK is not there, and the subscript if it is.

```
C EXAMINE CHARS TO FIND CLOOK
      IFIND=Ø
      DO 1Ø K=2Ø,1,-1
 1Ø IF(CLOOK.EQ.CHARS(K))IFIND=K
```

In searching for equality the .EQ. relational operator is safe. But what happens if CLOOK occurs more than once? Why has the DO-loop been run backwards?

EXAMPLE:

It is desired to sort the same array into alphabetical order. To be safe the functions for lexical comparison are used in the following program, which is for bubble sorting into alphabetical order. Bubble sorting was described earlier, in Chapter 11.

```
C COMMENCE SORTING
      NTOP=2Ø
 2Ø NSTOP=Ø
      DO 3Ø K=1,NTOP-1
         KEY1=CHARS(K)
         KEY2=CHARS(K+1)
         IF(KEY1.GT.KEY2) THEN
C SWITCH AND REMEMBER WHERE
            CHARS(K)=KEY2
            CHARS(K+1)=KEY1
            NSTOP=K
         END IF
 3Ø CONTINUE
      NTOP=NSTOP
      IF(NSTOP.GT.1)GO TO 2Ø
```

It has been seen in examples that character constants can be given names in PARAMETER statements. In a similar fashion, character variables can be given initial values in DATA statements. Recall that PARAMETER statements define constants whose values remain fixed in a particular program unit. The initial values given to variables in DATA statements, on the other hand, are often changed by the program as the variables are used.

DATA statements assign initial values to VARIABLES
PARAMETER statements assign forever values to CONSTANTS

In a DATA statement, one simply includes character names among the list of variables to be defined; it can be seen from Fig. 16.1 that the DATA statement follows the specification statements and the PARAMETER statements. Therefore the type, character length, array sizes, and all constants are defined before the DATA statement.

EXAMPLE:

```
PARAMETER(LEN=4)
CHARACTER CHAR*(LEN),BIT1,BIT2
DATA CHAR/'FOUR'/
DATA BIT1,BIT2/'A','B'/
```

In this example, everything was the correct length.

EXAMPLE:

Here is an ape-like example with long arms and short legs.

```
CHARACTER*8 ARM,LEG
DATA ARM/'MUCH TOO LONG'/
DATA LEG/'SHORT'/
```

The character variable ARM has to be truncated and is given the value

```
MUCH TOO
```

while the data given for LEG has to be ranged left and padded with blanks to be

```
SHORT___   ←
```
　　　　　　　　　　3 blanks

EXAMPLE:

An array can be filled but one separate character constant must be given for each array element:

```
CHARACTER CRAY(3)*3
DATA CRAY/'ONE','TWO','THREE'/
```

What values do the elements of CRAY have?

EXAMPLE:

```
CHARACTER AYES(10),STARS(100)
DATA AYES,STARS/10*'A',100*'*'/
```

EXAMPLE:

Here is a program fragment to convert an integer into its hexadecimal equivalent. Recall from Chapter 3 that numbers are often represented in the Octal (base 8) number system by computer people because a given octal number corresponds to three binary bits. Many computers are organized around groups of eight bits (called 'bytes') and for this reason a lot of computer people also use the hexadecimal (base 16) number system. Now in base 16 you run out of digits at 9, and so the digits missing are called A to F as in Table 16.3. Note that the hexadecimal number 10 has decimal value 16. This little program assumes that it is converting a positive number lying in the range 0-FFFF (decimal 0-65535). The base conversion is done by remaindering as before, but the hexadecimal digits are taken from the character array DIGITS to form the four digit hexadecimal result HEX.

Decimal Number	Hexadecimal Equivalent		Decimal Number	Hexadecimal Equivalent
0	0	.	8	8
1	1	.	9	9
2	2	.	10	A
3	3	.	11	B
4	4	.	12	C
5	5	.	13	D
6	6	.	14	E
7	7	.	15	F

Table 16.3. Hexadecimal representation of numbers.

A substring is a piece of a character variable. Anywhere in FORTRAN that a character variable name can be used, a substring can also be referred to.* Formally, a substring is a contiguous portion of a character datum - memorize that for cocktail party use.

A substring is written

$$variable \ (e1:e2)$$

or

$$array[(subscript)](e1:e2)$$

e1 and e2 are integer expressions whose values delineate the substring. The first character in the substring is at position e1, and the last at e2. Clearly it is necessary that

$$1 \le e1 \le e2 \le length$$

for the substring to make any sense. The value of the substring itself is therefore a string of characters from within a character variable or array element.

```
C DECIMAL-HEXADECIMAL CONVERSION
C
      CHARACTER DIGITS(0:15),HEX(4)
      DATA DIGITS/'0','1','2','3',
     +            '4','5','6','7',
     +            '8','9','A','B',
     +            'C','D','E','F'/
   10 PRINT*,'GIVE DECIMAL NUMBER'
   20 PRINT*,'IN RANGE 0 - 65536'
      READ*,I
      IF(I.LT.0) GO TO 20
      IF(I.GT.65536) GO TO 20
C CONVERT THIS NUMBER
      DO 30 K=4,1,-1
         IQUOT=I/16
         IREM=I-IQUOT*16
         HEX(K)=DIGITS(IREM)
   30 I=IQUOT
      PRINT*,HEX
      GO TO 10
      END
```

---

*Actually by closely reading the FORTRAN 77 standard it seems that the substring is omitted from the list of things that can appear on the right hand side of a statement function. It is not forbidden - just not allowed. I wonder how this will work in practice.

EXAMPLE:

```
CHARACTER STRING*6,STRANG*4
DATA STRING/'STRONG'/
        :
        :
STRANG=STRING(2:5)
```

STRANG is assigned the value

TRON

from characters 2-4 of STRING.

EXAMPLE:

```
CHARACTER*6 ROTAS(6)
CHARACTER*6 FIRST,OUTPT
DATA FIRST/'ABCDEF'/
DO 10 K=1,6
10 ROTAS(K)=FIRST(K:6)//FIRST(1:K)
PRINT*,ROTAS
END
```

Notice the truncation of the result, particularly when K=1 and K=6. Do you know what this does? Run it.

If e1 is not given, 1 is assumed; if e2 is not given, the right hand end is assumed.

EXAMPLE:
Run this:

```
CHARACTER PART*8,WHOLE*8
DATA WHOLE/'ALL THIS'/
DO 10 K=1,8
    PART=WHOLE(:K)
10 PRINT*,PART
END
```

EXAMPLE:
Run this:

```
CHARACTER PART*8,WHOLE*8
DATA WHOLE/'ALL THIS'/
DO 10 K=1,8
    PART=WHOLE(K:)
10 PRINT*,PART
END
```

EXAMPLE:

```
STRUNG(:)
```

refers to the entire variable STRUNG.

EXAMPLE:
The most basic steps in text editing are locating and replacing character substrings in text. In this program fragment, a long character string called TEXT is searched using the intrinsic function INDEX to find if a substring identical to OLD occurs. If it does, the string NEW replaces it in TEXT.

```
CHARACTER OLD*4,NEW*4,TEXT*80
        :
        :    old, new, text
        :    are defined
        :
C REPLACE OLD WITH NEW AT FIRST
C OCCURRENCE IN TEXT
    ISTAR=INDEX(TEXT,OLD)
    TEXT=TEXT(1:ISTAR-1)//NEW
                //TEXT(ISTAR+4)
        :
        :
```

There is a complication in the 'definition status' of character variables or array elements. Because only part of a character string may be defined, a character variable at any point in a program may be partly defined and partly undefined. Trouble will result from an attempt to refer to an undefined part.

EXAMPLE:

```
CHARACTER GEORGE*8
GEORGE(4:)='RIGHT'
```

defines only characters 4-8 in GEORGE. Unless characters 1-3 are later defined, they cannot be referred to. Therefore

```
PRINT*,GEORGE(5:6)
```

is perfectly acceptable but

```
PRINT*,GEORGE
```

invites disaster unless an intervening process has defined the remaining characters in GEORGE.

EXAMPLE:
Substrings can be defined in DATA statements:

```
CHARACTER DANGER*1Ø
DATA DANGER(4:1Ø)/'CAREFUL'/
```

Again part of DANGER is undefined.

The COMMON and EQUIVALENCE statements can be used to associate character variables and arrays with each other in an identical manner to real and integer quantities. Substrings cannot be associated, except of course as a result of associating the variables in which they occur. The storage arrangement of characters in particular computers is not specified. For this reason, it is forbidden to associate character entities with anything else. Therefore, if any groups of variables associated through EQUIVALENCE statements are of type CHARACTER then they must all be. Therefore

```
CHARACTER*4 ARAY(1Ø),BRAY(5),RAY
EQUIVALENCE (ARAY,BRAY,RAY)
EQUIVALENCE (INT,REAL)
```

is correct whereas

```
CHARACTER*4 ARAY(1Ø),BRAY(5),RAY
DIMENSION X(5)
EQUIVALENCE (ARAY,RAY,X)
EQUIVALENCE (BRAY,INT)
```

is wrong.

Furthermore a particular COMMON area must consist entirely of character entities if any are character. For this reason it is necessary to form separate COMMON blocks for character data. In

```
CHARACTER*8 THESE,THOSE,THEM
COMMON/CHARS/THESE(1Ø),THOSE,THEM
COMMON/OTHERS/ INPUT(25),XFACT(4)
```

the COMMON block /CHARS/ is used for characters only, and the COMMON block /OTHERS/ has reals and integers in it. The restriction applies equally to blank COMMON;

```
CHARACTER*4 SILLY,NUTTY
COMMON LARGE(1ØØ),SILLY(5)
COMMON ZAPPO,NUTTY
```

is not allowed.

16.5 Character functions and text editing

As would be expected, the FORTRAN language allows character entities to be passed as arguments to FUNCTION and SUBROUTINE subprograms. The language also provides for the creation of external functions that are of type CHARACTER.

A character function subprogram is like any other, except that its first line is

CHARACTER[*length] FUNCTION name

As with characters in main programs, this function has a length associated with it, which is either a positive nonzero integer constant expression, or 1 by default. It can also be given a length of (*) as will be seen, which allows the program referring to a character function to dictate the length. The length must be given in the CHARACTER FUNCTION statement; it cannot be specified by a separate CHARACTER statement. Fig.16.1 gave the rules for statement ordering in a subprogram.

Naturally enough, every variable and dummy argument of the subprogram has a type, and so a CHARACTER statement must identify those which are of type character.

EXAMPLE:
Here the editing facility is made into a function. The first occurrence of the string OLD in TEXT is replaced by NEW.

```
      CHARACTER*12Ø FUNCTION
     +          EDIT(TEXT,OLD,NEW)
C
C REPLACE THE FIRST OCCURRENCE
C    OF OLD IN TEXT BY NEW
C
      CHARACTER*8 OLD,NEW,TEXT*12Ø
      ISTAR=INDEX(TEXT,OLD)
      EDIT=TEXT(1:ISTAR-1)//NEW//
     +          TEXT(ISTAR+8:)
      END
```

As required in a FUNCTION subprogram the result is assigned to EDIT within the function.

To use this in a main program, one could write

```
    CHARACTER*120 TEXT,EDIT
    CHARACTER*8 OLD,NEW
10  PRINT*,'ENTER A LINE OF TEXT'
    READ*,TEXT
    PRINT*,'ENTER STRING TO'
    PRINT*,'REPLACE, 8 CHARS'
    READ*,OLD
    PRINT*,'ENTER REPLACEMENT'
    PRINT*,'STRING, 8 CHARS'
    READ*,NEW
    TEXT=EDIT(TEXT,OLD,NEW)
    PRINT*,TEXT
    GO TO 10
    END
```

Note here that the name EDIT has been declared as a character entity - this is essential, otherwise the main program would think it was dealing with a real function. Try this. The input data must be given in apostrophes, as explained in Section 16.7.

Whenever dummy arguments are of fixed length, as in these examples, the actual arguments are adjusted to that length when the function is used, by ranging left and truncating or by padding with blanks as necessary.

For convenience, FORTRAN 77 permits character functions to be written with assumed lengths for both character function names and dummy arguments. In both cases the lengths can be given as (*), in which case the program will figure out for itself what lengths to use when the function is referred to.

EXAMPLE:
Our editing function is more general if the actual lengths of TEXT, OLD, and NEW are not constrained, and if the function itself is given an assumed length.

```
    CHARACTER*(*) FUNCTION
+            EDIT(TEXT,OLD,NEW)
C
C REPLACE THE FIRST OCCURRENCE
C    OF OLD IN TEXT BY NEW
C
    CHARACTER TEXT*(*)
    CHARACTER OLD*(*),NEW*(*)
    EDIT=TEXT
    LENTH=LEN(OLD)
    ISTAR=INDEX(TEXT,OLD)
    IF(ISTAR.EQ.0) RETURN
    EDIT=TEXT(1:ISTAR-1)//NEW//
+            TEXT(ISTAR+LENTH:)
    END
```

There are three situations, therefore, in which the length can be given as (*). In any program unit, a length of (*) can be used if a later PARAMETER statement assigns a constant value to that symbolic name. In a function or a subroutine, an assumed length of (*) can also be given to character dummy arguments. Also, the name of the character function can itself be given an assumed length in the CHARACTER FUNCTION statement.

EXAMPLES:
In a main program, the only use of a character length of (*) is in connection with a PARAMETER statement.

```
    CHARACTER MESSG*(*)
    PARAMETER (MESSG='HELLO')
```

In any subprogram the length (*) could also be used for the name of a dummy argument.

```
    SUBROUTINE CRUMB(SCRAP)
    CHARACTER SCRAP*(*),CHCON*(*)
    PARAMETER (CHCON='FIXED')
```

In a FUNCTION subprogram, the function name itself can be given an assumed length:

```
    CHARACTER*(*) FUNCTION
                CLOWN(FUNNY)
    CHARACTER*(*) FUNNY
              :
              :
```

Some rules governing the use of character functions:

(i) It is necessary that the character function and the program referring to it must agree on the lengths of the function and its arguments. If a length of (*) is given, this agreement will always occur.

(ii) In a character function, all entries are of type CHARACTER and the same length as the function. A program using multiple entries to a character function must conform to this.

(iii) Within a function, a character dummy argument with a length of (*) cannot be used as an operand for concatenation, except in a character assignment statement, as occurred in the function EDIT used as an example above. This means, for example, that an assumed length character dummy argument may not be used in an expression which becomes the actual argument of a further function reference.

```
FUNCTION SILLY(CHAR)
CHARACTER CHAR*(*),OUTPT*8
CHARACTER CON*8,FUNC
          :
          :
OUTPT=FUNC(OUTPT//CHAR)
          :
          :   (illegal)
```

nope! not allowed

EXAMPLE:
The function EDIT has been improved to make the lengths of its arguments assumed, and worked out when it is called. The main program can be re-written to let both OLD and NEW be variable in length, and not the same length, so that this is a perfectly general editing operation. When OLD is entered, one wishes to establish its length. It is most common to delimit fragments of text using recognizable characters. Indeed it is rather clever to take the first character as the delimiter, and look to see where that character next occurs. Everything in between must be the desired character string. For example

```
/STRING/
```

is delineated by slashes, and the part of interest is

```
STRING
```

Here is an integer function which works out the length of the string of interest. The first character is the delimiter, and the desired string is everything between it and its next appearance.

```
      FUNCTION IWINK(STRING)
C
C INTEGER FUNCTION TO WINKLE OUT
C THE BIT OF STRING BETWEEN TWO
C DELIMITERS. THE FIRST CHARACTER
C OF STRING IS THE DELIMITER
C AND IWINK IS THE INDEX OF
C THE NEXT OCCURRENCE OF THE
C SAME DELIMITER. ZERO MEANS
C IT DOES NOT OCCUR AGAIN.
C
      CHARACTER STRING*(*),DELIM
C GET FIRST CHARACTER
      DELIM=STRING
C FIND NEXT OCCURRENCE
      IWINK=INDEX(STRING(2:),DELIM)
      END
```

Using this function, the editing procedure becomes very general indeed:

```
      CHARACTER*(*) FUNCTION
     +          EDIT(TEXT,OLD,NEW)
C
C REPLACE THE FIRST OCCURRENCE
C    OF OLD IN TEXT BY NEW
C
      CHARACTER TEXT*(*)
      CHARACTER OLD*(*),NEW*(*)
      EDIT=TEXT
      LENTH=LEN(OLD)
      ISTAR=INDEX(TEXT,OLD)
      IF(ISTAR.EQ.0) RETURN
      EDIT=TEXT(1:ISTAR-1)//NEW//
     +          TEXT(ISTAR+LENTH:)
      END
```

How would you delete a string from TEXT using this? Try it out.

EXAMPLE:

Here is a function EDITAL, which re-places all occurrences of OLD by NEW in TEXT.

```
      CHARACTER*(*) FUNCTION
+              EDITAL(TEXT,OLD,NEW)
C
C REPLACES ALL OCCURRENCES
C  OF OLD IN TEXT BY NEW
C
      CHARACTER TEXT*(*)
      CHARACTER OLD*(*),NEW*(*)
      L=1
      EDITAL=TEXT
      LENTH=LEN(OLD)
      MENTH=LEN(NEW)
  1Ø  ISTAR=INDEX(TEXT(L:),OLD)
      IF(ISTAR.EQ.Ø)RETURN
      L=L+ISTAR-1
      EDITAL=TEXT(1:L-1)//NEW//
+                    TEXT(L+LENTH:)
      L=L+MENTH
      TEXT=EDITAL
      GO TO 1Ø
      END
```

Try it out.

16.6 Subroutines and typesetting

This section is intended to demonstrate the usefulness of subroutines in character manipulation by introducing the beginnings of what could be developed into a very useful project, that of the setting up and layout of printed text.

All the same considerations apply to the use of characters in subroutines as did with functions, except of course that a subroutine has no length associated with its name. Dummy arguments of a subroutine can be of type CHARACTER, and all the same rules apply to the lengths of these, and to what happens to actual arguments when the subroutine is called.

Word processing machines are these days a very common feature of offices. They permit letter-perfect printed material to be produced after the text has been entered and edited through a terminal. Most of the printers in these systems

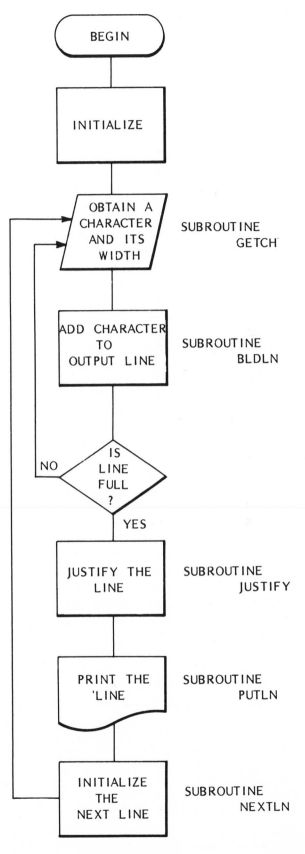

Fig. 16.2. Outline flowchart of a simple typesetting program.

have a fixed spacing of characters, and so even though the right and left margins can be aligned, or 'justified', the output is basically of typewriter quality because of the fixed spacing.

Here the next step upward in quality is considered. Computer terminals are available fairly widely with facilities to control the spacing of individual characters. These could be used for typesetting with margin justification using fully variable spacing of characters and of the spaces between words.

Consider a very simple system in which the printer is connected to a computer. The computer reads a text file and produces a typeset output. A FORTRAN 77 program does this by taking one character at a time and building up a line of output. When a line is full, the program must go back to the last space in the line, and expand it to fill out to its margins exactly. It can then be printed. The flowchart shown in Fig.16.2 describes the operation of the program in broad outline.

This main program serves to control the process, but all of the real work is done in subroutines. COMMON blocks will be used for communication of information that the main program needs to share with its subroutines. In the common block /TEXT/ is the line that is being built called THISLN. Remembering that common blocks may not mix character entities with other types, a separate block called /HORIZ/ is used for all the information about the horizontal layout and statistics of the line. Presumably, if paging and other features of vertical layout were to be added to the program, a block called /VERT/ could be added.

The information obtained from subroutine GETCH will be a new character, CHAR, and its width, IWIDE. In this program the information is passed directly to BLDLN. (As facilities are added to the program to control and modify the layout, it would be after GETCH that the facility to recognize commands would be added.)

Each character has a width - the letter m might be five units wide, n three units, and i one unit, for example. Three characters are special. The obvious special character is the space or blank. This is given a width that is the minimum permitted, and the blanks will later have their widths adjusted to achieve the margin justification. Another special character is the 'hard blank'. This is used to create a space whose width cannot be adjusted - for example it might stand for a fixed indentation or a space that you are later going to fill by hand with a special symbol that the printer doesn't have. In this example a * is used. This unfortunately means that the program as it stands will not print the character *. The third special character is an example of one with zero width, the 'permitted hyphen'. This is used to indicate where hyphens could be placed if necessary to break up long words. Here a + is used for this purpose. It would of course be better to use something more obscure.

The following information is passed in the common block /HORIZ/.

ILEFT = the position of the left margin.
IRIGHT = the position of the right margin.
KLAST = the pointer to the last character in THISLN.
LLAST = the total width of the line after the last character.
KFIRST = a pointer to the first character in the next line.
LINWID = the width between margins; actually IRIGHT-ILEFT.
LWIDS = the array of widths of characters in the present line.

The complete main program is

```
C MAIN PROGRAM FOR TYPESETTING
      CHARACTER CHAR,THISLN
      COMMON/TEXT/ THISLN(100)
      COMMON/HORIZ/ ILEFT,IRIGHT
      COMMON/HORIZ/ KLAST,LLAST
      COMMON/HORIZ/ LASTBK,LINWID
      COMMON/HORIZ/ LWIDES(100)
C INITIALIZE THE LINE STATUS
```

```
      ILEFT=0
      IRIGHT=60
      LINWID=IRIGHT-ILEFT
      KLAST=0
      LLAST=0
C OBTAIN A CHARACTER
   10 CALL GETCH(CHAR,IWIDE)
C ADD IT TO THE LINE
      CALL BLDLN(CHAR,IWIDE)
C GO BACK FOR MORE IF NOT FULL
      IF(LLAST.LT.LINWID) GO TO 10
      CALL JUSTIFY
      CALL PUTLN
      CALL NEXTLN
      GO TO 10
      END
```

Remember that this is a very simple example. As facilities are added, this main program could grow substantially. It would, however, be wrong to destroy the basic simplicity of the subroutines, and for that reason they have been given all the facilities which would be necessary for quite a comprehensive system.

Subroutine GETCH is probably machine dependent, and you will have to write this yourself to the following specification:

```
      SUBROUTINE GETCH(CHAR,IWIDE)
C OBTAIN NEXT CHARACTER, CHAR
C AND ITS WIDTH IWIDE FROM INPUT
C TEXT. THE HARD BLANK IS * AND
C IT CAN HAVE ANY WIDTH. THE
C PERMITTED HYPHEN IS + AND
C ITS WIDTH MUST BE ZERO.
C AN ACTUAL BLANK SHOULD HAVE
C THE MINIMUM PERMITTED WIDTH.
C
      CHARACTER CHAR
```

Subroutine BLDLN adds CHAR to the line. However a series of ordinary blanks should be reduced to one, as should a series of permitted hyphens. Blanks and permitted hyphens at the beginning of a line are deleted. Blanks and permitted hyphens may not follow each other. The indicators in the common block /HORIZ/ must be correctly set.

```
      SUBROUTINE BLDLN(CHAR,IWIDE)
C THIS ROUTINE ADDS A CHARACTER
C CHAR TO THE PRESENT LINE AND
C ADJUSTS THE LINE STATUS.
C
      CHARACTER CHAR,THISLN
      CHARACTER ISOFT,IBLANK
      CHARACTER CTEST
      COMMON/TEXT/ THISLN(100)
      COMMON/HORIZ/ ILEFT,IRIGHT
      COMMON/HORIZ/ KLAST,LLAST
      COMMON/HORIZ/ KFIRST,LINWID
      COMMON/HORIZ/ LWIDES(100)
      PARAMETER(ISOFT='+')
      PARAMETER(IBLANK=' ')
C
C IS THIS CHARACTER A BLANK
      IF(CHAR.EQ.IBLANK) THEN
C IGNORE IF BEGINNING OF LINE
      IF(KLAST.EQ.0) RETURN
C IGNORE IF PREVIOUS WAS BLANK
      CTEST=THISLN(KLAST)
      IF(CTEST.EQ.IBLANK) RETURN
C IGNORE IF PREVIOUS PERMITTED -
      IF(CTEST.EQ.ISOFT) RETURN
C IS THIS A PERMITTED HYPHEN
      ELSE IF(CHAR.EQ.ISOFT) THEN
C IGNORE IF BEGINNING OF LINE
      IF(KLAST.EQ.0)RETURN
C IGNORE IF PREVIOUS WAS BLANK
      CTEST=THISLN(KLAST)
      IF(CTEST.EQ.IBLANK) RETURN
C IGNORE IF PREVIOUS PERMITTED -
      IF(CTEST.EQ.ISOFT) RETURN
      END IF
C IF GET TO HERE, ADD IT ON
      LLAST=LLAST+IWIDE
      KLAST=KLAST+1
      THISLN(KLAST)=CHAR
      LWIDES(KLAST)=IWIDE
      END
```

If the line has over-run when the program returns from BLDLN, then it is time to justify and print it.

In JUSTIFY, the line is scanned backwards to the first blank or permitted hyphen. It is necessary to be careful that the true width of the hyphen does not push the line over the top. If the break is going to be a hyphen, it is put in. If there is no break, then the program fails to achieve justification and will print the line 'as is', thus over-running by one character.

Once the width of the line up to the break, MWIDTH, is established, then the number of ordinary blanks, NUMB, is counted before the break. The number of width units to add to each blank is IADD:

$$IGAP=LINWID-MWIDTH$$
$$IADD=IGAP/NUMBL$$

and in addition some blanks have to be increased by an additional unit. To do this, the first

$$IREST=IGAP-IADD*NUMBL$$

blanks are incremented. The line is then nearly ready to be printed. Here is JUSTIFY:

```
      SUBROUTINE JUSTIFY
C
C JUSTIFY THISLN TO MARGINS
C LINWID APART. LAST PERMITTED
C BREAK IS FOUND AND EARLIER
C SPACES ARE FILLED OUT.
C
      CHARACTER THISLN,IBLANK
      CHARACTER ISOFT,IHYPH
      CHARACTER CTEST
      PARAMETER(IBLANK=' ')
      COMMON/TEXT/ THISLN(100)
      COMMON/HORIZ/ ILEFT,IRIGHT
      COMMON/HORIZ/ KLAST,LLAST
      COMMON/HORIZ/ KFIRST,LINWID
      COMMON/HORIZ/ LWIDES(100)
C
C FIND LAST PERMITTED BREAK
      CALL PERMIT(MWIDE)
C IF NONE THE LINE WILL OVERRUN
      IF(KFIRST.EQ.KLAST) RETURN
C COUNT THE BLANKS TO KFIRST
      NUMBL=0
      DO 10 K=1,KFIRST
        CTEST=THISLN(K)
        IF(CTEST.EQ.IBLANK)
+             NUMBL=NUMBL+1
  10  CONTINUE
C AGAIN IF NONE, CAN'T JUSTIFY
      IF(NUMBL.EQ.0) RETURN
C HOW MUCH TO EXPAND LINE
      IGAP=LINWID-MWIDE
      IADD=IGAP/NUMBL
      IF(IADD.EQ.0) GO TO 30
```

```
C BLEND THE EXPANDED BLANKS IN
      DO 20 K=1,KFIRST
        CTEST=THISLN(K)
        IF(CTEST.EQ.IBLANK) THEN
          LWIDES(K)=LWIDES(K)+IADD
        END IF
  20  CONTINUE
C AND INCREMENT THE REMAINDER
  30  IREM=IGAP-IADD*NUMBL
      IDONE=0
      DO 40 K=1,KFIRST
        IF(THISLN(K).EQ.IBLANK)THEN
          IDONE=IDONE+1
          IF(IDONE.GT.IREM) RETURN
          LWIDES(K)=LWIDES(K)+1
        END IF
  40  CONTINUE
      END
```

The scan to find the last break is a separate subroutine, because it could be useful in other contexts:

```
      SUBROUTINE PERMIT(MWIDE)
C FIND LAST PERMITTED BREAK IN
C THISLN UP TO KLAST - THE LINE
C WIDTH IS RETURNED IN MWIDE.
C
      CHARACTER THISLN,IBLANK
      CHARACTER ISOFT,IHYPH
      CHARACTER CTEST
      COMMON/TEXT/ THISLN(100)
      COMMON/HORIZ/ ILEFT,IRIGHT
      COMMON/HORIZ/ KLAST,LLAST
      COMMON/HORIZ/ KFIRST,LINWID
      COMMON/HORIZ/ LWIDES(100)
      PARAMETER(IBLANK=' ')
      PARAMETER(ISOFT='+')
      PARAMETER(IHYPH='-')
      PARAMETER(LHYPH=2)
      KFIRST=KLAST
      MWIDE=LLAST
      DO 10 K=KLAST,1,-1
        CTEST=THISLN(K)
        MWIDE=MWIDE-LWIDES(K)
C IT MIGHT BE A BLANK
        IF(CTEST.EQ.IBLANK) THEN
          KFIRST=K-1
          RETURN
C IT MIGHT BE PERMITTED HYPHEN
        ELSE IF(CTEST.EQ.ISOFT)THEN
          NWIDE=MWIDE+LHYPH
          IF(NWIDE.LE.LINWID)THEN
            MWIDE=NWIDE
            LWIDES(K)=LHYPH
            THISLN(K)=IHYPH
```

```
            KFIRST=K
            RETURN
         END IF
      END IF
 10 CONTINUE
C IF IT GETS TO HERE, NO BREAK
      MWIDE=LLAST
      KFIRST=KLAST
      END
```

After JUSTIFY, PUTLN is called. This is probably machine dependent and is not given here. It must replace the hard blanks by ordinary blanks of the same width, and should also ignore permitted hyphens. It then prints the line, with ILEFT units of space at the beginning.

Finally, NEXTLN has to initialize the next line by transferring the leftovers from the previous one to the beginning of the next one. Blanks or permitted hyphens at the beginning are left out. The indicators in /HORIZ/ are set and the program is ready for more characters:

```
      SUBROUTINE NEXTLN
C ROUTINE TO BEGIN A NEW LINE
C BY CARRYING LEFTOVERS BACK
C TO BEGINNING OF NEW LINE.
C
      CHARACTER THISLN
      CHARACTER IBLANK,ISOFT
      CHARACTER CTEST
      COMMON/TEXT/ THISLN(100)
      COMMON/HORIZ/ ILEFT,IRIGHT
      COMMON/HORIZ/ KLAST,LLAST
      COMMON/HORIZ/ KFIRST,LINWID
      COMMON/HORIZ/ LWIDES(100)
      PARAMETER(IBLANK=' ')
      PARAMETER(ISOFT='+')
C
C ACCUMULATE THE NEW WIDTH
      LLAST=0
C POSSIBLY EMPTY NEW LINE
      KFIRST=KFIRST+1
      IF(KFIRST.GT.KLAST) THEN
         KLAST=0
         RETURN
      END IF
C THE FIRST CHARACTER MIGHT BE
C BLANK OR PERMITTED HYPHEN
      CTEST=THISLN(KFIRST)
```

```
      IF(CTEST.EQ.IBLANK.OR.
     +          CTEST.EQ.ISOFT)
     +             KFIRST=KFIRST+1
C AGAIN LINE COULD BE EMPTY
      IF(KFIRST.GT.KLAST) THEN
         KLAST=0
         RETURN
      END IF
C NOW CAN SAFELY COPY DOWN
      KNUM=0
      DO 10 K=KFIRST,KLAST
         KNUM=KNUM+1
         THISLN(KNUM)=THISLN(K)
         LWIDES(KNUM)=LWIDES(K)
         LLAST=LLAST+LWIDES(K)
 10   CONTINUE
      KLAST=KNUM
      END
```

It should be noted that although THISLN in this example has been a character array, it could as easily have been a single character variable, say of length 100, and all the manipulations could have been done as substrings.

16.7 Reading and printing characters

The examples of this Chapter have mostly made use of list-directed input and output in which the computer takes control of the layout. When printing in this way, the program has no control over the arrangement of items on the printed line. If a list-directed WRITE or PRINT statement

```
      PRINT*, list
```

or

```
      WRITE(6,*) list
```

has character values in its list, these are produced in the output.

If a list-directed READ statement

```
      READ*, list
```

has the names of character variables, arrays, or substrings in its list, it is necessary for the input to contain characters within apostrophes.

EXAMPLE:
In response to the request

```
      CHARACTER ALPHA*4
      READ*,X,ALPHA,I
```

the input

```
        3.14,'IT''S',73
```

would be allowed. Note that a desired apostrophe is represented by two in succession.

If the length of the input string is not exactly as expected, then the leftmost characters are taken and truncated or filled out with blanks, just as happens in any other manipulation.

EXAMPLE:
In response to

```
      CHARACTER*8 CHIN,TOES(1Ø)
      READ*,CHIN,TOES(3)(4:6)
```

the input

```
        'FIRST','SECOND'
```

defines the variable CHIN to be

```
      FIRST
           ↑         3 blanks
```

It also defines the array element substring TOES(3)(4:6) to be

```
      SEC
```

Note that TOES(3)(1:3) is not defined by this READ statement.

It may be recalled from Chapter 2 that blanks or commas are used to separate values in list-directed input, and a slash to terminate input, leaving the values undefined. Any of these characters – blank, comma, and slash – can appear in character input even though they are value separators. This is because the apostrophes take precedence.

EXAMPLE:
In response to

```
      CHARACTER SLASH
      READ*,SLASH
```

you provide

```
        '/'
```

which will define SLASH to have the character value

```
      /
```

whereas if you were to provide it without apostrophes, as

```
      /
```

it leaves SLASH unchanged – it could have a value defined earlier or it could be undefined.

Clearly formatted input and output has the advantage of allowing exact control of the layout, and this is often vital with character data. FORTRAN supports an editing style for characters called A-editing. The edit description

```
        [n]A[w]
```

specifies m character fields of width w in the FORMAT. This operates in the same way as was described in Chapter 5 for other types of editing; in particular, one-to-one correspondence of the types of the values in an input/output list is needed with the editing descriptions in the format specification.

EXAMPLE:
A particularly enjoyable subroutine is SPLOGE. Call it up at any time for a splodge of solid asterisks right across the printed page – this is very useful to separate blocks of output:

```
      SUBROUTINE SPLOGE
C PRINT A ROW OF STARS
      PRINT 1Ø
   1Ø FORMAT(1X,12Ø('*'))
      END
```

Of course you might want to change the line length, and the character used. So SPLAT, with its A-editing and implied DO-loop, is more versatile:

```
      SUBROUTINE SPLAT(CHAR,N)
C
C PRINT A ROW OF N REPETITIONS
C OF CHARACTER CHAR - MAX 120
      CHARACTER CHAR
      PRINT 10,(CHAR,I=1,N)
 10 FORMAT(1X,120A1)
      END
```

As would be expected, the width of the data field specified by A-editing interacts with the length of the character entity in the input/output list.

Firstly, if the width w is not specified in the FORMAT, then it is taken to be the length of the character entity.

EXAMPLE:
The statements

```
      CHARACTER THING(*)
      PARAMETER (THING='FOUR')
      PRINT 20,THING
 20 FORMAT(1XA)
```

will print four characters, and the input statement

```
      CHARACTER ENTITY*6
      READ '(A)', ENTITY
```

expects a six character input field.

If the width of the A description is less than the character length, then the familiar processing takes place; on output the leftmost characters are printed and on input the data are ranged left and filled with blanks.

EXAMPLE:
The statements

```
      PRINT 20,'CONSTANT'
 20 FORMAT(1XA5)
```

produce the output

```
      CONST
```

The statements

```
      CHARACTER TILLER*6
      READ'(A4)',TILLER
```

require four characters to be given as input. If this input were

```
      HELM
```

then the character variable TILLER is given the value

```
      HELM ↑   2 blanks
i.e. H E L M   blank blank.
```

A different thing would occur if the width w were greater than the length of the input/output. On input the rightmost characters are taken, and on output the character items are right justified.

EXAMPLE:
The statements

```
      CHARACTER MESSG*5
      DATA MESSG/'HELLO'/
      PRINT 10,MESSG
 10 FORMAT(1XA10)
```

print

```
           HELLO
         ↑
  5 blanks
```

The statements

```
      CHARACTER CORNER*4
      READ 10,CORNER
 10 FORMAT(A6)
```

require six characters to be given as input. If given the input

```
      ATTACK
```

the value assigned to CORNER is

```
      TACK
```

i.e. it contains no blanks.

16.8 Graph plotting

A very useful thing supported by the character facilities is the printing of graphs on a terminal or lineprinter. Simple graphs are extremely easy to prepare; they are plotted on their sides using a method very close to that of the subroutine SPLAT, described above. In fact, a solid graph could be done using SPLAT provided axes were not required.

EXAMPLE:
This program draws a ramp function on the printer using SPLAT:

```
C PROGRAM TO MAKE A SOLID RAMP
      CHARACTER STAR
      PARAMETER(STAR='*')
      DO 1Ø K=1,2Ø
        CALL SPLAT(STAR,K)
   1Ø CONTINUE
      END
```

EXERCISE:
Try it.

SPLAT achieved this pleasing result using an implied DO-loop in its PRINT statement. This idea can be used to print a conventional graph, if spaces are provided first using the implied DO-loop, and then the star.

EXAMPLE:
This program plots a graph of the function

$$f(x) = e^{-x^2/2}$$

which is a function often used, $\sqrt{2\pi}$ times the density of the normal distribution with zero mean and unit variance. The function is defined by a statement function. The scaling factor is established in the PARAMETER statement, which is also where the character constants used are established. By changing these two statements, any single valued function could be plotted. XSC is the difference between the x-values of successive lines of the plot. YSC is the multiplying constant that connects the y-values of the function to spaces on the printed line.

```
C PROGRAM TO PLOT A GRAPH
      CHARACTER PLUS,BLNK,STAR
      PARAMETER(PLUS='+',BLNK=' ')
      PARAMETER(STAR='*')
      PARAMETER(XSC=Ø.1)
      PARAMETER(YSC=4Ø.Ø)
```

```
      FUNC(X)=EXP(-X*X/2.Ø)
C FIRST PLOT A Y-AXIS
      PRINT 2Ø,(PLUS,K=1,45)
   2Ø FORMAT(1X,7ØA1)
C CALCULATE AND PLOT VALUES
      DO 5Ø P=1.Ø,2Ø.Ø
      ICOL=YSC*FUNC(P*XSC)-Ø.5
      PRINT 2Ø,PLUS,(BLNK,K=1,ICOL)
     +            ,STAR
   5Ø CONTINUE
      END
```

The graph from this program comes out sideways. Fig. 16.3 shows it as it is printed; you must rotate it through 90° anticlockwise to view it.

EXAMPLE:
Using much the same approach, a histogram can be prepared. The function RANDY was assigned as Problem 8.3, and gives random numbers whose expected distribution is rectangular, i.e. uniform between 0.0 and 1.0. Fig. 16.4 is the probability density function. In reality, RANDY should not give an exactly flat histogram for a finite number of tries - it would be very suspicious if it did because it is supposed to be random!

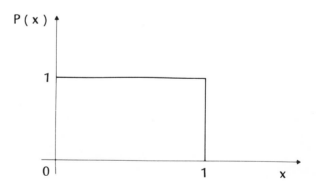

Fig. 16.4. Probability density function for a rectangular distribution.

For preparing a histogram, the array IHIST is used. Initially all entries are zero, but after each new random number is obtained the appropriate 'bin' of IHIST is incremented by one. The scaling between the random values and the corresponding subscript for IHIST is worked out. The number of trials is variable, as is the number of histogram bins to a maximum of 1000.

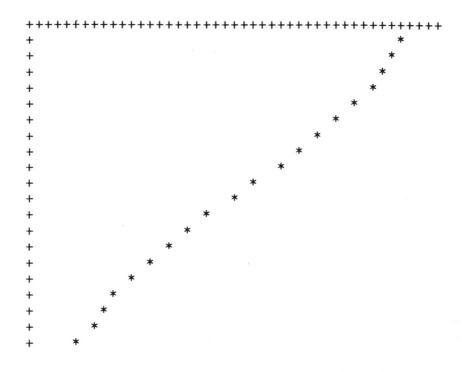

Fig.16.3. Printed output from a graph plotting program.

```
      DIMENSION IHIST(1001)
      CHARACTER STAR
      PARAMETER (STAR='*')
C REQUEST SIZE AND NO. OF TRIALS
  10  PRINT*,'HOW MANY BINS ?'
      READ*, NBINS
      PRINT*,'HOW MANY TRIALS ?'
      READ*,NTRYS
C ALL BINS INITIALLY ARE ZERO
      DO 20 K=1,NBINS
  20  IHIST(K)=0
C GET RANDOMS AND MAKE HISTOGRAM
      DO 30 K=1,NTRYS
         L=RANDY()*NBINS+1.0
         IHIST(L)=IHIST(L)+1
  30  CONTINUE
C WORK OUT SCALE FACTOR FROM
C THE EXPECTED NUMBER PER BIN
      EXPEC=REAL(NTRYS)/REAL(NBINS)
      SCALE=40.0/EXPEC
C NOW PRINT THE HISTOGRAM
      DO 50 K=1,NBINS
         IBIN=IHIST(K)*SCALE
         PRINT 40,(STAR,L=1,IBIN)
  40  FORMAT(1X,70A1)
  50  CONTINUE
      GO TO 10
      END
```

A typical run using this program is shown in Fig. 16.5.

A FORMAT feature not introduced earlier is the overprint facility. This applies to lineprinters, on which successive lines can be made to overstrike each other. Until now, the first space of an output line has been kept clear to avoid unwanted trouble with the carriage. However, on lineprinters that first space has the following meaning.

Character	Action (before printing)
Blank	Advance one space
0	Advance two spaces
1	Go to a new page
+	Overprint previous line

EXAMPLE:
A graph which has several symbols per line can be done in the same way very easily on a lineprinter using the overprint carriage control, even if the order of the symbols changes. Here is a program which prints a cycle of sin(x) and cos(x) together, along with an x-axis.

```
      HOW MANY BINS ?
    ? 25
      HOW MANY TRIALS ?
    ? 1000
      *****************************************
      *****************************************
      ******************************************
      ******************************************
      ********************************************
      ********************************
      *****************************************
      ******************************************
      *************************************************
      ******************************************
      ******************************************
      **********************************
      *****************************************
      *********************************
      *************************************
      ********************************************
      ****************************************
      ********************************************
      *****************************************
      ***********************************************
      ******************************
      **************************************
      ************************************
      **************************************
      **************************************
      HOW MANY BINS ?
    ? stop
```

Fig. 16.5. Printed histogram of 1000 numbers from a rectangular distribution, showing the dialogue with the program.

```
      CHARACTER IB,IS,IC,II
      PARAMETER(IB=' ',IS='S')
      PARAMETER(IC='C',II='I')
      XTOP=8.0*ATAN(1.0)
      DX=XTOP/24.0
      DO 60 X=0.0,XTOP,DX
C CALCULATE AND PRINT SINE
      ICOL=26.5+25.0*SIN(X)
      PRINT 10,(IB,L=1,ICOL),IS
 10 FORMAT(1X,80A1)
C NOW OVERPRINT COS AND AXIS
      ICOL=26.5+25.0*COS(X)
      PRINT 20,(IBL,L=1,ICOL),IC
      PRINT 20,(IB,L=1,25),II
 20 FORMAT('+',80A1)
 60 CONTINUE
      END
```

The graph is shown in Fig. 16.6. This same example may be used to show the second basic method of graph plotting - that of predefining the printed line in a character array.

EXAMPLE:

It may not be possible to use the overprint carriage control; for example on timesharing terminals. You could write a very messy program to sort out the order for printing things. Alternatively an array can be used to construct the line before it is printed. Here is the same example done in this way.

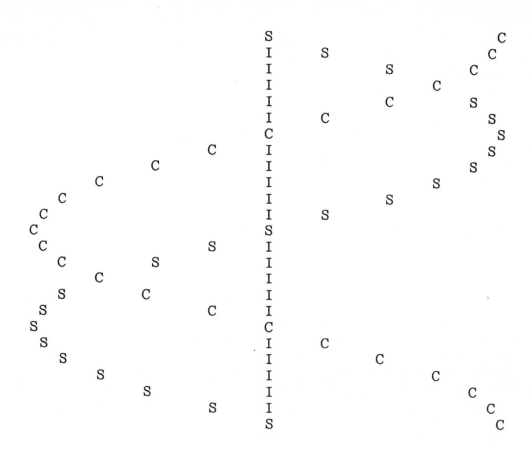

Fig.16.6. Printed graph using two symbols per line. The program must allow either symbol to occur first on the line. There are two basic methods for doing this.

```
      PROGRAM THING
C USES AN ARRAY TO PLOT A GRAPH
      CHARACTER LINE(70)
      CHARACTER IB,IS,IC,II
      PARAMETER(IB=' ',IS='S')
      PARAMETER(IC='C',II='I')
 10   FORMAT(1X,70A1)
      XTOP=8.0*ATAN(1.0)
      DX=XTOP/24.0
      DO 60 X=0.0,XTOP,DX
C FIRST CLEAR THE LINE
      DO 20 L=1,70
 20   LINE(L)=IB
C GET BOTH PRINT POSITIONS
      ICOLS=26.5+25.0*SIN(X)
      ICOLC=26.5+25.0*COS(X)
C PUT THEM IN ARRAY
      LINE(26)=II
      LINE(ICOLS)=IS
      LINE(ICOLC)=IC
      PRINT 10,LINE
 60   CONTINUE
      END
```

Which one of these programs actually printed Fig. 16.6?

Having arrived at the use of character arrays to predefine lines of output before printing, a number of new possibilities arise. Two are set as problems at the end of the Chapter and one is worked out here.

EXAMPLE:

How about printing that histogram the right way up? The same program can be used to define it all, but then it is printed from the top down. It is assumed here that the printer has 120 spaces across its width - one advantage of this number is that it has a large number of factors. The horizontal width that each bin will occupy is determined by dividing 120

```
  HOW MANY BINS ?
? 25
  HOW MANY TRIALS ?
? 1000
```

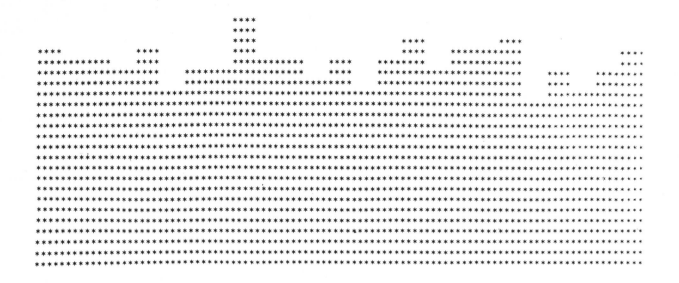

Fig. 16. 7. The histogram printed the other way up.

by NBINS to get NWIDE. The total
line width is then NBINS*NWIDE.

```
      DIMENSION IHIST(1001)
      CHARACTER LINE(120)
      CHARACTER STAR,BLANK,ICH
   PARAMETER(STAR='*',BLANK=' ')
C REQUEST SIZE AND NO. OF TRIALS
 10 PRINT*,'HOW MANY BINS ?'
      READ*, NBINS
      PRINT*,'HOW MANY TRIALS ?'
      READ*,NTRYS
C ALL BINS INITIALLY ARE ZERO
      DO 20 K=1,NBINS
 20 IHIST(K)=0
C GET RANDOMS AND MAKE HISTOGRAM
      DO 30 K=1,NTRYS
      L=RANDY()*NBINS+1.0
      IHIST(L)=IHIST(L)+1
 30 CONTINUE
C WORK OUT SCALE FACTOR FROM
C THE EXPECTED NUMBER PER BIN
```

```
      EXPEC=REAL(NTRYS)/REAL(NBINS)
      SCALE=EXPEC/20.0
C NOW PRINT THE HISTOGRAM
      NWIDE=120/NBINS
      LWIDE=NWIDE*NBINS
      DO 60 K=30,1,-1
C FILL OUT THE LINE
      LL=1
      DO 50 N=1,NBINS
      ITEST=K*SCALE
      ICH=BLANK
      IF(IHIST(N).GE.ITEST)ICH=STAR
      DO 50 L=1,NWIDE
      LINE(LL)=ICH
 50 LL=LL+1
 60 PRINT 70,(LINE(L),L=1,LWIDE)
 70 FORMAT(1X,120A1)
      GO TO 10
      END
```

An output is shown in Fig. 16.7.
What happens if you ask for more than
120 bins?

16.9 Character values as FORMAT

It is actually possible in FORTRAN 77 to use any character value as the FORMAT specifier for formatted input/output. The FORMAT specifier of a READ, WRITE, or PRINT statement can be:

(i) An *, which implies list-directed input/output

        PRINT*, INDEX

(ii) The label of a FORMAT statement

        READ 2Ø, JAWS
     2Ø FORMAT(I5)

(iii) A character constant

     PRINT'(1X,12Ø(''*''))'

or

     CHARACTER ZOWIE*(*)
     PARAMETER(ZOWIE='(1X,8F5.2)')
            ⋮
     PRINT ZOWIE, XRAY

(iv) A character variable or substring

     CHARACTER ZONK*1Ø
     DATA ZONK/'(1X,6F9.2)'/
            ⋮
     PRINT ZONK, XRAY

or

     CHARACTER*12 LAYOUT
     DATA LAYOUT/'(I3)(I4)(I5)'/
            ⋮
     PRINT LAYOUT(5:8) LUCKY

(v) A character array

     CHARACTER*4 FRAY(2)
     DATA FRAY/'(TRY',' ME)'/
            ⋮
     WRITE(7,FRAY)

This raises an interesting possibility, that of reading in the FORMAT specification when the program is run. Such a specifi-cation must include the parentheses which enclose the FORMAT specifier. As an example, a program could have

     CHARACTER FROTHY*8
     READ*, FROTHY
     PRINT FROTHY,'CLEVER ISN''T IT ?'

in which situation a valid character input in response to the READ could be

        '(8X,A17)'

16.10 Problems

PROBLEM 16.1:
Write an integer function called INHEX which reads in a hexadecimal number as a series of characters and converts it to a decimal integer, returning the value. Allow the input hexadecimal number to be variable in length; a person using your program may prefer to enter F for 15 rather than, for example, 000F.

PROBLEM 16.2:
Write a subroutine to sort a list of words into alphabetical order.

PROBLEM 16.3:
Write a subroutine to search a list of words which is in alphabetical order for a given word. Use a binary search.

PROBLEM 16.4:
Another basic editing operation is that of modifying selected parts of a line of text. Write a subroutine to do this interactively. It should first print the text to be modified. The person using the program then types his changes underneath. First of all make the sub-routine change only those parts of the line which have corresponding non-blank characters typed in. Then make it more sophisticated so that it can replace by blanks where desired, elim-inate parts of the text, and insert replacements.

PROBLEM 16.5:

Write a program that can reproduce a grey scale image on a printer. You are given an array of two dimensions containing integer values which represent the darkness of the picture. White is blank, slightly grey could be a minus, and so on. Do it by overprinting, using successively denser characters.

PROBLEM 16.6:

Develop a program for printing address labels. Special computer paper may be obtained, although it is a bit expensive, for printing sticky address labels. You will want to devise a convenient input format for addresses, and an attractive layout for the labels. Your program should first print a number of test labels so that the paper can be lined up properly. You then read in your addresses and print them beautifully. Do your Christmas cards this way.

PROBLEM 16.7

In Chapter 15 a subroutine was given for contour drawings. It is actually much easier to do on a lineprinter. You are given an array of two dimensions which represents the field to be contoured, as in Chapter 15. Using different symbols for the desired contour levels, build up the contour plot and print it one line at a time, using an array of one dimension to construct and print each new line in turn.

PROBLEM 16.8:

Write a program to assist an author in preparing an index for a book. He will wish to sit down at a terminal and scan through his book, entering each keyword as he finds it along with the page numbers. When he is finished, he types in 'finished' and the program sorts his keywords into alphabetical order. It then prints the keywords and the page numbers for him. After a quick edit by hand, the index is complete.

If you think that the program may be useful, you will want to enable the author to do his index in several sessions, so that he can have his new entries merged with his old ones which have been tucked away on a file. To do this, you will need to refer to later Chapters.

17
Other variable types

17.1 Introduction

In the early Chapters of this book, the distinctions between real and integer variables were carefully drawn, and then carried through the exposition of the many facilities of FORTRAN 77. It was assumed throughout that the type (real or integer) of a variable or a named constant was implied by the initial letter of the name. Then, in Chapter 16, a new type of variable - the CHARACTER type - was introduced, which somewhat overturned the earlier concept of implied type by requiring an explicit declaration of the type CHARACTER to be made in a CHARACTER statement.

In this Chapter, the full range of facilities for defining the type of a quantity will be introduced, along with several completely new types of data. It will be seen first of all that FORTRAN 77 includes a very flexible system which arranges for the type of any variable or named constant to be implied by its spelling. Effectively any letter of the alphabet can be made to imply any one type of data by using the IMPLICIT statement. Furthermore, it is possible to make an explicit definition of the type of a named quantity, which overrides the implicit type, using what is called a 'type statement'. The CHARACTER statement, which was introduced earlier, is an example of a type statement. The others are REAL, INTEGER, LOGICAL, DOUBLE PRECISION, and COMPLEX. Each of these defines a special type of data that can be used for meeting special requirements in a FORTRAN 77 program.

LOGICAL expressions were encountered in Chapter 6. It is possible to create logical variables which can have only the values .TRUE. or .FALSE., and these can be useful in decision making and in branching. There are also double precision variables or constants which are used to obtain increased accuracy or precision in calculations where the usual accuracy of the computer is insufficient. Likewise, FORTRAN 77 includes special facilities allowing convenient handling of complex numbers when defined as complex variables or constants. These new types of variables can be used in expressions, but the ways of combining them with each other and with real and integer variables are strictly defined. For these new types of variables, special built-in functions of various types with assorted types of arguments are provided, as will be seen.

In addition, it is sometimes convenient to pass the name of a subroutine or function to another subroutine or function, as an argument. For this reason a name can be declared to be the name of an external program using the EXTERNAL statement. In a similar way, the name of an intrinsic function can be passed if it has been identified in an INTRINSIC statement - although not all of the intrinsic functions qualify for this facility.

Finally, this Chapter ends with the complete rules for the ordering of statements in FORTRAN 77 programs.

17.2 Implicit definitions of type — the IMPLICIT statement

Up to this point it has been said that the type (real or integer) of a variable is given implicitly by the spelling of its name: I,J,K,L,M or N to begin integers and anything else for reals. The only exception has been that the CHARACTER statement overrides this implicit scheme. Now it will be shown that this scheme can be modified (or confirmed) by an IMPLICIT statement, which has the form:

    IMPLICIT type(letters) [,...]

Here, 'type' is one of the data types of FORTRAN 77, which are REAL, INTEGER, CHARACTER, LOGICAL, DOUBLE PRECISION and COMPLEX. These last three types are introduced in this Chapter. The 'letters' denote a list of single letters or a range of letters of the alphabet that become associated with a particular type, but only in the program unit where the IMPLICIT statement appears.

EXAMPLES:

In this first example will be seen two ways of specifying a range of letters, either singly, or with a minus sign between:

    IMPLICIT INTEGER(A,B,C,D)
    IMPLICIT REAL(E-Z)

The above statements would cause the main program or the subprogram which contain them to regard all names of quantities beginning with the letters A to D as integer and all the rest as real. It has overridden the normal convention for the letters I to N.

    IMPLICIT INTEGER(A-D)

The above example again defines names beginning with A,B,C or D as integers but leaves the rest of the alphabet untouched, so that

    A - D   implies integer
    E - H   implies real (by default)
    I - N   implies integer (by default)
    O - Z   implies real (by default)

These examples demonstrate that a range of letters can either be spelled out by listing the individual letters with commas between, or by using a minus sign between the letters at the ends of the range. The default, or normal, condition of FORTRAN is the same as the following IMPLICIT scheme:

    IMPLICIT REAL(A-H),INTEGER(I-N)
    IMPLICIT REAL(O-Z)

The other types of FORTRAN can be used. as well. The following example is self explanatory:

    IMPLICIT COMPLEX(C)
    IMPLICIT DOUBLE PRECISION(D,P)
    IMPLICIT LOGICAL(L)
    IMPLICIT CHARACTER(H)

For character data, the default length of a character quantity is 1. However, in the IMPLICIT statement the assumed length can be changed. This is very useful; the following statement causes all quantities beginning with the letter H to be of type CHARACTER and length 4:

    IMPLICIT CHARACTER*4(H)

The standard does not allow

    IMPLICIT CHARACTER*4

because it requires any type named in an IMPLICIT statement to have at least one letter associated with it. The length specification for characters given in an IMPLICIT statement may be any integer constant expression. It does not need to be enclosed in parentheses (brackets) as it did in the CHARACTER statement.

As will be seen in the sections which follow, any implicit scheme can be overridden (or else confirmed) by explicit declarations for particular names. The lengths can be overridden as well for CHARACTER quantities. If the following statements appear, all names beginning with Q are character quantities of length 6. In addition, PERV and STUB are of type CHARACTER with length 4, while QUER is also of type CHARACTER but of length 2:

    IMPLICIT CHARACTER*6 (Q)
    CHARACTER*4 PERV,STUB,QUER*2

The IMPLICIT statement has effect only within a particular program unit, i.e. a main program, a FUNCTION subprogram, a SUBROUTINE subprogram or a BLOCK DATA subprogram. It applies to variables (including dummy arguments of a sub-program), arrays, names of constants defined in PARAMETER statements, statement functions of the program unit, and the names of all external function references.

In the following example, CHUGG is the name of a function of type CHARACTER, and when the program is run, it will expect to be able to find a CHARACTER FUNCTION named CHUGG also of length 4.

```
      IMPLICIT CHARACTER*4(C)
            :
            :
      CLUNK=CHUGG(CLICK)
```

The following example does exactly the same thing without an IMPLICIT statement:

```
      CHARACTER*4 CLUNK,CHUGG,CLICK
            :
            :
      CLUNK=CHUGG(CLICK)
```

An IMPLICIT statement does not change the type of the intrinsic functions of FORTRAN. As an example, in a program with

```
      IMPLICIT INTEGER(C)
```

the CHAR function is still a character function of an integer argument.

Obviously, no contradictions are allowed. The specification which follows would be rejected:

```
      IMPLICIT REAL(A-M),COMPLEX(C)
```

17.3 Mixing IMPLICIT and PARAMETER statements

The IMPLICIT statement is a specification statement of FORTRAN. It belongs at the beginning of a program where it can be intermixed with the PARAMETER statements, but it must precede all other specification statements. Refer to Section 10 of this Chapter for the final word on the order of statements in FORTRAN 77 programs.

Because only real and integer types exist in the normal default condition of FORTRAN 77, it is only possible to use another type in a PARAMETER statement if an earlier IMPLICIT statement makes the type available. Only certain combinations of PARAMETER and IMPLICIT can be used. Remember:

(i) A symbolic name of a constant can only be used after the PARAMETER statement that defines it.

(ii) A symbolic constant whose type depends on an IMPLICIT statement cannot be defined until after the IMPLICIT statement.

Therefore there are some situations in which PARAMETER must precede IMPLICIT, and others in which IMPLICIT must precede PARAMETER. These can be demonstrated by a series of examples using the CHARACTER data type.

Character constants can be given symbolic names through PARAMETER statements. To do this, the type of the name must first be established by either a CHARACTER statement or an IMPLICIT statement. For example

```
      IMPLICIT CHARACTER*4 (F)
      PARAMETER(FIRST4='ABCD')
```

gives the symbolic name FIRST4 to the character constant whose value is ABCD. Throughout the same program unit FIRST4 stands only for that constant value and cannot be changed. In addition, any name beginning with the letter F is a character entity. The statements

```
      CHARACTER*4 FIRST4
      PARAMETER(FIRST4='ABCD')
```

have the same effect on FIRST4, but do not associate the type character with the letter F.

The rules permit the length to come from an earlier PARAMETER statement. Consider

```
PARAMETER(NUMS=5)
IMPLICIT CHARACTER*NUMS (S-Z)
PARAMETER(TODAY='SUNNY')
PRINT*,TODAY
```

which is correct.

There is a possible clash of lengths between the IMPLICIT statement and the PARAMETER statement. As before, this is resolved by ranging the character constant expression left and either truncating at the right end or filling out with blanks as necessary. In the statements

```
IMPLICIT CHARACTER(D)
PARAMETER(DULL='PQRS')
```

the length of DULL is 1 character (by default). Only the leftmost character from the constant expression 'PQRS' is taken in the PARAMETER statement and so the symbolic character constant DULL has the value P. In the statements

```
IMPLICIT CHARACTER*4(A,B)
PARAMETER(BRIGHT='RA')
```

the length of BRIGHT is 4 characters, but the PARAMETER statement defines only 2. Here the right hand end is filled with blanks, so the value assigned to BRIGHT is the same as

```
'RA  '
```

17.4 Explicit definitions of type — the REAL and INTEGER statements

In the early stages of this book, the type of a quantity was implied by the spelling of its name: I,J,K,L,M or N to begin integers and any other letter for reals. Then, in this Chapter, it was seen that an IMPLICIT statement could modify that scheme. Now it will be shown that the type of a quantity can be stated explicitly in a REAL or an INTEGER statement, and this overrides any implicit scheme that might be in force. REAL and INTEGER statements are called 'type statements'. The CHARACTER statement was also a type statement.

EXAMPLE:
The statements

```
REAL LUNG
INTEGER ZAP
```

define the quantity LUNG to be of type real and ZAP to be integer. In the statements

```
IMPLICIT REAL(I)
INTEGER ICICLE,COOL
REAL MOTHER
```

the IMPLICIT scheme makes most of the quantities beginning with I into reals, but the INTEGER statement has overridden this to make ICICLE and COOL into integer variables. The REAL statement forces MOTHER to be a real name.

Obviously it would be possible for a programmer to make very confusing programs by using IMPLICIT to modify the normal scheme for real and integer names and by overriding the implied spellings. Although these facilities can be very convenient, the best programmers do not mess about with the names of real and integer quantities.

REAL and INTEGER statements can be used to define the type of variable names, the names of symbolic constants, array names, function names, or the names of external programs. They cannot modify the type of an intrinsic function of FORTRAN 77. It is meaningless to attempt to assign a type to the name of a main program, a SUBROUTINE subprogram, or a BLOCK DATA subprogram. In fact it would not be allowed.

The REAL and INTEGER statements can also be used to define the dimension bounds of an array. The statements

```
PARAMETER(ISZ=5)
REAL XPART(0:20),YPART(0:20)
INTEGER IPROD(2*ISZ),LUNG(3*ISZ)
```

are exactly equivalent to

```
PARAMETER(ISZ=5)
DIMENSION XPART(0:20),YPART(0:20)
DIMENSION IPROD(2*ISZ),LUNG(3*ISZ)
```

The following statements

```
      REAL KWOTA(8),QUOTA(8)
      INTEGER YES(10),NO(10)
```

not only state the dimension bounds of four arrays but also force two changes of type. KWOTA becomes a real array and YES an integer one. This could not be accomplished by a single statement, but equivalent statements are

```
      REAL KWOTA
      INTEGER YES
      DIMENSION KWOTA(8),QUOTA(8)
      DIMENSION YES(10),NO(10)
```

This last example illustrates an important principle, that the type statements and the DIMENSION statement can be mixed together in virtually any combination. However, the declaration of the dimension bounds of an array can only occur once. Therefore it is possible to say

```
      PARAMETER(N=3)
      REAL ITEM(-N:N)
```

or to say the same thing by putting

```
      PARAMETER(N=3)
      DIMENSION ITEM(-N:N)
      REAL ITEM
```

in which it is noted that the type declaration can follow the declaration of the array bounds. It is not correct to put

```
      PARAMETER(N=3)
      REAL ITEM(-N:N)
      DIMENSION ITEM(-N:N)
```

in which the dimension bounds of ITEM are stated twice. A program containing the above would be rejected.

An EQUIVALENCE statement can cause variables or arrays to become associated, as in

```
REAL KWOTA(8),QUOTA(8)
INTEGER YES(10),NO(10)
EQUIVALENCE(KWOTA,QUOTA,YES,NO)
```

which compresses all the arrays into a single area, 10 locations long. (It will be recalled that characters can only be equivalenced to other characters.)

COMMON can also be involved. The very nasty example which follows produces the layout illustrated in Fig. 17.1. It would be bad style to create such an involved layout unnecessarily, i.e. unless really pushed for space:

```
REAL JOHN,LINDA,MARY
REAL IMPULS,FRED(7)
INTEGER IMPLIC(100),REFER,DAVID
INTEGER OUTPUT,INFER(10)
DIMENSION MARY(8),REFER(8)
DIMENSION EXPLIC(64),HERE(5)
COMMON XAVIER,INPUT,MARY
COMMON INFER,IMPULS(15),IMPLIC
EQUIVALENCE(JOHN,INPUT)
EQUIVALENCE(XAVIER,OUTPUT)
EQUIVALENCE(LINDA,MARY)
EQUIVALENCE(INFER,REFER)
EQUIVALENCE(IMPLIC(37),EXPLIC)
EQUIVALENCE(DAVID,HERE)
```

The COMMON, REAL, INTEGER, DIMENSION, and EQUIVALENCE statements can be mixed together in any order. However, it is suggested for good style that a programmer adopt as a matter of habit the following sequence:

(i) REAL, INTEGER or other type. Specify the dimensions in these statements unless the arrays are named in a COMMON statement.
(ii) DIMENSION if necessary, but why not give all dimension bounds either in a type statement or in a COMMON statement?
(iii) COMMON. For arrays in COMMON specify the dimension bounds in the COMMON statement.
(iv) EQUIVALENCE.

By following this scheme, the previous example begins to be readable:

```
REAL JOHN,LINDA,MARY,IMPULS
REAL FRED(7),HERE(5),EXPLIC(64)
INTEGER DAVID,OUTPUT,REFER(8)
COMMON XAVIER,INPUT,MARY(8)
COMMON INFER(10),IMPULS(15)
COMMON IMPLIC(100)
EQUIVALENCE(JOHN,INPUT)
EQUIVALENCE(XAVIER,OUTPUT)
EQUIVALENCE(LINDA,MARY)
EQUIVALENCE(INFER,REFER)
EQUIVALENCE(IMPLIC(37),EXPLIC)
EQUIVALENCE(DAVID,HERE)
```

However, it is still a pretty terrible choice of variable names.

The required order of statements in a FORTRAN 77 program is finally spelled out in Section 10 of this Chapter. However, whenever a program has a complicated data structure, it is best to follow a consistent scheme among type statements, COMMON, DIMENSION, and EQUIVALENCE as suggested above. Good programming is clear programming.

The type statements REAL and INTEGER can be used freely in functions and subroutines with or without adjustable or assumed size dimensions for arrays which are dummy arguments, just as in the DIMENSION statement. This usage was described in detail in Chapter 11. It must be recalled, however, that the actual arguments of a CALL statement and the dummy arguments in a SUB-ROUTINE statement must correspond in

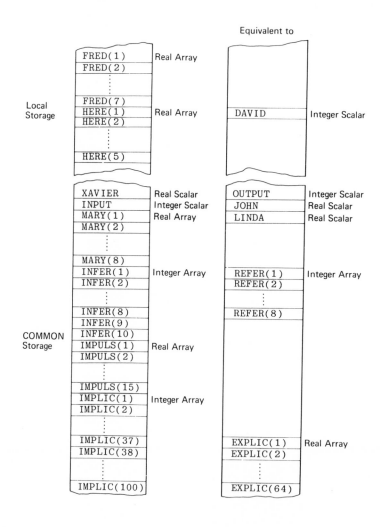

Fig. 17.1.   Storage arrangement arising from a combination of type, DIMENSION, COMMON, and EQUIVALENCE statements.

type. The same is true of the actual and dummy arguments in referencing a function. Because a subroutine or function is a separate program unit, the type of dummy arguments is taken to be that implied by their spelling. To change this an IMPLICIT statement or an explicit declaration in a type statement could be used. As before, adjustable dimensions may not be used with variables in COMMON.

The ability to change the type of a name also extends to statement functions and external functions. Suppose that an arithmetic statement function which is real is to be created which converts any angle in degrees to the equivalent in the range 0°-360° (called the principal angle). For reasons of his own a programmer wants to call this function MINE. To make this possible, use either

```
IMPLICIT REAL(M)
MINE(THETA)=MOD(THETA,36Ø.Ø)
```

or

```
REAL MINE
MINE(THETA)=MOD(THETA,36Ø.Ø)
```

In either case the arithmetic statement function MINE is a real function of a single real argument. The second version would be preferred unless it is necessary that all names beginning with M should be real.

The type of a function subprogram can also be controlled. A function for shifting the binary digits of an integer to the left might be called SHIFT. The programmer has to put

```
INTEGER SHIFT
```

in any program that refers to SHIFT, or else use an equivalent IMPLICIT statement. The integer function SHIFT can be created using the INTEGER FUNCTION statement, which declares the type of the function explicitly:

```
INTEGER FUNCTION SHIFT(I,ISHF)
C
C SHIFT I LEFT BY ISHF PLACES
C IF ISHF IS -VE GOES RIGHT
C WORKS FOR TWOS COMPLEMENT
```

```
IF(ISHF.LT.Ø) THEN
   SHIFT=(I-1)/2**(-ISHF)
ELSE
   SHIFT=I*2**ISHF
END IF
END
```

The above program does an arithmetic binary shift of the integer argument I by ISHF positions to the left (assuming that the computer uses twos complement arithmetic). If ISHF is negative, this is interpreted as a right shift by ABS(ISHF) positions.

There is also a similar REAL FUNCTION statement for an explicit declaration of the type of a real function subprogram, as in

```
REAL FUNCTION IDIOT(X)
```

For a function which has multiple entry points, the type of entry name must agree in the program which refers to it, and in the function itself. Either implicit or explicit means can be used. For example, in an integer function called REP, RAP is another integer entry point and ZUG is a real one. All three entry points have a single integer argument. The program using these functions might have

```
IMPLICIT INTEGER(R,S,T)
        :
        :
TUG=REP(NUG)
        :
        :
SLUG=RAP(NOG)
        :
        :
ZLEP=ZUG(NIG)
```

whereas the function itself might be

```
INTEGER FUNCTION REP(I)
INTEGER RAP
        :
        :
ENTRY RAP(J)
        :
        :
ENTRY ZUG(K)
        :
        :
```

It should be recalled, however, that in character functions all entry points must be of type character.

17.5 The LOGICAL type

A quantity can be declared to be of logical type by the LOGICAL statement. In the case of simple variables, simply write

    LOGICAL variable names

The LOGICAL statement belongs in the same position in a program as the other type statements. Refer to Section 10 of this Chapter for the definitive rules about the order of statements.

The specification that a particular quantity is logical is a complete one; the same variable cannot be real or integer or any other type at the same time. Since there is no implicit spelling for logical names by default, they can only exist if there is an IMPLICIT or LOGICAL statement to make it happen. The statement

    IMPLICIT LOGICAL(L)

causes all names of variables, arrays, symbolic constants, and functions to be of logical type if they start with the letter L - for only the program unit in which this statement appears.

Arrays can be of type logical, and so the specification of the dimension bounds for them can be given in the LOGICAL statement itself, or in the other ways described in Section 3 of this Chapter.

EXAMPLES:
(i) The statements

    PARAMETER (N=5)
    LOGICAL TRUTH,ANSWER(N+1:3*N)
    LOGICAL INCLU

define the variables TRUTH, ANSWER, and INCLU as being of type logical. ANSWER is an array of 10 logical values. None of the named quantities can appear in any other type statement. However, TRUTH and INCLU

could appear in DIMENSION or COMMON statements and so might be arrays themselves.

(ii) The statements

    DIMENSION LOGS(16),VALUES(20)
    LOGICAL LOGS

define a logical array LOGS of 16 logical values. The array VALUES is evidently real.

(iii) The statements

    COMMON BEANS(6),DECIDE
    DIMENSION WHY(2),PEAS(4)
    DIMENSION NUTS(4),LUCY(4)
    LOGICAL DECIDE,WHY
    LOGICAL WHERE(4),PARK
    EQUIVALENCE (BEANS,WHY)
    EQUIVALENCE (PEAS,LUCY,WHERE)
    EQUIVALENCE (NUTS,PARK)

define the storage layout illustrated in Fig.17.2. In an EQUIVALENCE statement, a logical value will take up the same amount of space as a real or integer value, as Fig.17.2 shows.

There are two possible logical constants, .TRUE. and .FALSE., whose values are self explanatory. Logical variables and constants can only be used in limited circumstances in a FORTRAN program. Together they can be combined into logical expressions using the logical operations .AND., .OR., .NOT., .EQV., and .NEQV., and with other variable types by means of the relational operators .GT., .GE., .LT., .LE., .EQ., and .NE.. These logical expressions are permitted only in the logical IF statement or in an assignment statement. Logical values can also be assigned to logical variables in DATA statements and logical quantities can be used in READ and WRITE statements.

A logical expression is something which is easily understood but more difficult to define precisely. First consider any relational expression:

    arithmetic relational arithmetic
    expression operator expression

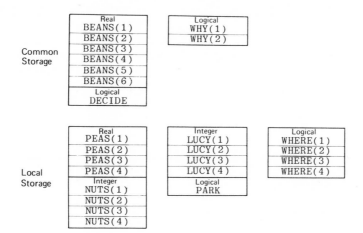

Fig. 17.2. A storage arrangement created by COMMON,
DIMENSION, LOGICAL, and EQUIVALENCE.

These arithmetic expressions can be of any of the types real, integer, complex, or double precision, except that complex expressions are permitted only for the operations .EQ. and .NE., and a relational expression may not be used to compare a double precision result with a complex result.

It is also possible to compare two expressions, both of type character, as was described in Chapter 16:

character   relational   character
expression   operator   expression

In either case, the result of a relational expression is of type logical, and when evaluated take one of the logical values .TRUE. or .FALSE..

A logical expression is then some combination of logical values using the available logical operators, which produce the results defined by the 'truth table' of Fig. 17.3. As can be seen, the .NEQV. operator is the one often known as the exclusive OR operation, and .EQV. is its inverse.

The logical operator .NOT. must be followed by a logical value, and all the other operators must be both preceded and followed by logical values. In the

Logical expression a	Logical operator	Logical expression b	Logical result
	.NOT.	.TRUE. .FALSE.	.FALSE. .TRUE.
.TRUE. .TRUE. .FALSE. .FALSE.	.AND.	.TRUE. .FALSE. .TRUE. .FALSE.	.TRUE. .FALSE. .FALSE. .FALSE.
.TRUE. .TRUE. .FALSE. .FALSE.	.OR.	.TRUE. .FALSE. .TRUE. .FALSE.	.TRUE. .TRUE. .TRUE. .FALSE.
.TRUE. .TRUE. .FALSE. .FALSE.	.EQV.	.TRUE. .FALSE. .TRUE. .FALSE.	.TRUE. .FALSE. .FALSE. .TRUE.
.TRUE. .TRUE. .FALSE. .FALSE.	.NEQV.	.TRUE. .FALSE. .TRUE. .FALSE.	.FALSE. .TRUE. .TRUE. .FALSE.

Fig. 17.3.   Truth table for the logical operations of FORTRAN 77.

absence of brackets, the hierarchy of all the various operators in FORTRAN is as follows:

```
( )
 **
* or /
+ or -
 //
.GT., .GE., .EQ., .LE., .LT., .NE.
.NOT.
.AND.
.OR.
.EQV. or .NEQV.
```

which could be summarized as

```
( )  Expression in Brackets
Arithmetic Operators
Character Operators
Relational Operators
Logical Operators
```

EXAMPLE:

```
LOGICAL ONE,TWO,THREE,FOUR
FOUT=ONE. OR. TWO. AND. THREE
```

means

```
LOGICAL ONE,TWO,THREE,FOUR
FOUT=ONE. OR. (TWO. AND. THREE)
```

Considering that .AND. is considered to be 'logical multiplication' in Boolean algebra, and .OR. is 'logical addition', the relative priority of the two operators is consistent with the priority of ordinary multiplication and addition. Logical expressions involving the operators .EQV. or .NEQV., which have equal priority, are evaluated from left to right.

A logical expression, which has the result either .TRUE. or .FALSE., is used in logical or block IF statements, ELSE IF statements, assignment statements, and the output statements PRINT or WRITE. It may not be used anywhere else. A logical expression involving only known constants, however, may appear in a PARAMETER statement. A logical variable or array name may appear in a READ statement. These are the only appearances that logical values can make in a FORTRAN program.

An assignment statement can be used:

```
logical    =  logical
variable      expression
```

Here, the logical expression is evaluated and the result, which is either .TRUE. or .FALSE., becomes the new value of the logical variable. No conversions are allowed - if the left hand side of an assignment statement is a logical variable, then the right hand side can only be a logical expression.

EXAMPLES:
(i)

```
JURY=. TRUE.
```

Here JURY must be a logical variable declared by an IMPLICIT assignment or in a LOGICAL statement, or else this statement could refer to the first item in a logical array called JURY. Either way, the value .TRUE. is assigned to it.

(ii)

```
SWITCH=A. GT. 4. Ø. OR. I. LT. 73
```

SWITCH must be logical, and A and I real, integer or double precision. SWITCH will be assigned the value .FALSE. unless either A is greater than 4.0 or I is less than 73.

(iii)

```
EOR=A. AND. . NOT. B. OR. . NOT. A. AND. B
```

Referring to the hierarchy of the operators, enthusiasts of Boolean algebra will notice that this is the expression for the exclusive OR operation, and is exactly the same as

```
EOR=A. NEQV. B
```

The exclusive OR of A and B will be formed. EOR, A, and B must all be of type logical.

The various forms of IF statement were described in Chapter 6. The logical IF

```
IF   logical    executable
     expression  statement
```

the block IF

        IF   logical   THEN
              expression

and the ELSE IF

        ELSE IF   logical   THEN
                  expression

The principal uses of logical values are in these statements.

Symbolic names can be given to logical constants through the PARAMETER statements - of course the only available values are .TRUE. and .FALSE..

EXAMPLES:

```
LOGICAL YES,NO,MAYBE(4)
PARAMETER(YES=.TRUE.,NO=.FALSE.)
```

A logical expression which involves only constant values is also possible:

```
LOGICAL UN,DEUX,TRAY
PARAMETER(X=4.3,I=2)
PARAMETER(UN=.TRUE.,DEUX=.FALSE.)
PARAMETER(TRAY=.NOT.X.GT.I.OR.UN)
```

which defines TRAY as the name of a constant of value .TRUE. - not a very useful thing to do actually.

Also, the type could be established by an IMPLICIT statement

```
IMPLICIT LOGICAL(L)
PARAMETER(LINGUS=.FALSE.)
```

after which nearly everything which begins with L will be taken as logical.

Logical variables or arrays can be given their initial values by a DATA statement:

```
LOGICAL QRAY(4),BEER
DATA QRAY/4*.TRUE./,BEER/.FALSE./
```

Logical values can be included in list-directed input or output statements. In a list-directed PRINT or WRITE statement, the computer will arrange to print T for .TRUE. and F for .FALSE. as required, but in its own way:

```
LOGICAL THIS,THAT,OTHER
        ⋮
        ⋮
PRINT*,THIS,THAT.OR.OTHER
```

In response to a list-directed READ statement, the input data to match a logical item in the list can be any item beginning with T or .T to stand for .TRUE. and with F or .F to stand for .FALSE.. For example in response to

```
IMPLICIT LOGICAL(T)
        ⋮
        ⋮
READ*,TDUM,TDEE
```

the data

        FRUE,TRALSE

could be given to define TDUM (standing for Tweedle DUM) as .FALSE. and TDEE (guess who?) as .TRUE..

For formatted input or output, there is a logical editing description, the L field, given by

        Lw

where w is the width of the field. In a FORMAT used by a WRITE or PRINT statement, the letter T for .TRUE. or F for .FALSE. would be printed right justified in the field. In response to a READ statement referring to fields of L format, the input should contain T, .T, F or .F as the first nonblank characters in the field. As an example, here is a program which gives the exclusive OR of two values:

```
      LOGICAL A,B,C
C READ IN A AND B
      READ 10,A,B
 10 FORMAT(2L10)
C ECHO THE INPUT
      PRINT 20,A,B
 20 FORMAT('A =',L2,'  B =',L2)
C FORM THE EXCLUSIVE OR
      C=A.NEQV.B
C AND PRINT THE RESULT
      PRINT 30,C
 30 FORMAT(' A.EOR.B =',L2)
      END
```

In response to the READ statement it could be given

TRILLY   FOLLY

and it would print as its result

A = T   B = F
A.EOR.B = T

EXAMPLE:
The binary half addition of two digits obeys the truth table shown by Fig. 17.4, so that if A and B are the inputs and SUM and CARRY are the outputs,

SUM = A.B + B.A
(A and not B or B and not A)

CARRY = A.B
(A and B)

The following subroutine will perform binary half addition on its arguments A and B, returning the result in SUM and CARRY.

```
SUBROUTINE HALFAD(A,B,SUM,CARRY)
LOGICAL A,B,SUM,CARRY
SUM=A.NEQV.B
CARRY=A.AND.B
END
```

Statement functions of type logical can be created; here one is defined for the NOR (not OR) operation. It is a logical function of two logical dummy arguments

```
LOGICAL NOR,X,Y,A,B
NOR(X,Y)=.NOT.(X.OR.Y)
```

Brackets are required in defining NOR because of the priority of the .NOT. operation. In the same program this function could be used in a statement like

IF(NOR(A,B)) THEN

It is also possible to make function subprograms of type LOGICAL, using the LOGICAL FUNCTION statement. Here is one for the NAND (not AND) operation

```
LOGICAL FUNCTION NAND(X,Y)
LOGICAL X,Y
NAND=.NOT.(X.AND.Y)
END
```

INPUTS		OUTPUTS	
A	B	SUM	CARRY
F	F	F	F
F	T	T	F
T	F	T	F
T	T	F	T

Fig. 17.4.   Truth   table   for   binary   half-addition.

Note that the name of the function is not repeated in the LOGICAL statement. In the statement which defines NAND, unnecessary brackets are used for clarity.

Any program which used this function would have to include an IMPLICIT or LOGICAL statement which specifies the type of NAND:

```
LOGICAL NAND,X,Y,Z
      :
      :
Z=NAND(NAND(X,NAND(X,Y)),
      NAND(Y,NAND(Y,NAND(X,Y))))
```

The reader may wish to amuse himself figuring out what this expression means.

There are no intrinsic functions of type logical in FORTRAN 77. As a final word about the logical type, it should be said that apart from relational expressions in IF statements, logical results are infrequently used. When structuring a normal FORTRAN program which does numerical calculations there is no real need for them. Although they can be used quite respectably in forming many of the program structures described in Chapter 9, they are just as likely to obscure the meaning of a program as they are to improve it. As with many facilities in FORTRAN, a program can create quite a mess by over-indulgence in the use of logical variables. Unless they aid program clarity or provide needed logical facilities, as in Boolean algebra, they should not be used.

17.6 The DOUBLE PRECISION type

A name can be defined as being of double precision type by the DOUBLE PRECISION statement:

DOUBLE PRECISION variable names

or by a scheme of implicit names, such as

IMPLICIT DOUBLE PRECISION(D)

The specification of double precision is a complete one; the same quantity cannot be of any other type. The DOUBLE PRECISION statement is a type statement and belongs at the head of a program unit in the order specified by the rules of Section 10 of this Chapter.

The purpose of double precision is to give a program the ability to calculate or accumulate results with more digits of accuracy than are normally available to real values. It is, however, slower than ordinary arithmetic and so should be used judiciously. In Chapter 4 a number of examples were shown in which a perfectly reasonable calculation was likely to be beyond the capabilities of a computer. By making selected variables or other quantities have extra precision, these problems can often be circumvented. In general, double precision will provide twice the number of significant digits in a machine. Double precision names can refer to arrays, and so the information about the dimension bounds can be included in the DOUBLE PRECISION statement, or through a COMMON or DIMENSION statement. The various combinations are the same as with the REAL and INTEGER statements. In using COMMON or EQUIVALENCE statements with double precision values, there arises a special complication because each double precision variable or array member takes twice as much space as a real or integer value. This must be allowed for when laying out COMMON and when using EQUIVALENCE.

EXAMPLE:

```
DOUBLE PRECISION PRECIS(4),DUBBL
INTEGER IRAY(1Ø)
COMMON SLUG(1Ø)
EQUIVALENCE(SLUG,PRECIS)
EQUIVALENCE(IRAY,DUBBL)
```

This storage arrangement is illustrated by Fig. 17.5.

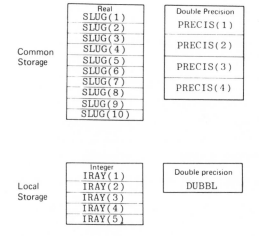

Fig. 17.5. Illustrating a storage arrangement using COMMON, DIMENSION, and DOUBLE PRECISION statements. Each double precision value takes twice the space of reals, integers, or logicals.

Constants of double precision are written in FORTRAN programs by using a form similar to the exponential form of a basic real constant but substituting the letter D to indicate double precision for the E. They are written as

real constant D exponent

or

integer constant D exponent

EXAMPLES:

2.73D-36

means 2.73×10^{-36} with double precision accuracy.

7D∅

means 7.0 with double precision accuracy.

A double precision constant can be given a symbolic name in a PARAMETER statement provided, as always, that the type is established beforehand.

EXAMPLE:

DOUBLE PRECISION PIE
PARAMETER(PIE=3.14159 26535
            89793 23846)

The value of PIE is defined to an accuracy not of 21 digits, but using those digits to whatever accuracy the machine may have available for double precision values. This will mean either that the given value could be truncated or that extra zeros could be added, depending on the machine.

IMPLICIT DOUBLE PRECISION(E)
PARAMETER(EBASE=2.71828 18284
            590̸45 23536)

Similarly EBASE is defined as the name of a double precision constant; this time all names beginning with E will be of type double precision in the particular program unit.

An initial value can be assigned to a double precision variable or array member in the DATA statement:

DOUBLE PRECISION X
DATA X/1.5D∅/

Double precision quantities can be used in expressions of FORTRAN in all the circumstances in which real values are allowed. Therefore in expressions real, integer, complex and double precision values can be mixed fully, with the one restriction that a double precision value can never be directly involved in an operation with a complex term, i.e. you cannot add, subtract, multiply, divide, or exponentiate a double precision value with a complex one, or vice versa. In Section 8 of this Chapter the rules governing the combinations of type are

described, including the method of predicting the type of a result where the terms are of mixed type. Because of the prohibition on using complex and double precision values together, they cannot be compared in an IF statement. This is because a relational expression

value 1   relational   value 2
            operator

has to be equivalent to

value 1 – value 2   relational   ∅
                      operator

because this is the way most computers would actually do it.

In assignment statements, once again any assignments are allowed involving the types real, integer, double precision and complex. Therefore in a statement like

variable = expression

the expression could be any one of the four arithmetic types, and a conversion is made, if necessary, before assignment. A conversion from double precision to something else would involve loss of precision. Similarly, converting anything else to double precision only adds on zeros.

For FORMAT-directed input and output a double precision editing description is available, the D description:

Dw.d

which is similar to the E description as used with real values. w is the total field width used for the value and d is the number of decimal digits expected. As with the E description, room is required for signs, exponents, and the letter D to be printed. Therefore for output w should be at least 7 greater than d.

For input, the value given can be in the form of any basic real constant, or any double precision constant. It can also be a simple number, in which case the computer assumes that it is a basic real constant with a decimal point implied before the last d digits. In fact the input data forms for F, E, or D editing are completely interchangeable.

List-directed input/output statements can also be used. For output the computer will print the values in D editing form, making its own arrangements for the digits and the exponent:

PRINT*,4.0D0*DATAN(1.0D0)

In response to a list-directed READ statement, double precision items can be given in either D, F, or E form, or as a string of digits in which case it is assumed to have no decimal places. To respond to

DOUBLE PRECISION EBASE
READ*,EBASE

one could put any of the forms

2.7D0
.271828E1
2.71828182845

to define EBASE. None of these forms are accurate of course; for 21 digits one would want

2.71828 18284 59045 23536

EXAMPLE:
This program calculates and prints the value of π to 30 significant digits. This assumes that double precision on the computer is 30 digits; it may actually be a lot less.

```
      DOUBLE PRECISION PIE
      PIE=4.0D0*DATAN(1.0D0)
      PRINT 20,PIE
   20 FORMAT(1X,D40.30)
      STOP
      END
```

EXERCISE:
Run the above program. Check the result against mathematical tables. This will tell you approximately the extent of double precision on your computer - but not exactly because the function DATAN which is used will not itself quite achieve the maximum possible precision.

In the example, all the constants in the arithmetic statement have been written carefully as double precision to ensure a double precision result. The function DATAN is a special, intrinsic double precision function for the arctangent. Because FORTRAN already knows that DATAN is of type double precision, it has not been necessary to declare it as such in the DOUBLE PRECISION statement. The double precision functions which are part of standard FORTRAN 77 are listed in Table 17.1.

If the generic name of the function is used, then the type of the argument may influence the type of the result. Therefore

DOUBLE PRECISION X
X=ATAN(1.0)

does not evaluate the arctangent to double precision - it will do it as a real and then convert the result to X by adding on extra zeros - probably not what the program wants. It is likely that the person who wrote this really wants

DOUBLE PRECISION X
X=ATAN(1.0D0)

or alternatively

DOUBLE PRECISION X
X=DATAN(1.0D0)

Considerable care is required to get results in double precision which actually have the extra digits required!

As would be expected, double precision statement functions and function subprograms can be defined.

EXAMPLES:
(i) The following program contains the double precision arithmetic statement function ANGL, which will convert its double precision argument in degrees to a double precision result in radians. Note that the function name, the name of its dummy argument and the names of the variables used with it have all been declared to be double precision.

```
DOUBLE PRECISION ANGL,X,Y,Z
ANGL(Z)=4D0*DATAN(1D0)*Z/180D0
   :
```

Generic Name	Specific Name	Meaning
DBLE(argument)		Convert to double precision. For complex argument takes real part.
INT(D)	IDINT(D)	Convert to integer.
REAL(D)	SNGL(D)	Convert to single precision real.
CMPLX(D)		Make complex, imaginary part $\emptyset.\emptyset$.
AINT(D)	DINT(D)	Truncate to integer part - result is double precision.
ANINT(D)	DNINT(D)	Round to nearest whole number - result is double precision.
NINT(D)	IDNINT(D)	Round to nearest whole number - result is integer.
ABS(D)	DABS(D)	Absolute value of D.
MOD(D1,D2)	DMOD(D1,D2)	Remainder D1-AINT(D1/D2)*D2.
DIM(D)	DDIM(D)	Positive difference D1-MIN(D1,D2).
SIGN(D1,D2)	DSIGN(D1,D2)	Transfer sign, (sign D2)*ABS(D1).
	DPROD(X1,X2)	Double precision product of reals.
MAX(D1,D2,...)	DMAX1(D1,D2,...)	Choose maximum value argument.
MIN(D1,D2,...)	DMIN1(D1,D2,...)	Choose minimum value argument.
SQRT(D)	DSQRT(D)	Square root.
EXP(D)	DEXP(D)	Exponential function e^D.
LOG(D)	DLOG(D)	Logarithm to base e, $\log_e D$.
LOG1$\emptyset$(D)	DLOG1$\emptyset$(D)	Logarithm to base 1$\emptyset$, $\log_{1\emptyset} D$.
SIN(D)	DSIN(D)	Sine of D, D in radians.
COS(D)	DCOS(D)	Cosine of D, D in radians.
TAN(D)	DTAN(D)	Tangent of D, D in radians.
ASIN(D)	DASIN(D)	Arcsin(D), $\emptyset \leq a \leq \pi$ with sin a = D.
ACOS(D)	DACOS(D)	Arccos(D), $\emptyset \leq a \leq \pi$ with cos a = D.
ATAN(D)	DATAN(D)	Arctan(D), $-\pi/2 \leq a \leq \pi/2$, tan a = D.
ATAN2(D1,D2)	DATAN2(D1,D2)	Arctan( ), $-\pi \leq a \leq \pi$, tan a = D2/D1.
SINH(D)	DSINH(D)	Hyperbolic sine, $(e^D - e^{-D})/2.\emptyset$.
COSH(D)	DCOSH(D)	Hyperbolic cosine, $(e^D + e^{-D})/2.\emptyset$.
TANH(D)	DTANH(D)	Hyperbolic tan, $(e^D - e^{-D})/(e^D + e^{-D})$.

Table 17.1. Intrinsic functions used with double precision data. All have double precision arguments except for DBLE and DPROD. If the generic name is used, the type of the result will be same as the type of the arguments except for the conversion functions. If the specific names are used the arguments must be double precision.

(ii) A double precision function is used in the following program to evaluate the power series for sin(x) until the next term contributes less than one part in 10^{-25} to the sum. This is assuming that the particular computer has double precision accuracy of at least 25 decimal digits; on some machines it could be a lot less. Note that the function name and variables used with it are declared in a DOUBLE PRECISION statement within the main program.

```
      DOUBLE PRECISION DSIN1,X,Y
C GET THE ANGLE IN DEGREES
 10 PRINT*,'ENTER THE ANGLE'
      READ*,X
C EVALUATE THE SINE
      Y=DSIN1(X)
C PRINT THE RESULT
      PRINT 20,X
 20 FORMAT('THE SINE OF',D20.10)
      PRINT 30,Y
 30 FORMAT('IS',D35.25)
      GO TO 10
      END
```

The sum for sin(x) with x in radians is

$$\sin(x) = x - \frac{x^3}{3!} + \frac{x^5}{5!} - \frac{x^7}{7!} + \ldots$$

which has a recurrence relation for the term of power n, t_n:

$$t_n = \frac{-x^2}{n(n-1)} t_{n-2}$$

$$\text{for } n = 3,5,7,\ldots$$

The function is as follows. It contains the double precision statement function DANGL. Note that the name of the function is not declared in the DOUBLE PRECISION statement – that is taken care of by the DOUBLE PRECISION FUNCTION statement. The double precision arithmetic has been very carefully organized.

```
      DOUBLE PRECISION FUNCTION DSIN1(D)
C
C FUNCTION FINDS SINE OF DOUBLE PRECISION
C ANGLE D TO DOUBLE PRECISION BY USING A
C                POWER SERIES
C
      IMPLICIT DOUBLE PRECISION(D)
      PARAMETER(DELTA=1D-25)
      DANGL(DUMMY)=4D0*ATAN(1D0)*DUMMY/180D0
C CONVERT THE ARGUMENT TO RADIANS
      DY=DANGL(D)
C INITIALIZE THE SUM
      DSUM=DY
      DYSQ=DY*DY
      DTERM=DY
      DNUM=3D0
C PERFORM THE RECURRENCE
 10 DTERM=-DTERM*DYSQ/DNUM/(DNUM-1D0)
      DSUM=DSUM+DTERM
C CHECK TO SEE IF FINISHED
      IF(DABS(DTERM/DSUM).LT.DELTA) THEN
         DSIN1=DSUM
         RETURN
      END IF
      DNUM=DNUM+2D0
      GO TO 10
      END
```

17.7   The COMPLEX type

Complex values, with real and imaginary parts, arise in many problems of science and engineering. A quantity can be defined as being of type complex by the COMPLEX statement:

COMPLEX names

or by an IMPLICIT scheme such as

IMPLICIT COMPLEX(C)

That a quantity is COMPLEX is a complete specification; it cannot be of any other type at the same time. Note particularly that it cannot be complex and double precision at the same time. There is no such thing as 'double precision complex' type.

A complex variable is, in effect, two real numbers, one standing for the real part and the other for the imaginary part of a complex number. Complex variables can be arrays, and so the dimension information can be included in the COMPLEX statement, or perhaps in other ways such as through COMMON or DIMENSION statements. Because a complex variable is a pair of numbers, it occupies twice as much storage as do reals, integers or logicals. Therefore, just as with double precision variables but for different reasons, double space has to be allowed for complex variables when laying out COMMON and when using EQUIVALENCE.

EXAMPLE:

```
COMPLEX RESPON,RATIO
INTEGER IMPULS(8)
DOUBLE PRECISION PRECIS(4)
COMMON RESPON(5)
EQUIVALENCE(RESPON,PRECIS)
EQUIVALENCE(IMPULS,RATIO)
```

The above layout in the memory of a computer is illustrated by Fig. 17.6.

Complex constants are written in FORTRAN programs as a pair of real numbers in parentheses (brackets) with a comma between. The numbers may be signed; the brackets are always required, regardless of context.

EXAMPLES:

$(1.\emptyset,1.\emptyset)$ is the complex number $1+j1$

$(\emptyset.\emptyset,1.414)$ is the complex number $j1.414$

$(-2.\emptyset,+1.\emptyset)$ is the complex number $-2+j1$

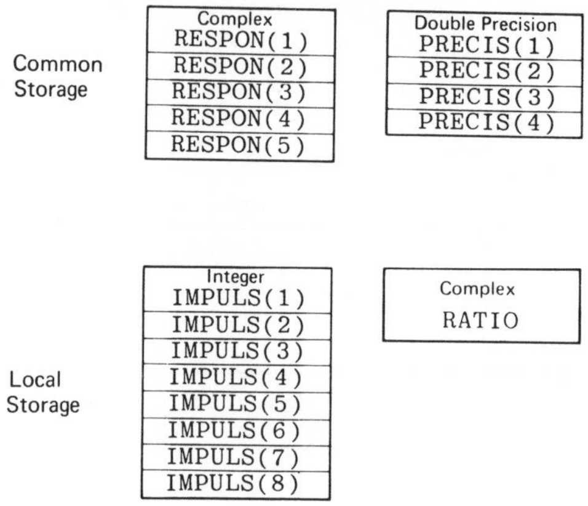

Fig. 17.6. Illustrating a storage arrangement using COMMON, DIMENSION, DOUBLE PRECISION, and COMPLEX. Each complex or double precision value takes twice the space of reals, integers, or logicals.

Complex constants can be given symbolic names in PARAMETER statements:

```
COMPLEX BRUCE,FRED
PARAMETER(BRUCE=(3.∅,4.∅))
PARAMETER(FRED=BRUCE)
```

However a complex constant cannot be formed using the names of real constants. This is illegal according to the FORTRAN 77 standard:

```
IMPLICIT COMPLEX(C)
PARAMETER(X=1.∅,Y=2.∅)
PARAMETER(CLUCK=(X,Y))
```

Complex quantities can be included in expressions of FORTRAN intermixed with real, integer and double precision values, except that an operation can never be performed directly between complex and double precision values (and as a consequence they cannot be compared in a relational expression). Furthermore in a relational expression a complex operand is only permitted when the relational operator is .EQ. or .NE., simply because the other relational operations are mathematically meaningless with a complex operand. In the next section of this Chapter the rules governing the combinations of variable types and the method of predicting the type of an expression are given.

Complex values can be assigned to complex variables or array elements. In the statement

```
complex variable = expression
```

the complex variable has the arithmetical result of the expression assigned to it. In the case of a real, integer, or double precision value, the imaginary part of the new complex value is taken as zero.

In a DATA statement, initial complex values can be assigned to variables or arrays, as for example in

```
COMPLEX OHMS
DATA OHMS/(1.0,1.0)/
```

For formatted input/output of complex values, two real editing descriptions are required for each complex item to be transferred (either F, E or G descriptions). The one-to-one correspondence between the READ, PRINT, or WRITE list and the FORMAT will be preserved by providing two real fields for every complex member of the list. The output will be two real numbers. Any of the allowed forms for real input can be used in response to a READ - recall that the inputs to F, D and E specifications are interchangeable.

Similarly, a complex value occurring in list-directed output will be printed as a pair of real values, with brackets around them and a comma between. In response to a list-directed READ statement, two numbers should be given in any of the permitted forms, as F, E or D fields or as an integer.

EXAMPLE:
  The second order differential equation

$$\frac{d^2 y}{dt^2} + 2\frac{dy}{dt} + y = x(t)$$

could describe the behaviour of a variety of systems, for example either the mechanical or electrical systems of Fig. 17.7. The complex ratio

$$\frac{Y(\omega)}{X(\omega)} = \frac{1}{-\omega^2 + 2j\omega + 1}$$

is called the frequency response of the system because it describes the relationship between input and output for sinusoidal excitation at a frequency of ω. The following program evaluates the frequency response for a given value of ω and prints it both as a complex number and in polar form (magnitude and phase).

```
      IMPLICIT COMPLEX(R)
      ANGL(R)=ATAN2(AIMAG(R),
     +                  REAL(R))
C GET THE DESIRED FREQUENCY
   10 PRINT*,'GIVE FREQ., RADIANS'
      READ*,W
C FIND RESPONSE AT FREQUENCY W
      RASP=CMPLX(-W*W+1.0,2.0*W)
      RESP=1.0/RASP
C ALSO GET MAGNITUDE AND PHASE
      XMAG=CABS(RESP)
      XPHA=ANGL(RESP)
C PRINT THE RESULTS
      PRINT 20,W
   20 FORMAT(' AT FREQ.',F8.2)
      PRINT 30,RESP
   30 FORMAT(' RESPONSE IS',2F8.2)
      PRINT*,' OR IN POLAR FORM'
      PRINT 40,XMAG
   40 FORMAT(' MAGNITUDE',F8.2)
      PRINT 50,XPHA
   50 FORMAT(' AND PHASE',F8.2)
      GO TO 10
      END
```

Here, AIMAG, REAL, CMPLX and CABS are intrinsic functions which deal with complex numbers in FORTRAN 77. Table 17.2 lists all the functions with either complex arguments or complex results. If generic names are used, the type of the result will depend on the type of the argument except for the type conversion functions. If the specific names are used, then the arguments must be of the specified type.

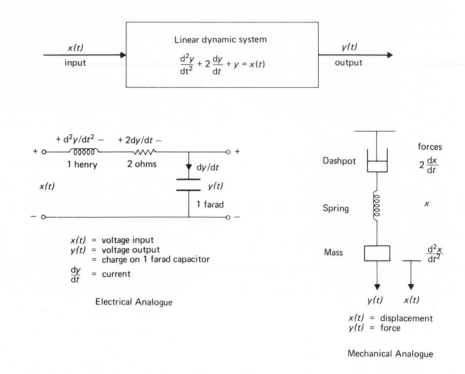

Electrical Analogue

$x(t)$ = voltage input
$y(t)$ = voltage output
     = charge on 1 farad capacitor
$\dfrac{dy}{dt}$ = current

Mechanical Analogue

$x(t)$ = displacement
$y(t)$ = force

Fig. 17.7. A linear dynamic system and two physical interpretations of it. The frequency response is calculated as an example of complex arithmetic in FORTRAN 77.

The statement function ANGL used in the above example is itself a real function of a complex dummy argument.

As might be expected, it is possible to define complex function subprograms and complex arithmetic statement functions; the following simple example has both.

EXAMPLE:

A complex function subprogram CARTES is used to convert complex numbers given in polar form by the real variables XMAG (magnitude) and XANG (phase in degrees) into a Cartesian complex number CMPLEX. The subprogram contains a complex arithmetic statement function RECT and a real arithmetic statement function ANGL.

Main program:

```
      COMPLEX CARTES,CMPLEX
      :
      :
      CMPLEX=CARTES(XMAG,XANG)
      :
      :
      END
```

function subprogram:

```
      COMPLEX FUNCTION CARTES(X,Y)
C
C GET RECTANGULAR CARTESIAN
C CO-ORDINATES OF NUMBER WITH
C REAL MAGNITUDE X AND REAL
C ANGLE Y (GIVEN IN DEGREES)
C
      COMPLEX RECT
      RECT(P,Q)=CMPLX(P*COS(Q),
     +                    P*SIN(Q)
      ANGL(Z)=4.*ATAN(1.)*Z/18Ø.
      CARTES=RECT(X,ANGL(Y))
      END
```

Generic Name	Specific Name	Meaning
CMPLX(A,B)		Complex number (A,B) - A and B must be same type.
CMPLX(A)		Complex number (A,$\emptyset$).
CMPLX(C)		Complex number C, i.e. do nothing.
INT(C)		Truncate real part to integer value.
REAL(C)		Take real part as real value.
DBLE(C)		Take real part as double precision.
ABS(C)	CABS(C)	$\text{SQRT}(\text{real part}^2 + \text{imag part}^2)$ - result is type real.
	AIMAG(C)	Take imaginary part - real value.
	CONJG(C)	Conjugate, (real part, -imag part).
SQRT(C)	CSQRT(C)	Square root of C, $C^{1/2}$.
EXP(C)	CEXP(C)	Exponential function e^C.
LOG(C)	CLOG(C)	Natural logarithm, $\log_e C$.
SIN(C)	CSIN(C)	Sine of C.
COS(C)	CCOS(C)	Cosine of C.

Table 17.2. Intrinsic functions used with complex data. C is a complex argument. A and B are arguments of any other type provided that in CMPLX(A,B), A and B are the same type. The functions REAL, ABS, and AIMAG have results of type real. The type of the conversion functions is obvious. All others give a complex result.

17.8 Combining different types — the rules

All the data types which occur in FOR-TRAN 77 have now been covered, and it is the purpose of this section to summarize the rules which govern their combination.

(i) Expressions

(a) An arithmetic expression which involves addition, subtraction, multiplication, division, and exponentiation can contain mixtures of real, integer, complex, and double precision values. All combinations are allowed except those between complex and double precision values. No arithmetic operation can be performed between a complex value and a double precision value.

(b) The type of an arithmetic expression depends on which operations are performed. The hierarchy of operations was described in Chapter 2. To determine the type of value that occurs in each stage of the evaluation of an arithmetic expression, first determine the order of the operations, then follow the evaluation through in the correct order.

If an operation is performed on two integers, the resulting value is of type integer.

If an operation is performed on two reals, or on a real and an integer, the resulting value is of type real.

If an operation is performed on two double precision values, or on a double precision and a real, or on a double precision and an integer, the resulting value is of type double precision.

If an operation is performed on two complex values, or a complex and a real, or a complex and an integer, the resulting value is of type complex.

This is summarized in Fig. 17.8.

(c) Logical expressions are formed in the manner described fully in Section 5 of this Chapter. There are no operations mixing logical values with values of any other type.

(d) Character expressions have been described in Chapter 16. There are no operations which intermix character entities with values of any other type.

(ii) Assignment Statements

    variable = expression

or

    array element = expression

(a) An arithmetic assignment consists of an expression of integer, real, double precision, or complex type, as described above, assigned to a variable or array element of any of these types.

(b) A logical expression may only be assigned to a variable or an array element of type logical.

(c) A character expression may only be assigned to a variable or array element or substring of type character.

(iii) EQUIVALENCE

(a) Character entities can be associated only with other character entities.

(b) Variables or arrays of all other types can be associated in any combinations. Every integer, or real, or logical value will take one unit of storage. Every complex or double precision value will take two units of storage.

	Integer	Real	Double Precision	Complex
Integer	Integer	Real	Double Precision	Complex
Real	Real	Real	Double Precision	Complex
Double Precision	Double Precision	Double Precision	Double Precision	/////////////////////
Complex	Complex	Complex	/////////////////////	Complex

Fig. 17.8. This shows the type of the result if values of various types are combined in any arithmetic operation.

(iv) Comparisons in Relational Expressions

(a) Integer, real, double precision and complex values can be compared in relational expressions in all combinations except that:

> only .EQ. and .NE. can be used with the complex type;
> complex values and double precision values can never be compared.

(b) Logical values cannot be compared in a relational expression - but of course the logical operators themselves cover all the necessary cases.

(c) Character entities can only be compared with character entities.

17.9 Subprogram names as arguments — the EXTERNAL and INTRINSIC statements

All the data types of FORTRAN are used in situations where a name stands for a value stored in the computer memory. The EXTERNAL or INTRINSIC statements are used (not very often) in the one situation where the name itself is the message. This is where the actual name of a function or subroutine is to be communicated to a subprogram as an argument, or where a programmer wishes to provide his own subprogram to replace an intrinsic function.

The EXTERNAL statement

> EXTERNAL names

indicates that the 'names' do not stand for values of any type, but are instead the actual names of functions or of subroutines. This means that such a name can be passed as the argument of a subprogram. The EXTERNAL statement belongs with the specification statements in a FORTRAN 77 program; the rules for ordering statements are given in the next section. A name can only appear in one EXTERNAL statement in a program unit. Such a name can only represent the name of an external subprogram, and so it cannot be dimensioned in the EXTERNAL statement, nor can it appear in PARAMETER, COMMON, DIMENSION, or EQUIVALENCE.

EXAMPLE:
One of the examples in Chapter 10 gave a complete subroutine for finding the area under a curve, i.e. numerical quadrature, by the trapezoidal rule. The subroutine STRAP itself called a function FUNC. The user provided the function subprogram FUNC.

It would be possible, by using an EXTERNAL statement, to make the name of the function a dummy argument of subroutine STRAP, as the listing shows.

In this program the external name FNAME is a dummy argument of the subroutine. Therefore every reference to the function FNAME is a reference to some function whose actual name is given by the subroutine CALL. In a main program one could write

```
EXTERNAL ACTUAL
    :
    :
CALL STRAP(Ø.,1.,ACTUAL,DELTA,
            ANS,1ØØ)
```

in which case the subroutine would find the area under the curve defined by an external function called ACTUAL.

In this example the type of ACTUAL is real. For function references the type of a function is important. For this reason, a name which appears in an EXTERNAL statement can be given a type through a type statement or an IMPLICIT statement.

EXAMPLE:
A character function ADDIT is to concatenate a string A with the result of an operation on a string B. There are various things which this operation might be, so the programmer makes an EXTERNAL name OPERA represent an external character function:

```
CHARACTER*8 FUNCTION ADDIT(A,B,
                           OPERA)
EXTERNAL OPERA
CHARACTER*4 A,B,OPERA
ADDIT=A//OPERA(B)
END
```

```
      SUBROUTINE STRAP(BOT,TOP,FNAME,DELTA,ANSWER,NSTRIP)
C
C SUBROUTINE FOR QUADRATURE BY TRAPEZOIDAL RULE
C INTEGRATES FUNCTION FROM BOT TO TOP, DOUBLING
C NUMBER OF STRIPS UNTIL ERROR IS LESS THAN DELTA
C THE USER SUPPLIES THE EXTERNAL FUNCTION FNAME
C
C BOT - INPUT VALUE, THE LOWER LIMIT OF INTEGRATION
C TOP - INPUT VALUE, THE UPPER LIMIT OF INTEGRATION
C FNAME - EXTERNAL VARIABLE GIVING THE NAME OF
C           THE FUNCTION TO BE INTEGRATED
C DELTA - INPUT VALUE, THE DESIRED ERROR BOUND
C ANSWER - OUTPUT VARIABLE, THE CALCULATED INTEGRAND
C NSTRIP - OUTPUT VARIABLE, THE NUMBER OF STRIPS USED
C
C SET UP LOCAL VARIABLES FOR EFFICIENCY
      XDELTA=4.0*DELTA
      XTOP=TOP
      XBOT=BOT
C INITIALIZE
      NST=1
      H=XTOP-XBOT
      SOLD=(FNAME(XBOT)+FNAME(XTOP))*H/2.0
C MAKE THE NEW SUM
   10 X=XBOT+H/2.0
      NST=NST*2
      SNEW=0.0
      DO 20 K=1,NST,2
         SNEW=SNEW+FNAME(X)
         X=X+H
   20 CONTINUE
C FORM NEW INTEGRAND AND ESTIMATE ERROR
      H=H/2.0
      SNEW=SNEW*H+SOLD/2.0
      CHANGE=ABS(SOLD-SNEW)
      SOLD=SNEW
C DO AGAIN WHILE ERROR.GT.4.0*DELTA
      IF(CHANGE.GT.XDELTA)GO TO 10
C FINISHED, RETURN RESULTS
      ANSWER=SOLD
      NSTRIP=NST
      END
```

In a main program one could write

```
CHARACTER*4 YES,NO,MAYBE
CHARACTER*4 NEVER,TAKE
CHARACTER*8 RESLT,MORE
EXTERNAL TAKE,GIVE
       :
       :
RESLT=ADDIT(YES,NO,TAKE)
MORE=ADDIT(MAYBE,NEVER,GIVE)
```

to force ADDIT to use the different external functions GIVE and TAKE in the two references to it.

If a program mentions the name of an intrinsic function in an EXTERNAL statement, then the programmer must intend to provide his own program to replace the intrinsic function.

EXAMPLE:
You could say

EXTERNAL SQRT

but you are then expected to provide your own external program SQRT. Usually a programmer would do this if he were intending to provide a straight replacement for the function SQRT:

XLEN=SQRT(X*X+Y*Y)

However, he could instead intend SQRT to be a subroutine:

CALL SQRT(arguments)

Either way, the intrinsic function SQRT is not available to any program unit that has in it

EXTERNAL SQRT

It is also possible to pass the name of an intrinsic function as an argument. Normally if a program contained

CALL THIS(ATAN)

ATAN would be the name of a real variable. However if it had an INTRINSIC statement

INTRINSIC ATAN

then the argument is the name of the intrinsic function ATAN.

EXAMPLE:
You can find the area under the ALOG function by having

INTRINSIC ALOG
CALL STRAP(1.,2.,ALOG,.01,ANS,20)

Note that in the function subprogram STRAP the name is still regarded as external.

The names of intrinsic functions for type conversion (INT, IFIX, IDINT, FLOAT, SNGL, REAL, DBLE, CMPLX, ICHAR, or CHAR), lexical relationships (LGE, LGT, LLE or LLT) and for choosing the largest or smallest value (MAX, MAX0, AMAX1,

DMAX1, AMAX0, MAX1, MIN, MIN0, AMIN1, DMIN1, AMIN0, or MIN1) must not be used as actual arguments - hence there is no point in using them in an INTRINSIC statement. A name cannot be both INTRINSIC and EXTERNAL in the same program unit.

17.10 The order of statements in FORTRAN 77 programs

Many statements have been introduced throughout this book whose order in a FORTRAN program is constrained. Here, the rules are summarized. Fig. 17.9 is the last word on statement ordering in a main program. Note that the PROGRAM statement, mentioned in this table, is a machine dependent statement which may or may not be required by a particular computer. The existence of this statement is allowed by the FORTRAN 77 standard, but its form is not specified.

In Section 4 of this Chapter, recommendations (but not rules) were made regarding the order of specification statements as an aid to program clarity.

Here is the list of the various kinds of statements:

(i) Specification statements:

DIMENSION
EQUIVALENCE
COMMON
Type statements
IMPLICIT
PARAMETER
EXTERNAL
INTRINSIC
SAVE

(ii) Type statements are a special category within the specification statements:

INTEGER
REAL
DOUBLE PRECISION
COMPLEX
LOGICAL
CHARACTER

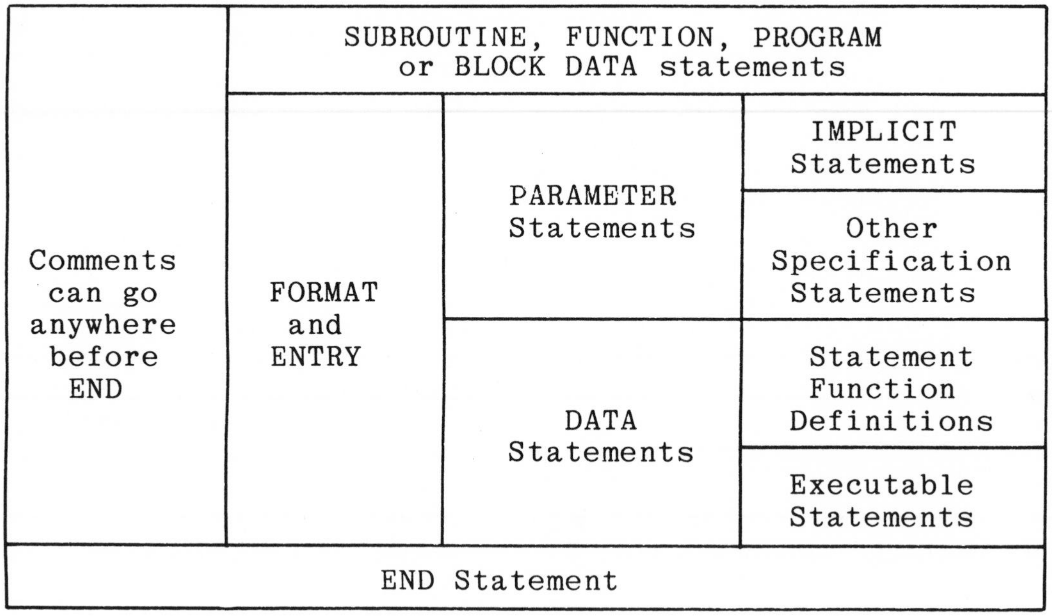

Comments can go anywhere before END	FORMAT and ENTRY	SUBROUTINE, FUNCTION, PROGRAM or BLOCK DATA statements		
		PARAMETER Statements	IMPLICIT Statements	
			Other Specification Statements	
		DATA Statements	Statement Function Definitions	
			Executable Statements	
END Statement				

Fig. 17.9. The definitive regulations about the order of statements in full FORTRAN 77.

(iii) Executable statements:

Assignment statements
ASSIGN
GO TO
Assigned GO TO
Computed GO TO
Arithmetic IF
Logical IF
Block IF
ELSE IF
ELSE
END IF
CONTINUE
STOP
PAUSE
DO
READ
WRITE
PRINT
REWIND
BACKSPACE

ENDFILE
OPEN
CLOSE
INQUIRE
CALL
RETURN
END

All statements not appearing in the list of executable statements are called non-executable statements. They are:

All specification statements
Statement function definitions
PROGRAM
FUNCTION
SUBROUTINE
ENTRY
BLOCK DATA
DATA
FORMAT

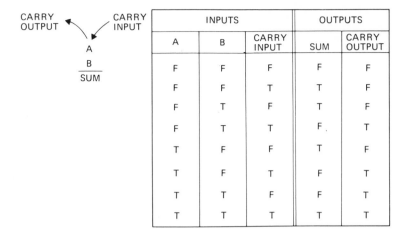

Fig.17.10. Truth table for full binary addition.

17.11 Problems

PROBLEM 17.1:

The Fig.17.10 illustrates a full binary adder with inputs A,B, and C (a carry input). Write a program to generate and print the sum and carry outputs using a function NOR(X,Y) defined as (.NOT.X.OR.Y) for all operations, i.e. once the NOR function has been defined, the other FORTRAN operations should not be used. Referring to Fig. 17.10,

$$S = A \oplus B \oplus C_{in}$$

where $A \oplus B$ = exclusive OR of A and B

$$C_{out} = (A \oplus B).C_{in} + A.B$$

Both these equations can be rewritten entirely in terms of the NOR operation.

PROBLEM 17.2:

The Newton-Raphson iteration for finding roots of an equation

$$f(x)=0$$

uses the recurrence

$$x_n = x_{n-1} - \frac{f(x_{n-1})}{f'(x_{n-1})}$$

where x_n is an improvement on the approximate root x_{n-1}. If the function is very flat near the root, then f(x) and f'(x) will be small and there could be some difficulty in evaluating f(x) and f'(x), and in calculating the new x_n using their ratio. Double precision arithmetic can help in such a situation.

By using the Newton-Raphson iteration to solve for g'(x)=0, locate the position and value of the minimum of g(x) for

(i) $g(x) = x^4 - 5.2x^3 + 10.14x^2$
$$-8.788x + 4.5561$$

(Answer 1.7 at x=1.3)

(ii) $g(x) = x^8 - 13.6\ x^7 + 80.92\ x^6$
$-275.128\ x^5 + 584.647x^4 - 795.1122x^3$
$+ 675.851932x^3 - 328.2709384x^2$
$$+ 71.0575441$$

Compare the success or otherwise of the solution with and without judicious use of double precision. Because double precision arithmetic is slow, only use it where necessary.

PROBLEM 17.3:

The discrete Fourier transform of a series of N real numbers X_0, X_1, ..., X_{N-1} is given by

$$Y_n = \frac{1}{N} \sum_{k=0}^{N-1} X_k \, e^{-\frac{j2\pi kn}{N}}$$

for n=0,1,...,N-1

where Y_n is complex. Write a complex function subprogram to provide Y_n for a given real array X of length N and a particular n.

The inverse transform

$$X_k = \sum_{n=0}^{N-1} Y_n \, e^{\frac{j2\pi kn}{N}}$$

for k=0,1,...,N-1

should convert the complex array Y of length N containing all the results Y_0, Y_1,...,Y_{N-1} back into the real number X_k. Write a real function subprogram to do this given the complex array Y, length N, and a particular k.

PROBLEM 17.4:
Write a subroutine for numerical quadrature by Simpson's rule of a function which is named as a dummy argument in the subroutine call:

CALL SIMP(X∅,X1,NSTEP,FUNC,ANS)

where
   X0 = lower limit of integration
   X1 = upper limit of integration
   NSTEP = the number of strips into which the interval (X0,X1) is to be divided. NSTEP should be an even number.
   FUNC = the name of the function to be evaluated
   ANS = the result of the integration

Simpson's rule was described earlier in Problem 7.4.

Using function subprograms to evaluate the functions, find to an accuracy of 0.1%

(i)

$$0.5 \; + \; \frac{1}{\sqrt{2\pi}} \int_0^1 e^{-x^2/2} \, dx$$

(Answer 0.8413)

(ii)

$$\int_0^{2\pi} \frac{dx}{\sqrt{1 - \frac{\sin^2 x}{4}}}$$

(Answer 1.686)

18

INPUT and OUTPUT — formatted and list - directed

18.1 Introduction

Quite a lot of basic information about input and output, either list-directed or under control of the FORMAT statement, was introduced gradually as it became necessary when using FORTRAN 77. This Chapter summarizes the techniques which have already been mentioned and completes the description of the sequential form of input and output using formatted and list-directed statements.

Strictly speaking, the list-directed form is a special case of the formatted form. Another form of input and output will be described in Chapter 19, and is called 'unformatted'. Also, the input and output forms introduced so far have been of the kind called 'sequential'. This term will be explained in this Chapter, and in Chapter 19 an alternative form called 'direct' will be introduced. To summarize, input and output can take place in formatted or unformatted form, and by sequential or direct methods. List-directed data transfers are a special case of the formatted form.

The reader will be familiar by now with the meaning of the terms input and output. Whenever a computer program demands to be given values through a READ statement, then to satisfy this demand input is given to the computer on cards or from a teletype, magnetic tape, disk or other medium. In fact, as will be seen in Chapter 19, the file from which the data is read can sometimes be an internal file, already somewhere in the memory of the computer. Similarly, every time a program gives values to a file in the outside world through a WRITE or PRINT statement, then the action is called output. Again,

it will be seen in Chapter 19 that an output statement can send data to an 'output' file that is actually inside the computer.

18.2 Records and sequential files

The basic unit of input or output is called a 'record'. A printed line of output is a record; so too is a single line of input from a terminal or a single card of input. However, records need not be fixed in length. Whenever a READ, or WRITE, or PRINT statement occurs, a new record of input or output begins. During the execution of an input or output transfer, however, additional records can begin. In a formatted transfer, new lines begin in various ways, as was described earlier and will be summarized again in the next section. This happens when a / (slash) occurs in a FORMAT, or when output continues after the end of a format specification is reached. Whenever this occurs, another new record is said to begin. Also, in list-directed output the computer decides for itself when to begin new lines. In list-directed input the user can do the same thing.

Remember:

(i) Each new line is a new record.
(ii) Each READ, WRITE, or PRINT begins a new record.
(iii) Additional new records may occur.

This concept becomes particularly useful when handling unformatted information, as described in Chapter 19, in which case the idea of a new line or card does not apply.

Many devices are "sequential" in nature. This means that a computer program can only access the records of a file in the natural sequence in which they occur. For example, after printing a line of output, a terminal is in the correct position to print the next line. Lines on a terminal are always printed in sequence. Lineprinters behave in the same way. So do card readers or punches - it is obvious that one card is taken after another in the correct order or sequence although it must be admitted that everyone puts a deck of cards in the wrong way around once in a while! A magnetic tape behaves the same way.

Perhaps this is obvious - the concept of a sequential file is not really very complicated. The difference between a sequential file and a "direct" file is important, however. In a direct file the computer can access any part of the file, in any order. After reading or writing a particular record, it can jump to another place. Ideally, a disk storage device behaves in this way. FORTRAN 77 has special facilities for "direct access" files and these are introduced in Chapter 19.

18.3 Formatted READ, WRITE, and PRINT statements

The fundamental input and output statements of FORTRAN 77 are the READ, WRITE, and PRINT statements. Their general form is:

$$\text{READ} \begin{pmatrix} \text{control} \\ \text{list} \end{pmatrix} \begin{bmatrix} \text{data} \\ \text{list} \end{bmatrix}$$

$$\text{READ} \quad \begin{matrix} \text{format} \\ \text{identifier} \end{matrix} \begin{bmatrix} , \text{ data} \\ \text{list} \end{bmatrix}$$

$$\text{WRITE} \begin{pmatrix} \text{control} \\ \text{list} \end{pmatrix} \begin{bmatrix} \text{data} \\ \text{list} \end{bmatrix}$$

$$\text{PRINT} \quad \begin{matrix} \text{format} \\ \text{identifier} \end{matrix} \begin{bmatrix} , \text{ data} \\ \text{list} \end{bmatrix}$$

The full range of facilities available in a "control list" is described in Chapter 19. For the purposes of this Chapter, a restricted form is discussed:

$$\text{READ} \begin{pmatrix} \text{unit} & , & \text{format} \\ \text{number} & & \text{identifier} \end{pmatrix} \begin{bmatrix} \text{data} \\ \text{list} \end{bmatrix}$$

$$\text{READ} \quad \begin{matrix} \text{format} \\ \text{identifier} \end{matrix} \begin{bmatrix} , \text{ data} \\ \text{list} \end{bmatrix}$$

$$\text{WRITE} \begin{pmatrix} \text{unit} & , & \text{format} \\ \text{number} & & \text{identifier} \end{pmatrix} \begin{bmatrix} \text{data} \\ \text{list} \end{bmatrix}$$

$$\text{PRINT} \quad \begin{matrix} \text{format} \\ \text{identifier} \end{matrix} \begin{bmatrix} , \text{ data} \\ \text{list} \end{bmatrix}$$

It will be recalled that items shown in square brackets are optional. A WRITE, or PRINT statement with no "data list" causes an empty record to be written - on a lineprinter or terminal this produces a blank line of output. Similarly, a READ statement with no data list skips over a record of input. The READ and PRINT statements without a "unit number" use what has been called in this text the "obvious device". This means the terminal in a timesharing system, and probably a cardreader and lineprinter in a batch system.

Traditionally, unit number 5 has been used for the obvious input unit, and unit number 6 for the obvious output device.

The "format identifier" can be given in one of three ways.

(i) By giving the label of a FORMAT statement from the same program unit directly, as in:

```
  WRITE(6,2Ø)
2Ø FORMAT('FORMAT SPECIFICATION')
```

or through assignment to an integer variable name:

```
      ASSIGN 1ØØ TO IFT
      :
      :
      PRINT IFT,X,Y,Z
      :
```

```
        :
 100 FORMAT(1X,3F10.5)
```

(ii) By giving a character string which specifies the format directly in the input/output statement, as a character string constant

```
 READ(5,'(2I10)')KLIP,KLOP
```

or as an expression,

```
CHARACTER STARS*(*)
PARAMETER(STARS='(80(''*'')//')
        :
        :
PRINT STARS//'1X,3I20)',J,K,L
```

(note that in a subprogram it must not involve concatenation of any dummy argument or function or entry name whose length specification is (*) in that subprogram).

Look at the above example carefully. The symbolic character constant STARS prints a whole row of asterisks plus one blank line as the first part of any format specification that is grafted on by concatenation. Note how the required parentheses around the format description are achieved. Perhaps this is too clever.

Allowed expressions include the symbolic name of a constant, as used above, the name of a variable or substring, or the name of a character array:

```
CHARACTER FIRMDT*20
DATA FIRMDT/'(''A FORMAT'')'/
        :
        :
PRINT FIRMDT
        :
        :
```

(iii) By giving an asterisk to specify list-directed processing, as in:

```
        WRITE(6,*) DATA
```

List-directed processing is a special case of formatted input or output and is discussed in Section 18.10.

Every format-directed statement begins a new record of input or output. Additional new records can begin as a result of the / description occurring in the format specification or as a result of repetition of the specification. Both these effects are described in Section 4 of this Chapter.

The "data list" of an input/output statement is a list of items to be read or written by the program. A format-directed statement refers to the format specification for the required layout of the record or records. It expects a one-to-one correspondence between the items in the list, and an appropriate format description, as described in the next section. If the data list consists of items of type real, integer, character, logical, or double precision which are not arrays, then the number of values transmitted is just the number of items in the list.

EXAMPLE:

```
        READ(5,21)X,Y,I,J
```

As long as the variables X, Y, I, J are real, integer, character, logical or double precision, then the input request is for four items which are to be provided on unit 5 according to the FORMAT statement numbered 21.

If complex numbers are involved, then care has to be taken to provide two values for each complex pair. Remember that both numbers in the pair are themselves real; there is no such thing as a complex integer.

EXAMPLE:

```
        REAL P,Q,R
        LOGICAL Y
        COMPLEX C,S
          :
          :
        PRINT 25,P,C,Q,Y,R,S
```

Eight values are printed according to the FORMAT numbered 25.

The items in an input list must be the names of quantities which it is sensible for an input statement to define, i.e. the name of a variable, an array or an element of an array. For character data the name of a substring is also allowed. It would obviously not be sensible to allow constants, or expressions involving operands or function references, in an input list.

An output list can, however, contain any of the items allowed for an input list, and in addition any expression at all except a character expression in a subprogram which involves concatenation of a dummy argument or function or entry name whose length specification was a (*).

```
CHARACTER CH1,CH2
       :
       :
PRINT 1Ø,EXP(I+3*J),CH1//CH2
```

This permits reverberations; a function reference could alter the value of an item which appears later in the list:

```
PRINT 2Ø,LIST(I),I
```

where LIST is a function which might be something like:

```
FUNCTION LIST(J)
LIST=7*J
J=J+3
END
```

The above is not really a very good idea.

With arrays, an item in the data list can either give a subscript, in which case it is clear that a single value is intended, or it can name the array without a subscript, causing the whole array to be transmitted.

EXAMPLE:

```
INTEGER MOM,DAD
COMPLEX KIDS
DIMENSION KIDS(3),XRAY(3,2)
          :
          :
PRINT 21,MOM,DAD,KIDS,XRAY(1,1)
```

Here nine values are printed - the integer values MOM and DAD, six real values representing the complex array KIDS, and the real value XRAY(1,1).

When dealing with multidimensional arrays it is important to know in what order the information is transmitted. Unfortunately it is not in the most obvious or convenient order. Perhaps the inventors of FORTRAN were mathematically illiterate, because arrays are transmitted with the first subscript varying most rapidly. For two dimensional arrays this means to a mathematician that the order of transmission is by columns, which is the transpose of what might be expected. The usual notation for an array having dimensions m rows and n columns is

$$
\begin{matrix}
a_{11} & a_{12} & a_{13} & \cdots & a_{1n} \\
a_{21} & a_{22} & a_{23} & & a_{2n} \\
\vdots & & & & \\
a_{m1} & a_{m2} & a_{m3} & & a_{mn}
\end{matrix}
$$

The FORTRAN statements

```
DIMENSION A(5,4)
READ(5,21) A
```

cause the 25 items of real data to be read down the columns:

$$a_{11}, a_{21}, a_{31}, a_{41}, a_{51}, a_{12}, \cdots \text{ etc}$$

This in itself is not so bad, but consider the statement

```
PRINT 27,A
27 FORMAT(1X,5F1Ø.5)
```

which will produce the highly confusing paper result:

$$
\begin{matrix}
a_{11} & a_{21} & a_{31} & a_{41} & a_{51} \\
a_{12} & a_{22} & a_{32} & a_{42} & a_{52} \\
a_{13} & a_{23} & a_{33} & a_{43} & a_{53} \\
a_{14} & a_{24} & a_{34} & a_{44} & a_{54} \\
a_{15} & a_{25} & a_{35} & a_{45} & a_{55}
\end{matrix}
$$

Always remember carefully that FORTRAN transmits arrays with the first subscript varying most rapidly; that is to say in column order.

This problem can be overcome using the implied DO-loop facility. The following is the sensible way to keep a matrix straight and is the usual practice:

```
DIMENSION A(5,5)
     :
     :
WRITE(6,51)((A(I,J),J=1,3),
                        I=1,3)
51 FORMAT(1X,3F10.5)
```

This prints the desired submatrix in the order

$$a_{11} \quad a_{12} \quad a_{13}$$
$$a_{21} \quad a_{22} \quad a_{23}$$
$$a_{31} \quad a_{32} \quad a_{33}$$

For comparison, the statement

```
PRINT 25,A
```

is the equivalent of

```
PRINT 25,((A(I,J),I=1,5),J=1,5)
```

An implied DO-loop can contain several items to be transmitted, and they need not all be subscripted. For example,

```
CHARACTER STAR
PARAMETER(STAR='*')
WRITE(6,33)(STAR,I=1,80)
33 FORMAT(1X,80A1)
```

or in general, any data list can include a sublist in parentheses:

$$\left(\begin{matrix} \text{data} \\ \text{list} \end{matrix}, \text{variable} = \begin{matrix}\text{first}\\\text{value}\end{matrix}, \begin{matrix}\text{last}\\\text{value}\end{matrix} \left[, \begin{matrix}\text{step}\\\text{value}\end{matrix}\right]\right)$$

EXAMPLE:
The statements

```
WRITE(6,90)(X,A(I),(B(I,J),
                    J=1,3),I=1,4)
90 FORMAT(1X,5F10.5)
```

produce an output arrangement like

$$x \quad a_1 \quad b_{11} \quad b_{12} \quad b_{13}$$
$$x \quad a_2 \quad b_{21} \quad b_{22} \quad b_{23}$$
$$x \quad a_3 \quad b_{31} \quad b_{32} \quad b_{33}$$
$$x \quad a_4 \quad b_{41} \quad b_{42} \quad b_{43}$$

This assumes that X is a scalar, A is an array of one dimension whose length is at least 4, and B is in two dimensions of at least 4 x 3.

This implied DO-loop works exactly the same way as an ordinary DO-loop. In particular it should be remembered that the number of repetitions of the loop is determined in advance. It is forbidden to have the DO-variable as an item in an input list, or any other variable which is associated with it through EQUIVALENCE or through COMMON. This means that it is possible to write

```
PRINT*,((I,J,I=1,30),J=1,30)
```

but it is wrong to have

```
READ(5,20)(KLOWN,KLOWN=1,6)
```

With an implied DO-loop, the number of kinds of reverberations or 'side effects' increases. In general, a programmer must use common sense in avoiding them. There is nothing wrong with having

```
READ(5,5)NUM,(XRAY(I),I=1,NUM)
```

but this next one is horrible:

```
PRINT 34,(YUCK(I),I=10,2,-2)
```

where the function YUCK tries to interfere with the loop variable. It won't work!

```
FUNCTION YUCK(I)
YUCK=I
I=I-1
END
```

18.4   Format descriptions

A format specification, always in parentheses, gives a description of the data editing to be performed in conjunction with a format-directed READ, WRITE, or PRINT statement. As discussed in the previous section, the format specification may be given either in a FORMAT statement, as in

```
label FORMAT('THIS IS A FORMAT')
```

or in some kind of character quantity

```
PRINT'('''THIS IS A FORMAT''')'
```

Format-directed input and output statements refer to a format specification for information about how the values are to be presented. As has been described earlier, a format specification consists of field descriptions of the data that is expected, and of other punctuation, which could be commas or colons to separate the fields, parentheses (brackets) to divide up up the specification, and slashes which indicate new lines or records. Remember that a FORMAT statement is not executed in the same way as, for example, is a WRITE statement, and it can therefore be placed virtually anywhere in a program unit before the END statement, as detailed in Chapter 17. There can be any number of different READ, WRITE, or PRINT statements which refer to the same format specification, unless of course the format is given as part of the statement itself.

Type of Datum	Appropriate Description
Integer	I
Real	F,E,D,or G
Double Precision	F,E,D,or G
Complex	Two descriptions, F,E,D,or G
Character	A
Logical	L

The specifications listed above must occur in one-to-one correspondence with items in the data list of the input/output statement. In the case of complex data, the two descriptions can be different and non-data descriptions can separate them, for example

```
COMPLEX CREEPY
     ⋮
     ⋮
   PRINT 2Ø,CREEPY
2Ø FORMAT(' REAL',F1Ø.2/,
          ' IMAG',E1Ø.2)
```

18.5   Descriptions for numeric fields

Here is a list of the descriptions which are available in format specifications for numeric fields.

(a) Integer - I

A field description of the form

$$[n]Iw[.d]$$

indicates that n consecutive integer fields are required, each with a width of w spaces and with at least d digits printed. Both n and d are optional and are taken as one if not given.

If d is not given,

$$Iw$$

the output field consists of an integer right justified in the field with leading blanks, although a zero value will be printed as zero. A minus sign right justified against the number will be given for negative values. The computer has the option of printing a plus sign for positive values unless an SS or SP edit description specifies otherwise. Sufficient space must be allowed for the value expected or a rude row of w asterisks will be all that is printed.

EXAMPLE:
  The statements

```
   DATA I,J,K,L/-99,Ø,75,1Ø23/
   WRITE(6,2Ø) L,K,J,I
2Ø FORMAT(SS,2I5,I2,I4)
```

will produce the printed line

  .1∅23   75 ∅ -99
  . . . .

where the dots indicate the printer spacing and are not a part of the printed output.

For output only, the optional value of d forces the printer to print enough leading zeros to ensure that at least d digits are printed:

$$Iw[.d]$$

EXAMPLE:
The statement

    PRINT'(SP,I5.3)',4

will print

   +∅∅4
  . . . . .

If d is given the value zero, then a zero data value produces only a blank field.

EXAMPLE:
The statement

    PRINT'(I4)',∅

prints the zero

    ∅
 . . . .

whereas this one

    PRINT'(I4.∅)',∅

produces

   . . . .

i.e. nothing at all.

For input given in response to an I specification, d is meaningless; it can be given but it will be ignored. The expected input is an integer value which must lie entirely within the field of w spaces. On many computers data need not be right justified because blanks in input fields are ignored, as in BN editing (Section 18.6). You can turn blanks into significant zeros with the BZ specification, or using a BLANK= control

directive for the file (Chapter 19). If you are unlucky, your computer will do this on preconnected files.

EXAMPLES:
In response to the statements

    READ(5,1∅)INTEG
 1∅ FORMAT(I5)

the value 300 is given as any of

  .3∅∅
 . . . . .
  3∅∅
 . . . . .
  3∅∅
 . . . . .

and the value 3 is given as any of

      3
 . . . . .
     3
 . . . . .
    3
 . . . . .
   3
 . . . . .
 3
 . . . . .

However, the zeros can be made significant by the description BZ. In response to

    READ(5,1∅)INTEG
 1∅ FORMAT(BZ,I5)

the value 300 could be any of

  .3∅∅
 . . . . .
   3∅
 . . . . .
   3 ∅
 . . . . .
   3
 . . . . .

but 3 can only be given as

    3
 . . . . .

(b) Real without exponent - F

The field description

   [n]Fw.d

indicates that n consecutive items are each real values occupying w spaces with d places of decimals. The n is optional and is taken as one if it is not given. This kind of field can be used for real or double precision data and for either or both of the two values that make up a complex datum. It is subject to the P scaling specification described in the next section.

As an output description, the F field causes a number to be printed right justified in the field of w spaces. It is rounded and scaled if a P scaling factor is in force, and will always be printed with d places of decimals. A minus sign will always be printed for negative numbers, and the plus sign for positive numbers may or may not be printed, depending on the whim of the computer. Leading zeros before the decimal place are not printed, except that the computer, at its discretion, may print one zero before the decimal point if the scaled value of the data is less than one. A zero must appear if there would otherwise be no digits in the field. All this means that w must be at least one greater than d for a positive number if no sign is expected, and would more usually be two greater.

EXAMPLES:
The statement

PRINT'(1X,F5.2)'4.Ø*ATAN(1.Ø)

will correctly print the result

3.14
• • • • •

but this one

PRINT'(1X,F5.2)',4ØØ.Ø*ATAN(1.Ø)

does not have enough room and will print

*****
• • • • •

which indicates that the data cannot be squeezed into the given field specification.

The printing of the sign can be controlled by the SS or SP descriptions described later in Section 18.6.

Input to an F field must fit entirely inside the field of w spaces and can be of any kind valid for real data. The interpretation of the data will be affected by any P-scaling that is in force and by the significance, or otherwise, of blanks as controlled by the BN or BZ descriptions (Section 18.6) or the BLANK= control directive for the file being read (Chapter 19).

The valid input forms are:

(i) An optional sign followed by digits which have a decimal point. The given decimal point overrides the format description, as in

READ(5,1Ø)PYE
1Ø FORMAT(F5.2)

to which the value 3.14 can be given as

3.142
• • • • •

(ii) As above but with no decimal point. In this case the value of d in the field description tells the machine where to place the decimal point in determining the value of the data. The rightmost d digits of the field constitute the fractional part of the number, with leading zeros if necessary. Blanks in the field are normally ignored. Therefore the statements

READ(5,1Ø)PYE
1Ø FORMAT(F5.2)

can be given the value 3.14 for PYE by any of

```
  314
• • • • •
  314
• • • • •
314
• • • • •
  3 14
• • • • •
 3 14
• • • • •
 3  14
• • • • •
```

and can be given the value .01 by any of

```
          1
    . . . . .
        1
    . . . . . .
      1
    . . . . .
    1
  . . . . . .
1
  . . . . .
```

It is possible to force the computer to regard blanks as significant zeros by using a BZ editing specification (Section 18.6) or by using a BLANK= control directive for the file being read (Chapter 19). With significant blanks, the statements

```
      READ(5,1Ø)SMAL
1Ø  FORMAT(BZ,F5.2)
```

have the value .01 given by

```
    1
  . . . . .
```

and .1 given by

```
      1
  . . . . .
```

which is completely different to the normal behaviour.

(iii) As above but with an integer exponent, either simply with a sign, as

$$3+1\emptyset$$

for the value 3.0×10^{10}, or with an E followed by an optionally signed integer exponent, as

```
3E1Ø
3E+1Ø
```

or else with a D followed by an optionally signed exponent, as

```
3D1Ø
3D+1Ø
```

In these exponents, again blanks are normally not significant but can be made so by the BZ description which is described in Section 18.6, as

```
      READ(5,12) SPEED
12  FORMAT(BZ,F8.2)
```

In this case the value 3.0×10^{10} can be given as

```
  3.ØE1Ø
. . . . . . .
```

whereas the input value

```
  3.ØE1Ø
. . . . . . . .
```

defines instead 3.0×10^{100} because of the placing of the exponent and the significance assigned to the blanks.

It is seen that an F field accepts as input any value in the F, D, E, or G forms. Indeed for input the field descriptions and data forms for F, D, E, and G are completely interchangeable.

(c) Real with exponent - E

The field description

$$[n]Ew.d[Ee]$$

indicates that n consecutive items are values, each occupying w spaces with d places of decimals and an exponent of e digits. The n is optional, and is taken as one if it is not given. This kind of field can be used for real or double precision data and for either or both of the two values that make up a complex datum. The P scaling specification as described in the next section can influence the number of digits.

As an output description, the E field causes numbers to be printed with exponents, right justified in the field of w spaces. A value is rounded, and for a P scaling factor of zero, which is normal, it is printed in the form:

$$[+][\emptyset].digits\ exponent$$

The computer has a number of options. Unless the SS or SP description is in force, it can include or omit a plus sign. It can also include or leave out the leading zero. There will always be d digits printed after the decimal point and the exponent will be a signed integer with or without the letter E. If an e specification is given, the exponent will have e digits; otherwise it will have either two or three, depending on the value of the exponent. If it has three digits, the letter E will not be printed.

Clearly, the computer has been given quite a lot of flexibility in arranging this output. The advantage of this form is that a very wide range of data values can be printed in a field of modest width. The disadvantage is that w must be quite a lot greater than d. For safety, always make w at least 7 greater than d if no value of e is given. If a value of e is given, make w at least e+5 greater than d.

EXAMPLES:

Using a field E15.5 the following numbers could be printed as shown:

Number	Printed Output
3×10^{10}	.... Ø.3ØØØØE+11
16.35×10^{-4}	.... Ø.1635ØE-Ø2
-7.32×10^{24}	.... -Ø.732ØØE+25
-4.28×10^{-15}	.... -Ø.428ØØE-14

However the computer has the option of leaving out the letter E and the leading zero. It has the option of adding a plus sign to the positive values unless the SP or SS description has removed this option.

Again using the field E15.5, the following numbers are printed out as shown:

Number	Printed Output
91.2×10^{361}	.... Ø.912ØØ+363
-373×10^{-132}	.... -Ø.373ØØ-135

Here, the computer will always leave out the letter E, and has the option of leaving out the leading zero. It could add the plus sign to the positive value.

Finally, a field E15.3E4 would produce:

Number	Printed Output
91.2×10^{361}	.... Ø.912+Ø363
16.35×10^{-4}	.... Ø.164-ØØØ2

In the above, the letter E is never printed. Notice the rounding. The computer has the option of deleting the leading zero and/or adding a plus sign to a positive number.

An impossible task assigned to an E specification will produce a row of asterisks. The statement

PRINT'(E1Ø.8)'3.ØE1Ø

produces

****

The input data to an E field can take any of the forms permitted for an F field, and described in detail earlier. Essentially on input the field descriptions and input data forms are interchangeable among the F, E, D and G fields.

(d) Real with exponent - D

In earlier versions of FORTRAN the D field was reserved for double precision data. In FORTRAN 77 the interchangeability of F, E, D and G fields makes it unnecessary in principle but it is included for compatibility. A user may still use it for double precision values for clarity. The field description

nDw.d

behaves exactly like the specification

nEw.d

for both input and output, except that the letter D is used. In FORTRAN 77, there is no form of the D description allowing the number of digits to be controlled.

(e) Real with exponent only if necessary - G

This clever editing description allows values to be printed out in a form without an exponent unless too many symbols are needed, when an exponent is added on at the end. The number of significant digits is specified and is always the same, and they always line up nicely in tables.

The field description

$$[n]Gw.d[Ee]$$

calls for n consecutive items to be values occupying a field of w spaces with d significant digits. An exponent of e digits is printed but only if necessary. The n is optional and if not given is taken as one. The e is also optional, and behaves as it did with the E description.

On output, a G field reserves space at the right hand end for the exponent, of 4 spaces if no e is given, or e+2 if e is given. This space is left blank if the computer is able to print the number without an exponent.

sign   d digits with   exponent if
(maybe) decimal point   necessary

Next to the space reserved for the exponent is a space of d digits plus a decimal point and optional sign. The computer will print the number with d significant digits if possible. Otherwise it will revert to a form exactly like:

$$[n]Ew.d[Ee]$$

Clearly the printed output depends on the value to be printed.

EXAMPLES:
Suppose the description is G15.5. For a small value, less than 0.1, the E form has to be used:

$$....\emptyset.12345E-\emptyset4$$
....

Recall that the computer has discretion in the E, and leading zero, and may have the option of a plus

sign for positive numbers unless an SS or SP description removes it.

For any value lying between 0.1 and 10**d, an F form can be used:

$$-\emptyset.62\emptyset\emptyset\emptyset$$
....
$$4379.1$$
....

In this case, the decimal point will appear where it belongs within the d significant digits.

When the value is 10**d or greater, the E form is again used:

$$....\emptyset.3\emptyset\emptyset\emptyset\emptyset E+11$$
....

A value of e will, of course, cause the number of digits in the exponent to vary. The size of the exponent will be either 4 or e+2, depending on whether e is specified. For safety, w should be at least 7 greater than d with no e given, or if e is given w should be at least e+5 greater than d.

A P scaling factor affects the printed output in the E form but not in the F form.

Input to a G field is the same as to an F, E or D field. Essentially, for the input of data, the field descriptions and data forms are interchangeable among the F, E, D and G fields.

(f) Hexadecimal fields - Z

This is not a standard feature, but it should be. All the numbers considered before have been decimal ones, but computers actually work in the binary system. Frequently a programmer may wish to see the binary equivalent of a data value, but a binary number of even modest size is very long. Many computers are organized internally into internal slices of memory of 8 bits, or one "byte". Half a byte is sometimes called a "nibble". Using four bits (one nibble) it is possible to count up to 16 and so the hexadecimal (base 16) number system is very important. In order to count up to 16 using single digits our number system is extended using letters. Hexadecimal to decimal conversion operates as follows:

Hexadecimal	Binary
0	0000
1	0001
2	0010
3	0011
4	0100
5	0101
6	0110
7	0111
8	1000
9	1001
A	1010
B	1011
C	1100
D	1101
E	1110
F	1111

and the next hexadecimal number is 10, which corresponds to 16 in decimal or 1000 in binary. Two hexadecimal digits make up one 8-bit byte.

EXAMPLE:
The decimal number 37 is equivalent to 00100101 in binary and 25 in hexadecimal. The hexadecimal version simply represents each group of four binary digits as a single hexadecimal digit, i.e.

$$\underset{2}{\underbrace{0010}} \qquad \underset{5}{\underbrace{0101}}$$

Some other numbers:

Hexadecimal		Binary		Decimal
1A	=	0001 1010	=	26
E3	=	1110 0011	=	243
FF	=	1111 1111	=	255

The format description (if allowed)

$$[\,n\,]Zd$$

indicates n consecutive items in the hexadecimal system, each with a field width of d digits. This could be done for real, double precision, or complex values. A machine might also permit character strings or logical values to be inspected in this way. It will be found that an integer value translates directly into its hexadecimal equivalent - including the complements of negative numbers if appropriate to the machine. Surprises will be in store with all other data types.

(g) Octal fields - O

This is not a standard feature. In some computers the internal organization of the machine is based on 6 bit units rather than 8 bit bytes. The octal system, base 8, requires three bits to count, and so a 6 bit unit could be made up of two octal digits. Humans also find it easier to manipulate octal mentally than hexadecimal. The octal to binary table is:

Octal	Binary
0	000
1	001
2	010
3	011
4	100
5	101
6	110
7	111

and the next octal number will be 10, corresponding to 8 in decimal notation or 1000 in binary.

EXAMPLE:
The number 37 in decimal is 100101 in binary and 45 in octal. The octal version simply represents groups of three binary digits as a single octal digit, i.e.

$$\underset{4}{\underbrace{100}} \quad \underset{5}{\underbrace{101}}$$

The format description (if allowed)

$$[\,n\,]Od$$

indicates n consecutive items in the octal system with a field width of d digits. This could be done for real, integer, double precision, or complex values. A machine may also allow character strings or logical values to be inspected in this way. It will be found that integer values translate directly into their octal equivalents - including the complement form of negative numbers if appropriate to the machine. Surprises will be in store with other data types.

18.6 Format descriptions affecting numeric fields

FORTRAN 77 provides three format editing descriptions which can be used to control the transmission of numeric values. On output, the printing (or otherwise) of a plus sign with positive values can be controlled by the SP or SS descriptions. For input, the BN or BZ descriptions can change the significance of blanks in an input field. For both input and output the P scaling facility can specify the placing of the decimal point in exponential forms of data, and can specify a scale factor for the input of data using the F description. Here is a description of these facilities.

(a) Printing of the plus sign - SP, SS, S

Normally the computer has the option to print or not to print the plus sign in front of positive values for all types of numbers. The SP description forces the computer to print signs with all values for the remainder of one complete format description.

EXAMPLES:

```
    PRINT 20,X,Y
20 FORMAT(1X,SP,2F10.5)
```

The values of X and Y will be printed with signs, whether positive or negative.

```
    PRINT 20,X,Y
20 FORMAT(1X,F10.5,SP,F10.5)
```

The computer has the option of leaving out the sign if X is positive, but the value of Y will be printed with a sign whatever its value.

Similarly the SS description means that the plus sign is to be suppressed.

EXAMPLE:

```
    PRINT 20,X,Y
20 FORMAT(1X,SS,F10.5,SP,F10.5)
```

The value of X will be printed with a sign if X is negative. The value of Y will always be printed with a sign.

The option of printing or not printing the sign is returned to the computer by the S description.

EXAMPLE:

```
    PRINT 20,X,Y
20 FORMAT(1X,SP,F10.5,S,F10.5)
```

The value of X will be printed with a sign. The computer has the option of leaving out the plus sign if Y is positive.

These descriptions have effect for only the format specification in which they appear.

EXAMPLE:

```
    PRINT 20,I,J
20 FORMAT(1X,SP,I5,SS,I5)
    PRINT 30,K,L
30 FORMAT(1X,2I5)
```

The value of I is printed with a sign. The value of J is printed without a sign if it is positive. The computer has the option of leaving out the sign if K and L are positive.

These facilities apply only on output, and are ignored (because they are meaningless) if they are present in a format specification used with a READ statement. They affect all the numeric editing descriptions: I, F, E, D and G. Note that when a format specification repeats (Section 9 of this Chapter) the latest SP, SS or S description remains in force.

(b) Blanks in input fields - BN and BZ
Normally a blank in an input field is ignored and a completely blank field means zero. This may not be true for preconnected files, and a BLANK= specifier in the OPEN statement can change this for a particular file, as described in Chapter 19.

Within each format specification the normal interpretation of blanks can be confirmed or changed by the BN and BZ descriptions.

The BN description forces blanks to be taken as 'null', i.e. ignored. This is the normal situation.

EXAMPLE:

```
      READ(5,1Ø)INTEG
 1Ø   FORMAT(BN,I4)
```

The value 30 could be presented to this statement in one of several ways:

$$
\begin{array}{c}
3Ø \\
3\ Ø \\
3\ \ Ø \\
3Ø \\
3\ Ø \\
3Ø
\end{array}
$$

The BZ description forces blanks to be regarded as zeros.

EXAMPLE:

```
      READ(5,1Ø)INTEG
 1Ø   FORMAT(BZ,I4)
```

Moving the same string of numbers about in the input field has a different meaning now:

Input Field	Value
3 Ø	300
3 Ø	3000
3Ø	300
3 Ø	3000
3Ø	3000

The interpretation of blanks can be switched during the execution of the format specification.

EXAMPLE:

```
      READ(5,3Ø)X,Y
 3Ø   FORMAT(BN,F5.Ø,BZ,F5.Ø)
```

In response to the above request, providing the following data

$$
\begin{array}{c}
3\ \ \ \ \ 3
\end{array}
$$

defines X=3.0 and Y=300.0.

Following the execution of an input statement, the normal state will be restored for the next input statement.

EXAMPLE:
Suppose for input unit number 5 blanks are normally ignored, as is usual in FORTRAN 77. Then in the statements

```
      READ(5,1Ø)MATT
 1Ø   FORMAT(BZ,I5)
      READ(5,2Ø)MARK
 2Ø   FORMAT(I5)
```

the input data for MATT has blanks interpreted as zeros and for MARK has blanks ignored.

When a format specification repeats because there are more items in the input/output list than there are format descriptions, the most recent BN or BZ description continues to apply (see Section 9 of this Chapter).

The BN and BZ descriptions affect input operations for the I, F, E, D and G field descriptions. For output they are ignored as being meaningless.

(c) Scaling of real values - P

The P scaling facility is useful when outputting values with E, D and G editing because it enables the program to alter the position of the decimal point. It also has an effect when input is given to an F, E, D or G description with no exponent. However, since it operates in completely different ways for input and output, it does tend to confuse programmers.

In the specification

$$kP$$

k is an integer constant scale factor, which may be signed. At the beginning of every format description, the scale factor is zero and to alter this requires a P description which takes effect for the duration of the format, unless of course it is changed again by another P description.

On input, any number that is given without an exponent to the F, E, D or G fields is multiplied by 10**k, so that the computer applies a scale factor to input data if there is no exponent in it. It does not scale data given with an exponent.

EXAMPLES:

```
    READ 35,X,Y
35 FORMAT(F5.Ø,2PF5.Ø)
```

The above statements could be given the following lines of data.

        1Ø   1Ø
. . . .

defines X=10.0, Y=1000.0 by scaling;

      1Ø 3.736
. . . .

defines X=10.0, Y=373.6 by scaling;

     1 Ø 4E1
. . . .

and defines X=10.0, Y=4.0 without scaling.

For output, the situation is reversed. P scaling has no effect on a value which is written out by using the F description, or by using the G description as long as it is not using an exponent. However it does affect the layout of any field which is printed with an exponent, which means the E and D forms always and the G form sometimes.

The normal position of the decimal point in a field with an exponent is before the first significant digit, as in:

```
  PRINT 2Ø,122.9
2Ø FORMAT(1X,E1Ø.3)
```

which prints

    Ø.123E+Ø3
. . . .

Using P scaling with a scale factor of k, the decimal point is moved k places to the right and the exponent is reduced by k, as in

```
  PRINT 2Ø,122.9
2Ø FORMAT(1X,2P,E1Ø.3)
```

which prints

    12.3E+Ø3
. . . .

As can be seen, the apparent value is not changed, only the layout. The difference between the effect of P scaling on input and on output is not completely logical. Actually, not many people use it.

Since k can be signed, the decimal point in an output field can be moved the other way, as in

```
  PRINT 2Ø,122.9
2Ø FORMAT(1X,-2P,E1Ø.3)
```

which prints

    Ø.ØØ1E+Ø5
. . . .

Note that in all of these examples of exponential form, the leading zero and optional sign are left to the discretion of the computer.

EXAMPLE:
Using a G field, the statement

```
  PRINT'(1X,2P,G12.4)',512.1
```

gives

      512.1
. . . .

while the statement

        PRINT'(1X,2P,G12.4)',12345.6

gives

            12.346E+Ø3
            ············

18.7 Other fields — L, X, A, and character constants

This section describes the format descriptions available for non-numeric data. The L description is used with data of type logical. The X description is used to insert blanks into a field. The A description is used for the input and output of character data from an input/output list. Character constants can also be inserted directly into a format description.

(a) Logical values - L

The field description

            [n]Lw

indicates that n consecutive items are logical values occupying w spaces each. The n is optional and is taken as one if it is not given. The L description can only be used in conjunction with an item of type logical.

On output, the single letters T for .TRUE. and F for .FALSE. are printed in the rightmost space of the field.

On input, the first nonblank characters in the field must be either T or .T to define a value as .TRUE., or F or .F for .FALSE. Everything else is ignored.

(b) Blank fields - X

The format description

            nX

indicates a field of n blanks.

On output n blanks are produced.

EXAMPLE:
    The statement

        PRINT'(1X,I3,3X,I3)',123,789

prints

            123   789
            ········

Recall that a lineprinter will regard the first character of output as a carriage control.

In an input record, a field of width n spaces is skipped over.

EXAMPLE:
    In response to

            CHARACTER A1*3,A3*5
            READ(5,2Ø)A1,A3
        2Ø FORMAT(A,3X,A)

you could give

            ONETWOTHREE

which defines A1 as 'ONE' and A3 as 'THREE'.

(c) Character strings - A

The specification

            [n]A[w]

indicates that n consecutive items are character strings occupying w spaces each. The n is optional and is taken as one if it is not given. The w is also optional, and if it is not given then the width is the length of the corresponding character item in the input/output list. The A description can only be used in conjunction with values of type character.

EXAMPLES:
    The statement

        PRINT'(1X,2A)','FIRST','SECOND'

prints

            FIRSTSECOND

The statements

            CHARACTER THYNG*6
            READ(5,1Ø)THYNG
        1Ø FORMAT(A)

expect a character value of length 6.

When w is given, the length of a character entity may not match it.

On output, if w is less than the length of the character string, the leftmost w characters will be printed.

EXAMPLE:
The statement

```
      PRINT 33,'TOOMUCH'
33 FORMAT(1X,A4)
```

prints

```
TOOM
```

On the other hand, if w is greater than the length of an output character string, the output is right justified in the field, preceded by blanks.

EXAMPLE:
The statement

```
      PRINT 35,'MORE','MORE'
35 FORMAT(1X,2A6)
```

prints

```
  MORE  MORE
..............
```

For input, if w is less than the length of the required character string, then additional blanks are used to fill up the string with trailing blanks.

EXAMPLE:
The statement

```
      CHARACTER*6 CHUGG
      READ(5,60)CHUGG
60 FORMAT(A4)
```

will fill out CHUGG with blanks. If the input were

```
LESSTHAN
```

then CHUGG would be given the value 'LESS ' with two trailing blanks.

Similarly, if w is greater than the length of the required character string in a READ statement, the rightmost w characters are used.

EXAMPLE:

```
      CHARACTER ALUGG*5
      READ(5,90)ALUGG
90 FORMAT(A9)
```

takes the rightmost five characters from the 9 character input field. If it were given as input

```
LEFTRIGHT
```

then ALUGG would be given the value 'RIGHT'.

(d) Character constants - apostrophes or H

A field description in apostrophes

```
'a character constant'
```

can be used only within a format description for output by a WRITE or PRINT statement. The character constant is written out.

EXAMPLE:
The statement

```
PRINT'(''HELLO SAILOR'')'
```

prints

```
HELLO SAILOR
```

Recall that apostophes can be inserted into character constants by doubling them.

EXAMPLE:
The statement

```
PRINT*,'TO GET '' PUT '''''
```

prints

```
TO GET ' PUT ''
```

An obsolete feature of FORTRAN IV which is supported by FORTRAN 77 is the H description. The field

nH

specifies that the n characters which follow the H are to be regarded as a character constant. This field can appear only within an output format description, and is similar to a field in apostrophes. If the H field is inside a character constant delimited by apostrophes, each apostrophe must be represented by two, which count as one when working out n. Otherwise you only need one. The disadvantage of the H field is that you have to spend time counting the characters in constants. So it is seldom used any more.

EXAMPLE:

```
   PRINT 5Ø
5Ø FORMAT(16H TO GET ' PUT '')
```

prints

```
        TO GET ' PUT ''
```

18.8 Field positioning — T, TL, TR

These format descriptions will cause the position of information in the field to jump back and forth. They can be used in a number of useful ways.

Strictly, the X field is a positional description. A field

nX

causes the next n spaces in a field to be skipped. The description for right tabulation

TRc

behaves similarly. The next input field occurs c positions to the right. Therefore

4X

has the same effect as

TR4

The description

TLc

causes a similar movement of c spaces left. This is most interesting, since it allows a line to be wholly or partially replaced on output, or re-read on input. If a TL description attempts to move further than the first space of line it moves only to the first space.

On output, a TL description can replace what was already there.

EXAMPLE:
The statements

```
   PRINT 99
99 FORMAT(' REPLACE',TL4,'THIS')
```

print

```
        REPTHIS
```

With input, a field can be re-read.

EXAMPLE:
The statements

```
        CHARACTER CHARX*6
        READ(5,25)X,CHARX
     25 FORMAT(F6.2,TL6,A)
```

cause the real value X and the character value CHARX to be read from the same field. Were the data

```
     +1.ØØØ
```

X has the value 1.0, and CHARX is the character string '+1.000'.

The description

Tc

will cause an immediate jump to output space c. Remember that X, TR, and TL cause tabulation which is relative to the present position, while T jumps to an absolute print position.

18.9 Punctuation and Format Repetitions

(a) Punctuation by commas

When a format specification contains a number of field descriptions and other specifiers, it is usual to separate all of them by commas; it is safest to do this always.

EXAMPLE:

66 FORMAT(1X,SP,'YOW',3I5,2F6.0)

However, the commas are not always necessary. According to the standard, the comma may be omitted between a P scaling description and a following F, E, D or G description:

2PF10.5,4PE15.6

Commas are not required before or after a slash:

PRINT'(//'NO COMMAS'//)'

Commas are not required before or after a colon:

200 FORMAT(F10.5:'THERE IS MORE')

(b) Punctuation by brackets - repetitions

So that groups of format descriptions may be repeated, FORTRAN 77 allows any number of paired brackets to occur which may be repeated by an integer repetition constant.

EXAMPLE:

127 FORMAT(1X,5(F10.5,I3))

takes care of five pairs of real and integer values in a line of 66 spaces.

If the data list of an input or output statement is not finished when the end of a format specification is encountered, then a new record begins and the format is repeated from the group ended by the last embedded right bracket, using its repeat factor if any.

If there are no embedded brackets, then the entire format specification is used again. This means that new lines of input or output will occur whenever the end of the format is reached.

EXAMPLE:
The statements

DIMENSION UNIT(3,3)
DATA UNIT/1.,3*0.,1.,3*0.,1./
PRINT88,((UNIT(I,J),J=1,3),
                          I=1,3)
88 FORMAT(1X,3F5.2)

write the values of the array on three lines in row order:

1.00 0.00 0.00
0.00 1.00 0.00
0.00 0.00 1.00

(c) Punctuation by slashes - new lines

A format specification can call for a new line to begin by using a slash (/). Recall that each new line is called a "record". Every READ, or WRITE, or PRINT statement begins a new record. Due to the way format descriptions are repeated, additional new records begin when the end of a format specification is reached and there are still more items to be transferred. The slash in a format is the third way of forcing a new record.

EXAMPLE:
To the previous example, a message could be added on its own line before the array is printed, and the array could be spaced out using additional new lines:

DIMENSION UNIT(3,3)
DATA UNIT/1.,3*0.,1.,3*0.,1./
PRINT 88,((UNIT(I,J),J=1,3),
                          I=1,3)
88 FORMAT(' UNIT MATRIX'//
          (1X,3F5.2))

whose output is

UNIT MATRIX

1.00 0.00 0.00
0.00 1.00 0.00
0.00 0.00 1.00

Note the useful effect of repeating the format specification from the first embedded bracket.

(d) Punctuation by colons – stopping a format

The way a format description starts and repeats has already been described. The colon can control how it ends. Normally a format carries on after the last item transferred until it finds an item describing a data field it does not need; then it stops.

EXAMPLES:
This program

```
   PRINT 20,1,2
20 FORMAT(1X,2I3,' THEN THIS',I4)
   END
```

prints the following

```
   1   2 THEN THIS
```

This program

```
      READ(5,10)I,J,K
10 FORMAT(3I5//)
```

skips two records of input, possibly cards.

This can be overridden by the colon. If there are still any items to be transferred, the colon has no effect. However if all the data items required by an input or output list have been completed the colon stops it.

EXAMPLE:
In the example

```
   REAL XES(5)
   DATA XES/1.0,2.0,3.0,4.0,5.0/
   PRINT 22,XES
22 FORMAT(F10.5:' MORE FOLLOWS')
   END
```

the output is

```
   1.00000 MORE FOLLOWS
   2.00000 MORE FOLLOWS
   3.00000 MORE FOLLOWS
   4.00000 MORE FOLLOWS
   5.00000
```

18.10   List-directed input and output

The list-directed input/output statement is actually a special case of formatted Input/output. If the format specification is simply an asterisk, then for output the computer arranges the data in any way convenient to itself, and for input the user is similarly given a free hand. This is very useful. List-directed statements can have a control information list, as described in Chapter 19. Without one, they are

```
READ(unit,*)[data list]

READ * [, data list]

WRITE(unit,*)[data list]

PRINT * [, data list]
```

In the READ and PRINT statements with no unit number given, the obvious unit is used. This would refer to the user's own timesharing terminal in an interactive session, or to the cardreader and lineprinter in a batch environment.

Whenever a list-directed WRITE or PRINT statement is used, the computer arranges the output itself and ensures that blank characters are always provided in each new line so that the correct carriage control is provided for single spacing of a lineprinter.

In response to a list-directed READ statement, the data must be given in the correct order and must be of the correct type, with all the data values separated either by a single comma or by one or more blanks. The various kinds of data that might be provided are:

(a) Integer. Provide an integer.

(b) Real or double precision. Provide any numeric constant without an exponent. If it is provided as an integer, the decimal point is taken at the end of it.

EXAMPLE:
In response to

```
READ *,I,X,Y
```

you could provide

$$34,4,4321.23$$

and this will define I=34, X=4.0 and Y=4321.23.

(c) Complex. Give two numeric values enclosed in parentheses with a comma between.

EXAMPLE:
In response to

```
COMPLEX C
READ *,C
```

you could put

$$(1.1,2.2)$$

(d) Logical. The given values must begin with T or .T (for .TRUE.) or F or .F (for .FALSE.).

(e) Characters. A character constant must be given enclosed in apostrophes. As in other situations, to include an apostrophe inside the constant, double apostrophes are required.

EXAMPLE:
In response to

```
CHARACTER MESSG*5
READ*,MESSG
```

you could provide

```
'ISN''T'
```

which defines MESSG to have the value

```
ISN'T
```

If the length of the character item in the data list of the READ statement does not match the length of the given constant, the computer takes what is given, left justifies it, and either truncates it or fills it with blanks to make it the correct length. This is exactly what happens in a character assignment statement, but it is not the same as reading using the A format description.

EXAMPLE:
In response to

```
CHARACTER CHUGG*4
READ*,CHUGG
```

you could give

```
'A'
```

in which case CHUGG is given the value 'A   ' with three trailing blanks. On the other hand, if you gave

```
'LEFTRIGHT'
```

then CHUGG is given the value 'LEFT'.

(f) Null fields. Any data list item can be left unchanged by giving it no value. Usually this is done by putting in commas to indicate clearly the null fields.

EXAMPLE:
In response to

```
DATA I,J,K/1,2,3/
READ *,I,J,K
```

you give

$$4,,2$$

which defines I=4, K=2 but leaves J unchanged as 2. To give a null value to I, put something like

$$,3,2$$

after which I is unchanged at 1, J=3, K=2. A null value leaves the list item unchanged. If it were undefined, it will remain undefined. Otherwise it continues to have the same value as before.

(g) No more input. Giving a slash as input at any stage terminates the request for input and leaves all the remaining items unchanged, as if a series of null values had been given.

EXAMPLE:
In response to

```
DATA I,J,K/1,2,3/
READ *,I,J,K
```

you could give

4/

which sets I=4 and leaves J=2 and K=3.

(h) Repeating fields. In list-directed input, an asterisk can be used to indicate the same value repeated, much as in a data statement.

EXAMPLE:
In response to

```
DATA I,J,K/1,2,3/
READ*,I,J,K
```

the data

3*4

defines I=J=K=4.

Null values can be repeated also. To the same example giving

2*,4

defines K=4, but I and J remain unchanged, with I=1, J=2.

19
Records and files

19.1 Sequential and direct files

The previous Chapter defined "records" of input and output to be the basic items by which data is transferred to and from the computer. In formatted and list-directed transfers, each READ, WRITE, or PRINT statement begins a new record, and additional new records could occur during input or output operations as described in the previous Chapter. The notion of a record was associated with lines of data for common input/output devices. In this Chapter, the idea of a record as an identifiable group of data becomes much more important as facilities are introduced which enable a computer program to manipulate the input/ouput devices in more general ways.

A collection of records read from or written to the same place is called a "file". Previously, programs have written records of data to a printer or terminal in sequence - such a file is called a "sequential file". Similarly input records from a cardreader or from a timesharing terminal form a sequential file. A digital tape on which records can be written, starting at the beginning and one after another, is also a sequential file.

The other kind of file is called a "direct" file. In a direct file, a program can jump immediately to a desired record; as an example, on a magnetic disk any desired record can be accessed at any time. A disk could also be a sequential file - but in FORTRAN 77 not at the same time as it is being a direct file. Some devices can only be used for one kind of file - for example cardreaders, lineprinters and timesharing terminals are usually sequential only, for obvious reasons. The files that are available, and the allowed methods of access, will depend on local arrangements in any individual computer system.

It will be seen in this Chapter that data can be transferred to and from sequential or direct access files in either formatted or "unformatted" form. The "unformatted" form is not the same as the list-directed form; unformatted data transfers will be introduced in Section 19.6. The records in any file must be either all formatted or all unformatted; no mixture is permitted. The main restrictions on direct access files are that list-directed formatting cannot be used, and that the record length has to be fixed. Therefore to be able to use a sequential file later as a direct access file, the length of the records have to be fixed and list-directed formatting cannot be used.

In this Chapter the reader will also learn how to make the most of the powerful input/output facilities by using the "control list" of READ and WRITE statements, and by using additional input/output statements which determine the status and position of a file. An "internal file" facility is also introduced - using this facility, character data can be transferred between character entities inside the machine.

19.2 More READ/WRITE facilities

The complete form of the READ, WRITE, and PRINT statements is:

$$\text{READ} \quad \begin{pmatrix} \text{control} \\ \text{list} \end{pmatrix} \begin{bmatrix} \text{data} \\ \text{list} \end{bmatrix}$$

$$\text{READ} \quad \begin{matrix} \text{format} \\ \text{identifier} \end{matrix} \begin{bmatrix} , \text{ data} \\ \text{list} \end{bmatrix}$$

$$\text{WRITE} \quad \begin{pmatrix} \text{control} \\ \text{list} \end{pmatrix} \begin{bmatrix} \text{data} \\ \text{list} \end{bmatrix}$$

$$\text{PRINT} \quad \begin{matrix} \text{format} \\ \text{identifier} \end{matrix} \begin{bmatrix} , \text{data} \\ \text{list} \end{bmatrix}$$

In Chapter 18 the special cases of formatted and list-directed transfers were considered. Here, the full range of available facilities is described.

A "control list" contains information about the destination and layout of the records to be transferred to or from a file. The list contains a number of items separated by commas. There must be at least one item which is a "unit specifier"; everything else is optional. The control list items can be as follows.

UNIT =   unit
            identifier

FMT =   format
            identifier

REC = record
         number

IOSTAT = integer variable
          or array element

END = label

ERR = label

(a) Unit Specifier

The unit specifier has the form

UNIT =   unit
           identifier

Every control list must contain exactly one unit specifier. If the optional UNIT= is omitted, the unit specifier must be the first item in the control list.

The "unit specifier" can be an integer expression:

READ(FMT=*,UNIT=5) XRAY

WRITE(6,'(''HELLO SAILOR'')')

or an asterisk to identify the obvious unit to be used for formatted sequential access, such as the cardreader or lineprinter in a batch system, or a user's timesharing terminal:

WRITE(*,'(''HELLO SAILOR'')')

It will be seen in Section 7 of this Chapter that the unit identifier can also be the name of an internal character quantity which makes up an internal file.

(b) Format Identifier

The format identifier is

FMT =   format
           identifier

At most one optional format identifier can be given in a control list. If none is given, then the record to be transferred is of the "unformatted" type to be described in Section 19.5. If one is given it can be one of the types described in Chapter 18:

(i) The label of a format statement or an integer variable name that has been assigned the label of a format statement.
(ii) A character quantity giving the format description.
(iii) An asterisk, specifying list-directed formatting.

Formatted and list-directed input and output were described in some detail in Chapter 18.

If the optional FMT= is omitted, the format specifier must be the second item in the control list, and the first item must have been a unit specifier without the optional UNIT= specifier.

(c) Record Number

At most one record number can be given:

REC = record
number

This specifier is used for direct access on a file which is connected for direct access. If no record number is given, then the input/output transfer will be sequential, and will read from or write to the next record in sequence on the input/output unit. Note, however, that sequential and direct transfers cannot be mixed without first closing and reopening the file - see Section 19.4.

If a record number is given, then the data is transferred to or from the desired record in a direct file. The record number can be any positive integer expression. Direct access input and output are described fully, with examples, in Section 19.3.

(d) Input/Output Status

A program can get information about the status of an input/output unit. The control list may contain at most one IOSTAT specifier:

IOSTAT = integer variable
or array elememt

For example:

READ(6,21,IOSTAT=J)

where J is the name of an integer variable. What happens depends on the choices made for an individual computer. The integer variable, J in the example, will be assigned a value according to the state of the file being accessed, as follows:

(i) A zero value if there is no error or end-of-file condition.
(ii) A positive integer value if an error occurs.
(iii) A negative integer value if there is no error but an end-of-file occurs.

(e) End-of-File Condition

It is possible that a READ statement could encounter the end of the information in a file, and that the program would want to know at what point this happened. The optional control list item

END = label

allows this to be done. Only one can be given. When a READ statement reaches the end-of-file without an error occurring, no more data is transferred; the IOSTAT variable will then be set (if it is there), and the program will jump to the statement in the same program unit whose label is given.

EXAMPLE:

```
1Ø  READ(73,END=2Ø)
    GO TO 1Ø
2Ø  PRINT*,'NO MORE DATA'
```

This little program reads the data from unit number 73 until there is no more data, when it prints NO MORE DATA.

EXERCISE:
In the above example, how would you count the number of records that were present on unit number 73?

In Section 19.5, it will be seen how a program which creates a file can indicate the end of that file.

(f) Error Condition

It is possible that some form of error could occur during an input/output transfer. This could be the programmer's fault, such as trying to read the wrong type of data with the wrong kind of format description, or using sequential access on a file presently intended for direct access, and in several other ways. It could also be the fault of the computer, as for example ripping up or misreading cards or magnetic tape. The IOSTAT parameter will tell the program what kind of error has taken place, although the exact interpretation of this information is likely to be different for every different computer. As with the end-of-file condition, it is possible to send the program to a statement in the same program unit. To do this give at most one error specifier:

ERR = label

When an error occurs, and there is an error specifier, the input/output transfer is terminated, the position of the file becomes unknown, the IOSTAT variable is set (if there was one), and the program jumps to the given label which must be in the same program unit. Note that if an error and an end-of-file occur together, the ERR= specifier will take priority if it is present.

19.3 Direct access files

A direct access file is one in which a computer program can read or write any desired record from the file. For example, magnetic disk storage is usually organized so that the computer can seek out and access any desired record at any time. Not all input/output devices can be used as direct access files. Each computer installation will have a number of devices available as direct and/or sequential files.

To achieve direct access, FORTRAN 77 uses the REC= specifier as described in the previous section. The first record in a file is record number 1, and data can be written to or read from any desired part of the file by specifying the record number.

A file cannot be available for direct access and sequential access at the same time. When a FORTRAN 77 program is executed, some files will be automatically "preconnected" for sequential or direct access. If a file is not connected, or is the wrong access type, then an OPEN statement can connect it for direct access provided that this is allowed for the particular device. The OPEN statement is described in the next section. Once connected, a file stays in the same form of access, and an error condition arises if the wrong form of access is used. However, a file can be later reconnected by an OPEN statement for a different kind of access, as described in Section 19.4.

In a direct access file, the physical records on the device used for the file are all of the same length. This length is the maximum number of characters that can be written or read by a formatted transfer, and to a certain extent it is controllable by the OPEN statement. Every record has a record number, and in the file the records occur in order. Therefore if a file created by direct access is later read by sequential access, the records will be found in order of their number, starting with record number 1. The records in any file must be either entirely written using format-directed statements, or entirely written using unformatted statements as described in Section 19.6. Formatted and unformatted records cannot be mixed in any kind of file. In direct access files list-directed formatting may not be used. Therefore if a file created by sequential access is later read by direct access, the records must all be the same length and not written by list-directed statements.

EXAMPLE:
Suppose your computer has unit number 7 preconnected as a direct access file with a maximum record length of 130 characters. You wish to read some data from unit 5 which is a sequential cardreader, and divide the even and odd numbered cards into the top and bottom halves of the new file. This reordering is illustrated by Fig. 19.1. If there are 64 records to reorganize, here is the program:

```
      CHARACTER DATA*80
      DO 10 KREC=1,64
      READ(5,'(A)') DATA
      LREC=1+KREC/2+32*MOD(KREC+1,2)
      WRITE(7,'(A)',REC=LREC) DATA
   10 CONTINUE
```

Quite clever, really. The key to the reordering is in the calculation of the new record number, LREC, from the original order in the sequential file. Whatever formatted data occurred in the deck of cards is now divided so that the odd numbered cards now occur in order before the even numbered ones on the new unit number 7, as in Fig. 19.1. You could now read them back and print their new order:

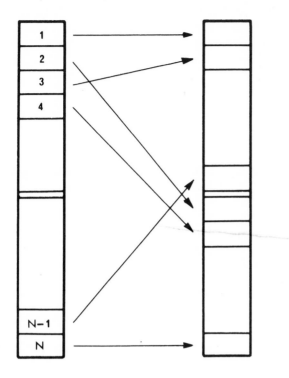

The above WRITE statement has written records 7, 9, and 11 in the direct access file on unit 10. Records 8 and 10 have been skipped over.

If a transfer calls for a record which is larger than the maximum permitted for the particular file, then an error has occurred (which could be detected by an IOSTAT= specifier). However, a transfer in either direction can use only part of a record as in the above examples.

Finally, it is common sense with any kind of file that it is only possible to read back what has actually been written. A program cannot expect to read values from a record that has not been written. In the program

```
SMART=1.0
DUMB=2.0
WRITE(16,REC=11) SMART
READ(16,REC=11) SMART,DUMB
```

DUMB would become undefined after the READ statement. Similarly if an 'empty' record is read, everything in the data list of the READ statement becomes undefined.

Fig. 19.1. Using a direct output file, even-odd reordering of a sequential input file is easily achieved.

```
      DO 20 MREC=1,64
      READ(7,'(A)',REC=MREC) DATA
      PRINT*, DATA
20    CONTINUE
      END
```

Note that because character type has been used, any formatted file could have been rearranged in this way. This same file could be reopened as a sequential file, and the data read back. This is used as an example in the next section.

If a formatted operation needs several records then several records of the direct access file are used.

EXAMPLE:

```
      INTEGER IRAY(3,3)
          :
          :
      WRITE(10,20,REC=7) IRAY
20    FORMAT(3I10/)
```

19.4 The properties of a file — INQUIRE, OPEN, and CLOSE

FORTRAN 77 has three auxiliary input/output statements. The INQUIRE statement can be used to discover all the properties of a file. The OPEN statement connects a file and can establish some of its properties. The CLOSE statement disconnects a file. These statements are described in this section, which begins with the INQUIRE statement.

A file can have a name which is known to the computer system. The INQUIRE statement can ask about a file by its name:

```
INQUIRE(FILE=name,enquiry list)
```

where the file name is given as any character expression in which trailing blanks are ignored, for example

```
INQUIRE(FILE='FRED',enquiry list)
```

The enquiry list is described below.

A file, whether or not it has a name, can be connected to a numbered input/output unit known to the program. This connection could be made automatically by the computer. It could alternatively be done by the OPEN statement described later in this section. An INQUIRE statement can refer to a file by its unit number instead of its name, as

```
INQUIRE(UNIT=number,enquiry list)
```

or

```
INQUIRE(number,enquiry list)
```

as in the example

```
INQUIRE(5,enquiry list)
```

In either form of the INQUIRE statement, the enquiry list asks for the facts about the file. An enquiry list can contain any of the following specifiers:

```
IOSTAT=
ERR=
EXIST=
OPENED=
NUMBER=
NAMED=
ACCESS=
SEQUENTIAL=
DIRECT=
FORM=
FORMATTED=
UNFORMATTED=
RECL=
NEXTREC=
BLANK=
```

Here, the enquiry specifiers are described in turn, as are all the possible properties of a file.

(a) IOSTAT=int

The presence of this specifier causes the status of the file to be indicated by 'int', which is an integer variable or integer array element. The value zero is returned if there is no error condition at present in the file. A positive integer value is returned if an error occurs. A negative value is returned if there is no error, but an end-of-file condition occurs.

```
    INQUIRE(23,IOSTAT=INK)
    IF(INK) 19,2Ø,21
2Ø          :
            :
```

Here, if there is no error condition on unit number 23, the program continues from label 20 because INK is set to zero. The program will jump to label 21 if there is an error and label 19 if there is no error but the file is positioned at the end.

(b) ERR=label

If an error condition has occurred, the program will jump immediately to the statement with the label "label", which must be in the same program unit.

(c) EXIST=log

This specifier enquires whether or not the file exists. Here "log" is a logical variable or array element. If the file exists, "log" is given the value .TRUE.. Otherwise, the file does not exist and the value .FALSE. is returned.

(d) OPENED=log

Some files may already be connected by the computer system to a program when it begins executing; the standard printer and input unit certainly will. Other files may have to be connected by an OPEN statement, described later in this section. Exactly what has to be done depends on the machine. Some computers automatically connect all the files, whereas others may require action from the program. The INQUIRE statement with an OPENED=log specifier will tell the program whether or not the file is presently connected. "log" is a logical variable or array element which is set to .TRUE. if it is connected, or to .FALSE. if it is not.

(e) NUMBER=int

This specifier causes the integer variable or array element "int" to be assigned the value of the unit number that is connected to the file; if none "int" becomes undefined. This is mainly useful for discovering the unit number of a named file.

(f) NAMED=log

The logical variable or array element "log" is assigned the value .TRUE. if the file in question has a name, otherwise .FALSE..

(g) To discover the name of a numbered file, use

NAME=char

Here, "char" is a character variable or array element that is assigned the name of a file as it is known to the computer system. This name may not be exactly the same as in the FILE= specifier, but it can be used as a FILE= specifier in an OPEN statement for the same file.

(h) ACCESS=char

This tells the program, through the character variable or array element "char", for what type of access the file is connected. However, if it is not connected, "char" becomes undefined, otherwise "char" is given a value which is either SEQUENTIAL or DIRECT.

(i) A program may wish to enquire, not about the present form of access, but about what forms of access are permitted. The specifier

SEQUENTIAL=char

will set the character variable or array element "char" to YES, NO, or UNKNOWN, according to whether sequential access is permitted for the file. This is not the same as asking for what form of access the file is presently connected.

In the same vein, the specifier

DIRECT=char

asks whether direct access is permitted for this file.

(j) FORM=char

This specifier uses the character variable or array element "char" to say whether the file is connected for use with formatted data or unformatted data. "char" is given the value FORMATTED or UNFORMATTED, whichever is appropriate. If the file is not connected, then "char" becomes (or remains) undefined.

(k) A program may enquire, not about the present type of data, but whether a particular type of data is permitted for the file. The specifier

FORMATTED=char

will use the character variable or array element "char" to say whether formatted data transfers are allowed on the file by assigning the value YES, NO, or UNKNOWN to "char". This is not the same as asking for what type of transfer the file is presently connected. Similarly

UNFORMATTED=char

asks whether unformatted transfers are allowed on this file.

(l) The record length of a direct access file is important. A program can give the enquiry specifier

RECL=int

which will cause the integer variable or integer array element "int" to be assigned the maximum record length if the file is connected for direct access. If the file is connected for sequential access, or if it is not connected at all, "int" becomes undefined.

(m) To discover the present position in a direct access file, use

NEXTREC=int

This is perhaps the most useful of the facilities of the INQUIRE statement. The integer variable or integer array member "int" is assigned the value of the next record in a direct access file. When such a file is first connected, the next record is record number 1. After a READ or WRITE to a direct access file in which the last record used is record number n, the next record is n+1.

EXAMPLE:

```
      INTEGER IRAY(3,3)
          :
          :
      WRITE(1Ø,2Ø,REC=7) IRAY
   2Ø FORMAT(3I1Ø/)
      INQUIRE(1Ø,NEXTREC=NEXT1)
```

NEXT1 is assigned the integer value 13. What would NEXT1 be if the FORMAT were:

```
   2Ø FORMAT(3I1Ø:/)
```

(n) The program can determine from the INQUIRE statement whether blanks are significant in formatted input fields from the file. The specifier

BLANK=char

sets the character variable or character array element "char" to either NULL or ZERO if the file is at present connected for formatted input/output. If it is not connected at all, or if it is connected for direct access, then "char" becomes undefined.

This parameter is of some importance in formatted input. Normally if a file is connected automatically for formatted transfers, blanks are interpreted as nulls, i.e. they have no meaning in numerical fields processed by editing descriptions in a format specification. However, it was seen in Chapter 18 that a BN or BZ editing specification could override this in an individual format. In the OPEN statement, which is described next, it is possible to change the normal interpretation of blanks.

The connection of a file may be done automatically by the computer system, or it may require the OPEN statement which is described here. The OPEN statement

OPEN([UNIT=]number,filespec list)

will connect the file and define its characteristics using the file specification list "filespec list".

The following are the available specifiers:

```
      IOSTAT=
      ERR=
      FILE=
      STATUS=
      ACCESS=
      FORM=
      RECL=
      BLANK=
```

The meaning of each specifier is listed below:

(a) IOSTAT=int

This specifier has the same meaning as it does in all the other input/output statements. Here "int" is an integer variable or integer array element to which the computer assigns a value according to the status of the file. If no error is detected in opening the file, "int" is assigned the value zero. If an error condition exists, "int" is given a positive value whose interpretation will vary between computer systems.

(b) ERR=label

If an error condition has occurred, the program will jump immediately to the statement with the label "label" which must be in the same program unit. This could happen, for example, if a program tries to open a file for direct access but direct access is not permitted for that file.

(c) FILE=char

When a file name is not given in an OPEN statement, the computer opens a file on some device of its choice, and the relationship between the unit numbers and the allowed form of access will depend on the computer installation. However, a program can specify the name of the file it wants opened, in the FILE= specifier. The "name" is a character expression giving the name of the file to be opened. Trailing blanks are disregarded.

(d) The STATUS= specifier allows the program to make a file one of several kinds:

STATUS=char

The character expression "char" states what kind of file the program desires, and can be OLD, NEW, SCRATCH, or UNKNOWN. Trailing blanks are ignored. The meaning of these is:

OLD The file must already exist in the computer system. The computer opens it.

NEW The file must not exist already. The computer creates and opens a new file.

SCRATCH Must not be specified for a named file. A scratch file is one that is discarded when closed by a CLOSE statement or when the program terminates.

UNKNOWN The computer decides what kind of file it is. If there is no STATUS= specifier, then a value of UNKNOWN is assumed.

(e) ACCESS=char

Ignoring trailing blanks, "char" must be a character expression which is either SEQUENTIAL or DIRECT. This specifies what kind of file is desired. If not given, SEQUENTIAL is assumed. For direct access of an existing file, direct access must be allowed otherwise an error condition is created.

EXAMPLE:
The direct access file created as an example in the previous section read data from a sequential file and rearranged their order on a new direct access file. Here is a program which takes no chances about the

characteristics of the files, and at the end reopens the file as a sequential file and copies it to a lineprinter.

```
CHARACTER DATA*8Ø
OPEN(1,STATUS='OLD')
OPEN(2,STATUS='NEW',ACCESS='DIRECT',
     RECL=8Ø,FORM='FORMATTED')
DO 1Ø KREC=1,64
   READ(1,'(A)')DATA
   LREC=1+KREC/2+32*MOD(KREC+1,2)
   WRITE(2,'(A)',REC=LREC)DATA
1Ø CONTINUE
CLOSE(2)
OPEN(2,STATUS='OLD')
DO 2Ø KREC=1,64
   READ(2,'(A)') DATA
   PRINT'(A)',DATA
2Ø CONTINUE
END
```

Because the record length has been kept constant in creating file number 2, it is possible to close it and reopen it as a sequential access file.

(f) The program specifies that the file is being connected either for formatted or for unformatted input by the FORM= specifier:

FORM=char

"char" is a character expression whose value when trailing blanks are removed is either FORMATTED or UNFORMATTED. If the specifier is not given, then it is assumed that a sequential file is formatted and that a direct access file is unformatted.

EXAMPLES: OPEN(2)

The file on unit 2 is sequential and formatted.

OPEN(25,FORM='UNFORMATTED')

The file on unit 25 is sequential and unformatted.

OPEN(7,ACCESS='DIRECT',RECL=13Ø)

The file on unit 7 is direct access and unformatted. Notice that the record length is given.

(g) The record length must be given for a direct access file:

RECL=int

Here "int" is an integer expression giving a positive value which is the record length of the file. For formatted records, this is the maximum permitted number of characters. For unformatted records the required length will vary between computer systems.

A record length must not be given for a sequential access file.

(h) The BLANK= specifier determines the interpretation of blanks in formatted numeric fields, as discussed in Chapter 18. It can only be given for a file being connected for formatted input/output, and has the form

BLANK=char

"char" is a character expression which is either NULL or ZERO depending on whether blanks are to be ignored or treated as zeros. (An all blank field is always taken to be zero.) If no BLANK= specifier is given, NULL is assumed.

When using an OPEN statement, it is important to know whether the file is already connected. If it is, then the file remains in the same position and only the BLANK= specifier can be changed. To make some significant change, the file should first be closed by a CLOSE statement and then reopened, as in the example given in connection with the ACCESS= specifier.

A file can only be connected to one unit number and a unit number can only be connected to one file. If a program tries to connect the same unit number to an additional file, then the first file is automatically closed. If a program tries to connect the same file to an additional unit number, an error occurs.

The CLOSE statement disconnects a file:

CLOSE([UNIT=]number,specifiers)

and the unit number "number" is disconnected. The possible specifiers are:

IOSTAT=
ERR=
STATUS=

(a) As in the other input/output statements, the specifier

IOSTAT=int

causes the integer variable or array element "int" to be assigned the value zero if no error exists on the file. If an error condition occurs, a positive value is assigned. The interpretation of this value depends on the computer system.

(b) When an error occurs, the specifier

ERR=label

causes the program to jump to the statement with the label "label", which must exist in the same program unit.

(c) The specifier

STATUS=char

tells the computer what to do with the file. The character expression "char" could have the values KEEP or DELETE.

KEEP The file continues to exist and could be reconnected. However, KEEP cannot be used with a file that was specified as a SCRATCH file in the OPEN statement - scratch files are always deleted.
DELETE The file ceases to exist.

If no STATUS= specifier is given, all files are kept except those which were designated as SCRATCH files when they were opened.

19.5 Sequential file manipulation — BACKSPACE, REWIND, and END FILE

Records are transferred between files and the computer by the READ, WRITE and PRINT statements. Earlier in this Chapter, the basic forms of access, sequential and direct, were described. The position of records in a direct access file are determined by the REC= specifier in these statements. In a sequential access file, the position of the file is determined by its past history. When a new file is created, the program initially starts at the first record, and sequential files are always written or read one record at a time, in order. However, an old file could be positioned anywhere when it is first connected by the OPEN statement, depending on where previous activity had left it. This section describes the methods of rewinding, backspacing, and marking the end of a sequential file. The BACK-SPACE, REWIND, and END FILE statements are used only with sequential files. An error condition occurs if an attempt is made to use them on a direct access file.

The most useful is the REWIND statement. At any time during processing a unit can be rewound to start either reading or writing again from the beginning. A file is rewound by the statement

REWIND number

or

$$\text{REWIND}\left([\text{UNIT}=]\text{number}\left[\begin{matrix},\text{control}\\ \text{list}\end{matrix}\right]\right)$$

The unit to be rewound is always given by its number, for example

```
REWIND 3
REWIND(UNIT=3)
REWIND(3)
```

and in addition two specifiers can be used:

```
IOSTAT=
ERR=
```

(a) IOSTAT=int

Just as with the other input/output statements, the IOSTAT= specifier sets the integer variable or integer array element "int" to zero if no error has occurred, or to a positive value if an error does occur. The interpretation of "int" depends on the computer installation but, for example, a particular value of "int" might be used to indicate an attempt to rewind a direct access file.

(b) ERR=label

If an error occurs on the file, the program will jump to the statement with the label "label". A useful example of this is given later in connection with the END FILE statement.

When the REWIND is executed, the unit is rewound to the beginning. As will be explained later, a user might have several groups of data on the unit separated by end-of-file markers. A file is rewound to the very beginning. If it was already at the beginning, it stays there - this is not an error.

(c) Reading files previously written

Given the ability to rewind a file, a programmer has to be aware of the conditions under which he can reread the information in the file. In a sequential file, the details of the READ must match the details of the WRITE which first created the file of data. This means that the occurrence of values according to their type (REAL, INTEGER, etc.), and that the order in which they occur must be the same. Furthermore, formatted records are only compatible with formatted records using an equi-valent format specification for each field. List-directed statements are com-patible with each other, and un-formatted records (described in Section 19.6) can only be read by unformatted READ statements. In every case the organization into **records** has to be compatible. Recall **that** every WRITE or PRINT statement **begins** a new record, and so does every READ statement. In the formatted case additional records can occur when format specifications are restarted or when a slash occurs in the format specification. It is up to the user to ensure that attempts to read data are compatible with the way the data has been written.

EXAMPLE:
Data is written according to

```
    DO 66 K=1,6
66  WRITE(1,70)I,J,X,Y
70  FORMAT(2I10,2F10.5)
```

The same program unit could recover it by a compatible READ statement:

```
      REWIND 1
      DO 88 K=1,6
   88 READ(1,7Ø)L,M,W,Z
```

However, because each READ statement begins a new record, partial records can be read:

```
      REWIND 1
      DO 91 K=1,6
   91 READ(1,95) L,M,W
   95 FORMAT(2I1Ø,F1Ø.5)
```

although here the FORMAT statement 70 would have done just as well. The first real value in each record is passed over.

EXAMPLE:
Data is written according to

```
      DIMENSION A(5,5)
            ⋮
            ⋮
      WRITE(3,1Ø)A
   1Ø FORMAT(25F5.Ø)
```

and can be recovered by

```
      REWIND 3
      READ(3,1Ø)A
```

EXAMPLE:
Data is written by

```
      DIMENSION A(5,5)
            ⋮
            ⋮
      WRITE(3,2Ø)A
   2Ø FORMAT(5F5.Ø)
```

and is contained in 5 records because of FORMAT repetition. It can then be reread by

```
      REWIND 3
      READ(3,2Ø)A
```

or by

```
      REWIND 3
      DO 3Ø K=1,5
   3Ø READ(3,2Ø)(A(L,K),L=1,5)
```

Note the order of subscripts. The upper 3x3 part could be accessed by

```
      REWIND 3
      DO 5Ø K=1,3
   5Ø READ(3,2Ø)(A(L,K),L=1,3)
```

which is the only way to do this. The last two elements of each column are passed over because each time statement 50 is executed a new record begins.

EXAMPLE:
Data is written by

```
      WRITE(9,9Ø)X,Y,Z
   9Ø FORMAT(F1Ø.5,F5.2/F1Ø.5)
```

and is therefore in two records. It could be recovered by

```
      REWIND 9
      READ(9,9Ø)X,Y,Z
```

or by

```
      REWIND 9
      READ(9,91)X,Y
      READ(9,91)Z
   91 FORMAT(F1Ø.5,F5.2)
```

and finally X and Z alone could be obtained by

```
      REWIND 9
      READ(9,91)X
      READ(9,91)Z
```

(d) Rewriting sequential files

When a unit is rewound to be rewritten, all the old data following the rewrite is lost, and programmers are sometimes deluded about what this means. On a sequential file, you can write, rewind, and reread. You can also write, rewind, and rewrite but you cannot follow this by another read. The sense of this is best explained in relation to magnetic tape. As shown in Fig.19.2, a tape is a sequential access device, which is to say the computer starts from the beginning and writes consecutively before rewinding and reading or rewriting. But there is no guarantee on rewriting that the new

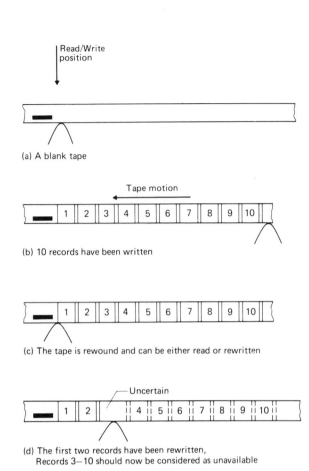

(a) A blank tape

(b) 10 records have been written

(c) The tape is rewound and can be either read or rewritten

(d) The first two records have been rewritten,
Records 3–10 should now be considered as unavailable

Fig. 19.2. On a sequential file, a READ cannot immediately follow a WRITE. This is illustrated for a magnetic tape. In (d) records 3–10 are unavailable. It would be possible to read records 1 or 2 after a BACKSPACE or REWIND.

information takes exactly the same physical space on the tape that the old information did, even if the FORMATs were identical. This is because the physical characteristics of the device - its start and stop time and the actual density of information written on the tape - will vary somewhat. So it is not safe to READ after WRITE without a REWIND. Put another way, if a unit is rewound and writing begins on it, it is best to consider all previous information on the unit to be lost.

EXAMPLE:
Write, rewind, and reread

```
        DO 31 K=1,10
31   WRITE(3,20)K
20   FORMAT(I10)
        REWIND 3
        DO 32 K=1,10
32   READ(3,20)K
```

EXAMPLE:
Write, rewind, rewrite

```
20   FORMAT(I10)
        DO 31 K=1,10
31   WRITE(3,20)K
        REWIND 3
        DO 32 K=1,2
32   WRITE(3,20)K
```

At this point it might be expected that a statement like

```
READ(3,20)I
```

would produce I=3. However it is not allowed. To play that kind of game, use a direct access device.

```
On a sequential file, never say
            WRITE then READ
without a REWIND in between.
```

The BACKSPACE statement

BACKSPACE unit number

or

$$\text{BACKSPACE} \left([\text{UNIT=}]\text{number} \left[, \begin{matrix} \text{control} \\ \text{list} \end{matrix} \right] \right)$$

causes the unit to be stepped back one record on the unit given by the "unit number". The control list items available are exactly as described for the REWIND statement. It is possible to have the sequence WRITE, BACKSPACE, READ, but then the next operation cannot be READ, for much the same reason as described above. It is not possible to backspace over records written using list-directed formatting.

EXAMPLE:
This is a permissible operation on a sequential file

```
      WRITE(9,9Ø)X,Y,Z
   9Ø FORMAT(F1Ø.5,F5.2/F1Ø.5)
      BACKSPACE 9
      READ(9,9Ø)P
```

whatever value was written as Z is read back into P. This cannot then be followed by another READ.

The END FILE statement causes a special mark to be written, specifying the end of a file of data:

END FILE unit number

or

$$\text{END FILE} \left([\text{UNIT}=]\text{number} \begin{bmatrix} ,\text{control} \\ \text{list} \end{bmatrix} \right)$$

where the control list is exactly as was described for the REWIND statement. These special marks are sometimes used in data processing to separate groups of records or data. In FORTRAN IV it was not possible to get past an end-of-file mark, but in FORTRAN 77 it is possible. This is because after a READ statement which encounters an end-of-file mark, a sequential unit is positioned after the end-of-file mark which could be at the beginning of a new group of data records. It is, of course, up to the user to organize his files, but here is a subroutine SKIP which skips over end-of-file marks:

```
      SUBROUTINE SKIP(N,IUNIT)
   C  SKIP N ENDFILES ON UNIT IUNIT
      DO 2Ø K=1,N
   1Ø READ(IUNIT,END=2Ø)
      GO TO 1Ø
   2Ø CONTINUE
      END
```

This subroutine skips over N end-of-file marks on the input/output unit IUNIT which is assumed to be connected and positioned at the desired point for skipping to begin.

As a final note to this section, it is worth pointing out again that FORTRAN does not automatically position a unit at a particular place at the beginning of a program. Particularly on a timesharing system it may be wise to REWIND units before processing; previous runs of the

same or other programs during a session or a complicated processing job may have left the files not rewound.

19.6   Unformatted input and output

Although introduced as the penultimate section of this text, and not given much space at that, this is a very useful facility particularly to advanced users. If a READ or WRITE statement does not include a format specifier, then that statement calls for "unformatted" data transfers. This should not be confused with list-directed transfers in which the format specifier is "*". Unformatted data is transferred in and out in a special code used by the computer system which is usually more efficient in its use of tape or disk space and faster than formatted or list-directed operations. It is achieved by using READ and WRITE statements without a format:

$$\text{READ} \begin{pmatrix} \text{control} \\ \text{list} \end{pmatrix} \begin{bmatrix} \text{data} \\ \text{list} \end{bmatrix}$$

$$\text{WRITE} \begin{pmatrix} \text{control} \\ \text{list} \end{pmatrix} \begin{bmatrix} \text{data} \\ \text{list} \end{bmatrix}$$

In the simplest form, only the unit number is given:

$$\text{READ(number)} \begin{bmatrix} \text{data list} \end{bmatrix}$$

$$\text{WRITE(number)} \begin{bmatrix} \text{data list} \end{bmatrix}$$

There are some devices for which unformatted transfers are inappropriate, for example lineprinters.

Unformatted transfers can be used with either direct access files or sequential files. However the same file cannot be a mixture of formatted and unformatted records. The computer system might preconnect some units for unformatted transfer - this will depend upon local arrangements - or a program may request unformatted files to be connected through an OPEN statement.

By default, direct access files are unformatted. Therefore the statement

```
OPEN(3,ACCESS='DIRECT',RECL=255)
```

connects unit 3 for unformatted direct
access transfers. The required record
length will depend upon the individual
computer system. Therefore to use unformatted direct access, a user will have to
get local information about this.

By default, sequential files are connected
for formatted transfers. Therefore, to use
a unit that is not preconnected by the
computer system for sequential unformatted transfers, it is necessary to put a
FORM= specifier in the OPEN statement, as
in

```
OPEN(73,FORM='UNFORMATTED')
```

which connects unit 73 for unformatted
sequential access. (It is sequential because
the ACCESS= specifier is not given.)

A statement

```
WRITE(unit number) data list
```

transfers the values named in the "data
list" to the unit number "unit number" in
exactly one record of the unformatted
form, sometimes called a "binary record".
With this kind of operation, it is still true
that each new READ or WRITE statement
begins a new record, but as there is
exactly one record for the entire data
list, it is much easier to figure out where
the program is in a file.

If such data is to be read by a READ
statement, then it is obvious that the
READ statement has to be unformatted as
well. In addition the information to be
read must follow the layout that was
used when it was written, and be in
one-to-one correspondence by type and
position. It was pointed out that when
rereading formatted records, the exact
format need not be used provided
appropriate fields matched the data; any
formatted data could be read as a
character string as an extreme example.
Here, with unformatted data, the rule is
more strict. Exactly the same type must
be used in corresponding positions of the
data list in the WRITE and READ
statements.

EXAMPLE:
Data is prepared by

```
DIMENSION A(5,5)
DIMENSION ROW(5),COL(5)
        :
        :
WRITE(63,REC=17) A
```

which generates a single unformatted
record on the direct access unit 63,
containing 25 real values. It could be
read by

```
READ(63,REC=17) A
```

in the same program unit. There is no
way of reading out of the middle of this
record, although the first column only
could be read by

```
READ(63,REC=17) COL
```

It will be recalled that to write in row
order, it is necessary to put

```
WRITE(63,REC=17)((A(I,J),J=1,5)
                ,I=1,5)
```

and then

```
READ(63,REC=17) ROW
```

would read back the first row.

EXAMPLE:
Data is prepared by

```
DIMENSION A(5,5)
        :
        :
DO 70 K=1,5
70 WRITE(11)(A(K,L),1=1,5)
```

It is in five records and can be read by

```
REWIND(11)
DO 91 K=1,5
91 READ(11)(A(K,L),L=1,8)
```

It is possible to BACKSPACE, REWIND,
and END FILE unformatted sequential files.

19.7 Internal files

A very limited internal file facility is available in FORTRAN 77 which allows a file of character data to exist inside the computer rather than on an external unit. The file actually consists of a character variable, substring, array or array element and can be transferred between other entities in the machine by sequential formatted input and output statements. If the file is a character variable, substring or array element, then the file has only one record, and the length of that record is the length of the character datum. If the file is a character array, then it has as many records as there are array elements and all the records are the same length: the length of one array element.

At the start of execution of a program, all internal files are positioned at the beginning. Records can be written to the file by sequential formatted WRITE statements, and read by sequential formatted READ statements. List-directed and unformatted transfers are not permitted.

To write a record, the WRITE statement simply gives the name of the character datum that constitutes the file as a unit specifier in place of a unit number:

```
CHARACTER*2Ø THING
        :
        :
    WRITE(THING,1Ø) X,Y
1Ø  FORMAT(2F1Ø.5)
```

It can be seen for the above example that, although the file holds only character quantities, any formatted data can be written to it. This is because formatted records actually consist of characters. If the record written is shorter than the record length of the file, the records are filled out with trailing blanks. If it is longer, it is chopped off. Writing data to an internal file causes records of that file to become defined. They can also be defined in other ways, as for example in the data list of ordinary READ statements or in assignment statements. And of course the file can be manipulated in the normal manner of character variables. This could be very

useful; external data could be read into a character variable which is preprocessed in some way and then read out of the character variable as numerical data by a formatted READ statement.

Once a record is defined it is possible to read it using a sequential formatted READ statement. Each such statement starts to read the internal file again from the beginning.

EXAMPLE:

In this program fragment, data is read into the character variable CDATA from unit 5. CDATA is then scanned one character at a time, and every blank is converted to a zero. The variable CDATA is then read as an internal file into the real array RDATA.

```
    REAL RDATA(1Ø)
    CHARACTER*8Ø CDATA
1Ø  READ(5,'(A)') CDATA
    DO 2Ø K=1,8Ø
    IF(CDATA(K:K).EQ.' ') THEN
        CDATA(K:K)='Ø'
    END IF
2Ø  CONTINUE
    READ(CDATA,3Ø)RDATA
3Ø  FORMAT(1ØF8.Ø)
```

A program is not allowed to use any of the statements for manipulating files with an internal file. You do not need REWIND or BACKSPACE because every READ of an internal file behaves as if it were rewound first. You may not use END FILE, OPEN, CLOSE or INQUIRE with an internal file.

Appendix

Shhh!

Here is the clever counting bit-reversal scrambling routine required to complete the fast Fourier transform program of Section 12.3. Why the secrecy? It gives away Problem 7.5.

```
      SUBROUTINE SCRAG(XRAY,N)
C SUBROUTINE TO SCRAMBLE THE REAL
C ARRAY XRAY INTO BIT-REVERSE
C ORDER BY BRENNER'S COUNTING METHOD-
C
C XRAY = REAL ARRAY LENGTH N WHICH
C          THIS ROUTINE SCRAMBLES
C    N = INTEGER VALUE, LENGTH OF
C          ARRAY AND REVERSAL MODULUS
C
      DIMENSION XRAY(0:N-1)
      NADDON=N/2
      KREVRS=0
      DO 20 KADDRS=1,N-2
C KREVRS IS THE BIT-REVERSE OF KADDRS
      ICARRY=NADDON
C FIX UP BIT REVERSE CARRIES
  10 IF(KREVRS.GE.ICARRY)THEN
        KREVRS=KREVRS-ICARRY
        ICARRY=ICARRY/2
        GO TO 10
      END IF
      KREVRS=KREVRS+ICARRY
      IF(KREVRS.LT.KADDRS)THEN
        T=XRAY(KADDRS)
        XRAY(KADDRS)=XRAY(KREVRS)
        XRAY(KREVRS)=T
      END IF
  20 CONTINUE
      END
```

Index